W9-CGQ-491

HoopStats

HoopStats

THE BASKETBALL ABSTRACT

Joshua Trupin
Gerald Secor Couzens

A BANTAM TRADE PAPERBACK

BANTAM BOOKS
New York • Toronto • London • Sydney • Auckland

Special thanks to
Michael Cruz of Graphic Arts Associates in Stamford, Connecticut,
who solved many major crises for us without complaint.

The authors believe all information
contained in this book
regarding NBA players and teams
was correct up to July 1, 1989
when it was sent to the printer.

HOOPSTATS
A Bantam Book / October 1989

All rights reserved.
Copyright © 1989 by Gerald Secor Couzens and Joshua Trupin.
Cover design copyright © 1989 by Rich Rossiter.
Cover photos copyright © 1989 by Focus on Sports.
No part of this book may be reproduced or transmitted
in any form or by any means, electronic or mechanical,
including photocopying, recording, or by any information
storage and retrieval system, without permission in writing from
the publisher.
For information address: Bantam Books.

Produced by M 'N O Production Services, Inc.

Library of Congress Cataloging-in-Publication Data

Trupin, Joshua.
HoopStats : the basketball abstract.

1. Basketball—United States—Records. 2. National
Basketball Association—History. I. Couzens, Gerald
Secor. II. Title.
GV885.55.T78 1989 796.323'0973'021   89-15192
ISBN 0-553-34769-1

Published simultaneously in the United States and Canada

Bantam Books are published by Bantam Books, a division of Bantam Doubleday Dell
Publishing Group, Inc. Its trademark, consisting of the words "Bantam Books" and
the portrayal of a rooster, is Registered in the U.S. Patent and Trademark Office and
in other countries. Marca Registrada. Bantam Books, 666 Fifth Avenue, New York,
New York 10103.

PRINTED IN THE UNITED STATES OF AMERICA

CWO 0 9 8 7 6 5 4 3 2 1

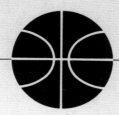

Contents

Introduction

Over the past few years, people have started to look more closely at sports. Not "look," in the sense of sitting in front of a cable box, flipping between kick boxing and cheerleading competitions, but look, in the sense of making sense out of everything. Bill James started it all. For years, his annual *Baseball Abstract* was the most radical trade paperback published in America. What other work so successfully challenged authority? It wasn't easy, having to look critically at a sport we thought we had known for all these years. His book opened everyone's eyes, whether or not those eyes liked what they saw.

Soon other writers arrived with new and very valuable research. Pete Palmer and John Thorn wrote *The Hidden Game of Baseball* (and Bob Carroll joined the gang for *The Hidden Game of Football*). The Elias Sports Bureau loosened up their grip on statistics a bit, and now put out *The Elias Baseball Analyst*. James puts his name on *The Great American Baseball Stat Book*, although if you look closely, Don Zminda really runs the show now. George Ignatin and Allen Barra put together the yearly *Football by the Numbers*.

These books are all well worth the investment for sports fans. However, there seemed to be something missing. We think basketball is the greatest stat sport on earth, yet the market has been strangely barren of anything groundbreaking. Sure, you can read ghostwritten autobiographies of your favorite coaches and players. But who wants to read about Pat Riley's championship season all over again, especially if you're a die-hard Celtics fan? We think that basketball fans deserve as good as or better than

baseball fans, and that's what we'll try to give you here. Lots of ideas are tossed about in the newspapers and on television about the NBA: The team with the best defense wins. It's impossible to win in Boston. A team's play tends to deteriorate the longer it stays out on the road. Anytime we hear such theories, we set out to see whether or not they're really true. Sometimes they are. Sometimes they're not. It's more fun when they're not, we admit it.

Instead of just accepting the view of the so-called experts in the media, we have attempted to look closely at the various issues in search of answers. Who knows? Maybe our questioning the authorities will lead to heightened hoop enlightenment, enhance your appreciation of this great game, and also make your visit to the Basketball Hall of Fame (all hoop nuts must go) much more worthwhile.

We're hoop junkies. Sometimes we get carried away, just like other fans. Sometimes we have preferences for a player or a team, although you won't often see it in here. What we have is a fierce interest in the NBA just like yours. We want to know *why* things happen the way they do, who was better in a particular play, and what wasn't what it seemed.

We want to make this a living book, however. If you don't agree with us, drop us a line care of the publisher! We've tried to keep an open mind through all of this. If there's something we've missed, tell us, and we'll give you credit.

You'll notice how complete our coverage of the season just past is. Our goal is to bring in-depth coverage to some of the league's burning questions,

together with a full statistical blanket of what's going on. It's usually easier to see trends when something is graphed out. Therefore, we've put in plenty of pictures for those of you who'd like a break from reading. Just flip through and see.

We don't have any tricks to doing all this. We use only homemade ingredients in this book. The stats you read here are compiled by us from extended box scores in your daily newspaper (the ones with individual assists, turnovers, and so on). We've taken them and embellished—added them up, sorted them, done whatever we needed to look at them clearly. It's all done on an IBM XT, using a spreadsheet and a word processor, with just a pinch of love for the game.

How is this book set up? Using a natural progression of studies, we first present articles dealing mainly with teams—home court advantage, predicting a team's future performance, and over- and underachieving groups in the league.

The best grist for arguments is found in the section where we rate players. We also study how they perform as they age, so you can see how and why Kareem started to slow down as he pushed 40. We even study the revenge factor in the NBA—how players do against their old teams.

Those sections are somewhat abstract, in that they could describe *any* season. So we move on into the 1988–89 season, giving you a breakdown of every team's performance, some comments, and a lot of information you haven't seen elsewhere. Then we turn the microscope on individuals, with short discussions of most of the league's players. It's

a rough job, but someone's gotta do it.

Why are we the ones to do it? Since this is the first year of our existence, we'd like to take this time to introduce ourselves. Gerald is the tall one, the one who's always on the phone trying to reach someone, somewhere, for a quote. He's written several other books, and if you want to learn how to *play* basketball instead of watch it, you could learn a lot from a copy of *Hoops!* Gerald is more of a straight basketball guy, having wandered all over Europe playing basketball before settling down to write a fitness column for *Newsday*. Josh has been known to wander from sport to sport (including two years managing the Yale hockey team, while compiling stats for about ten others in the Sports Information Office). He's the computer whiz who can take a pile of stats and make a picture worth a thousand numbers.

Before we begin this book, we just ask one thing of you. Please, *please* don't take this book and start betting on its contents. You can bet someone $5 that we said something, but *don't* use it to bet on anything in the future. We don't want to get letters saying that you lost $10,000 because we said Sacramento was 9–0 in their first home game and you bet them and lost. You've been warned. We feel gambling is set up for you to lose, not win, which is why everyone in Las Vegas drives big cars. One more time: If you're planning to gamble on the basis of some fact you found in here, don't. This is a book about looking at the past, not into the future. Keep your future by not getting involved with betting.

CHAPTER ONE

The Hallowed Halls

The Boston Celtics. The hallowed halls of the Boston Garden. Not to mention the hallowed mall surrounding their other home court, in Hartford. There seems to be a magic spell cast over all invaders of Beantown. How else can you explain their consistent home marks: 318–51 (.862) since 1980–81, no losing seasons at home since they went 16–21 in 1969–70? Obviously, the Celtic mystique permeates every plank of that parquet floor. Indeed, an unexplained force suffuses this grand old arena. Is any team more intimidating, more linked to their home court?

What is it about the Garden? Is it the ghosts of Cousy, Russell, and Havlicek? That intangible Celtic pride that's always being trumpeted? The lack of any air conditioning whatsoever in the building? The cheap seats up top from which you have *perfect* sight lines of exactly half the court? The Larry Bird/Crunch bar ads that permeate the place? Leprechauns?

Yeah, right. Leprechauns. There is nothing mystical about the Garden, in fact. True, there are several unusual characteristics to be found. All the stories about the awful dressing rooms? They're true. Imagine, if you will, a room too small for a basketball player to sit down in. Now make it 100 degrees. Not "new" heat, either, but "old" heat, the kind that feels like it's been there for twenty years. The Celtics organization uses every little psych-out it can to gain an edge on its opponents. The dressing rooms are just one factor. Another gripe you'll often hear from visitors is that the parquet floorboards are so loose that they're in danger of popping up at any time, hitting someone in the head much like a bad

F Troop joke. When they awarded Kareem a square of the floor during his retirement tour, it was widely reported that they didn't bother to replace it. Game-day practices? Sorry, the Bruins own the arena. The nearest a team will get to a court on game day is at nearby Hellenic College.

Obviously, all these little annoyances add up to quite a headache for the visiting team. A team is lucky to keep the score close for a half, and a coach often has difficulty getting his top seven or eight players some time late in the game. Or so you would think. The stats tell a different story. True, the Celtics do have a great home court tradition. And they do use every form of mental intimidation at their disposal. But the cause-and-effect relationship isn't as great as one might suppose. If you're looking for the single factor most responsible for their dominance, look no further than the strong teams they always field. In fact, *any* team with an overall record such as the Celtics have had will win as often at home as Boston does. Well, any team except the Lakers, but we'll get into that later.

Let's start by better defining our goals. We could try to find that magic number which is the much-discussed "home court edge," the amount by which a team will beat an equally talented team at home. We can also take a step back and try to find out how many games outstanding home play is worth to a team in a year. We'll do both, but let's start from the outside.

When trying to figure out the worth of the home court over a season, we have at least three ways to look at it. We can consider it as a straight compar-

ison (a team that went 34–7 at home, 14–27 on the road would be +20), a ratio (the same team would be .829 versus .341, or .488 better), or we can try to fit an equation to it (if we find that an average team wins 6 more than twice as many games at home as on the road). These three methods may seem trivial, but in effect make a big difference when we try to account for certain factors. We'll have more on this later.

As the league goes, it's often said that it's impossible to win on the road. Take, for instance, the 1987–88 San Antonio Spurs. They were 31–51 overall, buying them their lottery ticket. If you made the mistake of expecting them to play like a 31–51 team at home, however, you'd soon find out otherwise: they went 23–18 at home. The home court can make even the Kings look like kings, a team that went 24–58 overall, but 19–22 at home. And they were the fourth *worst* team in the league at home. But back to those Spurs. Teams play 41 games on the road, so the Spurs' home mark of 23–18 means that they ended up 8–33 on the road, sixth worst in the league. They won 15 more games at home than on the road—quite a large number when you have only 41 in the season. San Antonio wasn't one team, but two—a .195 team when playing on the road, but a very respectable .561 team when at home.

Isn't every team like this? Doesn't every team turn into a squad of jumbos when you toss them in front of ten thousand screaming fans? Well, yes and no. The better a team is, the better it will play at home. But a *team* makes the home court advantage, not the other way around. Sure, the Celtics are almost unbeatable at home. But that's because they're unbeatable, not because they're playing at home! The average NBA team over the past 5 years (1984–88) has won 66 more games at home than on the road. The Celts? Only 58. Game by game, the Celts have had, over the past 5 years, the second worst home court advantage in the league!

Actually, for this study, we ran the information two ways. In case you haven't noticed, the Lakers and Celtics just happen to be the two teams with the lowest-rated home court advantages. This gave us some doubt that the games-back method proved anything except which teams had the best records. After all, the more games you win, the more you'll win on the road, meaning the fewer games you can

be at home. Or something like that. Anyway, it didn't matter that the Clippers came in third; we had to make sure that these numbers truly measured a difference, rather than just reflecting overall performance.

So we measured the edge as a *percentage* of total wins. Instead of just being +58 games at home, the Celtics were 46.4% better at home over 5 years (183 wins at home versus 125 on the road). A funny thing happened here. The Celtics and Lakers still showed the smallest home court advantages. However, all the other teams jumped around. This could mean one of two things: (1) the home court edge is nullified by excellence, or (2) we're poor mathematicians.

We double-checked the math on the computer, so it's probably not the latter. But why would good teams tend toward lower home court advantages? Common wisdom decrees that if you can play .500 ball on the road, you'll be a pretty good team. Logic, however, finds that you'd have to be an excellent team to break even out there. In fact, only two teams, Boston and L.A., have been able to do it over the past 5 years. And every extra road win means that your home edge is one game smaller.

Is it really all that great a difference? You bet it is. The Lakers played only 29.3% better at home (172 wins to 133). The Suns won nearly 3 times as many home games over the same span, 128 to 45. The Lakers didn't play at home often enough to win that many more. If you take the straight comparison, you've biased against better teams. If a team wins 60 games, they *can't* do better than +22 at home, no matter what. If they win all their home games, they'll still win 19 on the road. A .500 team that won every game at home and none on the road would appear to be a better home team by 41 full games. It's probably preferable to the ratio method, which magnifies every win for a very poor team, especially one that wins only 3 or 4 games on the road. A team that wins 5 at home to 1 on the road is 400% better, while a team that wins 25 at home and 10 on the road is only 150% better. It is arguable which team really gets more of a kick at home.

So is there anything we can look for to explain *why* some teams are so much better at home? Actually, the question is a complex issue that combines, and must take into account, such very real-life problems as the rigors of travel (air and bus), dif-

ferent home court arenas, hometown fans, referees, the age of the player, the length of a road trip, and how many days off there are between games, as well as where a team is located geographically. How much time a team has off before its first game back home is also a consideration thrown into the hopper.

Take into account also the fact that basketball is the most physically demanding of any sport, and that it is the only pro sport played in all four seasons, from the season opening in October to the Championship final in the beginning of summer. Nonstop play will tear down the best-conditioned athletes. It's just a matter of time before the body and mind start to give out.

Why are teams better at home? In 1985–86 the Celtics went 40–1 (67–15 overall), establishing an NBA home court record in the process, eventually going on to wrest the Championship title from the Lakers. How can a team be so dominating over the course of 82 games? Many reasons are given by team general managers and coaches, the people in the know who regularly ponder the thought, especially as their team hustles off to the local airport in the middle of a snowstorm to start a six-city, eight-day cross-country jaunt. "It's really not the home court that's so difficult, it's the talent level of the home team," said Philadelphia GM John Nash. "For example, five years ago it wasn't tough to play in the Omni in Atlanta. But now that the Hawks are much tougher as a team, the Omni has become a tough place to play in."

Jerry West, Laker GM, admits to the existence of the home court dominance, but that's because any team that plays well will have an advantage. Says West, "Great players will play great everywhere they go, home or away." It's the average player who will play poorly on the road a lot of the time, West commented, and this is often the deciding difference between getting another notch in the win column and not.

Al Bianchi, the Knick General Manager, agrees with his West Coast counterpart. "It's what the seventh, eighth, or ninth man can do for you in a road game that will determine a game's outcome. I think bench players contribute more when they're playing at home than anywhere else," said Bianchi. In order to help overcome this, Bianchi picked up All-Star Kiki Vandeweghe from the Trail Blazers at mid-

season last year to ensure that the Knicks had more bona fide firepower coming off the bench, adding a player who wouldn't be affected by bombing away in the Palace in Auburn Hills, or at the Great Western Forum in Los Angeles.

Hometown teams can be tough, even the Clippers. "The hometown team is generally the aggressor," said Jack McCloskey, Piston GM. "They come out and play tough and have the fans backing them up. This certainly puts them in the driver's seat most of the time." In a perfect world, an NBA team (yes, this would include the Timberwolves, Heat, Magic, and Clippers) would win all 41 of their home games and lose each one on the road. It's not a perfect world, though (that might explain why Clipper guard Quintin Dailey ate his way off the team by packing on 30 extra pounds by midseason before being suspended and sent to a fat farm), and teams don't win all of their home games. "The difference is in the talent level of your team," said Phoenix team President Jerry Colangelo. "Coaching is important, too. However, the true mark of a competitive team is its ability to win on the road. You expect them to win at home. If they don't, you're in for a terrible season."

And it's expected in the NBA not only that you win at home, but, says Colangelo, that you do it so convincingly that no matter who you end up playing, you still dominate on your home court throughout the season.

The hometown fans have a definite positive effect on the players on the court—on the visitors as well. "Early in the existence of our franchise we didn't have a talented team," explained Norm Sonju, the General Manager of the Dallas Mavericks, "but since the crowd was always behind the team, it really bolstered the spirits of the players and helped them win some games.

"Unfortunately for the Mavs, though, the crowd also hyped up the competitive juices of such notables as Larry Bird, Magic Johnson, Kareem Abdul-Jabbar, and Michael Jordan," said Sonju. "It was our crowd that brought out the best in these players."

A boisterous home crowd does have an intimidating effect on the refs as well as the visiting players. "The refs may be tired and not as crisp after a grueling travel and game schedule," said Bob Whitsitt, the Seattle GM. "Even though they may have colds or flu, they'll still be out there."

And it's there on the court that the crowd can make its presence felt most on the men with the whistles. When comparing this sport to baseball, hockey, and football, Sacramento head coach Jerry Reynolds feels that the basketball crowd has more control over a game than in any other sport. "Each player has to play offense and defense," said Reynolds, "and he can easily go up a notch in performance with the help of the crowd." This "sixth player" also affects the officiating at times, says Reynolds.

"Some refs get heckled and worked over pretty well by the crowd," admitted Dave Checketts, GM of the Utah Jazz. "They end up protecting the hometown team's star player at times because of it, don't dare make a controversial call in the final seconds if the home team isn't winning, and wouldn't dare call a technical foul on a popular home coach.

"When we're on the road and I see certain refs on the floor," said Checketts, "you have to just hope that your team gets far enough ahead. It's really hard to believe that you'll have a shot to win with those refs out there unless you have that lead."

There are strong-willed refs who bend over backward in order not to be swayed by the reaction of the hometown fans. Typically, these are the men with seniority in the whistle-blowing ranks. But then there are those who seem to blow their whistles based on the noise level and crowd reactions. "When your team gets going at home, the crowd noise picks up, and this puts pressure on the refs," said Indiana Pacer GM Donnie Walsh.

A packed house can help get a home team steamrolling through a visiting team's defense. "When you're at home and on a roll offensively or defensively, the officials are less likely to put a damper on it," explained Jan Volk, GM of the Celtics. "But if the roll happens to be by a visiting team, the crowd suddenly gets very quiet, it starts to moan a lot, and the officials are affected. If you happen to be the visiting team, it's often very difficult to get that roll going."

The arena that a game is played in is often hyped as a game-winning factor. Sometimes this is true. "Whenever there's more talent on an opposing team, the arena they play in often becomes a difficult place," said Piston coach Chuck Daly. Daly feels that his team has historically had trouble at Portland's 12,666-seat Memorial Coliseum, and not

only because of the presence of Clyde Drexler, Jerome Kersey, and Kevin Duckworth. "The arena is small and the Portland fans are sitting almost right on the court," said Daly. "It's always a tough place to play."

Indeed it is. Over the past 15 seasons the Blazers, playing in their tiny gym (only the Salt Palace in Salt Lake City with 12,444 is smaller), have posted the best home court record in the NBA.

It was once estimated that a pro basketball player who runs up and down the court during the course of a 48-minute game will cover close to five miles. Physiologically, that's quite a demand on the heart and lungs, especially when you consider that the player is often sprinting, jumping high to shoot or block a shot, and also slamming into huge bodies while trying to get across the paint. Now take that superbly conditioned NBA player and fly him in for a game against the Jazz in Salt Lake City, where the altitude is 4,390 feet above sea level, or have him go play the Nuggets in Denver, the aptly named Mile High City (altitude 5,280 feet) and you're stacking the odds against the player turning in a stellar performance.

According to exercise experts, elevations at approximately 4,000 feet above sea level and below rarely have any effect on normally healthy adults. But as you start to go up in elevation and attempt to run and play basketball, oxygen supply is affected and overall performance levels begin to decline with the altitude.

Does altitude enter into the win-lose equation? It certainly does. "More than any other team in the NBA, it makes a difference whether you play Denver in Denver or at your own place," said Norm Sonju, the Dallas GM. "Altitude is definitely a factor to be considered in Denver. One day I went out for a jog there and felt as if the air was being sucked out of my lungs. The altitude really tires you out and can make you feel like you're 200 years old." For the visiting players, the effects are more marked.

"Whether or not altitude is a factor in Denver, we always tried to let the other team think that it was," said Carl Scheer, the GM at Denver for 10 seasons before moving on to a similar post with the near-sea-level Charlotte Hornets. Pete Babcock, the current Denver GM, feels that the altitude factor is slightly exaggerated in importance, but it still gives the Nuggets an advantage when visiting teams troop

into the McNichols Sports Arena—especially when they're lugging oxygen tanks, as the Lakers did several years ago in the playoffs.

"The altitude helps us more psychologically than physically," said Babcock. "Some players coming here think that they will play badly because they have trouble getting their second wind. Thinking like that can only help us, especially in the fourth quarter."

Teams generally have a difficult time when they have to play at altitude. "It usually takes at least one game to get used to it," said Dave Checketts of Utah, who points out that the only time a team has a chance to adapt is in the playoffs, when it might be in town for two or three days.

What do coaches do to prepare their teams for the altitude of Denver or Utah? Nothing, really. "I don't ever talk to the players about it," said Lenny Wilkens, the Cleveland head coach. Chuck Daly never brings up the altitude issue with his players, either. "Planting an idea like altitude in their heads is the worst thing a coach could ever do to his players," said Daly, whose Pistons posted a combined 1–1 road away record against Denver and Utah this past season. "What I do when we play in those cities is substitute earlier and try to get our player rotation going so the players will be fresh."

Even though the altitude poses problems for most visitors, Jerry Reynolds feels that his Sacramento Kings have more trouble trying to contain Alex English, Fat Lever, Walter Davis, and the Nuggets' nonstop running game than trying to catch their breath because of the altitude. Still, performance remains in favor of the players who live at altitude during the season. The combined Nuggets-Jazz home court record of 69–13 certainly seems to point in that direction.

When a player is about to play on a distant court, other factors enter into the equation, some only slightly. "Boston Garden is difficult to play in because of all the dead spots on the court," pointed out Bob Ferry, the Bullets GM. In addition to the court itself, Dave Checketts of Utah feels that the younger players are often intimidated just by being in Boston Garden. "They've grown up watching the Celtic games on TV and they've heard all about the mystique, the NBA championship banners, the retired uniforms, and Red Auerbach and his cigars. It makes a big impression on them at first."

The Great Western Fabulous Forum, home of the L.A. Lakers, is also a difficult arena, and not just because of the always tough Lakers. "When the players come in and see the stretch limos at the door and the Hollywood and television stars at courtside like Jack Nicholson, Michael Douglas, and Dyan Cannon, they're in awe," said Checketts. "To top it off, the Laker fans are a sarcastic bunch. If the Lakers are blowing us out of the gym, the fans become merciless with their comments. I'm positive that our player performance is affected by this. They pretend that they don't hear what's being said, but I'm sure that they do."

The NBA hometown version of "Abuse Your Guests" is especially popular at the Pistons' new arena, the Palace. Here Leon "The Barber" Bradley sits courtside right behind the visitors' bench and taunts every player who camps in front of him. Bradley, a 65-year-old former barber, has been harassing players for more than 20 years now, first in Cobo Arena, then the Pontiac Silverdome, and currently while perched in his $33-a-game seat in the Palace. If his beloved Pistons moved to Canada, Bradley would probably find a way to make the trip with them, because just as hard as a player strives to perfect his game, Bradley and many other NBA hometown razzers (the hairy ape in Phoenix, the vociferous Garment District basketball experts at Madison Square Garden) strive toward, even live for, making life miserable for visiting players.

The most important factor that has to be considered in the home court question is not so much the arena or the hoop nuts in the seats there, but the different effects of "The Road." For it is the road and all that it encompasses—airline and hotel food, short beds, little sleep, tremendous boredom, and long stays away from home—that will have the most negative impact on the performance of a visiting player and his team.

"It all comes down to a player's comfort zone," said Chuck Daly. "When a player is home, he eats well, sleeps in his own bed, knows where to park his car at the arena, greets the same people. It's not like that on the road, and it all adds up."

Take a player out of his comfort zone and send him from Washington to Atlanta, to Cleveland, down to Dallas, over to Los Angeles, and the mental and physical fatigue that overcomes a player becomes something to consider seriously, along

NBA Road Records
As Road Trips Progress

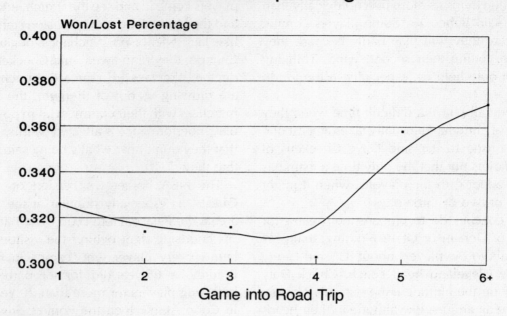

with jet lag, changing time zones, changing from 60-degree temperatures one day to ice and snow the next. Not to mention the effect Dominique Wilkins, Brad Daugherty, Rolando Blackman, and Magic Johnson can have on a player's psyche.

"The game beats you up," said Jerry Krause of the Chicago Bulls, "but travel beats you up, too. It really adds to a team's home court advantage when they get to play against a team that's in the midst of a long road trip."

"As a general rule," said Jan Volk of Boston, "the longer the road trip, the harder it gets for a team.

NBA Road Records
As Road Trips Wind Down

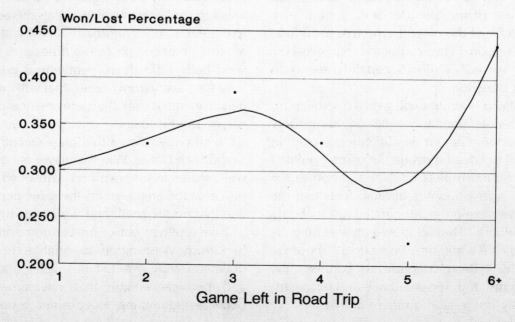

You're not only away from your home, but wherever you go, you are the enemy and the fans hate you. They boo you when you go on the court. They cheer when you miss a shot or make a bad play, and they're quiet when you do something nice. Go through 10 days like this, and it starts to take a cumulative toll on the players."

The charts on page 8 show how teams tend to weaken as they advance through road trips and home stands. The first two graphs show, in order, how teams do depending on how far they are into a road trip. The higher the game number, the longer they've been away from home. Conversely, we've also figured how teams play when they're getting closer to the end of a road trip, figuring that the last game of a trip would be the worst. The second chart shows how teams in their last road game play worse than during any other road games.

Back-to-back games and four games in five nights in different cities will also sap the strength of these NBA frequent-fliers. "Lobby time, all that standing around in airport and hotel lobbies, can make you tired," said Dave Checketts. "Even a short 90-minute flight can take it out of you. Planes are stressful for a lot of players."

"It's a killer if you have to play and try to be competitive when you've been on the road for a long time," said Jerry Colangelo of Phoenix. "Long road trips are unavoidable, but if the team could get a trip with a game on Tuesday, Thursday, Saturday, and Monday, with spacing in between left for travel and practice, that team would at least have a chance to be more competitive."

"We had the Knicks in Salt Lake City on the seventh game of a seven-game road trip last January," recalled Hot Rod Hundley, the Jazz TV color man. "The Knicks were still up by one at the half, even though the Jazz were playing great. At halftime, the coach switched strategies based on the fact that the Knicks *had* to be tired. When the Jazz came out in the second half they pressed the Knicks for the rest of the game."

Karl Malone led the Jazz in scoring that night with 41 points, as the Knicks were blown away by 23 points (127–104), suffering their worst defeat of the year. After five hours of airport lobby time and flying, the Knicks raced to their homes to catch up on sleep, slightly dazed after their 2–5 road performance.

Bob Whitsitt, the Seattle Supersonic General Manager, believes that scheduling is the biggest cause of a home court advantage. "If a team is tired and then has to travel all day, gets delayed by fog, snow, or ice, they can't be as competitive as you'd like them to be coming in to play a home team that's had a day's rest, has been waiting just for them, and has a packed arena to cheer them on, pumping juice into them from the start of the game to the end."

Whitsitt, whose team had three sets of back-to-back games on the road last season and played six games in eight days on one memorable March swing around the country, would like to see a rule change that allows for a day off between games played on the road. "It's only fair," said Whitsitt.

You can't always expect players to come into a gym and start firing up 20-footers with any degree of accuracy if they haven't had a chance to practice. Often they do, but not reliably. On road trips teams are forced to practice in strange surroundings, that is, when they can get a gym. If they're lucky, they get to shoot-around in the arena that they'll play in that night, but often not. It's usually a local high school or college gym that takes in the vagabonds. While the coach tries to make practices similar to those they have at home, it's usually not possible because there aren't enough baskets to work on all the drills he wants covered. So instead, coaches will run through some plays and have a shoot-around until the janitor comes to kick them out so the high school gym class can start.

Even though the NBA contract calls for first-class air travel for all flights over an hour (if there isn't enough space in first class, the players with least seniority in the league get bounced to coach, with an empty seat purchased next to them so they can stretch out), traveling around the country for 41 away games is not to be envied. "Travel starts to take its toll on the team after as little as two or three games," explained Mike Saunders, the Knick trainer and traveling secretary. "Following an away game that usually ends by 10 P.M., the players are out of the arena and back to their hotel by 11," said Saunders. "Since they're still wired and pumped from the game, they usually don't get to bed until 1 or 2 A.M.

"The NBA contract calls for teams to get the first available flight out the next morning in order not to

miss a game," said Saunders, "so the players have to get up at six, sometimes earlier, to make it to that plane."

In the NBA, a favorable travel schedule can make the difference between winning and losing. Put in a week of keeping to a nonstop road schedule and try to play championship ball at the same time. It's understandable why some visiting teams may appear sluggish, out of sync, or listless. While the Miami Heat stumbled toward one of the worst records in NBA history (15–67) and had no player averaging over 13 points a game ("We need to improve in so many areas—shooting, passing, rebounding," said coach Ron Rothstein. "I can't speculate how many of these players will be around in three years"), their travel schedule certainly didn't help the cold Heat.

The 1988–89 season saw the Heat in the Midwest Division regularly playing the likes of division powers Utah Jazz and Denver Nuggets, both located a half-continent away. On top of that, they had 4 six-day-plus trips out West and 10 back-to-backs, the home-and-away games on successive nights that can tire a player out very quickly.

The newcomers aren't the only ones complaining about their hellish travel woes. "We finished a game in Seattle and had to play two nights later in Miami," said Supersonic General Manager Bob Whitsitt. "The players all arrived at the airport at seven for our flight. The plan called for an afternoon arrival in Miami and then a shoot-around the next day.

"We got hit with snow and ice that morning at the airport," said Whitsitt. "Our flight was canceled, the airport was down to one runway, and we really had to push to get all of us on the 2 P.M. flight to Miami. With luck we took off, finally arriving in Miami at 1 A.M. We had spent the whole day traveling."

Any type of practice was out of the question for the Supersonics, and after sleeping in on game day, the Sonics went to play the cellar-dwelling Heat at the Miami Arena, barely eking out a 100–93 win. The next day started with a 5:30 wakeup call, and the tired Sonics moved on to Charlotte, losing to the Hornets that night 108–106. "It just caught up with us," said Seattle coach Bernie Bickerstaff. "We didn't have any legs at the end."

Seattle has it tough all season long as they move out from their outpost in the Pacific Northwest and head out on the road, switching planes as often as they change their socks. But other teams get stuck in traffic as well. After defeating the Bullets in double overtime 128–121, the Milwaukee Bucks had to leave the next morning to get back for a home game against Utah. Bad weather kept their plane from landing in Milwaukee, Green Bay, Madison, and Chicago. After landing in Grand Rapids, Michigan, and taking a bus, they finally arrived at their arena 15 minutes before tip-off, the end of a 10½-hour trip. The game had to be delayed more than an hour to let the Bucks get the blood circulating back in their legs. The Bucks eventually prevailed, 107–89.

The Detroit Pistons have found a surefire way to end all the road madness, but it's a solution that only a winner, or at least a possible contender, could try. In 1987 Piston owner Bill Davidson purchased from Don Carter, owner of the Dallas Mavs, a fifteen-year-old BAC 1-11 jet. The Mavs had chartered the jet from Carter to use in several playoff games instead of going the regularly scheduled airline route.

Piston General Manager Jack McCloskey had more far-sweeping plans for the jet. After having the interior stripped and outfitted with two seven-foot couches, oversize VCRs, and comfortable chairs, the plane was repainted in Piston team colors, christened Roundball One, and put into service as the Pistons' season-long jet. No longer did players have to be roused out of bed for early morning flights; gone were the long airport lobby waits with fans bugging players for autographs while they desperately tried to catch a snooze on the plastic chairs. The Pistons now leave when they want to, eat what they want to eat, and do it in comfort five miles up while looking at game videos and preparing to face their next opponent.

"In basketball, the name of the game is winning," said Jack McCloskey. "The way we look at it is that even just one more victory a year may make the difference between having a playoff advantage (where all the home playoff receipts go to the home team) and not having that advantage.

"Owning that plane escalates our travel costs by 100 percent," said McCloskey, "and you probably couldn't justify the cost of it to an accountant. Still, since we can travel when we want, we feel that, on the conservative side, owning the plane gives us an

NBA Home Records
As Home Stands Progress

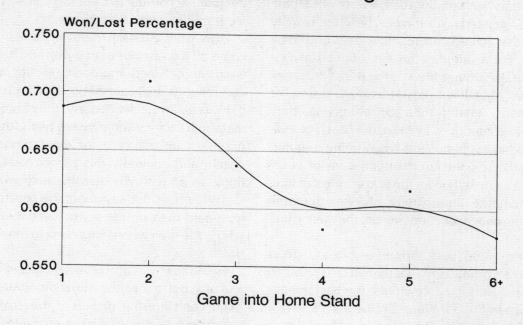

Won/Lost Percentage

Game into Home Stand

extra four wins every year. It also extends the playing careers of our players by a few years as well."

Adrian Dantley, the tenth leading scorer in NBA history, and the leading scorer for two seasons with the Pistons, was traded to Dallas in February of last season for moody small forward Mark Aguirre, the

Mavs' all-time scorer (13,390 in 8 seasons). The sudden trade triggered a boycott from Dantley, who not only wanted a new contract, but also wanted Mav owner Carter to buy his jet back from the Pistons. "There's no question that a private jet can add years to a guy's career," said Dantley. "I

NBA Home Records
As Home Stands Wind Down

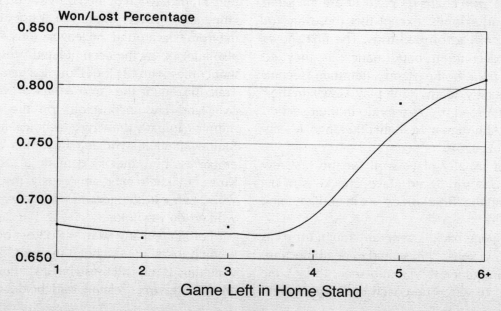

Won/Lost Percentage

Game Left in Home Stand

thought I was going to play 20 years in the NBA, but now I'm looking at 17 without that plane."

While most NBA teams play better at home, the great ones play well on the road, even with all the problems associated with travel. These are usually the teams that have been together as a unit for a long time. For example, the Cleveland Cavalier players average among the youngest in the league (27.38 years), but have played as a solid unit for three seasons, taking their drubbings as they matured into contenders. Even so, the coach of a talented team has his hands full when trying to pump up his squad before the fourth or fifth game of a five-game trip at a time when all the players are thinking about going home. Surprisingly, it's often the same problem the coach encounters on the first game back home.

"The first game back home is often a good chance for a visiting team that's had a day off to catch a win," said Jerry Reynolds, the Sacramento coach. Chicago Bull GM Jerry Krause agrees. "It's a bitch," said Krause. "The players automatically assume that they'll win because they're in front of their fans, and they end up not playing as hard as they should."

Harry Weltman, GM of the Nets, sees the first home game after a long trip as just a continuation of the last game on the road. "We often see a letdown, a loss of concentration, and we never really know what to expect from the team," said Weltman.

Do Weltman's views hold water? We created two studies to find out, and as it turns out, he's surprisingly accurate. The charts on page 11 are the same as the two earlier ones, except that these are for home stands instead of road trips. The first shows how teams decline in performance as they go deeper into their home stand after their second game. Surprisingly, teams don't play as well in their first game off a road trip as they do in their second game home. Although it's a slight difference, it's significant (about .025).

"Our team usually plays well for the first few games of a road trip," said Dave Checketts of his Jazz, "but then the 'Road Blues' set in and anything can happen.

"The first game back is generally tough for us as well," said Checketts. "I'm scared to death because the players are generally flat and seem to lack the effort needed to win. The coach has to give them

some Knute Rockne pep speech in the locker room. But often it isn't enough." The Jazz usually have trouble in the first half of their first game back from the road, according to Checketts. "The players realize it and recover. Sometimes."

How does a coach motivate a team that's just come off a disastrous road swing and has an equally tough home stand approaching? "It's a fairly difficult thing to do," said Kings coach Jerry Reynolds. "This is a players' league, and they know that. With their high salaries and pension plans, the tenth man on the team makes a lot more money than the coach, and generally this player has little, if anything, to do with whether the team wins or loses.

"What does this say about the coach, who is the least-paid man on the team," said Reynolds, "but who is the man who is supposed to have all the control?"

Every coach is at the mercy of his top players, and it's not a healthy situation, notes Reynolds. "You can't fire the players if they can't be motivated because they all have guaranteed contracts. And since you really don't have any voice in selecting the players you want on the team, if the ones you do have don't want to produce for you, it's you who gets fired. You can try to motivate them and rotate your talent, but it's really up to the players to win."

"The Road" and all the pressures associated with trying to win get not only to the players, but to coaches as well. Last season Jack Ramsay quit the Pacers after 20-plus years in the league and an NBA title. Frank Layden of the Jazz gave up the sidelines, citing among other things the abuse he was receiving from fans around the league. Jerry Reynolds was also affected by the accumulated stress and fatigue that comes with his job. During a game against the Trail Blazers at the Arco Arena, Reynolds keeled over and lay unconscious on the floor for six minutes, initially drawing a technical foul(!) from ref Blaine Reichelt, who felt Reynolds was trying to embarrass him after he'd made a call against the Kings. Reichelt later generously rescinded the T while two cardiologists in attendance at the game worked on Reynolds.

"I didn't feel any pain," said Reynolds later, after being hooked up to a heart monitor, "except when watching us miss all those layups." Reynolds recovered (it was stress-related, said the doctors, who had

Reynolds taken to a hospital) and eventually Sacramento won the game 112–111.

When the regular 82-game season finally comes to a close in late April and the 16 top teams move on to the playoff rounds, Part II of the NBA season begins in earnest. The home court advantage becomes less of an advantage. Last season all of the playoff teams finished with winning home records, posting an overall .797 winning record. In the playoffs the overall home court records were .548.

"You play several games in the same arena and have a chance to rest," said Stu Inman, the former Trail Blazer head coach and current director of player personnel for the Miami Heat, explaining the difference in regular season and playoff home court advantages. "With the equality that we have in the league, with all things being somewhat equal, it's just that much more difficult to win—anywhere."

We've taken the liberty of preparing a little chart listing the teams of the NBA in order of the home court advantage by games (see below). In addition, we've included a couple of other little fun facts.

Well, now, would you look at that! Denver made it right to the top of the list. Anyone here from the New York area? Remember when the Knicks lost out there in the early part of last season? There was

more than a bit of bitching and moaning about the disadvantages of playing in the rarefied air of the Mile High City. From the stats, however, it seems that the paranoia was justified, since it gets every team that goes out there.

The other teams at the top all play in somewhat out-of-the-way cities, such as Portland, Phoenix, San Antonio, and Seattle. Could travel weariness be the biggest factor in the home team's favor? It's one hypothesis to take seriously. There's another one that we've formulated, however.

Besides playing in the least accessible of the NBA cities, the top home court teams are also pretty much the only act in town. Even if you *do* consider Seattle a major-league baseball town, the top nine teams on this list share their market with a total of only nine other major sports franchises. In contrast, the bottom five teams each share their markets with squads in every other major sport! Fifteen sports teams in all, in only five towns. If one subscribes to the theory that the crowd is the sixth man on the court, it might make sense that the fans in Portland and San Antonio are able to give their teams much more undivided, if not rabid, attention. Anyway, it's worth thinking about. (For a more complete breakdown of the numbers, see the Appendix.)

Home Court Value

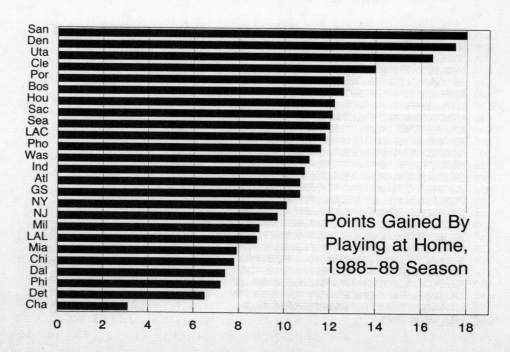

Points Gained By Playing at Home, 1988–89 Season

Team Competition
In NBA Cities

Team	NFL	MLB	NHL
Atlanta	X	X	
Boston	X	X	X
Charlotte			
Chicago	X	X	X
Cleveland	X	X	
Dallas	X	X	
Denver	X		
Detroit	X	X	X
Golden State	X	X	
Houston	X	X	
Indiana	X		
LA Clippers	X	X	X
LA Lakers	X	X	X
Miami	X		
Milwaukee	X	X	
New Jersey	X	X	X
New York	X	X	X
Philadelphia	X	X	X
Phoenix	X		
Portland			
Sacramento			
San Antonio			
Seattle	X	X	
Utah			
Washington	X		X

(NFL = football, MLB = baseball, NHL = hockey)

There's one little thing that you probably think we've forgotten. Although it doesn't make much of a difference when you're looking at the results for a season, certain elements out there might be concerned with the spread. Breakdowns get even more interesting here, although it helps the Boston mystique once again. In the 1988–89 season, Boston had a 7.1-point scoring margin at home and were outscored by 5.5 on the road, giving them a 12.6-point spread between home and road games. Divide that by two, and we find that the Celtics played 6.3 points per game better at home than they would have on a neutral court. Now for the surprises. Five teams outperformed Boston in this measure, raising their scoring edge by 7.9 ppg on average. Which teams led all others? Which teams pulled it off? Would you believe . . . Utah, San Antonio, and Denver? Well, believe it—it's true.

Another possibly interesting but unrelated statistic we found was that only four teams scored as much as or more than their opponents did on the road. Detroit (+2.8 on the road) and the Lakers (+2.7), the two-time finalists, were two of the four. The other teams were "upstarts" Phoenix and Cleveland. The Clippers and Nets did their fans proud, being the only non-expansion teams to be

Home/Away Scoring Edges

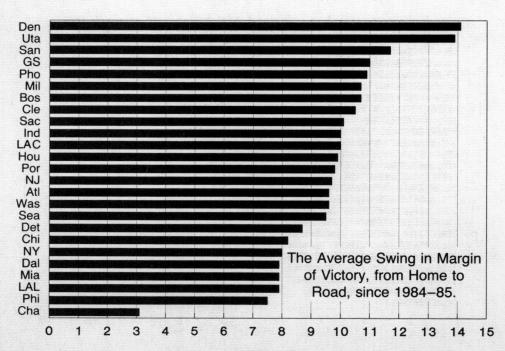

The Average Swing in Margin of Victory, from Home to Road, since 1984–85.

outscored at home. And what of the Lakers? Just about the only constant across the games and points studies were the two-time NBA champions. They were near the basement in points swing, and lead only Philly and Charlotte over the past five years. How does the best team in the league have the worst home court advantage? It's really bizarre, but then again, the Fabulous Forum fans (oops! the Great Western Forum fans) are known for their tranquillity.

THE MAGIC THAT IS THE GARDEN IN BOSTON

Boston Garden typically springs to mind when we think about home court advantages. Built in 1928, it is currently the oldest of the 26 NBA arenas. Although it seats only 14,890, the Celtic fans are rabid and absolutely fanatical about their team. Sixteen championship banners in 43 years gives them plenty to cheer about. By the start of the 1992 season there may still be only 16 banners hanging (unless management brings in a stronger supporting cast for Larry Bird), but the Garden will be no more. A new 20,000-seat, $85 million Garden will take the place of its predecessor. And the days of the 100-degree temperatures for playoff games, loose floorboards, obstructed views, and cramped locker rooms will come to an end.

GARDEN HIGHLIGHTS

November 16, 1946
The Celts with Connie Simmons (10.3 ppg that year—he might have fit in nicely with the low-scoring Heat) lose to the Toronto Huskies and had only a 14–16 home record, third worst in the 11-team league.

April 13, 1957
With Bill Russell playing in his first NBA Championships, Boston goes to two overtimes to beat the St. Louis Hawks for its first title.

June 8, 1986
Boston wins two of its home games, plus another one in Houston in the championship series, then

returns home to the Garden to trounce the Rockets 114–97 for its 16th NBA title.

ROAD WARRIORS

The NBA went to an 82-game schedule in the 1967–68 season. Here's a brief year-by-year look at some of the more notable road records posted by the teams on their 41-game journeys around the league.

1967–68 Boston, 20–16 on the road, 28–9 at home, 6–3 on neutral courts, defeats the Lakers by winning the deciding fourth game in Los Angeles.

1968–69 Celtics are so-so with a 21–19 road record, but win a two-pointer in Los Angeles in the seventh game of the Championships.

1969–70 The Knicks post a league-best 27–10 road record (30–11 home, 3–1 neutral), yet lose two of three in Los Angeles in the Championships. Take the Lakers 113–99 in the Garden for the title.

1970–71 Milwaukee, behind rookie Kareem Abdul-Jabbar and his 31.7 ppg average, goes 28–13 on the road and shuts out the Bullets 4–0 for its only NBA title.

1971–72 The Lakers post a 31–7 road record and roll past the Knicks 4–1 for the title.

1972–73 Boston has a 32–8 road record but loses to New York in the Eastern Conference finals as New York (21–18 on the road) goes on to defeat the Lakers 4–1 for the NBA crown.

1973–74 Milwaukee (24–6 road) and Boston (21–18 road) battle it out in a seven-game championship series won by the Celtics on the road, 102–87.

1974–75 Golden State takes a negative road record (17–24) but a high-powered offense (108.5 ppg, 30.6 coming from Rick Barry) and tramples the Washington Bullets (24–17 road) in four games for the Championship.

1975–76 Phoenix (15–26 road), the third best finisher in the Pacific Division and barely over the .500 mark, marches past Seattle and Golden State before losing 4–2 to the Celtics for the title.

1976–77 The Trail Blazers go 35–6 at home and lukewarm 14–27 on the road, but overpower Philadelphia for their only NBA crown.

1977–78 The Bullets (15–26 road) finish 8 games behind Central Division leader San Antonio

during regular-season play, but win the NBA title 4–3 from Seattle.

1978–79 The Supersonics lose 10 games at home, go 21–20 on the road during the regular season, winning their division title and putting the bite on the Bullets, 4–1, for the Championship.

1979–80 The Lakers post a league-best 37–4 home record, are tied for second best on the road with 23–18 with the Sixers, and beat the Sixers on the road 123–107 in the sixth game of the series for the title.

1980–81 The Celts post a 27–14 road record (35–6 at home) and roll past the Rockets (15–26 road) 4–2 for the title.

1981–82 Celts post league-best road record, 28–13, but lose to Philadelphia in Eastern Conference finals. Los Angeles took second best road record (27–14) and defeated Philadelphia (third best road record, 26–15) for the NBA title.

1982–83 The Sixers have league-best record (65–17), losing only 11 away from home en route to blanking the Lakers 4–0 for the title.

1983–84 Celtics lose 12 on the road, 8 at home. Come the playoffs, they go 3–7 on the road, but manage to take the title 4–3 from the Lakers.

1984–85 The Lakers have second best record overall (62–20, 15 road losses) and defeat Boston

4–2—the best road team in the league (28–13).

1985–86 The Celts lose 14 games on the road, 1 at home, and defeat the Rockets 4–2.

1986–87 Los Angeles has best road and home record (28–13, 37–4) and defeats Boston (22–19, 39–2) 4–2 for the title.

1987–88 Lakers lose 15 road games, 5 at home, while the Pistons lose 21 on the road and 7 at home. The Lakers prevail despite winning only 30% of their road playoff games (3–7) and win their fifth title of the decade.

The following are three more charts demonstrating the home court advantage. Chart 1 shows the home court winning percentage of all NBA teams, year by year, from the league's inception to the present. Note the steady decline of the advantage from 1951 to about 1970, as the league spread out and became bigger. In the seventies, the trend was reversed, as home court advantage took a decided upturn. After a brief correction (this is like the stock market, huh?), the advantage has been increasing at a more pronounced rate since 1981.

CHART 1

NBA Home Court Dominance
1947–Present

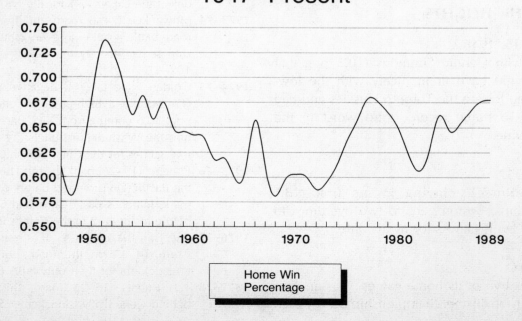

Home Win Percentage

Chart 2 illustrates those fun facts we mentioned earlier: a list of the only teams ever to play better on the road than at home.

CHART 2

Only six NBA teams since the league began have posted better records on the road than at home:

		Total			**Home**			**Road**			**Neutral**				
		W	L	Pct	W	L	Pct	W	L	Pct	W	L	Pct	GB	PctB
Bos	1975	60	22	732	28	13	683	32	9	780	0	0	0	-4	098
NY	1948	26	22	542	12	12	500	14	10	583	0	0	0	-2	083
NYN	1977	22	60	268	10	31	244	12	29	293	0	0	0	-2	049
NY	1968	43	39	524	20	17	541	21	16	568	2	6	250	-1	027
NY	1956	35	37	486	14	14	500	15	14	517	6	9	400	-1	017
Chi	1968	29	53	354	11	22	333	12	23	343	6	8	429	-1	010

In addition, these five teams each won more games on the road than at home, although each had a better home percentage (due to a difference in games played in each category):

		Total			**Home**			**Road**			**Neutral**			
		W	L	Pct	W	L	Pct	W	L	Pct	W	L	Pct	GB
Bos	1962	60	20	750	23	5	821	26	12	684	11	3	786	-3
Bos	1961	57	22	722	21	7	750	24	11	686	12	4	750	-3
Mil	1955	26	46	361	6	11	353	9	19	321	11	19	367	-3
Chi	1949	38	22	633	16	8	667	18	14	563	4	0	1000	-2
Cin	1969	41	41	500	15	13	536	16	21	432	10	7	588	-1

Chart 3 is a list of each team's road record in 1988–89, broken down by game into the trip.

CHART 3

Road Records, 1988-89 Season

			Game Into Roadtrip										
Team	Total		First		Second		Third		Fourth		Fifth		Sixth +
Atl	19	22	10	11	3	9	4	1	1	0	0	1	1	0
Bos	10	31	3	17	5	6	1	3	0	4	0	1	1	0
Cha	8	33	3	19	2	9	2	2	0	2	1	1	0	0
Chi	17	24	10	15	2	4	2	2	1	2	1	1	1	0
Cle	20	21	12	11	5	5	1	4	2	0	0	1	0	0
Dal	14	27	9	9	2	8	2	5	1	3	0	2	0	0
Den	9	32	4	16	1	7	2	4	1	3	1	2	0	0
Det	26	15	16	10	6	0	2	2	1	2	0	1	1	0
GS	14	27	6	15	1	7	3	2	1	2	2	0	1	1
Hou	14	27	8	10	4	7	1	4	1	3	0	2	0	1
Ind	8	33	4	17	2	7	1	4	1	4	0	1	0	0
LAC	4	37	2	16	1	9	0	5	1	4	0	2	0	1
LAL	22	19	13	7	3	6	3	2	2	1	1	1	0	2
Mia	3	38	2	16	0	9	1	5	0	5	0	2	0	1
Mil	18	23	9	14	4	5	3	2	1	1	1	0	0	1
NJ	9	32	6	15	1	10	1	3	0	3	1	1	0	0
NY	17	24	10	9	3	8	2	4	1	1	1	0	0	2
Phi	16	25	7	10	4	7	1	2	0	3	2	1	2	2
Pho	20	21	7	14	6	4	3	2	2	1	1	0	1	0
Por	11	30	5	14	2	9	1	4	1	2	2	0	0	1
Sac	6	35	3	15	2	9	1	5	0	3	0	1	0	2
San	3	38	2	18	1	11	0	6	0	2	0	1	0	0
Sea	16	25	13	7	2	8	1	4	0	3	0	2	0	1
Uta	17	24	4	12	6	5	2	4	1	2	3	0	1	1
Was	10	31	3	19	4	7	2	2	1	2	0	1	0	0
Total	331	694	171	336	72	176	42	83	20	58	17	25	9	16

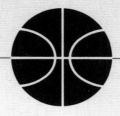

CHAPTER TWO

The Stats That Matter

If you want to figure out which team won a particular game, which *one* game stat would you want to know? Final rebounds? Assists? Of course not. The one stat you'd want to know is the final score. How does a team win a game, after all? When we posed this same question to the GMs and coaches around the league, we received a variety of responses. Sure, the final score is important, they all agreed, but other stats interest them, especially at halftime, because they clarify what their team is doing, what direction it's going in. "At halftime I want to know the field goal percentage by the opponent," said John Nash of Philadelphia. "This will tell me if my team is playing good defense."

"Turnovers and the number of foul shots are what I look at on the stat sheet," said Laker GM Jerry West. "That will indicate to me whether the team is concentrating. Also, these stats tell me whether the team has been aggressive and quick."

There's not one specific stat that Jack McCloskey of Detroit looks at. They all have importance to him, but one stat alone can't determine a clue to the final outcome. "In a game against Boston we shot 30 more times, had 20 more offensive rebounds, and still lost the game," he said.

While the final score is the final indicator of success, for Jan Volk of the Celtics, turnovers are a significant measure because they tell him how the Celts are doing offensively. The number of foul shots attempted also lets him know how aggressive the team is on offense, as well as how aggressive the

opponent is. "Stats are informative," said Volk, "but they can't be viewed in the abstract." (Author's note: In *this* Abstract they can!)

Jerry Krause of Chicago is far from being a stat freak. "You can take the sheet and wipe your a —— with it," said Krause. "Stats are deceptive. If I saw a game, I know what I saw and don't need a listing of performance breakdowns to tell me things. For example, stats aren't indicative of a player's value to the team. There's nothing on the typical stat sheet that counts the number of charges taken, or who dove for a loose ball, or who helped out on the fast break. I don't let stats influence me because they don't measure the heart of a player and what that player truly means to a team."

While an occasional hoop fan might look at the number of points scored in a game and be satisfied, others want more information. "Points are what I look at last," said Norm Sonju of the Mavericks. "I want to know how many turnovers we had, how many offensive rebounds, and what our total rebounds were. This will give me a pretty good idea of how aggressive the team is."

Dave Checketts doesn't look at stat sheets at halftime, but relies instead on the Utah Jazz shot chart for information because it lets him see clearly where the points are coming from on the court. "In theory, I'd like to see two thirds of our shots taken inside, one third outside," he said. "Twice as many shots inside the paint will give us a better chance to score and get to the free throw line. When you have play-

ers like Karl Malone and Thurl Bailey on your team, I want the ball going in to them most of the time." The NBA game is all inside, says Checketts, and teams that rely on the outside shot exclusively will die from it, too.

Carl Scheer of the Charlotte Hornets is a stat man, but at halftime he looks closely at the assist-to-turnover ratio and the total number of shots taken by both his Hornets and the opposition. "The team that can take 100 shots a game usually makes fewer turnovers, plays an up-tempo game, and shoots 45% or better," said Scheer. "If we can get off more shots than the opposition, we have a much better chance of winning."

Since the offensive system of the Denver Nuggets is geared to a running game, their strategy is to get off at least 10 more shots per game than their opposition. "We're not such a good shooting team, so we need that 10-shot cushion by the half," said Pete Babcock, the Nugget GM, who looks at the FGA stat very closely. "If we get off 20 more shots a game than the opponent, we generally win."

Turnovers are an area of consistent weakness for the Sacramento Kings, so coach Jerry Reynolds checks that stat at the half. "I hope the turnovers are caused because of our youth and the fact that the players are playing together for the first time," said Reynolds. "Time will tell."

According to Stu Inman, Miami's director of player personnel, free throws, more than any other stat, will give you a pretty good picture of what your team is doing. "The team that goes to the line the most usually wins a greater percentage of games," noted Inman. "I'm also big on steals. They show if a player is alert, hustles, is aggressive, and has made a commitment to play on the defensive end of the court."

Del Harris, coach of the Milwaukee Bucks, hardly gives the stat sheet a second glance at the half. "I basically know what went on in the game. I was there, I saw it, the players saw it, too. It's unnecessary."

Still, for the people who *weren't* there, and even for those who were at the game, stats do tell a story of their own. Yet despite the mountain of statistics you'll find in this book and elsewhere, there's only one final statistic that matters. A team wins a game by outscoring its opponents on game night.

Sure, other stats contribute mightily to the final score. But you'll never hear a sportscaster say "Sacramento outrebounded Boston 73–64 last night, raising their record to 12–54." You *might* hear, however, "Boston outscored Sacramento 143–107." If you tell us the number of points a team scores and allows in a single game, we betcha we'll be able to tell you the winner every time.

Usually, you'll find that something that happens in a particular game will hold true throughout a season. It won't work *exactly* the same way every time, but, for example, you can expect Michael Jordan to score about 35 points in a game. At the end of the season, his scoring average will be around 35.0. Sometimes he'll score 45, sometimes only 15.

Therefore, it would make sense to say that the easiest way to figure out a team's expected won-lost record would be to take into account the statistics that matter most in each win or loss. Those stats are, of course, points scored and points allowed. In a single game, a team can either go 1.000 (1–0) or .000 (0–1). However, over a full season, there are 82 games. Therefore, there are 82 possible final records, from 0–82 to 82–0.

This just makes things a little bit harder. If the Knicks, as they did in 1987–88, score around 105.5 points per game while allowing 106.0, does it mean they will go 0–82? Of course not. They scored about $1/2$ point less in an "average" game than they allowed. They obviously didn't lose 82 games by $1/2$ point each. Just as with Jordan's scoring, we can figure out, on average, what to expect from the Knicks given these numbers.

But how exactly are these numbers all related? In a single game, there can't be a tie. However, in a season, there can be a team with a 41–41 record. You would expect this team to score the same number of points as it gives up, since 41–41 means the team is about even with its competition. The number you get when you divide points against into points for should be 1.00 for this team (that is, if it scores 103.0/game and allows 103.0/game, the number would be 103.0/103.0, or 1.00). In this case, the team's winning percentage is exactly half of its PF/PA ratio.

Does this mean, then, that in order for a team to win 25% of its games, it should score only half as much as its opponents? Not at all. The worst team *ever* was the 1972–73 Philadelphia 76ers. Checking in at a measly 9–73, they still scored 90% as many points as their opponents. The difference

between a .500 team and a .110 team is . . . only 10 percent? How can this be?

The answer comes when you compare basketball to other sports. In baseball, hockey, and other one-point-at-a-time sports, teams take a close victory by a 1–0 score. When's the last time you saw a shutout in basketball? In basketball, a tight win is a 101–100 squeaker. While the final margin of victory is the same, the final *percentage* of victory isn't. An average baseball team scores around 4½ runs per game. One run more than that is a 22% difference! If your basketball team scores 100 points per game, and exceeds that by a single point, that's only a 1% edge. Basketball, then, is a much closer game, percentagewise, than low-scoring sports. If you take a 5–4 game in baseball, the smallest of margins, that would project to a 125–100 game in hoops. In which game would you be more likely to see the reserves get their time?

We've taken the records for each NBA team in the past decade, to try to find the correlation between a team's scoring ratio and its won-lost percentage. Making a chart with the team's won-lost record on the Y (vertical) axis and its scoring ratio on the X (horizontal) axis, we show this graph below.

We then used something called a least-squares fit, which is a way to find the equation that best describes a group of points. What we found was:

- A team whose scoring ratio is about .8628 should lose all its games.
- Every point the ratio goes up after .8628 increases the won-lost percentage by about 3.6266 points. If a team's scoring ratio is .8728, its won-lost percentage should be .036226. If a team's scoring ratio is .9 (90.0 for, 100.0 against), its won-lost percentage should be about .135. So a team that scores 90.0 ppg but allows 100.0 ppg should go 11–71 over an 82-game schedule.

So what we know is this: Barring luck or other factors, a team will always score at *least* 86% as many points as its opponents over the course of a season (86.28%, to be exact). Any team falling below this ratio will most likely not win a game, and even *with* the Clippers in the league, this isn't likely anytime soon. Anytime a team exceeds this ratio, each point above it will be worth about 3.6 points in its won-lost percentage, on up to a team whose ratio is 1.1385, who should be expected to win *all* its games. So all you really have to do is score 114 ppg and allow 100, and you'll be in the high seventies, winwise.

Is it formulas you want? Here you go. Just divide

Scoring Ratio vs. Won–Lost Record

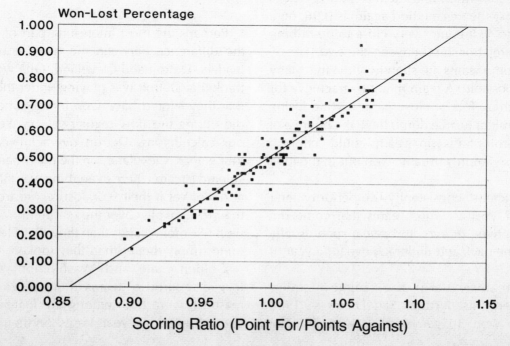

a team's PF by its PA (either the total points or average points per game will do, since the ratio will remain the same), and plug it into either of these two formulas:

(The math-freak version)

$$\text{Expected W–L Pct.} = 3.6266 \times (\text{PF/PA} - .8628)$$

(The English-equivalent, rest-of-us version)

Find a team's scoring ratio by dividing its points scored by its points allowed. From this number subtract .8628 and multiply the number you get by 3.6266. This will give you the team's expected won-lost percentage. If those numbers are too big, just use .86 and 3.6; you'll get close enough.

With all the teams we looked at—202 to be exact—there were only 9 teams that were more than 6 games off this formula; 163 teams were within 4 games of their predicted percentage. Why would these teams be off? Since the formula describes the teams as a whole, some fluctuation is probable. It's impossible to get an exact formula for anything more than 2 points, usually. Still, the correlation between the formula and actual performances (using the least-squares method again) is 0.96, on a scale of −1 to 1. It comes very close to describing perfectly the relationship between the two.

But still, some teams are slightly off. Why? Many reasons are possible. A team might overachieve for a while, winning lots of close games while losing blowouts. It might just be dumb luck, the bounce of a ball or the roll of a layup. Teams could "choke," although these failures usually even out in the long run.

Do any teams consistently outperform their expectations? Well . . . no. Teams that come out ahead over a two- or even three-year span usually fall back to the pack and underachieve for a year or two.

Which teams were the biggest over/underachievers this decade? San Diego in 1980 should have won 30 games; they won 38. The

Warriors were outscored by about 200 points in 1987, yet went 42–40 (7.3 games above expectations). On the flip side, two teams in 1986 were far ahead of all others in the decade in terms of failure. Seattle was outscored by only 8 points (8564–8572), yet finished *20* games under .500. At worst, they should have been 40–42. Milwaukee, that same year, had a scoring ratio of 1.086, exactly the same as the '87 Lakers. However, the Lakers won 65 games, the Bucks came away with only 57. Dumb luck or no dumb luck.

In 1988–89, here's how the league stacked up:

Team	PF	PA	PF/PA	Actual W	L	Expected W	L	+/-	
LAC	106.2	116.2	0.9139	21	61	15.2	66.8	5.8	*Better Than*
Det	106.6	100.8	1.0575	63	19	57.9	24.1	5.1	*Expected*
Was	108.3	110.4	0.9810	40	42	35.1	46.9	4.9	
Mia	97.8	109.0	0.8972	15	67	10.2	71.8	4.8	
GS	116.6	116.9	0.9974	43	39	40.0	42.0	3.0	
NJ	103.7	110.1	0.9419	26	56	23.5	58.5	2.5	
Chi	106.4	105.0	1.0133	47	35	44.8	37.2	2.2	
Cha	104.5	113.0	0.9248	20	62	18.4	63.6	1.6	
Hou	108.5	107.5	1.0093	45	37	43.6	38.4	1.4	
Phi	111.9	110.4	1.0136	46	36	44.8	37.2	1.2	
NY	116.7	112.9	1.0337	52	30	50.8	31.2	1.2	
Sac	105.5	111.0	0.9505	27	55	26.1	55.9	0.9	
Dal	103.5	104.7	0.9885	38	44	37.4	44.6	0.6	
San	105.5	112.8	0.9353	21	61	21.6	60.4	-0.6	
Den	118.0	116.3	1.0146	44	38	45.1	36.9	-1.1	
Ind	106.9	111.1	0.9622	28	54	29.6	52.4	-1.6	
Sea	112.1	109.2	1.0266	47	35	48.7	33.3	-1.7	
Bos	109.2	108.1	1.0102	42	40	43.8	38.2	-1.8	
Mil	108.9	105.3	1.0342	49	33	51.0	31.0	-2.0	
Atl	111.0	106.1	1.0462	52	30	54.5	27.5	-2.5	
LAL	114.7	107.5	1.0670	57	25	60.7	21.3	-3.7	
Uta	104.7	99.7	1.0502	51	31	55.7	26.3	-4.7	
Por	114.6	113.1	1.0133	39	43	44.7	37.3	-5.7	
Cle	108.8	101.2	1.0751	57	25	63.1	18.9	-6.1	*Worse Than*
Pho	118.6	110.9	1.0694	55	27	61.4	20.6	-6.4	*Expected*

Perhaps the most interesting part of this chart is the difference between the two Central Division leaders, Detroit and Cleveland. One would tend to think that Detroit was playing under their capacity, that they should have won more games than they did during the slow regular season. Yet, based on our calculations, Detroit *overachieved* by about four games. Cleveland, on the other hand, was considered a team where everything was falling right all at once. Yet if their won-lost record truly reflected their level of play over the season, they would have won 5½ more games than they did! Cleveland was, quite simply, better than they looked.

Golden State and Washington, two of the league's "surprise" teams (though for very different reasons), were both among the league's won-lost overachievers last year, based on their actual level

of play. The dregs of the league (Miami, Charlotte, the Clips, and the Nets) ended up near the top, too, which leads to the inference that the formula might be better suited for middleweight teams, rather than those on the edge of greatness or extinction. However, this is the first year for which we've noticed this effect. And the numbers for San Antonio were right on, while those for the Pacers swung wide in the *other* direction (they were better than they looked). So we wouldn't worry too much about the bum-bunching at the top. As they say, it'll all even out eventually.

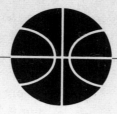

CHAPTER THREE

The Three-Point Shot

"There were three significant rule changes in the NBA game that were tremendous," noted Norm Sonju, the Dallas Mav GM. "First, there was the 24-second clock, which kept teams from sitting on the ball; second was widening the lane from twelve to sixteen feet; and third was the introduction of the three-point shot."

The NBA moved to the three-point shot in the 1979–80 season, and, although little used at first, and even now still not fully exploited, the three-pointer is slowly becoming an offensive staple and a surefire hit with the fans. "While not as important as the 24-second clock," said Sonju, "for the excitement value it can't be beat and I'm all for it."

Before the three came to the NBA, jump shooting was on its way to becoming a lost art. Not quite in the category of the set shot, but fast approaching it. The game was being played almost exclusively *inside* with the taller and stronger players demanding and getting the ball to power it up to the basket. Yawn. Shrug shoulders. "Yo! Hot dog over here!"

"Ten years ago it was a big man's game," admitted Dave Checketts of the Jazz. "Players no longer worked on their outside shooting or even golf during the off-season. Instead, they were in the weight room pumping iron to get stronger. In the end, it was the little guy who could shoot who lost out to these bruisers who could make a two-point shot with a higher degree of efficiency by just cramming it in the basket."

The impetus behind the move to Rollerball-style hoops was the high percentage of making the inside shot. For many coaches a "good shot" is one taken as close to the hoop as possible. Although not necessarily exciting hoops, what with guys throwing it down with their elbows, the inside game wins games for teams. Coaches, thirsting for more W's, keep ordering the ball passed into the hole. And for the most part, it will remain like this until some player comes along who can consistently prove he's capable of hitting more than half of his outside moonballs.

Luckily for the NBA hoop junkie, three-point marksmen like Trent Tucker, Reggie Miller, Danny Ainge, and Dale Ellis have helped change the "big man gets the rock" philosophy by canning canaries from the 23'9" stripe with enough regularity to make opposing coaches start to rethink their own offensive ways. "It's changed the game in a lot of ways that people don't yet realize," said Jerry West, one of the finest jump shooters in the history of the world. "I've seen the three-point shot make it very difficult for us at times to protect even sizable leads when we play against teams with the good three-point shooters."

Amen. It's pearls of wisdom like that that help explain why fans are now glued to their seats right to the last shot instead of bolting for the parking lot midway through the final period as they used to.

While West says that most teams haven't fully utilized the three, it won't be long before many start following the lead of the Knicks, a team that set the NBA standard in three-pointers attempted (1147, 15.1% of all their field goals) and connected (386, for a .337 3G%) this past season. "In the NBA, any team that does something new and is successful

Highest Ratio of Threes To Twos Taken, 1988-89

Player	Team	FG%	3G%	2:3
Tucker,Trent	NY	0.454	0.399	0.96
Adams,Michael	DEN	0.433	0.357	1.33
Cooper,Michael	LAL	0.431	0.381	1.35
Hodges,Craig	CHI	0.472	0.417	1.39
Brooks,Scott	PHI	0.420	0.359	1.42
Anderson,Richard	POR	0.417	0.348	1.47
Pressley,Harold	SAC	0.439	0.403	1.96
Floyd,Eric	HOU	0.443	0.373	2.06
Henderson,Gerald	PHI	0.414	0.308	2.25
Newman,Johnny	NY	0.475	0.338	2.33
Miller,Reggie	IND	0.479	0.402	2.41
Ainge,Danny	SAC	0.457	0.380	2.45
Berry,Ricky	SAC	0.450	0.406	2.54
McGee,Mike	NJ	0.473	0.365	2.60
Davis,Brad	DAL	0.483	0.317	2.75
Higgins,Rod	GS	0.476	0.393	2.77
Bol,Manute	GS	0.369	0.220	2.78
Paxson,John	CHI	0.480	0.338	2.86
Sikma,Jack	MIL	0.431	0.380	2.87
Harper,Derek	DAL	0.477	0.356	3.05
Jackson,Mark	NY	0.467	0.338	3.27
Price,Mark	CLE	0.526	0.441	3.77
Ellis,Dale	SEA	0.501	0.478	4.04
Morris,Chris	NJ	0.457	0.366	4.17
Porter,Terry	POR	0.471	0.361	4.23
Ehlo,Craig	CLE	0.475	0.390	4.24
Majerle,Dan	PHO	0.419	0.329	4.27
Griffith,Darrell	UTA	0.446	0.311	4.33
Williams,Reggie	LAC	0.438	0.288	4.71
Hawkins,Hersey	PHI	0.455	0.428	4.85
Skiles,Scott	IND	0.448	0.267	4.89
Wilkins,Gerald	NY	0.452	0.297	4.95

brings to the game. "It's a tremendous tool," said Sonju. "And it has a high degree of difficulty that has put fan interest at a high level every time that the shot is launched."

Once upon a time, the dunk once offered the pro game excitement and a display of athleticism unequaled anywhere else except in ballet. But for the most part now, a seven footer throwing one down and rattling the rim only brings yawns. So, what else is new? It's expected, it's a modern-day layup, for goodness' sake. Until the NBA raises the hoop to, say, eleven feet, there's no reason *not* to slam some down.

Most Points <u>Gained</u> By Taking Threes

Player	Team	3G%	2G%	Gain
Ellis,Dale	SEA	0.478	0.507	142.30
Pressley,Harold	SAC	0.403	0.457	87.52
Sundvold,Jon	MIA	0.522	0.444	62.26
Hawkins,Hersey	PHI	0.428	0.461	59.99
Sikma,Jack	MIL	0.380	0.449	51.98
Tucker,Trent	NY	0.399	0.512	50.68
Ainge,Danny	SAC	0.380	0.488	50.36
Floyd,Eric	HOU	0.373	0.478	48.12
Price,Mark	CLE	0.441	0.548	47.56
Berry,Ricky	SAC	0.406	0.467	45.61
Miller,Reggie	IND	0.402	0.511	44.60
Cooper,Michael	LAL	0.381	0.468	43.31
Adams,Michael	DEN	0.357	0.489	42.80
Hodges,Craig	CHI	0.417	0.512	40.68
Johnson,Eddie	PHO	0.413	0.509	37.74
Scott,Byron	LAL	0.399	0.508	34.74
Higgins,Rod	GS	0.393	0.505	28.19

Most Points <u>Lost</u> By Taking Threes

Player	Team	3G%	2G%	Loss
Humphries,Jay	MIL	0.266	0.516	-22.03
Person,Chuck	IND	0.307	0.519	-23.88
Maxwell,Vernon	SAN	0.248	0.466	-24.13
Johnson,Dennis	BOS	0.140	0.459	-24.92
Stockton,John	UTA	0.242	0.561	-26.09
Drexler,Clyde	POR	0.255	0.512	-27.57
Johnson,Earvin	LAL	0.314	0.548	-29.03
Jordan,Michael	CHI	0.265	0.554	-30.57
Mullin,Chris	GS	0.230	0.527	-36.49
Harper,Ron	CLE	0.250	0.540	-38.32
Barkley,Charles	PHI	0.219	0.635	-98.05

The players in the two lists above either gained or lost the most points by shooting three-pointers last year. All the Gainers added 25 or more points to their scoring totals, while all the Losers knocked off at least 20 points. The Gain/Loss number is figured by pretending all the player's three-pointers were shot as two-pointers at the higher 2G% rate, and finding the difference between the total number of points each would yield.

with it—it doesn't take long before you see copies of that success starting to pop out in the league," says West.

Harry Weltman, the Nets GM, feels that the three-pointer is here to stay, for the most part because of the college players now coming into the league. Currently, the college hoopsters take an average of 23.1 three-pointers a game, while shooting 37.6% from the (relatively close) 19'9" stripe. "Colleges now put a premium on shooting with their long shot, and this helps create shooting specialists," said Weltman. "Since the NBA is in essence what the colleges end up feeding you, you'll see that we're going to have a group of pro players who emphasize the long distance shot."

While the three-pointer may not be as important an offensive innovation in the NBA as the 24-second clock, Norm Sonju of Dallas contends that it's a close second for the excitement that it

The three-pointer, on the other hand, has quickly surpassed the dunk in both marquee value and fan appeal. The bomb, while not a high percentage shot, is still a skill shot, as opposed to the dunk's rather mundane and often characterless grunt, jump-in-your face movements that often go unseen because they happen so quickly. In addition, you don't *need* to hit them as well as a two, because you get more for them. If you're shooting, say, 50% from inside, you can get the same results by hitting 1/3 of your three-pointers. When they start falling, you can watch the opposing coach's face sag a bit in disbelief.

"When the ball is in the air for the three-pointer, you can hear the fans starting to yell 'Three!,' " said the Sonics' Bob Whitsett. "They go crazy if the shot goes in and moan when it's missed. It's like a home run in baseball, fireworks on the fourth of July. It's changed the game for the better, without a doubt."

Carl Scheer was GM of the Denver Nuggets when they played in the ABA, the renegade league where the long shot originated, and was with the team when the shot was first introduced to the NBA. "I remember the NBA committee meeting when the shot was being brought up for a vote," said Scheer. "Red Auerbach stood up and made an impassioned plea to forestall its introduction to the league based solely on tradition. 'If the three-point shot is allowed, should we give one point for a layup and four points for a shot from 30 feet?' he asked." Auerbach was never one to look a gift horse in the mouth, however, and the Celtics consistently led the league in the outside shot in its infancy, lighting them up more often than Red lit up his cigars.

"Notwithstanding, the shot was voted in that day," said Scheer, "and since then it's opened up the game tremendously by spreading the defenses. It's also made it truly a 48-minute game by always giving teams that last chance to shoot their way to victory."

If you watch games closely, you've probably noticed that pro defenses have evolved over the years. Teams now use what Phoenix GM Jerry Colangelo calls "trick defenses" that circumvent NBA defensive coverage guidelines. Teams are trapping, double teaming, and rotating so often, especially down low on the boxes, that many times it appears as if a zone is being played. Oftentimes it is.

In order to get away from this sticky defense and to force the defenders to cover more court (thereby keeping them "honest"), many teams have spread their offenses out on the perimeter. In the process they have made it a lot easier to get wide-open threes. With the "Bomb Squad" lining up at the three-point stripe and defenders hustling out to cover them, especially at the close of tight games, big men are suddenly finding themselves with fewer bodies draped over them down in the paint. The ball is flipped in to these giants, with the result being that fans are treated to a little more one-on-one play down low and less of the bruise-and-bang that had for too long been an NBA staple.

"We're in the entertainment business," said John Nash, the 76er GM. "And the three-point shot has really helped us in that regard. It may be devastating when it's used against you, but it's tremendous if you're the team behind." And that's what makes the bomb FANTASTIC!

Strategy-wise, the three was slow in acceptance. Despite an early "novelty" status, it is only in the past two years that it has been accepted in full. In the chart below, we can see how the increase in threes taken was slow at first but recently has undergone exponential growth (actually *more* than exponential—the line drawn from bar to bar shows what exponential growth would look like). Some teams have traditionally taken far more threes than others, too. Boston has traditionally been the league leader, although the Knicks' big season last year lifted them to third lifetime. Miami and Charlotte, the expansion teams, had only one year to play to accumulate the stats.

History Of The Three
League Totals Since 1980

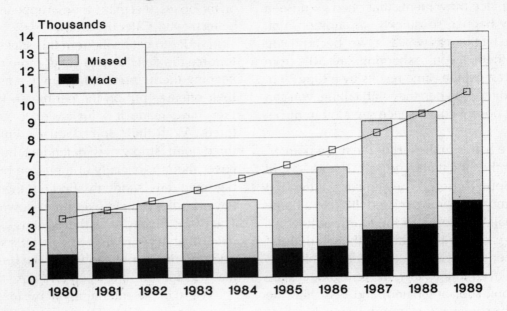

Three-Pointers By Team
1988-89

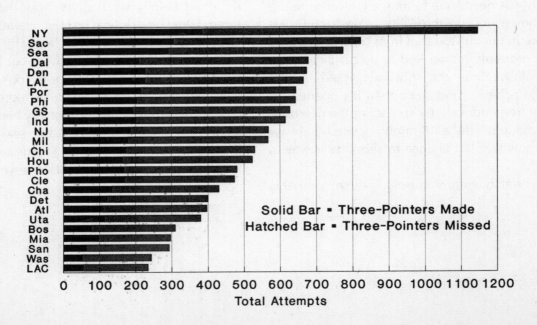

Most Three Point Attempts, 1988-89

Adams,Michael	DEN	465
Ellis,Dale	SEA	339
Ainge,Danny	SAC	305
Tucker,Trent	NY	296
Pressley,Harold	SAC	295
Floyd,Eric	HOU	292
Newman,Johnny	NY	287
Harper,Derek	DAL	278
McGee,Mike	NJ	255
Miller,Reggie	IND	244
Jackson,Mark	NY	240
Porter,Terry	POR	219
Sikma,Jack	MIL	216
Price,Mark	CLE	211
Cooper,Michael	LAL	210
Person,Chuck	IND	205

Highest Three-Point Pct., 1988-89

Player	Team	3GM	3GA	3G%
Sundvold,Jon	MIA	48	92	0.522
Hoppen,Dave	CHA	1	2	0.500
Wittman,Randy	IND	3	6	0.500
Sellers,Brad	CHI	3	6	0.500
Berry,Walter	HOU	1	2	0.500
Dumars,Joe	DET	14	29	0.483
Ellis,Dale	SEA	162	339	0.478
Cummings,Terry	MIL	7	15	0.467
Price,Mark	CLE	93	211	0.441
Hawkins,Hersey	PHI	71	166	0.428
Hodges,Craig	CHI	75	180	0.417
Johnson,Eddie	PHO	71	172	0.413
Berry,Ricky	SAC	65	160	0.406
Pressley,Harold	SAC	119	295	0.403
Miller,Reggie	IND	98	244	0.402
Bailey,Thurl	UTA	2	5	0.400

Most Three Pointers Made, 1988-89

Adams,Michael	DEN	166
Ellis,Dale	SEA	162
Pressley,Harold	SAC	119
Tucker,Trent	NY	118
Ainge,Danny	SAC	116
Floyd,Eric	HOU	109
Harper,Derek	DAL	99
Miller,Reggie	IND	98
Newman,Johnny	NY	97
Price,Mark	CLE	93
McGee,Mike	NJ	93
Sikma,Jack	MIL	82
Jackson,Mark	NY	81
Cooper,Michael	LAL	80
Porter,Terry	POR	79
Scott,Byron	LAL	77
Hodges,Craig	CHI	75

Three-Point Field Goal Attempts Per Game

Number Attempted

Team	1	2	3	4	5	6	7	8	9	10	11	12	13	14	15	16	17	18	19	20	Total
NY	0	0	0	0	0	0	2	2	3	4	8	10	16	5	10	6	6	1	3	6	1147
SAC	1	1	4	6	6	9	6	6	7	5	7	0	3	4	5	1	2	2	2	5	824
SEA	0	1	0	4	5	10	11	4	7	9	8	7	4	7	1	1	1	0	1	1	775
DAL	0	2	1	6	8	8	11	12	11	3	3	6	7	2	0	1	0	0	0	1	680
DEN	1	1	2	2	11	10	13	9	9	6	6	2	2	4	0	2	1	1	0	0	675
LAL	0	0	3	4	5	12	17	7	14	3	7	3	2	3	1	3	1	0	1	0	666
POR	4	6	3	7	8	3	7	9	8	7	4	5	2	3	1	3	1	0	1	0	645
PHI	2	5	4	6	7	8	5	11	6	5	4	7	6	3	0	0	2	0	0	0	644
GS	0	6	4	7	7	12	8	7	4	5	5	1	4	4	3	2	0	0	0	1	628
IND	2	1	5	7	11	11	10	9	9	2	5	3	2	1	2	0	1	0	0	1	615
NJ	0	1	5	8	11	10	15	13	7	6	4	0	0	2	0	0	0	0	0	0	568
MIL	1	8	5	8	5	10	10	8	5	4	4	7	2	2	0	1	0	0	0	0	567
CHI	1	3	8	10	12	12	10	10	5	2	3	2	2	1	1	0	0	0	0	0	530
HOU	3	4	13	10	5	14	6	7	2	4	8	3	1	0	1	1	0	0	0	0	523
PHO	3	9	11	7	12	9	13	1	7	3	1	1	2	2	0	1	0	0	0	0	481
CLE	3	4	5	18	11	10	10	5	9	1	1	3	1	0	0	0	0	0	0	0	474
CHA	2	5	14	15	14	6	11	3	4	4	3	0	0	0	0	0	0	0	0	0	430
DET	11	7	10	9	14	5	2	7	6	1	1	4	0	0	0	1	0	0	0	0	400
ATL	4	6	16	13	18	8	8	4	2	1	0	0	1	1	0	0	0	0	0	0	397
UTA	4	7	17	12	15	12	9	2	3	1	0	0	0	0	0	0	0	0	0	0	380
BOS	11	16	12	10	11	8	2	3	3	1	0	1	0	0	0	0	0	0	0	0	310
MIA	11	12	13	16	9	9	5	2	1	0	0	0	0	0	0	0	0	0	0	0	297
SAN	10	17	18	10	5	6	6	5	0	0	0	1	0	0	0	0	0	0	0	0	293
WAS	16	16	5	11	7	7	2	1	2	1	0	0	0	0	0	0	0	0	0	0	243
LAC	18	17	13	9	11	4	0	1	1	0	1	0	0	0	0	0	0	0	0	0	234

The numbers 1–20 are the amount of games in which a team attempted or made the cited number of 3-point shots. The total is derived by multiplying the number of games by the number of shots attempted or made in each column.

Three-Point Field Goals Made

Number Made

Team	1	2	3	4	5	6	7	8	9	10	11	12	13	14	15	16	17	18	19	20	Total
NY	4	10	14	12	17	7	5	4	4	2	2	0	0	0	0	0	0	0	0	0	386
SAC	8	15	15	10	4	5	7	2	2	0	2	0	1	0	0	1	0	0	0	0	307
SEA	8	13	22	13	5	12	4	2	0	0	0	0	0	0	0	0	0	0	0	0	293
DEN	15	20	16	11	12	1	1	1	0	0	0	0	0	0	0	0	0	0	0	0	228
LAL	14	20	12	14	5	4	1	2	1	0	0	0	0	0	0	0	0	0	0	0	227
POR	7	22	12	14	12	1	1	0	0	0	0	0	0	0	0	0	0	0	0	0	216
DAL	22	17	16	9	9	2	2	0	0	0	0	0	0	0	0	0	0	0	0	0	211
PHI	23	22	9	8	7	2	2	1	1	0	0	0	0	0	0	0	0	0	0	0	204
IND	18	16	18	10	4	3	0	0	1	0	1	0	0	0	0	0	0	0	0	0	202
GS	18	10	18	9	4	5	1	0	1	0	0	0	0	0	0	0	0	0	0	0	194
NJ	18	26	9	15	2	2	0	1	0	0	0	0	0	0	0	0	0	0	0	0	187
MIL	19	18	12	9	4	4	0	1	0	0	0	0	0	0	0	0	0	0	0	0	179
CHI	22	19	13	7	2	2	0	2	1	0	0	0	0	0	0	0	0	0	0	0	174
CLE	15	19	18	6	5	0	2	0	0	0	0	0	0	0	0	0	0	0	0	0	170
PHO	19	17	20	4	3	1	0	0	2	0	0	0	0	0	0	0	0	0	0	0	168
HOU	16	19	12	10	2	4	0	0	0	0	0	0	0	0	0	0	0	0	0	0	164
CHA	23	22	13	4	1	0	1	0	0	0	0	0	0	0	0	0	0	0	0	0	134
DET	26	14	7	4	2	2	1	0	0	0	0	0	0	0	0	0	0	0	0	0	120
UTA	32	22	7	3	1	0	0	0	0	0	0	0	0	0	0	0	0	0	0	0	114
ATL	25	22	7	5	0	0	0	0	0	0	0	0	0	0	0	0	0	0	0	0	110
MIA	26	15	9	1	2	0	0	0	0	0	0	0	0	0	0	0	0	0	0	0	97
BOS	25	13	5	3	0	0	0	0	0	0	0	0	0	0	0	0	0	0	0	0	78
SAN	28	8	2	2	1	0	0	0	0	0	0	0	0	0	0	0	0	0	0	0	63
LAC	26	6	4	1	0	0	0	0	0	0	0	0	0	0	0	0	0	0	0	0	54
WAS	17	9	2	1	1	0	0	0	0	0	0	0	0	0	0	0	0	0	0	0	52

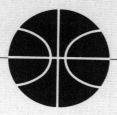

CHAPTER FOUR

HoopStat Grading System (HGS)

If you're flipping through this book before you buy it, chances are you opened to this section. Rating players is the most fundamental element of sports, but in most cases it is also the least scientific. Teams, can be measured by wins and playoff performance, but everyone has his own opinion about what makes a player great. Doubtless you've been party to the Eternal Debate. Although its focal point changes with the decades, it has remained with us since before there was an NBA. Today it can be summed up in just three words: Magic or Bird? Bird or Magic? Or Jordan? The debate can get very heated and very regional, yet you'll never see it become the subject of dispassionate discourse. But who needs objectivity? Magic is obviously the best—and he's got the Championship rings to prove it. Kurt Rambis has the same rings? Gee, forgot about that. Besides, Jordan's clearly the best—he was the best offensive *and* defensive player last year. He's young, too—his true greatness probably lies years ahead of him. But wouldn't you, deep down, rather have Bird on the court in that seventh game?

So what *does* make the best player? The one with the highest scoring average? Or the best "all-around" player? Are we looking at sweet moves? The guy who can move the ball better than anyone else? Or do we want the most deadly shooter? The hardest worker? The player who's been a winner ever since high school?

Earlier, we demonstrated that the easiest way to estimate a team's won-lost record is by its scoring ratio. Therefore, points scored and allowed are the single most important factors in winning. When a team scores only 90% as much as its opponents, you'll never see it go 65–17. No matter how much heart, tenacity, work ethic, or luck the players have, it just doesn't happen. All those qualities, if real, will show up in the statistics somewhere.

It's the same for a player as for a team. All the commonly named qualities of legendary players—clutch play, resolve, instinct, athleticism—will be translated somewhere into statistics, *if* they really are worth anything. A player who works harder than anyone else, will come up with the stats to prove it. This is true at least in a league like the NBA, where even the eighth or ninth man off the bench is often an excellent player. If we want to isolate the league's great players, we should look for the ones who create the most wins for their teams. Therefore, we should look for the ones who create the most points.

First, however, we have to consider one question. It's very basic, and seems intuitive, but you'd be surprised how little thought has been given to the answer. The question is what exactly earns points for a team? Now, most fans *have* thought about this in the abstract, if only to compare the statistics of unlike players. Who is more valuable, for instance: a player who scores 22.3 points per game with 2 rebounds, or one who pours in 22.0 per game, but pulls down 12 boards? All other stats

being equal, most fans would say the second player. After all, he grabs 10 extra rebounds per game, while scoring only 0.3 point fewer, or about one shot in two weeks. That one shot can't begin to compensate for the 10 rebounds, agreed?

If you *do* agree with the previous statement, you've already started to look at basketball in an analytical light. Let's consider it in more depth. How does a team score two points? On one level, the answer is simple. Somebody makes a basket. Two points. However, is this action worth the entire two points? True, the field goal puts the actual score on the board. But what about the perfect pass that sets it up? Shouldn't the big man, the one who wrestled on the floor for the rebound, get something for his effort? Isn't the entire offensive sequence that creates the basket worth two points?

If you concur that 10 rebounds are more valuable than 0.3 of a point, you've answered the last question yourself. If nothing but the shot mattered, then 0.3 of a point would be worth a million rebounds— and a million times nothing would still not equal 0.3. Rebounds are very obviously worth very much more than that; otherwise, no one would put out any effort for them. Although coaches say that "the only thing that matters is the W at the end," player statistics other than points scored have *some* team value.

The next question generates dozens of player rating systems, no two alike. How much is each stat worth? What happens when you compare a player with stats of 22.3 ppg and 2.0 rpg with a teammate who puts up 10.0 ppg/12.0 rpg? A fan can look at these numbers and identify the shooting guard and "big man." The same fan, however, can't tell whether the 10.0 rebounds are worth 12.3 points or not. Even if he can, he can't tell you *why* they are or aren't. Attempts usually revert to the logic of the Eternal Debate. Most rating systems don't even make an effort to find the value of stats versus one another, instead lumping them together and awarding one point for each: 1 rebound = 1 point = 1 assist = 1 block. Is one block, which might not even give the team possession, worth one assist, which ensures that the team scored? And what about all the other stats that proliferate in the NBA guides? Is there any way we can make sense out of all of them? Can we *really* attach specific worth to peripheral stats?

Hell, we're young and arrogant enough to give it a try. Pick a statistic out of the air. Did you choose blocked shots? If you didn't, try it again, since that's what we're going to explain right now. What does a blocked shot do? It converts the value of one shot from whatever it would be worth to zero. Often, it leads to a turnover (if the blocking team recovers). Sometimes, the shooting team gets it back for another possession.

If you don't have any other information, a shot will be worth about one point. A field goal attempt is good around 48% of the time. Broken down into two- and three-point shots, 94.3% of all shots are from two-point range, and they fall about 49% of a time. The remainder of shots, 5.7%, are for the three, but they fall only about 32% of the time. For every 1,000 shots, 943 are two-pointers, and of those, 49% are good, for a total of 924 points. In addition, there are 57 three-pointers, which will net about 55 points. Therefore, any random collection of 1,000 shots will produce about 979 points. Every one shot will produce .979 point for a team. Who wants to remember that number? Let's just say that a shot—or an offensive sequence culminating in a shot, to be specific—is worth about one point on average.

A block erases the one point the sequence is normally worth. However, we're missing one part of this equation. When a team misses a shot, it doesn't automatically mean that the offensive sequence's value is zero. Why is this? About a third of the time, a team will recover its own miss and set up again. How much will the following sequence be worth then? Normally, a team gets a shot off in about 80% to 85% of its possessions. If a shot is worth about one point, then a possession is worth about 80% of that, or .80 point.

A team recovers its own shot almost exactly 33% of the time. Each one of these offensive rebounds can be considered the start of a new possession (for both our purposes and the 24-second clock keeper's). Since each of *these* possessions is potentially worth about a point, a missed shot is worth one point, 33% of the time, or .33 point. In addition, players are often fouled coming down with the ball, or in the paint. This will increase the value of a missed shot sequence to around .40 point. A team will score a basket about once in five drives initially ending in a miss.

Of course, the missed shot itself is worth zilch, but the points that occur after it can be considered when we're looking for the value of an offensive sequence. When a ball is blocked, then, the shooting team loses the 1.0 points for the original shot (isolated from the entire scoring sequence), plus .40 of a point for the possible actions going on after a miss. Therefore, a blocked shot is worth about 1.4 defensive points.

Let's look at some other stats now. Instead of doing all the tedious math here, we'll describe the effect of a stat, followed by its point value.

Turnovers: A turnover ends an offensive possession, without regard for whether or not a shot would have been taken. Therefore it is worth, in negative, as much as a generic possession is worth—**0.8 point.**

Offensive Rebounds: An offensive rebound starts a possession that is slightly more valuable than a normal possession, since the ball is already downcourt, and turnover opportunities are fewer, and tip-ins more likely. When looked at in a team context, it's a negative statistic, since it always follows a missed shot sequence. However, solely in terms of its value in the current possession, it averages out to about **0.85 point.**

Defensive Rebounds: A defensive rebound is the opposite of an offensive rebound, and it will lessen your opponent's scoring by as many points as they could expect to stem from an offensive rebound. We already figured this number to be 0.85. However, the defense is usually in better position to grab the board, a fact reflected in the ratio of offensive to defensive rebounds leaguewide (1:2). When a defensive rebound starts a possession sequence, the team will score at the same rate as it would for any other series. Taking all these facts into account, a defensive rebound is worth about **0.5 point.**

Steals: A steal ends an opponent's sequence with a production of zero. Therefore, a steal should be worth as many points as one average offensive sequence would. Unlike a blocked shot, there is no guarantee that a shot will even be taken during the possession—the ball handler who had his pockets picked might have been preparing to pass the ball

into the third row, but never got the chance. So we decided to give it the same rating as a possession, plus a slight additional value, because it often leads to a less contested shot at the other end, for a total of **1.0 point.**

Assists: Since it leads directly to two points, an assist is extremely valuable. It means the shot *was* made. In fact, next to shots themselves, assists are more closely correlated to points scored than any other statistic. **1.0 point.**

Field Goals: Without field goals, no other statistic matters. In essence, the difference between a made field goal (which is 2.0 points) and a missed one (−0.6) will define the difference between an offensive sequence ending in a made field goal and one ending in a missed one. Since a successful play is worth two points (ignoring for now three-point plays), and an unsuccessful one is worth only one, the shot is worth **1.0 point.** Its value is equal to the difference between the two types of drives.

Missed Field Goals: A sequence ending in a field goal attempt is worth 1.0 point, and one ending in a missed attempt is worth 0.4. Missing your attempt, therefore, reduces the entire drive's average value by 0.6 points. Missed field goals, as calculated by FGA-FGM, are worth **−0.6 point** each.

Foul Shots: You're *always* supposed to make *all* your foul shots. In Norwalk, Connecticut, Calvin Murphy's hometown, this was the one thing all gym teachers taught. Day after day, week after week, we'd do foul shot drills. We'd line up after the dodge ball game to have shooting drills. We'd come in early from the soccer game for foul shooting practice.

In the NBA, however, players make about 75% of their foul shots. A foul shot is unique in basketball, since it is the only play that isn't part of an actual offensive sequence. Therefore, its worth isn't judged in terms of the final product, but is taken in and of itself. Since each free throw made is worth **1.0 point,** it seems logical to attach this value to the statistic.

Personal Fouls: The personal foul is another unique statistic. It's negative, but only in the same

way a sacrifice bunt is. In fact, it's often used to let the other team get only one point instead of two. Fouling is also a technique to get possession back. It can slow a fast break. There are so many potential positives to this negative that we hesitate to give it a value either way. Therefore, just as baseball leaves sacrifices out of batting averages, we will leave this out of our formula.

TO	=	−0.8 point
Off Reb	=	0.85 point
Block	=	1.4 points
Def Reb	=	0.5 point
Stl	=	1.0 point
Ast	=	1.0 point
FG made	=	1.4 point
FG miss	=	−0.6 point
FT made	=	1.0 point

So there you have what we consider to be fairly accurate values for the official NBA statistics. Possibly the numbers appear odd to you. You might not agree with them entirely, or even prefer other systems. The most enjoyable part of playing with stats is the ability to take a bunch of indisputable facts and turn them into unprovable conjecture. We

can't, at this time, say that a field goal isn't worth 1.3 points instead of 1.0. No one ever said this business would be easy, but our system seems reasonable.

The next question, of course, is how these values describe the true worth of actual players. On this page is listed the Official HoopStat Top 20 of the 1988–89 NBA season. The columns in the chart are, in order: player name, position, team, games played, minutes played, points per game played, points per 48 minutes, HoopStat Grade, and the difference between the HoopStat Grade and points per 48 minutes.

The scoring average that most people look at is points per game played. But if you don't know how long the player was in the game, it means nothing when used to describe how well he played. A scoring average of 10.5 points per game tells a far different story when describing the seventh man on the bench and the starting center. Instead, we try to describe players in terms of points scored per 48 minutes, which gets its own column in the chart below. This number is simply how many points a player would score were he in the game for all 48 minutes.

The final column, called "Gun," is the difference between a player's HGS (measured per 48 minutes), and scoring. The higher this number is, the lower the contribution of scoring toward his total grade.

THE 1988–89 HOOPSTAT TOP 20

HoopStat Top 20	Pos	Team	GP	Min	PPG	Pt/48	HGS	GUN
Michael Jordan	G	Chi	81	3255	32.5	38.8	39.1	0.3
Magic Johnson	G	LAL	77	2886	22.5	28.8	37.3	8.5
Akeem Olajuwon	C	Hou	82	3024	24.8	32.3	36.6	4.3
Charles Barkley	F	Phi	79	3088	25.8	31.7	35.0	3.3
Karl Malone	F	Uta	80	3126	29.1	35.7	32.8	−2.9
Patrick Ewing	C	NY	80	2896	22.7	30.1	32.6	2.5
John Stockton	G	Uta	82	3171	17.1	21.2	32.3	11.1
Clyde Drexler	G	Por	78	3066	27.2	33.2	31.9	−1.3
Kevin Johnson	G	Pho	81	3179	20.4	24.9	31.1	6.2
Fat Lever	G	Den	71	2745	19.8	24.6	29.8	5.2
Robert Parish	C	Bos	80	2840	18.6	25.1	29.3	4.2
Chris Mullin	G	GS	82	3093	26.5	33.8	29.1	−4.8
Moses Malone	C	Atl	81	2878	20.2	27.3	28.8	1.5
Larry Nance	F	Cle	73	2526	17.2	23.9	27.8	3.9
Benoit Benjamin	C	LAC	79	2585	16.4	24.1	27.7	3.6
Rod Strickland	G	NY	81	1358	8.9	25.5	27.0	1.5
John Williams	F	Was	82	2413	13.7	22.3	26.8	4.5
Tom Chambers	F	Pho	81	3002	25.7	33.3	26.8	−6.5
Ron Harper	F	Cle	82	2851	18.6	25.7	26.8	1.1
Kevin McHale	F	Bos	78	2876	22.5	29.3	26.8	−2.5

More simply, low numbers under "Gun" point out gunners (Karl Malone, Clyde Drexler, Chris Mullin, Tom Chambers), while high numbers represent the more "complete" player (Magic and Kevin Johnson, John Stockton, John Williams). The best part about the HGS system is that it doesn't favor skills found at one position—the top five have one player from each.

So, you say, why should we bother to use this system? Well, three reasons. First, HGS produces a number that can be compared to points per game. You know that 39.1 is a great scoring average; it's also a great HGS. Second, it doesn't discriminate. A player with good passing skills isn't rewarded more than a great scorer, or rebounder, or vice versa. In

fact, of the top twenty, there are eight guards, seven forwards, and five centers. The men you think of as superstars prove why, but the ones considered underrated (Kevin Johnson, Fat Lever) are given their due also. It's not a system where Danny Ainge ends up on top of the list and everyone wonders why.

The HGS will be used in upcoming sections to get a better handle on just how well certain players performed over the course of the year. We'll rank the players in the individual section with it, and toss around some other numbers. As a whole, the formula is subject to some minor revision (for instance, points scored might be worth only 1.35, not 1.4), but it's pretty solid as ratings go.

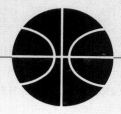

CHAPTER FIVE

Revenge Factors: Fact or Fantasy?

How many times has this happened to you? With nothing to do on a Tuesday night, you flip on a random cable channel. It happens to be WTBS, as it always is, and they're feeding you a game between two teams, neither of which are from Atlanta, neither of which you have seen play in years. Your first thought is, "Hmmm . . . when did they change their uniforms?" Your second thought is, "Hmmm . . . I thought Johnson used to play for the other team!"

But no sooner have you thought that than the color commentator remarks, "Johnson is playing against his ex-teammates tonight. He says it's just another game, but he has to be feeling some extra adrenaline out there tonight." The announcer, a 14-year veteran, would seem to know what he is talking about, wouldn't he? But then again, here's Mr. Journeyman on the court, committing his second consecutive three-seconds violation of the quarter as they cut back to the live action. Suddenly, Johnson is sitting on the visitor's bench again, hearing it from the coach. Never quite regaining his momentum, Johnson tosses in 1 for 8 the rest of the night.

Back to the broadcaster, though. Midway through the third quarter, the remote camera pans to a shot of Johnson sitting at the other end of the bench, chewing on a towel. "Case of nerves," speculates the announcer. "The first time back is always hard, you know." The play-by-play man doesn't have much insight to add to the issue, being a play-by-play man. You, the viewer, just sit back and

wonder whether Johnson's performance was any different from any other game he'd been in in the past four seasons. Of course, that doesn't make good copy, so it is glossed over by the media and others "in the know."

So who's right here? Does playing against one's old team tend to increase or decrease one's effort, or does it have no real effect? If it does have some bearing, is it the adrenaline produced by wanting to punish the owners for moving you? Is it because the player knows the other guys' moves? Is it just because the old team is lousy? Is it an overrated tool? Possibly. If the GM's are so savvy, they should know exactly what they were giving up, and hopefully know exactly what they're getting in return.

"You expect traded players to come back and do well against you," said Jan Volk, who sent three-point bomber Danny Ainge from Beantown to Sacramento at midseason. "The player just doesn't fall off the face of the earth because he's traded. If he didn't have any skills and value he wouldn't be tradable in the first place."

Jerry Krause has been the mastermind behind the many trades pulled off by the Bulls in the past four seasons, making approximately twice as many as the entire League total. Talk about rebuilding! Do the ex-Bulls come back to Chicago Stadium set on revenge? "I want them to do well. I expect them to do well," said Krause of the legion of Bulls alumni roaming the League. "But I don't necessarily want them to do well against us."

When a trade is made, explained Krause, both teams have to benefit from it. "It has to be equitable for both teams," said Krause, "or else if the other team comes out looking bad, you can never trade with them again."

Several years ago, Seattle and Dallas pulled off a trade sending Dale Ellis and his 7 ppg average to Seattle for Al Wood. In his first return to Seattle, Wood took revenge by hitting a three-pointer to end the half, ripping the cords for 25 points by game's end. "He was laughing at us," recalled Sonic GM, Bob Whitsitt. "But by the end of the season Al Wood was no longer on the Mavericks and Dale Ellis was averaging 25 points a game for us."

How did Tom Chambers, Seattle's 6'10" five-year vet and NBA All Star, do after coming back to Seattle with his new team, the Suns? He was a bit nervous. Air balls are uncommon for this 25 ppg bomber, but he threw up three that night against his old teammates.

Trades are made basically for three reasons. The needs of the club may start to change due to injury, age, and talent and a player or players are needed to shore up the weaknesses. Aging hits us all, and basketball players are not immune. As they get up in years and out of the "developmental stage" (26–28 years old), their perceived role may change on a club. While a player may be an aging starter on a middle-of-the pack team, if traded to a contender for the title this same player may be just what's needed to give 10–20 minutes a game and get them the championship.

The marketability of the player is also a big factor in whether he's trade bait. Does he have an attitude problem? Can he produce in the clutch games, or does he tend to do best during "garbage time?" Is there still room for improvement in his game or is he past his prime? Is he injury prone? These are just some of the factors to be considered before a player is shipped out or a new one welcomed to the team.

"It's not so much that the player you traded away comes back and has a great night," said Harry Weltman, the Nets GM who has welcomed many new people to the Nets in years past, "but more importantly that the player you picked up in the trade does a good job."

"A trade is a two-way street," pointed out Norm Sonju, who packaged nobody's favorite, Mark Aguirre, for Adrian Dantley of the Pistons shortly after the All-Star break. "Sometimes a player blossoms more in another system and will come back to score a lot against you. It's not really surprising "

Let's investigate the entire trade issue to see if there is a connection with a player returning to his old team and doing them in. We compiled a list of players who changed jerseys either during the 1988 or 1989 seasons. These are the players who have been traded or released by the old team, or claimed by the new. In all, there were 71 players, and we've gathered 143 games they played against their former employers for research. The players ranged from Tom Chambers and Moses Malone, two free agents, to Muggsy Bogues and Scott Hastings, both plucked off rosters by expansion teams, to Mark Aguirre and Adrian Dantley, traded for each other.

The players averaged 26 minutes per game they played, scoring about 11 points on average. They shot around 48.4%, close to average. However, where the players, as a group, didn't show much difference from other players, some individual performances certainly stood out.

Tom Chambers was easily the leader in scoring

BEST PERFORMANCES AGAINST OLD TEAMS, 1988–89

Date	For	Vs.	Player	Min	FGM	FGA	FG%	3GM	3GA	FTM	FTA	FT%	OR	TR	Ast	PF	St	TO	BK	Pts	HGS48
1/11	NJ	Phi	Hinson, R	24	4	6	0.667	0	0	5	6	0.833	4	8	2	3	2	2	5	13	48.4
12/10	GS	Was	Bol, M	23	1	4	0.250	0	0	3	5	0.600	2	9	2	4	0	0	9	5	46.7
3/29	Atl	Was	Malone, M	35	11	21	0.524	0	0	6	6	1.000	7	16	2	4	0	3	5	28	44.5
2/15	Pho	Sea	Chambers, T	38	12	16	0.750	2	2	9	10	0.900	1	8	4	3	2	2	2	35	44.1
1/16	Atl	Was	Malone, M	33	6	17	0.353	0	0	8	13	0.615	10	21	1	0	0	0	3	20	42.2
1/11	Cle	Pho	Nance, L	37	11	20	0.550	0	0	6	8	0.750	2	13	2	5	1	1	3	28	38.4
1/17	Sea	LAC	Cage, M	37	9	18	0.500	0	0	5	6	0.833	4	12	6	3	3	3	2	23	37.6
11/13	Sac	Hou	McCray, R	40	11	20	0.550	1	1	6	8	0.750	3	12	7	2	1	2	0	29	35.3
3/4	NY	Chi	Oakley, C	25	5	8	0.625	0	0	4	6	0.667	8	10	2	5	1	2	0	14	35.3
4/6	Pho	Sea	Chambers, T	42	11	18	0.611	0	1	10	11	0.909	2	12	4	4	1	6	2	32	35.3

WORST PERFORMANCES AGAINST OLD TEAMS, 1988–89

Date	For	Vs.	Player	Min.	FGM	FGA	FG%	3GM	3GA	FTM	FTA	FT%	OR	TR	Ast	PF	St	TO	BK	Pts	HGS48
2/19	Chi	Mil	Hodges, C	3	0	0	——	0	0	0	0	——	0	0	0	0	0	2	0	0	−25.6
4/2	Hou	Phi	McCormick, T	6	0	1	0.000	0	0	0	0	——	0	1	0	2	0	2	0	0	−13.6
4/19	Hou	San	Berry, W	6	1	2	0.500	0	0	0	0	——	1	1	0	1	0	3	0	2	−6.0
1/21	Chi	Pho	Hodges, C	17	0	3	0.000	0	1	0	0	——	1	2	1	1	0	2	0	0	−3.0
3/10	Cle	LAC	Valentine, A	5	0	0	——	0	0	0	0	——	0	0	0	1	0	0	0	0	0.0
3/14	Sac	Hou	Petersen, J	28	1	8	0.125	0	0	0	0	——	0	4	1	4	1	2	1	2	1.7
11/22	Was	Phi	Colter, S	24	1	2	0.500	0	0	0	0	——	1	2	2	4	0	4	0	2	1.9
2/15	Phi	Ind	Anderson, R	31	4	12	0.333	0	0	0	0	——	1	3	0	4	1	3	0	8	1.9
1/4	Chi	Was	Bogues, T	19	2	4	0.500	0	0	1	1	1.000	0	1	0	0	1	4	0	5	2.3
1/3	Dal	Sac	Tyler, T	4	1	2	0.500	0	0	0	1	0.000	0	2	0	1	0	2	0	2	2.4

Team Revenge

Team	Record, 1st			Record, 2nd		
	W	L	MV	W	L	MV
Cleveland	19	5	-1.7	4	1	9.6
LA Lakers	18	6	-2.1	4	2	8.2
Detroit	18	6	-3.8	3	3	3.2
Milwaukee	18	6	-2.4	3	3	1.3
Philadelphia	16	8	-3.7	4	4	1.5
Dallas	16	8	-2.3	1	7	-9.9
Golden State	15	9	-5.1	6	3	2.0
Denver	15	9	-5.2	5	4	3.3
Atlanta	15	9	-2.1	7	2	9.7
Houston	14	10	-3.8	4	6	-1.7
Chicago	14	10	-3.7	7	3	0.4
Phoenix	13	11	-4.6	9	2	9.8
New York	13	11	-4.0	9	2	5.5
Boston	12	12	-5.7	5	7	-0.9
New Jersey	12	12	-6.4	3	9	-8.1
Utah	11	13	-5.6	9	4	3.8
Seattle	10	14	-5.5	10	4	6.1
Portland	10	14	-6.7	6	8	0.1
LA Clippers	8	16	-12.2	3	13	-12.7
Washington	8	16	-9.9	8	8	-1.6
Indiana	7	17	-4.8	8	9	-2.5
Charlotte	6	18	-9.5	5	13	-8.8
San Antonio	6	18	-7.6	7	11	-3.9
Sacramento	4	20	-12.7	7	13	-4.4
Miami	2	22	-14.0	5	17	-8.6
League	**300**	**300**	**-5.80**	**142**	**158**	**-2.83**

This chart demonstrates just how teams do in their second meeting with teams which have knocked them off before. The first column shows each team's overall record against the league in their first meetings of the season. The second column shows the average scoring margin in the losses. The third column is each team's record in the second meeting of the year versus teams they had lost to the first time, and the final column is the average margin of victory/loss in all those games.

against his old team, putting in 30 points more than once. However, Roy Hinson and Manute Bol had the best overall performances against old teams. Hinson, on January 11, played only 24 minutes, but scored 13, with 8 rebounds and 5 blocks against Philly. His efforts, however, were wasted as the Nets lost by nine. Manute's performance against Washington on December 10, including nine blocks and rebounds, spurred the Warriors to a 109–102 victory.

Other players, however, weren't quite as fortunate against their old mates. Craig Hodges played for both Phoenix and Milwaukee in 1988 before being traded to Chicago. Against Phoenix, he played 17 minutes and did nothing except miss three shots, ending up with a – 3.0 HGS for the game. In February, he played Milwaukee and did even worse, seeing only three miutes of action and turning the ball over twice. For his efforts, Craig earned a game HGS of – 25.6.

What about longer performances though? Jim Petersen was looking to prove himself to Houston on March 14 when he took the court for the Kings. But in 28 minutes of play, he clanged to a 1 for 8 from the field, and picked up four fouls. Ron Anderson was usually looked at as a good pickup for Philly, and everyone wondered aloud how Indiana could have let him go. When his usually hot shooting went Arctic against them though, their doubts were no doubt lessened. His 4 for 12 shooting was one of the worst games he had all year.

How much respect did the ten players on the worst list get? They played a total of 197 minutes, but their opponents only bothered to guard them closely enough to send them to the line twice. In contrast, their frustration caused them to commit 18 fouls in the same span. Compare those numbers to the *best* performers, who drew 79 trips to the line, while being whistled only 33 times.

The biggest contributor to the revenge factor, it seems, is the relative talent of the player, although certainly some do rise to the occasion. A player's normal level seems to be magnified against his old team, to the point where top performers like Tom Chambers and Moses Malone look like monsters, while the dimmer lights of the league take the collar regularly, even more often than they normally do. The revenge factor acts as a magnifier, not a pull in one direction or the other.

Another facet of the revenge factor is *team* revenge. How many times have you seen a game hyped with the claim that one team is "looking for revenge" after an earlier setback?

It's always tricky to give a human emotional trait to an entire group, but athletic teams have a unique form of interpersonal psychology. There's only one way to find out how a team really bounces back from a loss, and that's to research it. In every game, there's a winner and a loser (moral victories aren't counted here), which means that every meeting, after the first, can be considered a grudge match of sorts.

When teams play each other for the second time, the team that lost the first game was 142–158. When you consider that the team that wins the first time is usually better overall, that's not an insignificant figure.

Which teams were able to create the mental edge to win the second game? Considering they had gone 0–11 against the teams the first time, both the Knicks and Suns managed to post 9–2 second meeting records against those teams. The Suns took special umbrage at being beaten, and whipped those teams by nearly 10 points in each of the return engagements. Seattle won more second chances than any other team, going 10–4. Only Dallas, New Jersey, and the Clippers, three teams which took a big plunge toward the end of the season, were beaten *more* badly the second time around.

So is there a team revenge factor? Much of the 142-game swing can be seen as a correction, since it often involved two even teams. However, a sample of 300 is significant enough to indicate that *something* is at work here.

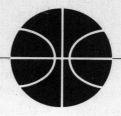

CHAPTER SIX

The NBA: A Team-by-Team Analysis

A LOOK BACK . . . A LOOK AHEAD . . .

Even before the season began, the scoreboard in the new Charlotte Coliseum crashed to the floor—not that they'd have much to put up on it in the way of points. Unfortunately, the board didn't keep track of attendance, which were the only numbers the Hornets could boast about. The Miami Heat gave team owner Billy Cunningham and friends some warmth under the collar by dropping their first 17 straight games and then remaining buried in the league cellar. With the Timberwolves and Magic debuting this year, the Heat may move up. Top pick Danny Manning of the Clippers held out for big bucks, finally joined the squad, and almost as quickly tore his cruciate ligaments on a drive to the hoop. Coach Gene Shue didn't faint, but this quirky accident spelled his demise.

King's coach Jerry Reynolds did faint (during a game against Portland) on the sidelines, and Frank Layden, the jovial GM/coach of the Jazz, left the coaching ranks at midseason, citing fan abuse, among other things. New Pacer coach Dick Versace didn't quit when his team was getting drubbed. He threw a chair instead and was fined by the league office.

Rod Thorne, NBA boxing commissioner, er, director of league operations, went over the video-tapes, and $124,000 was levied out in fines. The blood money all goes to charities. Players were suspended for fighting in a total of 14 games. Detroit's Isiah Thomas was sidelined for two games after fracturing his hand on Bill Cartwright, and Phoenix's Armon Gilliam received the same punishment for strangling Pearl Washington in the Heat locker room. The Detroit bad boys led the league in total fines with $30,000, more than twice as much as any other team. It's rumored that Piston bullies Rick Mahorn and Bill Laimbeer were seen with Hulk Hogan. Will they be joining the Hulkster in the next Wrestlemania Battle Royale or just continue their antics in the NBA? Stay tuned.

Larry Bird and his injured heels were operated on several games into the season, and he never returned to the Celtics. Will he come back as the Larry Bird of old—firing away and dishing off?—this remains the big Boston question mark.

One player who definitely won't be returning this year is 42-year-old Kareem Abdul-Jabbar. The Big Fellah—Rookie of the Year in 1970, 20 winning seasons, six-time league MVP—didn't stay too long or leave too early. His legacy of excellence will stand the test of future stars and of time itself.

Last season's final standings point out that times

are changing in the league. Detroit's walk-over of Boston and Chicago in the Eastern Conference playoffs and then their sweep in the finals against the Lakers point out that this is a team to be reckoned with. Last season, seven teams—the Suns, Lakers, Jazz, Pistons, Hawks, Cavs, and Knicks—won 50 or more games, with the Pistons winning a league-best 63. Again, any of these teams will be a legitimate contender for the title this season.

Detroit may just be the team to beat. Isiah Thomas will again direct operations with Joe Dumars assisting, while Mark "Trade Me" Aguirre is expected to do most of the offensive damage.

Not to dismiss the Lakers and their eight consecutive Pacific Division titles as has-beens because of Jabbar's retirement, but the Suns could be Division and possible Western Conference champs if Kevin Johnson, Tom Chambers, and Eddie Johnson can sustain their running offense and equal last year's 55–27 finish. Don Nelson's Warriors, a surprise last year in the playoffs after sending Utah home, could again be spoilers if Chris Mullin and Mitch Richmond keep up their offensive wizardry.

The Jazz, with Karl Malone, John Stockton, and Thurl Bailey roaming the court, should win the Midwest Division, but a resurgent Maverick team,

with a healthy Roy Tarpley and Rolando Balakman, may cause some problems.

David Robinson, the Navy's tallest sailor ever at 7–0, finally trades in his spit-polished shoes for high-tops this season. Larry Brown and the city of San Antonio couldn't be happier. Playmaker Alvin Robertson and center Cadillac Anderson were shipped out to the Bucks in exchange for high-scoring Terry Cummings. The Spurs should easily, if not dramatically, improve on their lowly 21–61 record.

Again, the Central Division is the toughest division in the league, if not in all of pro sports. Look for pitched battles between Detroit, Cleveland, Atlanta, and Milwaukee. Even the Pacers, dubbed the "new Cavaliers" with its young, talented team, could surprise people.

In the Atlantic Division it could be the Knicks once again as champs. But without Rick Pitino directing operations at the sideline, there are a lot of questions. Pat Ewing has to get the ball more often down in the paint, and somebody has to come through with consistent outside shooting—Kiki? The Sixers, meanwhile, who made the playoffs for the 13th time in 14 seasons, will again be carried by Charles Barkley. They are hoping that guard Hersey Hawkins gets over his phobia about shooting and begins to fire away as they think he can.

INTRODUCTION TO POWER CHARTS

We wanted to develop a graphic method to demonstrate a team's ups and downs over the course of a season. The Power Charts are the direct product of this desire. What they are, simply, is a way to show the level a team played at during any point in the season, and how its play improved or deteriorated over the course of the year.

The left axis (Y) is the team's level of play at any point during the year. The bottom axis (X) is the month. There are two lines on the graph, a solid line that goes up and down, and a straight dashed line. The dashed line is simply the trend a team's play followed over the course of a year. For instance, Atlanta appeared to be about a .640 team in the beginning of the season, but their play improved at the end, where they were playing nearly .700-quality ball. When the line goes upward over the course of a season, it means the team has shown overall improvement. When the line goes downward, it means the team is falling apart (see the Cleveland Power Chart). A steady line means the team was playing about the same in the beginning and at end of the season.

The wavy line shows all the ups and downs a team has taken during the season. If we were to draw it game by game, it would be far too jagged to show anything useful. Instead, what we've done is utilize a six-game moving average. Simply put, the position of the line at any time shows the team's quality of play over the previous six games. The wavier the line is, the more the team's play fluctuated over the course of the season. The smoother it is, the more consistency the team showed.

You might be asking just how we figured out where the line should go. Okay, we suppose we should let you in on it. Instead of just working with wins and losses, or even scoring margin, what we did was figure out the team's average points scored and allowed over the past six games, adjusted it for the home court advantage (which was 4.7112 in the NBA last year), and found the team's six-game scoring ratio. We then put that number into the formula for Expected Won-Lost Record that we derived earlier, and got their approximate level of play for the previous six games. If the number was above 1.000 or below .000 (which it was about once a year for some teams), we made those two values the upper and lower limits of the graph. We did that for all 82 games (the first 5 games just took all the games played up to that point), connected the dots, and smoothed the curve out a little so it was easier to look at. The result is the team's Power Chart.

ATLANTA HAWKS

In the first trade of the preseason of 1988–89, Atlanta dealt away Randy Wittman to get the now-departed Reggie Theus. Then, in August, they grabbed Moses Malone as an unrestricted free agent. Add these two to Dominique Wilkins, and suddenly the Hawks were up to their ears in ball hogs. Understandably, the team entered the season with a great deal of uncertainty. Would the league allow them to play home games with three balls at once? Would spontaneous pushing matches break out at halfcourt as the three of them scrambled after loose balls they could turn into their own fast breaks? Could the team survive three stars each trying to feel out his place in the offense? Would Ted Turner waste more draft choices on 7'7" centers from the Argentinian National Team? ("Get Russia on the blower—you won't *believe* this forward I saw at the Goodwill Games!")

Well, as luck would have it, the Big Three *did* get along together and showed that you could go whole hog on shooters, so to speak. The Hawks had problems throughout the year, but most of them were not of their own causing. Who could have predicted Cleveland's rise and be taken seriously? Who knew that Milwaukee would rebound from their death notices to become a power once again? And who knew that Kevin Willis would take the year off with a doctor's note? Among all these problems, the predicted selfishness of the Big Three never really materialized.

Each of the Three fell into well-defined roles early in the season and never much varied from them through the year. They combined for about 55% of the team's total shots, a number that stayed remarkably steady, as shown in the graph. Rarely did the Three exceed 60% of the team's total shots or drop below 50%.

So the next time someone comes up to you on the street and says, "Chemistry is everything on a ball team," agree with him if he doesn't look too dangerous. But remember, the Hawks showed last year that it's a lot easier to overcome on-court chemistry problems than off-court chemistry problems. Are you listening, Walter Berry?

Instead of worrying about sharing the ball, the Hawks should have kept their minds on consistency. For all their talent, they couldn't string together any prolonged high points. Sure, they took both the Lakers and the Cavs on the road, but what about those mental vacations in Charlotte and Miami? Their inconsistent play is highlighted in their power curve chart, where they clearly seem to

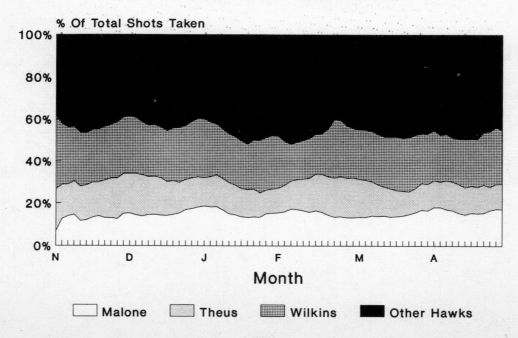

be spinning their wheels in reverse over the course of the season. Head coach Mike Fratello had high hopes last season that 6'10" Moses Malone would take the squad to the promised land. Malone, three-time league MVP, brought his lifetime (12-season) 23.6 ppg and intensity to the Hawks, but it wasn't enough as plans went awry. Instead of moving back to his natural forward spot with the addition of Malone, Kevin Willis, the 7' banger, went to the sidelines instead with a season-ending stress fracture. Chris Washburn, the 6'11" backup, never made it out of drug rehab, leaving Malone to toil under the boards all by himself. Dominique Wilkins, previously the Hawks one-man band, still led the team in minutes played, shots attempted (1756, .461), and scoring (26.7), seventh best in the league, but had to share the ball not only with Moses but with 6'7" guard Reggie Theus (15.8 ppg). Doc Rivers, 6'4" point guard, did a great job directing the ball distribution and had a team-high 525 assists, but the Hawks still fell to third in the Central Division behind the Pistons and the amazing Cavs. The end result: Two games better than 1987–88, but one spot lower in the standings.

This season, the loss of Theus to expansion and the return of Willis might be enough to inch the Hawks closer to Cleveland for second place in the division, but no further. On second thought, maybe getting Jorge Gonzalez from Argentina might not be such a bad idea.

Atlanta Hawks

	Home W	Home L	Road W	Road L
By Month				
November	5	0	3	6
December	8	2	3	1
January	5	1	2	6
February	5	1	4	3
March	4	4	3	4
April	6	0	4	2
Playoffs				
Home/Away	33	8	19	22
Overtime	1	0	1	3
Offense				
0-89	0	2	0	2
90-99	1	2	2	6
100-109	7	2	5	6
110-119	8	1	9	7
120-129	11	0	1	1
130-	6	1	2	0
Defense				
0-89	3	1	1	0
90-99	10	1	5	1
100-109	10	2	8	5
110-119	9	3	5	12
120-129	1	0	0	3
130-	0	1	0	1
Over/Under				
0-189	3	2	1	1
190-199	4	0	3	5
200-209	4	3	3	1
210-219	4	1	2	6
220-229	8	1	4	3
230-239	3	0	5	4
240-	7	1	1	2
Margin Of Victory				
0-3	5	4	5	5
4-6	1	0	1	3
7-10	6	2	7	7
11-15	5	2	2	3
16-20	8	0	2	2
21-	8	0	2	2
Field Goal Attempts				
0-69	0	0	1	0
70-79	2	2	0	0
80-89	17	3	11	12
90-99	13	3	6	9
100-109	1	0	1	1
110+	0	0	0	0
Field Goals Made				
0-34	1	2	2	2
35-39	5	4	2	9
40-44	12	1	10	10
45-49	9	1	4	1
50-54	6	0	1	0
55+	0	0	0	0
Field Goal Pct.				
.000-.399	2	2	0	5
.400-.424	1	1	1	4
.425-.449	3	2	2	6
.450-.474	5	2	4	5
.475-.499	4	0	3	0
.500-.524	7	0	7	2
.525-.549	6	1	2	0
.550-.574	1	0	0	0

	Home W	Home L	Road W	Road L
.575-.599	2	0	0	0
.600-	2	0	0	0
Opp. Field Goal Attempts				
0-69	1	0	1	0
70-79	4	2	2	5
80-89	17	4	6	11
90-99	9	1	8	5
100-109	2	1	2	0
110+	0	0	0	1
Opp. Field Goal Made				
0-34	4	2	2	0
35-39	11	0	9	4
40-44	14	3	7	7
45-49	4	2	1	7
50-54	0	1	0	4
55+	0	0	0	0
Opp. Field Goal Percentage				
.000-.399	2	0	3	0
.400-.424	7	1	4	2
.425-.449	10	0	3	2
.450-.474	5	1	6	2
.475-.499	3	2	1	2
.500-.524	1	2	0	5
.525-.549	2	1	1	5
.550-.574	2	0	0	3
.575-.599	1	1	1	1
.600-	0	0	0	0
Free Throw Attempts				
0-9	0	0	0	0
10-19	2	0	0	1
20-29	7	4	7	8
30-39	15	3	8	12
40-49	9	1	3	0
50+	0	0	1	1
Free Throws Made				
0-9	0	0	0	0
10-19	4	2	2	7
20-29	13	4	10	9
30-39	16	2	6	6
40-49	0	0	1	0
50+	0	0	0	0
Free Throw Pct.				
.000-.549	0	0	0	0
.550-.599	0	0	0	0
.600-.649	0	1	0	1
.650-.699	2	1	1	1
.700-.749	0	1	3	1
.750-.799	12	2	6	10
.800-.849	10	2	6	6
.850-.899	6	1	2	3
.900-.949	3	0	1	0
.950-	0	0	0	0
Opp. Free Throw Attempts				
0-9	0	0	0	0
10-19	4	2	3	2
20-29	14	5	7	9
30-39	13	1	6	10
40-49	2	0	3	1
50+	0	0	0	0
Opp. Free Throws Made				
0-9	0	0	0	0
10-19	12	3	7	5
20-29	16	5	7	15

	Home W	Home L	Road W	Road L
30-39	5	0	5	2
40-49	0	0	0	0
50+	0	0	0	0
Opp. Free Throw Pct.				
.000-.549	0	0	0	0
.550-.599	0	0	0	0
.600-.649	3	0	1	5
.650-.699	2	0	3	0
.700-.749	5	1	3	4
.750-.799	6	1	6	5
.800-.849	11	1	3	3
.850-.899	2	2	1	3
.900-.949	4	1	2	2
.950-	0	2	0	0
Offensive Rebounds				
0-9	2	0	1	2
10-14	3	2	8	3
15-19	16	4	5	14
20-24	10	1	5	3
25+	2	1	0	0
Total Rebounds				
0-39	1	0	1	1
40-44	1	1	0	3
45-49	6	1	6	5
50-54	0	0	0	0
55-59	20	5	8	10
60-64	3	1	3	2
65-	2	0	1	1
Opp. Offensive Rebounds				
0-9	3	0	1	2
10-14	10	6	7	9
15-19	11	2	6	10
20-24	6	0	4	1
25+	3	0	1	0
Opp. Total Rebounds				
0-39	3	0	0	0
40-44	7	1	2	1
45-49	3	2	4	3
50-54	0	0	0	0
55-59	20	5	8	13
60-64	0	0	5	3
65-	0	0	0	2
Offensive Rebound Pct.				
Below 25%	3	1	5	5
25-29.99%	4	2	5	7
30-34.99%	11	4	4	8
35-39.99%	6	1	3	2
40-44.99%	6	0	2	0
45% and up	3	0	0	0
Assists				
0-14	0	2	0	2
15-19	2	2	0	9
20-24	4	2	8	9
25-29	15	1	10	2
30-34	10	1	1	0
35+	2	0	0	0
Opp. Assists				
0-14	1	0	0	0
15-19	8	1	0	1
20-24	16	2	10	3
25-29	6	2	6	8
30-34	1	3	3	9
35+	1	0	0	1

	Home W	Home L	Road W	Road L
Edge In Assists				
Below -15	0	1	0	2
-10 to -14	0	0	0	12
-5 to -9	1	4	3	5
0 to -4	5	1	4	1
1-4	9	2	7	1
5-9	11	0	5	1
10-14	4	0	0	0
15-	3	0	0	0
Personal Fouls				
0-14	1	0	0	0
15-19	7	2	4	4
20-24	14	3	7	8
25-29	10	3	6	7
30-34	1	0	2	3
35+	0	0	0	0
Opp. Personal Fouls				
0-14	0	0	0	0
15-19	2	1	1	3
20-24	8	2	7	9
25-29	11	5	6	8
30-34	11	0	4	2
35+	1	0	1	0
Personal Fouls Edge				
Below -15	0	0	1	0
-10 to -14	6	0	2	1
-5 to -9	14	3	4	3
0 to -4	7	5	6	8
1-4	4	0	4	5
5-9	2	0	2	5
10-14	0	0	0	0
15+	0	0	0	0
Steals				
0-5	3	1	3	1
6-7	2	1	3	7
8-9	7	2	8	5
10-11	3	1	1	6
12-13	11	1	1	2
14+	7	2	3	1
Opp. Steals				
0-5	5	2	3	5
6-7	6	2	5	4
8-9	6	1	7	6
10-11	9	2	2	5
12-13	6	1	2	1
14+	1	0	0	1
Edge In Steals				
Below -7	1	0	1	1
-4 to -6	2	1	2	2
0 to -3	10	1	6	5
1-3	10	3	5	8
4-6	4	2	3	5
7-	6	1	2	1
Turnovers				
0-14	12	3	7	10
15-19	13	3	9	9
20-24	8	2	3	3
25-29	0	0	0	0
30-34	0	0	0	0
35+	0	0	0	0
Opp. Turnovers				
0-14	3	1	4	8
15-19	16	6	11	11

	Home W	L	Road W	L
20-24	10	1	2	3
25-29	3	0	2	0
30-34	0	0	0	0
35+	1	0	0	0
Edge In Turnovers				
Below -15	2	1	0	0
-10 to -14	2	0	2	0
-5 to -9	10	1	4	4
0 to -4	11	3	7	10
1- 4	5	1	4	5
5- 9	2	2	2	3
10-14	1	0	0	0
15+	0	0	0	0
Blocks				
1-2	2	0	2	5
3-4	5	2	6	5
5-6	7	4	4	7
7-8	12	2	3	3
9-10	5	0	3	1
11+	2	0	1	1

	Home W	L	Road W	L
Opp. Blocks				
0-2	14	2	4	3
3-4	10	2	4	8
5-6	5	0	8	6
7-8	2	4	1	1
9-10	2	0	2	3
11+	0	0	0	1
Edge In Blocks				
Below -7	0	0	0	1
-4 to -6	1	1	2	6
0 to -3	7	4	8	5
1-3	12	2	5	5
4-6	8	1	3	4
7+	5	0	1	1
Three-Pointers Attempted				
0-2	6	0	2	2
3-5	20	5	13	9
6-8	7	1	4	8
9-11	0	2	0	1
12-14	0	0	0	2
15+	0	0	0	0

	Home W	L	Road W	L
Three-Pointers Made				
0-2	26	8	17	19
3-5	7	0	2	3
6-8	0	0	0	0
9-11	0	0	0	0
12-14	0	0	0	0
15+	0	0	0	0
Three-Pointers Pct.				
.000-.099	9	6	8	7
.100-.149	2	0	1	4
.150-.199	1	0	0	2
.200-.249	0	1	1	1
.250-.299	2	0	3	2
.300-.349	10	1	3	2
.350-.399	0	0	1	1
.400-.449	0	0	0	0
.450-.499	0	0	0	0
.500-	9	0	2	3
Opp. Three-Point Attempts				
0-2	4	0	1	8
3-5	11	1	3	5
6-8	12	5	10	6

	Home W	L	Road W	L
9-11	4	1	2	1
12-14	2	0	1	2
15+	0	1	2	0
Opp. Three-Pointers Made				
0-2	24	4	14	19
3-5	7	4	3	1
6-8	2	0	2	2
9-11	0	0	0	0
12-14	0	0	0	0
15+	0	0	0	0
Opp. Three-Pointer Pct.				
.000-.099	17	3	6	10
.100-.149	4	1	6	1
.150-.199	1	0	2	1
.200-.249	3	1	0	0
.250-.299	0	1	1	1
.300-.349	1	0	2	4
.350-.399	0	0	1	0
.400-.449	2	1	0	0
.450-.499	0	0	0	0
.500-	5	1	1	5

Atlanta Hawks
1988–89 Power Chart

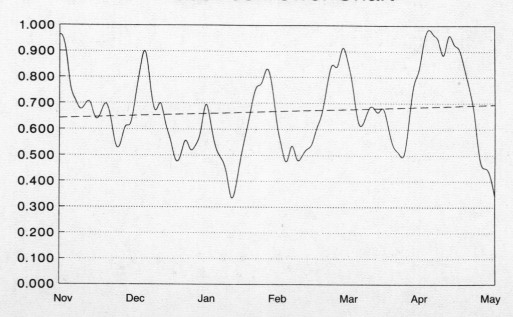

Atlanta Hawks

	GP	GS	Min	FGM	FGA	FG%	2GM	2GA	2G%	3GM	3GA	3G%	FTM	FTA	FT%	Off	Tot	Ast	PF	Stl	TO	Blk	Pts	HGS
John Battle	82	0	1672	287	628	0.457	276	594	0.465	11	34	0.324	194	238	0.815	30	110	140	125	42	104	9	779	640
Per GP			20.4	3.5	7.7		3.4	7.2		0.1	0.4		2.4	2.9		0.4	1.3	1.7	1.5	0.5	1.3	0.1	9.5	7.8
Per 48			34.8	8.2	18.0		7.9	17.1		0.3	1.0		5.6	6.8		0.9	3.2	4.0	3.6	1.2	3.0	0.3	22.4	18.4
Dudley Bradley	38	0	267	28	86	0.326	20	55	0.364	8	31	0.258	8	16	0.500	7	25	32	41	16	14	2	72	62
Per GP			7.0	0.7	2.3		0.5	1.4		0.2	0.8		0.2	0.4		0.2	0.7	0.8	1.1	0.4	0.4	0.1	1.9	1.6
Per 48			5.6	5.0	15.5		3.6	9.9		1.4	5.6		1.4	2.9		1.3	4.5	5.8	7.4	2.9	2.5	0.4	12.9	11.1
Antoine Carr	78	12	1488	226	470	0.481	226	469	0.482	0	1	0.000	130	152	0.855	106	168	274	221	31	82	62	582	617
Per GP			19.1	2.9	6.0		2.9	6.0		0.0	0.0		1.7	1.9		1.4	2.2	3.5	2.8	0.4	1.1	0.8	7.5	7.9
Per 48			31.0	7.3	15.2		7.3	15.1		0.0	0.0		4.2	4.9		3.4	5.4	8.8	7.1	1.0	2.6	2.0	18.8	19.9
Duane Ferrell	41	0	231	35	83	0.422	35	83	0.422	0	0	0.000	30	44	0.682	19	22	41	33	7	12	6	100	93
Per GP			5.6	0.9	2.0		0.9	2.0		0.0	0.0		0.7	1.1		0.5	0.5	1.0	0.8	0.2	0.3	0.1	2.4	2.3
Per 48			4.8	7.3	17.2		7.3	17.2		0.0	0.0		6.2	9.1		3.9	4.6	8.5	6.9	1.5	2.5	1.2	20.8	19.3
Jon Koncak	74	22	1531	141	269	0.524	141	266	0.530	0	3	0.000	63	114	0.553	147	306	453	238	54	60	98	345	661
Per GP			20.7	1.9	3.6		1.9	3.6		0.0	0.0		0.9	1.5		2.0	4.1	6.1	3.2	0.7	0.8	1.3	4.7	8.9
Per 48			31.9	4.4	8.4		4.4	8.3		0.0	0.1		2.0	3.6		4.6	9.6	14.2	7.5	1.7	1.9	3.1	10.8	20.7
Cliff Levingston	80	52	2184	300	568	0.528	299	563	0.531	1	5	0.200	133	191	0.696	194	304	498	270	97	104	71	734	897
Per GP			27.3	3.8	7.1		3.7	7.0		0.0	0.1		1.7	2.4		2.4	3.8	6.2	3.4	1.2	1.3	0.9	9.2	11.2
Per 48			45.5	6.6	12.5		6.6	12.4		0.0	0.1		2.9	4.2		4.3	6.7	10.9	5.9	2.1	2.3	1.6	16.1	19.7
Moses Malone	81	80	2878	538	1096	0.491	538	1084	0.496	0	12	0.000	561	711	0.789	386	570	956	154	79	245	100	1637	1727
Per GP			35.5	6.6	13.5		6.6	13.4		0.0	0.1		6.9	8.8		4.8	7.0	11.8	1.9	1.0	3.0	1.2	20.2	21.3
Per 48			60.0	9.0	18.3		9.0	18.1		0.0	0.2		9.4	11.9		6.4	9.5	15.9	2.6	1.3	4.1	1.7	27.3	28.8
Pace Mannion	5	0	18	2	6	0.333	2	4	0.500	0	2	0.000	0	0	0.000	0	2	2	2	2	3	0	4	3
Per GP			3.6	0.4	1.2		0.4	0.8		0.0	0.4		0.0	0.0		0.0	0.4	0.4	0.4	0.4	0.6	0.0	0.8	0.6
Per 48			0.4	5.3	16.0		5.3	10.7		0.0	5.3		0.0	0.0		0.0	5.3	5.3	5.3	5.3	8.0	0.0	10.7	8.0
Glenn Rivers	76	76	2462	371	816	0.455	328	692	0.474	43	124	0.347	247	287	0.861	89	197	286	263	181	158	39	1032	1308
Per GP			32.4	4.9	10.7		4.3	9.1		0.6	1.6		3.3	3.8		1.2	2.6	3.8	3.5	2.4	2.1	0.5	13.6	17.2
Per 48			51.3	7.2	15.9		6.4	13.5		0.8	2.4		4.8	5.6		1.7	3.8	5.6	5.1	3.5	3.1	0.8	20.1	25.5
Reggie Theus	82	82	2517	497	1067	0.466	480	1008	0.476	17	59	0.288	285	335	0.851	86	156	242	236	108	194	16	1296	1152
Per GP			30.7	6.1	13.0		5.9	12.3		0.2	0.7		3.5	4.1		1.0	1.9	3.0	2.9	1.3	2.4	0.2	15.8	14.0
Per 48			52.4	9.5	20.3		9.2	19.2		0.3	1.1		5.4	6.4		1.6	3.0	4.6	4.5	2.1	3.7	0.3	24.7	22.0
Ray Tolbert	51	0	341	40	95	0.421	40	95	0.421	0	0	0.000	23	37	0.622	31	57	88	55	13	35	13	103	120
Per GP			6.7	0.8	1.9		0.8	1.9		0.0	0.0		0.5	0.7		0.6	1.1	1.7	1.1	0.3	0.7	0.3	2.0	2.4
Per 48			7.1	5.6	13.4		5.6	13.4		0.0	0.0		3.2	5.2		4.4	8.0	12.4	7.7	1.8	4.9	1.8	14.5	16.9
Spud Webb	81	6	1219	133	290	0.459	132	269	0.491	1	21	0.048	52	60	0.867	21	102	123	104	70	83	6	319	509
Per GP			15.0	1.6	3.6		1.6	3.3		0.0	0.3		0.6	0.7		0.3	1.3	1.5	1.3	0.9	1.0	0.1	3.9	6.3
Per 48			25.4	5.2	11.4		5.2	10.6		0.0	0.8		2.0	2.4		0.8	4.0	4.8	4.1	2.8	3.3	0.2	12.6	20.0
Dominique Wilkins	80	80	2997	814	1756	0.464	785	1651	0.475	29	105	0.276	442	524	0.844	256	297	553	138	117	181	52	2099	1639
Per GP			37.5	10.2	21.9		9.8	20.6		0.4	1.3		5.5	6.5		3.2	3.7	6.9	1.7	1.5	2.3	0.6	26.2	20.5
Per 48			62.4	13.0	28.1		12.6	26.4		0.5	1.7		7.1	8.4		4.1	4.8	8.9	2.2	1.9	2.9	0.8	33.6	26.3

BOSTON CELTICS

The Celtics provided fans with lots of opportunities for analysis last year, if nothing else. Will Bird come back? If so, will he be ready to make a difference? Should they make the playoffs? Should they look to the lottery? Is D.J. through? Did they get the most of the Ainge trade? Will Bird's injury be a blessing in disguise, since it allowed young players to get some experience? Or did it take away the last chance for this once great group of veterans to win a championship?

How far did the Green Pride fall without Larry Bird? In the two years before he joined the team, the Celtics were 61–103 (.372). In the Bird era (excluding this past season), they have gone 550–188 (.745), with their worst record being 56–26 (.683) in 1982–83. Last year, of course, they dipped by 15 games, to 42–40. An average team. This past year offered a strong argument that Larry Bird is one of the biggest impact players of all time—second, maybe, only to Kareem Abdul-Jabbar. When you look at the team's fortunes immediately BL and AL (Before and After Larry), it's painfully clear how much he was missed.

Looking back now, it is obvious from the numbers that Bird wasn't playing on full throttle past the first two games or so. Usually a major force from the three-point area, he didn't attempt a single shot from outside all year. Could it have been his reluctance to jump on his tender feet? In his last two games, he wasn't awarded a single free throw, and had one offensive board. His shooting percentage went way down. Lack of aggressiveness? You make the call. Larry called the orthopedic surgeon.

Whether or not the Celtics fly this season depends a lot on Bird's 32-year-old, size-13½ feet. Last season, shortly after All-Everything signed his mega-contract and started forking it over to podia-trists, the hopes and fortunes of the Celts and rookie coach Jimmy Rodgers nose-dived. Their remaining long-range bomber, Danny "I was the first Bo Jackson" Ainge, and Brad Lohaus were shipped out at midseason to bring in some beef futures (Joe Kleine) and firepower (Ed Pinckney). The trade worked, at least at first, as the Celtics went on a 9–3 run. After everyone got adjusted, though, the Celts came back down to earth, realizing that the Bullets were feistily snapping at their heels. Imagine the indignation of having to fight for "their" playoff spot, one that is usually salted away by Christmas. Even earning it on the last day of the season might not have been the best of luck for the Irish. They ended the season 42–40, edging the Bullets for the final playoff spot, but losing a free pass to the lottery in the process. Hello, $32,500 playoff share. Goodbye, Sean Elliott. Len Bias. If only . . . If only . . .

Other teams stand to capitalize from the Celtics' loss of lottery, but they didn't bother shedding any tears for Bird's problems. Among the casualties of the year were a couple of Boston Garden streaks. Until this season, eight teams had never beaten the Celtics at home since Larry joined the squad. Well, three of those teams, Cleveland (11/22), Phoenix (1/4) and Indiana (1/11), broke the schneid, which was nearly offset by two new streaks inaugurated by Charlotte and Miami. Golden State, the Clippers, Sacramento, San Antonio, and Utah are still looking.

Want to join the Junior Paleontologists club? Just look at Boston's roster; you'll be able to dig up quite a few fossils. Robert Parish learned how to be *the* team leader last year, not just *a* team leader. If he can pick up where he left off last year, at age 35, the Celtics will have no problem in the middle.

Larry Bird's Season

Date	Opp	Min	FGM-A	3GM-A	FTM-A	Reb 0- T	As	PF	St	TO	Bk	Pts
11/04	NY	47	12-23	0-0	5-5	0- 5	5	4	2	1	4	29
11/05	PHI	31	13-22	0-0	1-1	1- 5	7	3	2	2	0	27
11/09	CHI	34	7-19	0-0	4-4	0-10	6	4	1	1	0	18
11/11	DET	35	8-14	0-0	8-9	0-10	6	2	1	1	1	24
11/12	MIL	26	6-19	0-0	0-0	0- 6	3	3	0	4	0	12
11/15	MIA	16	3- 7	0-0	0-0	0- 1	2	2	0	2	0	6

Boston Celtics
The Rise and Fall

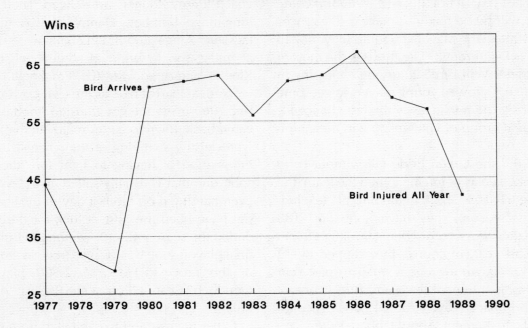

However, how much longer can you expect a 35-year-old to score 18.6 points per game and pull down 12½ rebounds? Far past the normal player's point of decline, he's now entering age's no-man's-land. Kevin McHale, who's starting to age as well, will have to produce his typical numbers of 22-plus points and 10 rebounds. Dennis Johnson was certainly no spring chicken on the court, often looking as if he were showing both his 34 years and some other players', too. He can't take over a game anymore, and his uncanny dominance at the end of games has shortened, from the last two minutes to the last five seconds. After he barely showed up with a 10.0 ppg average, look for his dominance to disappear completely, faster than you can say "Geritol."

And yet, the sun might still rise over the Charles River in the near future. The Celtics have quietly made some key acquisitions in the past two drafts. Their top choices, Reggie Lewis and Brian Shaw, have both stuck, and were two major reasons the Celts could even break .500. Expect even better things from Lewis (18.5 ppg) and Shaw, who made Ainge expendable. With a healthy Bird, an adequate backup for Parish, and more scoring from the bench, the Celts will push New York and Philly in the weak Atlantic Division. If those feet don't heal, though, and if the elders don't take their zinc to keep spry, it could be another season of discontent in Beantown.

Boston Celtics

	Home W	L	Road W	L
By Month				
November	6	3	2	4
December	4	2	1	5
January	6	2	1	6
February	3	1	3	6
March	10	0	1	4
April	3	1	2	6
Home/Away	32	9	10	31
Overtime	1	0	1	2
Offense				
0-89	0	1	1	3
90-99	0	0	1	5
100-109	7	6	3	11
110-119	16	2	4	10
120-129	8	0	1	2
130-	1	0	0	0
Defense				
0-89	1	1	2	0
90-99	8	0	5	4
100-109	16	2	3	7
110-119	7	4	0	9
120-129	0	2	0	4
130-	0	0	0	7
Over/Under				
0-189	0	1	1	3
190-199	2	0	3	4
200-209	6	1	2	3
210-219	7	3	2	7
220-229	10	2	1	2
230-239	6	2	1	4
240-	1	0	0	8
Margin Of Victory				
0-3	4	4	1	3
4-6	4	1	1	4
7-10	9	2	2	9
11-15	8	1	3	10
16-20	3	1	2	3
21-4	0	1	2	
Field Goal Attempts				
0-69	0	0	0	0
70-79	5	1	3	4
80-89	18	4	3	11
90-99	8	2	4	15
100-109	1	2	0	1
110+	0	0	0	0
Field Goals Made				
0-34	0	0	1	3
35-39	0	2	0	8
40-44	12	7	8	12
45-49	17	0	0	8
50-54	2	0	1	0
55+	1	0	0	0
Field Goal Pct.				
.000-.399	0	0	0	3
.400-.424	0	1	1	3
.425-.449	0	3	3	5
.450-.474	1	1	0	6
.475-.499	10	3	1	8
.500-.524	4	0	1	3
.525-.549	6	1	2	2
.550-.574	4	0	1	1
.575-.599	5	0	1	0
.600-	2	0	0	0

	Home W	L	Road W	L
Opp. Field Goal Attempts				
0-69	0	0	0	0
70-79	6	5	1	6
80-89	14	3	5	7
90-99	10	1	3	13
100-109	2	0	1	5
110+	0	0	0	0
Opp. Field Goal Made				
0-34	3	0	3	1
35-39	10	2	2	2
40-44	11	4	5	12
45-49	8	2	0	7
50-54	0	0	0	8
55+	0	1	0	1
Opp. Field Goal Percentage				
.000-.399	3	0	2	0
.400-.424	2	0	2	2
.425-.449	6	1	3	5
.450-.474	6	2	2	3
.475-.499	6	0	0	1
.500-.524	8	1	0	8
.525-.549	1	0	0	2
.550-.574	0	2	1	6
.575-.599	0	1	0	4
.600-	0	2	0	0
Free Throw Attempts				
0-9	0	0	0	0
10-19	3	1	1	3
20-29	13	5	5	14
30-39	12	3	3	12
40-49	4	0	1	2
50+	0	0	0	0
Free Throws Made				
0-9	1	0	0	0
10-19	7	5	4	13
20-29	18	3	3	14
30-39	6	1	3	4
40-49	0	0	0	0
50+	0	0	0	0
Free Throw Pct.				
.000-.549	1	0	0	1
.550-.599	0	0	0	2
.600-.649	2	0	1	0
.650-.699	2	0	0	2
.700-.749	1	4	2	4
.750-.799	8	2	4	5
.800-.849	12	1	3	11
.850-.899	4	1	0	3
.900-.949	2	1	0	3
.950-	0	0	0	0
Opp. Free Throw Attempts				
0-9	1	0	1	0
10-19	6	1	1	2
20-29	14	2	4	11
30-39	10	6	4	13
40-49	1	0	0	5
50+	0	0	0	0
Opp. Free Throws Made				
0-9	2	0	2	1
10-19	14	2	4	7
20-29	12	5	4	16
30-39	4	2	0	7
40-49	0	0	0	0
50+	0	0	0	0

	Home W	L	Road W	L
Opp. Free Throw Pct.				
.000-.549	1	0	1	0
.550-.599	0	1	1	1
.600-.649	2	0	1	1
.650-.699	3	0	0	3
.700-.749	5	1	1	5
.750-.799	8	3	2	9
.800-.849	8	2	3	6
.850-.899	2	0	1	4
.900-.949	3	1	0	2
.950-	0	1	0	0
Offensive Rebounds				
0-9	5	2	2	4
10-14	14	2	4	8
15-19	12	3	2	14
20-24	1	1	2	5
25+	0	1	0	0
Total Rebounds				
0-39	1	1	0	2
40-44	4	0	0	3
45-49	7	4	2	7
50-54	0	0	0	0
55-59	13	4	3	12
60-64	5	0	2	5
65-	2	0	3	2
Opp. Offensive Rebounds				
0-9	6	4	2	5
10-14	15	5	7	17
15-19	10	0	1	4
20-24	0	0	0	4
25+	1	0	0	1
Opp. Total Rebounds				
0-39	7	1	1	1
40-44	4	0	2	4
45-49	10	6	4	8
50-54	0	0	0	0
55-59	11	2	3	12
60-64	0	0	0	5
65-	0	0	0	1
Offensive Rebound Pct.				
Below 25%	8	3	3	10
25-29.99%	12	3	2	8
30-34.99%	6	2	4	8
35-39.99%	5	1	0	4
40-44.99%	1	0	1	1
45% and up	0	0	0	0
Assists				
0-14	0	0	0	3
15-19	0	0	0	6
20-24	1	4	7	10
25-29	10	2	2	6
30-34	15	3	1	6
35+	6	0	0	0
Opp. Assists				
0-14	0	0	1	0
15-19	6	1	2	1
20-24	11	3	3	9
25-29	10	3	3	9
30-34	4	1	1	9
35+	1	1	0	3
Edge In Assists				
Below -15	0	0	0	4
-10 to -14	1	2	0	2

	Home W	L	Road W	L
-5 to -9	1	1	1	7
0 to -4	4	0	4	13
1-4	8	3	2	3
5-9	7	1	3	1
10-14	8	2	0	1
15-	3	0	0	0
Personal Fouls				
0-14	0	0	1	0
15-19	5	2	3	2
20-24	19	4	2	16
25-29	8	2	4	12
30-34	0	1	0	1
35+	0	0	0	0
Opp. Personal Fouls				
0-14	0	0	0	0
15-19	3	0	2	5
20-24	12	6	5	16
25-29	14	2	1	8
30-34	3	1	2	2
35+	0	0	0	0
Personal Fouls Edge				
Below -15	0	0	0	0
-10 to -14	3	1	1	0
-5 to -9	8	0	4	3
0 to -4	12	3	0	15
1-4	5	5	3	6
5-9	4	0	2	7
10-14	0	0	0	0
15+	0	0	0	0
Steals				
0-5	5	4	1	8
6-7	8	0	5	8
8-9	7	3	3	8
10-11	5	2	0	5
12-13	2	0	1	2
14+	5	0	0	0
Opp. Steals				
0-5	5	1	2	0
6-7	7	3	0	8
8-9	9	2	1	5
10-11	3	3	3	8
12-13	7	0	2	6
14+	1	0	2	4
Edge In Steals				
Below -7	1	1	2	5
-4 to -6	4	1	3	9
0 to -3	10	3	2	12
1-3	9	2	2	5
4-6	6	2	1	0
7-	2	0	0	0
Turnovers				
0-14	17	5	3	8
15-19	11	4	3	15
20-24	4	0	3	7
25-29	0	0	1	1
30-34	0	0	0	0
35+	0	0	0	0
Opp. Turnovers				
0-14	15	4	6	19
15-19	12	3	3	10
20-24	3	2	1	1
25-29	2	0	0	1
30-34	0	0	0	0
35+	0	0	0	0

	Home W	L	Road W	L
Edge In Turnovers				
Below -15	0	0	0	0
-10 to -14	1	1	0	0
-5 to -9	7	1	1	2
0 to -4	10	3	1	3
1-4	8	3	4	11
5-9	5	0	2	12
10-14	1	1	1	2
15+	0	0	1	1
Blocks				
1-2	1	1	0	8
3-4	13	2	2	5
5-6	9	3	2	13
7-8	8	3	4	4
9-10	1	0	1	1
11+	0	0	1	0
Opp. Blocks				
0-2	10	2	2	3
3-4	9	3	3	9
5-6	9	2	4	5
7-8	3	1	1	10

	Home W	L	Road W	L
9-10	1	1	0	2
11+	0	0	0	2
Edge In Blocks				
Below -7	0	0	0	1
-4 to -6	3	1	1	5
0 to -3	7	4	1	15
1-3	14	2	4	8
4-6	8	2	3	2
7+	0	0	1	0
Three-Pointers Attempted				
0-2	15	2	3	11
3-5	12	5	6	10
6-8	4	0	1	8
9-11	1	2	0	1
12-14	0	0	0	1
15+	0	0	0	0
Three-Pointers Made				
0-2	28	7	9	30
3-5	4	2	1	1

	Home W	L	Road W	L
6-8	0	0	0	0
9-11	0	0	0	0
12-14	0	0	0	0
15+	0	0	0	0
Three-Pointers Pct.				
.000-.099	19	3	5	17
.100-.149	0	0	0	1
.150-.199	1	0	1	1
.200-.249	0	0	0	0
.250-.299	2	1	1	2
.300-.349	4	2	2	7
.350-.399	1	0	0	0
.400-.449	0	1	0	0
.450-.499	0	0	0	0
.500-	5	2	1	3
Opp. Three-Point Attempts				
0-2	2	4	3	8
3-5	12	2	4	12
6-8	11	2	2	6
9-11	3	1	1	0

	Home W	L	Road W	L
12-14	3	0	0	5
15+	1	0	0	0
Opp. Three-Pointers Made				
0-2	24	7	9	23
3-5	8	2	1	7
6-8	0	0	0	0
9-11	0	0	0	1
12-14	0	0	0	0
15+	0	0	0	0
Opp. Three-Pointer Pct.				
.000-.099	8	4	6	13
.100-.149	1	0	0	2
.150-.199	0	0	0	0
.200-.249	2	1	0	2
.250-.299	6	0	0	1
.300-.349	8	0	3	4
.350-.399	2	2	0	1
.400-.449	1	1	0	0
.450-.499	0	0	0	0
.500-	4	1	1	8

Boston Celtics
1988–89 Power Chart

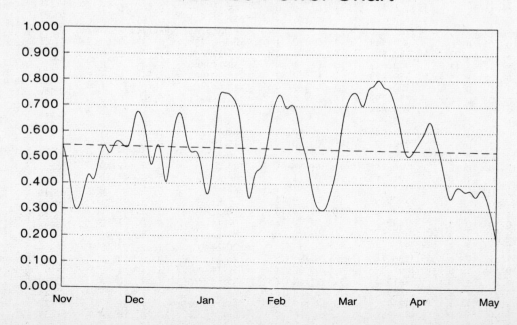

Boston Celtics

	GP	GS	Min	FGM	FGA	FG%	2GM	2GA	2G%	3GM	3GA	3G%	FTM	FTA	FT%	Off	Tot	Ast	PF	Stl	TO	Blk	Pts	HGS
Mark Acres	62	0	632	55	114	0.482	54	113	0.478	1	1	1.000	26	48	0.542	59	87	146	94	19	23	6	137	189
Per GP			10.2	0.9	1.8		0.9	1.8		0.0	0.0		0.4	0.8		1.0	1.4	2.4	1.5	0.3	0.4	0.1	2.2	3.0
Per 48			13.2	4.2	8.7		4.1	8.6		0.1	0.1		2.0	3.6		4.5	6.6	11.1	7.1	1.4	1.7	0.5	10.4	14.4
Danny Ainge	45	28	1349	271	589	0.460	213	434	0.491	58	155	0.374	114	128	0.891	37	117	154	108	52	82	1	714	595
Per GP			30.0	6.0	13.1		4.7	9.6		1.3	3.4		2.5	2.8		0.8	2.6	3.4	2.4	1.2	1.8	0.0	15.9	13.2
Per 48			28.1	9.6	21.0		7.6	15.4		2.1	5.5		4.1	4.6		1.3	4.2	5.5	3.8	1.9	2.9	0.0	25.4	21.2
Larry Bird	6	6	189	49	104	0.471	49	104	0.471	0	0	0.000	18	19	0.947	1	36	37	18	6	11	5	116	106
Per GP			31.5	8.2	17.3		8.2	17.3		0.0	0.0		3.0	3.2		0.2	6.0	6.2	3.0	1.0	1.8	0.8	19.3	17.7
Per 48			3.9	12.4	26.4		12.4	26.4		0.0	0.0		4.6	4.8		0.3	9.1	9.4	4.6	1.5	2.8	1.3	29.5	26.9
Otis Birdsong	13	0	108	18	36	0.500	17	33	0.515	1	3	0.333	0	2	0.000	4	9	13	10	3	12	1	37	26
Per GP			8.3	1.4	2.8		1.3	2.5		0.1	0.2		0.0	0.2		0.3	0.7	1.0	0.8	0.2	0.9	0.1	2.8	2.0
Per 48			2.3	8.0	16.0		7.6	14.7		0.4	1.3		0.0	0.9		1.8	4.0	5.8	4.4	1.3	5.3	0.4	16.4	11.6
Kevin Gamble	44	6	375	75	136	0.551	73	125	0.584	2	11	0.182	35	55	0.636	11	31	42	40	13	19	3	187	164
Per GP			8.5	1.7	3.1		1.7	2.8		0.0	0.3		0.8	1.3		0.3	0.7	1.0	0.9	0.3	0.4	0.1	4.3	3.7
Per 48			7.8	9.6	17.4		9.3	16.0		0.3	1.4		4.5	7.0		1.4	4.0	5.4	5.1	1.7	2.4	0.4	23.9	21.0
Ronnie Grandison	72	0	528	59	142	0.415	59	132	0.447	0	10	0.000	59	80	0.737	47	45	92	71	17	36	3	177	189
Per GP			7.3	0.8	2.0		0.8	1.8		0.0	0.1		0.8	1.1		0.7	0.6	1.3	1.0	0.2	0.5	0.0	2.5	2.6
Per 48			11.0	5.4	12.9		5.4	12.0		0.0	0.9		5.4	7.3		4.3	4.1	8.4	6.5	1.5	3.3	0.3	16.1	17.2
Dennis Johnson	72	72	2309	277	638	0.434	270	588	0.459	7	50	0.140	160	195	0.821	31	159	190	211	94	175	21	721	892
Per GP			32.1	3.8	8.9		3.8	8.2		0.1	0.7		2.2	2.7		0.4	2.2	2.6	2.9	1.3	2.4	0.3	10.0	12.4
Per 48			48.1	5.8	13.3		5.6	12.2		0.1	1.0		3.3	4.1		0.6	3.3	3.9	4.4	2.0	3.6	0.4	15.0	18.5
Joe Kleine	28	2	498	59	129	0.457	59	128	0.461	0	1	0.000	53	64	0.828	49	88	137	66	15	37	5	171	204
Per GP			17.8	2.1	4.6		2.1	4.6		0.0	0.0		1.9	2.3		1.8	3.1	4.9	2.4	0.5	1.3	0.2	6.1	7.3
Per 48			10.4	5.7	12.4		5.7	12.3		0.0	0.1		5.1	6.2		4.7	8.5	13.2	6.4	1.4	3.6	0.5	16.5	19.7
Reggie Lewis	81	57	2657	604	1242	0.486	601	1220	0.493	3	22	0.136	284	361	0.787	116	261	377	258	124	142	71	1495	1304
Per GP			32.8	7.5	15.3		7.4	15.1		0.0	0.3		3.5	4.5		1.4	3.2	4.7	3.2	1.5	1.8	0.9	18.5	16.1
Per 48			55.4	10.9	22.4		10.9	22.0		0.1	0.4		5.1	6.5		2.1	4.7	6.8	4.7	2.2	2.6	1.3	27.0	23.6
Brad Lohaus	48	15	738	117	270	0.433	117	266	0.440	0	4	0.000	35	46	0.761	47	95	142	101	21	49	26	269	262
Per GP			15.4	2.4	5.6		2.4	5.5		0.0	0.1		0.7	1.0		1.0	2.0	3.0	2.1	0.4	1.0	0.5	5.6	5.5
Per 48			15.4	7.6	17.6		7.6	17.3		0.0	0.3		2.3	3.0		3.1	6.2	9.2	6.6	1.4	3.2	1.7	17.5	17.0
Kevin McHale	78	74	2876	661	1211	0.546	661	1206	0.548	0	5	0.000	436	533	0.818	223	414	637	223	26	196	97	1758	1605
Per GP			36.9	8.5	15.5		8.5	15.5		0.0	0.1		5.6	6.8		2.9	5.3	8.2	2.9	0.3	2.5	1.2	22.5	20.6
Per 48			59.9	11.0	20.2		11.0	20.1		0.0	0.1		7.3	8.9		3.7	6.9	10.6	3.7	0.4	3.3	1.6	29.3	26.8
Robert Parish	80	80	2840	596	1045	0.570	596	1045	0.570	0	0	0.000	294	409	0.719	342	654	996	209	79	200	115	1486	1732
Per GP			35.5	7.4	13.1		7.4	13.1		0.0	0.0		3.7	5.1		4.3	8.2	12.4	2.6	1.0	2.5	1.4	18.6	21.6
Per 48			59.2	10.1	17.7		10.1	17.7		0.0	0.0		5.0	6.9		5.8	11.1	16.8	3.5	1.3	3.4	1.9	25.1	29.3
Jim Paxson	57	7	1138	202	445	0.454	198	421	0.470	4	24	0.167	84	103	0.816	18	56	74	96	38	57	8	492	375
Per GP			20.0	3.5	7.8		3.5	7.4		0.1	0.4		1.5	1.8		0.3	1.0	1.3	1.7	0.7	1.0	0.1	8.6	6.6
Per 48			23.7	8.5	18.8		8.4	17.8		0.2	1.0		3.5	4.3		0.8	2.4	3.1	4.0	1.6	2.4	0.3	20.8	15.8
Ed Pinckney	29	9	678	95	176	0.540	95	176	0.540	0	0	0.000	103	129	0.798	60	88	148	77	29	38	23	293	357
Per GP			23.4	3.3	6.1		3.3	6.1		0.0	0.0		3.6	4.4		2.1	3.0	5.1	2.7	1.0	1.3	0.8	10.1	12.3
Per 48			14.1	6.7	12.5		6.7	12.5		0.0	0.0		7.3	9.1		4.2	6.2	10.5	5.5	2.1	2.7	1.6	20.7	25.3
Ramon Rivas	28	0	91	12	31	0.387	12	30	0.400	0	1	0.000	16	25	0.640	9	15	24	21	4	9	1	40	38
Per GP			3.3	0.4	1.1		0.4	1.1		0.0	0.0		0.6	0.9		0.3	0.5	0.9	0.8	0.1	0.3	0.0	1.4	1.4
Per 48			1.9	6.3	16.4		6.3	15.8		0.0	0.5		8.4	13.2		4.7	7.9	12.7	11.1	2.1	4.7	0.5	21.1	20.0
Brian Shaw	82	54	2301	297	686	0.433	297	673	0.441	0	13	0.000	109	132	0.826	119	257	376	211	78	187	27	703	959
Per GP			28.1	3.6	8.4		3.6	8.2		0.0	0.2		1.3	1.6		1.5	3.1	4.6	2.6	1.0	2.3	0.3	8.6	11.7
Per 48			47.9	6.2	14.3		6.2	14.0		0.0	0.3		2.3	2.8		2.5	5.4	7.8	4.4	1.6	3.9	0.6	14.7	20.0
Kevin Upshaw	23	0	473	73	149	0.490	71	139	0.511	2	10	0.200	14	20	0.700	6	30	36	62	19	42	3	162	177
Per GP			20.6	3.2	6.5		3.1	6.0		0.1	0.4		0.6	0.9		0.3	1.3	1.6	2.7	0.8	1.8	0.1	7.0	7.7
Per 48			9.9	7.4	15.1		7.2	14.1		0.2	1.0		1.4	2.0		0.6	3.0	3.7	6.3	1.9	4.3	0.3	16.4	18.0

CHARLOTTE HORNETS

Charlotte fans realized early on what Minnesota Twins fans caught on to a long time ago: Screaming for three hours with no apparent provocation really psychs your team up, but more important, it makes for a great media event. Look! Rambis is taking his warmups off! Yeaaaaaaah! Isn't Muggsy cute out there? Yeaaaaaaaaaaah! Here comes a popcorn vendor! Yeaaaaaaaaaaaaah! Rex is tying his shoes! Yeaaaaaaaaaaaaaaaaaaaah!

In the beginning of the season, it got everyone pretty pumped, and the Hornets burned a few opponents early, establishing them as a team not to be taken lightly. However, the whole thing kind of fizzled later on in the season, as a prolonged slump finished off any realistic chances that Charlotte had to finish first in the Atlantic. Why the nose dive? It seems that teams didn't take them lightly—the second time around. But even though one would think that Charlotte became "super-charged" at home, no team had a smaller home-court advantage.

Of course, when a team goes 20–62 in their NBA debut, just about all you *can* talk about is their fans. Things pretty much have to get better in their second season, if only because *they* now can pick on two expansion teams (three if you count the

Clippers). They can aim for two goals next year: a better won-lost record, and even larger crowds at home. For the players as well as for the fans who packed the 23,500-seat Charlotte Coliseum 41 times to lead the league in attendance, the team's growing pains were cushioned somewhat by the deafening crowd noise. Unfortunately, many games were over by the end of the first quarter, when opponents scored over 35 points about twice a month. Things don't look much brighter in Dixie this season, except that the Hornets might still surprise a few teams, as they did last year. Team leader Kelly Tripucka (22.6, 13th best in league) will again vie for the ball with 6'5" Rex Chapman (16.9 ppg) and 33-year-old Robert Reid. But with no one even coming close to controlling the paint (Kurt Rambis, Earl Cureton, Tim Kempton, and Dave Hoppen do the best imitation), the Hornets will get pounded again. Look for slight improvement, but cellar status is imminent.

In December, *USA Today* ran a piece explaining that owner George Shinn held a pregame prayer right before the National Anthem at every game, "to thank God for his good fortune." The article was written with quotes from a team spokesman, pre-

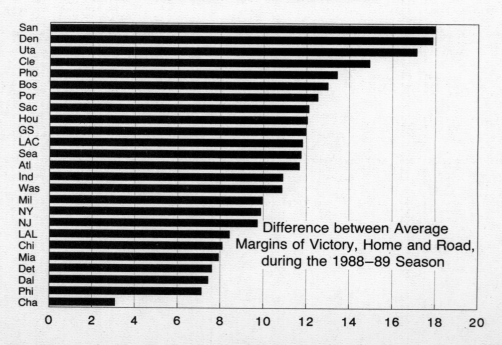

Charlotte Hornets

Difference between Average Margins of Victory, Home and Road, during the 1988–89 Season

sumably because Shinn, a 48-year-old business-man, was still recovering from a life-threatening brain seizure. The Lord doles out "good fortune" in mysterious ways.

Only in Charlotte: Earl Paula, a 5'7" Wrightsville, North Carolina, fan ended up in Wrongsville when he was caught in the Hornet locker room trying to suit up for the game against Cleveland. "I'm the only one who can stop Mark Price," he shouted as he was led away by the police. With Paula in the slammer, Price notched 20 against the Hornets. Coach Dick Harter only asked, "Why can't a 6'8" guy sneak into the locker room?" Word has it that Paula was later contacted by the Nets and offered a three-year no-cut deal on the spot, which fell through only when New Jersey couldn't figure out how to waste a draft choice on it.

Charlotte Hornets

By Month

	Home W	L	Road W	L
November	2	4	1	6
December	5	3	0	6
January	1	5	2	8
February	4	5	0	3
March	0	7	2	6
April	0	5	3	4
Home/Away	12	29	8	33
Overtime	0	2	1	1

Offense

	Home W	L	Road W	L
0-89	0	1	1	5
90-99	2	11	0	6
100-109	4	12	3	12
110-119	4	4	2	10
120-129	2	1	2	0
130-	0	0	0	0

Defense

	Home W	L	Road W	L
0-89	1	0	1	0
90-99	1	2	1	2
100-109	7	6	3	8
110-119	3	13	2	9
120-129	0	6	1	9
130-	0	2	0	5

Over/Under

	Home W	L	Road W	L
0-189	1	0	1	2
190-199	1	4	0	5
200-209	1	6	1	3
210-219	4	8	2	6
220-229	2	6	2	6
230-239	3	3	1	4
240-	0	2	1	7

Margin Of Victory

	Home W	L	Road W	L
0-3	6	2	3	2
4-6	1	5	3	3
7-10	1	9	1	9
11-15	4	6	0	6
16-20	0	2	1	4
21-	0	5	0	9

Field Goal Attempts

	Home W	L	Road W	L
0-69	0	0	0	0
70-79	1	0	0	3
80-89	1	13	3	13
90-99	10	12	4	14
100-109	0	4	1	3
110+	0	0	0	0

Field Goals Made

	Home W	L	Road W	L
0-34	0	1	0	4
35-39	2	6	1	9
40-44	5	19	2	11
45-49	5	3	3	9
50-54	0	0	2	0
55+	0	0	0	0

Field Goal Pct.

	Home W	L	Road W	L
.000-.399	0	1	1	4
.400-.424	1	6	0	5
.425-.449	1	5	0	7
.450-.474	3	10	2	5
.475-.499	3	4	1	4
.500-.524	3	2	2	3
.525-.549	1	1	1	2
.550-.574	0	0	0	3
.575-.599	0	0	1	0
.600-	0	0	0	0

Opp. Field Goal Attempts

	Home W	L	Road W	L
0-69	0	2	0	0
70-79	2	3	0	5
80-89	7	16	4	11
90-99	1	8	4	17
100-109	2	0	0	0
110+	0	0	0	0

Opp. Field Goal Made

	Home W	L	Road W	L
0-34	0	2	1	1
35-39	4	4	0	5
40-44	7	11	6	11
45-49	1	8	1	10
50-54	0	4	0	6
55+	0	0	0	0

Opp. Field Goal Percentage

	Home W	L	Road W	L
.000-.399	0	0	1	0
.400-.424	3	2	0	0
.425-.449	3	4	1	1
.450-.474	1	1	2	6
.475-.499	2	4	3	7
.500-.524	1	7	1	9
.525-.549	1	4	0	5
.550-.574	1	1	0	3
.575-.599	0	4	0	1
.600-	0	2	0	1

Free Throw Attempts

	Home W	L	Road W	L
0-9	0	1	1	0
10-19	0	9	1	7
20-29	6	11	4	16
30-39	5	7	2	10
40-49	1	1	0	0
50+	0	0	0	0

Free Throws Made

	Home W	L	Road W	L
0-9	0	3	1	2
10-19	6	14	3	17
20-29	4	11	4	13
30-39	2	1	0	1
40-49	0	0	0	0
50+	0	0	0	0

Free Throw Pct.

	Home W	L	Road W	L
.000-.549	1	0	0	0
.550-.599	0	1	0	1
.600-.649	1	1	0	3
.650-.699	1	4	0	1
.700-.749	2	9	0	4
.750-.799	3	7	4	8
.800-.849	2	2	1	9
.850-.899	1	3	3	4
.900-.949	0	1	0	2
.950-	1	1	0	1

Opp. Free Throw Attempts

	Home W	L	Road W	L
0-9	0	0	0	0
10-19	0	0	0	1
20-29	7	12	5	12
30-39	4	12	3	10
40-49	1	4	0	9
50+	0	1	0	1

Opp. Free Throws Made

	Home W	L	Road W	L
0-9	0	0	0	0
10-19	4	7	4	7
20-29	8	12	4	14
30-39	0	9	0	10
40-49	0	1	0	2
50+	0	0	0	0

Opp. Free Throw Pct.

	Home W	L	Road W	L
.000-.549	1	1	0	0
.550-.599	2	0	1	0
.600-.649	0	0	1	0
.650-.699	2	1	2	2
.700-.749	2	5	2	6
.750-.799	2	8	0	7
.800-.849	1	6	2	11
.850-.899	1	6	0	5
.900-.949	0	2	0	2
.950-1	0	0		

Offensive Rebounds

	Home W	L	Road W	L
0-9	0	4	1	6
10-14	5	10	4	14
15-19	7	13	2	9
20-24	0	2	1	4
25+	0	0	0	0

Total Rebounds

	Home W	L	Road W	L
0-39	0	5	0	3
40-44	0	4	0	8
45-49	4	6	4	4
50-54	0	0	0	0
55-59	4	13	3	17
60-64	3	1	0	1
65-1	0	1	0	

Opp. Offensive Rebounds

	Home W	L	Road W	L
0-9	2	3	0	2
10-14	4	17	4	11
15-19	3	6	3	19
20-24	3	3	0	1
25+	0	0	1	0

Opp. Total Rebounds

	Home W	L	Road W	L
0-39	0	0	0	0
40-44	0	1	1	3
45-49	4	7	0	3
50-54	0	0	0	0
55-59	5	11	4	15
60-64	2	8	2	8
65-1	2	1	4	

Offensive Rebound Pct.

	Home W	L	Road W	L
Below 25%	5	12	4	19
25-29.99%	4	11	1	9
30-34.99%	2	5	3	5
35-39.99%	1	1	0	0
40-44.99%	0	0	0	0
45% and up	0	0	0	0

Assists

	Home W	L	Road W	L
0-14	0	1	0	0
15-19	0	0	0	1
20-24	2	4	1	10
25-29	5	17	1	7
30-34	3	7	3	10
35+	2	0	3	5

Opp. Assists

	Home W	L	Road W	L
0-14	1	1	0	0
15-19	4	5	1	3
20-24	5	8	2	8
25-29	2	10	3	9
30-34	0	4	2	9
35+	0	1	0	4

Edge In Assists

	Home W	L	Road W	L
Below -15	0	0	0	0
-10 to -14	0	0	0	1

	Home W	L	Road W	L
-5 to -9	0	6	0	3
0 to -4	0	5	1	10
1-4	2	8	1	10
5-9	6	6	4	6
10-14	3	4	2	3
15-	1	0	0	0

Personal Fouls

	Home W	L	Road W	L
0-14	0	0	0	0
15-19	2	1	1	3
20-24	4	13	4	11
25-29	4	10	3	12
30-34	2	4	0	5
35+	0	1	0	2

Opp. Personal Fouls

	Home W	L	Road W	L
0-14	0	1	2	2
15-19	1	12	0	7
20-24	2	13	4	16
25-29	7	3	2	7
30-34	2	0	0	1
35+	0	0	0	0

Personal Fouls Edge

	Home W	L	Road W	L
Below -15	0	0	0	0
-10 to -14	1	0	0	0
-5 to -9	2	0	0	2
0 to -4	6	4	5	7
1-4	2	13	1	10
5-9	1	8	0	8
10-14	0	2	1	3
15+	0	2	1	3

Steals

	Home W	L	Road W	L
0-5	0	3	1	3
6-7	1	11	2	10
8-9	8	8	1	8
10-11	1	4	3	6
12-13	2	2	0	3
14+	0	1	1	3

Opp. Steals

	Home W	L	Road W	L
0-5	2	8	4	4
6-7	2	10	1	3
8-9	4	6	1	8
10-11	2	1	2	3
12-13	1	2	0	8
14+	1	2	0	7

Edge In Steals

	Home W	L	Road W	L
Below -7	0	1	0	4
-4 to -6	1	3	0	6
0 to -3	4	9	1	15
1-3	5	10	5	5
4-6	2	4	1	2
7-	0	2	1	1

Turnovers

	Home W	L	Road W	L
0-14	4	18	5	7
15-19	8	7	3	15
20-24	0	4	0	8
25-29	0	0	0	3
30-34	0	0	0	0
35+	0	0	0	0

Opp. Turnovers

	Home W	L	Road W	L
0-14	2	10	4	10
15-19	5	14	0	14
20-24	5	4	2	6
25-29	0	1	2	3
30-34	0	0	0	0
35+	0	0	0	0

	Home W	L	Road W	L
Edge In Turnovers				
Below -15	0	0	0	0
-10 to -14	0	1	1	3
-5 to -9	5	6	3	1
0 to -4	5	16	2	8
1-4	2	4	2	15
5-9	0	2	0	6
10-14	0	0	0	0
15+	0	0	0	0
Blocks				
1-2	6	11	2	13
3-4	2	11	5	13
5-6	4	5	0	4
7-8	0	2	1	3
9-10	0	0	0	0
11+	0	0	0	0
Opp. Blocks				
0-2	0	5	0	5
3-4	4	11	2	6
5-6	4	8	3	8
7-8	3	4	2	7

	Home W	L	Road W	L
9-10	1	1	0	6
11+	0	0	1	1
Edge In Blocks				
Below -7	1	0	1	3
-4 to -6	4	5	1	9
0 to -3	5	18	4	16
1-3	2	5	2	5
4-6	0	1	0	0
7+	0	0	0	0
Three-Pointers Attempted				
0-2	3	3	0	2
3-5	6	16	3	18
6-8	2	5	4	9
9-11	1	5	1	4
12-14	0	0	0	0
15+	0	0	0	0
Three-Pointers Made				
0-2	11	23	5	24
3-5	1	6	3	8

	Home W	L	Road W	L
6-8	0	0	0	1
9-11	0	0	0	0
12-14	0	0	0	0
15+	0	0	0	0
Three-Pointers Pct.				
.000-.099	6	10	2	11
.100-.149	1	1	0	3
.150-.199	0	0	0	1
.200-.249	0	0	0	1
.250-.299	1	4	0	0
.300-.349	3	10	1	6
.350-.399	1	0	1	3
.400-.449	0	1	0	2
.450-.499	0	0	1	0
.500-	0	3	3	7
Opp. Three-Point Attempts				
0-2	2	8	2	13
3-5	7	9	0	12
6-8	1	8	1	5
9-11	1	4	1	1

	Home W	L	Road W	L
12-14	0	0	4	2
15+	1	0	0	0
Opp. Three-Pointers Made				
0-2	10	25	4	28
3-5	2	4	3	5
6-8	0	0	1	0
9-11	0	0	0	0
12-14	0	0	0	0
15+	0	0	0	0
Opp. Three-Pointer Pct.				
.000-.099	5	13	4	19
.100-.149	2	1	0	0
.150-.199	1	3	1	2
.200-.249	1	2	0	2
.250-.299	0	0	0	1
.300-.349	1	6	2	2
.350-.399	0	0	1	0
.400-.449	1	2	0	2
.450-.499	0	0	0	0
.500-	1	2	0	5

Charlotte Hornets
1988–89 Power Chart

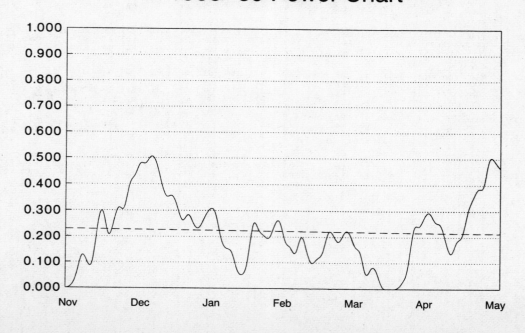

HoopStats

Charlotte Hornets

	GP	GS	Min	FGM	FGA	FG%	2GM	2GA	2G%	3GM	3GA	3G%	FTM	FTA	FT%	Off	Tot	Ast	PF	Stl	TO	Blk	Pts	HGS
Tyrone Bogues	79	21	1755	178	418	0.426	177	405	0.437	1	13	0.077	66	88	0.750	53	112	165	141	110	124	7	423	913
Per GP			22.2	2.3	5.3		2.2	5.1		0.0	0.2		0.8	1.1		0.7	1.4	2.1	1.8	1.4	1.6	0.1	5.4	11.6
Per 48			36.6	4.9	11.4		4.8	11.1		0.0	0.4		1.8	2.4		1.4	3.1	4.5	3.9	3.0	3.4	0.2	11.6	25.0
Rex Chapman	75	44	2219	526	1271	0.414	466	1080	0.431	60	191	0.314	155	195	0.795	74	113	187	167	71	113	25	1267	755
Per GP			29.6	7.0	16.9		6.2	14.4		0.8	2.5		2.1	2.6		1.0	1.5	2.5	2.2	0.9	1.5	0.3	16.9	10.1
Per 48			46.2	11.4	27.5		10.1	23.4		1.3	4.1		3.4	4.2		1.6	2.4	4.0	3.6	1.5	2.4	0.5	27.4	16.3
Earl Cureton	82	41	2047	233	465	0.501	233	464	0.502	0	1	0.000	66	123	0.537	188	300	488	230	50	114	61	532	737
Per GP			25.0	2.8	5.7		2.8	5.7		0.0	0.0		0.8	1.5		2.3	3.7	6.0	2.8	0.6	1.4	0.7	6.5	9.0
Per 48			42.6	5.5	10.9		5.5	10.9		0.0	0.0		1.5	2.9		4.4	7.0	11.4	5.4	1.2	2.7	1.4	12.5	17.3
Dell Curry	48	0	813	256	521	0.491	237	466	0.509	19	55	0.345	40	46	0.870	26	78	104	68	42	44	4	571	363
Per GP			16.9	5.3	10.9		4.9	9.7		0.4	1.1		0.8	1.0		0.5	1.6	2.2	1.4	0.9	0.9	0.1	11.9	7.6
Per 48			16.9	15.1	30.8		14.0	27.5		1.1	3.2		2.4	2.7		1.5	4.6	6.1	4.0	2.5	2.6	0.2	33.7	21.4
Rickey Green	33	2	370	57	132	0.432	56	127	0.441	1	5	0.200	13	14	0.929	4	19	23	16	18	28	0	128	138
Per GP			11.2	1.7	4.0		1.7	3.8		0.0	0.2		0.4	0.4		0.1	0.6	0.7	0.5	0.5	0.8	0.0	3.9	4.2
Per 48			7.7	7.4	17.1		7.3	16.5		0.1	0.6		1.7	1.8		0.5	2.5	3.0	2.1	2.3	3.6	0.0	16.6	17.9
Michael Holton	67	60	1696	215	504	0.427	212	490	0.433	3	14	0.214	120	143	0.839	30	75	105	165	66	119	12	553	722
Per GP			25.3	3.2	7.5		3.2	7.3		0.0	0.2		1.8	2.1		0.4	1.1	1.6	2.5	1.0	1.8	0.2	8.3	10.8
Per 48			35.3	6.1	14.3		6.0	13.9		0.1	0.4		3.4	4.0		0.8	2.1	3.0	4.7	1.9	3.4	0.3	15.7	20.4
Dave Hoppen	77	36	1419	199	353	0.564	198	351	0.564	1	2	0.500	101	139	0.727	123	261	384	239	25	77	21	500	572
Per GP			18.4	2.6	4.6		2.6	4.6		0.0	0.0		1.3	1.8		1.6	3.4	5.0	3.1	0.3	1.0	0.3	6.5	7.4
Per 48			29.6	6.7	11.9		6.7	11.9		0.0	0.1		3.4	4.7		4.2	8.8	13.0	8.1	0.8	2.6	0.7	16.9	19.3
Tim Kempton	79	0	1341	171	335	0.510	171	334	0.512	0	1	0.000	142	207	0.686	91	213	304	215	41	121	14	484	533
Per GP			17.0	2.2	4.2		2.2	4.2		0.0	0.0		1.8	2.6		1.2	2.7	3.8	2.7	0.5	1.5	0.2	6.1	6.7
Per 48			27.9	6.1	12.0		6.1	12.0		0.0	0.0		5.1	7.4		3.3	7.6	10.9	7.7	1.5	4.3	0.5	17.3	19.1
Greg Kite	12	12	213	16	30	0.533	16	30	0.533	0	0	0.000	6	10	0.600	15	38	53	43	4	12	8	38	64
Per GP			17.7	1.3	2.5		1.3	2.5		0.0	0.0		0.5	0.8		1.3	3.2	4.4	3.6	0.3	1.0	0.7	3.2	5.3
Per 48			4.4	3.6	6.8		3.6	6.8		0.0	0.0		1.4	2.3		3.4	8.6	11.9	9.7	0.9	2.7	1.8	8.6	14.4
Ralph Lewis	42	0	336	58	121	0.479	57	118	0.483	1	3	0.333	19	39	0.487	35	26	61	28	11	24	3	136	116
Per GP			8.0	1.4	2.9		1.4	2.8		0.0	0.1		0.5	0.9		0.8	0.6	1.5	0.7	0.3	0.6	0.1	3.2	2.8
Per 48			7.0	8.3	17.3		8.1	16.9		0.1	0.4		2.7	5.6		5.0	3.7	8.7	4.0	1.6	3.4	0.4	19.4	16.6
John Lowe	14	0	250	8	25	0.320	8	23	0.348	0	2	0.000	7	11	0.636	6	28	34	28	14	9	0	23	127
Per GP			17.9	0.6	1.8		0.6	1.6		0.0	0.1		0.5	0.8		0.4	2.0	2.4	2.0	1.0	0.6	0.0	1.6	9.1
Per 48			5.2	1.5	4.8		1.5	4.4		0.0	0.4		1.3	2.1		1.2	5.4	6.5	5.4	2.7	1.7	0.0	4.4	24.4
Kurt Rambis	75	75	2233	325	627	0.518	325	624	0.521	0	3	0.000	182	248	0.734	269	434	703	208	100	148	57	832	1122
Per GP			29.8	4.3	8.4		4.3	8.3		0.0	0.0		2.4	3.3		3.6	5.8	9.4	2.8	1.3	2.0	0.8	11.1	15.0
Per 48			46.5	7.0	13.5		7.0	13.4		0.0	0.1		3.9	5.3		5.8	9.3	15.1	4.5	2.1	3.2	1.2	17.9	24.1
Robert Reid	82	54	2152	519	1214	0.428	502	1162	0.432	17	52	0.327	152	196	0.776	82	220	302	235	53	106	20	1207	791
Per GP			26.2	6.3	14.8		6.1	14.2		0.2	0.6		1.9	2.4		1.0	2.7	3.7	2.9	0.6	1.3	0.2	14.7	9.6
Per 48			44.8	11.6	27.1		11.2	25.9		0.4	1.2		3.4	4.4		1.8	4.9	6.7	5.2	1.2	2.4	0.4	26.9	17.6
Brian Rowsom	34	0	517	80	162	0.494	79	161	0.491	1	1	1.000	65	81	0.802	56	81	137	69	10	18	12	226	252
Per GP			15.2	2.4	4.8		2.3	4.7		0.0	0.0		1.9	2.4		1.6	2.4	4.0	2.0	0.3	0.5	0.4	6.6	7.4
Per 48			10.8	7.4	15.0		7.3	14.9		0.1	0.1		6.0	7.5		5.2	7.5	12.7	6.4	0.9	1.7	1.1	21.0	23.4
Tom Tolbert	14	0	117	17	37	0.459	17	34	0.500	0	3	0.000	6	12	0.500	7	14	21	20	2	2	4	40	44
Per GP			8.4	1.2	2.6		1.2	2.4		0.0	0.2		0.4	0.9		0.5	1.0	1.5	1.4	0.1	0.1	0.3	2.9	3.1
Per 48			2.4	7.0	15.2		7.0	13.9		0.0	1.2		2.5	4.9		2.9	5.7	8.6	8.2	0.8	0.8	1.6	16.4	18.1
Kelly Tripucka	71	65	2302	568	1215	0.467	538	1131	0.476	30	84	0.357	440	508	0.866	79	188	267	196	88	236	16	1606	1154
Per GP			32.4	8.0	17.1		7.6	15.9		0.4	1.2		6.2	7.2		1.1	2.6	3.8	2.8	1.2	3.3	0.2	22.6	16.3
Per 48			48.0	11.8	25.3		11.2	23.6		0.6	1.8		9.2	10.6		1.6	3.9	5.6	4.1	1.8	4.9	0.3	33.5	24.1

CHICAGO BULLS

Does everyone have it straight? That Jordan's play was unselfish this year? We'll keep telling you if you don't. Jordan was getting his team into the flow all year. Michael didn't feel the pressure to do everything, so he got everyone else into the game so they'd all benefit. Michael switched to point guard to help the rest of the team get *just a bit more* into the flow of the game.

Now, if Jordan's being an unselfish player, is it that his teammates refuse to shoot, or that he's just unselfishly recognizing the need to take everyone else's shots for them? When you think of the most ultimately "selfish" players in the league, who comes to mind? (Bear in mind that by "selfish," we don't mean the guy takes everyone else's meal money, we mean he takes most of the team's shots.) You'd probably think Jordan and Charles Barkley were the most "selfish," and that Barkley might outshadow even Jordan when you looked at the percentage of total shots taken and points scored by the player versus the team. And yet . . .

It's not even close. Despite the unselfish play of Michael Jordan, Chicago led all teams in the difference between its first and second players' scoring averages. Was it close? About as close as your average Super Bowl.

As you can see, Chicago sported nearly a 20-point edge. The Philadelphia Barkleys were *fourth*. Utah, somewhat surprisingly, was in second place, yet Chicago's margin between first and second was greater than the difference between Utah's first- and fourth-place scorers (Karl Malone and Darrell Griffith), and greater than the *total* scoring average of Miami's leading scorer, Kevin Edwards!

There's a lot of muttering going on in Chicago— more, perhaps, than any other city except Indianapolis or Portland. Most of the grumbles involve 7'1" Bill "Mr. Elbows" Cartwright, who proved why he was the backup in New York. Cartwright thrilled the fans on the road often this season, averaging only 12.4 ppg (the same as Oakley!) and 6.6 rpg. He's not terrible, but all other NBA centers had better years. Not exactly the most vivacious of players, the entire trade for Cartwright was a bust in the eyes of the fans and many teammates, who'd just like to start fresh with a new center.

Horace Grant, the 6'10" second-year forward, filled the vacuum left when Oakley departed, pulling in a team-high 681 rebounds. Barring a suddenly accelerated aging process, he should continue to come into his own next year. Now, that

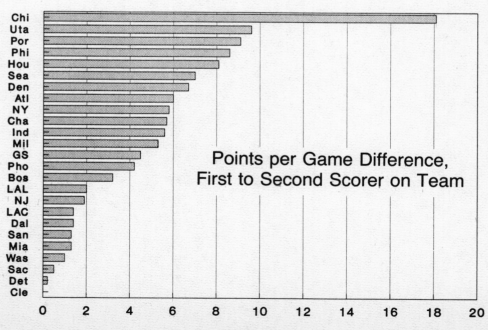

Chicago Bulls

Points per Game Difference,
First to Second Scorer on Team

center they need? Well Perdue, the seven-footer, could probably fit in there. But when a player is taken eleventh overall, you usually expect him to see more than 190 minutes of court time (about a minute for every 17 Jordan was out there). He received the least playing time of all first rounders, and only one more minute than Larry Bird had last year. Naturally, his scoring suffered, as he logged a high of 9 points—half as much as Jordan's low game of the year. Still, GM Jerry Krause expects great things of Perdue. Sooner would be preferable to later if the Bulls are going to get the much needed

help in the middle. Brad Sellers can surely block shots (he had a club-leading 69), but sweeping the boards is a skill you're born with more than learn, and Dave Corzine isn't going to suddenly acquire it at age 33.

Lack of rebounding on Cartwright's part and overall weak inside play will keep the Bulls from advancing past Detroit or Cleveland in Central, the NBA's current mega-division. And if, God forbid, Jordan suddenly went down, they'd be staring the lottery in the face.

Chicago Bulls

	Home W	L	Road W	L
By Month				
November	3	1	3	7
December	6	2	3	2
January	6	3	3	2
February	6	1	3	3
March	5	2	5	4
April	4	2	0	6
Playoffs				
Home/Away	30	11	17	24
Overtime	2	2	0	0
Offense				
0-89	0	3	0	1
90-99	1	5	0	11
100-109	13	2	7	8
110-119	10	1	8	3
120-129	6	0	1	1
130-	0	0	1	0
Defense				
0-89	3	0	1	0
90-99	11	2	3	1
100-109	11	7	10	11
110-119	3	2	3	5
120-129	2	0	0	7
130-	0	0	0	0
Over/Under				
0-189	1	2	1	1
190-199	5	2	0	3
200-209	8	5	6	9
210-219	6	0	5	3
220-229	7	2	3	4
230-239	1	0	1	2
240-	2	0	1	2
Margin Of Victory				
0-3	4	2	5	2
4-6	8	2	5	4
7-10	4	3	0	7
11-15	6	3	3	7
16-20	5	1	3	2
21-	3	0	1	2
Field Goal Attempts				
0-69	0	1	1	0
70-79	8	0	6	1
80-89	13	8	7	16
90-99	7	2	3	7
100-109	2	0	0	0
110+	0	0	0	0
Field Goals Made				
0-34	0	2	0	0
35-39	4	6	3	7
40-44	15	3	8	12
45-49	10	0	4	5
50-54	1	0	2	0
55+	0	0	0	0
Field Goal Pct.				
.000-.399	0	0	0	0
.400-.424	0	3	1	2
.425-.449	0	2	0	4
.450-.474	4	2	1	8
.475-.499	9	0	3	0
.500-.524	10	3	5	7
.525-.549	3	0	2	0
.550-.574	2	0	2	1

	Home W	L	Road W	L
.575-.599	2	1	1	1
.600-	0	0	2	0
Opp. Field Goal Attempts				
0-69	0	0	0	0
70-79	3	3	3	2
80-89	15	8	9	13
90-99	12	0	4	8
100-109	0	0	1	1
110+	0	0	0	0
Opp. Field Goal Made				
0-34	4	0	1	1
35-39	11	6	6	3
40-44	11	5	7	11
45-49	4	0	3	6
50-54	0	0	0	3
55+	0	0	0	0
Opp. Field Goal Pct.				
.000-.399	5	0	2	1
.400-.424	1	1	0	1
.425-.449	9	1	3	0
.450-.474	5	1	5	4
.475-.499	7	3	4	4
.500-.524	0	5	2	5
.525-.549	1	0	1	7
.550-.574	1	0	0	1
.575-.599	0	0	0	1
.600-	1	0	0	0
Free Throw Attempts				
0-9	0	0	0	1
10-19	1	5	2	8
20-29	15	3	10	12
30-39	12	2	5	3
40-49	2	0	0	0
50+	0	1	0	0
Free Throws Made				
0-9	0	0	0	1
10-19	13	6	6	15
20-29	12	4	9	8
30-39	5	0	2	0
40-49	0	1	0	0
50+	0	0	0	0
Free Throw Pct.				
.000-.549	0	0	0	0
.550-.599	1	0	0	1
.600-.649	0	2	0	0
.650-.699	4	1	1	2
.700-.749	3	2	0	3
.750-.799	5	4	4	10
.800-.849	9	2	3	4
.850-.899	5	0	8	2
.900-.949	2	0	1	2
.950-	1	0	0	0
Opp. Free Throw Attempts				
0-9	0	1	1	0
10-19	5	0	3	2
20-29	17	3	6	13
30-39	8	6	7	9
40-49	0	1	0	0
50+	0	0	0	0
Opp. Free Throws Made				
0-9	4	1	1	0
10-19	15	1	8	6
20-29	10	8	8	16

	Home W	L	Road W	L
30-39	1	1	0	2
40-49	0	0	0	0
50+	0	0	0	0
Opp. Free Throw Pct.				
.000-.549	1	0	1	0
.550-.599	2	0	0	0
.600-.649	2	0	1	0
.650-.699	4	0	3	2
.700-.749	4	2	1	5
.750-.799	11	2	6	6
.800-.849	3	2	2	6
.850-.899	2	4	1	3
.900-.949	1	1	2	2
.950-	0	0	0	0
Offensive Rebounds				
0-9	4	4	6	4
10-14	15	3	10	12
15-19	9	4	1	6
20-24	2	0	0	2
25+	0	0	0	0
Total Rebounds				
0-39	0	0	2	3
40-44	4	0	1	3
45-49	3	6	9	10
50-54	0	0	0	0
55-59	17	5	4	6
60-64	4	0	1	0
65-	2	0	0	2
Opp. Offensive Rebounds				
0-9	6	2	2	3
10-14	15	7	8	13
15-19	7	2	7	5
20-24	2	0	0	3
25+	0	0	0	0
Opp. Total Rebounds				
0-39	2	1	3	1
40-44	7	0	1	4
45-49	6	4	6	3
50-54	0	0	0	0
55-59	13	6	6	14
60-64	1	0	1	1
65-	1	0	0	1
Offensive Rebound Pct.				
Below 25%	11	5	8	10
25-29.99%	6	6	7	8
30-34.99%	12	0	2	3
35-39.99%	1	0	0	3
40-44.99%	0	0	0	0
45% and up	0	0	0	0
Assists				
0-14	0	0	0	0
15-19	0	1	2	1
20-24	1	4	4	11
25-29	16	6	5	9
30-34	9	0	5	3
35+	4	0	1	0
Opp. Assists				
0-14	0	0	1	0
15-19	5	0	1	2
20-24	9	3	7	9
25-29	12	3	5	5
30-34	3	5	2	6
35+	1	0	1	2

	Home W	L	Road W	L
Edge In Assists				
Below -15	0	0	0	0
-10 to -14	0	1	1	1
-5 to -9	3	5	1	5
0 to -4	1	3	5	10
1 to 4	10	1	3	4
5 to 9	8	1	5	3
10 to 14	7	0	2	1
15 and up	1	0	0	0
Personal Fouls				
0-14	1	1	0	0
15-19	8	1	3	2
20-24	14	4	8	14
25-29	7	3	5	7
30-34	0	1	1	1
35+	0	1	0	0
Opp. Personal Fouls				
0-14	0	2	0	3
15-19	9	3	5	6
20-24	10	1	7	11
25-29	8	4	3	4
30-34	3	0	2	0
35+	0	1	0	0
Personal Fouls Edge				
Below -15	0	0	0	0
-10 to -14	2	0	0	0
-5 to -9	9	0	3	1
0 to -4	8	3	3	5
1-4	6	5	9	6
5-9	5	2	2	10
10-14	0	1	0	2
15+	0	0	0	0
Steals				
0-5	3	3	1	3
6-7	4	2	5	6
8-9	7	2	3	8
10-11	7	3	6	4
12-13	6	1	2	3
14+	3	0	0	0
Opp. Steals				
0-5	6	3	5	1
6-7	6	3	3	6
8-9	8	3	4	7
10-11	6	0	3	4
12-13	4	1	0	3
14+	0	1	2	3
Edge In Steals				
Below -7	1	1	1	1
-4 to -6	2	1	2	5
0 to -3	8	5	5	13
1-3	10	1	4	3
4-6	4	3	3	1
7-	5	0	2	1
Turnovers				
0-14	12	5	5	9
15-19	18	3	8	8
20-24	0	2	3	7
25-29	0	1	1	0
30-34	0	0	0	0
35+	0	0	0	0
Opp. Turnovers				
0-14	14	7	6	14
15-19	12	4	7	10

	Home W	Home L	Road W	Road L
20-24	3	0	3	0
25-29	1	0	1	0
30-34	0	0	0	0
35+	0	0	0	0
Edge In Turnovers				
Below -15	0	0	1	0
-10 to -14	1	0	0	0
-5 to -9	5	0	2	1
0 to -4	12	6	6	8
1- 4	8	1	4	5
5- 9	4	3	3	8
10-14	0	1	1	2
15+	0	0	0	0
Blocks				
1-2	6	0	5	6
3-4	7	6	9	4
5-6	7	2	2	11
7-8	6	1	1	3
9-10	3	2	0	0
11+	1	0	0	0

	Home W	Home L	Road W	Road L
Opp. Blocks				
0-2	8	3	5	5
3-4	11	2	7	6
5-6	11	2	5	6
7-8	0	3	0	3
9-10	0	1	0	4
11+	0	0	0	0
Edge In Blocks				
Below -7	0	0	0	1
-4 to -6	2	1	0	4
0 to -3	11	6	12	12
1-3	9	1	5	4
4-6	5	2	0	2
7+	3	1	0	1
Three-Pointers Attempted				
0-2	1	0	1	2
3-5	14	2	6	8
6-8	8	6	7	11
9-11	5	1	2	2
12-14	2	2	1	0
15+	0	0	0	1

	Home W	Home L	Road W	Road L
Three-Pointers Made				
0-2	23	7	9	16
3-5	4	4	7	7
6-8	2	0	1	1
9-11	1	0	0	0
12-14	0	0	0	0
15+	0	0	0	0
Three-Pointers Pct.				
.000-.099	7	3	2	11
.100-.149	1	3	2	3
.150-.199	4	1	2	1
.200-.249	2	2	0	3
.250-.299	0	0	0	0
.300-.349	6	0	2	2
.350-.399	1	2	2	1
.400-.449	3	0	1	3
.450-.499	0	0	1	0
.500-	6	0	5	0
Opp. Three-Point Attempts				
0-2	4	2	2	3
3-5	3	5	3	9

	Home W	Home L	Road W	Road L
6-8	11	3	3	5
9-11	6	1	5	5
12-14	4	0	4	1
15+	2	0	0	1
Opp. Three-Pointers Made				
0-2	17	6	8	16
3-5	11	5	8	5
6-8	2	0	1	2
9-11	0	0	0	1
12-14	0	0	0	0
15+	0	0	0	0
Opp. Three-Pointer Pct.				
.000-.099	8	4	5	6
.100-.149	1	0	1	3
.150-.199	3	0	1	0
.200-.249	0	0	0	1
.250-.299	5	1	3	0
.300-.349	4	0	0	4
.350-.399	1	1	3	2
.400-.449	3	2	1	2
.450-.499	0	0	0	0
.500-	5	3	3	6

Chicago Bulls
1988–89 Power Chart

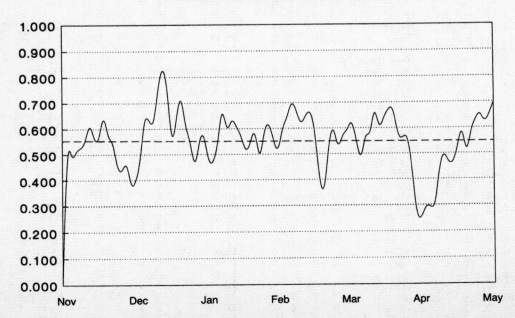

Chicago Bulls

	GP	GS	Min	FGM	FGA	FG%	2GM	2GA	2G%	3GM	3GA	3G%	FTM	FTA	FT%	Off	Tot	Ast	PF	Stl	TO	Blk	Pts	HGS
Bill Cartwright	78	76	2333	365	768	0.475	365	768	0.475	0	0	0.000	236	308	0.766	152	369	521	234	21	187	41	966	838
Per GP			29.9	4.7	9.8		4.7	9.8		0.0	0.0		3.0	3.9		1.9	4.7	6.7	3.0	0.3	2.4	0.5	12.4	10.7
Per 48			48.6	7.5	15.8		7.5	15.8		0.0	0.0		4.9	6.3		3.1	7.6	10.7	4.8	0.4	3.8	0.8	19.9	17.2
Dave Corzine	81	7	1483	203	440	0.461	201	432	0.465	2	8	0.250	71	96	0.740	92	223	315	134	29	93	41	479	518
Per GP			18.3	2.5	5.4		2.5	5.3		0.0	0.1		0.9	1.2		1.1	2.8	3.9	1.7	0.4	1.1	0.5	5.9	6.4
Per 48			30.9	6.6	14.2		6.5	14.0		0.1	0.3		2.3	3.1		3.0	7.2	10.2	4.3	0.9	3.0	1.3	15.5	16.8
Charles Davis	49	3	545	81	190	0.426	77	175	0.440	4	15	0.267	19	26	0.731	47	67	114	58	11	22	5	185	172
Per GP			11.1	1.7	3.9		1.6	3.6		0.1	0.3		0.4	0.5		1.0	1.4	2.3	1.2	0.2	0.4	0.1	3.8	3.5
Per 48			11.4	7.1	16.7		6.8	15.4		0.4	1.3		1.7	2.3		4.1	5.9	10.0	5.1	1.0	1.9	0.4	16.3	15.1
Horace Grant	79	79	2809	405	781	0.519	405	776	0.522	0	5	0.000	140	199	0.704	240	441	681	251	86	128	63	950	1146
Per GP			35.6	5.1	9.9		5.1	9.8		0.0	0.1		1.8	2.5		3.0	5.6	8.6	3.2	1.1	1.6	0.8	12.0	14.5
Per 48			58.5	6.9	13.3		6.9	13.3		0.0	0.1		2.4	3.4		4.1	7.5	11.6	4.3	1.5	2.2	1.1	16.2	19.6
Jack Haley	51	1	289	37	78	0.474	37	78	0.474	0	0	0.000	36	46	0.783	21	50	71	56	11	26	0	110	106
Per GP			5.7	0.7	1.5		0.7	1.5		0.0	0.0		0.7	0.9		0.4	1.0	1.4	1.1	0.2	0.5	0.0	2.2	2.1
Per 48			6.0	6.1	13.0		6.1	13.0		0.0	0.0		6.0	7.6		3.5	8.3	11.8	9.3	1.8	4.3	0.0	18.3	17.6
Craig Hodges	49	6	1112	187	394	0.475	116	226	0.513	71	168	0.423	45	53	0.849	21	63	84	82	41	52	4	490	375
Per GP			22.7	3.8	8.0		2.4	4.6		1.4	3.4		0.9	1.1		0.4	1.3	1.7	1.7	0.8	1.1	0.1	10.0	7.7
Per 48			23.2	8.1	17.0		5.0	9.8		3.1	7.3		1.9	2.3		0.9	2.7	3.6	3.5	1.8	2.2	0.2	21.2	16.2
Anthony Jones	8	0	65	5	15	0.333	5	14	0.357	0	1	0.000	2	2	1.000	4	4	8	7	2	1	1	12	15
Per GP			8.1	0.6	1.9		0.6	1.8		0.0	0.1		0.3	0.3		0.5	0.5	1.0	0.9	0.3	0.1	0.1	1.5	1.9
Per 48			1.4	3.7	11.1		3.7	10.3		0.0	0.7		1.5	1.5		3.0	3.0	5.9	5.2	1.5	0.7	0.7	8.9	11.1
Michael Jordan	81	81	3255	966	1795	0.538	940	1697	0.554	26	98	0.265	674	793	0.850	149	503	652	247	234	290	64	2632	2649
Per GP			40.2	11.9	22.2		11.6	21.0		0.3	1.2		8.3	9.8		1.8	6.2	8.0	3.0	2.9	3.6	0.8	32.5	32.7
Per 48			67.8	14.2	26.5		13.9	25.0		0.4	1.4		9.9	11.7		2.2	7.4	9.6	3.6	3.5	4.3	0.9	38.8	39.1
Ed Nealy	13	0	94	5	7	0.714	5	7	0.714	0	0	0.000	1	2	0.500	4	19	23	23	3	1	1	11	29
Per GP			7.2	0.4	0.5		0.4	0.5		0.0	0.0		0.1	0.2		0.3	1.5	1.8	1.8	0.2	0.1	0.1	0.8	2.2
Per 48			2.0	2.6	3.6		2.6	3.6		0.0	0.0		0.5	1.0		2.0	9.7	11.7	11.7	1.5	0.5	0.5	5.6	14.8
John Paxson	78	20	1738	246	513	0.480	201	380	0.529	45	133	0.338	31	36	0.861	13	81	94	162	53	71	6	568	579
Per GP			22.3	3.2	6.6		2.6	4.9		0.6	1.7		0.4	0.5		0.2	1.0	1.2	2.1	0.7	0.9	0.1	7.3	7.4
Per 48			36.2	6.8	14.2		5.6	10.5		1.2	3.7		0.9	1.0		0.4	2.2	2.6	4.5	1.5	2.0	0.2	15.7	16.0
Will Perdue	30	0	190	29	72	0.403	29	72	0.403	0	0	0.000	8	14	0.571	18	27	45	38	4	15	6	66	63
Per GP			6.3	1.0	2.4		1.0	2.4		0.0	0.0		0.3	0.5		0.6	0.9	1.5	1.3	0.1	0.5	0.2	2.2	2.1
Per 48			4.0	7.3	18.2		7.3	18.2		0.0	0.0		2.0	3.5		4.5	6.8	11.4	9.6	1.0	3.8	1.5	16.7	15.9
Scottie Pippen	73	56	2413	413	867	0.476	392	790	0.496	21	77	0.273	201	301	0.668	138	307	445	261	139	199	59	1048	1096
Per GP			33.1	5.7	11.9		5.4	10.8		0.3	1.1		2.8	4.1		1.9	4.2	6.1	3.6	1.9	2.7	0.8	14.4	15.0
Per 48			50.3	8.2	17.2		7.8	15.7		0.4	1.5		4.0	6.0		2.7	6.1	8.9	5.2	2.8	4.0	1.2	20.8	21.8
Dominick Pressley	3	0	17	1	6	0.167	1	4	0.250	0	2	0.000	0	0	0.000	0	1	1	2	0	0	0	2	3
Per GP			5.7	0.3	2.0		0.3	1.3		0.0	0.7		0.0	0.0		0.0	0.3	0.3	0.7	0.0	0.0	0.0	0.7	1.0
Per 48			0.4	2.8	16.9		2.8	11.3		0.0	5.6		0.0	0.0		0.0	2.8	2.8	5.6	0.0	0.0	0.0	5.6	8.5
Brad Sellers	80	25	1732	231	476	0.485	228	470	0.485	3	6	0.500	86	101	0.851	85	142	227	176	35	72	67	551	576
Per GP			21.6	2.9	5.9		2.8	5.9		0.0	0.1		1.1	1.3		1.1	1.8	2.8	2.2	0.4	0.9	0.8	6.9	7.2
Per 48			36.1	6.4	13.2		6.3	13.0		0.1	0.2		2.4	2.8		2.4	3.9	6.3	4.9	1.0	2.0	1.9	15.3	16.0
Sam Vincent	70	56	1703	274	566	0.484	272	549	0.495	2	17	0.118	106	129	0.822	35	156	191	124	53	142	10	656	711
Per GP			24.3	3.9	8.1		3.9	7.8		0.0	0.2		1.5	1.8		0.5	2.2	2.7	1.8	0.8	2.0	0.1	9.4	10.2
Per 48			35.5	7.7	16.0		7.7	15.5		0.1	0.5		3.0	3.6		1.0	4.4	5.4	3.5	1.5	4.0	0.3	18.5	20.0
David Wood	2	0	2	0	0	0.000	0	0	0.000	0	0	0.000	0	0	0.000	0	0	0	0	0	0	0	0	0
Per GP			1.0	0.0	0.0		0.0	0.0		0.0	0.0		0.0	0.0		0.0	0.0	0.0	0.0	0.0	0.0	0.0	0.0	0.0
Per 48			0.0	0.0	0.0		0.0	0.0		0.0	0.0		0.0	0.0		0.0	0.0	0.0	0.0	0.0	0.0	0.0	0.0	0.0

CLEVELAND CAVALIERS

I knew a guy at school who would work with his radio's antenna for hours, trying to pull in WWWE from Cleveland, 520 miles away. I couldn't understand why someone would put so much effort into getting a midseason Cavs game. Not the *new* Cavs, mind you. The old Cavs. The decrepit Cavs. The Cavs that traded away so many draft choices that they had to beg the league for more. The team that only a mother, or *true* fan, could love.

Fans like this—true fans—are the best reason a balanced league is better. Sure, it's great for television to have the Lakers and Celtics squaring off in the finals every season. Big cities mean big bucks. But for the sake of those fans out there who will do anything to listen to or watch their team through good and bad, there can be no argument that one- or two-team dominance is healthier for the league.

Unfortunately, no matter how *good* it might be for the league, teams like Cleveland have to be up to the task. The Cavs proved three things last year: you're only as good as your last playoff game, home court means nothing unless you take advantage of it, and Nature won't allow a team from Cleveland to get too far in any sport, no matter what their talents. Still, the fifth game against Chicago demonstrated the value of many things. The Cavaliers had the

most balanced starting lineup in the NBA. Yet in the end, they were beaten by the least balanced team in the league, whose star (Jordan) ran roughshod over a bench player (Ehlo). Perhaps team basketball is a noble goal, but having one player rise above the rest is too often the way teams win over the short haul.

It is too early to tell whether the devastating first-round playoff loss last year will do the Cavs good or bad. If they gain resolve from it, as the Pistons did last season from the Laker series, this team of the future will be ready to go now, several years ahead of GM Wayne Embry's schedule. Their starting lineup averaged 26.4 years of age last year, with only Larry Nance hitting the big three-oh. As mentioned before, however, the Cavaliers took the team concept to a fault last year. The Cavs have no superstars per se, but they have a number of players who could conceivably step forward to the task. Brad Daugherty had a puzzling season, falling off after his late-season injury. Suddenly he wasn't being mentioned in the same breath as Olajuwon and Ewing, but he still rated in the league's top five. Ron Harper showed some flashes of creative genius last year, and Mark Price solidified his reputation as a top point guard, although when you think of the top five in the league, you consider Magic and Kevin

Cleveland Cavaliers

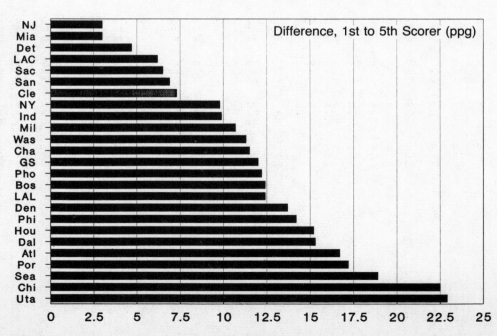

Difference, 1st to 5th Scorer (ppg)

Johnson, John Stockton, Isiah Thomas, Doc Rivers, and Mark Jackson. Can Price crack the league's top five? He might squeak past Rivers and Jackson, but it would be iffy at best. As a cog in this team, however, Price is just what's needed. Larry Nance could be a simply terrifying shot blocker at times, and his overall game was strong enough to push him high up in the ratings for forwards.

All in all, the Cavs are a bunch of nice, unselfish players who work so well together that they appear to be a clone of the mid-1980s Celtics, though the Cavs are much more of a suburban team. While one player like Jordan *does* take a team a long way, there aren't that many Jordans around. If you can't find one, you're much better off having five good players. Whom could you key in on when you played the Cavs? Their scoring attack was the best balanced in the league last year. When you look at the difference between first and fifth scorers in the league, only Detroit is more jam-packed at the top, among good teams.

Defense is a top Cavalier priority, and it shows. They held the opposition to under 100 points 42 times, and in games where they harassed opponents into shooting under 50%, they went 50–16. Last season was disappointing, but one could also argue that had a mere mortal received the ball in the last seconds, the Cavs would have been at least to the Eastern Conference finals. This season, a year older, Cleveland has no reason, indeed no excuse, to end their season any time before June. And way ahead of schedule.

Cleveland Cavaliers

By Month	Home W	L	Road W	L
November	4	1	4	2
December	8	1	5	1
January	7	0	4	4
February	8	0	2	3
March	5	1	4	7
April	5	1	1	4
Playoffs				
Home/Away	37	4	20	21
Overtime	1	0	0	2

Offense	Home W	L	Road W	L
0-89	0	0	1	2
90-99	1	2	3	6
100-109	10	2	8	10
110-119	15	0	5	3
120-129	9	0	2	0
130-	2	0	1	0

Defense	Home W	L	Road W	L
0-89	4	0	2	0
90-99	21	1	11	3
100-109	8	1	4	9
110-119	4	2	2	4
120-129	0	0	1	5
130-	0	0	0	0

Over/Under	Home W	L	Road W	L
0-189	2	0	3	3
190-199	6	1	3	2
200-209	10	1	7	6
210-219	9	1	2	4
220-229	4	1	3	2
230-239	4	0	1	4
240-	2	0	1	0

Margin Of Victory	Home W	L	Road W	L
0-3	1	1	5	6
4-6	3	1	3	3
7-10	3	1	5	4
11-15	6	0	5	5
16-20	12	1	1	2
21-	12	1	1	1

Field Goal Attempts	Home W	L	Road W	L
0-69	0	0	1	2
70-79	8	1	5	7
80-89	18	2	10	5
90-99	9	1	4	5
100-109	2	0	0	2
110+	0	0	0	0

Field Goals Made	Home W	L	Road W	L
0-34	0	0	2	3
35-39	8	3	4	9
40-44	13	1	10	7
45-49	5	0	2	1
50-54	8	0	2	1
55+	3	0	0	0

Field Goal Pct.	Home W	L	Road W	L
.000-.399	1	0	2	2
.400-.424	0	1	1	1
.425-.449	0	2	0	2
.450-.474	3	0	5	9
.475-.499	6	1	2	3
.500-.524	10	0	3	0
.525-.549	3	0	3	1
.550-.574	9	0	0	2
.575-.599	2	0	3	1
.600-	3	0	1	0

Opp. Field Goal Attempts	Home W	L	Road W	L
0-69	1	0	0	0
70-79	3	1	2	1
80-89	14	2	13	6
90-99	12	1	2	13
100-109	7	0	2	1
110+	0	0	1	0

Opp. Field Goal Made	Home W	L	Road W	L
0-34	3	0	2	1
35-39	13	1	5	2
40-44	15	2	11	9
45-49	5	1	2	7
50-54	1	0	0	2
55+	0	0	0	0

Opp. Field Goal Percentage	Home W	L	Road W	L
.000-.399	2	0	1	1
.400-.424	12	0	4	0
.425-.449	5	0	5	5
.450-.474	8	0	6	1
.475-.499	6	2	1	7
.500-.524	4	0	2	4
.525-.549	0	1	0	1
.550-.574	0	1	1	1
.575-.599	0	0	0	1
.600-	0	0	0	0

Free Throw Attempts	Home W	L	Road W	L
0-9	0	0	0	0
10-19	1	0	2	1
20-29	13	2	7	13
30-39	19	2	11	6
40-49	3	0	0	1
50+	1	0	0	0

Free Throws Made	Home W	L	Road W	L
0-9	0	0	0	0
10-19	9	1	7	10
20-29	20	3	11	9
30-39	7	0	2	2
40-49	1	0	0	0
50+	0	0	0	0

Free Throw Pct.	Home W	L	Road W	L
.000-.549	0	0	0	1
.550-.599	4	0	0	0
.600-.649	5	1	0	4
.650-.699	3	0	1	2
.700-.749	3	1	8	5
.750-.799	9	0	4	7
.800-.849	10	0	3	2
.850-.899	3	0	3	0
.900-.949	0	2	1	0
.950-	0	0	0	0

Opp. Free Throw Attempts	Home W	L	Road W	L
0-9	0	0	0	0
10-19	14	1	8	5
20-29	22	3	11	13
30-39	1	0	1	3
40-49	0	0	0	0
50+	0	0	0	0

Opp. Free Throws Made	Home W	L	Road W	L
0-9	6	0	2	0
10-19	25	4	13	11
20-29	6	0	5	10
30-39	0	0	0	0
40-49	0	0	0	0
50+	0	0	0	0

Opp. Free Throw Pct.	Home W	L	Road W	L
.000-.549	1	0	0	0
.550-.599	1	0	0	0
.600-.649	7	0	1	0
.650-.699	5	0	1	1
.700-.749	6	1	4	2
.750-.799	2	1	2	8
.800-.849	6	2	6	4
.850-.899	7	0	4	3
.900-.949	2	0	2	2
.950-	0	0	0	1

Offensive Rebounds	Home W	L	Road W	L
0-9	7	0	8	4
10-14	18	2	9	12
15-19	10	2	3	4
20-24	2	0	0	1
25+	0	0	0	0

Total Rebounds	Home W	L	Road W	L
0-39	0	0	0	1
40-44	3	0	3	2
45-49	8	2	7	8
50-54	0	0	0	0
55-59	20	1	8	9
60-64	4	1	1	1
65-	2	0	1	0

Opp. Offensive Rebounds	Home W	L	Road W	L
0-9	5	2	4	1
10-14	10	1	7	8
15-19	17	1	5	7
20-24	4	0	2	5
25+	1	0	2	0

Opp. Total Rebounds	Home W	L	Road W	L
0-39	2	0	3	0
40-44	4	2	1	3
45-49	10	0	7	3
50-54	0	0	0	0
55-59	18	2	8	12
60-64	2	0	1	2
65-	1	0	0	1

Offensive Rebound Pct.	Home W	L	Road W	L
Below 25%	13	1	10	11
25-29.99%	12	1	5	7
30-34.99%	9	2	3	2
35-39.99%	2	0	2	1
40-44.99%	1	0	0	0
45% and up	0	0	0	0

Assists	Home W	L	Road W	L
0-14	0	0	1	0
15-19	0	0	1	4
20-24	4	0	8	7
25-29	9	3	7	8
30-34	13	1	2	2
35+	11	0	1	0

Opp. Assists	Home W	L	Road W	L
0-14	1	0	1	0
15-19	5	0	2	1
20-24	13	2	10	7
25-29	11	2	4	7
30-34	5	0	3	5
35+	2	0	1	0

Edge In Assists	Home W	L	Road W	L
Below -15	0	0	0	0
-10 to -14	1	0	0	1
-5 to -9	4	0	2	7
0 to -4	2	1	7	9
1-4	4	2	7	3
5-9	13	1	3	1
10-14	9	0	1	0
15-	4	0	0	0

Personal Fouls	Home W	L	Road W	L
0-14	6	0	2	0
15-19	18	0	8	8
20-24	12	4	9	10
25-29	1	0	1	3
30-34	0	0	0	0
35+	0	0	0	0

Opp. Personal Fouls	Home W	L	Road W	L
0-14	0	0	0	0
15-19	3	1	1	6
20-24	16	2	10	8
25-29	11	1	8	7
30-34	6	0	1	0
35+	1	0	0	0

Personal Fouls Edge	Home W	L	Road W	L
Below -15	2	0	2	0
-10 to -14	9	0	2	0
-5 to -9	12	0	4	6
0 to -4	12	2	10	9
1-4	2	2	2	2
5-9	0	0	0	4
10-14	0	0	0	0
15+	0	0	0	0

Steals	Home W	L	Road W	L
0-5	2	0	4	2
6-7	5	1	3	6
8-9	8	1	6	5
10-11	6	0	2	3
12-13	9	2	2	5
14+	7	0	3	0

Opp. Steals	Home W	L	Road W	L
0-5	13	0	5	2
6-7	5	2	5	1
8-9	8	1	7	4
10-11	7	0	2	6
12-13	1	1	1	7
14+	3	0	0	1

Edge In Steals	Home W	L	Road W	L
Below -7	1	0	0	3
-4 to -6	2	0	3	1
0 to -3	7	2	3	12
1-3	8	1	9	3
4-6	12	1	2	1
7-	7	0	3	1

Turnovers	Home W	L	Road W	L
0-14	14	1	10	5
15-19	17	3	6	9
20-24	5	0	3	6
25-29	1	0	1	1
30-34	0	0	0	0
35+	0	0	0	0

Opp. Turnovers	Home W	L	Road W	L
0-14	5	1	6	10
15-19	19	2	7	8

	Home W L	Road W L
20-24	9 1	5 3
25-29	4 0	2 0
30-34	0 0	0 0
35+	0 0	0 0

Edge In Turnovers

	Home W L	Road W L
Below -15	1 0	1 0
-10 to -14	6 0	1 0
-5 to -9	9 2	3 2
0 to -4	12 1	7 5
1-4	7 1	4 6
5-9	2 0	3 6
10-14	0 0	1 2
15+	0 0	0 0

Blocks

	Home W L	Road W L
1-2	3 1	3 2
3-4	3 0	4 2
5-6	4 2	3 6
7-8	10 0	7 5
9-10	9 1	3 4
11+	8 0	0 2

Opp. Blocks

	Home W L	Road W L
0-2	11 0	5 2
3-4	13 2	3 11
5-6	6 1	10 3
7-8	4 0	2 4
9-10	3 1	0 10
11+	0 0	0 1

Edge In Blocks

	Home W L	Road W L
Below -7	0 1	0 0
-4 to -6	2 0	2 0
0 to -3	4 0	3 7
1-3	11 3	12 7
4-6	10 0	2 6
7+	10 0	1 1

Three-Pointers Attempted

	Home W L	Road W L
0-2	3 0	5 0
3-5	17 2	10 5
6-8	10 1	5 9
9-11	7 0	0 4
12-14	0 1	0 3
15+	0 0	0 0

Three-Pointers Made

	Home W L	Road W L
0-2	25 2	14 10
3-5	11 2	6 10
6-8	1 0	0 1
9-11	0 0	0 0
12-14	0 0	0 0
15+	0 0	0 0

Three-Pointers Pct.

	Home W L	Road W L
.000-.099	13 2	9 1
.100-.149	3 0	0 1
.150-.199	0 0	0 2
.200-.249	1 1	1 0
.250-.299	4 0	2 1
.300-.349	5 0	1 2
.350-.399	0 0	2 2
.400-.449	2 0	0 5
.450-.499	1 0	0 0
.500-	8 1	5 7

Opp. Three-Point Attempts

	Home W L	Road W L
0-2	8 0	3 6
3-5	7 2	5 6
6-8	13 1	9 5

	Home W L	Road W L
9-11	4 0	3 4
12-14	3 1	0 0
15+	2 0	0 0

Opp. Three-Pointers Made

	Home W L	Road W L
0-2	28 2	10 13
3-5	4 1	10 8
6-8	5 1	0 0
9-11	0 0	0 0
12-14	0 0	0 0
15+	0 0	0 0

Opp. Three-Pointer Pct.

	Home W L	Road W L
.000-.099	13 1	7 10
.100-.149	2 0	0 1
.150-.199	4 0	1 0
.200-.249	1 0	0 0
.250-.299	5 1	1 2
.300-.349	3 0	0 3
.350-.399	4 0	2 0
.400-.449	2 0	1 0
.450-.499	0 0	1 1
.500-	3 2	7 4

Cleveland Cavaliers
1988–89 Power Chart

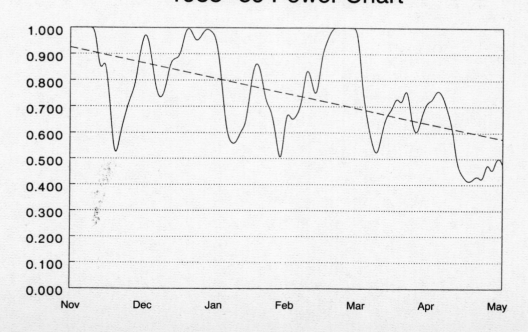

Cleveland Cavaliers

	GP	GS	Min	FGM	FGA	FG%	2GM	2GA	2G%	3GM	3GA	3G%	FTM	FTA	FT%	Off	Tot	Ast	PF	Stl	TO	Blk	Pts	HGS
Brad Daugherty	78	78	2821	544	1012	0.538	543	1009	0.538	1	3	0.333	386	524	0.737	167	551	718	175	61	230	40	1475	1502
Per GP			36.2	7.0	13.0		7.0	12.9		0.0	0.0		4.9	6.7		2.1	7.1	9.2	2.2	0.8	2.9	0.5	18.9	19.3
Per 48			58.8	9.3	17.2		9.2	17.2		0.0	0.1		6.6	8.9		2.8	9.4	12.2	3.0	1.0	3.9	0.7	25.1	25.6
Chris Dudley	61	2	544	73	168	0.435	73	167	0.437	0	1	0.000	39	107	0.364	72	85	157	82	11	44	23	185	217
Per GP			8.9	1.2	2.8		1.2	2.7		0.0	0.0		0.6	1.8		1.2	1.4	2.6	1.3	0.2	0.7	0.4	3.0	3.6
Per 48			11.3	6.4	14.8		6.4	14.7		0.0	0.1		3.4	9.4		6.4	7.5	13.9	7.2	1.0	3.9	2.0	16.3	19.1
Craig Ehlo	82	4	1867	249	524	0.475	210	424	0.495	39	100	0.390	71	117	0.607	100	195	295	161	110	116	19	608	747
Per GP			22.8	3.0	6.4		2.6	5.2		0.5	1.2		0.9	1.4		1.2	2.4	3.6	2.0	1.3	1.4	0.2	7.4	9.1
Per 48			38.9	6.4	13.5		5.4	10.9		1.0	2.6		1.8	3.0		2.6	5.0	7.6	4.1	2.8	3.0	0.5	15.6	19.2
Ron Harper	82	82	2851	587	1149	0.511	558	1033	0.540	29	116	0.250	323	430	0.751	122	287	409	224	185	230	74	1526	1593
Per GP			34.8	7.2	14.0		6.8	12.6		0.4	1.4		3.9	5.2		1.5	3.5	5.0	2.7	2.3	2.8	0.9	18.6	19.4
Per 48			59.4	9.9	19.3		9.4	17.4		0.5	2.0		5.4	7.2		2.1	4.8	6.9	3.8	3.1	3.9	1.2	25.7	26.8
Phil Hubbard	31	0	191	28	63	0.444	28	63	0.444	0	0	0.000	17	25	0.680	14	26	40	20	6	9	0	73	70
Per GP			6.2	0.9	2.0		0.9	2.0		0.0	0.0		0.5	0.8		0.5	0.8	1.3	0.6	0.2	0.3	0.0	2.4	2.3
Per 48			4.0	7.0	15.8		7.0	15.8		0.0	0.0		4.3	6.3		3.5	6.5	10.1	5.0	1.5	2.3	0.0	18.3	17.6
Randolph Keys	42	0	331	74	172	0.430	73	162	0.451	1	10	0.100	20	29	0.690	23	33	56	52	12	21	6	169	123
Per GP			7.9	1.8	4.1		1.7	3.9		0.0	0.2		0.5	0.7		0.5	0.8	1.3	1.2	0.3	0.5	0.1	4.0	2.9
Per 48			6.9	10.7	24.9		10.6	23.5		0.1	1.5		2.9	4.2		3.3	4.8	8.1	7.5	1.7	3.0	0.9	24.5	17.8
Larry Nance	73	72	2526	496	920	0.539	496	916	0.541	0	4	0.000	267	334	0.799	156	425	581	186	57	117	206	1259	1463
Per GP			34.6	6.8	12.6		6.8	12.5		0.0	0.1		3.7	4.6		2.1	5.8	8.0	2.5	0.8	1.6	2.8	17.2	20.0
Per 48			52.6	9.4	17.5		9.4	17.4		0.0	0.1		5.1	6.3		3.0	8.1	11.0	3.5	1.1	2.2	3.9	23.9	27.8
Mark Price	75	74	2728	529	1006	0.526	436	795	0.548	93	211	0.441	263	292	0.901	48	178	226	98	115	212	7	1414	1433
Per GP			36.4	7.1	13.4		5.8	10.6		1.2	2.8		3.5	3.9		0.6	2.4	3.0	1.3	1.5	2.8	0.1	18.9	19.1
Per 48			56.8	9.3	17.7		7.7	14.0		1.6	3.7		4.6	5.1		0.8	3.1	4.0	1.7	2.0	3.7	0.1	24.9	25.2
Wayne Rollins	60	2	583	62	138	0.449	62	137	0.453	0	1	0.000	12	19	0.632	37	102	139	89	11	22	38	136	201
Per GP			9.7	1.0	2.3		1.0	2.3		0.0	0.0		0.2	0.3		0.6	1.7	2.3	1.5	0.2	0.4	0.6	2.3	3.3
Per 48			12.1	5.1	11.4		5.1	11.3		0.0	0.1		1.0	1.6		3.0	8.4	11.4	7.3	0.9	1.8	3.1	11.2	16.5
Mike Sanders	82	82	2102	332	733	0.453	329	723	0.455	3	10	0.300	97	135	0.719	99	208	307	230	89	104	32	764	693
Per GP			25.6	4.0	8.9		4.0	8.8		0.0	0.1		1.2	1.6		1.2	2.5	3.7	2.8	1.1	1.3	0.4	9.3	8.5
Per 48			43.8	7.6	16.7		7.5	16.5		0.1	0.2		2.2	3.1		2.3	4.7	7.0	5.3	2.0	2.4	0.7	17.4	15.8
Darnell Valentine	77	4	1086	136	319	0.426	133	305	0.436	3	14	0.214	91	112	0.812	22	81	103	88	57	83	7	366	405
Per GP			14.1	1.8	4.1		1.7	4.0		0.0	0.2		1.2	1.5		0.3	1.1	1.3	1.1	0.7	1.1	0.1	4.8	5.3
Per 48			22.6	6.0	14.1		5.9	13.5		0.1	0.6		4.0	5.0		1.0	3.6	4.6	3.9	2.5	3.7	0.3	16.2	17.9
John Williams	82	10	2125	356	700	0.509	355	696	0.510	1	4	0.250	235	314	0.748	175	302	477	188	77	102	134	948	1118
Per GP			25.9	4.3	8.5		4.3	8.5		0.0	0.0		2.9	3.8		2.1	3.7	5.8	2.3	0.9	1.2	1.6	11.6	13.6
Per 48			44.3	8.0	15.8		8.0	15.7		0.0	0.1		5.3	7.1		4.0	6.8	10.8	4.2	1.7	2.3	3.0	21.4	25.3

DALLAS MAVERICKS

In six months, the Mavericks went from the heights of the NBA to the depths. The 1987–88 season ended with the Mavs, one of the most physically talented teams, losing out in the final minutes to the Lakers in the Western Conference finals. They were ready to take it one step further last year. Then Tarpley needed a knee 'scope. No problem. When he got back, they'd be okay. Then he got back. Then he left again, a victim of drug abuse. The Mavs were in trouble. No problem, though; the backups were adequate. Then James Donaldson and Bill Wennington went down in the same week. Problems. Rolando Blackman lost a few games due to injury. More problems. Mark Aguirre in general. Big problems.

It all combined to hit Dallas hard, in the loss column. The losses they sustained knocked as many games off their record as Larry Bird's injury did in Boston. Each team was 15 games worse off, tied for most in the league. The difference between Dallas and Portland, teams tied with 53 wins last year, was that the Blazers lost only 14 games off their record and beat the Mavs out by a game for the final playoff spot.

The nightmare just wouldn't stop in 1988–89. It was as if they moved the Reunion Arena to Elm Street. A 4–11 January tied a club record for losses in the month, and that performance was followed up with a 3–14 March that included a nifty 12-game losing streak. This was the first year since the franchise was founded that it didn't move forward in some way, mostly due to the absence of the key players for long periods. The absence of Tarpley, the 1987–88 NBA "Sixth Man" of the Year winner, allowed the opposition to run wild in the middle.

The biggest positive surrounding the team last year was the departure of Mark Aguirre. Let's face it. It was no secret that the Mavs were relieved, to a man, to be rid of Aguirre. After years of tolerance toward his petty behavior, the coaches he'd run out of town, the refusal to play, the night of February 15 was a time of catharsis for the other players. "You just can't let your teammates down, and he let us down a lot," claimed Rolando Blackman. "Sometimes Mark would just loaf around," added James Donaldson. Derek Harper told the world that the Mavs "were an uptight team for sure with him around." But players aren't paid for personality, they're paid for their performance. Which team got the better of this trade in the short run? The Pistons certainly got the younger player, and although a

Dallas Mavericks

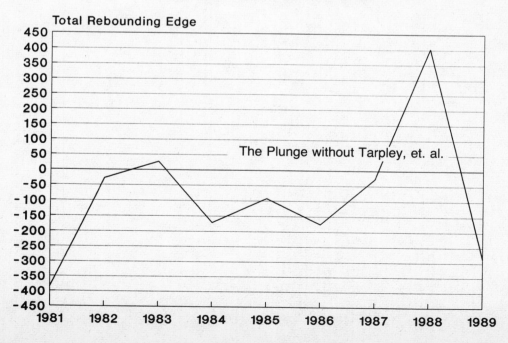

Total Rebounding Edge

The Plunge without Tarpley, et. al.

true statistician decries intangibles, Isiah should have a steadying influence on Mark. Isn't it more important that the Mavericks now feel better about themselves?

Aguirre's scoring dropped after the trade (from 29.9 to 25.0), but Dantley's stayed about the same. Dantley's shooting took a plunge, however, from .521 to .462. He obviously didn't feel comfortable after the trade (his first game back was 0 for 7).

The Mavs were hurt far more up the middle than anywhere else with their injuries. Scoring and rebounding both took a pummeling last season, and the domination Dallas showed on the boards for the first time in their history two years ago quickly reversed itself last year, giving them their worst rebounding margin since their inaugural season. In the chart on the previous page, you can see just how badly their rebounding plummeted in the midst of their losses.

This season, the 7'0", 256-pound Tarpley, the heart of the team, will return. It is to be hoped that he'll be free of his drug and knee problems (in that order). If he can pick up where he left off, intimidating, patrolling the middle, and sweeping the boards, it would be greatly appreciated by coach MacLeod. Guard Derek Harper has to make improvements in his play of last year, while silent Sam Perkins (15.0 ppg) has to become more active in the offense.

Dallas Mavericks

	Home W	L	Road W	L
By Month				
November	7	3	2	1
December	4	3	4	2
January	4	3	0	8
February	4	2	4	3
March	2	2	1	12
April	3	4	3	1
Playoffs				
Home/Away	24	17	14	27
Overtime	0	1	2	1
Offense				
0-89	0	2	0	4
90-99	5	8	2	11
100-109	5	5	6	8
110-119	9	2	5	2
120-129	4	0	1	2
130-	1	0	0	0
Defense				
0-89	5	0	3	0
90-99	11	1	4	5
100-109	5	6	3	8
110-119	3	8	4	9
120-129	0	2	0	3
130-	0	0	0	2
Over/Under				
0-189	4	1	2	5
190-199	5	2	2	3
200-209	4	6	4	5
210-219	6	5	2	8
220-229	2	3	3	3
230-239	2	0	0	1
240-	1	0	1	2
Margin Of Victory				
0-3	3	3	3	6
4-6	6	1	3	1
7-10	3	3	4	6
11-15	4	5	1	7
16-20	5	2	3	2
21-	3	3	0	5
Field Goal Attempts				
0-69	1	0	0	0
70-79	7	2	5	5
80-89	12	9	6	17
90-99	4	5	2	5
100-109	0	1	1	0
110+	0	0	0	0
Field Goals Made				
0-34	3	3	0	4
35-39	5	7	8	14
40-44	11	7	4	5
45-49	2	0	2	4
50-54	3	0	0	0
55+	0	0	0	0
Field Goal Pct.				
.000-.399	0	4	0	4
.400-.424	0	4	0	2
.425-.449	3	1	2	8
.450-.474	4	6	2	4
.475-.499	2	0	4	4
.500-.524	8	2	2	3
.525-.549	4	0	3	1
.550-.574	1	0	0	1

	Home W	L	Road W	L
.575-.599	1	0	0	0
.600-	1	0	1	0
Opp. Field Goal Attempts				
0-69	0	0	0	1
70-79	4	5	1	4
80-89	7	3	6	14
90-99	9	5	5	5
100-109	4	4	2	3
110+	0	0	0	0
Opp. Field Goal Made				
0-34	4	1	0	1
35-39	6	2	7	7
40-44	11	5	6	9
45-49	3	7	1	5
50-54	0	1	0	4
55+	0	1	0	1
Opp. Field Goal Percentage				
.000-.399	7	1	3	1
.400-.424	3	2	0	1
.425-.449	3	0	3	3
.450-.474	5	4	5	2
.475-.499	3	2	1	5
.500-.524	1	3	2	8
.525-.549	2	3	0	1
.550-.574	0	1	0	4
.575-.599	0	1	0	1
.600-	0	0	0	1
Free Throw Attempts				
0-9	0	0	0	0
10-19	1	4	1	2
20-29	10	9	6	17
30-39	11	4	6	8
40-49	2	0	1	0
50+	0	0	0	0
Free Throws Made				
0-9	0	2	0	1
10-19	4	6	2	13
20-29	17	9	8	11
30-39	3	0	4	2
40-49	0	0	0	0
50+	0	0	0	0
Free Throw Pct.				
.000-.549	0	0	0	0
.550-.599	1	0	1	1
.600-.649	0	1	0	1
.650-.699	1	2	0	4
.700-.749	5	3	0	5
.750-.799	5	4	4	4
.800-.849	3	5	6	9
.850-.899	7	1	1	1
.900-.949	2	1	2	2
.950-	0	0	0	0
Opp. Free Throw Attempts				
0-9	0	0	0	0
10-19	6	3	1	3
20-29	17	7	8	16
30-39	1	6	5	7
40-49	0	1	0	1
50+	0	0	0	0
Opp. Free Throws Made				
0-9	2	0	1	1
10-19	15	8	8	13
20-29	7	6	5	9

	Home W	L	Road W	L
30-39	0	3	0	4
40-49	0	0	0	0
50+	0	0	0	0
Opp. Free Throw Pct.				
.000-.549	1	0	0	0
.550-.599	3	0	1	3
.600-.649	2	0	2	3
.650-.699	4	4	4	2
.700-.749	3	2	3	2
.750-.799	4	4	3	6
.800-.849	5	3	1	2
.850-.899	2	3	0	5
.900-.949	0	1	0	3
.950-	0	0	0	1
Offensive Rebounds				
0-9	3	4	4	7
10-14	14	5	7	14
15-19	7	7	3	5
20-24	0	1	0	1
25+	0	0	0	0
Total Rebounds				
0-39	1	0	1	2
40-44	3	6	3	7
45-49	2	6	4	8
50-54	0	0	0	0
55-59	13	4	4	8
60-64	3	1	0	2
65-	2	0	2	0
Opp. Offensive Rebounds				
0-9	3	1	3	3
10-14	7	7	2	15
15-19	8	5	8	6
20-24	5	4	1	2
25+	1	0	0	1
Opp. Total Rebounds				
0-39	1	0	0	0
40-44	3	0	1	1
45-49	1	2	3	2
50-54	0	0	0	0
55-59	17	8	8	19
60-64	2	5	2	3
65-	0	2	0	2
Offensive Rebound Pct.				
Below 25%	8	7	10	17
25-29.99%	10	7	2	6
30-34.99%	4	3	0	3
35-39.99%	1	0	2	1
40-44.99%	1	0	0	0
45% and up	0	0	0	0
Assists				
0-14	0	0	0	2
15-19	2	5	4	9
20-24	6	9	5	13
25-29	10	3	4	3
30-34	4	0	0	0
35+	2	0	1	0
Opp. Assists				
0-14	0	0	0	0
15-19	3	0	2	2
20-24	7	3	6	7
25-29	11	6	4	12
30-34	3	7	2	4
35+	0	1	0	2

	Home W	L	Road W	L
Edge In Assists				
Below -15	0	2	1	4
-10 to -14	0	6	0	3
-5 to -9	2	2	3	9
0 to -4	7	6	4	9
1-4	6	1	2	1
5-9	7	0	4	1
10-14	2	0	0	0
15-	0	0	0	0
Personal Fouls				
0-14	0	1	0	1
15-19	8	3	5	9
20-24	13	9	6	13
25-29	3	3	2	4
30-34	0	1	1	0
35+	0	0	0	0
Opp. Personal Fouls				
0-14	0	0	0	0
15-19	3	5	1	10
20-24	12	5	7	14
25-29	8	7	4	3
30-34	1	0	2	0
35+	0	0	0	0
Personal Fouls Edge				
Below -15	1	0	0	0
-10 to -14	1	1	2	0
-5 to -9	4	2	2	5
0 to -4	15	6	5	9
1-4	2	6	5	9
5-9	1	2	0	4
10-14	0	0	0	0
15+	0	0	0	0
Steals				
0-5	8	5	3	5
6-7	9	6	5	9
8-9	4	4	3	8
10-11	2	0	1	4
12-13	1	2	2	1
14+	0	0	0	0
Opp. Steals				
0-5	8	3	1	4
6-7	3	5	6	6
8-9	4	3	4	7
10-11	6	5	1	6
12-13	2	1	1	3
14+	1	0	1	1
Edge In Steals				
Below -7	1	1	2	2
-4 to -6	7	2	0	5
0 to -3	6	9	4	11
1-3	6	2	5	5
4-6	3	3	3	4
7-	1	0	0	0
Turnovers				
0-14	11	11	6	13
15-19	8	4	5	12
20-24	4	2	3	1
25-29	1	0	0	1
30-34	0	0	0	0
35+	0	0	0	0
Opp. Turnovers				
0-14	17	8	6	13
15-19	3	9	7	14

	Home W	L	Road W	L
20-24	3	0	1	0
25-29	1	0	0	0
30-34	0	0	0	0
35+	0	0	0	0
Edge In Turnovers				
Below -15	0	0	0	0
-10 to -14	1	0	0	1
-5 to -9	2	4	1	3
0 to -4	8	5	6	7
1-4	8	6	4	11
5-9	3	2	2	3
10-14	2	0	1	2
15+	0	0	0	0
Blocks				
1-2	1	1	1	6
3-4	3	4	4	12
5-6	3	4	4	8
7-8	7	4	3	0
9-10	6	2	2	1
11+	4	2	0	0

	Home W	L	Road W	L
Opp. Blocks				
0-2	5	2	3	7
3-4	8	6	6	6
5-6	8	4	3	6
7-8	3	5	0	6
9-10	0	0	2	2
11+	0	0	0	0
Edge In Blocks				
Below -7	0	0	0	2
-4 to -6	0	0	1	2
0 to -3	6	5	4	15
1-3	7	8	7	6
4-6	3	2	2	2
7+	8	2	0	0
Three-Pointers Attempted				
0-2	2	0	0	0
3-5	5	1	2	7
6-8	9	6	7	9
9-11	3	6	3	5
12-14	5	2	2	6
15+	0	2	0	0

	Home W	L	Road W	L
Three-Pointers Made				
0-2	10	8	6	20
3-5	13	8	8	5
6-8	1	1	0	2
9-11	0	0	0	0
12-14	0	0	0	0
15+	0	0	0	0
Three-Pointers Pct.				
.000-.099	3	3	1	5
.100-.149	3	5	0	8
.150-.199	2	0	0	2
.200-.249	0	0	0	2
.250-.299	3	1	3	2
.300-.349	6	1	2	6
.350-.399	3	2	1	1
.400-.449	0	3	3	0
.450-.499	0	0	0	1
.500-	4	2	4	0
Opp. Three-Point Attempts				
0-2	5	0	1	2
3-5	9	6	7	11

	Home W	L	Road W	L
6-8	6	5	4	6
9-11	4	4	0	6
12-14	0	0	1	2
15+	0	2	1	0
Opp. Three-Pointers Made				
0-2	21	6	12	16
3-5	3	8	1	10
6-8	0	3	1	1
9-11	0	0	0	0
12-14	0	0	0	0
15+	0	0	0	0
Opp. Three-Pointer Pct.				
.000-.099	8	4	5	5
.100-.149	3	3	1	2
.150-.199	0	2	2	0
.200-.249	1	0	0	2
.250-.299	5	1	2	3
.300-.349	4	1	2	3
.350-.399	2	0	0	0
.400-.449	1	0	2	5
.450-.499	0	0	0	0
.500-	0	6	0	7

Dallas Mavericks
1988–89 Power Chart

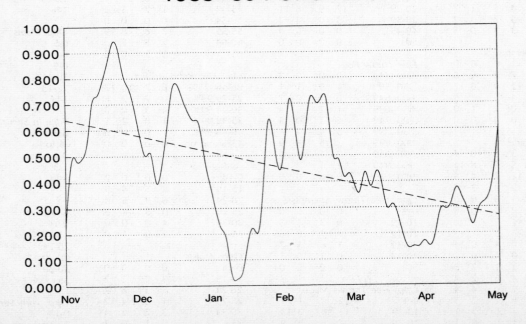

Dallas Mavericks

	GP	GS	Min	FGM	FGA	FG%	2GM	2GA	2G%	3GM	3GA	3G%	FTM	FTA	FT%	Off	Tot	Ast	PF	Stl	TO	Blk	Pts	HGS
Mark Aguirre	44	44	1529	373	829	0.450	344	730	0.471	29	99	0.293	178	244	0.730	90	145	235	128	29	140	29	953	722
Per GP			34.7	8.5	18.8		7.8	16.6		0.7	2.3		4.0	5.5		2.0	3.3	5.3	2.9	0.7	3.2	0.7	21.7	16.4
Per 48			31.9	11.7	26.0		10.8	22.9		0.9	3.1		5.6	7.7		2.8	4.6	7.4	4.0	0.9	4.4	0.9	29.9	22.7
Steve Alford	9	0	38	3	11	0.273	3	9	0.333	0	2	0.000	1	2	0.500	0	3	3	3	1	1	0	7	11
Per GP			4.2	0.3	1.2		0.3	1.0		0.0	0.2		0.1	0.2		0.0	0.3	0.3	0.3	0.1	0.1	0.0	0.8	1.2
Per 48			0.8	3.8	13.9		3.8	11.4		0.0	2.5		1.3	2.5		0.0	3.8	3.8	3.8	1.3	1.3	0.0	8.8	13.9
Uwe Blab	37	0	208	24	52	0.462	24	52	0.462	0	0	0.000	20	25	0.800	11	33	44	36	3	14	13	68	85
Per GP			5.6	0.6	1.4		0.6	1.4		0.0	0.0		0.5	0.7		0.3	0.9	1.2	1.0	0.1	0.4	0.4	1.8	2.3
Per 48			4.3	5.5	12.0		5.5	12.0		0.0	0.0		4.6	5.8		2.5	7.6	10.2	8.3	0.7	3.2	3.0	15.7	19.6
Rolando Blackman	78	78	2946	594	1249	0.476	564	1164	0.485	30	85	0.353	316	370	0.854	70	203	273	137	65	164	20	1534	1165
Per GP			37.8	7.6	16.0		7.2	14.9		0.4	1.1		4.1	4.7		0.9	2.6	3.5	1.8	0.8	2.1	0.3	19.7	14.9
Per 48			61.4	9.7	20.4		9.2	19.0		0.5	1.4		5.1	6.0		1.1	3.3	4.4	2.2	1.1	2.7	0.3	25.0	19.0
Adrian Dantley	31	25	1081	212	459	0.462	212	458	0.463	0	1	0.000	204	263	0.776	64	89	153	87	20	82	7	628	494
Per GP			34.9	6.8	14.8		6.8	14.8		0.0	0.0		6.6	8.5		2.1	2.9	4.9	2.8	0.6	2.6	0.2	20.3	15.9
Per 48			22.5	9.4	20.4		9.4	20.3		0.0	0.0		9.1	11.7		2.8	4.0	6.8	3.9	0.9	3.6	0.3	27.9	21.9
Brad Davis	78	4	1395	183	379	0.483	151	278	0.543	32	101	0.317	99	123	0.805	14	94	108	151	48	93	18	497	537
Per GP			17.9	2.3	4.9		1.9	3.6		0.4	1.3		1.3	1.6		0.2	1.2	1.4	1.9	0.6	1.2	0.2	6.4	6.9
Per 48			29.1	6.3	13.0		5.2	9.6		1.1	3.5		3.4	4.2		0.5	3.2	3.7	5.2	1.7	3.2	0.6	17.1	18.5
James Donaldson	53	53	1746	193	337	0.573	193	337	0.573	0	0	0.000	95	124	0.766	158	412	570	111	24	83	81	481	728
Per GP			32.9	3.6	6.4		3.6	6.4		0.0	0.0		1.8	2.3		3.0	7.8	10.8	2.1	0.5	1.6	1.5	9.1	13.7
Per 48			36.4	5.3	9.3		5.3	9.3		0.0	0.0		2.6	3.4		4.3	11.3	15.7	3.1	0.7	2.3	2.2	13.2	20.0
Derek Harper	81	81	2968	538	1127	0.477	439	849	0.517	99	278	0.356	229	284	0.806	46	182	228	219	172	205	41	1404	1394
Per GP			36.6	6.6	13.9		5.4	10.5		1.2	3.4		2.8	3.5		0.6	2.2	2.8	2.7	2.1	2.5	0.5	17.3	17.2
Per 48			61.8	8.7	18.2		7.1	13.7		1.6	4.5		3.7	4.6		0.7	2.9	3.7	3.5	2.8	3.3	0.7	22.7	22.5
Tony Jones	25	0	131	24	64	0.375	20	49	0.408	4	15	0.267	12	14	0.857	10	10	20	13	9	4	2	64	57
Per GP			5.2	1.0	2.6		0.8	2.0		0.2	0.6		0.5	0.6		0.4	0.4	0.8	0.5	0.4	0.2	0.1	2.6	2.3
Per 48			2.7	8.8	23.5		7.3	18.0		1.5	5.5		4.4	5.1		3.7	3.7	7.3	4.8	3.3	1.5	0.7	23.5	20.9
Sam Perkins	78	77	2860	445	959	0.464	438	921	0.476	7	38	0.184	274	329	0.833	232	456	688	224	76	137	92	1171	1236
Per GP			36.7	5.7	12.3		5.6	11.8		0.1	0.5		3.5	4.2		3.0	5.8	8.8	2.9	1.0	1.8	1.2	15.0	15.8
Per 48			59.6	7.5	16.1		7.4	15.5		0.1	0.6		4.6	5.5		3.9	7.7	11.5	3.8	1.3	2.3	1.5	19.7	20.7
Detlef Schrempf	37	1	845	112	263	0.426	110	247	0.445	2	16	0.125	127	161	0.789	56	110	166	118	24	56	9	353	374
Per GP			22.8	3.0	7.1		3.0	6.7		0.1	0.4		3.4	4.4		1.5	3.0	4.5	3.2	0.6	1.5	0.2	9.5	10.1
Per 48			17.6	6.4	14.9		6.2	14.0		0.1	0.9		7.2	9.1		3.2	6.2	9.4	6.7	1.4	3.2	0.5	20.1	21.2
Roy Tarpley	19	6	591	131	242	0.541	131	241	0.544	0	1	0.000	66	96	0.687	77	141	218	70	28	45	30	328	370
Per GP			31.1	6.9	12.7		6.9	12.7		0.0	0.1		3.5	5.1		4.1	7.4	11.5	3.7	1.5	2.4	1.6	17.3	19.5
Per 48			12.3	10.6	19.7		10.6	19.6		0.0	0.1		5.4	7.8		6.3	11.5	17.7	5.7	2.3	3.7	2.4	26.6	30.1
Terry Tyler	70	11	1057	169	360	0.469	168	351	0.479	1	9	0.111	47	62	0.758	74	135	209	90	24	51	39	386	377
Per GP			15.1	2.4	5.1		2.4	5.0		0.0	0.1		0.7	0.9		1.1	1.9	3.0	1.3	0.3	0.7	0.6	5.5	5.4
Per 48			22.0	7.7	16.3		7.6	15.9		0.0	0.4		2.1	2.8		3.4	6.1	9.5	4.1	1.1	2.3	1.8	17.5	17.1
Bill Wennington	65	9	1074	119	275	0.433	118	266	0.444	1	9	0.111	61	82	0.744	85	201	286	211	16	58	35	300	371
Per GP			16.5	1.8	4.2		1.8	4.1		0.0	0.1		0.9	1.3		1.3	3.1	4.4	3.2	0.2	0.9	0.5	4.6	5.7
Per 48			22.4	5.3	12.3		5.3	11.9		0.0	0.4		2.7	3.7		3.8	9.0	12.8	9.4	0.7	2.6	1.6	13.4	16.6
Morton Wiley	51	1	408	46	114	0.404	40	90	0.444	6	24	0.250	13	16	0.812	13	34	47	61	25	34	6	111	147
Per GP			8.0	0.9	2.2		0.8	1.8		0.1	0.5		0.3	0.3		0.3	0.7	0.9	1.2	0.5	0.7	0.1	2.2	2.9
Per 48			8.5	5.4	13.4		4.7	10.6		0.7	2.8		1.5	1.9		1.5	4.0	5.5	7.2	2.9	4.0	0.7	13.1	17.3
Herb Williams	30	20	903	78	197	0.396	78	195	0.400	0	2	0.000	43	68	0.632	48	149	197	80	15	41	54	199	290
Per GP			30.1	2.6	6.6		2.6	6.5		0.0	0.1		1.4	2.3		1.6	5.0	6.6	2.7	0.5	1.4	1.8	6.6	9.7
Per 48			18.8	4.1	10.5		4.1	10.4		0.0	0.1		2.3	3.6		2.6	7.9	10.5	4.3	0.8	2.2	2.9	10.6	15.4

DENVER NUGGETS

Two seasons ago, the Nuggets and their chaotic "passing-game" offense devised by Doug Moe won 54 games and the Midwest Division title. Last season the team showed its age, winning only 44 games and finishing up third in the division.

To win with Moe's seemingly unstructured passing-game offense, you have to have players who can, you know, actually *make* the occasional basket. For an offensive team such as Denver, a shooting percentage of .468 is poison. It tied the Nuggets with Golden State and San Antonio for sixth worst in the entire league, placing them ahead of only New Jersey, Miami, Charlotte, Sacramento, and Washington. What common thread can we find with all these teams? No, not the word "powerhouse." The word "lottery" is the one that comes to mind. Of the eight worst-shooting teams in the league, only Denver and Golden State squeaked into the playoffs. Interestingly, Denver and Golden State were one-two in the league in field goals *attempted*. Evidently coaches Moe and Nelson had a similar offensive philosophy—that if you throw enough times at the wall . . . well, you know the rest. And judging from their shooting percentages, what they threw up there really wasn't worth watching.

Normally, it would make sense that the team which takes more shots scores more, and wins the game. However, with the foul Nuggets shooting (as opposed to the foul-shooting Nuggets), the relationship didn't quite hold up. In nearly every game, Denver hoisted up more shots than their opponents, yet lost almost half of those contests. In fact, the most remarkable facet of Denver's game was that the *fewer* shots they outshot their opponents by, the greater their average margin of victory. When the relationship is found, there is a slight but definite trend, as shown in the chart below. Their break-even point is about 9 shots—when they outshoot their opponents by 9, they break even, on average. (The line on the chart shows the relationship between shots taken margin and scoring margin: scoring margin goes up as shooting margin goes down.)

It's strange, but what does it mean? Possibly that when the Nuggets fall behind, they get taken out of their game, and everyone starts taking shots they have no business taking. Indeed, had Denver shot 10 points better, for a just-average .478, they would have scored an additional 162 points. It wasn't just one player laying the foundation of bricks, either. The poor shooting was basically a team-wide phe-

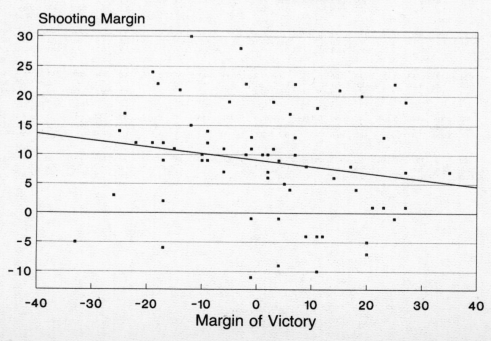

Denver Nuggets

nomenon. Even including the scrubs, Denver only had one player shooting .500 or better for the season—Danny Schayes. Every other team save Washington had at least two; Cleveland's *entire starting five* shot 50% or better. When you have a team this cold, you had better be able to win once in a while when you score under 110 points. Denver did it three times all year, while losing 18 times.

Denver had over a 5 point edge at home in the first quarter, running and scoring early while their opponents left their lungs at the hotel. However, where you'd expect the games to get worse as the game wore on and the opponents wore out, the opposite occurred. You'd expect that visitors would have their worst problems in the fourth quarter when they were out of oxygen, yet the Nuggets' fourth-quarter edge was only about 1½ points at home, the lowest of any quarter.

The Nuggets needed that home edge, too, because on the road they didn't do much of anything, with a record of 9–32. Only New Jersey, Charlotte, Indiana, San Antonio, Miami, Sacramento, and the L.A. Clippers had equal or worse road records. Notice something about *this* group of teams? (Hint: see the lowest shooting percentages, above.)

While the Nuggets were all tossing up bricks, they were also balanced in their attack when the ball fell for them. Thirty-five-year-old Alex English, the seventh leading scorer in NBA history, knocked in 27.1 ppg, sixth best in the league. Fat Lever (19.8 ppg), 5'10" Michael Adams (18.5 ppg), Walter Davis (15.6 ppg), and Danny Schayes (12.8 ppg) came across with the rest of the scoring output, 117.8 ppg, the second highest team average in the league. But obviously scoring isn't enough. The Nuggets have to be in trouble if they continue to rely on 175-pound Fat Lever to lead them in rebounds (662), assists (559), and steals (195), as well as to chip in his 20 points every game. If they're going to make a move on Utah, Houston, or Dallas this year, somebody else is going to have to help out Lever.

HoopStats

Denver Nuggets

	Home W	L	Road W	L
By Month				
November	8	1	1	3
December	5	2	3	5
January	4	2	1	9
February	8	0	0	4
March	5	0	3	6
April	5	1	1	5
Playoffs				
Home/Away	35	6	9	32
Overtime	1	1	1	3
Offense				
0-89	0	0	0	1
90-99	0	1	0	4
100-109	3	2	0	10
110-119	11	1	3	13
120-129	10	1	2	1
130-	11	1	4	3
Defense				
0-89	1	0	0	0
90-99	3	0	1	0
100-109	16	0	2	4
110-119	9	3	2	7
120-129	5	2	2	16
130-	1	1	2	5
Over/Under				
0-189	0	0	0	0
190-199	1	0	0	2
200-209	3	1	0	3
210-219	6	0	2	2
220-229	7	2	1	6
230-239	5	0	2	12
240-	13	3	4	7
Margin Of Victory				
0-3	5	2	2	7
4-6	7	0	0	5
7-10	4	2	2	4
11-15	4	1	3	4
16-20	4	1	1	6
21-	11	0	1	6
Field Goal Attempts				
0-69	0	0	0	0
70-79	0	0	0	0
80-89	6	0	0	6
90-99	14	1	5	10
100-109	14	2	4	12
110+	1	3	0	4
Field Goals Made				
0-34	0	0	0	1
35-39	4	1	0	9
40-44	5	2	1	5
45-49	11	2	3	12
50-54	9	0	4	4
55+	6	1	1	1
Field Goal Pct.				
.000-.399	0	2	0	6
.400-.424	1	2	0	8
.425-.449	6	0	0	5
.450-.474	5	1	1	7
.475-.499	4	0	4	1
.500-.524	11	1	2	3
.525-.549	5	0	1	2
.550-.574	1	0	0	0

	Home W	L	Road W	L
.575-.599	2	0	1	0
.600-	0	0	0	0
Opp. Field Goal Attempts				
0-69	0	0	0	0
70-79	7	0	0	2
80-89	9	1	6	12
90-99	13	3	0	15
100-109	5	1	3	2
110+	1	1	0	1
Opp. Field Goal Made				
0-34	1	0	0	0
35-39	9	0	1	2
40-44	16	2	2	8
45-49	5	1	5	9
50-54	3	3	1	11
55+	1	0	0	2
Opp. Field Goal Percentage				
.000-.399	4	0	0	0
.400-.424	4	0	1	0
.425-.449	4	0	0	1
.450-.474	7	1	0	4
.475-.499	4	2	2	5
.500-.524	7	1	3	8
.525-.549	3	2	3	7
.550-.574	1	0	0	1
.575-.599	0	0	0	3
.600-	1	0	0	3
Free Throw Attempts				
0-9	0	0	0	0
10-19	2	1	0	9
20-29	13	4	5	13
30-39	15	1	3	9
40-49	5	0	1	1
50+	0	0	0	0
Free Throws Made				
0-9	0	0	0	1
10-19	8	3	4	18
20-29	19	2	3	10
30-39	8	1	1	3
40-49	0	0	1	0
50+	0	0	0	0
Free Throw Pct.				
.000-.549	0	0	0	0
.550-.599	0	0	0	1
.600-.649	2	0	0	4
.650-.699	4	1	1	3
.700-.749	4	0	0	6
.750-.799	10	0	1	4
.800-.849	7	3	3	9
.850-.899	6	1	2	2
.900-.949	1	1	1	3
.950-	1	0	1	0
Opp. Free Throw Attempts				
0-9	0	0	0	0
10-19	1	0	0	0
20-29	11	2	5	10
30-39	16	3	2	13
40-49	7	0	2	8
50+	0	1	0	1
Opp. Free Throws Made				
0-9	0	0	0	0
10-19	13	1	2	5
20-29	15	4	5	17

	Home W	L	Road W	L
30-39	7	0	2	10
40-49	0	1	0	0
50+	0	0	0	0
Opp. Free Throw Pct.				
.000-.549	2	0	0	0
.550-.599	1	1	0	2
.600-.649	2	0	0	5
.650-.699	6	0	1	3
.700-.749	11	2	2	5
.750-.799	3	1	3	6
.800-.849	10	2	2	8
.850-.899	0	0	1	1
.900-.949	0	0	0	2
.950-	0	0	0	0
Offensive Rebounds				
0-9	1	1	1	2
10-14	20	2	4	12
15-19	9	2	3	14
20-24	5	0	1	2
25+	0	1	0	2
Total Rebounds				
0-39	0	0	0	1
40-44	2	0	1	3
45-49	4	0	2	4
50-54	0	0	0	0
55-59	14	3	6	19
60-64	11	3	0	3
65-	4	0	0	2
Opp. Offensive Rebounds				
0-9	6	3	1	10
10-14	10	0	5	9
15-19	13	2	2	10
20-24	5	1	0	2
25+	1	0	1	1
Opp. Total Rebounds				
0-39	1	0	0	0
40-44	1	0	1	0
45-49	7	0	0	0
50-54	0	0	0	0
55-59	11	3	6	18
60-64	9	1	1	6
65-	6	2	1	8
Offensive Rebound Pct.				
Below 25%	16	4	4	20
25-29.99%	12	1	2	6
30-34.99%	5	0	3	6
35-39.99%	1	1	0	0
40-44.99%	1	0	0	0
45% and up	0	0	0	0
Assists				
0-14	0	0	0	2
15-19	0	1	0	3
20-24	9	4	0	8
25-29	10	0	4	10
30-34	12	1	4	4
35+	4	0	1	5
Opp. Assists				
0-14	2	0	0	0
15-19	7	0	0	0
20-24	18	2	0	5
25-29	7	2	4	11
30-34	1	2	5	10
35+	0	0	0	6

	Home W	L	Road W	L
Edge In Assists				
Below -15	0	0	0	2
-10 to -14	0	0	0	5
-5 to -9	1	2	1	9
0 to -4	4	3	4	8
1-4	4	1	3	3
5-9	15	0	3	3
10-14	5	0	0	2
15-	6	0	1	0
Personal Fouls				
0-14	0	0	0	0
15-19	1	0	0	0
20-24	17	3	6	12
25-29	11	2	1	15
30-34	5	1	2	4
35+	1	0	0	1
Opp. Personal Fouls				
0-14	0	0	0	1
15-19	4	1	1	5
20-24	7	3	3	13
25-29	15	2	4	12
30-34	9	0	0	1
35+	0	0	1	0
Personal Fouls Edge				
Below -15	0	0	0	0
-10 to -14	1	0	0	0
-5 to -9	7	0	1	1
0 to -4	13	1	5	9
1-4	9	3	2	12
5-9	5	2	1	8
10-14	0	0	0	2
15+	0	0	0	0
Steals				
0-5	2	0	0	3
6-7	8	2	2	6
8-9	7	2	2	5
10-11	4	2	2	12
12-13	7	0	1	4
14+	7	0	2	2
Opp. Steals				
0-5	9	2	1	7
6-7	5	1	5	6
8-9	11	1	2	4
10-11	7	0	1	7
12-13	1	0	0	5
14+	2	2	0	3
Edge In Steals				
Below -7	0	1	0	2
-4 to -6	1	1	0	3
0 to -3	12	1	2	9
1-3	9	1	3	9
4-6	8	2	3	7
7-	5	0	1	2
Turnovers				
0-14	16	4	8	13
15-19	13	2	1	13
20-24	6	0	0	4
25-29	0	0	0	2
30-34	0	0	0	0
35+	0	0	0	0
Opp. Turnovers				
0-14	6	1	1	5
15-19	8	3	3	13

	Home W	L	Road W	L
20-24	13	1	5	10
25-29	6	1	0	3
30-34	2	0	0	1
35+	0	0	0	0
Edge In Turnovers				
Below -15	3	0	0	0
-10 to -14	9	0	1	4
-5 to -9	6	4	4	7
0 to -4	14	1	4	14
1-4	3	0	0	3
5-9	0	0	0	3
10-14	0	1	0	1
15+	0	0	0	0
Blocks				
1-2	5	0	3	7
3-4	6	1	2	9
5-6	10	2	2	8
7-8	10	2	1	5
9-10	3	1	1	2
11+	1	0	0	1

	Home W	L	Road W	L
Opp. Blocks				
0-2	3	0	0	3
3-4	9	1	3	10
5-6	11	1	4	7
7-8	8	2	2	4
9-10	4	1	0	4
11+	0	1	0	4
Edge In Blocks				
Below -7	0	1	0	4
-4 to -6	5	0	3	4
0 to -3	13	3	3	14
1-3	11	2	3	7
4-6	5	0	0	3
7+	1	0	0	0
Three-Pointers Attempted				
0-2	1	0	1	0
3-5	8	0	2	5
6-8	18	2	4	8
9-11	7	1	2	11
12-14	0	2	0	6
15+	1	1	0	2

	Home W	L	Road W	L
Three-Pointers Made				
0-2	17	2	5	16
3-5	18	3	4	14
6-8	0	1	0	2
9-11	0	0	0	0
12-14	0	0	0	0
15+	0	0	0	0
Three-Pointers Pct.				
.000-.099	4	1	1	2
.100-.149	2	0	0	2
.150-.199	1	0	0	5
.200-.249	1	0	0	1
.250-.299	5	2	2	5
.300-.349	5	1	3	7
.350-.399	5	0	1	4
.400-.449	2	0	0	2
.450-.499	1	0	0	2
.500-	9	2	2	2
Opp. Three-Point Attempts				
0-2	5	0	0	8
3-5	13	3	7	12

	Home W	L	Road W	L
6-8	13	3	1	6
9-11	1	0	1	3
12-14	2	0	0	3
15+	1	0	0	0
Opp. Three-Pointers Made				
0-2	27	4	8	21
3-5	6	2	1	7
6-8	2	0	0	4
9-11	0	0	0	0
12-14	0	0	0	0
15+	0	0	0	0
Opp. Three-Pointer Pct.				
.000-.099	9	2	3	9
.100-.149	2	0	2	0
.150-.199	4	1	0	3
.200-.249	0	0	0	0
.250-.299	3	0	1	0
.300-.349	8	2	3	7
.350-.399	0	0	0	1
.400-.449	1	0	0	0
.450-.499	0	0	0	0
.500-	8	1	0	12

Denver Nuggets
1988–89 Power Chart

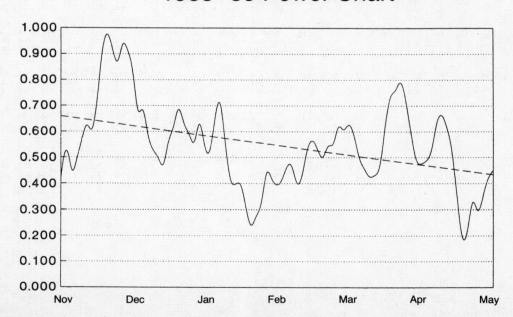

Denver Nuggets

	GP	GS	Min	FGM	FGA	FG%	2GM	2GA	2G%	3GM	3GA	3G%	FTM	FTA	FT%	Off	Tot	Ast	PF	Stl	TO	Blk	Pts	HGS
Michael Adams	77	77	2787	468	1082	0.433	302	617	0.489	166	465	0.357	322	393	0.819	71	212	283	149	166	180	11	1424	1303
Per GP			36.2	6.1	14.1		3.9	8.0		2.2	6.0		4.2	5.1		0.9	2.8	3.7	1.9	2.2	2.3	0.1	18.5	16.9
Per 48			58.1	8.1	18.6		5.2	10.6		2.9	8.0		5.5	6.8		1.2	3.7	4.9	2.6	2.9	3.1	0.2	24.5	22.4
Darwin Cook	30	4	386	71	163	0.436	69	153	0.451	2	10	0.200	17	22	0.773	13	35	48	44	28	26	6	161	148
Per GP			12.9	2.4	5.4		2.3	5.1		0.1	0.3		0.6	0.7		0.4	1.2	1.6	1.5	0.9	0.9	0.2	5.4	4.9
Per 48			8.0	8.8	20.3		8.6	19.0		0.2	1.2		2.1	2.7		1.6	4.4	6.0	5.5	3.5	3.2	0.7	20.0	18.4
Wayne Cooper	79	72	1865	220	444	0.495	219	440	0.498	1	4	0.250	79	106	0.745	212	407	619	302	36	73	211	520	987
Per GP			23.6	2.8	5.6		2.8	5.6		0.0	0.1		1.0	1.3		2.7	5.2	7.8	3.8	0.5	0.9	2.7	6.6	12.5
Per 48			38.9	5.7	11.4		5.6	11.3		0.0	0.1		2.0	2.7		5.5	10.5	15.9	7.8	0.9	1.9	5.4	13.4	25.4
Walter Davis	81	0	1857	536	1076	0.498	516	1007	0.512	20	69	0.290	175	199	0.879	41	110	151	187	72	132	5	1267	855
Per GP			22.9	6.6	13.3		6.4	12.4		0.2	0.9		2.2	2.5		0.5	1.4	1.9	2.3	0.9	1.6	0.1	15.6	10.6
Per 48			38.7	13.9	27.8		13.3	26.0		0.5	1.8		4.5	5.1		1.1	2.8	3.9	4.8	1.9	3.4	0.1	32.7	22.1
Wayne Engelstad	11	0	50	11	29	0.379	11	29	0.379	0	0	0.000	6	10	0.600	5	11	16	12	1	3	0	28	26
Per GP			4.5	1.0	2.6		1.0	2.6		0.0	0.0		0.5	0.9		0.5	1.0	1.5	1.1	0.1	0.3	0.0	2.5	2.4
Per 48			1.0	10.6	27.8		10.6	27.8		0.0	0.0		5.8	9.6		4.8	10.6	15.4	11.5	1.0	2.9	0.0	26.9	25.0
Alex English	82	82	2990	924	1881	0.491	922	1873	0.492	2	8	0.250	325	379	0.858	148	178	326	174	66	198	12	2175	1567
Per GP			36.5	11.3	22.9		11.2	22.8		0.0	0.1		4.0	4.6		1.8	2.2	4.0	2.1	0.8	2.4	0.1	26.5	19.1
Per 48			62.3	14.8	30.2		14.8	30.1		0.0	0.1		5.2	6.1		2.4	2.9	5.2	2.8	1.1	3.2	0.2	34.9	25.2
David Greenwood	29	3	491	62	148	0.419	62	148	0.419	0	0	0.000	48	71	0.676	48	116	164	78	17	35	28	172	251
Per GP			16.9	2.1	5.1		2.1	5.1		0.0	0.0		1.7	2.4		1.7	4.0	5.7	2.7	0.6	1.2	1.0	5.9	8.7
Per 48			10.2	6.1	14.5		6.1	14.5		0.0	0.0		4.7	6.9		4.7	11.3	16.0	7.6	1.7	3.4	2.7	16.8	24.5
Bill Hanzlik	41	0	701	66	151	0.437	65	146	0.445	1	5	0.200	68	87	0.782	18	75	93	82	25	53	5	201	238
Per GP			17.1	1.6	3.7		1.6	3.6		0.0	0.1		1.7	2.1		0.4	1.8	2.3	2.0	0.6	1.3	0.1	4.9	5.8
Per 48			14.6	4.5	10.3		4.5	10.0		0.1	0.3		4.7	6.0		1.2	5.1	6.4	5.6	1.7	3.6	0.3	13.8	16.3
Alfred Hughes	26	1	224	28	64	0.437	21	42	0.500	7	22	0.318	7	12	0.583	6	13	19	30	17	11	2	70	82
Per GP			8.6	1.1	2.5		0.8	1.6		0.3	0.8		0.3	0.5		0.2	0.5	0.7	1.2	0.7	0.4	0.1	2.7	3.2
Per 48			4.7	6.0	13.7		4.5	9.0		1.5	4.7		1.5	2.6		1.3	2.8	4.1	6.4	3.6	2.4	0.4	15.0	17.6
Jerome Lane	54	1	550	109	256	0.426	109	249	0.438	0	7	0.000	43	112	0.384	87	113	200	105	20	50	4	261	283
Per GP			10.2	2.0	4.7		2.0	4.6		0.0	0.1		0.8	2.1		1.6	2.1	3.7	1.9	0.4	0.9	0.1	4.8	5.2
Per 48			11.5	9.5	22.3		9.5	21.7		0.0	0.6		3.8	9.8		7.6	9.9	17.5	9.2	1.7	4.4	0.3	22.8	24.7
Lafayette Lever	71	71	2745	558	1221	0.457	535	1155	0.463	23	66	0.348	270	344	0.785	187	475	662	178	195	157	20	1409	1705
Per GP			38.7	7.9	17.2		7.5	16.3		0.3	0.9		3.8	4.8		2.6	6.7	9.3	2.5	2.7	2.2	0.3	19.8	24.0
Per 48			57.2	9.8	21.4		9.4	20.2		0.4	1.2		4.7	6.0		3.3	8.3	11.6	3.1	3.4	2.7	0.3	24.6	29.8
Calvin Natt	14	0	168	22	50	0.440	22	49	0.449	0	1	0.000	22	31	0.710	12	34	46	13	6	11	1	66	69
Per GP			12.0	1.6	3.6		1.6	3.5		0.0	0.1		1.6	2.2		0.9	2.4	3.3	0.9	0.4	0.8	0.1	4.7	4.9
Per 48			3.5	6.3	14.3		6.3	14.0		0.0	0.3		6.3	8.9		3.4	9.7	13.1	3.7	1.7	3.1	0.3	18.9	19.7
Blair Rasmussen	77	22	1308	257	577	0.445	257	577	0.445	0	0	0.000	69	81	0.852	105	182	287	194	29	49	41	583	514
Per GP			17.0	3.3	7.5		3.3	7.5		0.0	0.0		0.9	1.1		1.4	2.4	3.7	2.5	0.4	0.6	0.5	7.6	6.7
Per 48			27.2	9.4	21.2		9.4	21.2		0.0	0.0		2.5	3.0		3.9	6.7	10.5	7.1	1.1	1.8	1.5	21.4	18.9
Danny Schayes	76	64	1917	317	607	0.522	314	598	0.525	3	9	0.333	332	402	0.826	142	358	500	320	42	160	81	969	1034
Per GP			25.2	4.2	8.0		4.1	7.9		0.0	0.1		4.4	5.3		1.9	4.7	6.6	4.2	0.6	2.1	1.1	12.7	13.6
Per 48			39.9	7.9	15.2		7.9	15.0		0.1	0.2		8.3	10.1		3.6	9.0	12.5	8.0	1.1	4.0	2.0	24.3	25.9
Elston Turner	78	12	1746	151	353	0.428	149	346	0.431	2	7	0.286	33	56	0.589	109	178	287	209	90	60	8	337	501
Per GP			22.4	1.9	4.5		1.9	4.4		0.0	0.1		0.4	0.7		1.4	2.3	3.7	2.7	1.2	0.8	0.1	4.3	6.4
Per 48			36.4	4.2	9.7		4.1	9.5		0.1	0.2		0.9	1.5		3.0	4.9	7.9	5.7	2.5	1.6	0.2	9.3	13.8
Jay Vincent	5	1	95	13	38	0.342	12	36	0.333	1	2	0.500	5	9	0.556	2	16	18	11	1	5	1	32	21
Per GP			19.0	2.6	7.6		2.4	7.2		0.2	0.4		1.0	1.8		0.4	3.2	3.6	2.2	0.2	1.0	0.2	6.4	4.2
Per 48			2.0	6.6	19.2		6.1	18.2		0.5	1.0		2.5	4.5		1.0	8.1	9.1	5.6	0.5	2.5	0.5	16.2	10.6

DETROIT PISTONS

Seriously, who cares how much people hate a team if they're this good? Just about the only thing the Pistons lost last season was the attendance record to Charlotte. In capturing their second Central Division title, they recorded a club-record 63 wins, showing the mindset of champions by gearing up for the playoffs with a 16–1 March, tying the 1971–72 Lakers for the most victories in a month. They were well nigh unbeatable at home (37–4, including 21–0 to close the season), and on the road, they were tops in the league with a 26–15 record, four games ahead of the Lakers. Eight teams had fewer wins at home than the Pistons had on the road. Think they're going to sell the jet back to Dallas like Adrian Dantley wants them to? The only minus we can see on this team is that they lost too many games to fights last year.

A nasty bunch of baseline-to-baseline players, the Pistons held opponents to 100.8 points per outing, second only to the Utah Jazz (99.7 ppg). Although they weren't a high-scoring bunch by any means (106.6 ppg, only 15th best in the league), they were a good offensive team, shooting at a .494 clip, fifth best in the NBA. The Pistons' defense was a good demonstration of how little you can know about a team, despite the best intentions of statistics. They grabbed a league-low 522 steals, and blocked more shots than only six teams. But, again, only Utah held their opponents to a lower shooting percentage from the floor.

And when their opponents missed? Only three teams grabbed a higher percentage of the total defensive rebound chances than Detroit's .698 — Boston, Chicago, and (oddly) New Jersey. (The defensive rebound percentage is figured by the formula: OReb/(OReb + Opponents' DReb)) Once you missed the shot, you didn't get it back. Detroit proved that you don't have to force turnovers to be an excellent defensive team.

More remarkable numbers: The Pistons were 36–2 when holding their opponents under 100 points; perhaps the number of times they did it is even more interesting than the fact that they were 34 games over when they did it. They lost only 1 game in 10 when they led after three quarters, yet won about 60 percent when they trailed. They held their opponents under 20 points in a quarter over 50 times, by far a league-high. Basically, they made their opponents' offenses look like Miami's (on a good night). Their dominance at home could

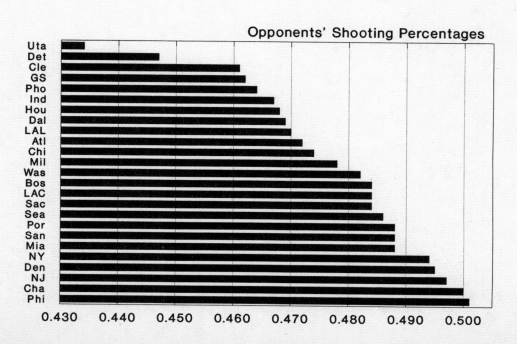

Detroit Pistons

Opponents' Shooting Percentages

be summed up with their first/second-half scoring averages: they outscored opponents by over 7 points in the first half, under 2 in the second half as they coasted home. Garbage time came early in more than a few games.

Scrappy? To go with the wins, the Pistons doubled their league-leading total of the previous season by racking up $26,500 in fines for fighting. Rick Mahorn, all 6'10" of him, set a league record in February for elbowing when he nailed Mark Price of the Cavs in the head at midcourt. He was fined $5,000, while Price, stunned from the blow, saw his shooting percentage go down steadily after the incident. Not to be outdone, team captain Isiah Thomas was docked two days' pay and lost for several

games after fighting and breaking his hand on Bill Cartwright's body. And who can forget Bill Laimbeer's bad luck as he broke his own Ironman streak thanks to a one-game suspension?

The Pistons this year are once again talented and 10-deep. Joe Dumars, MVP in the championship series and soon to be an All-Star, Dennis Rodman, the league's best sixth man, Vinnie "Mr. Offense" Johnson, Bill "Mr. Bully" Laimbeer, and John "Mr. Funny" Salley are ready for another run at the title.

Mark Aguirre, picked up in a daring midseason trade that sent Adrian Dantley to Dallas, was still on his best behavior and came through with 15.5 ppg, a personal low. But when it means a championship, who can complain?

Detroit Pistons

	Home W	L	Road W	L
By Month				
November	4	1	7	2
December	6	1	3	3
January	7	2	1	4
February	4	0	4	3
March	9	0	7	1
April	7	0	4	2
Playoffs				
Home/Away	37	4	26	15
Overtime	1	0	3	1
Offense				
0-89	0	1	0	2
90-99	7	1	4	6
100-109	15	0	6	5
110-119	12	2	11	2
120-129	2	0	5	0
130-	1	0	0	0
Defense				
0-89	8	1	3	1
90-99	18	0	7	0
100-109	9	1	13	5
110-119	2	1	3	6
120-129	0	0	0	3
130-	0	1	0	0
Over/Under				
0-189	7	1	3	1
190-199	8	1	1	1
200-209	12	0	7	4
210-219	4	0	6	6
220-229	4	1	6	1
230-239	1	0	2	1
240-	1	1	1	1
Margin Of Victory				
0-3	3	1	3	3
4-6	6	0	6	1
7-10	8	2	6	2
11-15	10	0	5	3
16-20	6	0	5	4
21-	4	1	1	2
Field Goal Attempts				
0-69	1	0	0	0
70-79	12	0	10	1
80-89	14	3	13	8
90-99	10	1	3	4
100-109	0	0	0	2
110+	0	0	0	0
Field Goals Made				
0-34	2	2	2	1
35-39	8	0	5	8
40-44	17	1	9	5
45-49	8	1	8	1
50-54	2	0	2	0
55+	0	0	0	0
Field Goal Pct.				
.000-.399	0	2	0	0
.400-.424	2	0	1	8
.425-.449	5	0	3	1
.450-.474	6	0	2	3
.475-.499	2	1	3	1
.500-.524	9	0	2	1
.525-.549	8	1	6	0
.550-.574	3	0	4	0

	Home W	L	Road W	L
.575-.599	1	0	5	1
.600-	1	0	0	0
Opp. Field Goal Attempts				
0-69	0	0	0	1
70-79	4	1	7	4
80-89	24	1	9	7
90-99	8	2	10	2
100-109	1	0	0	1
110+	0	0	0	0
Opp. Field Goal Made				
0-34	8	1	5	1
35-39	16	1	13	3
40-44	12	1	7	9
45-49	1	1	1	2
50-54	0	0	0	0
55+	0	0	0	0
Opp. Field Goal Percentage				
.000-.399	8	1	5	1
.400-.424	9	0	5	1
.425-.449	7	0	7	1
.450-.474	8	2	4	3
.475-.499	2	0	3	3
.500-.524	2	0	1	2
.525-.549	1	1	1	2
.550-.574	0	0	0	1
.575-.599	0	0	0	0
.600-	0	0	0	1
Free Throw Attempts				
0-9	0	0	0	0
10-19	3	1	2	2
20-29	19	1	10	7
30-39	12	2	10	5
40-49	3	0	4	1
50+	0	0	0	0
Free Throws Made				
0-9	0	0	0	0
10-19	13	2	8	8
20-29	20	2	11	6
30-39	4	0	7	1
40-49	0	0	0	0
50+	0	0	0	0
Free Throw Pct.				
.000-.549	0	0	0	1
.550-.599	0	0	0	0
.600-.649	2	0	1	2
.650-.699	2	0	2	4
.700-.749	8	1	2	4
.750-.799	11	1	6	3
.800-.849	10	1	9	1
.850-.899	4	0	5	0
.900-.949	0	1	1	0
.950-	0	0	0	0
Opp. Free Throw Attempts				
0-9	0	0	0	0
10-19	10	0	3	0
20-29	21	2	10	4
30-39	6	2	8	6
40-49	0	0	4	5
50+	0	0	1	0
Opp. Free Throws Made				
0-9	1	0	0	0
10-19	22	2	8	0
20-29	13	1	12	10

	Home W	L	Road W	L
30-39	1	1	5	5
40-49	0	0	1	0
50+	0	0	0	0
Opp. Free Throw Pct.				
.000-.549	1	0	0	0
.550-.599	0	0	0	0
.600-.649	3	0	2	0
.650-.699	4	0	0	2
.700-.749	6	0	5	1
.750-.799	7	1	7	2
.800-.849	9	1	9	5
.850-.899	2	0	1	3
.900-.949	4	2	1	1
.950-	1	0	1	1
Offensive Rebounds				
0-9	2	0	4	1
10-14	23	1	13	5
15-19	7	2	9	7
20-24	5	1	0	1
25+	0	0	0	1
Total Rebounds				
0-39	0	0	1	1
40-44	3	0	2	2
45-49	9	1	6	0
50-54	0	0	0	0
55-59	12	3	16	8
60-64	9	0	1	3
65-	4	0	0	1
Opp. Offensive Rebounds				
0-9	7	1	4	1
10-14	14	2	8	9
15-19	12	1	11	5
20-24	4	0	3	0
25+	0	0	0	0
Opp. Total Rebounds				
0-39	2	0	1	0
40-44	13	1	4	0
45-49	12	2	8	4
50-54	0	0	0	0
55-59	7	1	12	9
60-64	2	0	1	2
65-	1	0	0	0
Offensive Rebound Pct.				
Below 25%	7	0	10	4
25-29.99%	9	1	9	3
30-34.99%	16	2	5	6
35-39.99%	4	1	1	2
40-44.99%	0	0	0	0
45% and up	1	0	1	0
Assists				
0-14	0	1	0	0
15-19	1	1	6	2
20-24	15	1	4	10
25-29	15	0	12	2
30-34	5	0	4	0
35+	1	1	0	1
Opp. Assists				
0-14	1	0	0	0
15-19	10	0	6	3
20-24	19	2	13	5
25-29	6	2	5	5
30-34	1	0	2	2
35+	0	0	0	0

	Home W	L	Road W	L
Edge In Assists				
Below -15	0	0	0	0
-10 to -14	0	1	0	0
-5 to -9	3	0	3	5
0 to -4	7	2	10	5
1-4	11	0	3	3
5-9	11	1	5	2
10-14	5	0	3	0
15-	0	0	2	0
Personal Fouls				
0-14	0	0	0	0
15-19	14	1	2	1
20-24	19	2	8	3
25-29	4	1	11	6
30-34	0	0	3	4
35+	0	0	2	1
Opp. Personal Fouls				
0-14	0	0	0	0
15-19	4	0	1	0
20-24	16	2	10	6
25-29	13	1	6	6
30-34	3	1	5	2
35+	1	0	4	0
Personal Fouls Edge				
Below -15	0	0	0	0
-10 to -14	5	1	0	0
-5 to -9	10	0	7	1
0 to -4	16	1	11	5
1-4	6	2	7	5
5-9	0	0	1	1
10-14	0	0	0	3
15+	0	0	0	0
Steals				
0-5	14	3	11	7
6-7	9	0	10	3
8-9	6	1	3	2
10-11	6	0	1	2
12-13	2	0	1	0
14+	0	0	0	1
Opp. Steals				
0-5	8	1	11	1
6-7	10	1	4	2
8-9	10	0	6	5
10-11	5	2	2	3
12-13	1	0	2	3
14+	3	0	1	1
Edge In Steals				
Below -7	3	2	1	2
-4 to -6	5	0	9	4
0 to -3	16	1	7	7
1-3	11	1	7	5
4-6	2	0	3	0
7-	0	0	1	2
Turnovers				
0-14	12	1	9	2
15-19	20	2	13	8
20-24	3	1	4	4
25-29	2	0	0	1
30-34	0	0	0	0
35+	0	0	0	0
Opp. Turnovers				
0-14	16	2	16	7
15-19	11	2	7	4

	Home W	L	Road W	L
20-24	8	0	3	2
25-29	2	0	0	2
30-34	0	0	0	0
35+	0	0	0	0

Edge In Turnovers

	Home W	L	Road W	L
Below -15	0	0	0	0
-10 to -14	0	0	0	2
-5 to -9	8	1	3	1
0 to -4	10	0	9	0
1- 4	11	1	5	6
5- 9	5	1	9	4
10-14	3	1	0	2
15+	0	0	0	0

Blocks

	Home W	L	Road W	L
1-2	3	1	5	2
3-4	11	3	5	5
5-6	14	0	9	6
7-8	6	0	6	2
9-10	2	0	1	0
11+	1	0	0	0

Opp. Blocks

	Home W	L	Road W	L
0-2	10	2	5	2
3-4	11	2	12	2
5-6	11	0	6	6
7-8	4	0	2	3
9-10	0	0	1	2
11+	1	0	0	0

Edge In Blocks

	Home W	L	Road W	L
Below -7	1	0	1	0
-4 to -6	2	0	1	2
0 to -3	11	2	10	10
1-3	15	1	7	2
4-6	6	1	7	1
7+	2	0	0	0

Three-Pointers Attempted

	Home W	L	Road W	L
0-2	12	1	8	1
3-5	12	1	12	8
6-8	9	2	1	2
9-11	3	0	2	3
12-14	1	0	3	0
15+	0	0	0	1

Three-Pointers Made

	Home W	L	Road W	L
0-2	32	3	20	11
3-5	5	1	4	3
6-8	0	0	2	1
9-11	0	0	0	0
12-14	0	0	0	0
15+	0	0	0	0

Three-Pointers Pct.

	Home W	L	Road W	L
.000-.099	16	2	13	5
.100-.149	5	0	1	1
.150-.199	1	1	0	0
.200-.249	2	0	1	1
.250-.299	0	0	0	0
.300-.349	8	0	2	4
.350-.399	3	1	3	2
.400-.449	0	0	1	0
.450-.499	0	0	0	0
.500-	2	0	5	2

Opp. Three-Point Attempts

	Home W	L	Road W	L
0-2	4	1	3	1
3-5	9	1	8	5
6-8	12	0	6	6
9-11	8	0	7	2
12-14	3	0	2	1
15+	1	2	0	0

Opp. Three-Pointers Made

	Home W	L	Road W	L
0-2	27	2	20	11
3-5	8	0	6	4
6-8	2	0	0	0
9-11	0	2	0	0
12-14	0	0	0	0
15+	0	0	0	0

Opp. Three-Pointer Pct.

	Home W	L	Road W	L
.000-.099	12	1	7	5
.100-.149	6	1	4	1
.150-.199	7	0	3	2
.200-.249	1	0	2	1
.250-.299	1	0	2	1
.300-.349	2	0	4	1
.350-.399	2	0	0	2
.400-.449	0	0	0	0
.450-.499	1	0	0	0
.500-	5	2	4	2

Detroit Pistons
1988–89 Power Chart

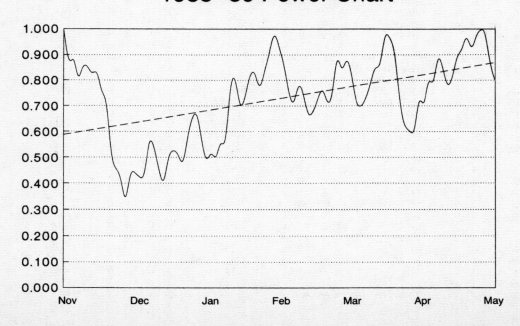

Detroit Pistons

	GP	GS	Min	FGM	FGA	FG%	2GM	2GA	2G%	3GM	3GA	3G%	FTM	FTA	FT%	Off	Tot	Ast	PF	Stl	TO	Blk	Pts	HGS
Mark Aguirre	36	32	1068	213	441	0.483	191	366	0.522	22	75	0.293	110	149	0.738	56	95	151	101	16	68	7	558	427
Per GP			29.7	5.9	12.2		5.3	10.2		0.6	2.1		3.1	4.1		1.6	2.6	4.2	2.8	0.4	1.9	0.2	15.5	11.9
Per 48			22.2	9.6	19.8		8.6	16.4		1.0	3.4		4.9	6.7		2.5	4.3	6.8	4.5	0.7	3.1	0.3	25.1	19.2
Adrian Dantley	42	42	1341	258	495	0.521	258	495	0.521	0	0	0.000	256	305	0.839	53	111	164	99	23	81	6	772	635
Per GP			31.9	6.1	11.8		6.1	11.8		0.0	0.0		6.1	7.3		1.3	2.6	3.9	2.4	0.5	1.9	0.1	18.4	15.1
Per 48			27.9	9.2	17.7		9.2	17.7		0.0	0.0		9.2	10.9		1.9	4.0	5.9	3.5	0.8	2.9	0.2	27.6	22.7
Darryl Dawkins	14	0	48	9	19	0.474	9	19	0.474	0	0	0.000	9	18	0.500	3	4	7	13	0	4	1	27	19
Per GP			3.4	0.6	1.4		0.6	1.4		0.0	0.0		0.6	1.3		0.2	0.3	0.5	0.9	0.0	0.3	0.1	1.9	1.4
Per 48			1.0	9.0	19.0		9.0	19.0		0.0	0.0		9.0	18.0		3.0	4.0	7.0	13.0	0.0	4.0	1.0	27.0	19.0
Fennis Dembo	31	0	74	14	42	0.333	14	38	0.368	0	4	0.000	8	10	0.800	8	15	23	15	1	7	0	36	25
Per GP			2.4	0.5	1.4		0.5	1.2		0.0	0.1		0.3	0.3		0.3	0.5	0.7	0.5	0.0	0.2	0.0	1.2	0.8
Per 48			1.5	9.1	27.2		9.1	24.6		0.0	2.6		5.2	6.5		5.2	9.7	14.9	9.7	0.6	4.5	0.0	23.4	16.2
Joe Dumars	69	67	2409	456	903	0.505	442	874	0.506	14	29	0.483	260	306	0.850	57	115	172	103	63	178	5	1186	1054
Per GP			34.9	6.6	13.1		6.4	12.7		0.2	0.4		3.8	4.4		0.8	1.7	2.5	1.5	0.9	2.6	0.1	17.2	15.3
Per 48			50.2	9.1	18.0		8.8	17.4		0.3	0.6		5.2	6.1		1.1	2.3	3.4	2.1	1.3	3.5	0.1	23.6	21.0
James Edwards	76	1	1254	211	422	0.500	211	420	0.502	0	2	0.000	133	194	0.686	68	163	231	226	13	72	31	555	489
Per GP			16.5	2.8	5.6		2.8	5.5		0.0	0.0		1.8	2.6		0.9	2.1	3.0	3.0	0.2	0.9	0.4	7.3	6.4
Per 48			26.1	8.1	16.2		8.1	16.1		0.0	0.1		5.1	7.4		2.6	6.2	8.8	8.7	0.5	2.8	1.2	21.2	18.7
Steve Harris	3	0	7	1	4	0.250	1	4	0.250	0	0	0.000	2	2	1.000	0	2	2	1	1	0	0	4	4
Per GP			2.3	0.3	1.3		0.3	1.3		0.0	0.0		0.7	0.7		0.0	0.7	0.7	0.3	0.3	0.0	0.0	1.3	1.3
Per 48			0.1	6.9	27.4		6.9	27.4		0.0	0.0		13.7	13.7		0.0	13.7	13.7	6.9	6.9	0.0	0.0	27.4	27.4
Vinnie Johnson	82	21	2073	462	996	0.464	449	952	0.472	13	44	0.295	193	263	0.734	109	146	255	155	72	105	17	1130	939
Per GP			25.3	5.6	12.1		5.5	11.6		0.2	0.5		2.4	3.2		1.3	1.8	3.1	1.9	0.9	1.3	0.2	13.8	11.5
Per 48			43.2	10.7	23.1		10.4	22.0		0.3	1.0		4.5	6.1		2.5	3.4	5.9	3.6	1.7	2.4	0.4	26.2	21.7
Bill Laimbeer	81	81	2640	449	900	0.499	419	813	0.515	30	87	0.345	178	212	0.840	138	638	776	259	51	131	100	1106	1236
Per GP			32.6	5.5	11.1		5.2	10.0		0.4	1.1		2.2	2.6		1.7	7.9	9.6	3.2	0.6	1.6	1.2	13.7	15.3
Per 48			55.0	8.2	16.4		7.6	14.8		0.5	1.6		3.2	3.9		2.5	11.6	14.1	4.7	0.9	2.4	1.8	20.1	22.5
John Long	24	0	152	19	40	0.475	19	40	0.475	0	0	0.000	11	13	0.846	2	9	11	16	0	9	2	49	42
Per GP			6.3	0.8	1.7		0.8	1.7		0.0	0.0		0.5	0.5		0.1	0.4	0.5	0.7	0.0	0.4	0.1	2.0	1.8
Per 48			3.2	6.0	12.6		6.0	12.6		0.0	0.0		3.5	4.1		0.6	2.8	3.5	5.1	0.0	2.8	0.6	15.5	13.3
Rick Mahorn	72	61	1795	203	393	0.517	203	391	0.519	0	2	0.000	116	155	0.748	141	355	496	206	40	97	66	522	697
Per GP			24.9	2.8	5.5		2.8	5.4		0.0	0.0		1.6	2.2		2.0	4.9	6.9	2.9	0.6	1.3	0.9	7.3	9.7
Per 48			37.4	5.4	10.5		5.4	10.5		0.0	0.1		3.1	4.1		3.8	9.5	13.3	5.5	1.1	2.6	1.8	14.0	18.6
Pace Mannion	5	0	14	2	2	1.000	2	2	1.000	0	0	0.000	0	0	0.000	0	3	3	3	1	0	0	4	5
Per GP			2.8	0.4	0.4		0.4	0.4		0.0	0.0		0.0	0.0		0.0	0.6	0.6	0.6	0.2	0.0	0.0	0.8	1.0
Per 48			0.3	6.9	6.9		6.9	6.9		0.0	0.0		0.0	0.0		0.0	10.3	10.3	10.3	3.4	0.0	0.0	13.7	17.1
Dennis Rodman	82	8	2207	316	531	0.595	310	506	0.613	6	25	0.240	97	155	0.626	327	445	772	292	55	126	76	735	1070
Per GP			26.9	3.9	6.5		3.8	6.2		0.1	0.3		1.2	1.9		4.0	5.4	9.4	3.6	0.7	1.5	0.9	9.0	13.0
Per 48			46.0	6.9	11.5		6.7	11.0		0.1	0.5		2.1	3.4		7.1	9.7	16.8	6.4	1.2	2.7	1.7	16.0	23.3
Jim Rowinski	6	0	8	0	2	0.000	0	2	0.000	0	0	0.000	4	4	1.000	0	2	2	0	0	0	0	4	4
Per GP			1.3	0.0	0.3		0.0	0.3		0.0	0.0		0.7	0.7		0.0	0.3	0.3	0.0	0.0	0.0	0.0	0.7	0.7
Per 48			0.2	0.0	12.0		0.0	12.0		0.0	0.0		24.0	24.0		0.0	12.0	12.0	0.0	0.0	0.0	0.0	24.0	24.0
John Salley	67	21	1458	166	333	0.498	166	331	0.502	0	2	0.000	135	195	0.692	134	201	335	197	40	100	72	467	617
Per GP			21.8	2.5	5.0		2.5	4.9		0.0	0.0		2.0	2.9		2.0	3.0	5.0	2.9	0.6	1.5	1.1	7.0	9.2
Per 48			30.4	5.5	11.0		5.5	10.9		0.0	0.1		4.4	6.4		4.4	6.6	11.0	6.5	1.3	3.3	2.4	15.4	20.3
Isiah Thomas	80	76	2924	569	1227	0.464	536	1106	0.485	33	121	0.273	287	351	0.818	49	224	273	209	133	296	20	1458	1430
Per GP			36.5	7.1	15.3		6.7	13.8		0.4	1.5		3.6	4.4		0.6	2.8	3.4	2.6	1.7	3.7	0.3	18.2	17.9
Per 48			60.9	9.3	20.1		8.8	18.2		0.5	2.0		4.7	5.8		0.8	3.7	4.5	3.4	2.2	4.9	0.3	23.9	23.5
Michael Williams	49	0	358	47	129	0.364	45	120	0.375	2	9	0.222	31	47	0.660	9	18	27	44	13	42	3	127	118
Per GP			7.3	1.0	2.6		0.9	2.4		0.0	0.2		0.6	1.0		0.2	0.4	0.6	0.9	0.3	0.9	0.1	2.6	2.4
Per 48			7.5	6.3	17.3		6.0	16.1		0.3	1.2		4.2	6.3		1.2	2.4	3.6	5.9	1.7	5.6	0.4	17.0	15.8

GOLDEN STATE WARRIORS

This past year, the Warriors were slightly lucky to have a 43–39 record, since they were outscored by about 0.3 points per game. A major factor in their luck seemed to be their style of play, which could best be described as high-octane. They were involved in 30 games where the combined score was over 240. Games were always wide open going into the fourth—they were trailing after three quarters in about half their games. Leads meant nothing. Take a look at some of the scores below.

SOME GOLDEN STATE GAMES (HOME TEAM FIRST)

Date	Home		Visitor	
3/01	GS	121	LAL	142
3/04	Sac	143	GS	155
3/21	Por	127	GS	151
3/23	Pho	154	GS	124
3/25	GS	104	Hou	144
3/31	GS	134	NY	114

And that's just in March, after they got a bit leg-weary. They could win big, lose big, or just score big and keep it close. Just think what they could have done without a healthy Ralph Sampson!

True, the Warriors had many factors involved in their upswing, but was it an improvement or a correction? This year will be the big test. Three years ago, Golden State was 42–40 before the bottom dropped out. Last year they rebounded, and due credit was given to Don Nelson for his role in the team's progress. Now, far be it from us to write anything otherwise, even though he *was* the only coach who didn't want to talk to us (well, he *did* wish us luck before hanging up on us), but when you have a team that drops by 22 games one year, there's a good chance that it'll rebound by at least a few of those the next, no matter who's coaching. Twenty-two games is a large quantity. When Philly went 9–73 in 1972–73, that was only a 21-game drop, and it was followed by a 16-game recovery. Of the 15 teams that have experienced 20-game drops, only 2 have not bounced back at all the next year. Most of them get about 16 games back, and make further gains in years two and three.

Only 4 teams in history fell further than Golden State did in 1987–88. Of all teams that have dropped by 20 or more games, however, the Warriors experienced the largest bounce-back in NBA history last year, about 7 games more than you'd normally expect by looking at what others have done. Of all these teams, only Golden State has gained back its full loss in a single year.

Yet they didn't change their look all that much. Mitch Richmond was the consensus rookie of the year, but he was the only real addition, unless you count the overrated Manute Bol. What couldn't

BIGGEST ONE-YEAR DROPS/REBOUNDS

Team	Yr	Year		Drop		Reb'd		Drop	Reb'd
		W	L	W	L	W	L		
Hou	1982	46	36	14	68	29	53	32	15
SF	1964	48	32	17	63	35	45	31	18
NY	1984	47	35	24	58	23	59	23	−1
Chi	1975	47	35	24	58	44	38	23	20
GS	*1987*	42	40	20	62	43	39	22	23
Pro	1947	28	32	6	42	12	48	22	6
Sea	1980	56	26	34	48	52	30	22	18
StL	1961	51	28	29	51	48	32	22	19
Mil	1974	59	23	38	44	38	44	21	0
Sea	1972	47	35	26	56	36	46	21	10
Was	1947	49	11	28	20	38	22	21	10
Phi	1972	30	52	9	73	25	57	21	16
Phi	1952	33	33	12	57	29	43	21	17
Hou	1977	49	33	28	54	47	35	21	19
LAC	1986	32	50	12	70	17	65	20	5
Avg		44.3	33.4	21.4	54.9	34.4	43.7	22.9	13

have been predicted is how Chris Mullin returned and thrived after his serious alcohol problems. His speedy adaptation to a new position, forward, earned him All-Star status. Nelson got a lot out of his players, perhaps more than people thought they were capable of. In addition to Mullin, who was 5th in the league in scoring, Richmond logged in at 16th best. No matter what you hear, though, don't believe that Manute Bol's three-point shooting is anything more than a freak show. He lost 16.97 points by shooting the long bombs, most in the league among centers. The loss was more than offset by his 4.31 blocks per game (which led the league), but no matter how great the threes might look, they just don't help. (Chris Mullin lost over 36 points by trying the three, so Manute needn't feel all that bad.)

Rod Higgins and Winston Garland were decent but not outrageous players. Higgins drew much of his strength from three-point range, hitting for a .393 average (12th best in the league). Garland picked off well over two passes a game, putting him in the league's top ten. The big difference between the 1988 and 1989 seasons was the offense, which improved by 9.6 ppg to 116.6, fourth best in the league. Ironically, the defense actually got worse last year, by 1.6 ppg. Still, an 8-point swing isn't chopped liver, and it translated to a 23-game difference in the win column over the previous season.

So, you ask, can they continue their progress, and possibly become the 1990s equivalent of Nelson's 1980s Bucks? Everyone's fairly young, so there's a good chance they can take another step forward next year. They'll still probably be lodged in third place, behind the Suns and Lakers, but it sure beats last. If someone wakes up Ralph Sampson, who was a shadow of his former self last year (is he too thin to cast a shadow these days?), the Warriors could really get it going. His scoring dropped from 19.3 to 6.2, so just about anything over 10.0 next year will put him in serious consideration for the Comeback Player award. Wish the Warriors luck, and pray that Mullin will be able to weather the many sober St. Patrick's Days ahead as well as he has so far.

Golden State Warriors

	Home W	L	Road W	L
By Month				
November	3	3	3	4
December	4	1	1	6
January	7	1	4	4
February	5	0	4	2
March	7	3	2	7
April	3	4	0	4
Playoffs				
Home/Away	29	12	14	27
Overtime	2	2	2	2
Offense				
0-89	0	1	0	0
90-99	0	0	0	4
100-109	5	5	2	12
110-119	7	3	4	7
120-129	7	3	5	4
130-	10	0	3	0
Defense				
0-89	0	0	0	0
90-99	3	1	3	0
100-109	9	1	3	3
110-119	13	5	7	8
120-129	2	2	0	7
130-	2	3	1	9
Over/Under				
0-189	0	1	0	0
190-199	0	0	1	0
200-209	3	1	1	5
210-219	5	1	2	3
220-229	4	4	3	4
230-239	5	0	2	4
240-	12	5	5	11
Margin Of Victory				
0-3	3	1	2	5
4-6	3	3	4	4
7-10	10	4	3	2
11-15	7	2	2	4
16-20	1	1	1	4
21-	5	1	2	8
Field Goal Attempts				
0-69	0	0	0	0
70-79	1	0	0	1
80-89	6	1	3	3
90-99	10	3	7	13
100-109	10	5	4	7
110+	2	3	0	3
Field Goals Made				
0-34	0	1	0	0
35-39	1	2	1	4
40-44	8	4	5	14
45-49	10	4	2	7
50-54	5	1	4	2
55+	5	0	2	0
Field Goal Pct.				
.000-.399	0	2	0	4
.400-.424	1	5	0	4
.425-.449	5	1	3	4
.450-.474	5	1	4	10
.475-.499	4	3	2	2
.500-.524	5	0	1	3
.525-.549	5	0	1	0
.550-.574	2	0	3	0

	Home W	L	Road W	L
.575-.599	1	0	0	0
.600-	1	0	0	0
Opp. Field Goal Attempts				
0-69	0	0	0	0
70-79	0	0	0	3
80-89	4	5	5	2
90-99	11	3	4	8
100-109	11	4	4	12
110+	3	0	1	2
Opp. Field Goal Made				
0-34	0	0	1	0
35-39	7	1	3	2
40-44	10	5	5	4
45-49	9	3	4	11
50-54	3	1	1	6
55+	0	2	0	4
Opp. Field Goal Percentage				
.000-.399	3	1	1	0
.400-.424	8	1	3	2
.425-.449	6	1	6	4
.450-.474	7	2	2	2
.475-.499	4	2	0	6
.500-.524	1	2	2	5
.525-.549	0	0	0	6
.550-.574	0	1	0	2
.575-.599	0	2	0	0
.600-	0	0	0	0
Free Throw Attempts				
0-9	0	0	0	0
10-19	1	0	2	4
20-29	12	10	5	16
30-39	12	1	4	4
40-49	4	1	3	3
50+	0	0	0	0
Free Throws Made				
0-9	0	0	0	0
10-19	4	4	4	16
20-29	17	7	6	7
30-39	8	1	4	4
40-49	0	0	0	0
50+	0	0	0	0
Free Throw Pct				
.000-.549	0	1	0	0
.550-.599	1	0	0	0
.600-.649	0	0	1	1
.650-.699	1	1	2	6
.700-.749	1	1	0	3
.750-.799	3	3	3	6
.800-.849	13	3	5	8
.850-.899	7	3	3	1
.900-.949	2	0	0	1
.950-	1	0	0	1
Opp. Free Throw Attempts				
0-9	1	0	0	0
10-19	5	0	1	2
20-29	6	8	3	8
30-39	16	2	9	11
40-49	1	2	1	6
50+	0	0	0	0
Opp. Free Throws Made				
0-9	1	0	0	0
10-19	8	4	4	7
20-29	16	5	8	11

	Home W	L	Road W	L
30-39	4	3	2	9
40-49	0	0	0	0
50+	0	0	0	0
Opp. Free Throw Pct				
.000-.549	0	0	0	0
.550-.599	2	0	0	0
.600-.649	1	1	1	1
.650-.699	5	0	3	4
.700-.749	5	0	3	2
.750-.799	6	4	4	6
.800-.849	7	5	1	8
.850-.899	1	2	1	6
.900-.949	1	0	0	0
.950-	1	0	1	0
Offensive Rebounds				
0-9	2	0	2	1
10-14	12	4	4	12
15-19	9	2	5	9
20-24	4	2	3	5
25+	2	4	0	0
Total Rebounds				
0-39	0	0	0	0
40-44	1	0	0	4
45-49	1	0	2	2
50-54	0	0	0	0
55-59	11	8	8	15
60-64	8	2	3	4
65-	8	2	1	2
Opp. Offensive Rebounds				
0-9	0	2	1	1
10-14	8	7	0	5
15-19	8	2	9	10
20-24	10	1	2	7
25+	3	0	2	4
Opp. Total Rebounds				
0-39	0	0	0	0
40-44	2	0	1	1
45-49	1	1	1	0
50-54	0	0	0	0
55-59	15	8	6	8
60-64	4	1	2	6
65-	7	2	4	12
Offensive Rebound Pct.				
Below 25%	11	3	6	12
25-29.99%	5	4	3	7
30-34.99%	7	2	5	5
35-39.99%	4	3	0	3
40-44.99%	2	0	0	0
45% and up	0	0	0	0
Assists				
0-14	0	0	0	1
15-19	1	4	4	6
20-24	8	6	3	9
25-29	12	2	4	9
30-34	4	0	1	2
35+	4	0	2	0
Opp. Assists				
0-14	0	0	0	0
15-19	2	0	2	1
20-24	14	2	7	5
25-29	8	6	1	7
30-34	4	1	4	7
35+	1	3	0	7

	Home W	L	Road W	L
Edge In Assists				
Below -15	0	2	0	3
-10 to -14	2	2	2	6
-5 to -9	4	6	1	8
0 to -4	4	1	6	5
1-4	5	1	2	4
5-9	9	0	1	0
10-14	4	0	0	1
15-	1	0	2	0
Personal Fouls				
0-14	1	0	0	0
15-19	5	3	2	3
20-24	14	4	4	12
25-29	8	4	5	9
30-34	1	1	3	3
35+	0	0	0	0
Opp. Personal Fouls				
0-14	0	0	0	1
15-19	2	1	2	8
20-24	11	7	6	10
25-29	11	4	2	7
30-34	5	0	2	0
35+	0	0	2	1
Personal Fouls Edge				
Below -15	2	0	0	0
-10 to -14	1	0	0	0
-5 to -9	7	1	4	2
0 to -4	10	5	7	8
1-4	6	3	0	9
5-9	3	3	1	5
10-14	0	0	2	2
15+	0	0	0	1
Steals				
0-5	1	1	0	4
6-7	4	3	1	4
8-9	4	2	3	8
10-11	10	5	5	5
12-13	5	1	2	2
14+	5	0	3	4
Opp. Steals				
0-5	1	1	1	3
6-7	6	2	2	5
8-9	7	2	4	2
10-11	2	2	1	6
12-13	8	3	2	7
14+	5	2	4	4
Edge In Steals				
Below -7	1	2	0	3
-4 to -6	5	4	4	7
0 to -3	7	2	2	7
1-3	10	2	5	3
4-6	4	1	2	5
7-	2	1	1	2
Turnovers				
0-14	5	2	2	8
15-19	14	8	6	8
20-24	9	2	2	7
25-29	1	0	4	2
30-34	0	0	0	2
35+	0	0	0	0
Opp. Turnovers				
0-14	3	3	1	7
15-19	12	8	3	11

	Home W L	Road W L
20-24	10 1	8 6
25-29	2 0	2 2
30-34	1 0	0 1
35+	1 0	0 0

Edge In Turnovers

	Home W L	Road W L
Below -15	1 0	0 0
-10 to -14	2 0	0 1
-5 to -9	7 2	5 4
0 to -4	11 2	3 8
1-4	7 6	4 7
5-9	1 2	2 4
10-14	0 0	0 2
15+	0 0	0 1

Blocks

	Home W L	Road W L
1-2	1 0	0 2
3-4	2 1	0 3
5-6	7 4	3 8
7-8	6 4	2 10
9-10	8 2	5 0
11+	5 1	4 4

Opp. Blocks

	Home W L	Road W L
0-2	3 1	1 5
3-4	10 4	6 4
5-6	11 5	1 6
7-8	3 1	3 3
9-10	1 0	2 2
11+	1 1	1 7

Edge In Blocks

	Home W L	Road W L
Below -7	0 1	0 2
-4 to -6	1 0	0 4
0 to -3	7 3	2 9
1-3	7 1	5 5
4-6	8 6	6 4
7+	6 1	1 3

Three-Pointers Attempted

	Home W L	Road W L
0-2	4 0	2 2
3-5	5 2	4 7
6-8	11 2	6 8
9-11	6 2	1 5
12-14	2 1	1 5
15+	1 5	0 0

Three-Pointers Made

	Home W L	Road W L
0-2	16 2	9 17
3-5	11 7	4 9
6-8	2 3	0 1
9-11	0 0	1 0
12-14	0 0	0 0
15+	0 0	0 0

Three-Pointers Pct

	Home W L	Road W L
.000-.099	11 0	5 9
.100-.149	5 1	0 2
.150-.199	0 0	3 0
.200-.249	0 0	0 0
.250-.299	0 4	0 4
.300-.349	6 2	3 7
.350-.399	2 2	0 1
.400-.449	2 2	0 4
.450-.499	1 0	0 0
.500-	2 1	3 0

Opp. Three-Point Attempts

	Home W L	Road W L
0-2	1 2	2 2
3-5	8 0	3 4
6-8	6 5	2 7

	Home W L	Road W L
9-11	4 1	1 7
12-14	4 1	3 2
15+	6 3	3 5

Opp. Three-Pointers Made

	Home W L	Road W L
0-2	13 6	7 13
3-5	11 2	5 10
6-8	4 2	1 3
9-11	0 2	1 0
12-14	1 0	0 0
15+	0 0	0 1

Opp. Three-Pointer Pct

	Home W L	Road W L
.000-.099	4 1	1 4
.100-.149	1 0	3 1
.150-.199	5 1	0 1
.200-.249	2 1	0 2
.250-.299	1 0	2 5
.300-.349	5 4	4 5
.350-.399	4 0	2 3
.400-.449	2 2	1 2
.450-.499	1 0	0 0
.500-	4 3	1 4

Golden State Warriors
1988–89 Power Chart

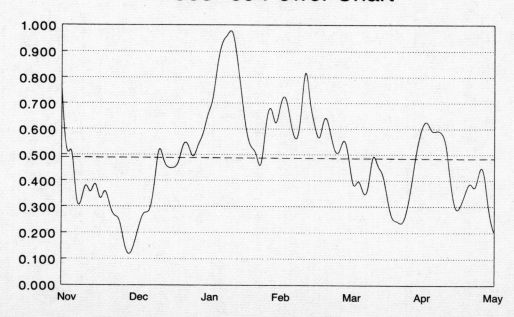

Golden State Warriors

	GP	GS	Min	FGM	FGA	FG%	2GM	2GA	2G%	3GM	3GA	3G%	FTM	FTA	FT%	Off	Tot	Ast	PF	Stl	TO	Blk	Pts	HGS
Steve Alford	57	3	868	145	313	0.463	125	260	0.481	20	53	0.377	49	59	0.831	10	59	69	54	44	44	3	359	285
Per GP				15.2	2.5	5.5		2.2	4.6		0.4	0.9		0.9	1.0		0.2	1.0	1.2	0.9	0.8	0.8	0.1	6.3	5.0
Per 48				18.1	8.0	17.3		6.9	14.4		1.1	2.9		2.7	3.3		0.6	3.3	3.8	3.0	2.4	2.4	0.2	19.9	15.8
Manute Bol	80	4	1769	127	344	0.369	107	253	0.423	20	91	0.220	40	66	0.606	116	346	462	226	11	82	339	314	806
Per GP				22.1	1.6	4.3		1.3	3.2		0.3	1.1		0.5	0.8		1.4	4.3	5.8	2.8	0.1	1.0	4.2	3.9	10.1
Per 48				36.9	3.4	9.3		2.9	6.9		0.5	2.5		1.1	1.8		3.1	9.4	12.5	6.1	0.3	2.2	9.2	8.5	21.9
Tellis Frank	32	2	245	34	91	0.374	34	90	0.378	0	1	0.000	39	51	0.765	26	35	61	59	13	29	6	107	105
Per GP				7.7	1.1	2.8		1.1	2.8		0.0	0.0		1.2	1.6		0.8	1.1	1.9	1.8	0.4	0.9	0.2	3.3	3.3
Per 48				5.1	6.7	17.8		6.7	17.6		0.0	0.2		7.6	10.0		5.1	6.9	12.0	11.6	2.5	5.7	1.2	21.0	20.6
Winston Garland	79	79	2661	466	1074	0.434	456	1031	0.442	10	43	0.233	203	251	0.809	101	227	328	216	175	188	13	1145	1238
Per GP				33.7	5.9	13.6		5.8	13.1		0.1	0.5		2.6	3.2		1.3	2.9	4.2	2.7	2.2	2.4	0.2	14.5	15.7
Per 48				55.4	8.4	19.4		8.2	18.6		0.2	0.8		3.7	4.5		1.8	4.1	5.9	3.9	3.2	3.4	0.2	20.7	22.3
Michael Graham	7	0	22	3	10	0.300	3	10	0.300	0	0	0.000	2	4	0.500	8	3	11	6	0	2	0	8	9
Per GP				3.1	0.4	1.4		0.4	1.4		0.0	0.0		0.3	0.6		1.1	0.4	1.6	0.9	0.0	0.3	0.0	1.1	1.3
Per 48				0.5	6.5	21.8		6.5	21.8		0.0	0.0		4.4	8.7		17.5	6.5	24.0	13.1	0.0	4.4	0.0	17.5	19.6
Rod Higgins	81	1	1887	301	633	0.476	235	465	0.505	66	168	0.393	188	229	0.821	111	265	376	172	39	78	40	856	830
Per GP				23.3	3.7	7.8		2.9	5.7		0.8	2.1		2.3	2.8		1.4	3.3	4.6	2.1	0.5	1.0	0.5	10.6	10.2
Per 48				39.3	7.7	16.1		6.0	11.8		1.7	4.3		4.8	5.8		2.8	6.7	9.6	4.4	1.0	2.0	1.0	21.8	21.1
Shelton Jones	2	0	13	3	5	0.600	3	5	0.600	0	0	0.000	0	0	0.000	2	0	2	0	3	1	0	6	9
Per GP				6.5	1.5	2.5		1.5	2.5		0.0	0.0		0.0	0.0		1.0	0.0	1.0	0.0	1.5	0.5	0.0	3.0	4.5
Per 48				0.3	11.1	18.5		11.1	18.5		0.0	0.0		0.0	0.0		7.4	0.0	7.4	0.0	11.1	3.7	0.0	22.2	33.2
Ben McDonald	11	0	103	13	19	0.684	13	19	0.684	0	0	0.000	9	15	0.600	4	8	12	11	4	3	0	35	38
Per GP				9.4	1.2	1.7		1.2	1.7		0.0	0.0		0.8	1.4		0.4	0.7	1.1	1.0	0.4	0.3	0.0	3.2	3.5
Per 48				2.1	6.1	8.9		6.1	8.9		0.0	0.0		4.2	7.0		1.9	3.7	5.6	5.1	1.9	1.4	0.0	16.3	17.7
Chris Mullin	82	82	3093	830	1630	0.509	807	1530	0.527	23	100	0.230	493	553	0.892	152	331	483	178	176	298	39	2176	1877
Per GP				37.7	10.1	19.9		9.8	18.7		0.3	1.2		6.0	6.7		1.9	4.0	5.9	2.2	2.1	3.6	0.5	26.5	22.9
Per 48				64.4	12.9	25.3		12.5	23.7		0.4	1.6		7.7	8.6		2.4	5.1	7.5	2.8	2.7	4.6	0.6	33.8	29.1
Mitch Richmond	79	79	2717	649	1386	0.468	616	1296	0.475	33	90	0.367	410	506	0.810	158	310	468	220	82	270	13	1741	1384
Per GP				34.4	8.2	17.5		7.8	16.4		0.4	1.1		5.2	6.4		2.0	3.9	5.9	2.8	1.0	3.4	0.2	22.0	17.5
Per 48				56.6	11.5	24.5		10.9	22.9		0.6	1.6		7.2	8.9		2.8	5.5	8.3	3.9	1.4	4.8	0.2	30.8	24.5
Ralph Sampson	61	36	1086	164	365	0.449	161	357	0.451	3	8	0.375	62	95	0.653	105	202	307	170	31	90	62	393	484
Per GP				17.8	2.7	6.0		2.6	5.9		0.0	0.1		1.0	1.6		1.7	3.3	5.0	2.8	0.5	1.5	1.0	6.4	7.9
Per 48				22.6	7.2	16.1		7.1	15.8		0.1	0.4		2.7	4.2		4.6	8.9	13.6	7.5	1.4	4.0	2.7	17.4	21.4
Larry Smith	80	78	1897	219	397	0.552	219	397	0.552	0	0	0.000	18	58	0.310	272	380	652	248	61	116	52	456	798
Per GP				23.7	2.7	5.0		2.7	5.0		0.0	0.0		0.2	0.7		3.4	4.8	8.1	3.1	0.8	1.4	0.6	5.7	10.0
Per 48				39.5	5.5	10.0		5.5	10.0		0.0	0.0		0.5	1.5		6.9	9.6	16.5	6.3	1.5	2.9	1.3	11.5	20.2
Otis Smith	80	5	1597	311	715	0.435	304	679	0.448	7	36	0.194	174	218	0.798	128	202	330	165	88	136	40	803	752
Per GP				20.0	3.9	8.9		3.8	8.5		0.1	0.4		2.2	2.7		1.6	2.5	4.1	2.1	1.1	1.7	0.5	10.0	9.4
Per 48				33.3	9.3	21.5		9.1	20.4		0.2	1.1		5.2	6.6		3.8	6.1	9.9	5.0	2.6	4.1	1.2	24.1	22.6
John Starks	36	0	316	51	125	0.408	41	99	0.414	10	26	0.385	34	52	0.654	15	26	41	36	23	39	3	146	110
Per GP				8.8	1.4	3.5		1.1	2.8		0.3	0.7		0.9	1.4		0.4	0.7	1.1	1.0	0.6	1.1	0.1	4.1	3.1
Per 48				6.6	7.7	19.0		6.2	15.0		1.5	3.9		5.2	7.9		2.3	3.9	6.2	5.5	3.5	5.9	0.5	22.2	16.7
John Stroeder	4	0	20	2	5	0.400	2	5	0.400	0	0	0.000	0	0	0.000	5	9	14	1	0	2	2	4	14
Per GP				5.0	0.5	1.3		0.5	1.3		0.0	0.0		0.0	0.0		1.3	2.3	3.5	0.3	0.0	0.5	0.5	1.0	3.5
Per 48				0.4	4.8	12.0		4.8	12.0		0.0	0.0		0.0	0.0		12.0	21.6	33.6	2.4	0.0	4.8	4.8	9.6	33.6
Terry Teagle	66	41	1569	409	859	0.476	407	847	0.481	2	12	0.167	182	225	0.809	110	153	263	173	79	114	17	1002	762
Per GP				23.8	6.2	13.0		6.2	12.8		0.0	0.2		2.8	3.4		1.7	2.3	4.0	2.6	1.2	1.7	0.3	15.2	11.5
Per 48				32.7	12.5	26.3		12.5	25.9		0.1	0.4		5.6	6.9		3.4	4.7	8.0	5.3	2.4	3.5	0.5	30.7	23.3
Jerome Whitehead	5	0	52	3	6	0.500	3	6	0.500	0	0	0.000	1	2	0.500	0	5	5	8	1	2	0	7	7
Per GP				10.4	0.6	1.2		0.6	1.2		0.0	0.0		0.2	0.4		0.0	1.0	1.0	1.6	0.2	0.4	0.0	1.4	1.4
Per 48				1.1	2.8	5.5		2.8	5.5		0.0	0.0		0.9	1.8		0.0	4.6	4.6	7.4	0.9	1.8	0.0	6.5	6.5

HOUSTON ROCKETS

Maybe they *should* have tried to get Calvin Murphy back after the All-Star Legends game. After a promising start, leading the division for much of the first half of the season, the Rockets foundered down the stretch, and when the dust cleared, they landed 6 games behind Utah in the Midwest, just one game out of third. The only thing that stands out when you look at Houston's breakdowns is that nothing stands out. This is an average, average team. Olajuwon is, to put it kindly to the other eleven players, the whole team. His defense produces more points for his team than any other NBA star. He's their leader in just about every category. His biggest negative? Well, if we have to find one, he *is* 1 for 19 over his career from three-point range.

Oddly enough, though, he didn't play the most

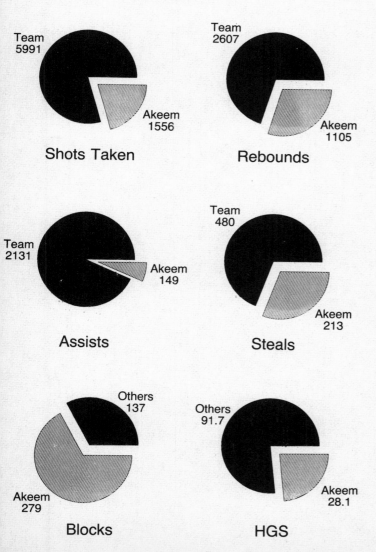

Shots Taken
Team 5991
Akeem 1556

Rebounds
Team 2607
Akeem 1105

Assists
Team 2131
Akeem 149

Steals
Team 480
Akeem 213

Blocks
Others 137
Akeem 279

HGS
Others 91.7
Akeem 28.1

minutes for the Rockets. Otis Thorpe beat him by about 90 minutes for the season, and both started all 82 games. Sleepy Floyd was third in minutes, but second in HGS. Beyond these three, the team was a study in ordinariness. If you had to rate this team on a scale of one to ten, they'd be "the perfect five." Houston is falling into the same trap as Chicago: assuming that one player will take up all the slack, and not worrying as much about the supporting cast. Compare Olajuwon and Jordan to Magic Johnson, for instance. You can easily ask how much the former two are worth, since their teams aren't all that hot, while Los Angeles is. However, the Lakers have surrounded Magic with far better supporting talent.

In contrast, to Magic, Akeem is the proverbial big fish in a small pond. Even when Ralph Sampson haunted the halls of the Summit, Olajuwon dominated every statistical category. Now that Sampson's gone, Akeem is even bigger.

There's a major problem when one person dominates the play of a team to this extent. If you can stop him, you've pretty much stopped the whole squad. Most teams could afford to double-team Akeem to an extent that would be too dangerous on a Magic or Bird. As a result, he had to fight for everything against two players and ended up with over 70 more personal fouls than Otis Thorpe. He fouled out 10 times and drew 8 technicals, many undoubtedly due to frustration. When Walter Berry is one of your most productive players, you better go out and sign some more talent, if only because Walter's not going to last for more than a year or two. So here's the deal. Go sign Calvin. Trade Walter Berry to Milan. See if Olajuwon has any tall cousins back home. But do *something* to stop this mediocrity.

On the other hand (we know we're waffling here), maybe all they need is a year of stability. They *were* learning along with a first-year coach in Chaney. No one really knew what to expect from one game to the next. Would they blow away teams by 40 or would they be whipping boys for a night? Thorpe's production fell by 5.5 pp48 last year, and he'll need to return to his level of old (he's a lifetime 25.2 pp48 scorer). His rebounding has also fallen by over a full board per 48 minutes, from 13.1 lifetime to 12.0 last year.

Sleepy Floyd boosted his playmaking in a big way last year. A lifetime 9.43 ap48 man, he dished off 12.1 last year. Of course, he was the only player with no real competition from Akeem, who was the Rockets' own version of a black hole—basketballs disappeared inside to him, never to be seen again by teammates. He only trailed Floyd by 9.7 ap48 last year. Mike Woodson used to play for the Nets. If you really want to know more, he shot a woeful 43.8% from the field, which meant that Houston's starting guards shot a total of .441, despite a decent .367 three-point mark. Second-year guard Derrick Chievous was an early crowd favorite, but lagged as the season went on. He only had a 9.3 ppg average, but was the second best scorer in terms of minutes played, with 23.4 pp48. Scoring was all he did, however, as his HGS was a weak 17.6.

If this team is going to go anywhere, the supporting cast will all have to exceed last year's output to take some of the pressure off Olajuwon down low. There are a lot of ifs here, and a lot of guys are being counted on to come through with near-career seasons, but after a year of play under Chaney, the Rockets this season could have the stability needed to challenge Utah for the Midwest crown and hold off a resurgent Dallas. Or, they could give San Antonio reason to hope. If nothing changes on the team, they're a cinch for a 41–41 record.

Houston Rockets

	Home W	L	Road W	L
By Month				
November	6	3	3	3
December	7	0	2	5
January	5	2	2	4
February	4	1	2	5
March	7	2	1	6
April	2	2	4	4
Playoffs				
Home/Away	31	10	14	27
Overtime	1	1	2	2
Offense				
0-89	1	1	0	2
90-99	2	3	4	8
100-109	9	1	4	10
110-119	6	4	4	7
120-129	11	1	2	0
130-	2	0	0	0
Defense				
0-89	2	0	3	0
90-99	9	2	4	3
100-109	12	2	4	3
110-119	6	3	3	8
120-129	2	3	0	13
130-	0	0	0	0
Over/Under				
0-189	2	1	3	2
190-199	1	1	4	2
200-209	9	2	0	5
210-219	4	0	2	4
220-229	5	2	4	4
230-239	6	3	1	10
240-	4	1	0	0
Margin Of Victory				
0-3	5	5	4	5
4-6	5	2	2	3
7-10	8	1	3	6
11-15	6	1	4	4
16-20	4	1	0	6
21-	3	0	1	3
Field Goal Attempts				
0-69	0	0	0	1
70-79	7	1	4	3
80-89	8	5	6	11
90-99	14	3	2	8
100-109	2	1	2	4
110+	0	0	0	0
Field Goals Made				
0-34	1	1	2	3
35-39	8	1	4	11
40-44	6	4	4	9
45-49	12	3	4	3
50-54	2	1	0	1
55+	2	0	0	0
Field Goal Pct.				
.000-.399	2	0	0	5
.400-.424	1	2	1	5
.425-.449	3	1	1	3
.450-.474	5	2	6	5
.475-.499	5	3	2	5
.500-.524	7	1	2	2
.525-.549	2	0	1	2
.550-.574	4	1	0	0

	Home W	L	Road W	L
.575-.599	2	0	1	0
.600-	0	0	0	0
Opp. Field Goal Attempts				
0-69	0	0	0	0
70-79	2	4	2	5
80-89	13	1	6	12
90-99	11	3	5	8
100-109	4	2	0	2
110+	1	0	1	0
Opp. Field Goal Made				
0-34	3	2	1	0
35-39	8	2	5	6
40-44	13	1	7	11
45-49	6	4	1	8
50-54	1	1	0	2
55+	0	0	0	0
Opp. Field Goal Percentage				
.000-.399	4	0	3	1
.400-.424	3	0	1	0
.425-.449	6	2	2	3
.450-.474	7	3	5	6
.475-.499	6	1	1	5
.500-.524	2	3	1	8
.525-.549	0	1	0	0
.550-.574	2	0	1	1
.575-.599	0	0	0	1
.600-	1	0	0	2
Free Throw Attempts				
0-9	0	0	0	0
10-19	1	2	1	4
20-29	8	5	5	10
30-39	14	3	6	9
40-49	7	0	2	4
50+	1	0	0	0
Free Throws Made				
0-9	0	0	0	0
10-19	5	7	3	10
20-29	15	3	8	13
30-39	10	0	3	4
40-49	1	0	0	0
50+	0	0	0	0
Free Throw Pct.				
.000-.549	1	0	0	0
.550-.599	0	1	0	0
.600-.649	1	1	0	3
.650-.699	5	0	2	1
.700-.749	7	4	2	8
.750-.799	9	2	3	9
.800-.849	4	2	4	6
.850-.899	3	0	1	0
.900-.949	1	0	2	0
.950-	0	0	0	0
Opp. Free Throw Attempts				
0-9	0	0	0	0
10-19	3	0	5	1
20-29	19	5	6	6
30-39	6	4	1	17
40-49	2	1	2	2
50+	1	0	0	1
Opp. Free Throws Made				
0-9	2	0	2	0
10-19	12	4	6	3
20-29	15	4	5	17

	Home W	L	Road W	L
30-39	2	2	1	6
40-49	0	0	0	1
50+	0	0	0	0
Opp. Free Throw Pct.				
.000-.549	2	0	1	0
.550-.599	1	0	0	0
.600-.649	5	1	1	1
.650-.699	3	0	1	1
.700-.749	4	1	5	4
.750-.799	5	1	2	8
.800-.849	10	3	4	10
.850-.899	1	2	0	3
.900-.949	0	0	0	0
.950-	0	0	0	0
Offensive Rebounds				
0-9	2	2	2	4
10-14	14	4	6	10
15-19	9	3	4	8
20-24	5	1	2	4
25+	1	0	0	1
Total Rebounds				
0-39	0	0	0	1
40-44	2	2	1	4
45-49	4	2	2	6
50-54	0	0	0	0
55-59	12	3	7	11
60-64	5	3	2	3
65-	8	0	2	2
Opp. Offensive Rebounds				
0-9	5	2	4	8
10-14	12	5	2	6
15-19	12	2	6	9
20-24	2	1	1	4
25+	0	0	1	0
Opp. Total Rebounds				
0-39	1	0	0	0
40-44	2	2	4	2
45-49	4	0	4	7
50-54	0	0	0	0
55-59	20	8	3	9
60-64	2	0	2	5
65-	2	0	1	4
Offensive Rebound Pct.				
Below 25%	9	4	4	11
25-29.99%	14	3	2	7
30-34.99%	5	2	6	7
35-39.99%	2	1	0	2
40-44.99%	1	0	2	0
45% and up	0	0	0	0
Assists				
0-14	0	0	2	0
15-19	6	1	1	7
20-24	10	3	4	9
25-29	8	3	6	6
30-34	5	3	1	5
35+	2	0	0	0
Opp. Assists				
0-14	0	0	0	0
15-19	7	2	2	0
20-24	11	3	8	7
25-29	10	4	4	12
30-34	3	1	0	6
35+	0	0	0	2

	Home W	L	Road W	L
Edge In Assists				
Below -15	0	0	0	1
-10 to -14	1	1	1	4
-5 to -9	5	0	0	7
0 to -4	6	4	3	10
1-4	9	3	6	1
5-9	6	0	3	3
10-14	2	2	1	1
15-	2	0	0	0
Personal Fouls				
0-14	1	0	0	0
15-19	5	0	2	1
20-24	16	3	6	6
25-29	5	7	5	15
30-34	2	0	0	5
35+	2	0	1	0
Opp. Personal Fouls				
0-14	0	0	1	1
15-19	3	2	0	5
20-24	9	5	5	10
25-29	10	3	5	8
30-34	7	0	3	3
35+	2	0	0	0
Personal Fouls Edge				
Below -15	1	0	0	0
-10 to -14	2	0	0	0
-5 to -9	7	1	3	2
0 to -4	15	3	6	5
1-4	4	2	2	7
5-9	1	3	3	10
10-14	1	1	0	3
15+	0	0	0	0
Steals				
0-5	2	2	1	6
6-7	2	1	2	5
8-9	7	2	3	5
10-11	6	4	5	2
12-13	7	1	3	4
14+	7	0	0	5
Opp. Steals				
0-5	2	1	2	3
6-7	6	2	2	3
8-9	6	1	4	8
10-11	7	1	3	4
12-13	4	1	3	6
14+	6	4	0	3
Edge In Steals				
Below -7	0	2	0	3
-4 to -6	3	2	1	3
0 to -3	13	3	5	9
1-3	8	1	5	8
4-6	6	1	2	2
7-	1	1	1	2
Turnovers				
0-14	5	2	2	4
15-19	17	3	7	11
20-24	5	3	3	7
25-29	3	2	2	4
30-34	1	0	0	0
35+	0	0	0	1
Opp. Turnovers				
0-14	6	3	3	9
15-19	10	5	7	12

	Home W L	Road W L
20-24	10 2	3 5
25-29	5 0	1 1
30-34	0 0	0 0
35+	0 0	0 0

Edge In Turnovers

	Home W L	Road W L
Below -15	0 0	0 0
-10 to -14	1 0	0 1
-5 to -9	5 0	2 0
0 to -4	13 5	3 7
1-4	6 2	5 9
5-9	5 2	3 6
10-14	1 1	1 2
15+	0 0	0 2

Blocks

	Home W L	Road W L
1-2	3 2	2 5
3-4	5 1	4 6
5-6	9 3	2 7
7-8	7 2	2 4
9-10	6 2	1 4
11+	1 0	3 1

Opp. Blocks

	Home W L	Road W L
0-2	4 3	4 4
3-4	12 2	3 3
5-6	9 2	4 9
7-8	4 3	1 3
9-10	2 0	0 6
11+	0 0	2 2

Edge In Blocks

	Home W L	Road W L
Below -7	1 0	2 2
-4 to -6	1 1	0 3
0 to -3	10 3	6 14
1-3	11 4	1 5
4-6	7 1	1 3
7+	1 1	4 0

Three-Pointers Attempted

	Home W L	Road W L
0-2	4 0	2 1
3-5	14 5	5 4
6-8	8 0	5 14
9-11	4 3	1 6
12-14	1 1	1 1
15+	0 1	0 1

Three-Pointers Made

	Home W L	Road W L
0-2	21 6	9 18
3-5	8 4	4 8
6-8	2 0	1 1
9-11	0 0	0 0
12-14	0 0	0 0
15+	0 0	0 0

Three-Pointers Pct.

	Home W L	Road W L
.000-.099	13 6	3 9
.100-.149	1 0	0 0
.150-.199	1 0	1 2
.200-.249	1 0	0 0
.250-.299	0 1	0 3
.300-.349	6 2	4 6
.350-.399	0 0	1 4
.400-.449	1 0	1 1
.450-.499	0 1	0 0
.500-	8 0	4 2

Opp. Three-Point Attempts

	Home W L	Road W L
0-2	1 2	0 7
3-5	11 3	7 8

	Home W L	Road W L
6-8	8 2	3 7
9-11	8 1	3 0
12-14	2 2	1 5
15+	1 0	0 0

Opp. Three-Pointers Made

	Home W L	Road W L
0-2	21 3	8 17
3-5	8 5	6 8
6-8	2 2	0 1
9-11	0 0	0 1
12-14	0 0	0 0
15+	0 0	0 0

Opp. Three-Pointer Pct.

	Home W L	Road W L
.000-.099	13 2	4 8
.100-.149	3 0	1 1
.150-.199	1 0	1 1
.200-.249	0 0	1 0
.250-.299	4 0	0 0
.300-.349	2 1	2 6
.350-.399	1 2	0 2
.400-.449	1 1	1 2
.450-.499	0 0	0 0
.500-	6 4	4 7

Houston Rockets
1988–89 Power Chart

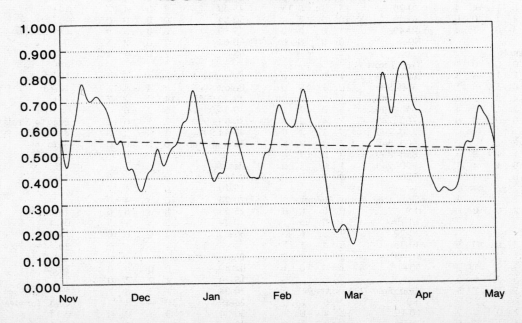

Houston Rockets

	GP	GS	Min	FGM	FGA	FG%	2GM	2GA	2G%	3GM	3GA	3G%	FTM	FTA	FT%	Off	Tot	Ast	PF	Stl	TO	Blk	Pts	HGS
Walter Berry	40	14	799	146	270	0.541	145	268	0.541	1	2	0.500	57	80	0.712	54	98	152	114	19	49	35	350	368
Per GP			20.0	3.6	6.8		3.6	6.7		0.0	0.0		1.4	2.0		1.3	2.4	3.8	2.8	0.5	1.2	0.9	8.8	9.2
Per 48			16.6	8.8	16.2		8.7	16.1		0.1	0.1		3.4	4.8		3.2	5.9	9.1	6.8	1.1	2.9	2.1	21.0	22.1
Tony Brown	14	0	91	14	45	0.311	12	36	0.333	2	9	0.222	6	8	0.750	7	8	15	14	3	7	0	36	19
Per GP			6.5	1.0	3.2		0.9	2.6		0.1	0.6		0.4	0.6		0.5	0.6	1.1	1.0	0.2	0.5	0.0	2.6	1.4
Per 48			1.9	7.4	23.7		6.3	19.0		1.1	4.7		3.2	4.2		3.7	4.2	7.9	7.4	1.6	3.7	0.0	19.0	10.0
Derrick Chievous	81	1	1539	277	634	0.437	272	610	0.446	5	24	0.208	191	244	0.783	114	142	256	161	48	136	11	750	564
Per GP			19.0	3.4	7.8		3.4	7.5		0.1	0.3		2.4	3.0		1.4	1.8	3.2	2.0	0.6	1.7	0.1	9.3	7.0
Per 48			32.1	8.6	19.8		8.5	19.0		0.2	0.7		6.0	7.6		3.6	4.4	8.0	5.0	1.5	4.2	0.3	23.4	17.6
Eric Floyd	82	82	2789	396	893	0.443	287	601	0.478	109	292	0.373	261	309	0.845	48	258	306	196	125	253	10	1162	1328
Per GP			34.0	4.8	10.9		3.5	7.3		1.3	3.6		3.2	3.8		0.6	3.1	3.7	2.4	1.5	3.1	0.1	14.2	16.2
Per 48			58.1	6.8	15.4		4.9	10.3		1.9	5.0		4.5	5.3		0.8	4.4	5.3	3.4	2.2	4.4	0.2	20.0	22.9
Buck Johnson	68	51	1860	274	519	0.528	273	510	0.535	1	9	0.111	101	134	0.754	115	172	287	213	65	113	34	650	674
Per GP			27.4	4.0	7.6		4.0	7.5		0.0	0.1		1.5	2.0		1.7	2.5	4.2	3.1	1.0	1.7	0.5	9.6	9.9
Per 48			38.8	7.1	13.4		7.0	13.2		0.0	0.2		2.6	3.5		3.0	4.4	7.4	5.5	1.7	2.9	0.9	16.8	17.4
Frank Johnson	66	0	868	105	242	0.434	104	236	0.441	1	6	0.167	75	93	0.806	21	57	78	91	41	99	0	286	325
Per GP			13.2	1.6	3.7		1.6	3.6		0.0	0.1		1.1	1.4		0.3	0.9	1.2	1.4	0.6	1.5	0.0	4.3	4.9
Per 48			18.1	5.8	13.4		5.8	13.1		0.1	0.3		4.1	5.1		1.2	3.2	4.3	5.0	2.3	5.5	0.0	15.8	18.0
Allen Leavell	55	3	627	65	188	0.346	60	147	0.408	5	41	0.122	44	60	0.733	13	40	53	61	25	62	5	179	202
Per GP			11.4	1.2	3.4		1.1	2.7		0.1	0.7		0.8	1.1		0.2	0.7	1.0	1.1	0.5	1.1	0.1	3.3	3.7
Per 48			13.1	5.0	14.4		4.6	11.3		0.4	3.1		3.4	4.6		1.0	3.1	4.1	4.7	1.9	4.7	0.4	13.7	15.5
Tim McCormick	81	0	1257	169	351	0.481	169	347	0.487	0	4	0.000	87	129	0.674	87	174	261	193	18	69	23	425	424
Per GP			15.5	2.1	4.3		2.1	4.3		0.0	0.0		1.1	1.6		1.1	2.1	3.2	2.4	0.2	0.9	0.3	5.2	5.2
Per 48			26.2	6.5	13.4		6.5	13.3		0.0	0.2		3.3	4.9		3.3	6.6	10.0	7.4	0.7	2.6	0.9	16.2	16.2
Chuck Nevitt	43	0	228	27	62	0.435	27	62	0.435	0	0	0.000	11	16	0.687	16	47	63	51	5	22	29	65	96
Per GP			5.3	0.6	1.4		0.6	1.4		0.0	0.0		0.3	0.4		0.4	1.1	1.5	1.2	0.1	0.5	0.7	1.5	2.2
Per 48			4.8	5.7	13.1		5.7	13.1		0.0	0.0		2.3	3.4		3.4	9.9	13.3	10.7	1.1	4.6	6.1	13.7	20.2
Akeem Olajuwon	82	82	3024	790	1556	0.508	790	1546	0.511	0	10	0.000	454	652	0.696	338	767	105	329	213	275	279	2034	2304
Per GP			36.9	9.6	19.0		9.6	18.9		0.0	0.1		5.5	8.0		4.1	9.4	1.3	4.0	2.6	3.4	3.4	24.8	28.1
Per 48			63.0	12.5	24.7		12.5	24.5		0.0	0.2		7.2	10.3		5.4	12.2	1.7	5.2	3.4	4.4	4.4	32.3	36.6
Purvis Short	65	16	1157	198	480	0.412	189	447	0.423	9	33	0.273	77	88	0.875	65	114	179	116	41	70	13	482	407
Per GP			17.8	3.0	7.4		2.9	6.9		0.1	0.5		1.2	1.4		1.0	1.8	2.8	1.8	0.6	1.1	0.2	7.4	6.3
Per 48			24.1	8.2	19.9		7.8	18.5		0.4	1.4		3.2	3.7		2.7	4.7	7.4	4.8	1.7	2.9	0.5	20.0	16.9
Bernard Thompson	23	0	222	20	59	0.339	20	57	0.351	0	2	0.000	22	26	0.846	9	19	28	33	13	19	1	62	56
Per GP			9.7	0.9	2.6		0.9	2.5		0.0	0.1		1.0	1.1		0.4	0.8	1.2	1.4	0.6	0.8	0.0	2.7	2.4
Per 48			4.6	4.3	12.8		4.3	12.3		0.0	0.4		4.8	5.6		1.9	4.1	6.1	7.1	2.8	4.1	0.2	13.4	12.1
Otis Thorpe	82	82	3135	521	961	0.542	521	959	0.543	0	2	0.000	328	450	0.729	272	515	787	259	84	225	37	1370	1440
Per GP			38.2	6.4	11.7		6.4	11.7		0.0	0.0		4.0	5.5		3.3	6.3	9.6	3.2	1.0	2.7	0.5	16.7	17.6
Per 48			65.3	8.0	14.7		8.0	14.7		0.0	0.0		5.0	6.9		4.2	7.9	12.0	4.0	1.3	3.4	0.6	21.0	22.0
Mike Woodson	81	79	2259	410	936	0.438	379	847	0.447	31	89	0.348	195	237	0.823	51	143	194	195	89	135	18	1046	780
Per GP			27.9	5.1	11.6		4.7	10.5		0.4	1.1		2.4	2.9		0.6	1.8	2.4	2.4	1.1	1.7	0.2	12.9	9.6
Per 48			47.1	8.7	19.9		8.1	18.0		0.7	1.9		4.1	5.0		1.1	3.0	4.1	4.1	1.9	2.9	0.4	22.2	16.6

INDIANA PACERS

Every year, at least one team earns the label "Biggest Disaster Story," and this year Indiana nudged out the Clippers by a nose for the honors. At least the Pacers *used* to be good. The Pacers earned their stripes last season as they (a) went through three coaches (Jack Ramsay, Mel Daniels, George Irvine) before settling on former Piston assistant Dick Versace; (b) had one disgruntled player quit (guard Scott Skiles) and then come back; (c) had another threaten to quit (forward Chuck Person) after many of the losses, not to mention (d) putting the rest of the team down after several losses. Add it all up, put it on a court, and you come up with a 28–54 team, down 10 wins from the year before.

Despite the losses due to injury, the Pacers were surprisingly decent defensively, which bodes well for their future. They held opponents under 100 points 11 times; they won 10 of those games. Of course, *they* were held under 100 points 24 times, losing 22. Still, it seems their needs lie more along the lines of firepower than defense.

With center-forward Steve Stipanovich lost to injuries, Rik Smits, the 7'4" rookie from the Netherlands, was thrown to the wolves in his first year. Although he looked at times as if he were wearing wooden clogs, he made steady progress through the season, contributing 1.84 blocks per game (10th in the league) and 11.7 ppg. However, Smits, along with many of the other Pacers, had a curious tendency to commit fouls. Lots and lots of fouls. Three Pacers led their positions in total disqualifications during the season (Smits with 14, Person with 12, LaSalle Thompson with 6 in 33 games for Indiana, 12 overall).

In fact, the Pacers led the entire league in disqualifications by a huge margin. They had 48 DQs; the Lakers, on the other end of the spectrum, had 2. Even the second-place team, Miami, had over a fifth fewer foul-outs.

Why do some teams pick up foul-outs, anyway? It seems that the poorer teams are whistled out more often, but if that *is* true, why? Is it that their skills are not refined to the point where they can reach in without fouling? Or do they have fewer stars who get the calls going their way? Is it frustration? If so, why did New Jersey have only 12 players pick up 6 fouls in a game? Do shorter teams need to foul more to make up for their lack of height? Then why did Rik Smits have so many? Charlotte and Washington,

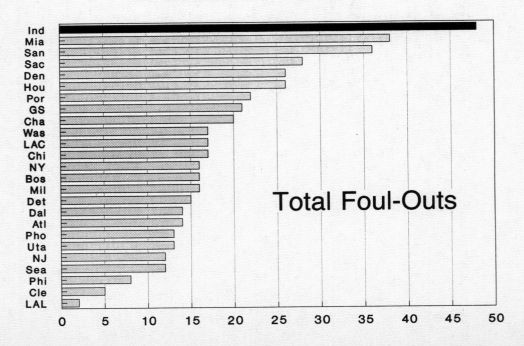

Indiana Pacers

Total Foul-Outs

two of the shortest teams around, were in the very middle of the pack in DQs. We have no idea why. All we know is that the Pacers must learn how to keep better track of their personals.

Things *could* be worse, though. The Pacers do have the Hornets to look forward to in their division next year. Hopefully, Steve Stipanovich will return, bringing his 13.2 ppg and 7.8 rpg to the team. The Pacers are looking to move him to forward, and a front court consisting of Stipo, Smits, and Chuck Person could conceivably erase many of the problems Indiana had last year. Person's foul trouble kept him missing from the fourth quarter of quite a few games last year, but having another healthy body to muscle out defenders should really help.

At least the management is showing healthy signs of making an effort. They shopped around before the trading deadline last year, and came up with LaSalle Thompson, who sweeps the boards better than most. Detlef Schrempf relieved the inside pressure with his outside range last year, and Reggie Miller is certainly no slouch. If their offense matures to the point where it complements their defense, the Pacers might even sneak up on the Bucks. Small consolation in a state used to basketball excellence, but let's take things one step at a time.

Indiana Pacers

	Home W	L	Road W	L
By Month				
November	2	4	0	8
December	3	4	0	6
January	5	3	1	6
February	2	3	1	6
March	5	4	3	4
April	3	3	3	3
Playoffs				
Home/Away	20	21	8	33
Overtime	0	1	3	2
Offense				
0-89	0	2	0	0
90-99	1	6	1	14
100-109	6	9	1	9
110-119	8	3	2	10
120-129	5	1	3	0
130-	0	0	1	0
Defense				
0-89	3	0	1	0
90-99	6	1	0	0
100-109	7	8	3	8
110-119	3	8	2	13
120-129	1	3	2	7
130-	0	1	0	5
Over/Under				
0-189	1	2	1	0
190-199	3	1	0	3
200-209	3	7	0	6
210-219	8	4	2	8
220-229	2	3	1	6
230-239	2	1	2	6
240-	1	3	2	4
Margin Of Victory				
0-3	2	4	4	5
4-6	2	3	1	2
7-10	8	7	2	9
11-15	5	3	0	5
16-20	1	3	1	5
21-	2	1	0	7
Field Goal Attempts				
0-69	1	0	1	0
70-79	7	6	3	4
80-89	7	11	1	19
90-99	4	4	2	9
100-109	1	0	1	1
110+	0	0	0	0
Field Goals Made				
0-34	0	3	1	1
35-39	6	7	2	12
40-44	7	10	0	15
45-49	5	1	5	5
50-54	2	0	0	0
55+	0	0	0	0
Field Goal Pct.				
.000-.399	0	1	0	1
.400-.424	0	4	1	2
.425-.449	2	3	0	7
.450-.474	3	1	0	9
.475-.499	3	4	1	4
.500-.524	3	6	3	6
.525-.549	2	2	0	3
.550-.574	2	0	1	1

	Home W	L	Road W	L
.575-.599	3	0	0	0
.600-	2	0	2	0
Opp. Field Goal Attempts				
0-69	1	0	0	0
70-79	1	4	0	3
80-89	7	10	3	9
90-99	8	6	2	17
100-109	3	1	2	4
110+	0	0	1	0
Opp. Field Goal Made				
0-34	2	2	1	0
35-39	8	5	3	7
40-44	7	10	2	8
45-49	2	4	0	14
50-54	1	0	2	4
55+	0	0	0	0
Opp. Field Goal Percentage				
.000-.399	2	0	1	2
.400-.424	8	2	3	1
.425-.449	2	2	3	3
.450-.474	5	6	0	9
.475-.499	0	6	0	4
.500-.524	2	2	1	9
.525-.549	0	2	0	1
.550-.574	1	0	0	3
.575-.599	0	1	0	1
.600-	0	0	0	0
Free Throw Attempts				
0-9	0	0	0	0
10-19	2	3	1	5
20-29	8	9	3	19
30-39	8	8	3	6
40-49	2	1	1	3
50+	0	0	0	0
Free Throws Made				
0-9	0	0	0	1
10-19	7	8	2	16
20-29	9	10	5	14
30-39	4	3	1	2
40-49	0	0	0	0
50+	0	0	0	0
Free Throw Pct				
.000-.549	0	1	0	0
.550-.599	0	0	0	2
.600-.649	0	3	0	1
.650-.699	2	2	0	3
.700-.749	5	1	0	5
.750-.799	5	3	2	7
.800-.849	3	6	1	7
.850-.899	3	4	3	6
.900-.949	1	1	2	2
.950-	1	0	0	0
Opp. Free Throw Attempts				
0-9	1	0	0	0
10-19	2	0	0	1
20-29	9	5	3	9
30-39	6	12	5	16
40-49	2	4	0	5
50+	0	0	0	0
Opp. Free Throws Made				
0-9	1	0	0	0
10-19	9	0	2	6
20-29	8	15	5	15

	Home W	L	Road W	L
30-39	2	6	1	11
40-49	0	0	0	1
50+	0	0	0	0
Opp. Free Throw Pct				
.000-.549	2	0	0	2
.550-.599	2	0	0	0
.600-.649	3	1	0	1
.650-.699	1	2	1	2
.700-.749	0	3	1	2
.750-.799	8	4	3	5
.800-.849	3	6	1	13
.850-.899	1	5	1	6
.900-.949	0	0	1	1
.950-	0	0	0	1
Offensive Rebounds				
0-9	5	1	3	9
10-14	7	12	2	13
15-19	6	6	3	7
20-24	2	2	0	4
25+	0	0	0	0
Total Rebounds				
0-39	0	0	2	3
40-44	4	3	1	2
45-49	2	5	1	9
50-54	0	0	0	0
55-59	9	13	3	14
60-64	3	0	1	2
65-	2	0	0	3
Opp. Offensive Rebounds				
0-9	2	1	0	2
10-14	7	9	1	13
15-19	8	9	3	12
20-24	2	2	3	4
25+	1	0	1	2
Opp. Total Rebounds				
0-39	1	1	0	0
40-44	4	2	0	1
45-49	3	1	2	6
50-54	0	0	0	0
55-59	11	17	5	18
60-64	0	0	0	7
65-	1	0	1	1
Offensive Rebound Pct.				
Below 25%	7	10	4	18
25-29.99%	6	5	1	9
30-34.99%	4	2	3	4
35-39.99%	3	4	0	2
40-44.99%	0	0	0	0
45% and up	0	0	0	0
Assists				
0-14	0	0	0	1
15-19	2	4	0	6
20-24	4	9	2	14
25-29	7	6	3	8
30-34	7	2	2	4
35+	0	0	1	0
Opp. Assists				
0-14	1	0	0	0
15-19	3	5	2	2
20-24	12	9	2	5
25-29	3	7	3	15
30-34	1	0	0	8
35+	0	0	1	3

	Home W	L	Road W	L
Edge In Assists				
Below -15	0	0	0	1
-10 to -14	0	0	0	7
-5 to -9	0	4	2	12
0 to -4	4	6	1	4
1-4	7	8	1	8
5-9	6	3	2	1
10-14	2	0	2	0
15-	1	0	0	0
Personal Fouls				
0-14	2	0	0	0
15-19	2	0	1	1
20-24	7	3	4	9
25-29	7	13	3	13
30-34	2	5	0	8
35+	0	0	0	2
Opp. Personal Fouls				
0-14	0	1	0	0
15-19	3	1	0	6
20-24	5	5	2	11
25-29	10	10	3	13
30-34	2	4	3	3
35+	0	0	0	0
Personal Fouls Edge				
Below -15	1	0	0	0
-10 to -14	0	0	1	0
-5 to -9	5	1	2	2
0 to -4	5	12	3	8
1-4	6	4	2	9
5-9	3	2	0	12
10-14	0	1	0	2
15+	0	1	0	0
Steals				
0-5	6	6	0	12
6-7	6	8	2	9
8-9	5	3	5	9
10-11	2	3	1	3
12-13	1	1	0	0
14+	0	0	0	0
Opp. Steals				
0-5	1	1	0	2
6-7	4	3	2	6
8-9	5	4	2	5
10-11	6	5	2	6
12-13	2	4	1	6
14+	2	4	1	8
Edge In Steals				
Below -7	3	7	1	10
-4 to -6	4	3	0	9
0 to -3	9	5	6	8
1-3	4	6	1	5
4-6	0	0	0	1
7-	0	0	0	0
Turnovers				
0-14	7	2	0	1
15-19	8	10	4	18
20-24	3	5	3	9
25-29	2	4	1	5
30-34	0	0	0	0
35+	0	0	0	0
Opp. Turnovers				
0-14	9	10	3	17
15-19	10	7	4	15

	Home W L	Road W L
20-24	1 4	1 1
25-29	0 0	0 0
30-34	0 0	0 0
35+	0 0	0 0

Edge In Turnovers

	Home W L	Road W L
Below -15	0 0	0 0
-10 to -14	0 0	0 0
-5 to -9	2 0	0 0
0 to -4	6 6	2 5
1-4	5 4	2 11
5-9	4 9	4 12
10-14	3 1	0 4
15+	0 1	0 1

Blocks

	Home W L	Road W L
1-2	3 4	3 1
3-4	6 5	2 11
5-6	6 8	3 10
7-8	4 3	0 4
9-10	1 0	0 7
11+	0 1	0 0

Opp. Blocks

	Home W L	Road W L
0-2	4 5	2 4
3-4	10 10	4 6
5-6	2 5	1 11
7-8	3 0	0 5
9-10	1 0	1 4
11+	0 1	0 3

Edge In Blocks

	Home W L	Road W L
Below -7	0 1	0 1
-4 to -6	3 2	0 5
0 to -3	4 5	5 13
1-3	11 9	2 7
4-6	2 3	1 7
7+	0 1	0 0

Three-Pointers Attempted

	Home W L	Road W L
0-2	3 0	0 0
3-5	6 4	1 12
6-8	6 9	2 13
9-11	3 4	2 7
12-14	1 3	1 1
15+	1 1	2 0

Three-Pointers Made

	Home W L	Road W L
0-2	11 12	2 20
3-5	7 8	4 13
6-8	1 1	1 0
9-11	1 0	1 0
12-14	0 0	0 0
15+	0 0	0 0

Three-Pointers Pct

	Home W L	Road W L
.000-.099	2 4	0 11
.100-.149	0 5	0 4
.150-.199	1 1	1 2
.200-.249	0 0	0 1
.250-.299	0 2	1 3
.300-.349	7 3	1 5
.350-.399	1 0	1 2
.400-.449	1 1	2 1
.450-.499	0 0	0 0
.500-	8 5	2 4

Opp. Three-Point Attempts

	Home W L	Road W L
0-2	1 5	0 8
3-5	8 5	2 9
6-8	5 6	0 9
9-11	5 3	1 3
12-14	1 2	2 3
15+	0 0	3 1

Opp. Three-Pointers Made

	Home W L	Road W L
0-2	15 17	3 22
3-5	5 4	4 10
6-8	0 0	1 0
9-11	0 0	0 1
12-14	0 0	0 0
15+	0 0	0 0

Opp. Three-Pointer Pct

	Home W L	Road W L
.000-.099	6 7	2 10
.100-.149	2 1	0 6
.150-.199	0 2	0 1
.200-.249	1 1	1 0
.250-.299	5 3	1 1
.300-.349	1 2	1 3
.350-.399	0 2	0 0
.400-.449	4 1	3 7
.450-.499	0 0	0 0
.500-	1 2	0 5

Indiana Pacers
1988–89 Power Chart

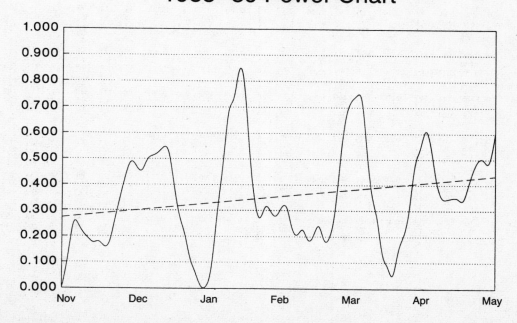

Indiana Pacers

	GP	GS	Min	FGM	FGA	FG%	2GM	2GA	2G%	3GM	3GA	3G%	FTM	FTA	FT%	Off	Tot	Ast	PF	Stl	TO	Blk	Pts	HGS
Greg Dreiling	53	4	396	43	77	0.558	43	77	0.558	0	0	0.000	43	64	0.672	39	53	92	100	5	39	11	129	150
Per GP			7.5	0.8	1.5		0.8	1.5		0.0	0.0		0.8	1.2		0.7	1.0	1.7	1.9	0.1	0.7	0.2	2.4	2.8
Per 48			8.2	5.2	9.3		5.2	9.3		0.0	0.0		5.2	7.8		4.7	6.4	11.2	12.1	0.6	4.7	1.3	15.6	18.2
Vern Fleming	76	69	2552	419	814	0.515	416	791	0.526	3	23	0.130	243	304	0.799	85	225	310	212	77	192	12	1084	1212
Per GP			33.6	5.5	10.7		5.5	10.4		0.0	0.3		3.2	4.0		1.1	3.0	4.1	2.8	1.0	2.5	0.2	14.3	15.9
Per 48			53.2	7.9	15.3		7.8	14.9		0.1	0.4		4.6	5.7		1.6	4.2	5.8	4.0	1.4	3.6	0.2	20.4	22.8
Anthony Frederick	46	0	313	63	125	0.504	61	120	0.508	2	5	0.400	24	34	0.706	26	26	52	59	14	34	6	152	125
Per GP			6.8	1.4	2.7		1.3	2.6		0.0	0.1		0.5	0.7		0.6	0.6	1.1	1.3	0.3	0.7	0.1	3.3	2.7
Per 48			6.5	9.7	19.2		9.4	18.4		0.3	0.8		3.7	5.2		4.0	4.0	8.0	9.0	2.1	5.2	0.9	23.3	19.2
Stuart Gray	72	0	783	72	153	0.471	72	152	0.474	0	1	0.000	44	64	0.687	84	161	245	128	11	48	21	188	279
Per GP			10.9	1.0	2.1		1.0	2.1		0.0	0.0		0.6	0.9		1.2	2.2	3.4	1.8	0.2	0.7	0.3	2.6	3.9
Per 48			16.3	4.4	9.4		4.4	9.3		0.0	0.1		2.7	3.9		5.1	9.9	15.0	7.8	0.7	2.9	1.3	11.5	17.1
John Long	44	1	767	128	319	0.401	120	299	0.401	8	20	0.400	59	63	0.937	16	50	66	68	29	48	1	323	219
Per GP			17.4	2.9	7.3		2.7	6.8		0.2	0.5		1.3	1.4		0.4	1.1	1.5	1.5	0.7	1.1	0.0	7.3	5.0
Per 48			16.0	8.0	20.0		7.5	18.7		0.5	1.3		3.7	3.9		1.0	3.1	4.1	4.3	1.8	3.0	0.1	20.2	13.7
Reggie Miller	74	70	2536	398	831	0.479	300	587	0.511	98	244	0.402	287	340	0.844	73	219	292	170	93	143	29	1181	1002
Per GP			34.3	5.4	11.2		4.1	7.9		1.3	3.3		3.9	4.6		1.0	3.0	3.9	2.3	1.3	1.9	0.4	16.0	13.5
Per 48			52.8	7.5	15.7		5.7	11.1		1.9	4.6		5.4	6.4		1.4	4.1	5.5	3.2	1.8	2.7	0.5	22.4	19.0
Richard Morton	2	0	11	3	4	0.750	3	4	0.750	0	0	0.000	0	0	0.000	0	0	0	2	0	1	0	6	4
Per GP			5.5	1.5	2.0		1.5	2.0		0.0	0.0		0.0	0.0		0.0	0.0	0.0	1.0	0.0	0.5	0.0	3.0	2.0
Per 48			0.2	13.1	17.5		13.1	17.5		0.0	0.0		0.0	0.0		0.0	0.0	0.0	8.7	0.0	4.4	0.0	26.2	17.5
Chuck Person	80	79	3012	711	1453	0.489	648	1248	0.519	63	205	0.307	243	307	0.792	144	372	516	285	83	308	18	1728	1252
Per GP			37.6	8.9	18.2		8.1	15.6		0.8	2.6		3.0	3.8		1.8	4.6	6.4	3.6	1.0	3.8	0.2	21.6	15.6
Per 48			62.7	11.3	23.2		10.3	19.9		1.0	3.3		3.9	4.9		2.3	5.9	8.2	4.5	1.3	4.9	0.3	27.5	20.0
Detlef Schrempf	32	12	1005	162	315	0.514	157	296	0.530	5	19	0.263	146	189	0.772	70	159	229	102	29	77	10	475	494
Per GP			31.4	5.1	9.8		4.9	9.2		0.2	0.6		4.6	5.9		2.2	5.0	7.2	3.2	0.9	2.4	0.3	14.8	15.4
Per 48			20.9	7.7	15.0		7.5	14.1		0.2	0.9		7.0	9.0		3.3	7.6	10.9	4.9	1.4	3.7	0.5	22.7	23.6
Scott Skiles	80	13	1571	198	442	0.448	178	367	0.485	20	75	0.267	130	144	0.903	21	128	149	151	64	177	2	546	658
Per GP			19.6	2.5	5.5		2.2	4.6		0.3	0.9		1.6	1.8		0.3	1.6	1.9	1.9	0.8	2.2	0.0	6.8	8.2
Per 48			32.7	6.0	13.5		5.4	11.2		0.6	2.3		4.0	4.4		0.6	3.9	4.6	4.6	2.0	5.4	0.1	16.7	20.1
Rik Smits	82	71	2041	386	746	0.517	386	745	0.518	0	1	0.000	184	256	0.719	185	315	500	310	37	130	151	956	1038
Per GP			24.9	4.7	9.1		4.7	9.1		0.0	0.0		2.2	3.1		2.3	3.8	6.1	3.8	0.5	1.6	1.8	11.7	12.7
Per 48			42.5	9.1	17.5		9.1	17.5		0.0	0.0		4.3	6.0		4.4	7.4	11.8	7.3	0.9	3.1	3.6	22.5	24.4
Everette Stephens	35	0	209	23	72	0.319	21	62	0.339	2	10	0.200	17	22	0.773	11	12	23	22	9	29	4	65	64
Per GP			6.0	0.7	2.1		0.6	1.8		0.1	0.3		0.5	0.6		0.3	0.3	0.7	0.6	0.3	0.8	0.1	1.9	1.8
Per 48			4.4	5.3	16.5		4.8	14.2		0.5	2.3		3.9	5.1		2.5	2.8	5.3	5.1	2.1	6.7	0.9	14.9	14.7
LaSalle Thompson	33	29	1053	169	314	0.538	169	314	0.538	0	0	0.000	75	93	0.806	104	222	326	132	33	62	39	413	499
Per GP			31.9	5.1	9.5		5.1	9.5		0.0	0.0		2.3	2.8		3.2	6.7	9.9	4.0	1.0	1.9	1.2	12.5	15.1
Per 48			21.9	7.7	14.3		7.7	14.3		0.0	0.0		3.4	4.2		4.7	10.1	14.9	6.0	1.5	2.8	1.8	18.8	22.7
Wayman Tisdale	48	5	1326	285	564	0.505	285	560	0.509	0	4	0.000	198	250	0.792	99	211	310	181	35	107	32	768	688
Per GP			27.6	5.9	11.7		5.9	11.7		0.0	0.1		4.1	5.2		2.1	4.4	6.5	3.8	0.7	2.2	0.7	16.0	14.3
Per 48			27.6	10.3	20.4		10.3	20.3		0.0	0.1		7.2	9.0		3.6	7.6	11.2	6.6	1.3	3.9	1.2	27.8	24.9
Sedrick Toney	2	0	9	1	5	0.200	1	2	0.500	0	3	0.000	0	1	0.000	1	1	2	1	0	2	0	2	-1
Per GP			4.5	0.5	2.5		0.5	1.0		0.0	1.5		0.0	0.5		0.5	0.5	1.0	0.5	0.0	1.0	0.0	1.0	-0.5
Per 48			0.2	5.3	26.7		5.3	10.7		0.0	16.0		0.0	5.3		5.3	5.3	10.7	5.3	0.0	10.7	0.0	10.7	-5.3
Herb Williams	46	46	1567	244	542	0.450	244	539	0.453	0	3	0.000	90	126	0.714	87	309	396	156	31	108	80	578	626
Per GP			34.1	5.3	11.8		5.3	11.7		0.0	0.1		2.0	2.7		1.9	6.7	8.6	3.4	0.7	2.3	1.7	12.6	13.6
Per 48			32.6	7.5	16.6		7.5	16.5		0.0	0.1		2.8	3.9		2.7	9.5	12.1	4.8	0.9	3.3	2.5	17.7	19.2
Randy Wittman	33	11	704	80	169	0.473	79	167	0.473	1	2	0.500	12	19	0.632	20	34	54	31	13	20	2	173	183
Per GP			21.3	2.4	5.1		2.4	5.1		0.0	0.1		0.4	0.6		0.6	1.0	1.6	0.9	0.4	0.6	0.1	5.2	5.5
Per 48			14.7	5.5	11.5		5.4	11.4		0.1	0.1		0.8	1.3		1.4	2.3	3.7	2.1	0.9	1.4	0.1	11.8	12.5

LOS ANGELES CLIPPERS

How do you build a winning team? You bite the bullet, trade for the future, amass some draft picks, wait, and hope. The Clippers gathered six first-round draft choices over two years, assembled a young team, and waited. Don Sterling was so optimistic two years ago that he took out full-page ads promising the NBA title this coming season. Well? Think they're still on target?

The Clippers did exactly what they wanted to do. They patiently built from the draft. And they're still badly deficient. It all boils down to two possible explanations: either they're victims of incredibly bad management, or an ancient Indian curse. How else to explain this team? They got the best player in the country, Danny Manning, and he played nearly a quarter of a season before his career-threatening injury. Quintin Dailey showed up one day, and had somehow gained thirty-odd pounds. How does this happen without anyone noticing? Seriously, did he just walk in one day, looking like he had just eaten a basketball? Why didn't he receive some friendly guidance from the coaching staff, such as "Put the Big Mac down, Quintin"? Were the coaches just worried about keeping their hands out of the way when they sat next to him at the training table? Did

Charles Smith personally insult the Indian high priestess, finishing up the season with strep throat, food poisoning, sore ankles, a sprained wrist, and a bruised hip? What can you do when Reggie Williams refuses to enter a game? (Reggie was the perfect example of the rat trying to jump off the sinking ship.) If only the Clippers weren't locked in with him, he would soon be a vague and distant memory for this team.

What's the best way to react to these misfortunes? Of course! Fire the coach! After Danny Manning went down, and the Clippers were 7–19, Gene Shue got the axe. Could he have done any better? Could anyone? Although Manning's injury sealed the team's fate, he wasn't going to be as valuable as Larry Bird, and the Celtics managed to finish around .500 in his absence, with a geriatric squad. You can't blame the coach for everything, especially when you have management who can't even find a permanent practice court for the team.

About the only positive for the Clippers was the play of their big man, Benoit Benjamin. Decent seven-footers are hard to find, and Benoit, still only 24 years old, had his career year in 1989. Despite a history as an NBA question mark who once

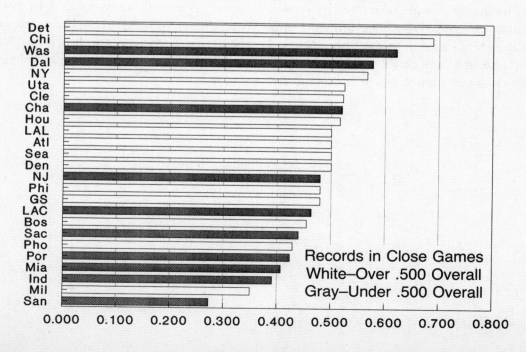

showed up to a game with two left sneakers, Benjamin lost 15 pounds under the new Casey regime, and boosted his scoring and rebounding to 16.4 and 8.7. If only every year were an option year . . . We fully expect him to revert to his form of old when he gets his new contract. Casey's discipline seemed to do a lot of players good, discipline-wise if not record-wise. Even Quintin Dailey, who himself shed 30 pounds (and he didn't even give birth). More than any other player on this team, Dailey needs to learn to reach inside himself for the mental toughness to make it big. If the Clippers are smart, they'll forget about their parade of candidates for the job, and just sign one coach to a long-term contract so he can build a system around the talents he's been given.

One of the enduring sports myths is that bad teams don't win the close games. In truth, when you look at the record, you'll never be able to tell a good team from a bad one on the basis of their record in close games. There's one simple reason for this: in a close game, anyone has a chance to win. It can be decided by luck. A team has to be good to win a blowout. They can be lucky and win a squeaker.

Take these Clippers, for instance. They actually went 13–15 in games decided by six points or fewer, which makes it sound like they're not bad down the stretch. However, you need to look further than that. In games decided by 16 or more points, good old-fashioned blowouts, they were 1–30. They let the other team beat them by sixteen points about twice every five games, but were only able to do it once all season to their opponents, a 111–19 win against Miami on the second day of the season. Which is the sign of the better team? The one who can crush you, or the one who can squeak by you half the time? Forget records in close games. They tell you nothing about how good a team is.

So are the Clippers still on schedule to cop the NBA crown this year? Forget it. They will be odds on favorites to improve on their dismal 21–61 record. Chances are, they won't be the first team to lose to both Orlando and Minneapolis, as they did to Miami and Charlotte. However, the question marks are overwhelming. So much depends on Manning's return to form after his surgery. Charles Smith and Ken Norman should be real players if they continue to work hard, and don't get down on their situation too badly. Gary Grant can't be considered a bona fide offensive threat, and a two-guard is a glaring need. Thirty wins isn't out of the question by any means, but Manning has to live up to his billing before this team can even dream about the playoffs.

It would help if they got out of Los Angeles, too. They're never going to establish a fan base there. Who's going to get excited about this team when the Lakers are firmly entrenched? And yet, Stirling turned down $30 million to move the team to a brand new arena in Anaheim. Is there something he sees that we don't? What, was he afraid to compromise the droves of loyal fans in LA? When a team is treated like a second-class citizen in a city, they're more likely to play like they are second class, and that's not a good precedent to set for a youthful bunch. You only need to look to the cable deals each team has signed to know where this city's hearts lie. The Lakers are shown on "Prime Ticket," while the Clippers appear on "Cable Z Channel."

Los Angeles Clippers

	Home W	L	Road W	L
By Month				
November	5	1	1	7
December	3	3	1	7
January	0	5	0	9
February	1	6	0	8
March	5	4	1	3
April	3	5	1	3
Playoffs				
Home/Away	17	24	4	37
Overtime	2	3	0	2
Offense				
0-89	0	2	0	3
90-99	0	3	1	11
100-109	5	13	0	16
110-119	7	3	3	6
120-129	3	1	0	1
130-	2	2	0	0
Defense				
0-89	0	1	0	0
90-99	2	1	2	0
100-109	6	7	2	3
110-119	6	6	0	17
120-129	3	5	0	10
130-	0	4	0	7
Over/Under				
0-189	0	2	1	0
190-199	1	1	0	2
200-209	3	1	1	6
210-219	2	10	1	9
220-229	5	2	1	8
230-239	3	3	0	7
240-	3	5	0	5
Margin Of Victory				
0-3	7	5	1	2
4-6	4	6	1	2
7-10	3	3	0	4
11-15	3	1	1	8
16-20	0	6	1	8
21-	0	3	0	13
Field Goal Attempts				
0-69	0	0	0	0
70-79	2	3	1	2
80-89	6	8	2	12
90-99	8	9	1	19
100-109	1	3	0	3
110+	0	1	0	1
Field Goals Made				
0-34	0	3	0	0
35-39	0	1	1	13
40-44	5	13	0	15
45-49	8	4	3	7
50-54	4	3	0	2
55+	0	0	0	0
Field Goal Pct.				
.000-.399	0	2	0	1
.400-.424	0	1	0	10
.425-.449	1	3	0	6
.450-.474	1	7	1	8
.475-.499	4	3	0	5
.500-.524	0	4	1	3
.525-.549	8	3	0	3
.550-.574	1	0	1	1

	Home W	L	Road W	L
.575-.599	1	1	0	0
.600-	1	0	1	0
Opp. Field Goal Attempts				
0-69	0	0	0	0
70-79	1	2	0	0
80-89	5	4	1	8
90-99	8	13	3	19
100-109	2	4	0	10
110+	1	1	0	0
Opp. Field Goal Made				
0-34	1	0	0	0
35-39	4	2	3	1
40-44	3	9	1	11
45-49	5	6	0	14
50-54	4	6	0	9
55+	0	1	0	2
Opp. Field Goal Percentage				
.000-.399	1	0	2	1
.400-.424	1	0	0	1
.425-.449	2	3	1	5
.450-.474	4	3	1	6
.475-.499	5	10	0	9
.500-.524	4	3	0	5
.525-.549	0	3	0	6
.550-.574	0	1	0	2
.575-.599	0	1	0	2
.600-	0	0	0	0
Free Throw Attempts				
0-9	0	0	0	1
10-19	1	4	0	11
20-29	8	10	2	16
30-39	6	7	2	8
40-49	1	3	0	1
50+	1	0	0	0
Free Throws Made				
0-9	0	1	0	2
10-19	7	10	0	22
20-29	9	10	4	12
30-39	0	3	0	1
40-49	1	0	0	0
50+	0	0	0	0
Free Throw Pct.				
.000-.549	0	0	0	2
.550-.599	1	1	0	4
.600-.649	2	2	2	5
.650-.699	2	5	0	9
.700-.749	4	4	0	6
.750-.799	4	6	1	4
.800-.849	3	5	0	4
.850-.899	1	1	0	0
.900-.949	0	0	1	1
.950-	0	0	0	2
Opp. Free Throw Attempts				
0-9	0	1	0	0
10-19	3	5	0	2
20-29	8	6	3	16
30-39	4	9	0	12
40-49	2	3	1	7
50+	0	0	0	0
Opp. Free Throws Made				
0-9	1	1	0	0
10-19	8	9	3	10
20-29	6	11	0	18

	Home W	L	Road W	L
30-39	2	3	1	9
40-49	0	0	0	0
50+	0	0	0	0
Opp. Free Throw Pct.				
.000-.549	1	0	0	0
.550-.599	1	0	0	0
.600-.649	0	1	0	2
.650-.699	3	1	1	4
.700-.749	3	5	3	4
.750-.799	4	6	0	15
.800-.849	2	6	0	9
.850-.899	1	5	0	3
.900-.949	2	0	0	0
.950-	0	0	0	0
Offensive Rebounds				
0-9	4	4	0	8
10-14	4	8	4	10
15-19	7	7	0	13
20-24	2	4	0	6
25+	0	1	0	0
Total Rebounds				
0-39	0	2	0	1
40-44	3	2	0	2
45-49	2	4	1	7
50-54	0	0	0	0
55-59	7	10	3	22
60-64	2	2	0	4
65-	3	4	0	1
Opp. Offensive Rebounds				
0-9	2	0	0	1
10-14	7	9	0	11
15-19	4	10	3	14
20-24	3	5	1	10
25+	1	0	0	1
Opp. Total Rebounds				
0-39	0	0	0	0
40-44	1	0	0	1
45-49	6	3	1	2
50-54	0	0	0	0
55-59	7	12	2	16
60-64	3	8	0	7
65-	0	1	1	11
Offensive Rebound Pct.				
Below 25%	6	7	2	20
25-29.99%	4	10	1	11
30-34.99%	7	4	1	1
35-39.99%	0	2	0	5
40-44.99%	0	1	0	0
45% and up	0	0	0	0
Assists				
0-14	0	0	1	0
15-19	0	1	1	3
20-24	1	5	1	17
25-29	4	7	1	10
30-34	8	10	0	5
35+	4	1	0	2
Opp. Assists				
0-14	0	0	1	0
15-19	0	0	0	0
20-24	5	4	2	2
25-29	6	7	1	15
30-34	4	10	0	12
35+	2	3	0	8

	Home W	L	Road W	L
Edge In Assists				
Below-15	0	1	0	2
-10 to -14	0	0	0	7
-5 to -9	2	9	1	13
0 to -4	3	3	2	7
1-4	3	7	1	5
5-9	6	3	0	2
10-14	3	1	0	1
15-	0	0	0	0
Personal Fouls				
0-14	0	2	0	0
15-19	5	4	1	5
20-24	5	8	2	15
25-29	6	7	0	10
30-34	1	3	1	7
35+	0	0	0	0
Opp. Personal Fouls				
0-14	0	1	0	2
15-19	1	2	1	15
20-24	10	9	1	10
25-29	3	10	2	8
30-34	1	2	0	2
35+	2	0	0	0
Personal Fouls Edge				
Below-15	0	1	0	0
-10 to -14	2	0	0	1
-5 to -9	3	6	1	3
0 to -4	8	8	1	9
1-4	1	4	2	10
5-9	3	4	0	8
10-14	0	1	0	5
15+	0	0	0	1
Steals				
0-5	0	4	1	0
6-7	4	3	0	11
8-9	1	8	0	5
10-11	4	5	0	7
12-13	5	2	2	8
14+	3	2	1	6
Opp. Steals				
0-5	2	1	0	1
6-7	2	3	0	2
8-9	6	7	1	5
10-11	1	3	0	4
12-13	3	5	2	14
14+	3	5	1	11
Edge In Steals				
Below-7	0	3	0	7
-4 to -6	3	6	1	6
0 to -3	6	9	2	14
1-3	3	4	1	8
4-6	3	1	0	2
7-	2	1	0	0
Turnovers				
0-14	3	4	0	4
15-19	7	11	2	9
20-24	6	8	1	11
25-29	0	0	1	11
30-34	1	1	0	2
35+	0	0	0	0
Opp. Turnovers				
0-14	3	12	0	7
15-19	8	8	2	15

	Home W	L	Road W	L
20-24	5	4	2	12
25-29	1	0	0	2
30-34	0	0	0	1
35+	0	0	0	0
Edge In Turnovers				
Below-15	1	0	0	0
-10 to -14	0	0	0	0
-5 to -9	2	2	0	4
0 to -4	4	4	2	7
1- 4	8	7	1	9
5- 9	1	8	1	12
10-14	1	3	0	3
15+	0	0	0	2
Blocks				
1-2	0	1	0	7
3-4	2	4	0	6
5-6	5	5	1	19
7-8	4	5	2	2
9-10	1	5	1	2
11+	5	4	0	1

	Home W	L	Road W	L
Opp. Blocks				
0-2	1	2	0	4
3-4	2	2	2	7
5-6	5	7	1	9
7-8	5	4	1	7
9-10	2	6	0	7
11+	2	3	0	3
Edge In Blocks				
Below-7	0	0	0	3
-4 to -6	3	6	0	6
0 to -3	6	5	1	17
1-3	2	9	3	8
4-6	4	3	0	2
7+	2	1	0	1
Three-Pointers Attempted				
0-2	15	11	3	13
3-5	2	12	1	18
6-8	0	1	0	4
9-11	0	0	0	2
12-14	0	0	0	0
15+	0	0	0	0

	Home W	L	Road W	L
Three-Pointers Made				
0-2	17	23	4	33
3-5	0	1	0	4
6-8	0	0	0	0
9-11	0	0	0	0
12-14	0	0	0	0
15+	0	0	0	0
Three-Pointers Pct.				
.000-.099	13	19	4	19
.100-.149	0	0	0	1
.150-.199	1	0	0	3
.200-.249	0	0	0	0
.250-.299	0	0	0	0
.300-.349	1	3	0	9
.350-.399	0	0	0	3
.400-.449	0	0	0	0
.450-.499	0	0	0	0
.500-	2	2	0	2
Opp. Three-Point Attempts				
0-2	2	2	1	3
3-5	4	9	1	10

	Home W	L	Road W	L
6-8	5	6	2	10
9-11	2	5	0	10
12-14	3	1	0	3
15+	1	1	0	1
Opp. Three-Pointers Made				
0-2	11	15	4	17
3-5	5	6	0	17
6-8	1	3	0	3
9-11	0	0	0	0
12-14	0	0	0	0
15+	0	0	0	0
Opp. Three-Pointer Pct.				
.000-.099	4	7	2	7
.100-.149	1	3	1	1
.150-.199	1	1	1	2
.200-.249	0	0	0	1
.250-.299	0	1	0	3
.300-.349	5	5	0	6
.350-.399	1	0	0	3
.400-.449	3	1	0	3
.450-.499	0	0	0	1
.500-	2	6	0	10

Los Angeles Clippers
1988–89 Power Chart

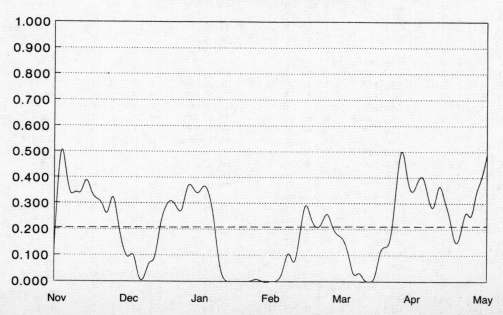

Los Angeles Clippers

	GP	GS	Min	FGM	FGA	FG%	2GM	2GA	2G%	3GM	3GA	3G%	FTM	FTA	FT%	Off	Tot	Ast	PF	Stl	TO	Blk	Pts	HGS
Ken Bannister	9	2	130	22	36	0.611	22	35	0.629	0	1	0.000	30	53	0.566	6	27	33	17	7	8	2	74	77
Per GP			14.4	2.4	4.0		2.4	3.9		0.0	0.1		3.3	5.9		0.7	3.0	3.7	1.9	0.8	0.9	0.2	8.2	8.6
Per 48			2.7	8.1	13.3		8.1	12.9		0.0	0.4		11.1	19.6		2.2	10.0	12.2	6.3	2.6	3.0	0.7	27.3	28.4
Benoit Benjamin	79	62	2585	491	907	0.541	491	905	0.543	0	2	0.000	317	426	0.744	164	532	696	221	57	237	221	1299	1494
Per GP			32.7	6.2	11.5		6.2	11.5		0.0	0.0		4.0	5.4		2.1	6.7	8.8	2.8	0.7	3.0	2.8	16.4	18.9
Per 48			53.9	9.1	16.8		9.1	16.8		0.0	0.0		5.9	7.9		3.0	9.9	12.9	4.1	1.1	4.4	4.1	24.1	27.7
Quintin Dailey	69	51	1722	448	964	0.465	447	955	0.468	1	9	0.111	217	286	0.759	69	137	206	152	90	122	6	1114	817
Per GP			25.0	6.5	14.0		6.5	13.8		0.0	0.1		3.1	4.1		1.0	2.0	3.0	2.2	1.3	1.8	0.1	16.1	11.8
Per 48			35.9	12.5	26.9		12.5	26.6		0.0	0.3		6.0	8.0		1.9	3.8	5.7	4.2	2.5	3.4	0.2	31.1	22.8
Tom Garrick	71	20	1499	176	359	0.490	176	346	0.509	0	13	0.000	102	127	0.803	37	119	156	141	78	116	9	454	570
Per GP			21.1	2.5	5.1		2.5	4.9		0.0	0.2		1.4	1.8		0.5	1.7	2.2	2.0	1.1	1.6	0.1	6.4	8.0
Per 48			31.2	5.6	11.5		5.6	11.1		0.0	0.4		3.3	4.1		1.2	3.8	5.0	4.5	2.5	3.7	0.3	14.5	18.3
Grant Gondrezick	27	0	244	38	95	0.400	35	84	0.417	3	11	0.273	26	40	0.650	15	21	36	36	13	17	1	105	103
Per GP			9.0	1.4	3.5		1.3	3.1		0.1	0.4		1.0	1.5		0.6	0.8	1.3	1.3	0.5	0.6	0.0	3.9	3.8
Per 48			5.1	7.5	18.7		6.9	16.5		0.6	2.2		5.1	7.9		3.0	4.1	7.1	7.1	2.6	3.3	0.2	20.7	20.3
Gary Grant	71	48	1924	361	830	0.435	356	808	0.441	5	22	0.227	119	162	0.735	81	157	238	170	144	258	9	846	947
Per GP			27.1	5.1	11.7		5.0	11.4		0.1	0.3		1.7	2.3		1.1	2.2	3.4	2.4	2.0	3.6	0.1	11.9	13.3
Per 48			40.1	9.0	20.7		8.9	20.2		0.1	0.5		3.0	4.0		2.0	3.9	5.9	4.2	3.6	6.4	0.2	21.1	23.6
Greg Kite	58	12	729	49	121	0.405	49	121	0.405	0	0	0.000	14	31	0.452	66	124	190	118	23	46	46	112	237
Per GP			12.6	0.8	2.1		0.8	2.1		0.0	0.0		0.2	0.5		1.1	2.1	3.3	2.0	0.4	0.8	0.8	1.9	4.1
Per 48			15.2	3.2	8.0		3.2	8.0		0.0	0.0		0.9	2.0		4.3	8.2	12.5	7.8	1.5	3.0	3.0	7.4	15.6
Rob Lock	20	0	110	9	32	0.281	9	32	0.281	0	0	0.000	12	15	0.800	14	18	32	15	3	13	4	30	34
Per GP			5.5	0.4	1.6		0.4	1.6		0.0	0.0		0.6	0.8		0.7	0.9	1.6	0.8	0.1	0.6	0.2	1.5	1.7
Per 48			2.3	3.9	14.0		3.9	14.0		0.0	0.0		5.2	6.5		6.1	7.9	14.0	6.5	1.3	5.7	1.7	13.1	14.8
Danny Manning	26	18	950	177	358	0.494	176	353	0.499	1	5	0.200	79	103	0.767	70	101	171	89	44	93	25	434	414
Per GP			36.5	6.8	13.8		6.8	13.6		0.0	0.2		3.0	4.0		2.7	3.9	6.6	3.4	1.7	3.6	1.0	16.7	15.9
Per 48			19.8	8.9	18.1		8.9	17.8		0.1	0.3		4.0	5.2		3.5	5.1	8.6	4.5	2.2	4.7	1.3	21.9	20.9
Norm Nixon	53	30	1318	153	370	0.414	145	341	0.425	8	29	0.276	48	65	0.738	13	65	78	69	46	118	0	362	466
Per GP			24.9	2.9	7.0		2.7	6.4		0.2	0.5		0.9	1.2		0.2	1.2	1.5	1.3	0.9	2.2	0.0	6.8	8.8
Per 48			27.5	5.6	13.5		5.3	12.4		0.3	1.1		1.7	2.4		0.5	2.4	2.8	2.5	1.7	4.3	0.0	13.2	17.0
Ken Norman	80	79	3020	638	1271	0.502	634	1250	0.507	4	21	0.190	170	270	0.630	245	422	667	223	106	206	65	1450	1412
Per GP			37.7	8.0	15.9		7.9	15.6		0.0	0.3		2.1	3.4		3.1	5.3	8.3	2.8	1.3	2.6	0.8	18.1	17.6
Per 48			62.9	10.1	20.2		10.1	19.9		0.1	0.3		2.7	4.3		3.9	6.7	10.6	3.5	1.7	3.3	1.0	23.0	22.4
Charles Smith	71	56	2161	435	877	0.496	435	874	0.498	0	3	0.000	285	393	0.725	173	292	465	273	68	146	89	1155	1101
Per GP			30.4	6.1	12.4		6.1	12.3		0.0	0.0		4.0	5.5		2.4	4.1	6.5	3.8	1.0	2.1	1.3	16.3	15.5
Per 48			45.0	9.7	19.5		9.7	19.4		0.0	0.1		6.3	8.7		3.8	6.5	10.3	6.1	1.5	3.2	2.0	25.7	24.5
Eric White	37	0	434	62	119	0.521	62	119	0.521	0	0	0.000	34	42	0.810	34	36	70	39	10	26	1	158	141
Per GP			11.7	1.7	3.2		1.7	3.2		0.0	0.0		0.9	1.1		0.9	1.0	1.9	1.1	0.3	0.7	0.0	4.3	3.8
Per 48			9.0	6.9	13.2		6.9	13.2		0.0	0.0		3.8	4.6		3.8	4.0	7.7	4.3	1.1	2.9	0.1	17.5	15.6
Kevin Williams	9	0	114	14	32	0.437	14	32	0.437	0	0	0.000	6	8	0.750	9	11	20	17	5	10	3	34	46
Per GP			12.7	1.6	3.6		1.6	3.6		0.0	0.0		0.7	0.9		1.0	1.2	2.2	1.9	0.6	1.1	0.3	3.8	5.1
Per 48			2.4	5.9	13.5		5.9	13.5		0.0	0.0		2.5	3.4		3.8	4.6	8.4	7.2	2.1	4.2	1.3	14.3	19.4
Reggie Williams	63	17	1303	260	594	0.438	230	490	0.469	30	104	0.288	92	122	0.754	70	109	179	182	81	114	29	642	503
Per GP			20.7	4.1	9.4		3.7	7.8		0.5	1.7		1.5	1.9		1.1	1.7	2.8	2.9	1.3	1.8	0.5	10.2	8.0
Per 48			27.1	9.6	21.9		8.5	18.1		1.1	3.8		3.4	4.5		2.6	4.0	6.6	6.7	3.0	4.2	1.1	23.7	18.5
Joe Wolf	66	15	1450	170	402	0.423	168	388	0.433	2	14	0.143	44	64	0.687	83	188	271	152	32	94	16	386	400
Per GP			22.0	2.6	6.1		2.5	5.9		0.0	0.2		0.7	1.0		1.3	2.8	4.1	2.3	0.5	1.4	0.2	5.8	6.1
Per 48			30.2	5.6	13.3		5.6	12.8		0.1	0.5		1.5	2.1		2.7	6.2	9.0	5.0	1.1	3.1	0.5	12.8	13.2
Dave Popson	10	0	68	11	25	0.440	11	25	0.440	0	0	0.000	1	2	0.500	5	11	16	9	1	6	2	23	23
Rob Rose	2	0	3	0	1	0.000	0	1	0.000	0	0	0.000	0	0	0.000	1	1	2	0	0	0	0	0	1
Barry Sumpter	1	0	1	0	1	0.000	0	1	0.000	0	0	0.000	0	0	0.000	0	0	0	0	0	0	0	0	-1
Ennis Whatley	8	0	90	12	33	0.364	12	33	0.364	0	0	0.000	10	11	0.909	2	14	16	15	7	11	1	34	45

LOS ANGELES LAKERS

The Lakers have gotten old. Despite the fact that they still won last year, the team is looking more and more like the recent Celtics, content to rely increasingly upon a strong starting five (Jabbar, Johnson, Worthy, Scott, Green). The fact that Jabbar was still in there for most of the minutes at center showed up in the final team stats, which were somewhat soft up the middle. The Lakers were out-blocked, 432–421, and out-offensive-rebounded 1178–1094. Still, they outscored their opponents by about 7.2 ppg, no mean feat when you consider that the Detroit Pistons, the league's new "power team," had only a 5.8-ppg scoring margin. Everything considered, the Lakers played the second best ball in the league, as only Cleveland had a better (7.6) margin, and we're sure the Cavs would have traded a little bit of that margin to have beaten Chicago.

The Lakers' large margin was generated by the team's many blowouts. Good teams usually win games big, and the Lakers were certainly no exception: they were 44–12 in games decided by 7 or more points, only 13–13 in closer match-ups.

The Lakers will be losing a player who will be a unanimous choice for Hall of Fame the first day he's eligible. No, don't worry, Orlando Woolridge isn't going anywhere. Kareem declined just as much as people said last year, but in most cases, his season last year was certainly not out of line with the rest of his career. With every other team, we've included one chart. This isn't an average team, however, and Kareem was no average player. Following these comments, you'll find each of Kareem's career statistics charted through his career.

In Kareem's last season, the Lakers (57–25) won their eighth consecutive Pacific title as Magic Johnson (more than 20 triple doubles) orchestrated the team to the top of the division heap, 2 games ahead of the surprising Phoenix Suns. If it weren't for a disastrous road start early in the season, the Lakers almost certainly would have had another 60-win season. Byron Scott (19.6 ppg/26.7 pp48, 231 assists) teamed with the Magic man to form one of the top guard combinations in the league and should do the same this year. Jabbar's meager offerings (10.1 ppg, the lowest of his life, grade school included) were barely bolstered by understudy Mychal Thompson (can we really call him an understudy? He played 299 more minutes). They only produced 19.3 points per 48 minutes shared, not good for the center position. Therein lies the problem for the Lakers this year: who's going to plug up the middle? Thompson, at 34, is no spring chicken, and he's not known as a scorer or a stopper. Without a quality-time center, the Lakers are in danger of dropping a rung below teams with dominators up the middle. They won't exactly become a Charlotte or Washington right away, but the difference will be noticeable. Although Magic's had some experience at center, he's needed too much at the point to send him down low—especially since they need help at guard, too. Super-sub Michael Cooper had a measly 16.7 HGS last season, and may be burned out. A. C. Green continues to improve and impress, upping his scoring to 13.3 ppg, fourth on the team, although his scoring rate was only seventh on the team (20.8 pp48). He led the team off the boards, however, and was the only Laker semi-regular to grab 90% as many rebounds as field goal attempts. James Worthy was the team's second best player last year, but with Jabbar gone, he'll have to beef up his rebounding to take some of the pressure off Magic (second in rebounding on the team last year). As the Lakers move for their ninth straight division title with Magic running the show, the big question is: Will they have enough to hold off Phoenix, Seattle, and Golden State? Never count a champion out, whether or not they've won it in the past year.

Kareem Abdul-Jabbar
Career Statistics

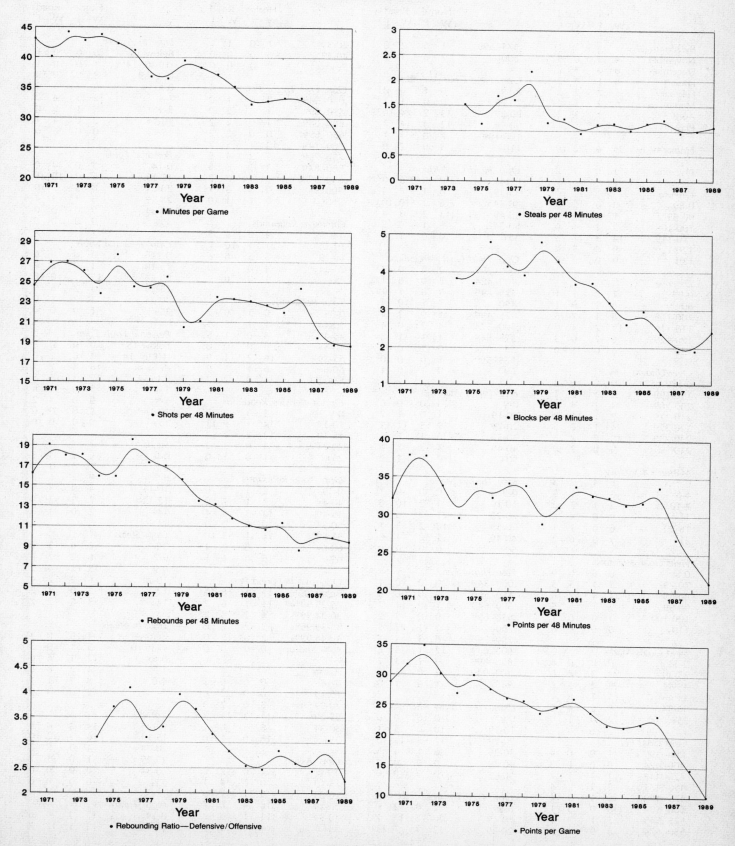

- Minutes per Game
- Steals per 48 Minutes
- Shots per 48 Minutes
- Blocks per 48 Minutes
- Rebounds per 48 Minutes
- Points per 48 Minutes
- Rebounding Ratio—Defensive/Offensive
- Points per Game

Los Angeles Lakers

	Home W	L	Road W	L
By Month				
November	4	0	6	3
December	6	0	3	7
January	8	1	3	2
February	5	2	2	2
March	6	2	5	2
April	6	1	3	3
Playoffs				
Home/Away	35	6	22	19
Overtime	1	0	1	2
Offense				
0-89	0	0	0	3
90-99	1	1	0	7
100-109	2	2	4	6
110-119	14	3	11	3
120-129	9	0	5	0
130-	9	0	2	0
Defense				
0-89	1	0	1	1
90-99	8	1	9	1
100-109	8	1	7	5
110-119	13	2	4	9
120-129	5	2	0	3
130-	0	0	1	0
Over/Under				
0-189	0	0	0	4
190-199	1	1	1	1
200-209	4	1	4	4
210-219	7	1	11	2
220-229	4	1	2	5
230-239	10	2	2	3
240-	9	0	2	0
Margin Of Victory				
0-3	6	4	3	3
4-6	3	1	1	5
7-10	2	1	7	2
11-15	9	0	4	6
16-20	6	0	1	1
21-	9	0	6	2
Field Goal Attempts				
0-69	0	0	0	0
70-79	2	1	5	3
80-89	21	4	12	10
90-99	9	1	5	5
100-109	3	0	0	1
110+	0	0	0	0
Field Goals Made				
0-34	0	0	0	4
35-39	3	3	4	8
40-44	9	2	5	6
45-49	15	1	8	1
50-54	6	0	4	0
55+	2	0	1	0
Field Goal Pct.				
.000-.399	1	0	0	4
.400-.424	0	0	0	3
.425-.449	1	1	1	2
.450-.474	2	3	2	4
.475-.499	5	1	3	4
.500-.524	8	0	3	1
.525-.549	7	1	7	1
.550-.574	8	0	3	0
.575-.599	1	0	2	0
.600-	2	0	1	0
Opp. Field Goal Attempts				
0-69	0	1	0	0
70-79	0	0	1	1
80-89	13	2	4	10
90-99	12	3	14	7
100-109	7	0	1	1
110+	3	0	2	0
Opp. Field Goal Made				
0-34	0	0	0	0
35-39	8	1	8	3
40-44	8	2	10	10
45-49	13	2	3	4
50-54	6	1	0	2
55+	0	0	1	0
Opp. Field Goal Percentage				
.000-.399	2	0	0	1
.400-.424	5	0	8	1
.425-.449	5	0	1	1
.450-.474	7	1	10	4
.475-.499	7	0	2	4
.500-.524	4	2	0	4
.525-.549	4	1	1	2
.550-.574	0	1	0	1
.575-.599	1	0	0	0
.600-	0	1	0	1
Free Throw Attempts				
0-9	0	0	0	0
10-19	1	0	1	2
20-29	9	3	11	11
30-39	20	1	7	6
40-49	5	2	2	0
50+	0	0	1	0
Free Throws Made				
0-9	0	0	0	1
10-19	3	2	10	8
20-29	21	2	6	9
30-39	10	2	5	1
40-49	1	0	1	0
50+	0	0	0	0
Free Throw Pct.				
.000-.549	0	0	0	1
.550-.599	0	0	0	0
.600-.649	1	0	1	2
.650-.699	0	0	3	2
.700-.749	2	1	2	5
.750-.799	8	3	4	1
.800-.849	12	1	5	6
.850-.899	9	1	3	2
.900-.949	2	0	3	0
.950-	1	0	1	0
Opp. Free Throw Attempts				
0-9	0	0	0	0
10-19	10	0	5	1
20-29	17	5	13	10
30-39	8	1	4	8
40-49	0	0	0	0
50+	0	0	0	0
Opp. Free Throws Made				
0-9	2	0	1	0
10-19	20	2	13	7
20-29	12	4	7	11
30-39	1	0	1	1
40-49	0	0	0	0
50+	0	0	0	0
Opp. Free Throw Pct.				
.000-.549	2	0	1	0
.550-.599	1	0	2	0
.600-.649	1	0	2	2
.650-.699	10	0	2	2
.700-.749	10	1	5	2
.750-.799	5	2	4	5
.800-.849	3	1	0	5
.850-.899	3	1	2	2
.900-.949	0	0	3	1
.950-	0	1	1	0
Offensive Rebounds				
0-9	4	0	5	5
10-14	21	1	10	7
15-19	5	5	6	6
20-24	4	0	1	0
25+	1	0	0	1
Total Rebounds				
0-39	0	1	0	2
40-44	1	1	3	1
45-49	8	0	1	5
50-54	0	0	0	0
55-59	16	3	11	9
60-64	6	1	5	0
65-	4	0	2	2
Opp. Offensive Rebounds				
0-9	3	3	2	0
10-14	14	1	9	13
15-19	13	2	7	4
20-24	4	0	3	2
25+	1	0	1	0
Opp. Total Rebounds				
0-39	2	1	1	0
40-44	3	1	7	0
45-49	13	3	6	4
50-54	0	0	0	0
55-59	16	1	5	10
60-64	1	0	2	4
65-	0	0	1	1
Offensive Rebound Pct.				
Below 25%	13	1	8	13
25-29.99%	11	1	6	2
30-34.99%	6	2	4	2
35-39.99%	3	2	2	2
40-44.99%	2	0	2	0
45% and up	0	0	0	0
Assists				
0-14	0	0	0	1
15-19	0	0	2	6
20-24	3	0	2	8
25-29	11	3	11	3
30-34	8	3	6	1
35+	13	0	1	0
Opp. Assists				
0-14	1	0	2	0
15-19	0	0	4	1
20-24	9	1	7	6
25-29	10	4	6	7
30-34	11	1	3	3
35+	4	0	0	2
Edge In Assists				
Below-15	0	0	0	1
-10 to -14	1	0	0	1
-5 to -9	3	0	2	10
0 to -4	6	2	5	4
1-4	12	3	4	2
5-9	5	1	6	0
10-14	8	0	4	1
15-	0	0	1	0
Personal Fouls				
0-14	3	0	4	0
15-19	16	2	10	5
20-24	8	3	5	10
25-29	8	1	3	4
30-34	0	0	0	0
35+	0	0	0	0
Opp. Personal Fouls				
0-14	0	0	0	0
15-19	3	0	6	3
20-24	15	2	9	10
25-29	13	2	6	6
30-34	3	2	1	0
35+	1	0	0	0
Personal Fouls Edge				
Below-15	0	0	0	0
-10 to -14	4	0	2	0
-5 to -9	16	3	7	3
0 to -4	12	3	9	8
1-4	3	0	1	6
5-9	0	0	3	2
10-14	0	0	0	0
15+	0	0	0	0
Steals				
0-5	6	1	3	6
6-7	7	0	3	2
8-9	9	2	6	5
10-11	4	0	3	3
12-13	7	3	3	3
14+	2	0	4	0
Opp. Steals				
0-5	2	0	3	2
6-7	6	2	2	4
8-9	13	2	4	5
10-11	6	2	7	4
12-13	5	0	4	2
14+	3	0	2	2
Edge In Steals				
Below-7	4	0	0	1
-4 to -6	5	1	6	3
0 to -3	12	1	6	6
1-3	4	2	6	8
4-6	8	2	1	1
7-	2	0	3	0
Turnovers				
0-14	14	3	4	6
15-19	16	3	12	10
20-24	4	0	5	2
25-29	1	0	1	1
30-34	0	0	0	0
35+	0	0	0	0
Opp. Turnovers				
0-14	17	3	9	8
15-19	13	1	12	7

	Home W L	Road W L		Home W L	Road W L		Home W L	Road W L		Home W L	Road W L
20-24	4 2	1 4	*Opp. Blocks*			*Three-Pointers Made*			6-8	7 1	7 5
25-29	1 0	0 0	0-2	5 1	5 2	0-2	17 4	10 12	9-11	4 1	3 3
30-34	0 0	0 0	3-4	13 2	5 5	3-5	14 2	8 7	12-14	8 1	3 2
35+	0 0	0 0	5-6	6 2	5 5	6-8	3 0	4 0	15+	2 0	2 0
			7-8	7 0	3 2	9-11	1 0	0 0			
Edge In Turnovers			9-10	3 1	4 3	12-14	0 0	0 0	*Opp. Three-Pointers Made*		
Below-15	0 0	0 0	11+	1 0	0 2	15+	0 0	0 0	0-2	20 4	14 12
-10 to -14	0 1	0 0							3-5	11 1	7 4
-5 to -9	7 0	1 3	*Edge In Blocks*			*Three-Pointers Pct.*			6-8	4 1	1 3
0 to -4	12 1	4 7	Below-7	2 0	1 3	.000-.099	4 3	3 4	9-11	0 0	0 0
1- 4	7 4	9 5	-4 to -6	1 1	3 2	.100-.149	1 0	2 1	12-14	0 0	0 0
5- 9	8 0	8 3	0 to -3	15 3	7 9	.150-.199	4 1	2 3	15+	0 0	0 0
10-14	1 0	0 1	1-3	8 2	6 5	.200-.249	2 0	1 0			
15+	0 0	0 0	4-6	7 0	2 0	.250-.299	3 1	1 5	*Opp. Three-Pointer Pct.*		
			7+	2 0	3 0	.300-.349	6 0	2 1	.000-.099	9 1	7 7
Blocks						.350-.399	0 1	0 2	.100-.149	1 0	2 1
1-2	4 2	6 6	*Three-Pointers Attempted*			.400-.449	7 0	3 2	.150-.199	6 1	2 2
3-4	7 3	5 6	0-2	0 0	0 0	.450-.499	0 0	0 0	.200-.249	3 0	1 0
5-6	11 1	4 5	3-5	7 0	4 1	.500-	8 0	8 1	.250-.299	0 0	1 0
7-8	6 0	4 2	6-8	13 3	11 9				.300-.349	5 0	4 4
9-10	5 0	1 0	9-11	10 2	4 8	*Opp. Three-Point Attempts*			.350-.399	0 0	2 0
11+	2 0	2 0	12-14	4 1	2 1	0-2	5 1	2 2	.400-.449	4 2	1 1
			15+	1 0	1 0	3-5	9 2	5 7	.450-.499	1 1	2 0
									.500-	6 1	0 4

Los Angeles Lakers
1988–89 Power Chart

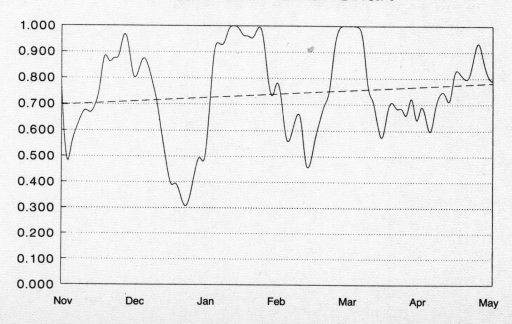

Los Angeles Lakers

	GP	GS	Min	FGM	FGA	FG%	2GM	2GA	2G%	3GM	3GA	3G%	FTM	FTA	FT%	Off	Tot	Ast	PF	Stl	TO	Blk	Pts	HGS
Kareem Abdul-Jabbar	74	74	1695	313	659	0.475	313	656	0.477	0	3	0.000	122	165	0.739	103	231	334	196	38	95	85	748	711
Per GP			22.9	4.2	8.9		4.2	8.9		0.0	0.0		1.6	2.2		1.4	3.1	4.5	2.6	0.5	1.3	1.1	10.1	9.6
Per 48			35.3	8.9	18.7		8.9	18.6		0.0	0.1		3.5	4.7		2.9	6.5	9.5	5.6	1.1	2.7	2.4	21.2	20.1
Tony Campbell	63	2	787	158	345	0.458	156	324	0.481	2	21	0.095	70	83	0.843	53	77	130	108	37	62	6	388	305
Per GP			12.5	2.5	5.5		2.5	5.1		0.0	0.3		1.1	1.3		0.8	1.2	2.1	1.7	0.6	1.0	0.1	6.2	4.8
Per 48			16.4	9.6	21.0		9.5	19.8		0.1	1.3		4.3	5.1		3.2	4.7	7.9	6.6	2.3	3.8	0.4	23.7	18.6
Michael Cooper	80	13	1943	213	494	0.431	133	284	0.468	80	210	0.381	81	93	0.871	33	158	191	186	75	94	32	587	676
Per GP			24.3	2.7	6.2		1.7	3.5		1.0	2.6		1.0	1.2		0.4	2.0	2.4	2.3	0.9	1.2	0.4	7.3	8.4
Per 48			40.5	5.3	12.2		3.3	7.0		2.0	5.2		2.0	2.3		0.8	3.9	4.7	4.6	1.9	2.3	0.8	14.5	16.7
A.C. Green	82	82	2510	401	758	0.529	397	741	0.536	4	17	0.235	282	359	0.786	258	481	739	171	94	117	55	1088	1269
Per GP			30.6	4.9	9.2		4.8	9.0		0.0	0.2		3.4	4.4		3.1	5.9	9.0	2.1	1.1	1.4	0.7	13.3	15.5
Per 48			52.3	7.7	14.5		7.6	14.2		0.1	0.3		5.4	6.9		4.9	9.2	14.1	3.3	1.8	2.2	1.1	20.8	24.3
Earvin Johnson	77	77	2886	579	1137	0.509	520	949	0.548	59	188	0.314	513	563	0.911	111	496	607	172	138	305	22	1730	2244
Per GP			37.5	7.5	14.8		6.8	12.3		0.8	2.4		6.7	7.3		1.4	6.4	7.9	2.2	1.8	4.0	0.3	22.5	29.1
Per 48			60.1	9.6	18.9		8.6	15.8		1.0	3.1		8.5	9.4		1.8	8.2	10.1	2.9	2.3	5.1	0.4	28.8	37.3
Jeff Lamp	37	0	176	27	69	0.391	25	65	0.385	2	4	0.500	4	5	0.800	6	28	34	27	8	16	2	60	49
Per GP			4.8	0.7	1.9		0.7	1.8		0.1	0.1		0.1	0.1		0.2	0.8	0.9	0.7	0.2	0.4	0.1	1.6	1.3
Per 48			3.7	7.4	18.8		6.8	17.7		0.5	1.1		1.1	1.4		1.6	7.6	9.3	7.4	2.2	4.4	0.5	16.4	13.4
Mark McNamara	39	0	318	32	64	0.500	32	64	0.500	0	0	0.000	49	78	0.628	38	62	100	51	4	24	3	113	137
Per GP			8.2	0.8	1.6		0.8	1.6		0.0	0.0		1.3	2.0		1.0	1.6	2.6	1.3	0.1	0.6	0.1	2.9	3.5
Per 48			6.6	4.8	9.7		4.8	9.7		0.0	0.0		7.4	11.8		5.7	9.4	15.1	7.7	0.6	3.6	0.5	17.1	20.7
David Rivers	47	0	440	49	122	0.402	48	117	0.410	1	5	0.200	35	42	0.833	13	30	43	50	23	61	9	134	179
Per GP			9.4	1.0	2.6		1.0	2.5		0.0	0.1		0.7	0.9		0.3	0.6	0.9	1.1	0.5	1.3	0.2	2.9	3.8
Per 48			9.2	5.3	13.3		5.2	12.8		0.1	0.5		3.8	4.6		1.4	3.3	4.7	5.5	2.5	6.7	1.0	14.6	19.5
Byron Scott	74	73	2605	588	1198	0.491	511	1005	0.508	77	193	0.399	195	226	0.863	72	230	302	181	111	157	27	1448	1083
Per GP			35.2	7.9	16.2		6.9	13.6		1.0	2.6		2.6	3.1		1.0	3.1	4.1	2.4	1.5	2.1	0.4	19.6	14.6
Per 48			54.3	10.8	22.1		9.4	18.5		1.4	3.6		3.6	4.2		1.3	4.2	5.6	3.3	2.0	2.9	0.5	26.7	20.0
Mychal Thompson	80	8	1994	291	521	0.559	291	520	0.560	0	1	0.000	156	230	0.678	157	310	467	224	58	97	59	738	825
Per GP			24.9	3.6	6.5		3.6	6.5		0.0	0.0		1.9	2.9		2.0	3.9	5.8	2.8	0.7	1.2	0.7	9.2	10.3
Per 48			41.5	7.0	12.5		7.0	12.5		0.0	0.0		3.8	5.5		3.8	7.5	11.2	5.4	1.4	2.3	1.4	17.8	19.9
Orlando Woolridge	74	0	1491	231	494	0.468	231	493	0.469	0	1	0.000	253	343	0.738	81	189	270	130	30	103	65	715	679
Per GP			20.1	3.1	6.7		3.1	6.7		0.0	0.0		3.4	4.6		1.1	2.6	3.6	1.8	0.4	1.4	0.9	9.7	9.2
Per 48			31.1	7.4	15.9		7.4	15.9		0.0	0.0		8.1	11.0		2.6	6.1	8.7	4.2	1.0	3.3	2.1	23.0	21.9
James Worthy	81	81	2960	702	1282	0.548	700	1259	0.556	2	23	0.087	251	321	0.782	169	320	489	175	108	182	56	1657	1518
Per GP			36.5	8.7	15.8		8.6	15.5		0.0	0.3		3.1	4.0		2.1	4.0	6.0	2.2	1.3	2.2	0.7	20.5	18.7
Per 48			61.7	11.4	20.8		11.4	20.4		0.0	0.4		4.1	5.2		2.7	5.2	7.9	2.8	1.8	3.0	0.9	26.9	24.6

MIAMI HEAT

Can anyone here play this game? In Miami, the heart of the Sunshine State, the Heat never quite saw the light at the end of the tunnel and finished up a dismal 15–67 with a ragtag collection of players. Perhaps their season was summed up when Armon Gilliam strode into their locker room in the last week of the season to lay a beating on Pearl Washington. Can you see him getting past the door in, say, Detroit or Los Angeles? He'd be eating his teeth for lunch if he tried such a stunt.

Cheer up, Heat fans. The good news is the Heat were no worse than the Mavericks were in their first season. The bad news is Dallas didn't have to compete against three other expansion teams for forthcoming help, and if they finished last, they were assured the first pick (unlike the current draft lottery situation). You knew they were going to be bad. They didn't disappoint, finishing last in the league in scoring and field goal accuracy. The way they were manhandled by opponents, by the time they limped to the free throw line, they were too bruised and battered to take advantage of gifts, and finished last in free throw accuracy as well. When you look at the final numbers, you realize just how bad an offensive team this was, very likely the worst ever. The Heat have no bona fide scorer, rebounder, or bench. Rookie guard Kevin Edwards led the team in scoring with a gaudy 13.8 ppg, the lowest team high in the NBA since the introduction of the 24-second clock in 1954–55. Rony Seikaly is what is known as a short 6'11", and his 549 rebounds and 10.9 ppg bore out that assessment. He couldn't even start consistently for an expansion team.

The Heat's players were in a unique situation–as they lost and lost, the media pressure increased. Fans and writers alike seemed to want them to lose more games. The dark side of human nature is drawn to badness, and everybody likes to see the worst team ever in a sport. If nothing else, it makes good copy. The Heat were really no worse than the Clippers (without Manning), but they had the bad fortune to have their dry spell from the start of the season. Fortunately for the good city of Miami, the Heat pulled safely out of reach of the 1973 Sixers with quite a few games left to go, so that even if more games had been canceled on account of riots, they'd be okay.

During their long streak, however, they really were an awful team. Despite Ron Rothstein's claims that the team could have pulled out five or six games in the stretch, those games were products of them being closer than they should have been, not

Miami Heat

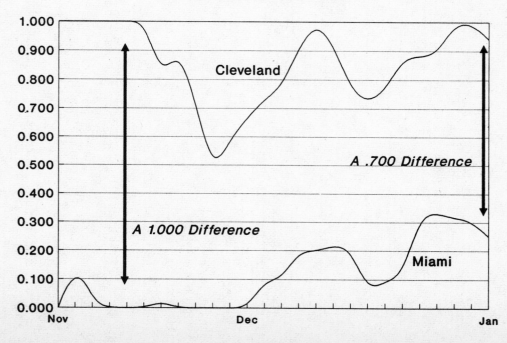

victims of hard luck. When they lost by six, it meant they were overplaying and normally would have lost by 12, not the other way around. Over the course of the losing streak, their scoring ratio projected them to be a .000 team. Perfection. To further dramatize how poorly they played, just look at the power charts for the first twenty games of Miami's season, compared with Cleveland's for the same period.

Last season the Heat were young (average 26.5 years of age) and inexperienced. This season, expect to see a big change. They'll be young, inexperienced, and playing in the Atlantic Division. After a couple more years of shuffling around, Miami and Orlando will end up there for good in 1991, feuling what could become one of the NBA's best natural rivalries. (Warning: compulsory "Heat" joke coming up.) If the team is going to catch fire,

er, spark, this year, look for improvement in the team's nucleus of Kevin Edwards, 6'8" forward Grant Long, Seikaly, and 6'7" Billy Thompson. Of course, it would help if someone could hit over half their field goals. The only bright light from the field was rookie guard Jon Sundvold, who led the league in three-point accuracy with .522 (48 for 92) after pouting that he should have been invited to the All-Star festivities to shoot them. Considering they found room for Russians, he was right. Billy Thompson was an adequate shot blocker, knocking back 1.33 shots a game to rank 15th best in the league. But don't expect a miracle here as happened in Milwaukee all those years ago. Seikaly and Edwards are nowhere near Jabbar and Robertson, and you only see luck like that once in a lifetime.

Miami Heat

	Home W	Home L	Road W	Road L
By Month				
November	0	6	0	6
December	2	6	1	6
January	1	5	0	8
February	4	5	0	4
March	4	4	1	7
April	1	3	1	7
Playoffs				
Home/Away	12	29	3	38
Overtime	3	2	0	0
Offense				
0-89	0	4	1	13
90-99	0	11	1	14
100-109	7	11	1	9
110-119	3	3	0	1
120-129	1	0	0	1
130-	1	0	0	0
Defense				
0-89	2	1	2	0
90-99	2	2	0	8
100-109	5	13	1	8
110-119	2	5	0	18
120-129	0	6	0	3
130-	1	2	0	1
Over/Under				
0-189	2	2	2	10
190-199	0	5	0	5
200-209	3	10	0	7
210-219	3	3	1	8
220-229	1	5	0	7
230-239	2	2	0	0
240-	1	2	0	1
Margin Of Victory				
0-3	6	3	2	1
4-6	2	6	1	6
7-10	1	7	0	6
11-15	0	3	0	4
16-20	1	3	0	7
21-	2	7	0	14
Field Goal Attempts				
0-69	0	1	0	0
70-79	1	2	2	8
80-89	7	13	1	16
90-99	4	11	0	12
100-109	0	2	0	2
110+	0	0	0	0
Field Goals Made				
0-34	0	1	0	7
35-39	3	15	2	18
40-44	6	8	1	9
45-49	1	5	0	3
50-54	2	0	0	1
55+	0	0	0	0
Field Goal Pct.				
.000-.399	0	6	0	7
.400-.424	1	3	0	12
.425-.449	0	5	0	5
.450-.474	3	5	1	7
.475-.499	4	3	2	1
.500-.524	2	4	0	2
.525-.549	0	3	0	3
.550-.574	1	0	0	1

	Home W	Home L	Road W	Road L
.575-.599	1	0	0	0
.600-	0	0	0	0
Opp. Field Goal Attempts				
0-69	1	1	0	1
70-79	0	9	2	8
80-89	4	11	0	23
90-99	6	7	1	5
100-109	1	1	0	1
110+	0	0	0	0
Opp. Field Goal Made				
0-34	2	3	3	3
35-39	3	7	0	8
40-44	6	9	0	16
45-49	0	4	0	9
50-54	0	5	0	2
55+	1	1	0	0
Opp. Field Goal Percentage				
.000-.399	2	1	1	0
.400-.424	2	0	0	1
.425-.449	2	3	1	10
.450-.474	1	5	1	5
.475-.499	4	6	0	6
.500-.524	0	5	0	4
.525-.549	1	4	0	5
.550-.574	0	2	0	4
.575-.599	0	1	0	1
.600-	0	2	0	2
Free Throw Attempts				
0-9	0	0	0	1
10-19	1	7	0	8
20-29	4	16	2	20
30-39	3	6	1	7
40-49	3	0	0	2
50+	1	0	0	0
Free Throws Made				
0-9	0	3	0	4
10-19	3	17	2	20
20-29	6	9	1	14
30-39	3	0	0	0
40-49	0	0	0	0
50+	0	0	0	0
Free Throw Pct.				
.000-.549	0	3	0	6
.550-.599	0	1	0	2
.600-.649	1	2	0	2
.650-.699	1	6	0	14
.700-.749	5	9	1	5
.750-.799	3	6	1	4
.800-.849	1	1	1	4
.850-.899	1	1	0	1
.900-.949	0	0	0	0
.950-	0	0	0	0
Opp. Free Throw Attempts				
0-9	0	0	0	0
10-19	1	1	0	2
20-29	4	11	2	11
30-39	6	14	0	16
40-49	1	3	1	8
50+	0	0	0	1
Opp. Free Throws Made				
0-9	0	0	0	0
10-19	5	4	1	8
20-29	6	20	1	22

	Home W	Home L	Road W	Road L
30-39	1	5	1	8
40-49	0	0	0	0
50+	0	0	0	0
Opp. Free Throw Pct.				
.000-.549	0	0	0	0
.550-.599	1	0	0	0
.600-.649	1	1	0	4
.650-.699	2	3	0	2
.700-.749	2	3	1	8
.750-.799	3	7	1	10
.800-.849	3	7	1	9
.850-.899	0	5	0	4
.900-.949	0	3	0	0
.950-	0	0	0	1
Offensive Rebounds				
0-9	1	2	1	3
10-14	2	6	1	13
15-19	8	14	1	14
20-24	1	5	0	7
25+	0	2	0	1
Total Rebounds				
0-39	0	1	0	2
40-44	1	2	1	4
45-49	1	8	1	7
50-54	0	0	0	0
55-59	8	14	1	17
60-64	1	2	0	6
65-	1	2	0	2
Opp. Offensive Rebounds				
0-9	0	3	0	0
10-14	4	16	2	21
15-19	7	7	1	16
20-24	1	3	0	1
25+	0	0	0	0
Opp. Total Rebounds				
0-39	0	1	0	0
40-44	0	3	0	5
45-49	2	9	0	4
50-54	0	0	0	0
55-59	9	12	3	20
60-64	0	3	0	6
65-	1	1	0	3
Offensive Rebound Pct.				
Below 25%	1	6	1	11
25-29.99%	4	5	2	14
30-34.99%	6	11	0	6
35-39.99%	0	3	0	7
40-44.99%	1	4	0	0
45% and up	0	0	0	0
Assists				
0-14	0	1	0	1
15-19	0	2	0	11
20-24	3	14	1	12
25-29	6	10	2	12
30-34	0	2	0	2
35+	3	0	0	0
Opp. Assists				
0-14	1	1	0	0
15-19	2	6	0	3
20-24	6	10	2	8
25-29	2	8	0	17
30-34	0	2	1	9
35+	1	2	0	1

	Home W	Home L	Road W	Road L
Edge In Assists				
Below -15	0	0	0	2
-10 to -14	0	2	0	7
-5 to -9	0	2	0	9
0 to -4	2	11	2	12
1-4	3	7	0	5
5-9	3	4	1	3
10-14	4	3	0	0
15-	0	0	0	0
Personal Fouls				
0-14	0	0	0	0
15-19	0	3	1	2
20-24	6	11	1	12
25-29	4	12	0	12
30-34	2	2	1	10
35+	0	1	0	2
Opp. Personal Fouls				
0-14	0	4	0	4
15-19	1	4	1	10
20-24	4	16	1	11
25-29	3	3	1	12
30-34	3	2	0	0
35+	1	0	0	1
Personal Fouls Edge				
Below -15	0	0	0	0
-10 to -14	0	0	0	0
-5 to -9	3	3	1	1
0 to -4	7	2	0	6
1-4	1	14	1	9
5-9	1	5	1	14
10-14	0	5	0	6
15+	0	0	0	2
Steals				
0-5	2	5	0	5
6-7	0	10	0	7
8-9	2	10	1	9
10-11	2	1	0	9
12-13	4	2	1	2
14+	2	1	1	6
Opp. Steals				
0-5	0	2	1	2
6-7	3	4	0	4
8-9	1	4	2	5
10-11	3	8	0	8
12-13	1	6	0	6
14+	4	5	0	13
Edge In Steals				
Below -7	0	6	0	12
-4 to -6	4	9	0	4
0 to -3	2	9	0	9
1-3	5	2	1	8
4-6	0	3	2	4
7-	1	0	0	1
Turnovers				
0-14	1	2	0	5
15-19	4	9	3	9
20-24	4	15	0	12
25-29	3	3	0	7
30-34	0	0	0	4
35+	0	0	0	1
Opp. Turnovers				
0-14	2	7	0	9
15-19	1	13	1	15

	Home W	L	Road W	L
20-24	5	7	1	11
25-29	4	2	1	2
30-34	0	0	0	1
35+	0	0	0	0

Edge In Turnovers

	Home W	L	Road W	L
Below -15	0	0	0	0
-10 to -14	0	0	1	1
-5 to -9	2	3	0	4
0 to -4	5	4	2	10
1-4	4	13	0	8
5-9	1	8	0	6
10-14	0	1	0	6
15+	0	0	0	3

Blocks

	Home W	L	Road W	L
1-2	1	3	0	6
3-4	2	13	0	15
5-6	3	5	0	11
7-8	2	6	3	4
9-10	3	2	0	2
11+	1	0	0	0

Opp. Blocks

	Home W	L	Road W	L
0-2	0	2	0	4
3-4	2	4	1	1
5-6	3	9	1	13
7-8	4	6	1	12
9-10	1	6	0	5
11+	2	2	0	3

Edge In Blocks

	Home W	L	Road W	L
Below -7	0	2	0	8
-4 to -6	1	7	0	7
0 to -3	8	13	1	14
1-3	3	6	1	8
4-6	0	1	1	0
7+	0	0	0	1

Three-Pointers Attempted

	Home W	L	Road W	L
0-2	7	5	2	13
3-5	3	17	1	17
6-8	2	6	0	8
9-11	0	1	0	0
12-14	0	0	0	0
15+	0	0	0	0

Three-Pointers Made

	Home W	L	Road W	L
0-2	10	24	3	33
3-5	2	5	0	5
6-8	0	0	0	0
9-11	0	0	0	0
12-14	0	0	0	0
15+	0	0	0	0

Three-Pointers Pct.

	Home W	L	Road W	L
.000-.099	6	10	2	16
.100-.149	0	1	0	1
.150-.199	0	0	0	0
.200-.249	0	0	0	0
.250-.299	0	1	0	3
.300-.349	3	9	0	5
.350-.399	0	0	0	1
.400-.449	0	0	0	0
.450-.499	0	0	0	0
.500-	3	8	1	12

Opp. Three-Point Attempts

	Home W	L	Road W	L
0-2	1	8	1	7
3-5	5	8	1	18

	Home W	L	Road W	L
6-8	4	10	0	7
9-11	0	2	1	4
12-14	2	1	0	1
15+	0	0	0	1

Opp. Three-Pointers Made

	Home W	L	Road W	L
0-2	8	18	2	26
3-5	4	10	1	10
6-8	0	0	0	2
9-11	0	1	0	0
12-14	0	0	0	0
15+	0	0	0	0

Opp. Three-Pointer Pct.

	Home W	L	Road W	L
.000-.099	5	11	3	18
.100-.149	0	0	0	0
.150-.199	1	1	0	0
.200-.249	1	0	0	0
.250-.299	0	1	0	2
.300-.349	2	6	0	3
.350-.399	1	0	0	3
.400-.449	1	5	0	5
.450-.499	0	0	0	1
.500-	1	5	0	6

Miami Heat
1988–89 Power Chart

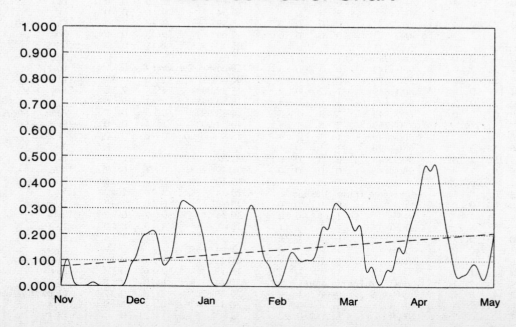

Miami Heat

	GP	GS	Min	FGM	FGA	FG%	2GM	2GA	2G%	3GM	3GA	3G%	FTM	FTA	FT%	Off	Tot	Ast	PF	Stl	TO	Blk	Pts	HGS
Pat Cummings	53	28	1096	197	394	0.500	197	392	0.503	0	2	0.000	72	97	0.742	84	197	281	160	29	111	18	466	412
Per GP				20.7	3.7	7.4		3.7	7.4		0.0	0.0		1.4	1.8		1.6	3.7	5.3	3.0	0.5	2.1	0.3	8.8	7.8
Per 48				22.8	8.6	17.3		8.6	17.2		0.0	0.1		3.2	4.2		3.7	8.6	12.3	7.0	1.3	4.9	0.8	20.4	18.0
Kevin Edwards	79	62	2349	470	1105	0.425	460	1068	0.431	10	37	0.270	144	193	0.746	85	177	262	154	138	243	26	1094	911
Per GP				29.7	5.9	14.0		5.8	13.5		0.1	0.5		1.8	2.4		1.1	2.2	3.3	1.9	1.7	3.1	0.3	13.8	11.5
Per 48				48.9	9.6	22.6		9.4	21.8		0.2	0.8		2.9	3.9		1.7	3.6	5.4	3.1	2.8	5.0	0.5	22.4	18.6
Sylvester Gray	55	15	1220	167	398	0.420	166	394	0.421	1	4	0.250	105	156	0.673	117	169	286	144	36	102	24	440	489
Per GP				22.2	3.0	7.2		3.0	7.2		0.0	0.1		1.9	2.8		2.1	3.1	5.2	2.6	0.7	1.9	0.4	8.0	8.9
Per 48				25.4	6.6	15.7		6.5	15.5		0.0	0.2		4.1	6.1		4.6	6.6	11.3	5.7	1.4	4.0	0.9	17.3	19.2
Scott Hastings	75	6	1206	143	328	0.436	134	300	0.447	9	28	0.321	90	107	0.841	72	159	231	203	32	68	41	385	414
Per GP				16.1	1.9	4.4		1.8	4.0		0.1	0.4		1.2	1.4		1.0	2.1	3.1	2.7	0.4	0.9	0.5	5.1	5.5
Per 48				25.1	5.7	13.1		5.3	11.9		0.4	1.1		3.6	4.3		2.9	6.3	9.2	8.1	1.3	2.7	1.6	15.3	16.5
Grant Long	82	73	2431	336	692	0.486	336	687	0.489	0	5	0.000	305	406	0.751	240	306	546	337	122	201	48	977	1096
Per GP				29.6	4.1	8.4		4.1	8.4		0.0	0.1		3.7	5.0		2.9	3.7	6.7	4.1	1.5	2.5	0.6	11.9	13.4
Per 48				50.6	6.6	13.7		6.6	13.6		0.0	0.1		6.0	8.0		4.7	6.0	10.8	6.7	2.4	4.0	0.9	19.3	21.6
Todd Mitchell	22	0	320	41	88	0.466	41	88	0.466	0	0	0.000	36	60	0.600	17	30	47	49	15	29	2	118	109
Per GP				14.5	1.9	4.0		1.9	4.0		0.0	0.0		1.6	2.7		0.8	1.4	2.1	2.2	0.7	1.3	0.1	5.4	5.0
Per 48				6.7	6.1	13.2		6.1	13.2		0.0	0.0		5.4	9.0		2.5	4.5	7.0	7.3	2.3	4.3	0.3	17.7	16.3
Craig Neal	32	0	341	34	88	0.386	26	63	0.413	8	25	0.320	13	21	0.619	4	14	18	46	15	40	4	89	113
Per GP				10.7	1.1	2.8		0.8	2.0		0.3	0.8		0.4	0.7		0.1	0.4	0.6	1.4	0.5	1.3	0.1	2.8	3.5
Per 48				7.1	4.8	12.4		3.7	8.9		1.1	3.5		1.8	3.0		0.6	2.0	2.5	6.5	2.1	5.6	0.6	12.5	15.9
Dave Popson	7	0	38	5	15	0.333	5	15	0.333	0	0	0.000	1	2	0.500	7	4	11	8	0	4	1	11	10
Per GP				5.4	0.7	2.1		0.7	2.1		0.0	0.0		0.1	0.3		1.0	0.6	1.6	1.1	0.0	0.6	0.1	1.6	1.4
Per 48				0.8	6.3	18.9		6.3	18.9		0.0	0.0		1.3	2.5		8.8	5.1	13.9	10.1	0.0	5.1	1.3	13.9	12.6
Ron Seikaly	78	62	1962	333	744	0.448	332	740	0.449	1	4	0.250	181	354	0.511	204	345	549	258	46	199	96	848	823
Per GP				25.2	4.3	9.5		4.3	9.5		0.0	0.1		2.3	4.5		2.6	4.4	7.0	3.3	0.6	2.6	1.2	10.9	10.6
Per 48				40.9	8.1	18.2		8.1	18.1		0.0	0.1		4.4	8.7		5.0	8.4	13.4	6.3	1.1	4.9	2.3	20.7	20.1
John Shasky	65	4	944	121	248	0.488	121	246	0.492	0	2	0.000	115	167	0.689	96	136	232	94	14	46	13	357	375
Per GP				14.5	1.9	3.8		1.9	3.8		0.0	0.0		1.8	2.6		1.5	2.1	3.6	1.4	0.2	0.7	0.2	5.5	5.8
Per 48				19.7	6.2	12.6		6.2	12.5		0.0	0.1		5.8	8.5		4.9	6.9	11.8	4.8	0.7	2.3	0.7	18.2	19.1
Rory Sparrow	80	79	2613	444	982	0.452	426	908	0.469	18	74	0.243	94	107	0.879	55	161	216	168	104	201	17	1000	916
Per GP				32.7	5.5	-12.3		5.3	11.3		0.2	0.9		1.2	1.3		0.7	2.0	2.7	2.1	1.3	2.5	0.2	12.5	11.4
Per 48				54.4	8.2	18.0		7.8	16.7		0.3	1.4		1.7	2.0		1.0	3.0	4.0	3.1	1.9	3.7	0.3	18.4	16.8
Jon Sundvold	68	8	1338	307	675	0.455	259	583	0.444	48	92	0.522	47	57	0.825	18	69	87	78	27	85	1	709	403
Per GP				19.7	4.5	9.9		3.8	8.6		0.7	1.4		0.7	0.8		0.3	1.0	1.3	1.1	0.4	1.3	0.0	10.4	5.9
Per 48				27.9	11.0	24.2		9.3	20.9		1.7	3.3		1.7	2.0		0.6	2.5	3.1	2.8	1.0	3.0	0.0	25.4	14.5
Anthony Taylor	21	7	368	60	151	0.397	60	149	0.403	0	2	0.000	24	32	0.750	11	23	34	37	22	20	5	144	130
Per GP				17.5	2.9	7.2		2.9	7.1		0.0	0.1		1.1	1.5		0.5	1.1	1.6	1.8	1.0	1.0	0.2	6.9	6.2
Per 48				7.7	7.8	19.7		7.8	19.4		0.0	0.3		3.1	4.2		1.4	3.0	4.4	4.8	2.9	2.6	0.7	18.8	17.0
Bill Thompson	79	58	2272	349	716	0.487	349	713	0.489	0	3	0.000	156	224	0.696	241	331	572	260	56	189	105	854	1023
Per GP				28.8	4.4	9.1		4.4	9.0		0.0	0.0		2.0	2.8		3.1	4.2	7.2	3.3	0.7	2.4	1.3	10.8	12.9
Per 48				47.3	7.4	15.1		7.4	15.1		0.0	0.1		3.3	4.7		5.1	7.0	12.1	5.5	1.2	4.0	2.2	18.0	21.6
Kelvin Upshaw	9	0	144	26	63	0.413	25	58	0.431	1	5	0.200	4	6	0.667	4	9	13	18	7	13	0	57	43
Per GP				16.0	2.9	7.0		2.8	6.4		0.1	0.6		0.4	0.7		0.4	1.0	1.4	2.0	0.8	1.4	0.0	6.3	4.8
Per 48				3.0	8.7	21.0		8.3	19.3		0.3	1.7		1.3	2.0		1.3	3.0	4.3	6.0	2.3	4.3	0.0	19.0	14.3
Dwayne Washington	54	8	1070	164	382	0.429	163	368	0.443	1	14	0.071	82	104	0.788	49	74	123	101	73	122	4	411	466
Per GP				19.8	3.0	7.1		3.0	6.8		0.0	0.3		1.5	1.9		0.9	1.4	2.3	1.9	1.4	2.3	0.1	7.6	8.6
Per 48				22.3	7.4	17.1		7.3	16.5		0.0	0.6		3.7	4.7		2.2	3.3	5.5	4.5	3.3	5.5	0.2	18.4	20.9
Clint Wheeler	8	0	143	24	42	0.571	24	42	0.571	0	0	0.000	8	10	0.800	5	7	12	9	8	6	0	56	63
Per GP				17.9	3.0	5.3		3.0	5.3		0.0	0.0		1.0	1.3		0.6	0.9	1.5	1.1	1.0	0.8	0.0	7.0	7.9
Per 48				3.0	8.1	14.1		8.1	14.1		0.0	0.0		2.7	3.4		1.7	2.3	4.0	3.0	2.7	2.0	0.0	18.8	21.1

MILWAUKEE BUCKS

Once the Central Division's perennial powerhouse, the proud Bucks have given way to the younger upstarts in Detroit, Cleveland, and Chicago. Although they notched their tenth straight winning season last year (49–33), for the second year they failed to win 50 games. One thing maturity has in its favor is that it helps develop a sense of appreciation. Last season the Bucks set an NBA record for team free-throw shooting. Their 82.073% accuracy broke a 14-year record previously held by Kansas City–Omaha (82.054%).

Things didn't break evenly for the Bucks all year. They were involved in 8 close games; they lost 7 of them. They outscored their opponents on average 108.9–105.3, and finished with a 49–33 record, but drew Atlanta in the first round, a team they had gone 0–6 against during the season. They disposed of the Hawks, then drew the Pistons in the next round. Their scoring margin was 6th best in the league; their won-lost record was 8th.

Super forward Terry Cummings returned to the form of old, leading the team in minutes (2824), points scored (1829) as well as points per 48 minutes (31.1), rebounds (650), and blocks (72). All, save rebounding, were personal bests for him.

He's taking Rese stats now to San Antonio. Sidney Moncrief, 32, continued his accelerated aging process, missing 20 games and finishing up with only 22.6 pp48, the lowest of his career. Once a perennial All-Star, he's been hobbled by injuries recently, and his best days are probably behind him. At season's end the Bucks refused to re-sign him and he'll be wearing a new uniform in the '90s. Jack Sikma, at 34, is the least prototypical of any center in the league. Although he slumped to fewer than 20 points per 48 minutes, he roamed out in the high-post area, making him the only real three-point threat amongst centers (and don't tell us how swell Manute Bol was!). Sikma tossed up 215 of them, as he appeared to be undergoing mid-life crisis. Center or forward? Center or forward? He improved his overall game by over 53 points by taking threes, although most coaches would just as soon not have their 7' center cop this honor. Paul Pressey, although he scored 12.1 ppg, was an effective big guard, leading the team in assists and rating the second highest HGS (23.1) on the team. Randy Breuer was like the proverbial 7'4" tree that fell in the forest—no one heard from him all year. He only scored 4.2 ppg, but that was deceiving, since he

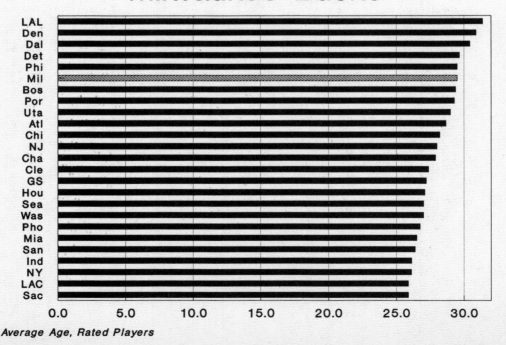

Average Age, Rated Players

only got 10.7 minutes per GP to gather points. In actuality, he scored 18.7 pp48, higher than Pressey managed in much greater action.

Guard Ricky Pierce only started four games, yet was the second most productive scorer for the Bucks last season, with 17.6 ppg/30.4 pp48. He was the third most productive player overall, with a 23.0 HGS. Larry Krystkowiak, is a 6'10" forward-center workhorse, and at 26 years old, he promises to improve in the next two or three years. Still, he has room to improve. That is, if he is able to rehab his damaged knee. Although a solid addition, his 19.9

HGS was only tenth of the seventeen players who put on a Buck uniform last year. The team, as a whole, is a mix of players on their way out and others on the way in. They include Alvin Robertson and Greg Anderson from the Spurs, and hopefully oft-injured Jeff Grayer. If the latter come through, Milwaukee could fend off a collapse for another season or two. By then, if they find some rebounding and young legs, they might be in a position to keep their heads above water. If not, well, they could be headed for their first losing season in a long, long time.

Milwaukee Bucks

By Month

	Home W	L	Road W	L
November	5	2	1	3
December	5	3	4	3
January	6	0	6	3
February	5	1	2	3
March	8	1	2	6
April	2	3	3	5
Playoffs				
Home/Away	31	10	18	23
Overtime	1	0	1	0

Offense

	Home W	L	Road W	L
0-89	0	0	0	1
90-99	2	6	0	8
100-109	7	2	7	10
110-119	11	2	8	4
120-129	10	0	3	0
130-	1	0	0	0

Defense

	Home W	L	Road W	L
0-89	3	0	1	0
90-99	8	1	6	1
100-109	16	5	6	6
110-119	4	4	4	10
120-129	0	0	1	6
130-	0	0	0	0

Over/Under

	Home W	L	Road W	L
0-189	2	0	1	0
190-199	5	2	2	5
200-209	3	4	5	3
210-219	7	2	2	5
220-229	9	1	5	6
230-239	4	1	1	4
240-	1	0	2	0

Margin Of Victory

	Home W	L	Road W	L
0-3	1	2	0	5
4-6	1	2	5	4
7-10	11	3	4	2
11-15	8	2	4	5
16-20	5	1	4	4
21-	5	0	1	3

Field Goal Attempts

	Home W	L	Road W	L
0-69	0	0	1	1
70-79	2	3	1	3
80-89	12	1	9	12
90-99	17	5	7	7
100-109	0	1	0	0
110+	0	0	0	0

Field Goals Made

	Home W	L	Road W	L
0-34	0	2	0	3
35-39	6	7	0	9
40-44	13	1	11	9
45-49	10	0	6	2
50-54	1	0	1	0
55+	1	0	0	0

Field Goal Pct.

	Home W	L	Road W	L
.000-.399	3	3	0	2
.400-.424	0	2	0	6
.425-.449	6	2	2	4
.450-.474	4	3	3	7
.475-.499	5	0	4	1
.500-.524	4	0	3	2
.525-.549	4	0	3	1
.550-.574	4	0	1	0
.575-.599	0	0	1	0
.600-	1	0	1	0

Opp. Field Goal Attempts

	Home W	L	Road W	L
0-69	0	1	0	0
70-79	7	3	3	7
80-89	16	6	8	13
90-99	6	0	5	3
100-109	2	0	2	0
110+	0	0	0	0

Opp. Field Goal Made

	Home W	L	Road W	L
0-34	5	2	3	1
35-39	15	1	5	4
40-44	6	6	8	11
45-49	5	1	2	4
50-54	0	0	0	3
55+	0	0	0	0

Opp. Field Goal Percentage

	Home W	L	Road W	L
.000-.399	4	1	5	1
.400-.424	5	0	3	0
.425-.449	6	0	3	1
.450-.474	7	0	2	0
.475-.499	3	2	2	3
.500-.524	1	3	2	6
.525-.549	3	2	1	5
.550-.574	1	0	0	1
.575-.599	1	1	0	4
.600-	0	1	0	2

Free Throw Attempts

	Home W	L	Road W	L
0-9	0	0	0	0
10-19	5	0	2	2
20-29	10	6	8	12
30-39	11	4	6	7
40-49	5	0	2	2
50+	0	0	0	0

Free Throws Made

	Home W	L	Road W	L
0-9	0	0	0	1
10-19	7	2	6	8
20-29	14	8	8	10
30-39	10	0	4	4
40-49	0	0	0	0
50+	0	0	0	0

Free Throw Pct.

	Home W	L	Road W	L
.000-.549	0	0	0	1
.550-.599	0	0	0	0
.600-.649	0	0	0	0
.650-.699	0	0	1	3
.700-.749	3	1	1	1
.750-.799	5	1	6	5
.800-.849	8	6	6	6
.850-.899	6	1	3	2
.900-.949	8	1	1	5
.950-	1	0	0	0

Opp. Free Throw Attempts

	Home W	L	Road W	L
0-9	0	0	0	0
10-19	4	0	2	2
20-29	14	4	9	8
30-39	12	5	7	10
40-49	1	1	0	3
50+	0	0	0	0

Opp. Free Throws Made

	Home W	L	Road W	L
0-9	0	0	0	0
10-19	14	2	7	7
20-29	16	4	8	8
30-39	1	4	3	8
40-49	0	0	0	0
50+	0	0	0	0

Opp. Free Throw Pct.

	Home W	L	Road W	L
.000-.549	0	0	0	0
.550-.599	0	0	0	0
.600-.649	0	0	2	2
.650-.699	6	1	4	1
.700-.749	7	1	3	2
.750-.799	8	2	1	8
.800-.849	2	4	5	5
.850-.899	8	1	2	3
.900-.949	0	1	1	2
.950-	0	0	0	0

Offensive Rebounds

	Home W	L	Road W	L
0-9	4	0	5	2
10-14	14	5	8	10
15-19	10	3	4	9
20-24	3	2	1	0
25+	0	0	0	2

Total Rebounds

	Home W	L	Road W	L
0-39	0	0	0	3
40-44	2	0	4	4
45-49	7	6	5	8
50-54	0	0	0	0
55-59	17	4	5	8
60-64	3	0	3	0
65-	2	0	1	0

Opp. Offensive Rebounds

	Home W	L	Road W	L
0-9	5	1	0	2
10-14	18	8	6	13
15-19	8	1	10	6
20-24	0	0	2	1
25+	0	0	0	1

Opp. Total Rebounds

	Home W	L	Road W	L
0-39	3	1	1	0
40-44	3	0	1	0
45-49	10	3	7	9
50-54	0	0	0	0
55-59	13	5	7	12
60-64	2	1	2	2
65-	0	0	0	0

Offensive Rebound Pct.

	Home W	L	Road W	L
Below 25%	12	3	10	12
25-29.99%	8	2	2	5
30-34.99%	9	4	4	3
35-39.99%	2	1	2	1
40-44.99%	0	0	0	2
45% and up	0	0	0	0

Assists

	Home W	L	Road W	L
0-14	0	0	0	0
15-19	0	1	1	7
20-24	6	5	9	9
25-29	13	4	5	7
30-34	10	0	3	0
35+	2	0	0	0

Opp. Assists

	Home W	L	Road W	L
0-14	0	0	1	0
15-19	3	2	4	1
20-24	12	2	8	4
25-29	12	4	3	7
30-34	2	2	1	7
35+	2	0	1	4

Edge In Assists

	Home W	L	Road W	L
Below -15	0	0	0	1
-10 to -14	0	1	1	7
-5 to -9	0	2	2	7
0 to -4	9	4	4	4
1-4	12	2	2	3
5-9	8	1	7	1
10-14	2	0	1	0
15-	0	0	1	0

Personal Fouls

	Home W	L	Road W	L
0-14	0	0	0	0
15-19	7	1	3	2
20-24	12	3	7	10
25-29	11	5	8	8
30-34	1	1	0	2
35+	0	0	0	1

Opp. Personal Fouls

	Home W	L	Road W	L
0-14	1	0	0	1
15-19	4	0	4	3
20-24	12	7	5	9
25-29	10	3	7	10
30-34	4	0	2	0
35+	0	0	0	0

Personal Fouls Edge

	Home W	L	Road W	L
Below -15	0	0	1	0
-10 to -14	2	0	0	0
-5 to -9	5	0	0	1
0 to -4	12	5	9	12
1-4	9	2	6	3
5-9	3	3	2	5
10-14	0	0	0	2
15+	0	0	0	0

Steals

	Home W	L	Road W	L
0-5	2	0	0	2
6-7	4	7	4	5
8-9	7	1	5	5
10-11	5	0	2	6
12-13	5	1	4	4
14+	8	1	3	1

Opp. Steals

	Home W	L	Road W	L
0-5	4	0	4	3
6-7	4	3	3	6
8-9	11	4	7	3
10-11	8	3	1	4
12-13	2	0	2	6
14+	2	0	1	1

Edge In Steals

	Home W	L	Road W	L
Below -7	1	0	1	0
-4 to -6	1	1	1	3
0 to -3	10	5	4	9
1-3	9	2	4	7
4-6	4	1	5	4
7-	6	1	3	0

Turnovers

	Home W	L	Road W	L
0-14	8	3	7	9
15-19	18	5	8	11
20-24	3	2	2	1
25-29	1	0	1	2
30-34	1	0	0	0
35+	0	0	0	0

Opp. Turnovers

	Home W	L	Road W	L
0-14	4	0	5	6
15-19	8	7	8	12

	Home W L	Road W L		Home W L	Road W L		Home W L	Road W L		Home W L	Road W L
20-24	12 2	5 5	Opp. Blocks			Three-Pointers Made			6-8	6 4	7 5
25-29	5 1	0 0	0-2	8 2	1 2	0-2	20 6	13 13	9-11	8 1	1 0
30-34	2 0	0 0	3-4	10 4	5 1	3-5	10 2	4 9	12-14	2 0	5 1
35+	0 0	0 0	5-6	10 2	7 7	6-8	1 2	1 1	15+	0 0	0 3
			7-8	3 1	3 6	9-11	0 0	0 0			
Edge In Turnovers			9-10	0 0	2 5	12-14	0 0	0 0	Opp. Three-Pointers Made		
Below -15	2 0	0 0	11+	0 1	0 2	15+	0 0	0 0	0-2	19 7	13 15
-10 to -14	4 2	1 0							3-5	11 3	3 4
-5 to -9	9 2	5 5	Edge In Blocks			Three-Pointers Pct.			6-8	1 0	2 2
0 to -4	9 3	6 12	Below -7	0 2	0 5	.000-.099	10 3	4 4	9-11	0 0	0 2
1-4	3 2	4 4	-4 to -6	2 0	5 7	.100-.149	2 1	0 2	12-14	0 0	0 0
5-9	4 1	2 0	0 to -3	15 7	6 8	.150-.199	3 1	3 1	15+	0 0	0 0
10-14	0 0	0 2	1-3	10 1	5 2	.200-.249	0 0	0 1			
15+	0 0	0 0	4-6	2 0	2 1	.250-.299	1 0	1 3	Opp. Three-Pointer Pct.		
			7+	2 0	0 0	.300-.349	5 2	4 5	.000-.099	11 3	4 4
Blocks						.350-.399	3 1	1 2	.100-.149	1 0	1 0
1-2	7 6	2 7	Three-Pointers Attempted			.400-.449	3 1	0 3	.150-.199	2 0	3 1
3-4	11 3	8 9	0-2	4 0	5 2	.450-.499	0 0	0 0	.200-.249	1 0	1 2
5-6	10 1	4 6	3-5	10 1	5 2	.500-	4 1	5 2	.250-.299	2 1	1 1
7-8	1 0	2 1	6-8	9 4	6 9				.300-.349	4 2	3 4
9-10	2 0	2 0	9-11	4 1	2 6	Opp. Three-Point Attempts			.350-.399	2 1	0 0
11+	0 0	0 0	12-14	4 3	0 4	0-2	6 0	1 4	.400-.449	1 0	1 2
			15+	0 1	0 0	3-5	9 5	4 10	.450-.499	1 0	0 0
									.500-	6 3	4 9

Milwaukee Bucks
1988–89 Power Chart

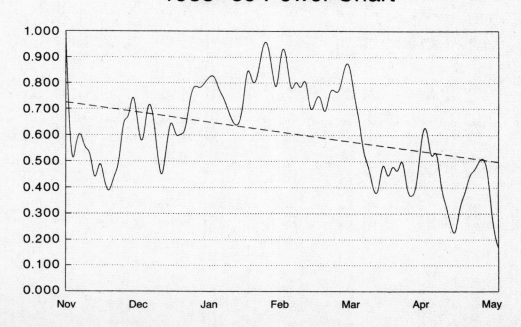

Milwaukee Bucks

	GP	GS	Min	FGM	FGA	FG%	2GM	2GA	2G%	3GM	3GA	3G%	FTM	FTA	FT%	Off	Tot	Ast	PF	Stl	TO	Blk	Pts	HGS
Randy Breuer	48	4	513	86	179	0.480	86	179	0.480	0	0	0.000	28	51	0.549	51	84	135	59	9	29	37	200	238
Per GP			10.7	1.8	3.7		1.8	3.7		0.0	0.0		0.6	1.1		1.1	1.8	2.8	1.2	0.2	0.6	0.8	4.2	5.0
Per 48			10.7	8.0	16.7		8.0	16.7		0.0	0.0		2.6	4.8		4.8	7.9	12.6	5.5	0.8	2.7	3.5	18.7	22.3
Tony Brown	29	0	274	36	73	0.493	34	66	0.515	2	7	0.286	18	23	0.783	15	14	29	28	12	10	4	92	97
Per GP			9.4	1.2	2.5		1.2	2.3		0.1	0.2		0.6	0.8		0.5	0.5	1.0	1.0	0.4	0.3	0.1	3.2	3.3
Per 48			5.7	6.3	12.8		6.0	11.6		0.4	1.2		3.2	4.0		2.6	2.5	5.1	4.9	2.1	1.8	0.7	16.1	17.0
Terry Cummings	80	78	2824	730	1563	0.467	723	1548	0.467	7	15	0.467	362	460	0.787	281	369	650	265	106	201	69	1829	1547
Per GP			35.3	9.1	19.5		9.0	19.3		0.1	0.2		4.5	5.8		3.5	4.6	8.1	3.3	1.3	2.5	0.9	22.9	19.3
Per 48			58.8	12.4	26.6		12.3	26.3		0.1	0.3		6.2	7.8		4.8	6.3	11.0	4.5	1.8	3.4	1.2	31.1	26.3
Mark Davis	31	0	251	48	97	0.495	47	88	0.534	1	9	0.111	26	32	0.812	15	21	36	38	13	12	5	123	111
Per GP			8.1	1.5	3.1		1.5	2.8		0.0	0.3		0.8	1.0		0.5	0.7	1.2	1.2	0.4	0.4	0.2	4.0	3.6
Per 48			5.2	9.2	18.5		9.0	16.8		0.2	1.7		5.0	6.1		2.9	4.0	6.9	7.3	2.5	2.3	1.0	23.5	21.2
Mike Dunleavy	2	0	5	1	2	0.500	0	0	0.000	1	2	0.500	0	0	0.000	0	0	0	0	0	0	0	3	1
Per GP			2.5	0.5	1.0		0.0	0.0		0.5	1.0		0.0	0.0		0.0	0.0	0.0	0.0	0.0	0.0	0.0	1.5	0.5
Per 48			0.1	9.6	19.2		0.0	0.0		9.6	19.2		0.0	0.0		0.0	0.0	0.0	0.0	0.0	0.0	0.0	28.8	9.6
Jeff Grayer	11	2	200	32	73	0.438	32	71	0.451	0	2	0.000	17	20	0.850	14	21	35	15	10	19	1	81	78
Per GP			18.2	2.9	6.6		2.9	6.5		0.0	0.2		1.5	1.8		1.3	1.9	3.2	1.4	0.9	1.7	0.1	7.4	7.1
Per 48			4.2	7.7	17.5		7.7	17.0		0.0	0.5		4.1	4.8		3.4	5.0	8.4	3.6	2.4	4.6	0.2	19.4	18.7
Rickey Green	30	0	501	72	132	0.545	70	126	0.556	2	6	0.333	17	19	0.895	7	39	46	19	22	33	2	163	211
Per GP			16.7	2.4	4.4		2.3	4.2		0.1	0.2		0.6	0.6		0.2	1.3	1.5	0.6	0.7	1.1	0.1	5.4	7.0
Per 48			10.4	6.9	12.6		6.7	12.1		0.2	0.6		1.6	1.8		0.7	3.7	4.4	1.8	2.1	3.2	0.2	15.6	20.2
Tito Horford	25	0	112	15	46	0.326	15	46	0.326	0	0	0.000	12	19	0.632	9	13	22	14	1	15	7	42	30
Per GP			4.5	0.6	1.8		0.6	1.8		0.0	0.0		0.5	0.8		0.4	0.5	0.9	0.6	0.0	0.6	0.3	1.7	1.2
Per 48			2.3	6.4	19.7		6.4	19.7		0.0	0.0		5.1	8.1		3.9	5.6	9.4	6.0	0.4	6.4	3.0	18.0	12.9
Jay Humphries	73	50	2220	345	714	0.483	320	620	0.516	25	94	0.266	129	158	0.816	70	119	189	187	142	158	5	844	937
Per GP			30.4	4.7	9.8		4.4	8.5		0.3	1.3		1.8	2.2		1.0	1.6	2.6	2.6	1.9	2.2	0.1	11.6	12.8
Per 48			46.3	7.5	15.4		6.9	13.4		0.5	2.0		2.8	3.4		1.5	2.6	4.1	4.0	3.1	3.4	0.1	18.2	20.3
Larry Krystkowiak	80	77	2472	362	766	0.473	358	754	0.475	4	12	0.333	289	351	0.823	198	412	610	219	93	146	9	1017	1023
Per GP			30.9	4.5	9.6		4.5	9.4		0.0	0.1		3.6	4.4		2.5	5.1	7.6	2.7	1.2	1.8	0.1	12.7	12.8
Per 48			51.5	7.0	14.9		7.0	14.6		0.1	0.2		5.6	6.8		3.8	8.0	11.8	4.3	1.8	2.8	0.2	19.7	19.9
Paul Mokeski	74	0	690	59	164	0.360	52	138	0.377	7	26	0.269	40	51	0.784	63	124	187	153	29	39	21	165	238
Per GP			9.3	0.8	2.2		0.7	1.9		0.1	0.4		0.5	0.7		0.9	1.7	2.5	2.1	0.4	0.5	0.3	2.2	3.2
Per 48			14.4	4.1	11.4		3.6	9.6		0.5	1.8		2.8	3.5		4.4	8.6	13.0	10.6	2.0	2.7	1.5	11.5	16.6
Sidney Moncrief	62	50	1594	261	532	0.491	236	459	0.514	25	73	0.342	205	237	0.865	46	126	172	114	65	92	12	752	706
Per GP			25.7	4.2	8.6		3.8	7.4		0.4	1.2		3.3	3.8		0.7	2.0	2.8	1.8	1.0	1.5	0.2	12.1	11.4
Per 48			33.2	7.9	16.0		7.1	13.8		0.8	2.2		6.2	7.1		1.4	3.8	5.2	3.4	2.0	2.8	0.4	22.6	21.3
Ricky Pierce	75	4	2078	527	1018	0.518	519	982	0.529	8	36	0.222	255	297	0.859	82	115	197	193	77	108	18	1317	997
Per GP			27.7	7.0	13.6		6.9	13.1		0.1	0.5		3.4	4.0		1.1	1.5	2.6	2.6	1.0	1.4	0.2	17.6	13.3
Per 48			43.3	12.2	23.5		12.0	22.7		0.2	0.8		5.9	6.9		1.9	2.7	4.6	4.5	1.8	2.5	0.4	30.4	23.0
Paul Pressey	67	62	2170	307	648	0.474	295	593	0.497	12	55	0.218	187	241	0.776	73	189	262	221	119	184	44	815	1041
Per GP			32.4	4.6	9.7		4.4	8.9		0.2	0.8		2.8	3.6		1.1	2.8	3.9	3.3	1.8	2.7	0.7	12.2	15.5
Per 48			45.2	6.8	14.3		6.5	13.1		0.3	1.2		4.1	5.3		1.6	4.2	5.8	4.9	2.6	4.1	1.0	18.0	23.0
Fred Roberts	71	3	1251	155	319	0.486	152	305	0.498	3	14	0.214	104	129	0.806	68	141	209	126	36	80	23	417	421
Per GP			17.6	2.2	4.5		2.1	4.3		0.0	0.2		1.5	1.8		1.0	2.0	2.9	1.8	0.5	1.1	0.3	5.9	5.9
Per 48			26.1	5.9	12.2		5.8	11.7		0.1	0.5		4.0	4.9		2.6	5.4	8.0	4.8	1.4	3.1	0.9	16.0	16.2
Jack Sikma	80	80	2587	360	835	0.431	278	619	0.449	82	216	0.380	266	294	0.905	141	482	623	300	85	146	60	1068	1187
Per GP			32.3	4.5	10.4		3.5	7.7		1.0	2.7		3.3	3.7		1.8	6.0	7.8	3.8	1.1	1.8	0.8	13.3	14.8
Per 48			53.9	6.7	15.5		5.2	11.5		1.5	4.0		4.9	5.5		2.6	8.9	11.6	5.6	1.6	2.7	1.1	19.8	22.0
Andre Turner	4	0	13	3	6	0.500	3	6	0.500	0	0	0.000	0	0	0.000	0	3	3	2	2	4	0	6	3
Per GP			3.3	0.8	1.5		0.8	1.5		0.0	0.0		0.0	0.0		0.0	0.8	0.8	0.5	0.5	1.0	0.0	1.5	0.8
Per 48			0.3	11.1	22.2		11.1	22.2		0.0	0.0		0.0	0.0		0.0	11.1	11.1	7.4	7.4	14.8	0.0	22.2	11.1

The Nets' home court problems last year were a matter of denial. If *you* had 41 games in New Jersey, would *you* let it sink in that, yes, this is your home? Evidently, the team refused to admit that the Meadowlands actually was their home, and usually played there as if it were just another stop on the road trip of life. New Jersey isn't really a fun place, and for all its natural beauty, the only part of it you're ever likely to see is the thin strip surrounding the turnpike. To think of *that* as your home can be somewhat disheartening.

Listen, I know New Jersey doesn't like its image. But just think about this: the only time I can recall my father hitting me was when I was sixteen. We were in a rental car without air conditioning, on a 90-degree day, going down the New Jersey Turnpike. I started to open my window for some air, right around exit 16 (the Meadowlands), and he clobbered me. But it was too late. Far too late. We ended up mouth-breathing straight to the Pennsylvania state line.

Anyway, the Nets played countless games in front of crowds that made it look as if East Rutherford were going through a measles quarantine. The combination of lack of identity along with the monster image of another local team pretty much sapped the fans away. A filler story in a local paper described the Nets Fan Club, which gives bonus points toward prizes to its members if they just go to a game, or wear a Nets cap, or *anything!* One of the members was docked points when he showed up for a Nets Fan Club official function wearing a Celtics jacket. Yes, even members of their own Fan Club don't root for them.

One of the big reasons for the home court advantage is that refs will give the home team the benefit of the doubt, consciously or not, when it comes to close calls. The home team will very often end up with more foul shots than the visitors. Do the sparse crowds in the Meadowlands contribute negatively to this factor, giving them a lower free-throw edge at home than other teams?

You think the foul shots would have helped the Nets? They need a lot more than that, and they're not going to get it anytime soon. Although they made progress in 1988–89, they have almost no hope of improving much further. Their first round draft choice was traded away for Orlando Woolridge, who then left for L.A., so they didn't get much value from him last year. The only player who would be moderately attractive to another team is Buck Williams. He's been around so long, he remembers when the Nets were good. Unfortunately, the 6'8" forward had his worst season last year, dropping to 13.0 ppg and 6.9 rpg.

Who can they recycle? When your Ironman is Roy Hinson (their scoring and minutes leader), there's not much room to grow. Hinson also placed second in rebounding behind Buck, and led the team with 121 blocked shots. Chris Morris can be left to develop, hopefully, after a promising 14.1 rookie season at forward. Know any teams looking for a .419 shooting guard? If so, they could swing a deal for Dennis Hopson. Otherwise, the Nets are stuck with him for at least another year. Who taught this guy to shoot from the outside anyway, Manute Bol? Joe Barry Carroll has to stop finding himself in sick bay for just one season. ("Medic! Medic! I jammed my finger!") He was mildly effective when he was in, but with complaints ranging from gastroenteritis to bad hands to what some cynical fans call "a case of double hypochondria," the Nets sorely missed his talents up the middle. About the only chance for improvement overall is if JBC plays well and often.

Beyond that, however, the only hope the Nets have are to either strike gold with their draft choice, or to bundle up some of their players as bodies in a trade for someone young and decent. About all they'll be able to do with the talent they have is make more trades on the scale of the Gminski/Coleman for Hinson/McCormick trade of two years ago. Although the Nets, at 26–56, showed a seven-game improvement over the previous campaign, they still had no cohesion, played worse as the season dragged on, and showed no promise for the future. Washington could very well be a coming team, and Boston can't be expected to hover below .500 again. Unless one of these two teams plummets, the Nets will find themselves lodged so firmly in fifth place in the weakened Atlantic Division that their only battle will be to avoid the humiliation of looking up and seeing Miami ahead of them.

New Jersey Nets

	Home W	L	Road W	L
By Month				
November	3	4	4	5
December	4	6	1	2
January	2	4	3	4
February	3	3	1	7
March	3	4	0	9
April	2	3	0	5
Home/Away	17	24	9	32
Overtime	3	1	1	0
Offense				
0-89	0	1	0	2
90-99	2	12	1	17
100-109	2	9	5	8
110-119	10	1	1	5
120-129	3	1	1	0
130-	0	0	1	0
Defense				
0-89	0	0	0	0
90-99	3	3	5	2
100-109	8	11	1	10
110-119	5	6	1	8
120-129	1	4	2	7
130-	0	0	0	5
Over/Under				
0-189	1	2	0	2
190-199	1	7	2	6
200-209	1	5	3	6
210-219	6	2	1	6
220-229	3	6	0	5
230-239	4	1	1	2
240-	1	1	2	5
Margin Of Victory				
0-3	4	6	3	2
4-6	3	3	2	2
7-10	6	8	4	7
11-15	3	4	0	8
16-20	1	3	0	4
21-	0	0	0	9
Field Goal Attempts				
0-69	0	0	0	0
70-79	3	1	4	3
80-89	6	14	4	14
90-99	8	8	0	13
100-109	0	1	1	2
110+	0	0	0	0
Field Goals Made				
0-34	0	4	0	5
35-39	5	6	3	12
40-44	4	12	3	11
45-49	7	2	1	4
50-54	1	0	2	0
55+	0	0	0	0
Field Goal Pct.				
.000-.399	0	5	0	7
.400-.424	0	1	0	4
.425-.449	1	9	0	5
.450-.474	4	4	2	10
.475-.499	3	2	1	0
.500-.524	5	2	4	4
.525-.549	2	0	1	2
.550-.574	1	1	1	0
.575-.599	1	0	0	0
.600-	0	0	0	0
Opp. Field Goal Attempts				
0-69	0	1	0	0
70-79	1	4	1	4
80-89	9	12	3	19
90-99	5	7	5	4
100-109	2	0	0	5
110+	0	0	0	0
Opp. Field Goals Made				
0-34	0	0	1	1
35-39	6	4	3	5
40-44	6	13	3	8
45-49	5	5	1	10
50-54	0	2	1	5
55+	0	0	0	3
Opp. Field Goal Percentage				
.000-.399	0	0	0	0
.400-.424	2	0	4	1
.425-.449	4	2	0	2
.450-.474	4	4	1	6
.475-.499	3	3	1	8
.500-.524	3	4	2	1
.525-.549	0	6	0	3
.550-.574	1	5	1	7
.575-.599	1	0	0	1
.600-	0	0	0	3
Free Throw Attempts				
0-9	0	0	0	0
10-19	1	3	0	8
20-29	8	12	3	17
30-39	6	7	5	5
40-49	2	2	1	1
50+	0	0	0	1
Free Throws Made				
0-9	0	0	0	3
10-19	4	15	2	20
20-29	9	6	5	6
30-39	4	3	2	3
40-49	0	0	0	0
50+	0	0	0	0
Free Throw Pct.				
.000-.549	0	2	1	3
.550-.599	0	1	0	2
.600-.649	0	5	0	4
.650-.699	4	4	1	5
.700-.749	3	4	4	6
.750-.799	2	3	0	7
.800-.849	4	3	2	3
.850-.899	2	1	1	2
.900-.949	2	1	0	0
.950-	0	0	0	0
Opp. Free Throw Attempts				
0-9	0	0	0	0
10-19	1	4	1	4
20-29	10	11	4	13
30-39	6	8	3	11
40-49	0	1	1	4
50+	0	0	0	0
Opp. Free Throws Made				
0-9	0	0	0	0
10-19	8	15	5	11
20-29	7	6	3	15
30-39	2	3	1	6
40-49	0	0	0	0
50+	0	0	0	0
Opp. Free Throw Pct.				
.000-.549	0	0	0	0
.550-.599	2	0	0	2
.600-.649	1	1	1	2
.650-.699	2	1	1	2
.700-.749	2	2	2	6
.750-.799	3	12	2	7
.800-.849	6	4	3	7
.850-.899	1	3	0	3
.900-.949	0	1	0	2
.950-0		0	0	1
Offensive Rebounds				
0-9	3	3	2	2
10-14	7	9	5	12
15-19	5	5	1	14
20-24	1	6	1	4
25+	1	1	0	0
Total Rebounds				
0-39	1	1	0	0
40-44	2	2	1	4
45-49	0	5	2	9
50-54	0	0	0	0
55-59	9	9	4	15
60-64	1	5	2	2
65-4	2	0	2	
Opp. Offensive Rebounds				
0-9	4	11	2	1
10-14	6	10	5	20
15-19	7	3	1	5
20-24	0	0	1	5
25+	0	0	0	1
Opp. Total Rebounds				
0-39	0	1	0	1
40-44	1	5	1	1
45-49	7	6	1	5
50-54	0	0	0	0
55-59	9	9	7	19
60-64	0	2	0	4
65-0	1	0	2	
Offensive Rebound Pct.				
Below 25%	5	9	7	11
25-29.99%	5	6	0	10
30-34.99%	5	5	2	9
35-39.99%	0	3	0	2
40-44.99%	2	1	0	0
45% and up	0	0	0	0
Assists				
0-14	0	1	0	2
15-19	4	10	3	7
20-24	5	11	3	16
25-29	6	2	2	5
30-34	2	0	1	1
35+	0	0	0	1
Opp. Assists				
0-14	1	0	0	0
15-19	4	5	1	1
20-24	4	9	0	3
25-29	7	8	6	15
30-34	1	2	2	7
35+	0	0	0	6
Edge In Assists				
Below -15	0	0	0	2
-10 to -14	0	2	0	7
-5 to -9	3	9	4	14
0 to -4	6	7	5	5
1-4	3	6	0	2
5-9	4	0	0	2
10-14	1	0	0	0
15-	0	0	0	0
Personal Fouls				
0-14	0	0	0	1
15-19	2	4	0	4
20-24	5	12	5	14
25-29	9	6	3	11
30-34	1	2	1	2
35+	0	0	0	0
Opp. Personal Fouls				
0-14	0	1	0	1
15-19	3	6	1	14
20-24	7	14	1	13
25-29	6	2	4	2
30-34	0	1	3	0
35+	1	0	0	2
Personal Fouls Edge				
Below -15	0	0	0	0
-10 to -14	0	0	0	2
-5 to -9	5	1	1	1
0 to -4	2	9	4	6
1-4	4	9	4	10
5-9	6	4	0	9
10-14	0	1	0	3
15+	0	0	0	1
Steals				
0-5	1	5	1	6
6-7	2	5	2	3
8-9	5	4	2	8
10-11	4	3	3	6
12-13	3	4	1	4
14+	2	3	0	5
Opp. Steals				
0-5	1	6	1	4
6-7	2	4	3	4
8-9	7	7	3	8
10-11	3	3	2	4
12-13	4	0	0	6
14+	0	4	0	6
Edge In Steals				
Below -7	0	1	0	2
-4 to -6	1	5	1	6
0 to -3	9	5	4	13
1-3	3	5	2	5
4-6	2	4	2	6
7-	2	4	0	0
Turnovers				
0-14	5	9	2	8
15-19	4	9	7	10
20-24	7	4	0	9
25-29	1	2	0	4
30-34	0	0	0	1
35+	0	0	0	0
Opp. Turnovers				
0-14	5	11	4	11
15-19	7	7	3	14

	Home W L	Road W L
20-24	4 4	2 4
25-29	0 2	0 3
30-34	1 0	0 0
35+	0 0	0 0

Edge In Turnovers

	Home W L	Road W L
Below -15	0 1	0 0
-10 to -14	1 0	0 0
-5 to -9	3 4	2 1
0 to -4	5 11	3 13
1-4	4 3	2 7
5-9	4 3	2 10
10-14	0 0	0 1
15+	0 2	0 0

Blocks

	Home W L	Road W L
1-2	1 1	4 6
3-4	3 6	2 14
5-6	5 8	3 4
7-8	2 7	0 5
9-10	6 2	0 2
11+	0 0	0 1

Opp. Blocks

	Home W L	Road W L
0-2	2 1	3 1
3-4	4 3	5 5
5-6	5 9	0 12
7-8	4 8	1 10
9-10	1 1	0 2
11+	1 2	0 2

Edge In Blocks

	Home W L	Road W L
Below -7	0 0	0 3
-4 to -6	1 4	1 9
0 to -3	8 15	2 12
1-3	4 3	5 4
4-6	3 2	1 4
7+	1 0	0 0

Three-Pointers Attempted

	Home W L	Road W L
0-2	0 0	0 1
3-5	8 8	3 5
6-8	4 12	5 17
9-11	5 3	1 8
12-14	0 1	0 1
15+	0 0	0 0

Three-Pointers Made

	Home W L	Road W L
0-2	9 17	6 21
3-5	7 7	3 9
6-8	1 0	0 2
9-11	0 0	0 0
12-14	0 0	0 0
15+	0 0	0 0

Three-Pointers Pct.

	Home W L	Road W L
.000-.099	4 4	1 4
.100-.149	1 3	0 6
.150-.199	0 1	0 0
.200-.249	0 3	0 2
.250-.299	4 2	1 5
.300-.349	0 4	2 3
.350-.399	0 1	1 1
.400-.449	3 0	2 4
.450-.499	0 0	0 1
.500-	5 6	2 6

Opp. Three-Point Attempts

	Home W L	Road W L
0-2	4 7	0 9
3-5	5 9	2 10

	Home W L	Road W L
6-8	2 3	2 5
9-11	3 3	3 3
12-14	3 1	1 3
15+	0 1	1 2

Opp. Three-Pointers Made

	Home W L	Road W L
0-2	12 15	4 23
3-5	5 9	4 7
6-8	0 0	1 2
9-11	0 0	0 0
12-14	0 0	0 0
15+	0 0	0 0

Opp. Three-Pointer Pct.

	Home W L	Road W L
.000-.099	9 7	1 17
.100-.149	3 0	0 0
.150-.199	0 0	0 0
.200-.249	0 1	1 2
.250-.299	0 1	1 0
.300-.349	0 2	4 7
.350-.399	3 4	0 3
.400-.449	1 1	0 1
.450-.499	0 0	0 0
.500-	1 8	2 2

New Jersey Nets
1988–89 Power Chart

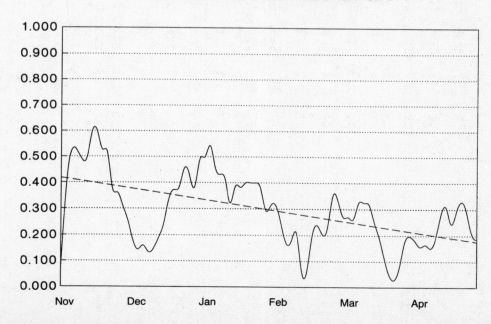

New Jersey Nets

	GP	GS	Min	FGM	FGA	FG%	2GM	2GA	2G%	3GM	3GA	3G%	FTM	FTA	FT%	Off	Tot	Ast	PF	Stl	TO	Blk	Pts	HGS
John Bagley	68	20	1642	200	481	0.416	189	427	0.443	11	54	0.204	89	123	0.724	36	108	144	117	74	159	5	500	630
Per GP			24.1	2.9	7.1		2.8	6.3		0.2	0.8		1.3	1.8		0.5	1.6	2.1	1.7	1.1	2.3	0.1	7.4	9.3
Per 48			34.2	5.8	14.1		5.5	12.5		0.3	1.6		2.6	3.6		1.1	3.2	4.2	3.4	2.2	4.6	0.1	14.6	18.4
Joe Barry Carroll	64	62	1996	363	810	0.448	363	810	0.448	0	0	0.000	176	220	0.800	118	355	473	193	71	143	81	902	869
Per GP			31.2	5.7	12.7		5.7	12.7		0.0	0.0		2.8	3.4		1.8	5.5	7.4	3.0	1.1	2.2	1.3	14.1	13.6
Per 48			41.6	8.7	19.5		8.7	19.5		0.0	0.0		4.2	5.3		2.8	8.5	11.4	4.6	1.7	3.4	1.9	21.7	20.9
Walter Berry	29	17	556	108	231	0.468	108	231	0.468	0	0	0.000	43	63	0.683	32	83	115	69	10	40	13	259	205
Per GP			19.2	3.7	8.0		3.7	8.0		0.0	0.0		1.5	2.2		1.1	2.9	4.0	2.4	0.3	1.4	0.4	8.9	7.1
Per 48			11.6	9.3	19.9		9.3	19.9		0.0	0.0		3.7	5.4		2.8	7.2	9.9	6.0	0.9	3.5	1.1	22.4	17.7
Ron Cavenall	5	0	16	2	3	0.667	2	3	0.667	0	0	0.000	2	5	0.400	0	2	2	2	0	2	2	6	6
Per GP			3.2	0.4	0.6		0.4	0.6		0.0	0.0		0.4	1.0		0.0	0.4	0.4	0.4	0.0	0.4	0.4	1.2	1.2
Per 48			0.3	6.0	9.0		6.0	9.0		0.0	0.0		6.0	15.0		0.0	6.0	6.0	6.0	0.0	6.0	6.0	18.0	18.0
Lester Conner	82	63	2532	309	676	0.457	296	639	0.463	13	37	0.351	212	269	0.788	100	255	355	132	180	180	5	843	1284
Per GP			30.9	3.8	8.2		3.6	7.8		0.2	0.5		2.6	3.3		1.2	3.1	4.3	1.6	2.2	2.2	0.1	10.3	15.7
Per 48			52.7	5.9	12.8		5.6	12.1		0.2	0.7		4.0	5.1		1.9	4.8	6.7	2.5	3.4	3.4	0.1	16.0	24.3
Corey Gaines	32	0	337	27	64	0.422	26	59	0.441	1	5	0.200	12	16	0.750	3	16	19	27	15	20	1	67	106
Per GP			10.5	0.8	2.0		0.8	1.8		0.0	0.2		0.4	0.5		0.1	0.5	0.6	0.8	0.5	0.6	0.0	2.1	3.3
Per 48			7.0	3.8	9.1		3.7	8.4		0.1	0.7		1.7	2.3		0.4	2.3	2.7	3.8	2.1	2.8	0.1	9.5	15.1
Roy Hinson	82	39	2542	495	1024	0.483	495	1022	0.484	0	2	0.000	318	420	0.757	152	370	522	298	34	164	122	1308	1152
Per GP			31.0	6.0	12.5		6.0	12.5		0.0	0.0		3.9	5.1		1.9	4.5	6.4	3.6	0.4	2.0	1.5	16.0	14.0
Per 48			53.0	9.3	19.3		9.3	19.3		0.0	0.0		6.0	7.9		2.9	7.0	9.9	5.6	0.6	3.1	2.3	24.7	21.8
Dennis Hopson	62	36	1551	299	714	0.419	295	687	0.429	4	27	0.148	186	219	0.849	91	111	202	150	71	102	30	788	623
Per GP			25.0	4.8	11.5		4.8	11.1		0.1	0.4		3.0	3.5		1.5	1.8	3.3	2.4	1.1	1.6	0.5	12.7	10.0
Per 48			32.3	9.3	22.1		9.1	21.3		0.1	0.8		5.8	6.8		2.8	3.4	6.3	4.6	2.2	3.2	0.9	24.4	19.3
Bill Jones	37	0	307	50	102	0.490	50	101	0.495	0	1	0.000	29	43	0.674	20	27	47	38	15	17	6	129	128
Per GP			8.3	1.4	2.8		1.4	2.7		0.0	0.0		0.8	1.2		0.5	0.7	1.3	1.0	0.4	0.5	0.2	3.5	3.5
Per 48			6.4	7.8	15.9		7.8	15.8		0.0	0.2		4.5	6.7		3.1	4.2	7.3	5.9	2.3	2.7	0.9	20.2	20.0
Keith Lee	57	4	840	109	258	0.422	109	256	0.426	0	2	0.000	53	71	0.746	73	186	259	138	19	51	33	271	338
Per GP			14.7	1.9	4.5		1.9	4.5		0.0	0.0		0.9	1.2		1.3	3.3	4.5	2.4	0.3	0.9	0.6	4.8	5.9
Per 48			17.5	6.2	14.7		6.2	14.6		0.0	0.1		3.0	4.1		4.2	10.6	14.8	7.9	1.1	2.9	1.9	15.5	19.3
Mike McGee	80	49	2027	434	917	0.473	341	662	0.515	93	255	0.365	77	144	0.535	73	116	189	184	80	124	12	1038	628
Per GP			25.3	5.4	11.5		4.3	8.3		1.2	3.2		1.0	1.8		0.9	1.4	2.4	2.3	1.0	1.5	0.1	13.0	7.8
Per 48			42.2	10.3	21.7		8.1	15.7		2.2	6.0		1.8	3.4		1.7	2.7	4.5	4.4	1.9	2.9	0.3	24.6	14.9
Chris Morris	76	48	2096	414	905	0.457	350	730	0.479	64	175	0.366	182	254	0.717	188	209	397	250	102	190	60	1074	884
Per GP			27.6	5.4	11.9		4.6	9.6		0.8	2.3		2.4	3.3		2.5	2.8	5.2	3.3	1.3	2.5	0.8	14.1	11.6
Per 48			43.7	9.5	20.7		8.0	16.7		1.5	4.0		4.2	5.8		4.3	4.8	9.1	5.7	2.3	4.4	1.4	24.6	20.2
Charles Shackleford	60	0	484	83	171	0.485	83	170	0.488	0	1	0.000	21	42	0.500	50	103	153	71	15	27	18	187	218
Per GP			8.1	1.4	2.8		1.4	2.8		0.0	0.0		0.3	0.7		0.8	1.7	2.5	1.2	0.3	0.4	0.3	3.1	3.6
Per 48			10.1	8.2	17.0		8.2	16.9		0.0	0.1		2.1	4.2		5.0	10.2	15.2	7.0	1.5	2.7	1.8	18.5	21.6
Buck Williams	74	72	2446	373	702	0.531	373	699	0.534	0	3	0.000	213	320	0.666	249	447	696	223	61	142	36	959	1049
Per GP			33.1	5.0	9.5		5.0	9.4		0.0	0.0		2.9	4.3		3.4	6.0	9.4	3.0	0.8	1.9	0.5	13.0	14.2
Per 48			51.0	7.3	13.8		7.3	13.7		0.0	0.1		4.2	6.3		4.9	8.8	13.7	4.4	1.2	2.8	0.7	18.8	20.6
Kevin Williams	41	0	433	67	168	0.399	66	162	0.407	1	6	0.167	40	51	0.784	19	31	50	74	25	42	8	175	143
Per GP			10.6	1.6	4.1		1.6	4.0		0.0	0.1		1.0	1.2		0.5	0.8	1.2	1.8	0.6	1.0	0.2	4.3	3.5
Per 48			9.0	7.4	18.6		7.3	18.0		0.1	0.7		4.4	5.7		2.1	3.4	5.5	8.2	2.8	4.7	0.9	19.4	15.9

NEW YORK KNICKS

For a good portion of the season, the Knicks looked like they might just be good enough to cruise to the conference finals, if not further. They were regularly dispatching foes at MSG, and they were okay on the road. The comparisons started with the Knicks of the early '70s. Early season trepidation slowly but surely melted away, and you could almost feel the mood in the city become more expectant, and suddenly the championship was by no means out of the picture.

Then came the slump. Mark Jackson's knee had to be 'scoped. While he was out, the team went 6–4 with Rod Strickland at the point. Not great, but not terrible. Around the same time, Kiki Vandeweghe joined the team. Dissatisfaction was fomented all over the place. Charles Oakley was upset that he was losing 30 seconds a game to the newcomer. Everyone wondered which one of them would be the odd man out come expansion draft time. Then their three-point shooting went cold. We got a whiff of some internal muttering. Many problems could be summed up by pinpointing the cause: the Knicks, simply, thought they were better than they really were.

They tailspun into the playoffs, losing 11 of their last 21. With a week left, they geared up for the playoffs by losing to Charlotte. They hit the playoffs at a crawl, and continued to putter through, taking out an inferior 76ers team in three games, but by a total of only eight points. They waved a broom around, cheered that they'd be playing Chicago instead of Cleveland, and got their butts kicked by Jordan and Co. End of season.

Although they were much improved, they still have some growing to do. In particular, one thing that made fans grind their teeth once the team started losing was their propensity for strange shot selections. Charles Oakley decided he should be shooting threes. Mark Jackson wanted to be the hero once too often, actually getting himself booed in the Garden after rushing a potential game winner against Chicago (which then won in OT). All year long, the Knicks were the recipients of a lot of ink regarding their three-point production, how they were on a record pace, and how important it was to their offense. Well, at times it was, but the volume of their shots was being confused with the worth of them. In fact, New York was a mediocre three-point shooting team, which showed a net loss through its use. Fourteen other teams gained more offense with

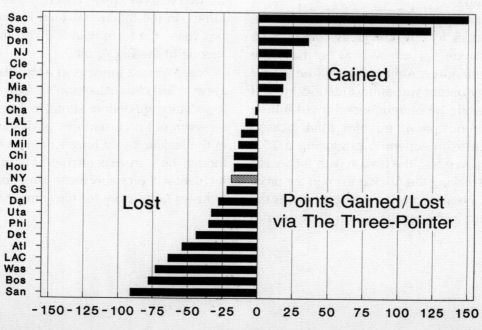

New York Knicks

the three, and the Knicks lost a total of 19 points compared to what they would have done had those shots been taken as twos.

Despite the playoff disappointment, the season was one of the more exciting in recent years for Knicks fans. I (Josh) had to listen to most of their games on the radio, since the cable company serving my area refused to carry their games on moral grounds—they owned a competing network that showed the Nets. From what I heard and Gerald saw, however, the Knicks could well be ready to advance to the upper ranks of the league this year, after winning their first Atlantic Division title since 1970–71. In the past two seasons the Knicks have made successive 14-game improvements, in part because of their scrambling, trapping defense. Last year they forced 20.6 turnovers a game and the Knicks finished up at 52–30, 16–3 when they forced over 25 turnovers. The team had been remarkably lucky with injuries for the past two seasons until Jackson went down, but if they can continue without anyone going down, this season should be slightly better. Patrick Ewing is the second best center in the league today, and has finally reached the level of play expected of him when he graduated Georgetown. He's the hub of the team's offense and defense, and played the most minutes on the team, taking the most shots (1282), and registering the best shooting percentage (.567) for 22.7 ppg, 12th best in the league. In addition, he pulled down 9.3 rpg and swatted away 281 shots, third best in the league.

Newly acquired Charles Oakley was one of the biggest differences for the Knicks this year, as he made the big trade pay off even as he made the Knicks into contenders. Although he hit only 12.9 ppg, his scoring output was almost identical to Bill Cartwright's, while he outrebounded Invisi-Bill by nearly 5.2 rebounds per 48 minutes. Mark Jackson usually ran the team superbly, producing a 25.5 HGS, placing seventh in the league with 8.6 assists per game, and making the All-Star team in the process. However, he all too often thought he was the best point guard in the league, when there are still

a few (Magic and Kevin Johnson, Stockton, Isiah Thomas) we would place him behind. Rookie Rod Strickland played when Jackson sat, started when he missed 10 games with knee trouble and actually produced more with a 27.0 HGS. It was generally felt, however, that Jackson was a better leader on the court, getting other players into the flow when they needed it most. If they're going to keep Strickland around (and it would be a mistake to banish him), look for them to be on the court together more often next year.

Beyond that, the Knicks have a lot of good role players. Johnny Newman was the team's second most prolific scorer, at 26.6 pp48, but his future is up in the air with the acquisition of Kiki Vandeweghe. Gerald Wilkins and Trent Tucker were okay as a platoon at shooting guard. Wilkins gave you a bit less than his scoring average would indicate, while Tucker, the team elder, gave you a bit more. Tucker usually drew the tough defensive assignments, and his presence often calmed an excitable Knicks locker room.

A lot depends on what the Knicks have learned from the Chicago series, where the Bulls pretty much demonstrated where New York could put their brooms. If they can get Kiki into the flow, and realize what they have to do to win, the Knicks will be ready to take their next big step. Winning the Atlantic will be a probability, and making it to the Eastern Conference finals is not out of the question.

A last thought: In Pitino's first, and, it turns out, last two years as Knicks coach, the team has won 90 games. In the much maligned Hubie Brown's first two years, the team won 91. You just can't please anyone in the Big Apple.

Pete Myers, a midseason acquisition, demanded a seat in first class at Jackson's expense. (NBA Player Association guidelines stipulate that first-class seats be given out on a seniority basis.) Myers *has* been in the league a year longer than Jackson, and even though he's an expendable twelfth man, and the incident will probably make him more expendable, it'll be a good story for his grandchildren.

New York Knicks

	Home W	L	Road W	L
By Month				
November	4	1	5	4
December	8	0	1	5
January	6	0	4	6
February	6	0	3	2
March	8	3	2	4
April	3	2	2	3
Home/Away	35	6	17	24
Overtime	2	0	2	1
Offense				
0-89	1	0	0	0
90-99	1	2	1	1
100-109	4	1	3	10
110-119	8	3	4	8
120-129	14	0	7	3
130-	7	0	2	2
Defense				
0-89	2	0	0	0
90-99	3	0	4	0
100-109	12	1	5	4
110-119	13	2	5	6
120-129	5	2	3	9
130-	0	1	0	5
Over/Under				
0-189	1	0	1	0
190-199	2	0	1	0
200-209	3	2	2	2
210-219	3	0	3	4
220-229	6	1	2	4
230-239	9	2	3	6
240-	11	1	5	8
Margin Of Victory				
0-3	5	0	3	7
4-6	6	1	3	5
7-10	8	2	5	5
11-15	5	2	3	4
16-20	6	1	2	1
21-	5	0	1	2
Field Goal Attempts				
0-69	0	0	0	0
70-79	1	0	1	2
80-89	9	0	8	6
90-99	16	6	4	10
100-109	9	0	4	4
110+	0	0	0	2
Field Goals Made				
0-34	1	0	0	0
35-39	2	1	4	4
40-44	11	3	5	7
45-49	9	2	5	9
50-54	12	0	2	4
55+	0	0	1	0
Field Goal Pct.				
.000-.399	1	0	1	1
.400-.424	2	1	0	5
.425-.449	4	1	3	5
.450-.474	8	2	1	2
.475-.499	7	2	4	2
.500-.524	3	0	3	4
.525-.549	6	0	3	2
.550-.574	2	0	1	2

	Home W	L	Road W	L
.575-.599	2	0	1	0
.600-	0	0	0	1
Opp. Field Goal Attempts				
0-69	0	0	0	0
70-79	3	0	1	2
80-89	11	3	10	13
90-99	16	3	4	8
100-109	5	0	2	1
110+	0	0	0	0
Opp. Field Goals Made				
0-34	1	0	1	0
35-39	6	0	3	2
40-44	16	3	7	4
45-49	8	2	3	14
50-54	4	1	3	3
55+	0	0	0	1
Opp. Field Goal Percentage				
.000-.399	2	0	2	0
.400-.424	2	0	0	0
.425-.449	7	0	1	0
.450-.474	8	2	3	2
.475-.499	4	1	3	4
.500-.524	8	1	4	6
.525-.549	2	1	2	3
.550-.574	1	1	2	6
.575-.599	1	0	0	2
.600-	0	0	0	1
Free Throw Attempts				
0-9	0	0	1	0
10-19	1	0	1	4
20-29	13	5	6	10
30-39	18	1	7	10
40-49	2	0	2	0
50+	1	0	0	0
Free Throws Made				
0-9	0	0	1	0
10-19	7	5	4	13
20-29	23	1	9	9
30-39	4	0	3	2
40-49	1	0	0	0
50+	0	0	0	0
Free Throw Pct.				
.000-.549	0	0	0	0
.550-.599	2	0	0	2
.600-.649	1	2	1	1
.650-.699	2	1	2	6
.700-.749	4	2	0	6
.750-.799	8	1	8	7
.800-.849	13	0	3	1
.850-.899	3	0	1	1
.900-.949	2	0	1	0
.950-	0	0	1	0
Opp. Free Throw Attempts				
0-9	1	0	0	0
10-19	4	0	3	0
20-29	19	4	8	7
30-39	9	1	6	13
40-49	1	1	0	4
50+	1	0	0	0
Opp. Free Throws Made				
0-9	1	0	0	0
10-19	17	2	8	3
20-29	14	3	9	14

	Home W	L	Road W	L
30-39	3	1	0	7
40-49	0	0	0	0
50+	0	0	0	0
Opp. Free Throw Pct.				
.000-.549	1	0	0	0
.550-.599	2	0	0	1
.600-.649	2	0	2	1
.650-.699	5	0	3	3
.700-.749	6	1	2	2
.750-.799	9	2	2	5
.800-.849	2	1	6	7
.850-.899	7	2	1	4
.900-.949	1	0	1	1
.950-	0	0	0	0
Offensive Rebounds				
0-9	2	0	1	1
10-14	11	0	6	12
15-19	16	4	9	6
20-24	4	1	1	3
25+	2	1	0	2
Total Rebounds				
0-39	1	0	0	1
40-44	2	0	1	4
45-49	5	2	4	5
50-54	0	0	0	0
55-59	16	3	9	11
60-64	8	1	3	2
65-	3	0	0	1
Opp. Offensive Rebounds				
0-9	2	0	1	5
10-14	15	3	8	9
15-19	11	2	6	8
20-24	5	1	2	1
25+	2	0	0	1
Opp. Total Rebounds				
0-39	0	0	0	0
40-44	1	0	2	4
45-49	9	1	5	3
50-54	0	0	0	0
55-59	19	4	8	10
60-64	4	1	2	3
65-	2	0	0	4
Offensive Rebound Pct.				
Below 25%	8	0	1	10
25-29.99%	9	1	5	5
30-34.99%	11	4	11	6
35-39.99%	4	0	0	2
40-44.99%	3	1	0	1
45% and up	0	0	0	0
Assists				
0-14	0	0	0	0
15-19	1	1	4	6
20-24	9	2	6	8
25-29	11	3	5	8
30-34	10	0	1	1
35+	4	0	1	1
Opp. Assists				
0-14	0	0	0	0
15-19	1	0	2	0
20-24	11	1	3	2
25-29	10	3	6	11
30-34	10	2	4	6
35+	3	0	2	5

	Home W	L	Road W	L
Edge In Assists				
Below -15	0	0	1	4
-10 to -14	3	1	1	5
-5 to -9	5	1	4	6
0 to -4	9	4	6	8
1 to 4	6	0	2	0
5 to 9	9	0	3	1
10 to 14	3	0	0	0
15 and up	0	0	0	0
Personal Fouls				
0-14	1	0	0	0
15-19	3	0	2	0
20-24	13	3	9	8
25-29	15	2	3	11
30-34	2	1	3	5
35+	1	0	0	0
Opp. Personal Fouls				
0-14	0	0	1	1
15-19	6	3	2	6
20-24	17	2	7	7
25-29	8	1	3	9
30-34	4	0	4	1
35+	0	0	0	0
Personal Fouls Edge				
Below -15	0	0	0	0
-10 to -14	0	0	0	0
-5 to -9	8	0	3	1
0 to -4	8	0	6	5
1 to 4	12	2	4	5
5 to 9	5	3	2	10
10 to 14	2	1	2	3
15+	0	0	0	0
Steals				
0-5	0	0	1	4
6-7	1	0	5	1
8-9	6	4	2	4
10-11	6	2	3	6
12-13	10	0	3	6
14+	12	0	3	3
Opp. Steals				
0-5	7	0	2	4
6-7	5	1	5	4
8-9	9	0	3	6
10-11	3	2	3	4
12-13	4	1	3	2
14+	7	2	1	4
Edge In Steals				
Below -7	1	1	1	3
-4 to -6	3	1	3	3
0 to -3	6	3	4	2
1 to 3	10	1	3	9
4 to 6	7	0	3	5
7-	8	0	3	2
Turnovers				
0-14	5	1	3	4
15-19	10	0	7	10
20-24	15	3	7	8
25-29	5	2	0	1
30-34	0	0	0	1
35+	0	0	0	0
Opp. Turnovers				
0-14	0	1	3	5
15-19	9	4	6	11

	Home W	L	Road W	L
20-24	13	1	5	5
25-29	12	0	2	3
30-34	1	0	1	0
35+	0	0	0	0

Edge In Turnovers

	Home W	L	Road W	L
Below -15	1	0	0	0
-10 to -14	2	0	1	0
-5 to -9	12	0	3	5
0 to -4	14	2	6	7
1 to 4	4	1	3	5
5 to 9	1	3	3	4
10 to 14	1	0	1	3
15+	0	0	0	0

Blocks

	Home W	L	Road W	L
1-2	5	0	1	3
3-4	8	3	4	8
5-6	9	2	5	7
7-8	5	1	6	4
9-10	7	0	1	0
11+	1	0	0	2

Opp. Blocks

	Home W	L	Road W	L
0-2	8	1	4	2
3-4	10	3	4	7
5-6	14	1	4	3
7-8	0	0	4	4
9-10	2	1	1	5
11+	1	0	0	3

Edge In Blocks

	Home W	L	Road W	L
Below -7	1	0	0	4
-4 to -6	3	1	1	3
0 to -3	9	2	6	8
1 to 3	12	2	7	8
4 to 6	7	1	3	1
7+	3	0	0	0

Three-Pointers Attempted

	Home W	L	Road W	L
0-2	0	0	0	0
3-5	0	0	0	0
6-8	2	0	0	2
9-11	7	1	4	3
12-14	15	1	5	10
15+	11	4	8	9

Three-Pointers Made

	Home W	L	Road W	L
0-2	5	2	2	6
3-5	20	3	10	10
6-8	7	0	3	6
9-11	3	1	2	2
12-14	0	0	0	0
15+	0	0	0	0

Three-Pointers Pct.

	Home W	L	Road W	L
.000-.099	3	1	2	1
.100-.149	1	0	0	0
.150-.199	3	3	3	6
.200-.249	4	0	0	2
.250-.299	5	1	1	3
.300-.349	4	0	3	2
.350-.399	4	1	1	3
.400-.449	2	0	3	4
.450-.499	1	0	0	1
.500-	8	0	4	2

Opp. Three-Point Attempts

	Home W	L	Road W	L
0-2	1	0	2	3
3-5	15	1	5	7
6-8	9	3	7	9
9-11	8	1	2	4
12-14	1	1	1	1
15+	1	0	0	0

Opp. Three-Pointers Made

	Home W	L	Road W	L
0-2	25	3	13	15
3-5	9	3	4	8
6-8	1	0	0	1
9-11	0	0	0	0
12-14	0	0	0	0
15+	0	0	0	0

Opp. Three-Pointer Pct.

	Home W	L	Road W	L
.000-.099	9	2	4	6
.100-.149	5	0	3	0
.150-.199	2	3	1	2
.200-.249	1	0	1	0
.250-.299	2	0	0	3
.300-.349	7	0	2	3
.350-.399	4	0	1	1
.400-.449	2	0	3	6
.450-.499	2	0	0	0
.500-	1	1	2	3

New York Knicks
1988–89 Power Chart

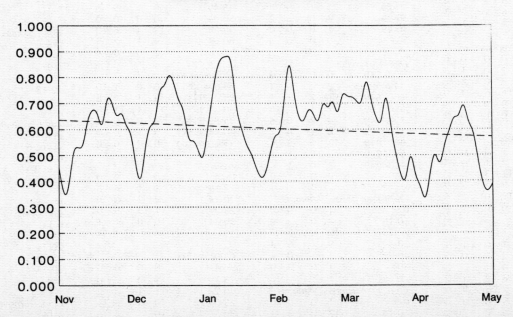

New York Knicks

	GP	GS	Min	FGM	FGA	FG%	2GM	2GA	2G%	3GM	3GA	3G%	FTM	FTA	FT%	Off	Tot	Ast	PF	Stl	TO	Blk	Pts	HGS
Greg Butler	33	0	140	20	48	0.417	20	45	0.444	0	3	0.000	16	20	0.800	9	19	28	28	1	17	2	56	37
Per GP			4.2	0.6	1.5		0.6	1.4		0.0	0.1		0.5	0.6		0.3	0.6	0.8	0.8	0.0	0.5	0.1	1.7	1.1
Per 48				2.9	6.9	16.5	6.9	15.4		0.0	1.0		5.5	6.9		3.1	6.5	9.6	9.6	0.3	5.8	0.7	19.2	12.7
Patrick Ewing	80	80	2896	727	1282	0.567	727	1276	0.570	0	6	0.000	361	484	0.746	213	527	740	311	117	266	274	1815	1966
Per GP			36.2	9.1	16.0		9.1	15.9		0.0	0.1		4.5	6.0		2.7	6.6	9.2	3.9	1.5	3.3	3.4	22.7	24.6
Per 48			60.3	12.0	21.2		12.0	21.1		0.0	0.1		6.0	8.0		3.5	8.7	12.3	5.2	1.9	4.4	4.5	30.1	32.6
Sidney Green	82	0	1277	194	422	0.460	194	419	0.463	0	3	0.000	129	170	0.759	157	237	394	172	47	125	18	517	564
Per GP			15.6	2.4	5.1		2.4	5.1		0.0	0.0		1.6	2.1		1.9	2.9	4.8	2.1	0.6	1.5	0.2	6.3	6.9
Per 48			26.6	7.3	15.9		7.3	15.7		0.0	0.1		4.8	6.4		5.9	8.9	14.8	6.5	1.8	4.7	0.7	19.4	21.2
Mark Jackson	72	72	2477	479	1025	0.467	398	785	0.507	81	240	0.337	180	258	0.698	106	235	341	163	139	226	7	1219	1318
Per GP			34.4	6.7	14.2		5.5	10.9		1.1	3.3		2.5	3.6		1.5	3.3	4.7	2.3	1.9	3.1	0.1	16.9	18.3
Per 48			51.6	9.3	19.9		7.7	15.2		1.6	4.7		3.5	5.0		2.1	4.6	6.6	3.2	2.7	4.4	0.1	23.6	25.5
Pete Myers	29	0	230	25	61	0.410	25	59	0.424	0	2	0.000	31	44	0.705	12	11	23	41	17	19	2	81	111
Per GP			7.9	0.9	2.1		0.9	2.0		0.0	0.1		1.1	1.5		0.4	0.4	0.8	1.4	0.6	0.7	0.1	2.8	3.8
Per 48			4.8	5.2	12.7		5.2	12.3		0.0	0.4		6.5	9.2		2.5	2.3	4.8	8.6	3.5	4.0	0.4	16.9	23.2
Johnny Newman	81	80	2336	455	957	0.475	358	670	0.534	97	287	0.338	286	351	0.815	93	113	206	259	111	151	23	1293	942
Per GP			28.8	5.6	11.8		4.4	8.3		1.2	3.5		3.5	4.3		1.1	1.4	2.5	3.2	1.4	1.9	0.3	16.0	11.6
Per 48			48.7	9.3	19.7		7.4	13.8		2.0	5.9		5.9	7.2		1.9	2.3	4.2	5.3	2.3	3.1	0.5	26.6	19.4
Charles Oakley	82	82	2604	426	835	0.510	414	787	0.526	12	48	0.250	197	255	0.773	343	518	861	270	104	248	14	1061	1211
Per GP			31.8	5.2	10.2		5.0	9.6		0.1	0.6		2.4	3.1		4.2	6.3	10.5	3.3	1.3	3.0	0.2	12.9	14.8
Per 48			54.2	7.9	15.4		7.6	14.5		0.2	0.9		3.6	4.7		6.3	9.5	15.9	5.0	1.9	4.6	0.3	19.6	22.3
Rod Strickland	81	10	1358	265	567	0.467	246	508	0.484	19	59	0.322	172	231	0.745	51	109	160	142	98	147	3	721	763
Per GP			16.8	3.3	7.0		3.0	6.3		0.2	0.7		2.1	2.9		0.6	1.3	2.0	1.8	1.2	1.8	0.0	8.9	9.4
Per 48			28.3	9.4	20.0		8.7	18.0		0.7	2.1		6.1	8.2		1.8	3.9	5.7	5.0	3.5	5.2	0.1	25.5	27.0
Trent Tucker	81	24	1824	263	579	0.454	145	283	0.512	118	296	0.399	43	55	0.782	55	121	176	163	88	59	6	687	510
Per GP			22.5	3.2	7.1		1.8	3.5		1.5	3.7		0.5	0.7		0.7	1.5	2.2	2.0	1.1	0.7	0.1	8.5	6.3
Per 48			38.0	6.9	15.2		3.8	7.4		3.1	7.8		1.1	1.4		1.4	3.2	4.6	4.3	2.3	1.6	0.2	18.1	13.4
Kiki Vandeweghe	27	0	502	97	209	0.464	94	199	0.472	3	10	0.300	51	56	0.911	15	21	36	38	12	23	7	248	181
Per GP			18.6	3.6	7.7		3.5	7.4		0.1	0.4		1.9	2.1		0.6	0.8	1.3	1.4	0.4	0.9	0.3	9.2	6.7
Per 48			10.5	9.3	20.0		9.0	19.0		0.3	1.0		4.9	5.4		1.4	2.0	3.4	3.6	1.1	2.2	0.7	23.7	17.3
Kenny Walker	79	2	1163	174	356	0.489	169	336	0.503	5	20	0.250	66	85	0.776	101	129	230	187	41	43	45	419	456
Per GP			14.7	2.2	4.5		2.1	4.3		0.1	0.3		0.8	1.1		1.3	1.6	2.9	2.4	0.5	0.5	0.6	5.3	5.8
Per 48			24.2	7.2	14.7		7.0	13.9		0.2	0.8		2.7	3.5		4.2	5.3	9.5	7.7	1.7	1.8	1.9	17.3	18.8
Eddie Wilkins	71	2	584	114	245	0.465	114	244	0.467	0	1	0.000	61	111	0.550	72	76	148	110	10	56	16	289	236
Per GP			8.2	1.6	3.5		1.6	3.4		0.0	0.0		0.9	1.6		1.0	1.1	2.1	1.5	0.1	0.8	0.2	4.1	3.3
Per 48			12.2	9.4	20.1		9.4	20.1		0.0	0.1		5.0	9.1		5.9	6.2	12.2	9.0	0.8	4.6	1.3	23.8	19.4
Gerald Wilkins	81	58	2414	462	1023	0.452	411	851	0.483	51	172	0.297	186	246	0.756	95	149	244	166	115	169	22	1161	936
Per GP			29.8	5.7	12.6		5.1	10.5		0.6	2.1		2.3	3.0		1.2	1.8	3.0	2.0	1.4	2.1	0.3	14.3	11.6
Per 48			50.3	9.2	20.3		8.2	16.9		1.0	3.4		3.7	4.9		1.9	3.0	4.9	3.3	2.3	3.4	0.4	23.1	18.6

PHILADELPHIA 76ERS

Okay, so the Sixers were swept out of the playoffs in the first round. So the last image of the team the fans saw was that of Charles Barkley lying motionless on the Spectrum floor for upward of fifteen minutes after a gut-wrenching loss to the Knicks. So the city of Philadelphia's fans proved once again how wildly supportive they are of successful basketball, leaving only 9,000 tickets unsold by twelve hours before the game. If nothing else, management can be heartened by the fact that they played equally well as, if not better than, the division champions in the best-of-five series.

As three-game sweeps go, this one was very even. Normally, teams are swept when they are badly outmanned, but in this series, the *total* three-game margin of victory for the Knicks was 8 points. In the history of the NBA, there has *never* been a closer best-of-five playoff sweep.

A sweep's a sweep, but they deserved better—from fate, and from their hometown fans. (In case you're interested, the old best-of-five sweep record was in 1961, when Syracuse beat Philly 3–0 with a total margin of victory of 12 points.)

Not only did the Sixers match up well with the Knicks in the playoffs, they actually took the season series, 4–2, including one game that broke the Knicks' 26-game home winning streak. Unfortunately, these successes were combined with embarrassing losses to Charlotte (three times), San Antonio, and a particularly nasty late-season 42-point blowout in Atlanta. The Sixers used an up-tempo offense (111.9 ppg, 7th best; 34–9 when scoring over 110 points) and hung on as All-Star forward Charles Barkley (25.8 ppg, 8th; .579 field goal accuracy, 2nd; and 12.5 rpg, 2nd) dragged them on his massive shoulders into second place in the Atlantic Division. Unlike the case in many up-tempo offenses, however, they were helped by sure hands (as a team, they averaged only 14.8 turn-overs per game, a league low). Center Mike Gminski, who we maintain looks more and more like pop star George Michael every time we see him, came through with his biggest offensive output of his nine-year career (17.2 ppg), rookie Hersey Hawkins, somewhat inconsistent (his 3 for 24 playoff slump being a prime example), at least lived up to his billing by canning 15.1 ppg, letting fly with a team-high 166 shots from three-point land to spread out the defense. Six-seven forward Ron Anderson, picked up from Indiana, was a pleasant surprise, as he banged home 16.2 ppg coming off the bench. The late addition of 6'6" small forward Derek Smith also gave the team more depth. Team captain Mo Cheeks, the 34-year-old war-horse, finished up his 11th season playing the fewest minutes in his career, but still came through with 11.6 ppg. If Barkley's bad back doesn't act up, if the Sixers get some more production from the point guard (Cheeks was the player voted "Most Widely Known As Underrated" last year), and get more power out of Christian Welp at backup center, the Sixers can again hope for a second-place division finish behind the Knicks. And hey, let's see some fans out there next year, okay?

The up-tempo game the Sixers played also utilized an effective clear-out game all season. They were consistently outrebounded, outshot, and outblocked. They were the only team that allowed their opponents to shoot over .500 from the field. Their opponents did better in both shots taken and percentage made. Yet the Sixers scored about 1.5 ppg more than their opponents.

How does this happen? A quick glance at the statistics shows one glaring plus on the Sixers' side. Because their opponents committed 263 more personal fouls, Philadelphia received 481 more free throws than they gave, making 405 of them. This trade-off, being outmuscled but drawing fouls,

THE CLOSEST NBA PLAYOFF SWEEPS

Year	Series Best of	Result	Total Margin	High Margin
1957	3	Minneapolis 2, Ft. Worth 0	6	4
1989	5	New York 3, Phil. 0	8	6
1975	7	Golden St. 4, Wash. 0	16	8

Philadelphia 76ers

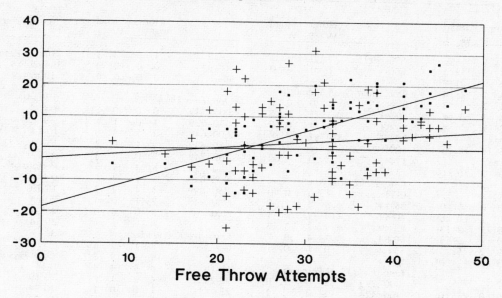

• Free Throws Margin   + Margin of Victory

worked well enough to give them a slight scoring edge. Who says that numbers don't tell a story? You see those stats, and you can almost hear Barkley taunting the guy who'd just knocked him on his back as he stepped up to the line to shoot two.

Oddly enough, though this was their major edge and Barkley the major recipient of the abuse up the middle, the team's fate wasn't often decided by how many free throws he was awarded. In fact, the correlation between his free-throw attempts and the team's margin of victory was about as close to none as you can get (about 0.05, to be exact). In fact, the Sixers' winning play depended much more on holding their opponents to few free throws rather than getting a lot for themselves. The break-even point was about 24—Philly had a better chance of winning when they could hold their opponents under this number of attempts, as seen in the graph above.

Sure bet: Jim Lynam will have less hair than Red Auerbach within about the next ten years. Next time you see the Sixers, check out his bald spot in progress. Trust us on this.

Philadelphia 76ers

By Month

	Home W	Home L	Road W	Road L
November	10	2	1	3
December	3	2	2	7
January	5	1	4	4
February	3	2	3	3
March	6	3	3	4
April	3	1	3	4

	Home W	Home L	Road W	Road L
Home/Away	*30*	*11*	*16*	*25*
Overtime	*3*	*2*	*0*	*0*

Offense

	Home W	Home L	Road W	Road L
0-89	0	0	0	0
90-99	0	1	2	6
100-109	8	7	2	13
110-119	10	1	5	3
120-129	9	2	5	3
130-	3	0	2	0

Defense

	Home W	Home L	Road W	Road L
0-89	0	0	1	0
90-99	8	0	2	1
100-109	9	3	10	7
110-119	11	4	3	8
120-129	1	4	0	7
130-	1	0	0	2

Over/Under

	Home W	Home L	Road W	Road L
0-189	0	0	1	1
190-199	4	0	2	3
200-209	3	1	1	2
210-219	5	4	0	6
220-229	7	1	8	7
230-239	7	3	3	3
240-	4	2	1	3

Margin Of Victory

	Home W	Home L	Road W	Road L
0-3	6	1	3	4
4-6	2	6	1	2
7-10	8	1	5	9
11-15	10	0	2	6
16-20	1	3	3	2
21-	3	0	2	2

Field Goal Attempts

	Home W	Home L	Road W	Road L
0-69	0	0	0	0
70-79	2	0	2	5
80-89	14	3	8	13
90-99	12	8	6	6
100-109	1	0	0	1
110+	1	0	0	0

Field Goals Made

	Home W	Home L	Road W	Road L
0-34	1	0	2	1
35-39	3	4	1	13
40-44	11	3	6	7
45-49	10	3	4	4
50-54	4	1	3	0
55+	1	0	0	0

Field Goal Pct.

	Home W	Home L	Road W	Road L
.000-.399	0	1	0	0
.400-.424	3	3	1	4
.425-.449	5	1	2	6
.450-.474	3	2	3	3
.475-.499	7	2	0	5
.500-.524	4	1	5	5
.525-.549	2	0	2	1
.550-.574	3	1	3	0
.575-.599	2	0	0	1
.600-	1	0	0	0

Opp. Field Goal Attempts

	Home W	Home L	Road W	Road L
0-69	1	0	0	0
70-79	3	1	0	5
80-89	13	4	8	10
90-99	10	4	7	8
100-109	1	2	1	2
110+	2	0	0	0

Opp. Field Goal Made

	Home W	Home L	Road W	Road L
0-34	1	0	0	0
35-39	5	0	2	3
40-44	14	4	9	5
45-49	9	2	5	9
50-54	1	4	0	7
55+	0	1	0	1

Opp. Field Goal Percentage

	Home W	Home L	Road W	Road L
.000-.399	2	0	1	0
.400-.424	1	0	0	2
.425-.449	6	0	0	0
.450-.474	5	1	4	1
.475-.499	4	1	5	4
.500-.524	6	3	6	3
.525-.549	2	3	0	7
.550-.574	3	2	0	2
.575-.599	1	1	0	4
.600-	0	0	0	2

Free Throw Attempts

	Home W	Home L	Road W	Road L
0-9	0	0	1	0
10-19	2	1	0	2
20-29	12	5	4	12
30-39	9	5	6	11
40-49	7	0	5	0
50+	0	0	0	0

Free Throws Made

	Home W	Home L	Road W	Road L
0-9	0	0	1	1
10-19	8	5	2	7
20-29	14	5	9	13
30-39	8	1	4	4
40-49	0	0	0	0
50+	0	0	0	0

Free Throw Pct.

	Home W	Home L	Road W	Road L
.000-.549	0	0	0	0
.550-.599	0	1	0	0
.600-.649	0	1	0	2
.650-.699	4	2	3	3
.700-.749	5	2	0	3
.750-.799	12	3	3	3
.800-.849	5	2	3	6
.850-.899	2	0	5	4
.900-.949	2	0	1	4
.950-	0	0	1	0

Opp. Free Throw Attempts

	Home W	Home L	Road W	Road L
0-9	0	1	0	0
10-19	9	1	7	5
20-29	14	7	8	8
30-39	6	2	1	11
40-49	1	0	0	1
50+	0	0	0	0

Opp. Free Throws Made

	Home W	Home L	Road W	Road L
0-9	1	1	2	1
10-19	16	3	11	9
20-29	12	7	3	12
30-39	1	0	0	3
40-49	0	0	0	0
50+	0	0	0	0

Opp. Free Throw Pct.

	Home W	Home L	Road W	Road L
.000-.549	0	0	0	1
.550-.599	1	0	1	1
.600-.649	2	1	3	0
.650-.699	5	1	0	2
.700-.749	5	0	3	3
.750-.799	6	3	4	5
.800-.849	6	1	3	7
.850-.899	3	4	2	3
.900-.949	2	1	0	3
.950-	0	0	0	0

Offensive Rebounds

	Home W	Home L	Road W	Road L
0-9	2	1	2	6
10-14	15	3	9	12
15-19	8	5	4	4
20-24	4	2	1	2
25+	1	0	0	1

Total Rebounds

	Home W	Home L	Road W	Road L
0-39	0	0	0	4
40-44	3	2	2	4
45-49	4	2	3	7
50-54	0	0	0	0
55-59	19	6	10	10
60-64	2	0	1	0
65-	2	1	0	0

Opp. Offensive Rebounds

	Home W	Home L	Road W	Road L
0-9	3	3	3	4
10-14	11	4	4	13
15-19	11	3	7	6
20-24	4	1	1	2
25+	1	0	1	0

Opp. Total Rebounds

	Home W	Home L	Road W	Road L
0-39	2	0	1	2
40-44	9	1	3	3
45-49	6	2	3	4
50-54	0	0	0	0
55-59	8	6	8	13
60-64	4	2	0	2
65-	1	0	1	1

Offensive Rebound Pct.

	Home W	Home L	Road W	Road L
Below 25%	8	3	4	13
25-29.99%	9	5	6	8
30-34.99%	6	2	4	2
35-39.99%	5	1	1	1
40-44.99%	2	0	1	1
45% and up	0	0	0	0

Assists

	Home W	Home L	Road W	Road L
0-14	0	0	0	1
15-19	1	0	4	7
20-24	2	4	5	7
25-29	15	4	3	7
30-34	10	3	4	3
35+	2	0	0	0

Opp. Assists

	Home W	Home L	Road W	Road L
0-14	0	0	0	0
15-19	0	0	4	1
20-24	9	2	4	2
25-29	13	4	6	9
30-34	6	2	2	10
35+	2	3	0	3

Edge In Assists

	Home W	Home L	Road W	Road L
Below -15	0	0	0	2
-10 to -14	0	1	2	4
-5 to -9	6	6	1	11
0 to -4	8	1	6	7
1-4	8	3	3	0
5-9	3	0	2	1
10-14	4	0	2	0
15-	1	0	0	0

Personal Fouls

	Home W	Home L	Road W	Road L
0-14	0	2	2	0
15-19	11	2	7	7
20-24	13	4	5	9
25-29	4	2	2	8
30-34	2	1	0	1
35+	0	0	0	0

Opp. Personal Fouls

	Home W	Home L	Road W	Road L
0-14	0	0	1	0
15-19	3	1	0	5
20-24	10	5	8	12
25-29	12	5	3	8
30-34	4	0	4	0
35+	1	0	0	0

Personal Fouls Edge

	Home W	Home L	Road W	Road L
Below -15	1	0	0	0
-10 to -14	3	2	4	0
-5 to -9	12	3	6	6
0 to -4	8	2	5	8
1-4	4	4	1	8
5-9	2	0	0	1
10-14	0	0	0	2
15+	0	0	0	0

Steals

	Home W	Home L	Road W	Road L
0-5	3	3	3	6
6-7	7	2	6	5
8-9	6	5	0	7
10-11	8	1	3	5
12-13	2	0	1	2
14+	4	0	3	0

Opp. Steals

	Home W	Home L	Road W	Road L
0-5	8	2	4	4
6-7	6	2	3	7
8-9	6	4	5	7
10-11	7	2	4	3
12-13	1	1	0	3
14+	2	0	0	1

Edge In Steals

	Home W	Home L	Road W	Road L
Below -7	0	0	0	1
-4 to -6	5	2	3	4
0 to -3	5	6	4	14
1-3	10	1	3	3
4-6	7	2	3	2
7-	3	0	3	1

Turnovers

	Home W	Home L	Road W	Road L
0-14	14	8	12	8
15-19	13	3	4	13
20-24	2	0	0	4
25-29	1	0	0	0
30-34	0	0	0	0
35+	0	0	0	0

Opp. Turnovers

	Home W	Home L	Road W	Road L
0-14	8	5	7	14
15-19	15	6	4	8

	Home W	Home L	Road W	Road L
20-24	6	0	3	3
25-29	1	0	2	0
30-34	0	0	0	0
35+	0	0	0	0

Edge In Turnovers

	Home W	Home L	Road W	Road L
Below -15	0	0	1	0
-10 to -14	1	0	0	0
-5 to -9	10	2	6	3
0 to -4	7	5	2	7
1-4	8	4	6	8
5-9	4	0	1	5
10-14	0	0	0	2
15+	0	0	0	0

Blocks

	Home W	Home L	Road W	Road L
1-2	3	2	1	11
3-4	12	2	8	11
5-6	7	4	7	2
7-8	1	3	0	1
9-10	4	0	0	0
11+	3	0	0	0

Opp. Blocks

	Home W	Home L	Road W	Road L
0-2	5	1	1	2
3-4	8	3	5	9
5-6	8	3	4	11
7-8	4	4	5	0
9-10	3	0	0	2
11+	2	0	1	1

Edge In Blocks

	Home W	Home L	Road W	Road L
Below -7	1	0	1	3
-4 to -6	1	1	2	4
0 to -3	15	7	8	12
1-3	8	2	5	6
4-6	4	1	0	0
7+	1	0	0	0

Three-Pointers Attempted

	Home W	Home L	Road W	Road L
0-2	4	0	2	1
3-5	11	1	1	5
6-8	5	3	6	10
9-11	4	3	4	4
12-14	5	3	3	5
15+	1	1	0	0

Three-Pointers Made

	Home W	Home L	Road W	Road L
0-2	21	8	7	16
3-5	6	2	8	8
6-8	3	1	0	1
9-11	0	0	1	0
12-14	0	0	0	0
15+	0	0	0	0

Three-Pointers Pct.

	Home W	Home L	Road W	Road L
.000-.099	6	2	4	6
.100-.149	0	0	3	3
.150-.199	2	3	0	2
.200-.249	1	1	2	2
.250-.299	3	0	0	1
.300-.349	9	2	2	2
.350-.399	0	0	2	5
.400-.449	1	2	0	0
.450-.499	0	0	0	2
.500-	8	1	3	2

Opp. Three-Point Attempts

	Home W	Home L	Road W	Road L
0-2	4	2	2	10
3-5	9	3	6	7

	Home W	Home L	Road W	Road L
6-8	9	4	4	4
9-11	5	0	1	1
12-14	2	2	1	3
15+	1	0	2	0

Opp. Three-Pointers Made

	Home W	Home L	Road W	Road L
0-2	20	8	12	17
3-5	8	3	3	6
6-8	1	0	1	2
9-11	1	0	0	0
12-14	0	0	0	0
15+	0	0	0	0

Opp. Three-Pointer Pct.

	Home W	Home L	Road W	Road L
.000-.099	9	3	5	12
.100-.149	2	0	2	2
.150-.199	1	0	1	0
.200-.249	0	0	0	0
.250-.299	1	0	2	0
.300-.349	3	3	2	1
.350-.399	2	0	0	1
.400-.449	5	3	2	1
.450-.499	0	0	0	0
.500-	7	2	2	8

Philadelphia 76ers
1988–89 Power Chart

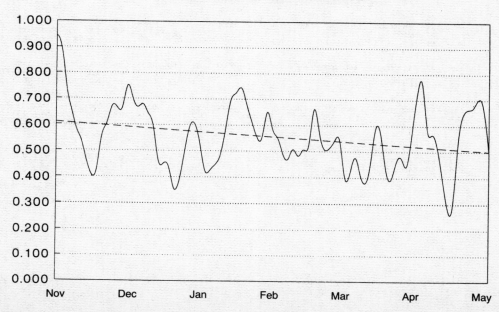

Philadelphia 76ers

	GP	GS	Min	FGM	FGA	FG%	2GM	2GA	2G%	3GM	3GA	3G%	FTM	FTA	FT%	Off	Tot	Ast	PF	Stl	TO	Blk	Pts	HGS
Ron Anderson	82	12	2623	566	1152	0.491	564	1141	0.494	2	11	0.182	196	229	0.856	167	239	406	166	71	122	23	1330	1043
Per GP			32.0	6.9	14.0		6.9	13.9		0.0	0.1		2.4	2.8		2.0	2.9	5.0	2.0	0.9	1.5	0.3	16.2	12.7
Per 48			54.6	10.4	21.1		10.3	20.9		0.0	0.2		3.6	4.2		3.1	4.4	7.4	3.0	1.3	2.2	0.4	24.3	19.1
Charles Barkley	79	79	3088	700	1208	0.579	665	1048	0.635	35	160	0.219	602	799	0.753	403	583	986	261	126	254	66	2037	2251
Per GP			39.1	8.9	15.3		8.4	13.3		0.4	2.0		7.6	10.1		5.1	7.4	12.5	3.3	1.6	3.2	0.8	25.8	28.5
Per 48			64.3	10.9	18.8		10.3	16.3		0.5	2.5		9.4	12.4		6.3	9.1	15.3	4.1	2.0	3.9	1.0	31.7	35.0
Scott Brooks	82	6	1367	156	371	0.420	101	218	0.463	55	153	0.359	61	69	0.884	19	75	94	116	69	65	3	428	531
Per GP			16.7	1.9	4.5		1.2	2.7		0.7	1.9		0.7	0.8		0.2	0.9	1.1	1.4	0.8	0.8	0.0	5.2	6.5
Per 48			28.5	5.5	13.0		3.5	7.7		1.9	5.4		2.1	2.4		0.7	2.6	3.3	4.1	2.4	2.3	0.1	15.0	18.6
Maurice Cheeks	71	70	2298	336	696	0.483	335	683	0.490	1	13	0.077	151	195	0.774	39	144	183	114	105	116	17	824	1093
Per GP			32.4	4.7	9.8		4.7	9.6		0.0	0.2		2.1	2.7		0.5	2.0	2.6	1.6	1.5	1.6	0.2	11.6	15.4
Per 48			47.9	7.0	14.5		7.0	14.3		0.0	0.3		3.2	4.1		0.8	3.0	3.8	2.4	2.2	2.4	0.4	17.2	22.8
Ben Coleman	58	11	703	117	241	0.485	117	241	0.485	0	0	0.000	61	77	0.792	49	128	177	120	10	48	18	295	270
Per GP			12.1	2.0	4.2		2.0	4.2		0.0	0.0		1.1	1.3		0.8	2.2	3.1	2.1	0.2	0.8	0.3	5.1	4.7
Per 48			14.6	8.0	16.5		8.0	16.5		0.0	0.0		4.2	5.3		3.3	8.7	12.1	8.2	0.7	3.3	1.2	20.1	18.4
Mike Gminski	82	82	2739	556	1166	0.477	556	1160	0.479	0	6	0.000	297	341	0.871	213	556	769	142	46	129	103	1409	1393
Per GP			33.4	6.8	14.2		6.8	14.1		0.0	0.1		3.6	4.2		2.6	6.8	9.4	1.7	0.6	1.6	1.3	17.2	17.0
Per 48			57.1	9.7	20.4		9.7	20.3		0.0	0.1		5.2	6.0		3.7	9.7	13.5	2.5	0.8	2.3	1.8	24.7	24.4
Hersey Hawkins	79	79	2572	442	971	0.455	371	805	0.461	71	166	0.428	241	290	0.831	51	174	225	184	120	158	37	1196	957
Per GP			32.6	5.6	12.3		4.7	10.2		0.9	2.1		3.1	3.7		0.6	2.2	2.8	2.3	1.5	2.0	0.5	15.1	12.1
Per 48			53.6	8.2	18.1		6.9	15.0		1.3	3.1		4.5	5.4		1.0	3.2	4.2	3.4	2.2	2.9	0.7	22.3	17.9
Gerald Henderson	65	0	986	144	348	0.414	111	241	0.461	33	107	0.308	104	127	0.819	17	51	68	121	42	73	3	425	350
Per GP			15.2	2.2	5.4		1.7	3.7		0.5	1.6		1.6	2.0		0.3	0.8	1.0	1.9	0.6	1.1	0.0	6.5	5.4
Per 48			20.5	7.0	16.9		5.4	11.7		1.6	5.2		5.1	6.2		0.8	2.5	3.3	5.9	2.0	3.6	0.1	20.7	17.0
Shelton Jones	42	34	577	81	179	0.453	81	178	0.455	0	1	0.000	50	67	0.746	24	71	95	50	16	39	13	212	197
Per GP			13.7	1.9	4.3		1.9	4.2		0.0	0.0		1.2	1.6		0.6	1.7	2.3	1.2	0.4	0.9	0.3	5.0	4.7
Per 48			12.0	6.7	14.9		6.7	14.8		0.0	0.1		4.2	5.6		2.0	5.9	7.9	4.2	1.3	3.2	1.1	17.6	16.4
Pete Myers	4	0	40	6	12	0.500	6	12	0.500	0	0	0.000	2	4	0.500	3	7	10	3	3	4	0	14	15
Per GP			10.0	1.5	3.0		1.5	3.0		0.0	0.0		0.5	1.0		0.8	1.8	2.5	0.8	0.8	1.0	0.0	3.5	3.8
Per 48			0.8	7.2	14.4		7.2	14.4		0.0	0.0		2.4	4.8		3.6	8.4	12.0	3.6	3.6	4.8	0.0	16.8	18.0
Cliff Robinson	14	13	416	90	187	0.481	90	186	0.484	0	1	0.000	32	44	0.727	19	56	75	37	17	34	2	212	169
Per GP			29.7	6.4	13.4		6.4	13.3		0.0	0.1		2.3	3.1		1.4	4.0	5.4	2.6	1.2	2.4	0.1	15.1	12.1
Per 48			8.7	10.4	21.6		10.4	21.5		0.0	0.1		3.7	5.1		2.2	6.5	8.7	4.3	2.0	3.9	0.2	24.5	19.5
Jim Rowinski	3	0	7	1	2	0.500	1	2	0.500	0	0	0.000	1	2	0.500	1	2	3	0	0	0	0	3	4
Per GP			2.3	0.3	0.7		0.3	0.7		0.0	0.0		0.3	0.7		0.3	0.7	1.0	0.0	0.0	0.0	0.0	1.0	1.3
Per 48			0.1	6.9	13.7		6.9	13.7		0.0	0.0		6.9	13.7		6.9	13.7	20.6	0.0	0.0	0.0	0.0	20.6	27.4
Derek Smith	36	18	695	105	220	0.477	101	204	0.495	4	16	0.250	65	93	0.699	31	55	86	100	24	44	15	279	275
Per GP			19.3	2.9	6.1		2.8	5.7		0.1	0.4		1.8	2.6		0.9	1.5	2.4	2.8	0.7	1.2	0.4	7.8	7.6
Per 48			14.5	7.3	15.2		7.0	14.1		0.3	1.1		4.5	6.4		2.1	3.8	5.9	6.9	1.7	3.0	1.0	19.3	19.0
Bob Thornton	54	0	449	47	111	0.423	46	108	0.426	1	3	0.333	32	60	0.533	36	56	92	87	9	23	7	127	134
Per GP			8.3	0.9	2.1		0.9	2.0		0.0	0.1		0.6	1.1		0.7	1.0	1.7	1.6	0.2	0.4	0.1	2.4	2.5
Per 48			9.4	5.0	11.9		4.9	11.5		0.1	0.3		3.4	6.4		3.8	6.0	9.8	9.3	1.0	2.5	0.7	13.6	14.3
Christian Welp	72	0	843	99	222	0.446	99	221	0.448	0	1	0.000	48	73	0.658	59	134	193	176	22	42	41	246	305
Per GP			11.7	1.4	3.1		1.4	3.1		0.0	0.0		0.7	1.0		0.8	1.9	2.7	2.4	0.3	0.6	0.6	3.4	4.2
Per 48			17.6	5.6	12.6		5.6	12.6		0.0	0.1		2.7	4.2		3.4	7.6	11.0	10.0	1.3	2.4	2.3	14.0	17.4
David Wingate	33	6	372	54	115	0.470	52	109	0.477	2	6	0.333	27	34	0.794	12	25	37	43	9	35	2	137	146
Per GP			11.3	1.6	3.5		1.6	3.3		0.1	0.2		0.8	1.0		0.4	0.8	1.1	1.3	0.3	1.1	0.1	4.2	4.4
Per 48			7.8	7.0	14.8		6.7	14.1		0.3	0.8		3.5	4.4		1.5	3.2	4.8	5.5	1.2	4.5	0.3	17.7	18.8

PHOENIX SUNS

Two years ago, the Suns won 28 games, finishing a mere 34 games back in the Pacific Division. After this, their worst showing in two decades, it was painfully obvious that something had to be done to revive this once powerful franchise. They'd been decimated by drugs, bad luck, and general aging and were nearly driven out of Arizona. A new arena? Forget it, guys. Fans became as rare as sub-90-degree days.

With nothing to lose, management did the only thing left to it: a major housecleaning. But unlike New Jersey and the Los Angeles Clippers, whose housecleanings look as if they were performed by Alice from *The Brady Bunch*, Phoenix actually worked constructively toward success. Cotton Fitzsimmons was brought in to coach (yet again), and Tom Chambers, the first NBA "true" free agent, was lured from Seattle as a forward/center, in the hopes he'd provide his accustomed scoring touch and be the team's mainstay. Cotton needed a point guard, too, and was bailed out (sorry) by 6'2" point guard Kevin Johnson, who was one of the top ten players in the whole league. He was third in assists per game (12.2), and became the fifth 10-20 man in NBA history when he notched more than 10 assists and 20 points a game. The other four are a select

crowd, too: Magic Johnson, Isiah Thomas, Nate Archibald, and Oscar Robertson. After being packaged by Cleveland in the Larry Nance trade two years ago, and raising his scoring average by about 8 points last year, K.J. ranks as not only one of the most improved players in the league, but one of the best, period.

Scorers, scorers, scorers. The Suns increased their offensive production by 10.1 points per game, ranking first overall with 118.6 ppg. Chambers, a malcontent with the Sonics, kept his mouth shut and came through even better than expected (his 25.7 ppg was 9th best in the league), while 6'7" forward Eddie Johnson was the highest-scoring sixth man in the league, at 21.5 ppg. Dan Majerle, a 6'5" guard picked up in the draft, must have felt snake-bitten last year, as he missed much of the season to mono and its complications. Armon Gilliam's 16 points per game didn't hurt the attack either. Do they like to run? In one March showdown against the Warriors they scored 87 points in the first half, 2 points shy of the NBA record en route to a 154–124 victory. It looked as if they were playing the East All-Stars again.

In the Golden State fiasco, the Suns outshot the Warriors, .581 to .416. In most of their wins,

Phoenix Suns

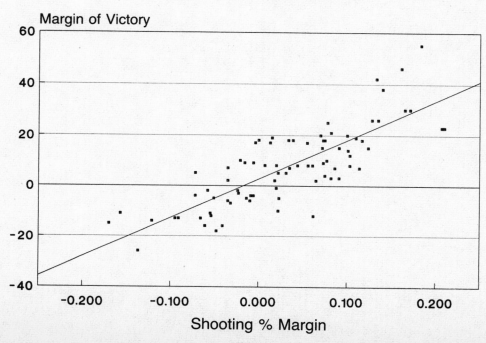

Phoenix outshot the competition. In fact, the correlation was so great, you could pretty much say that when they shot better, they'd win, and vice versa. The chart below clearly demonstrates this trend—the lower line, marked FG% Margin, shows the relationship between the margin of victory in Phoenix games and the percentage by which the Suns outshoot their opponents. As one gets higher, so does the other, and almost without exception, when one is positive, so is the other (outshooting = outscoring).

The top line is the Suns' field goal percentage, showing that the better they shoot as a team, the more they win by. The line's not as steep as the lower one, which means that while there's still a correlation, it's just not as strong.

The Suns put up some offensive numbers not seen since the high-scoring Nuggets were in their heyday. They were held under 20 points in a quarter fewer than 10 times, while scoring over 35 in a quarter over 60 times, both league bests. Unlike the offense of the Nuggets and Warriors, the Suns' was a high-percentage game and nearly always outshot their opponents. In fact, their accuracy was the major key to their victory.

As good teams are wont to do, the Suns blew out their opponents by 16 or more points 26 times, falling victim to the same only 4. As run-and-gun teams are prone to do, the Suns had only two games all year where the combined score fell below 200 points, losing to Milwaukee 100–93 and beating Utah 104–87.

If the Suns can continue forward where they left off last year, the weaker Lakers could fall prey to the heavy ballistics Phoenix employs. If everyone stays healthy, first place in the division is not out of the picture by a long shot. But just remember, a year ago the Suns *were* the long shots.

Phoenix Suns

	Home W	L	Road W	L
By Month				
November	4	2	2	5
December	8	0	2	4
January	6	1	4	3
February	7	1	1	4
March	7	1	5	5
April	3	1	6	0
Playoffs				
Home/Away	35	6	20	21
Overtime	1	1	0	1
Offense				
0-89	0	0	0	0
90-99	0	0	0	3
100-109	3	2	2	4
110-119	12	2	9	7
120-129	10	2	8	5
130-	10	0	1	2
Defense				
0-89	2	0	1	0
90-99	11	0	3	0
100-109	13	0	8	2
110-119	4	3	6	5
120-129	4	2	2	7
130-	1	1	0	7
Over/Under				
0-189	0	0	0	0
190-199	1	0	0	1
200-209	6	0	3	1
210-219	7	1	4	2
220-229	10	2	5	3
230-239	4	1	4	5
240-	7	2	4	9
Margin Of Victory				
0-3	2	3	3	1
4-6	3	1	1	7
7-10	8	0	7	2
11-15	3	1	2	8
16-20	9	1	4	2
21-	10	0	3	1
Field Goal Attempts				
0-69	0	0	0	0
70-79	1	0	1	0
80-89	15	4	7	7
90-99	14	1	8	7
100-109	5	1	3	6
110+	0	0	1	1
Field Goals Made				
0-34	0	0	0	1
35-39	3	1	2	5
40-44	11	3	5	3
45-49	9	2	9	7
50-54	10	0	3	4
55+	2	0	1	1
Field Goal Pct.				
.000-.399	0	2	0	2
.400-.424	0	0	0	4
.425-.449	2	0	1	2
.450-.474	7	0	1	2
.475-.499	5	1	6	5
.500-.524	10	1	7	3
.525-.549	2	0	2	0
.550-.574	5	2	1	2

	Home W	L	Road W	L
.575-.599	3	0	1	1
.600-	1	0	1	0
Opp. Field Goal Attempts				
0-69	0	0	0	0
70-79	1	0	0	1
80-89	9	3	4	3
90-99	18	3	7	15
100-109	6	0	7	2
110+	1	0	2	0
Opp. Field Goal Made				
0-34	3	0	0	0
35-39	13	0	4	0
40-44	10	3	10	3
45-49	7	1	5	10
50-54	2	2	1	6
55+	0	0	0	2
Opp. Field Goal Percentage				
.000-.399	7	0	6	0
.400-.424	9	0	4	0
.425-.449	5	0	3	0
.450-.474	5	2	1	3
.475-.499	4	1	3	3
.500-.524	4	0	2	3
.525-.549	0	2	1	7
.550-.574	1	1	0	5
.575-.599	0	0	0	0
.600-	0	0	0	0
Free Throw Attempts				
0-9	0	0	0	0
10-19	1	0	1	2
20-29	10	3	10	9
30-39	17	1	8	7
40-49	6	2	1	3
50+	1	0	0	0
Free Throws Made				
0-9	1	0	0	0
10-19	3	1	5	7
20-29	19	3	11	12
30-39	12	2	4	2
40-49	0	0	0	0
50+	0	0	0	0
Free Throw Pct				
.000-.549	0	0	0	0
.550-.599	2	0	0	0
.600-.649	0	0	0	0
.650-.699	1	0	3	2
.700-.749	6	0	2	3
.750-.799	11	3	6	6
.800-.849	8	1	4	7
.850-.899	7	0	4	2
.900-.949	0	2	0	1
.950-	0	0	1	0
Opp. Free Throw Attempts				
0-9	0	0	0	0
10-19	6	1	0	1
20-29	19	2	17	4
30-39	7	2	1	15
40-49	3	1	2	1
50+	0	0	0	0
Opp. Free Throws Made				
0-9	0	0	0	0
10-19	18	1	12	2
20-29	15	5	6	16

	Home W	L	Road W	L
30-39	2	0	2	3
40-49	0	0	0	0
50+	0	0	0	0
Opp. Free Throw Pct				
.000-.549	0	0	0	0
.550-.599	0	0	1	2
.600-.649	6	0	0	1
.650-.699	9	0	4	3
.700-.749	3	2	4	2
.750-.799	5	0	4	5
.800-.849	8	2	5	5
.850-.899	2	2	2	1
.900-.949	2	0	0	2
.950-	0	0	0	0
Offensive Rebounds				
0-9	2	1	4	4
10-14	20	3	11	9
15-19	9	1	5	5
20-24	4	0	0	3
25+	0	1	0	0
Total Rebounds				
0-39	0	0	0	0
40-44	1	0	0	4
45-49	3	2	3	4
50-54	0	0	0	0
55-59	21	4	12	11
60-64	5	0	2	2
65-	5	0	3	0
Opp. Offensive Rebounds				
0-9	4	2	2	1
10-14	10	3	4	9
15-19	19	0	8	9
20-24	0	1	3	1
25+	2	0	3	1
Opp. Total Rebounds				
0-39	1	0	0	0
40-44	4	0	0	2
45-49	2	4	3	3
50-54	0	0	0	0
55-59	24	2	12	6
60-64	4	0	4	3
65-	0	0	1	7
Offensive Rebound Pct.				
Below 25%	17	4	10	12
25-29.99%	6	1	7	5
30-34.99%	8	0	2	2
35-39.99%	3	1	1	2
40-44.99%	1	0	0	0
45% and up	0	0	0	0
Assists				
0-14	0	0	0	0
15-19	3	0	1	4
20-24	0	2	6	9
25-29	8	2	7	5
30-34	18	2	4	1
35+	6	0	2	2
Opp. Assists				
0-14	0	0	0	0
15-19	7	0	1	0
20-24	15	1	8	2
25-29	7	4	9	5
30-34	5	0	2	10
35+	1	1	0	4

	Home W	L	Road W	L
Edge In Assists				
Below -15	0	0	0	1
-10 to -14	1	0	2	6
-5 to -9	2	1	0	7
0 to -4	4	4	8	5
1-4	9	1	3	0
5-9	5	0	5	2
10-14	10	0	1	0
15-	4	0	1	0
Personal Fouls				
0-14	1	0	0	0
15-19	7	0	1	2
20-24	16	4	12	6
25-29	10	1	7	7
30-34	1	1	0	5
35+	0	0	0	1
Opp. Personal Fouls				
0-14	1	0	0	0
15-19	0	0	2	5
20-24	14	3	7	7
25-29	13	3	10	5
30-34	7	0	1	3
35+	0	0	0	1
Personal Fouls Edge				
Below -15	0	0	0	0
-10 to -14	4	0	1	0
-5 to -9	10	2	3	4
0 to -4	14	2	10	3
1-4	5	1	5	5
5-9	2	1	1	8
10-14	0	0	0	1
15+	0	0	0	0
Steals				
0-5	5	3	5	3
6-7	6	0	5	5
8-9	9	1	3	4
10-11	7	1	4	6
12-13	3	1	2	2
14+	5	0	1	1
Opp. Steals				
0-5	8	1	5	5
6-7	14	1	5	5
8-9	6	2	7	3
10-11	5	1	1	4
12-13	2	1	2	3
14+	0	0	0	1
Edge In Steals				
Below -7	0	1	1	2
-4 to -6	3	2	3	3
0 to -3	10	1	5	7
1-3	13	0	7	2
4-6	4	1	3	6
7-	5	1	1	1
Turnovers				
0-14	15	1	11	6
15-19	15	4	8	8
20-24	5	1	1	7
25-29	0	0	0	0
30-34	0	0	0	0
35+	0	0	0	0
Opp. Turnovers				
0-14	8	4	9	5
15-19	15	1	7	11

	Home W	L	Road W	L
20-24	9	1	4	4
25-29	2	0	0	1
30-34	1	0	0	0
35+	0	0	0	0

Edge In Turnovers

	Home W	L	Road W	L
Below -15	2	0	0	0
-10 to -14	5	0	0	1
-5 to -9	7	1	5	5
0 to -4	8	1	6	3
1-4	13	2	5	5
5-9	0	2	4	7
10-14	0	0	0	0
15+	0	0	0	0

Blocks

	Home W	L	Road W	L
1-2	4	1	5	4
3-4	10	2	3	10
5-6	10	3	6	3
7-8	4	0	5	2
9-10	5	0	1	1
11+	2	0	0	1

Opp. Blocks

	Home W	L	Road W	L
0-2	13	2	3	0
3-4	9	0	5	4
5-6	10	2	2	6
7-8	2	1	8	5
9-10	1	0	1	4
11+	0	1	1	2

Edge In Blocks

	Home W	L	Road W	L
Below -7	1	1	2	3
-4 to -6	0	0	1	4
0 to -3	10	3	12	10
1-3	15	2	1	3
4-6	5	0	3	0
7+	4	0	1	1

Three-Pointers Attempted

	Home W	L	Road W	L
0-2	6	0	4	2
3-5	15	3	8	4
6-8	9	0	4	10
9-11	3	2	3	3
12-14	1	1	1	2
15+	1	0	0	0

Three-Pointers Made

	Home W	L	Road W	L
0-2	23	2	12	15
3-5	10	4	7	6
6-8	1	0	0	0
9-11	1	0	1	0
12-14	0	0	0	0
15+	0	0	0	0

Three-Pointers Pct

	Home W	L	Road W	L
.000-.099	10	1	6	4
.100-.149	2	0	3	1
.150-.199	0	0	0	2
.200-.249	0	1	0	0
.250-.299	3	0	0	1
.300-.349	6	0	2	7
.350-.399	0	1	0	2
.400-.449	3	0	2	0
.450-.499	0	0	0	0
.500-	11	3	7	4

Opp. Three-Point Attempts

	Home W	L	Road W	L
0-2	5	0	1	3
3-5	5	2	9	4
6-8	16	4	4	6
9-11	7	0	3	5
12-14	1	0	0	2
15+	1	0	3	1

Opp. Three-Pointers Made

	Home W	L	Road W	L
0-2	24	2	17	8
3-5	9	4	3	12
6-8	2	0	0	1
9-11	0	0	0	0
12-14	0	0	0	0
15+	0	0	0	0

Opp. Three-Pointer Pct

	Home W	L	Road W	L
.000-.099	9	0	6	6
.100-.149	3	0	2	0
.150-.199	3	0	0	1
.200-.249	2	0	1	0
.250-.299	5	1	1	1
.300-.349	5	0	9	0
.350-.399	5	0	1	2
.400-.449	1	0	0	3
.450-.499	2	0	0	3
.500-	0	5	0	5

Phoenix Suns
1988–89 Power Chart

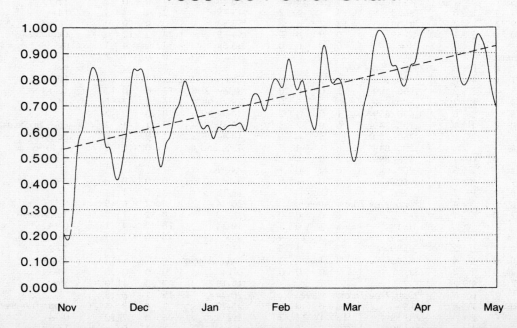

Phoenix Suns

	GP	GS	Min	FGM	FGA	FG%	2GM	2GA	2G%	3GM	3GA	3G%	FTM	FTA	FT%	Off	Tot	Ast	PF	Stl	TO	Blk	Pts	HGS
Tom Chambers	81	81	3002	774	1643	0.471	746	1557	0.479	28	86	0.326	509	598	0.851	143	541	684	271	87	231	55	2085	1673
Per GP			37.1	9.6	20.3		9.2	19.2		0.3	1.1		6.3	7.4		1.8	6.7	8.4	3.3	1.1	2.9	0.7	25.7	20.7
Per 48			62.5	12.4	26.3		11.9	24.9		0.4	1.4		8.1	9.6		2.3	8.7	10.9	4.3	1.4	3.7	0.9	33.3	26.8
Tyrone Corbin	77	30	1655	245	453	0.541	245	451	0.543	0	2	0.000	141	179	0.788	176	222	398	222	82	92	13	631	764
Per GP			21.5	3.2	5.9		3.2	5.9		0.0	0.0		1.8	2.3		2.3	2.9	5.2	2.9	1.1	1.2	0.2	8.2	9.9
Per 48			34.5	7.1	13.1		7.1	13.1		0.0	0.1		4.1	5.2		5.1	6.4	11.5	6.4	2.4	2.7	0.4	18.3	22.2
Winston Crite	2	0	6	0	3	0.000	0	3	0.000	0	0	0.000	0	0	0.000	1	0	1	1	0	1	0	0	-2
Per GP			3.0	0.0	1.5		0.0	1.5		0.0	0.0		0.0	0.0		0.5	0.0	0.5	0.5	0.0	0.5	0.0	0.0	-1.0
Per 48			0.1	0.0	24.0		0.0	24.0		0.0	0.0		0.0	0.0		8.0	0.0	8.0	8.0	0.0	8.0	0.0	0.0	-16.0
Mark Davis	2	0	7	1	5	0.200	1	4	0.250	0	1	0.000	2	2	1.000	1	0	1	1	0	0	0	4	2
Per GP			3.5	0.5	2.5		0.5	2.0		0.0	0.5		1.0	1.0		0.5	0.0	0.5	0.5	0.0	0.0	0.0	2.0	1.0
Per 48			0.1	6.9	34.3		6.9	27.4		0.0	6.9		13.7	13.7		6.9	0.0	6.9	6.9	0.0	0.0	0.0	27.4	13.7
T.R. Dunn	34	1	321	12	35	0.343	12	35	0.343	0	0	0.000	9	12	0.750	30	30	60	35	12	6	1	33	86
Per GP			9.4	0.4	1.0		0.4	1.0		0.0	0.0		0.3	0.4		0.9	0.9	1.8	1.0	0.4	0.2	0.0	1.0	2.5
Per 48			6.7	1.8	5.2		1.8	5.2		0.0	0.0		1.3	1.8		4.5	4.5	9.0	5.2	1.8	0.9	0.1	4.9	12.9
Kenny Gattison	2	0	9	0	1	0.000	0	1	0.000	0	0	0.000	1	2	0.500	0	1	1	0	0	0	0	1	1
Per GP			4.5	0.0	0.5		0.0	0.5		0.0	0.0		0.5	1.0		0.0	0.5	0.5	0.0	0.0	0.0	0.0	0.5	0.5
Per 48			0.2	0.0	5.3		0.0	5.3		0.0	0.0		5.3	10.7		0.0	5.3	5.3	0.0	0.0	0.0	0.0	5.3	5.3
Armon Gilliam	74	60	2120	468	930	0.503	468	930	0.503	0	0	0.000	240	323	0.743	165	376	541	176	53	140	27	1176	977
Per GP			28.6	6.3	12.6		6.3	12.6		0.0	0.0		3.2	4.4		2.2	5.1	7.3	2.4	0.7	1.9	0.4	15.9	13.2
Per 48			44.2	10.6	21.1		10.6	21.1		0.0	0.0		5.4	7.3		3.7	8.5	12.2	4.0	1.2	3.2	0.6	26.6	22.1
Craig Hodges	10	0	92	16	36	0.444	12	24	0.500	4	12	0.333	3	4	0.750	2	3	5	8	2	5	0	39	23
Per GP			9.2	1.6	3.6		1.2	2.4		0.4	1.2		0.3	0.4		0.2	0.3	0.5	0.8	0.2	0.5	0.0	3.9	2.3
Per 48			1.9	8.3	18.8		6.3	12.5		2.1	6.3		1.6	2.1		1.0	1.6	2.6	4.2	1.0	2.6	0.0	20.3	12.0
Jeff Hornacek	78	73	2487	440	889	0.495	413	808	0.511	27	81	0.333	147	178	0.826	75	191	266	188	130	109	8	1054	1172
Per GP			31.9	5.6	11.4		5.3	10.4		0.3	1.0		1.9	2.3		1.0	2.4	3.4	2.4	1.7	1.4	0.1	13.5	15.0
Per 48			51.8	8.5	17.2		8.0	15.6		0.5	1.6		2.8	3.4		1.4	3.7	5.1	3.6	2.5	2.1	0.2	20.3	22.6
Eddie Johnson	70	7	2043	608	1226	0.496	537	1054	0.509	71	172	0.413	215	248	0.867	91	215	306	200	47	122	7	1502	1001
Per GP			29.2	8.7	17.5		7.7	15.1		1.0	2.5		3.1	3.5		1.3	3.1	4.4	2.9	0.7	1.7	0.1	21.5	14.3
Per 48			42.6	14.3	28.8		12.6	24.8		1.7	4.0		5.1	5.8		2.1	5.1	7.2	4.7	1.1	2.9	0.2	35.3	23.5
Kevin Johnson	81	81	3179	570	1128	0.505	568	1106	0.514	2	22	0.091	510	578	0.882	46	294	340	226	135	322	24	1652	2061
Per GP			39.2	7.0	13.9		7.0	13.7		0.0	0.3		6.3	7.1		0.6	3.6	4.2	2.8	1.7	4.0	0.3	20.4	25.4
Per 48			66.2	8.6	17.0		8.6	16.7		0.0	0.3		7.7	8.7		0.7	4.4	5.1	3.4	2.0	4.9	0.4	24.9	31.1
Steve Kerr	26	0	157	20	46	0.435	12	29	0.414	8	17	0.471	6	9	0.667	3	14	17	12	7	6	0	54	54
Per GP			6.0	0.8	1.8		0.5	1.1		0.3	0.7		0.2	0.3		0.1	0.5	0.7	0.5	0.3	0.2	0.0	2.1	2.1
Per 48			3.3	6.1	14.1		3.7	8.9		2.4	5.2		1.8	2.8		0.9	4.3	5.2	3.7	2.1	1.8	0.0	16.5	16.5
Andrew Lang	62	25	526	60	117	0.513	60	117	0.513	0	0	0.000	39	60	0.650	54	93	147	112	17	28	48	159	252
Per GP			8.5	1.0	1.9		1.0	1.9		0.0	0.0		0.6	1.0		0.9	1.5	2.4	1.8	0.3	0.5	0.8	2.6	4.1
Per 48			11.0	5.5	10.7		5.5	10.7		0.0	0.0		3.6	5.5		4.9	8.5	13.4	10.2	1.6	2.6	4.4	14.5	23.0
Dan Majerle	54	5	1354	181	432	0.419	154	350	0.440	27	82	0.329	78	127	0.614	62	147	209	139	63	49	14	467	480
Per GP			25.1	3.4	8.0		2.9	6.5		0.5	1.5		1.4	2.4		1.1	2.7	3.9	2.6	1.2	0.9	0.3	8.6	8.9
Per 48			28.2	6.4	15.3		5.5	12.4		1.0	2.9		2.8	4.5		2.2	5.2	7.4	4.9	2.2	1.7	0.5	16.6	17.0
Ed Nealy	30	0	164	8	29	0.276	8	27	0.296	0	2	0.000	3	7	0.429	18	37	55	22	4	6	0	19	43
Per GP			5.5	0.3	1.0		0.3	0.9		0.0	0.1		0.1	0.2		0.6	1.2	1.8	0.7	0.1	0.2	0.0	0.6	1.4
Per 48			3.4	2.3	8.5		2.3	7.9		0.0	0.6		0.9	2.0		5.3	10.8	16.1	6.4	1.2	1.8	0.0	5.6	12.6
Tim Perry	62	15	614	108	202	0.535	107	198	0.540	1	4	0.250	40	65	0.615	61	71	132	47	19	36	32	257	275
Per GP			9.9	1.7	3.3		1.7	3.2		0.0	0.1		0.6	1.0		1.0	1.1	2.1	0.8	0.3	0.6	0.5	4.1	4.4
Per 48			12.8	8.4	15.8		8.4	15.5		0.1	0.3		3.1	5.1		4.8	5.6	10.3	3.7	1.5	2.8	2.5	20.1	21.5
Mark West	82	32	2019	243	372	0.653	243	372	0.653	0	0	0.000	108	202	0.535	167	382	549	273	35	103	187	594	957
Per GP			24.6	3.0	4.5		3.0	4.5		0.0	0.0		1.3	2.5		2.0	4.7	6.7	3.3	0.4	1.3	2.3	7.2	11.7
Per 48			42.1	5.8	8.8		5.8	8.8		0.0	0.0		2.6	4.8		4.0	9.1	13.1	6.5	0.8	2.4	4.4	14.1	22.8

PORTLAND TRAIL BLAZERS

Well, the Trail Blazers finally figured out a way to get rid of their second-place jinx. After coming in second to the Lakers every year, seemingly, since time began, the Blazers pulled it all together last year and finally managed to finish fifth instead. The same team that was called "Talent Blazers" in an early-season article came in with a disappointing 39–43 record (14 games off the previous season). Their rosy forecasts were torn asunder by the young team's dissension over distribution of minutes, the loss of lifetime 23.7-ppg scorer Kiki Vandeweghe to a chronic bad back and finally to the Knicks, and the problems between coach Mike Schuler and his disgruntled troops, All-Star Clyde Drexler in particular. Schuler, the former coach of the year, was given the pink slip midway through the season, and replaced by Rick Adelman. He'd lost control of many of the players, some of whom found out that if they didn't like something going on, they could take it upstairs to owner Paul Allen. When players know they'll be received by an owner, why bother with the coach anymore? Reports placed Drexler and Vandeweghe at the owner's house, having private shoot-arounds with him during the off-season.

There was more controversy in Portland than any time since Bill Walton led them to a championship.

We got the brunt of it in New York, as the Vandeweghe affair was plastered through the tabloids from the pre-season until the trading deadline. Would they make the trade? Would he decide his back was healed enough to play for Schuler? When the Knicks played in Portland, Schuler apparently said "screw everyone," and kept Kiki glued to the bench for all but five minutes. Punish the Knicks, punish Kiki, punish the Blazers. Completely inexplicable, and the whole issue eventually became just a boring headache for everyone here in New York, and we can just imagine how bad it must have gotten in Oregon.

The Blazers were a quick running team, bringing home the second most rebounds in the league (45.9 rpg), behind only the Warriors. All-Stars Kevin Duckworth and Clyde Drexler combined with Jerome Kersey for just under half the team's rebounds (49.9%, to be exact), while point guard Terry Porter had his best season among the grumblings chipped in with 367 boards of his own.

The offense showed flashes of brilliance all season, only being held under 100 points 12 times. They frequently blew people out, winning by 20 or more 9 times, impressive numbers even with the Clippers in your division.

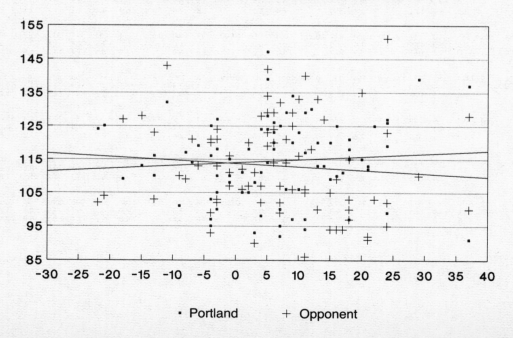

Portland Trail Blazers

• Portland   + Opponent

And yet it was their defense that controlled game outcomes. More so than most other teams, the Blazers won and lost pretty much independently of their offensive production. When they scored between 110 and 129 points they went only 26–23, not a good mark for anyone. They were a bit worse when they scored fewer than 110 (7–19), a bit better when they scored more than 129 (6–1). The defense, on the other hand, was a major factor in the outcome. When they held their opponents under 100, they went 11–2. When they allowed their opponents over 120, they were 8–22, a much more pronounced split in defense than offense.

The chart on the previous page bears out that difference, if you look at it the right way. The line that slopes downward describes an average Portland performance. As expected, the more points an opponent scores (as shown on the left margin), the greater Portland's margin of defeat (shown on the bottom). The other line shows Portland's scoring, which increases in step with their total margin of victory. When you compare the two lines, however,

the defensive one is much steeper. This shows that the relationship between Portland's defensive showing and margin of victory is much more pronounced than it is with their offense. In other words, the Blazers suffer more from each extra point allowed than they gain from each point scored.

The Blazers managed to make the playoffs, but only after a ridiculous "shoot-out" with Dallas, with neither team playing like they wanted to make it. Although Portland got in, the only team with a losing record to do so, they were bumped out in the round of 16 for the fourth straight year. Portland would look to be in better shape than Dallas for next season. After a season to forgive (perhaps), forget, and regroup, the Blazers should improve on last year's dismal effort. If 7'1" Sam Bowie can spend a year out of the emergency ward, and 6'9" forward Mark Bryant can improve into a premier sixth man, he'd be icing on the cake. Still, it will be an uphill division battle, with even the Clippers, of all teams, sniping at them.

Portland Trail Blazers

	Home W	Home L	Road W	Road L
By Month				
November	6	1	1	6
December	5	0	4	4
January	5	4	1	4
February	3	3	2	4
March	3	3	2	9
April	6	2	1	3
Playoffs				
Home/Away	*28*	*13*	*11*	*30*
Overtime	*3*	*1*	*1*	*0*
Offense				
0-89	0	0	0	0
90-99	2	1	1	8
100-109	1	3	3	7
110-119	10	8	3	6
120-129	9	0	4	9
130-	6	1	0	0
Defense				
0-89	1	0	0	0
90-99	8	1	2	1
100-109	10	1	6	8
110-119	3	4	1	6
120-129	4	6	2	9
130-	2	1	0	6
Over/Under				
0-189	2	0	0	0
190-199	0	1	1	3
200-209	5	1	2	3
210-219	5	1	2	6
220-229	5	2	3	4
230-239	3	6	1	2
240-	8	2	2	12
Margin Of Victory				
0-3	1	5	3	6
4-6	6	2	4	6
7-10	2	2	1	9
11-15	6	3	1	4
16-20	6	1	0	2
21-	7	0	2	3
Field Goal Attempts				
0-69	0	0	1	0
70-79	0	1	0	0
80-89	9	3	1	6
90-99	11	6	8	10
100-109	6	3	1	13
110+	2	0	0	1
Field Goals Made				
0-34	0	0	2	2
35-39	1	4	0	5
40-44	6	4	4	8
45-49	9	3	3	10
50-54	10	2	2	5
55+	2	0	0	0
Field Goal Pct.				
.000-.399	0	1	0	5
.400-.424	1	2	1	3
.425-.449	3	3	0	7
.450-.474	0	3	4	3
.475-.499	7	1	4	6
.500-.524	9	2	1	4
.525-.549	5	0	1	2
.550-.574	2	1	0	0

	Home W	Home L	Road W	Road L
.575-.599	1	0	0	0
.600-	0	0	0	0
Opp. Field Goal Attempts				
0-69	0	0	0	0
70-79	2	2	0	3
80-89	11	8	4	11
90-99	10	3	6	12
100-109	5	0	1	4
110+	0	0	0	0
Opp. Field Goal Made				
0-34	0	0	1	2
35-39	12	2	1	3
40-44	5	4	4	10
45-49	10	6	5	8
50-54	1	1	0	3
55+	0	0	0	4
Opp. Field Goal Percentage				
.000-.399	2	0	1	1
.400-.424	5	1	0	1
.425-.449	5	1	2	3
.450-.474	6	0	3	4
.475-.499	3	2	2	8
.500-.524	3	4	3	5
.525-.549	2	1	0	0
.550-.574	2	1	0	3
.575-.599	0	3	0	3
.600-	0	0	0	2
Free Throw Attempts				
0-9	0	0	0	0
10-19	1	0	2	6
20-29	13	8	2	15
30-39	8	3	4	8
40-49	4	2	3	1
50+	2	0	0	0
Free Throws Made				
0-9	0	0	0	3
10-19	9	6	3	14
20-29	12	5	4	12
30-39	7	2	4	1
40-49	0	0	0	0
50+	0	0	0	0
Free Throw Pct.				
.000-.549	0	0	0	1
.550-.599	3	1	0	2
.600-.649	2	1	0	0
.650-.699	5	4	0	7
.700-.749	6	1	4	5
.750-.799	6	2	2	7
.800-.849	4	3	4	4
.850-.899	2	0	1	2
.900-.949	0	0	0	2
.950-	0	1	0	0
Opp. Free Throw Attempts				
0-9	0	0	0	0
10-19	7	0	1	0
20-29	10	4	5	12
30-39	9	6	4	14
40-49	2	3	1	2
50+	0	0	0	2
Opp. Free Throws Made				
0-9	2	0	0	0
10-19	11	2	3	6
20-29	13	7	7	15

	Home W	Home L	Road W	Road L
30-39	1	3	1	7
40-49	1	1	0	2
50+	0	0	0	0
Opp. Free Throw Pct.				
.000-.549	1	0	0	0
.550-.599	1	1	0	1
.600-.649	2	0	2	0
.650-.699	1	2	3	3
.700-.749	7	2	2	2
.750-.799	8	2	1	10
.800-.849	4	3	3	7
.850-.899	4	3	0	3
.900-.949	0	0	0	3
.950-	0	0	0	1
Offensive Rebounds				
0-9	2	1	1	1
10-14	8	6	3	8
15-19	15	2	3	11
20-24	2	4	4	4
25+	1	0	0	6
Total Rebounds				
0-39	0	0	0	0
40-44	0	0	1	3
45-49	3	2	0	3
50-54	0	0	0	0
55-59	12	10	5	18
60-64	6	1	4	2
65-	7	0	1	4
Opp. Offensive Rebounds				
0-9	6	2	1	2
10-14	10	8	5	15
15-19	9	3	2	9
20-24	3	0	3	4
25+	0	0	0	0
Opp. Total Rebounds				
0-39	0	0	0	0
40-44	3	1	0	0
45-49	6	2	2	5
50-54	0	0	0	0
55-59	14	9	8	12
60-64	5	1	1	9
65-	0	0	0	4
Offensive Rebound Pct.				
Below 25%	8	5	2	7
25-29.99%	5	2	3	11
30-34.99%	11	4	3	5
35-39.99%	2	2	3	2
40-44.99%	1	0	0	5
45% and up	1	0	0	0
Assists				
0-14	0	0	0	0
15-19	1	1	0	2
20-24	4	4	4	13
25-29	10	7	4	6
30-34	11	0	2	5
35+	2	1	1	4
Opp. Assists				
0-14	1	0	0	0
15-19	8	1	1	1
20-24	11	7	5	4
25-29	7	4	4	11
30-34	1	1	1	7
35+	0	0	0	7

	Home W	Home L	Road W	Road L
Edge In Assists				
Below-15	0	0	0	3
-10 to -14	0	0	0	1
-5 to -9	2	1	2	6
0 to -4	2	7	2	10
1-4	6	1	3	9
5-9	10	3	3	1
10-14	5	0	1	0
15-	3	1	0	0
Personal Fouls				
0-14	1	0	0	0
15-19	7	0	1	3
20-24	9	4	7	13
25-29	7	3	3	10
30-34	3	5	0	3
35+	1	1	0	1
Opp. Personal Fouls				
0-14	0	0	0	1
15-19	1	1	1	6
20-24	14	8	5	13
25-29	8	1	4	9
30-34	4	2	1	1
35+	1	1	0	0
Personal Fouls Edge				
Below-15	0	0	0	0
-10 to -14	2	0	0	0
-5 to -9	8	0	3	3
0 to -4	8	5	5	2
1-4	8	3	2	12
5-9	2	5	1	9
10-14	0	0	0	4
15+	0	0	0	0
Steals				
0-5	1	0	1	1
6-7	2	3	4	4
8-9	7	6	0	12
10-11	7	1	1	5
12-13	6	3	3	4
14+	5	0	2	4
Opp. Steals				
0-5	5	1	1	6
6-7	8	3	1	3
8-9	5	2	3	8
10-11	5	4	5	6
12-13	2	1	1	2
14+	3	2	0	5
Edge In Steals				
Below-7	0	2	1	1
-4 to -6	2	0	0	3
0 to -3	10	4	3	8
1-3	4	6	4	10
4-6	8	1	2	7
7-	4	0	1	1
Turnovers				
0-14	10	3	2	10
15-19	9	6	6	10
20-24	8	3	3	8
25-29	1	0	0	2
30-34	0	1	0	0
35+	0	0	0	0
Opp. Turnovers				
0-14	2	2	2	4
15-19	13	6	5	15

	Home W	L	Road W	L
20-24	6	5	3	11
25-29	4	0	1	0
30-34	1	0	0	0
35+	2	0	0	0
Edge In Turnovers				
Below-15	2	0	0	0
-10 to -14	2	0	1	0
-5 to -9	7	3	1	6
0 to -4	9	4	5	14
1- 4	8	4	3	5
5- 9	0	1	1	5
10-14	0	1	0	0
15+	0	0	0	0
Blocks				
1-2	6	3	0	11
3-4	10	5	1	5
5-6	8	3	3	5
7-8	2	1	5	8
9-10	0	1	1	1
11+	2	0	1	0

	Home W	L	Road W	L
Opp. Blocks				
0-2	14	3	0	4
3-4	7	6	4	10
5-6	3	3	5	7
7-8	3	0	2	5
9-10	0	1	0	3
11+	1	0	0	1
Edge In Blocks				
Below-7	1	0	0	2
-4 to -6	2	2	1	6
0 to -3	7	5	2	12
1-3	13	5	5	5
4-6	4	0	3	4
7+	1	1	0	1
Three-Pointers Attempted				
0-2	6	1	2	1
3-5	5	1	3	9
6-8	9	1	5	4
9-11	5	6	0	8
12-14	2	3	1	4
15+	1	1	0	4

	Home W	L	Road W	L
Three-Pointers Made				
0-2	14	4	7	17
3-5	14	9	4	11
6-8	0	0	0	2
9-11	0	0	0	0
12-14	0	0	0	0
15+	0	0	0	0
Three-Pointers Pct.				
.000-.099	7	3	3	7
.100-.149	0	0	0	1
.150-.199	0	2	0	1
.200-.249	0	1	0	3
.250-.299	1	1	1	1
.300-.349	2	0	0	3
.350-.399	4	1	2	5
.400-.449	9	2	3	6
.450-.499	0	2	0	0
.500-	5	1	2	3
Opp. Three-Point Attempts				
0-2	2	0	3	7
3-5	9	2	4	6

	Home W	L	Road W	L
6-8	11	4	2	9
9-11	3	5	1	4
12-14	1	1	0	2
15+	2	1	1	2
Opp. Three-Pointers Made				
0-2	21	1	9	16
3-5	4	11	2	12
6-8	3	1	0	0
9-11	0	0	0	2
12-14	0	0	0	0
15+	0	0	0	0
Opp. Three-Pointer Pct.				
.000-.099	10	1	3	8
.100-.149	0	0	0	0
.150-.199	0	0	0	1
.200-.249	2	0	0	0
.250-.299	0	2	1	2
.300-.349	7	3	4	5
.350-.399	2	0	0	1
.400-.449	3	1	1	3
.450-.499	2	1	0	1
.500-	2	5	2	9

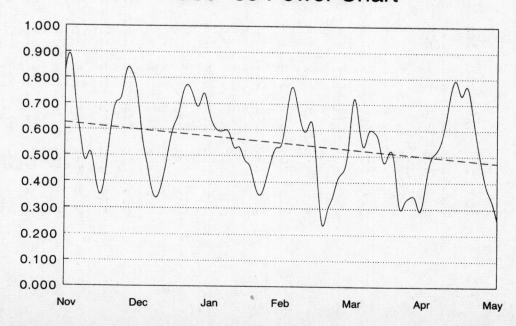

Portland Trail Blazers
1988–89 Power Chart

Portland Trail Blazers

	GP	GS	Min	FGM	FGA	FG%	2GM	2GA	2G%	3GM	3GA	3G%	FTM	FTA	FT%	Off	Tot	Ast	PF	Stl	TO	Blk	Pts	HGS
Richard Anderson	72	3	1082	145	348	0.417	96	207	0.464	49	141	0.348	32	37	0.865	62	169	231	100	44	54	12	371	366
Per GP			15.0	2.0	4.8		1.3	2.9		0.7	2.0		0.4	0.5		0.9	2.3	3.2	1.4	0.6	0.8	0.2	5.2	5.1
Per 48				22.5	6.4	15.4	4.3	9.2		2.2	6.3		1.4	1.6		2.8	7.5	10.2	4.4	2.0	2.4	0.5	16.5	16.2
Sam Bowie	20	0	412	69	153	0.451	64	146	0.438	5	7	0.714	28	49	0.571	36	70	106	43	8	33	26	171	194
Per GP			20.6	3.4	7.6		3.2	7.3		0.3	0.3		1.4	2.4		1.8	3.5	5.3	2.1	0.4	1.6	1.3	8.5	9.7
Per 48				8.6	8.0	17.8	7.5	17.0		0.6	0.8		3.3	5.7		4.2	8.2	12.3	5.0	0.9	3.8	3.0	19.9	22.6
Adrian Branch	67	4	811	202	436	0.463	195	405	0.481	7	31	0.226	87	120	0.725	63	69	132	99	45	64	3	498	375
Per GP			12.1	3.0	6.5		2.9	6.0		0.1	0.5		1.3	1.8		0.9	1.0	2.0	1.5	0.7	1.0	0.0	7.4	5.6
Per 48				16.9	12.0	25.8	11.5	24.0		0.4	1.8		5.1	7.1		3.7	4.1	7.8	5.9	2.7	3.8	0.2	29.5	22.2
Mark Bryant	56	32	803	120	247	0.486	120	247	0.486	0	0	0.000	40	69	0.580	65	114	179	144	20	41	7	280	274
Per GP			14.3	2.1	4.4		2.1	4.4		0.0	0.0		0.7	1.2		1.2	2.0	3.2	2.6	0.4	0.7	0.1	5.0	4.9
Per 48				16.7	7.2	14.8	7.2	14.8		0.0	0.0		2.4	4.1		3.9	6.8	10.7	8.6	1.2	2.5	0.4	16.7	16.4
Clyde Drexler	78	78	3066	829	1672	0.496	802	1566	0.512	27	106	0.255	438	548	0.799	289	326	615	269	213	250	53	2123	2039
Per GP			39.3	10.6	21.4		10.3	20.1		0.3	1.4		5.6	7.0		3.7	4.2	7.9	3.4	2.7	3.2	0.7	27.2	26.1
Per 48				63.9	13.0	26.2	12.6	24.5		0.4	1.7		6.9	8.6		4.5	5.1	9.6	4.2	3.3	3.9	0.8	33.2	31.9
Kevin Duckworth	79	79	2662	554	1161	0.477	554	1159	0.478	0	2	0.000	324	428	0.757	246	389	635	300	55	200	49	1432	1164
Per GP			33.7	7.0	14.7		7.0	14.7		0.0	0.0		4.1	5.4		3.1	4.9	8.0	3.8	0.7	2.5	0.6	18.1	14.7
Per 48				55.5	10.0	20.9	10.0	20.9		0.0	0.0		5.8	7.7		4.4	7.0	11.5	5.4	1.0	3.6	0.9	25.8	21.0
Rolando Ferreira	12	0	34	1	18	0.056	1	18	0.056	0	0	0.000	7	8	0.875	4	9	13	7	0	6	1	9	4
Per GP			2.8	0.1	1.5		0.1	1.5		0.0	0.0		0.6	0.7		0.3	0.8	1.1	0.6	0.0	0.5	0.1	0.8	0.3
Per 48				0.7	1.4	25.4	1.4	25.4		0.0	0.0		9.9	11.3		5.6	12.7	18.4	9.9	0.0	8.5	1.4	12.7	5.6
Steve Johnson	72	11	1477	296	565	0.524	296	565	0.524	0	0	0.000	129	245	0.527	135	223	358	254	20	140	44	721	683
Per GP			20.5	4.1	7.8		4.1	7.8		0.0	0.0		1.8	3.4		1.9	3.1	5.0	3.5	0.3	1.9	0.6	10.0	9.5
Per 48				30.8	9.6	18.4	9.6	18.4		0.0	0.0		4.2	8.0		4.4	7.2	11.6	8.3	0.6	4.5	1.4	23.4	22.2
Caldwell Jones	72	40	1279	77	183	0.421	77	182	0.423	0	1	0.000	48	61	0.787	88	212	300	166	24	83	85	202	409
Per GP			17.8	1.1	2.5		1.1	2.5		0.0	0.0		0.7	0.8		1.2	2.9	4.2	2.3	0.3	1.2	1.2	2.8	5.7
Per 48				26.6	2.9	6.9	2.9	6.8		0.0	0.0		1.8	2.3		3.3	8.0	11.3	6.2	0.9	3.1	3.2	7.6	15.3
Jerome Kersey	76	76	2716	533	1137	0.469	527	1116	0.472	6	21	0.286	258	372	0.694	246	383	629	277	137	167	83	1330	1405
Per GP			35.7	7.0	15.0		6.9	14.7		0.1	0.3		3.4	4.9		3.2	5.0	8.3	3.6	1.8	2.2	1.1	17.5	18.5
Per 48				56.6	9.4	20.1	9.3	19.7		0.1	0.4		4.6	6.6		4.3	6.8	11.1	4.9	2.4	3.0	1.5	23.5	24.8
Craig Neal	21	0	159	11	35	0.314	9	26	0.346	2	9	0.222	1	2	0.500	3	8	11	24	9	14	0	25	38
Per GP			7.6	0.5	1.7		0.4	1.2		0.1	0.4		0.0	0.1		0.1	0.4	0.5	1.1	0.4	0.7	0.0	1.2	1.8
Per 48				3.3	3.3	10.6	2.7	7.8		0.6	2.7		0.3	0.6		0.9	2.4	3.3	7.2	2.7	4.2	0.0	7.5	11.5
Terry Porter	81	81	3102	540	1146	0.471	461	927	0.497	79	219	0.361	272	324	0.840	85	282	367	187	146	248	8	1431	1606
Per GP			38.3	6.7	14.1		5.7	11.4		1.0	2.7		3.4	4.0		1.0	3.5	4.5	2.3	1.8	3.1	0.1	17.7	19.8
Per 48				64.6	8.4	17.7	7.1	14.3		1.2	3.4		4.2	5.0		1.3	4.4	5.7	2.9	2.3	3.8	0.1	22.1	24.9
Jerry Sichting	25	1	390	46	104	0.442	43	92	0.467	3	12	0.250	7	8	0.875	9	20	29	17	15	25	0	102	108
Per GP			15.6	1.8	4.2		1.7	3.7		0.1	0.5		0.3	0.3		0.4	0.8	1.2	0.7	0.6	1.0	0.0	4.1	4.3
Per 48				8.1	5.7	12.8	5.3	11.3		0.4	1.5		0.9	1.0		1.1	2.5	3.6	2.1	1.8	3.1	0.0	12.6	13.3
Brooke Steppe	27	2	242	33	78	0.423	28	69	0.406	5	9	0.556	32	37	0.865	13	19	32	32	11	13	1	103	90
Per GP			9.0	1.2	2.9		1.0	2.6		0.2	0.3		1.2	1.4		0.5	0.7	1.2	1.2	0.4	0.5	0.0	3.8	3.3
Per 48				5.0	6.5	15.5	5.6	13.7		1.0	1.8		6.3	7.3		2.6	3.8	6.3	6.3	2.2	2.6	0.2	20.4	17.9
Kiki Vandeweghe	18	1	432	103	217	0.475	87	179	0.486	16	38	0.421	29	33	0.879	11	24	35	40	7	18	4	251	158
Per GP			24.0	5.7	12.1		4.8	9.9		0.9	2.1		1.6	1.8		0.6	1.3	1.9	2.2	0.4	1.0	0.2	13.9	8.8
Per 48				9.0	11.4	24.1	9.7	19.9		1.8	4.2		3.2	3.7		1.2	2.7	3.9	4.4	0.8	2.0	0.4	27.9	17.6
Clint Wheeler	20	0	211	21	45	0.467	21	44	0.477	0	1	0.000	7	10	0.700	12	7	19	17	19	18	0	49	73
Per GP			10.5	1.0	2.3		1.0	2.2		0.0	0.0		0.3	0.5		0.6	0.3	0.9	0.8	0.9	0.9	0.0	2.4	3.6
Per 48				4.4	4.8	10.2	4.8	10.0		0.0	0.2		1.6	2.3		2.7	1.6	4.3	3.9	4.3	4.1	0.0	11.1	16.6
Danny Young	48	2	952	115	250	0.460	98	202	0.485	17	48	0.354	50	64	0.781	17	57	74	50	55	45	3	297	319
Per GP			19.8	2.4	5.2		2.0	4.2		0.4	1.0		1.0	1.3		0.4	1.2	1.5	1.0	1.1	0.9	0.1	6.2	6.6
Per 48				19.8	5.8	12.6	4.9	10.2		0.9	2.4		2.5	3.2		0.9	2.9	3.7	2.5	2.8	2.3	0.2	15.0	16.1

For a team that hasn't had a fifty-win season since their coach was playing in JuCo, the Kings are starting to show guarded optimism. There's not a single player left from the 1986–87 season, and the Kings made several bold moves during the season last year, sweeping out Joe Kleine, LaSalle Thompson, Ed Pinckney, and Derek Smith for Danny Ainge, Wayman Tisdale, and Brad Lohaus. Ainge and Tisdale ended the season 1–2 in points per 48 minutes for the Kings, with 26.5 and 26.6, respectively. The flux this team incurred was perhaps no better demonstrated than by the fact that their top five players started a total of only 264 games, by far the lowest in the league (New Jersey, at 294, was second worst—see the chart that appears with the Seattle comments).

If only the lack of continuity was their worst problem. Sacramento did quite well in defensive battles (they were 8–10 in games where under 200 points were scored), but when the score escalated, they were lost (8–27 when over 220 points were totaled in the game). In many of the looser games, they started to shoot before they could see the whites of the net, producing some truly putrid performances. Our personal favorites were: 24 for 80 (November 8 vs. Seattle), 29 for 83 (December 7 vs. Miami), 27 for 87 (November 12 vs. Dallas), and perhaps the silliest performance of this or any season, a 26 for 91 effort in a 34-point loss to an under-matched Utah team on December 3 (only 20 shots below .500!). By the way, in that Dallas game, the Kings went 17 for 29 from the stripe, losing by 40. Some teams set 120 points as a goal. Some try to hold opponents under 100. At times, the Kings seemed to be aiming for 30 shots made.

Only the Heat shot worse from the field than the Kings, although Sacramento shot fouls better than ten other teams. When a team is a significantly worse team from the field than the line, it often means that something other than aim is at fault, such as poor shot selection, lack of muscle, or poor offensive meshing. A lot of the Kings' poor aim could well be caused by their uncertainty, not being sure where teammates were, not knowing them well enough to give them the pick, not meshing well enough to work the ball around for the best possible shot. Their only big offensive positive was their three-point game, where they tried more shots than any team but the Knicks, and made a greater percentage than anyone but Seattle. A training camp together, with time for new coach-for-life Jerry Reynolds to implement a strategy based

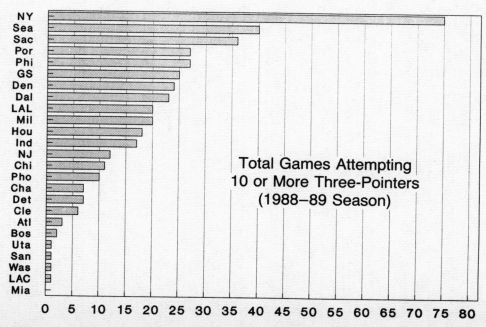

Sacramento Kings

Total Games Attempting
10 or More Three-Pointers
(1988–89 Season)

around the team's talents, and the Kings could actually be in a position to build on a halfway decent nucleus. With the continued progress of Ricky Berry and Vinnie Del Negro, and a good turnout by their draft choices, they should be looking down at least one or two other teams in the division for a change.

Listen, if they can keep this current team together, for the most part, over the next season, they should be much improved. Things look good for the future, since the front office refuses to panic like too many struggling franchises do. Bill Russell calmed everyone's fears by not returning to the sidelines, where he's proven to be ineffective in relating to players. Instead, Reynolds was given a long-term contract, perhaps just a bit out of sympathy, but also showing that the Kings have made a refreshing commitment to their future.

Everyone knows about the discovery of Reynolds' humorous streak after his courtside collapse. Our favorite line was when he said his biggest scare was "the thought of Billy Jones (the Kings' trainer) giving me mouth to mouth resuscitation. Death is preferable." Reynolds is a lot like Frank Layden—he realizes the insignificant place basketball occupies in the universe, but it doesn't mean that winning doesn't eat at him badly. He won't end the season with champagne this year, but his team will start to gel. Can they make .500? Probably not for another year. Can they make the playoffs? Iffy. Will they do better than last year? Certainly. There are two more expansion teams to pick on, if all else fails.

Sacramento Kings

	Home W	L	Road W	L
By Month				
November	2	4	0	5
December	3	2	1	8
January	4	3	2	7
February	2	6	1	4
March	5	5	1	5
April	5	0	1	6
Playoffs				
Home/Away	21	20	6	35
Overtime	0	1	0	2
Offense				
0-89	0	4	0	4
90-99	2	8	2	8
100-109	7	3	1	11
110-119	5	4	3	7
120-129	5	1	0	3
130-	2	0	0	2
Defense				
0-89	3	0	0	0
90-99	10	4	2	1
100-109	3	5	3	5
110-119	4	8	1	13
120-129	1	1	0	12
130-	0	2	0	4
Over/Under				
0-189	3	3	0	3
190-199	3	4	2	0
200-209	3	4	0	7
210-219	6	1	2	6
220-229	1	6	2	7
230-239	3	0	0	5
240-	2	2	0	7
Margin Of Victory				
0-3	3	3	4	3
4-6	3	1	1	7
7-10	3	7	1	3
11-15	6	1	0	9
16-20	2	3	0	7
21-	4	5	0	6
Field Goal Attempts				
0-69	0	0	0	0
70-79	1	2	1	4
80-89	9	7	1	15
90-99	8	9	4	13
100-109	3	2	0	3
110+	0	0	0	0
Field Goals Made				
0-34	1	5	1	5
35-39	5	4	0	9
40-44	5	9	5	10
45-49	7	2	0	8
50-54	3	0	0	3
55+	0	0	0	0
Field Goal Pct.				
.000-.399	1	4	1	6
.400-.424	2	7	2	1
.425-.449	3	1	1	5
.450-.474	4	2	1	4
.475-.499	3	3	0	7
.500-.524	4	1	1	6
.525-.549	3	2	0	4
.550-.574	1	0	0	2

	Home W	L	Road W	L
.575-.599	0	0	0	0
.600-	0	0	0	0
Opp. Field Goal Attempts				
0-69	0	0	0	0
70-79	3	5	0	1
80-89	5	10	2	14
90-99	7	3	2	13
100-109	5	2	2	6
110+	1	0	0	1
Opp. Field Goal Made				
0-34	3	0	0	0
35-39	11	3	2	3
40-44	2	9	2	10
45-49	5	6	1	12
50-54	0	2	0	8
55+	0	1	0	2
Opp. Field Goal Percentage				
.000-.399	7	0	1	2
.400-.424	3	0	2	1
.425-.449	5	0	0	0
.450-.474	4	3	1	2
.475-.499	1	2	2	7
.500-.524	1	4	0	10
.525-.549	0	7	0	6
.550-.574	0	2	0	4
.575-.599	0	0	0	3
.600-	0	2	0	0
Free Throw Attempts				
0-9	0	1	0	1
10-19	3	5	2	7
20-29	11	8	1	20
30-39	5	5	2	6
40-49	2	1	1	1
50+	0	0	0	0
Free Throws Made				
0-9	0	1	0	3
10-19	8	10	2	18
20-29	11	8	3	12
30-39	2	1	1	1
40-49	0	0	0	1
50+	0	0	0	0
Free Throw Pct.				
.000-.549	0	0	0	0
.550-.599	0	1	0	2
.600-.649	2	0	0	2
.650-.699	1	4	0	7
.700-.749	4	2	0	7
.750-.799	7	9	1	4
.800-.849	4	1	1	4
.850-.899	1	1	4	9
.900-.949	2	1	0	0
.950-	0	1	0	0
Opp. Free Throw Attempts				
0-9	0	0	0	0
10-19	1	5	1	3
20-29	16	10	3	14
30-39	3	4	2	13
40-49	1	1	0	4
50+	0	0	0	1
Opp. Free Throws Made				
0-9	1	0	1	0
10-19	9	13	2	8
20-29	10	6	3	21

	Home W	L	Road W	L
30-39	1	1	0	6
40-49	0	0	0	0
50+	0	0	0	0
Opp. Free Throw Pct.				
.000-.549	1	0	0	0
.550-.599	0	0	0	0
.600-.649	1	1	0	1
.650-.699	6	6	1	5
.700-.749	4	1	2	5
.750-.799	5	6	2	10
.800-.849	2	4	1	9
.850-.899	2	2	0	2
.900-.949	0	0	0	3
.950-	0	0	0	0
Offensive Rebounds				
0-9	2	1	0	5
10-14	9	9	3	18
15-19	7	10	3	11
20-24	3	0	0	1
25+	0	0	0	0
Total Rebounds				
0-39	0	1	0	2
40-44	2	4	0	6
45-49	0	4	1	9
50-54	0	0	0	0
55-59	10	9	1	15
60-64	4	2	2	3
65-	5	0	2	0
Opp. Offensive Rebounds				
0-9	2	7	0	5
10-14	7	7	2	14
15-19	6	6	3	10
20-24	5	0	1	6
25+	1	0	0	0
Opp. Total Rebounds				
0-39	0	0	0	0
40-44	0	3	0	4
45-49	1	3	1	4
50-54	0	0	0	0
55-59	15	9	3	16
60-64	2	2	2	5
65-	3	3	0	6
Offensive Rebound Pct.				
Below 25%	8	7	3	23
25-29.99%	8	11	1	8
30-34.99%	3	2	2	2
35-39.99%	1	0	0	1
40-44.99%	1	0	0	0
45% and up	0	0	0	1
Assists				
0-14	0	3	0	0
15-19	3	4	1	7
20-24	4	8	1	12
25-29	8	4	4	9
30-34	5	1	0	7
35+	1	0	0	0
Opp. Assists				
0-14	1	0	0	0
15-19	7	3	0	1
20-24	7	6	4	2
25-29	6	7	0	14
30-34	0	3	2	15
35+	0	1	0	3

	Home W	L	Road W	L
Edge In Assists				
Below-15	0	2	0	0
-10 to -14	0	1	1	7
-5 to -9	1	7	0	11
0 to -4	1	6	1	10
1-4	4	3	2	6
5-9	12	1	2	1
10-14	3	0	0	0
15-	0	0	0	0
Personal Fouls				
0-14	0	0	0	0
15-19	3	9	2	4
20-24	13	9	3	15
25-29	4	1	1	11
30-34	1	1	0	4
35+	0	0	0	1
Opp. Personal Fouls				
0-14	0	0	1	1
15-19	5	7	1	9
20-24	8	9	0	20
25-29	3	2	4	4
30-34	5	2	0	1
35+	0	0	0	0
Personal Fouls Edge				
Below-15	0	0	0	0
-10 to -14	0	1	0	0
-5 to -9	5	4	0	2
0 to -4	7	9	4	8
1-4	5	3	1	10
5-9	4	2	1	13
10-14	0	1	0	2
15+	0	0	0	0
Steals				
0-5	6	5	3	10
6-7	3	4	1	7
8-9	5	9	1	11
10-11	3	1	1	3
12-13	2	1	0	2
14+	2	0	0	2
Opp. Steals				
0-5	2	2	1	1
6-7	5	6	2	6
8-9	7	5	1	11
10-11	4	3	1	6
12-13	2	2	1	5
14+	1	2	0	6
Edge In Steals				
Below-7	2	2	1	5
-4 to -6	4	4	1	10
0 to -3	8	8	2	12
1-3	3	3	0	7
4-6	2	3	2	0
7-	2	0	0	1
Turnovers				
0-14	6	12	3	11
15-19	12	3	3	9
20-24	3	5	0	12
25-29	0	0	0	2
30-34	0	0	0	0
35+	0	0	0	1
Opp. Turnovers				
0-14	8	8	3	16
15-19	6	11	2	14

	Home W	L	Road W	L
20-24	3	1	1	4
25-29	4	0	0	1
30-34	0	0	0	0
35+	0	0	0	0
Edge In Turnovers				
Below-15	0	0	0	0
-10 to -14	3	0	0	1
-5 to -9	2	5	1	1
0 to -4	7	8	3	10
1- 4	5	4	2	8
5- 9	3	2	0	9
10-14	1	1	0	5
15+	0	0	0	1
Blocks				
1-2	2	3	1	10
3-4	5	8	1	11
5-6	4	8	2	10
7-8	4	0	1	3
9-10	3	1	0	0
11+	3	0	1	1

	Home W	L	Road W	L
Opp. Blocks				
0-2	3	3	0	9
3-4	6	3	1	8
5-6	7	4	1	4
7-8	5	9	3	7
9-10	0	1	1	3
11+	0	0	0	4
Edge In Blocks				
Below-7	0	0	0	2
-4 to -6	0	6	1	2
0 to -3	6	10	4	21
1-3	10	2	1	8
4-6	3	1	0	1
7+	2	1	0	1
Three-Pointers Attempted				
0-2	1	0	1	0
3-5	3	4	0	9
6-8	3	7	0	11
9-11	4	3	4	8
12-14	3	3	0	1
15+	7	3	1	6

	Home W	L	Road W	L
Three-Pointers Made				
0-2	3	11	3	16
3-5	9	7	1	12
6-8	4	2	2	6
9-11	4	0	0	0
12-14	0	0	0	1
15+	1	0	0	0
Three-Pointers Pct.				
.000-.099	3	4	2	6
.100-.149	0	0	0	2
.150-.199	1	1	0	3
.200-.249	0	0	1	2
.250-.299	0	4	0	2
.300-.349	3	7	1	3
.350-.399	2	1	0	5
.400-.449	2	1	0	6
.450-.499	2	1	0	1
.500-	8	1	2	5
Opp. Three-Point Attempts				
0-2	3	2	1	7
3-5	4	7	1	9

	Home W	L	Road W	L
6-8	6	6	1	5
9-11	4	4	2	10
12-14	4	1	0	2
15+	0	0	1	2
Opp. Three-Pointers Made				
0-2	13	12	4	23
3-5	8	7	2	9
6-8	0	0	0	3
9-11	0	1	0	0
12-14	0	0	0	0
15+	0	0	0	0
Opp. Three-Pointer Pct.				
.000-.099	6	5	2	7
.100-.149	3	2	1	2
.150-.199	1	1	0	2
.200-.249	1	0	0	3
.250-.299	5	2	1	5
.300-.349	1	1	2	8
.350-.399	1	1	0	1
.400-.449	0	0	0	1
.450-.499	1	2	0	0
.500-	2	6	0	6

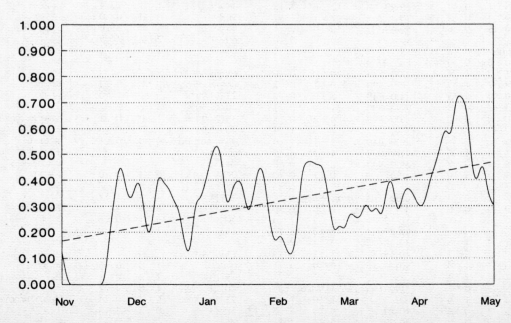

Sacramento Kings
1988–89 Power Chart

Sacramento Kings

	GP	GS	Min	FGM	FGA	FG%	2GM	2GA	2G%	3GM	3GA	3G%	FTM	FTA	FT%	Off	Tot	Ast	PF	Stl	TO	Blk	Pts	HGS
Danny Ainge	28	26	1028	209	462	0.452	151	312	0.484	58	150	0.387	91	112	0.812	34	67	101	78	41	63	7	567	482
Per GP			36.7	7.5	16.5		5.4	11.1		2.1	5.4		3.3	4.0		1.2	2.4	3.6	2.8	1.5	2.3	0.3	20.2	17.2
Per 48			21.4	9.8	21.6		7.1	14.6		2.7	7.0		4.2	5.2		1.6	3.1	4.7	3.6	1.9	2.9	0.3	26.5	22.5
Mike Allen	7	0	43	8	19	0.421	8	18	0.444	0	1	0.000	1	2	0.500	3	4	7	7	1	2	1	17	11
Per GP			6.1	1.1	2.7		1.1	2.6		0.0	0.1		0.1	0.3		0.4	0.6	1.0	1.0	0.1	0.3	0.1	2.4	1.6
Per 48			0.9	8.9	21.2		8.9	20.1		0.0	1.1		1.1	2.2		3.3	4.5	7.8	7.8	1.1	2.2	1.1	19.0	12.3
Ricky Berry	64	21	1406	255	567	0.450	190	407	0.467	65	160	0.406	131	166	0.789	57	140	197	197	37	82	22	706	501
Per GP			22.0	4.0	8.9		3.0	6.4		1.0	2.5		2.0	2.6		0.9	2.2	3.1	3.1	0.6	1.3	0.3	11.0	7.8
Per 48			29.3	8.7	19.4		6.5	13.9		2.2	5.5		4.5	5.7		1.9	4.8	6.7	6.7	1.3	2.8	0.8	24.1	17.1
Vinnie Del Negro	80	2	1556	239	503	0.475	233	483	0.482	6	20	0.300	85	100	0.850	48	123	171	160	65	65	14	569	602
Per GP			19.4	3.0	6.3		2.9	6.0		0.1	0.3		1.1	1.3		0.6	1.5	2.1	2.0	0.8	0.8	0.2	7.1	7.5
Per 48			32.4	7.4	15.5		7.2	14.9		0.2	0.6		2.6	3.1		1.5	3.8	5.3	4.9	2.0	2.0	0.4	17.6	18.6
Ben Gillery	24	0	84	6	19	0.316	6	19	0.316	0	0	0.000	13	23	0.565	7	16	23	29	2	5	4	25	33
Per GP			3.5	0.3	0.8		0.3	0.8		0.0	0.0		0.5	1.0		0.3	0.7	1.0	1.2	0.1	0.2	0.2	1.0	1.4
Per 48			1.8	3.4	10.9		3.4	10.9		0.0	0.0		7.4	13.1		4.0	9.1	13.1	16.6	1.1	2.9	2.3	14.3	18.9
Michael Jackson	14	0	70	9	24	0.375	7	18	0.389	2	6	0.333	1	3	0.333	1	3	4	12	3	4	0	21	18
Per GP			5.0	0.6	1.7		0.5	1.3		0.1	0.4		0.1	0.2		0.1	0.2	0.3	0.9	0.2	0.3	0.0	1.5	1.3
Per 48			1.5	6.2	16.5		4.8	12.3		1.4	4.1		0.7	2.1		0.7	2.1	2.7	8.2	2.1	2.7	0.0	14.4	12.3
Joe Kleine	47	11	913	116	303	0.383	116	302	0.384	0	1	0.000	81	88	0.920	75	166	241	126	18	67	18	313	303
Per GP			19.4	2.5	6.4		2.5	6.4		0.0	0.0		1.7	1.9		1.6	3.5	5.1	2.7	0.4	1.4	0.4	6.7	6.4
Per 48			19.0	6.1	15.9		6.1	15.9		0.0	0.1		4.3	4.6		3.9	8.7	12.7	6.6	0.9	3.5	0.9	16.5	15.9
Brad Lohaus	29	10	476	93	216	0.431	92	209	0.440	1	7	0.143	46	57	0.807	37	77	114	60	9	28	30	233	218
Per GP			16.4	3.2	7.4		3.2	7.2		0.0	0.2		1.6	2.0		1.3	2.7	3.9	2.1	0.3	1.0	1.0	8.0	7.5
Per 48			9.9	9.4	21.8		9.3	21.1		0.1	0.7		4.6	5.7		3.7	7.8	11.5	6.1	0.9	2.8	3.0	23.5	22.0
Rodney McCray	68	65	2435	340	729	0.466	335	707	0.474	5	22	0.227	169	234	0.722	143	371	514	120	57	168	35	854	983
Per GP			35.8	5.0	10.7		4.9	10.4		0.1	0.3		2.5	3.4		2.1	5.5	7.6	1.8	0.8	2.5	0.5	12.6	14.5
Per 48			50.7	6.7	14.4		6.6	13.9		0.1	0.4		3.3	4.6		2.8	7.3	10.1	2.4	1.1	3.3	0.7	16.8	19.4
Jim Petersen	66	40	1633	278	606	0.459	278	598	0.465	0	8	0.000	115	154	0.747	121	292	413	236	47	147	68	671	662
Per GP			24.7	4.2	9.2		4.2	9.1		0.0	0.1		1.7	2.3		1.8	4.4	6.3	3.6	0.7	2.2	1.0	10.2	10.0
Per 48			34.0	8.2	17.8		8.2	17.6		0.0	0.2		3.4	4.5		3.6	8.6	12.1	6.9	1.4	4.3	2.0	19.7	19.5
Ed Pinckney	51	24	1334	224	446	0.502	224	440	0.509	0	6	0.000	177	221	0.801	106	195	301	125	54	81	43	625	668
Per GP			26.2	4.4	8.7		4.4	8.6		0.0	0.1		3.5	4.3		2.1	3.8	5.9	2.5	1.1	1.6	0.8	12.3	13.1
Per 48			27.8	8.1	16.0		8.1	15.8		0.0	0.2		6.4	8.0		3.8	7.0	10.8	4.5	1.9	2.9	1.5	22.5	24.0
Harold Pressley	80	36	2257	383	873	0.439	264	578	0.457	119	295	0.403	96	123	0.780	216	269	485	216	92	124	76	981	929
Per GP			28.2	4.8	10.9		3.3	7.2		1.5	3.7		1.2	1.5		2.7	3.4	6.1	2.7	1.1	1.5	0.9	12.3	11.6
Per 48			47.0	8.1	18.6		5.6	12.3		2.5	6.3		2.0	2.6		4.6	5.7	10.3	4.6	2.0	2.6	1.6	20.9	19.8
Derek Smith	29	20	600	111	276	0.402	108	261	0.414	3	15	0.200	64	95	0.674	30	51	81	64	19	44	8	289	226
Per GP			20.7	3.8	9.5		3.7	9.0		0.1	0.5		2.2	3.3		1.0	1.8	2.8	2.2	0.7	1.5	0.3	10.0	7.8
Per 48			12.5	8.9	22.1		8.6	20.9		0.2	1.2		5.1	7.6		2.4	4.1	6.5	5.1	1.5	3.5	0.6	23.1	18.1
Kenny Smith	81	81	3145	547	1183	0.462	501	1055	0.475	46	128	0.359	263	357	0.737	49	177	226	173	102	249	7	1403	1311
Per GP			38.8	6.8	14.6		6.2	13.0		0.6	1.6		3.2	4.4		0.6	2.2	2.8	2.1	1.3	3.1	0.1	17.3	16.2
Per 48			65.5	8.3	18.1		7.6	16.1		0.7	2.0		4.0	5.4		0.7	2.7	3.4	2.6	1.6	3.8	0.1	21.4	20.0
LaSalle Thompson	43	42	1276	247	536	0.461	247	535	0.462	0	1	0.000	152	188	0.809	120	272	392	153	46	117	55	646	636
Per GP			29.7	5.7	12.5		5.7	12.4		0.0	0.0		3.5	4.4		2.8	6.3	9.1	3.6	1.1	2.7	1.3	15.0	14.8
Per 48			26.6	9.3	20.2		9.3	20.1		0.0	0.0		5.7	7.1		4.5	10.2	14.7	5.8	1.7	4.4	2.1	24.3	23.9
Wayman Tisdale	31	30	1108	247	472	0.523	247	472	0.523	0	0	0.000	119	160	0.744	88	211	299	109	20	65	20	613	559
Per GP			35.7	8.0	15.2		8.0	15.2		0.0	0.0		3.8	5.2		2.8	6.8	9.6	3.5	0.6	2.1	0.6	19.8	18.0
Per 48			23.1	10.7	20.4		10.7	20.4		0.0	0.0		5.2	6.9		3.8	9.1	13.0	4.7	0.9	2.8	0.9	26.6	24.2
Randy Wittman	31	2	416	50	117	0.427	48	113	0.425	2	4	0.500	16	22	0.727	6	20	26	12	10	12	0	118	93
Per GP			13.4	1.6	3.8		1.5	3.6		0.1	0.1		0.5	0.7		0.2	0.6	0.8	0.4	0.3	0.4	0.0	3.8	3.0
Per 48			8.7	5.8	13.5		5.5	13.0		0.2	0.5		1.8	2.5		0.7	2.3	3.0	1.4	1.2	1.4	0.0	13.6	10.7

SAN ANTONIO SPURS

It wasn't a fun year deep in the heart of Texas. Not much had been expected of the Spurs, but why accentuate that fact by thinking "wait till next year" before this year has even started? San Antonio is praying that David Robinson is truly the savior he has been made out to be. If he isn't, well, we're looking at some problems down the road.

For most of the campaign, the Spurs wandered aimlessly, perhaps running plays designed for when David Robinson joins the team. In addition, they've hired a coach known for leaving teams in the lurch (see: UCLA 1980, New Jersey 1983, Kansas 1988). As soon as a better offer comes around, expect to see Larry Brown take off. If he follows form, expect him to get an offer halfway through a first-round playoff game, and not come out after halftime.

The Spurs weren't the worst team last season, but they were far closer to the basement than the penthouse. For all his problems, Larry Brown is widely considered one of the best coaches on earth. Yet under his tutelage, the Spurs dropped 10 more games than their previous season, which itself was no great shakes. The last time this team won more than half its games was 1983, which was the fifth year they had won 50 or more since 1975. Since

then, they've had five losing seasons, and one where they reached .500 (1985, the last year of George Gervin's slippage). Their 21–61 record was also their worst record in the franchise history. No matter what you think of Brown morally, there's no way you can blame this whole thing on him, as it seemed many had started to do. When you have average players who then get hurt, things like this happen. The absence of three-time All-Star guard Alvin Robertson, center Petur Gudmundsson (who, after two knee operations still couldn't clear anything but waivers), and guard Johnny Dawkins contributed to the problems.

The Spurs were a worse team on the road (3–38, minus 16.5 scoring margin) than even the Heat (3–38, minus 14.6 scoring margin). Do you realize what this means? Read that once more. The Heat played better on the road than the Spurs did. Their offense was one of the worst in the league, managing to score fewer than 100 points 25 times. Miami turned that trick 44 times, and Sacramento did 28 times, but on the other end of the spectrum, the Suns were only held under 100 three times all year. When you can't score, you can't mount many furious rallies. In fact, most of the Spurs' rallies were

San Antonio Spurs

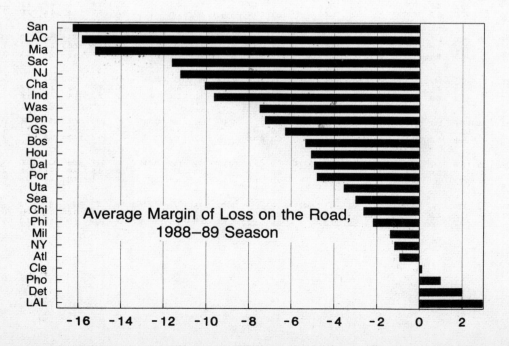

Average Margin of Loss on the Road, 1988–89 Season

better described as "piqued" than "furious." They shot 50 percent on the road only 7 times, going 2–5. They outfouled their opponents 54 times (going 10–44), indicating they constantly played from behind.

What they couldn't do in the field, they did even worse from the line. They were so bad from the stripe that they should seriously have considered declining some of the penalties and taken the yards instead. When the bricks cleared, the Spurs checked in at .698 from the foul line, the only team below .700, and a full .104 below the Bucks. How much did the foul shooting hurt them? When you're losing games by an average of 8 points, as they were, even those foul shots won't help. But it wasn't the final nail in the coffin as much as one symptom of overall shoddy play. Correcting any one these symptoms wouldn't have made a difference.

There were so many things wrong with this team that it's hard to know where to start. They shot a league-worst .215 from three-point territory, and rebounded better than only four teams. Considering that they missed so many shots, giving them more offensive rebound opportunities, their defensive rebounding must have been bad. It was, worse even than the woeful Hornets. The only thing that kept them from sinking further than they did was the fact that opponents tended to play down to their level—the Spurs were first in steals in the league, but also second in turnovers. These games were slop fests.

Alvin Robertson, when he played, did more than any other Spur, finishing with a 26.0 HGS despite only averaging 17.3 ppg. He's a Buck this season. Willie Anderson was one of the other bright spots at the HemisFair, justifying his top round draft choice by becoming the Spurs best scorer (26.4 pp48), and being outshadowed as a playmaker only by the multi-year All-Star Robertson. Vernon Maxwell,

another rookie guard, produced a fair 18.0 HGS, but shot only .432 from the field. Sixteen percent of his shots were three-point attempts, which cost him badly. Had he taken only twos, he would have scored 24 more points, raising his scoring average from 11.7 to 12.0. Okay, maybe it didn't hurt him badly, but it didn't help. If he can shoot more than .466 from two-point range, he'll become a productive pro.

Only one player was on the court for all 82 games last year, 6'10" power forward Greg Anderson. His weakness? He shot .503 from the field, but .514 from the line. Had he shot .698 (the team average—forget about the league average), he would have added 74 points to his totals. Maybe he'll perform better in Milwaukee. Had Johnny Dawkins shot the league average of 47.7% from the field, he'd have increased his production by 26 points. We've already found 124 points the Spurs could have added, by just being average. These points would have added 1.5 ppg to the team's scoring average, changing the team's scoring margin to − 5.8. Not great, but last year they projected to a .263 team. With those points, they'd be at least a .311 squad, giving them four or five more wins.

As we said before, David Robinson better be ready to play, since those plays are already being run for him. Everyone in San Antonio is hoping that Robinson will have an instant impact in the paint, where he'll clog up the middle, grab rebounds, and fill up the basket. It might be asking too much, too soon of the former number one pick from the U.S. Naval Academy. If everyone remains healthy this season, the Spurs should at least fend off the Hornets and the Timberwolves in the Midwest. If the losses start to pile up at a fast clip, however, we could see a new coach in here before too long.

San Antonio Spurs

	Home W	Home L	Road W	Road L
By Month				
November	4	3	1	5
December	2	5	0	7
January	4	4	1	6
February	0	3	1	9
March	6	2	0	8
April	2	6	0	3
Playoffs				
Home/Away	*18*	*23*	*3*	*38*
Overtime	*0*	*2*	*0*	*1*
Offense				
0-89	0	3	0	3
90-99	1	6	0	12
100-109	2	9	3	14
110-119	9	4	0	7
120-129	5	1	0	2
130-	1	0	0	0
Defense				
0-89	2	0	0	0
90-99	4	3	0	1
100-109	9	9	3	5
110-119	3	7	0	14
120-129	0	4	0	11
130-	0	0	0	7
Over/Under				
0-189	1	3	0	0
190-199	2	3	0	3
200-209	0	3	3	6
210-219	4	7	0	6
220-229	6	3	0	14
230-239	4	3	0	4
240-	1	1	0	5
Margin Of Victory				
0-3	1	2	1	4
4-6	2	8	2	2
7-10	2	6	0	4
11-15	5	7	0	8
16-20	5	0	0	9
21-	3	0	0	11
Field Goal Attempts				
0-69	0	0	0	0
70-79	1	2	0	0
80-89	7	12	2	18
90-99	10	7	0	13
100-109	0	2	1	7
110+	0	0	0	0
Field Goals Made				
0-34	0	1	0	3
35-39	0	6	0	13
40-44	4	13	3	13
45-49	9	2	0	8
50-54	5	1	0	1
55+	0	0	0	0
Field Goal Pct.				
.000-.399	0	2	0	5
.400-.424	0	2	0	12
.425-.449	0	3	1	3
.450-.474	2	7	0	6
.475-.499	3	2	0	7
.500-.524	3	7	2	4
.525-.549	6	0	0	1
.550-.574	2	0	0	0

	Home W	Home L	Road W	Road L
.575-.599	1	0	0	0
.600-	1	0	0	0
Opp. Field Goal Attempts				
0-69	0	1	0	0
70-79	3	4	1	3
80-89	11	9	0	18
90-99	4	7	1	11
100-109	0	2	1	5
110+	0	0	0	1
Opp. Field Goal Made				
0-34	1	1	0	0
35-39	13	6	2	5
40-44	2	7	1	13
45-49	2	9	0	13
50-54	0	0	0	5
55+	0	0	0	2
Opp. Field Goal Percentage				
.000-.399	2	0	1	2
.400-.424	2	1	0	1
.425-.449	2	2	0	0
.450-.474	8	4	1	4
.475-.499	1	8	0	7
.500-.524	0	5	1	13
.525-.549	2	1	0	7
.550-.574	1	2	0	2
.575-.599	0	0	0	2
.600-	0	0	0	0
Free Throw Attempts				
0-9	0	0	0	0
10-19	1	3	0	2
20-29	9	14	2	17
30-39	5	5	1	16
40-49	2	1	0	3
50+	1	0	0	0
Free Throws Made				
0-9	0	2	0	1
10-19	8	9	2	15
20-29	8	11	1	21
30-39	2	1	0	1
40-49	0	0	0	0
50+	0	0	0	0
Free Throw Pct				
.000-.549	0	0	0	4
.550-.599	2	1	0	4
.600-.649	5	8	1	5
.650-.699	4	1	0	5
.700-.749	2	6	1	7
.750-.799	3	1	1	8
.800-.849	1	4	0	2
.850-.899	0	2	0	3
.900-.949	1	0	0	0
.950-	0	0	0	0
Opp. Free Throw Attempts				
0-9	0	0	0	0
10-19	1	1	0	1
20-29	7	10	3	9
30-39	6	8	0	16
40-49	4	4	0	11
50+	0	0	0	1
Opp. Free Throws Made				
0-9	0	0	0	0
10-19	6	5	1	3
20-29	9	13	2	19

	Home W	Home L	Road W	Road L
30-39	3	5	0	15
40-49	0	0	0	1
50+	0	0	0	0
Opp. Free Throw Pct				
.000-.549	0	0	0	0
.550-.599	0	0	0	0
.600-.649	1	1	0	2
.650-.699	4	4	1	2
.700-.749	3	2	0	4
.750-.799	2	6	1	14
.800-.849	3	6	1	9
.850-.899	4	2	0	5
.900-.949	1	2	0	2
.950-	0	0	0	0
Offensive Rebounds				
0-9	0	4	0	2
10-14	7	7	1	9
15-19	8	9	1	18
20-24	3	2	1	7
25+	0	1	0	2
Total Rebounds				
0-39	1	1	0	2
40-44	1	8	0	1
45-49	0	4	1	7
50-54	0	0	0	0
55-59	11	7	1	18
60-64	2	1	1	7
65-	3	2	0	3
Opp. Offensive Rebounds				
0-9	1	3	0	0
10-14	10	8	0	14
15-19	7	9	1	19
20-24	0	2	1	5
25+	0	1	1	0
Opp. Total Rebounds				
0-39	2	1	0	0
40-44	1	0	0	1
45-49	4	4	1	3
50-54	0	0	0	0
55-59	10	12	1	19
60-64	1	1	0	9
65-	0	5	1	6
Offensive Rebound Pct.				
Below 25%	4	11	0	11
25-29.99%	6	5	1	13
30-34.99%	5	4	1	9
35-39.99%	3	1	1	2
40-44.99%	0	2	0	2
45% and up	0	0	0	1
Assists				
0-14	0	0	0	1
15-19	0	5	0	4
20-24	4	12	1	15
25-29	7	4	2	15
30-34	5	1	0	1
35+	2	1	0	2
Opp. Assists				
0-14	4	2	0	0
15-19	6	3	0	2
20-24	5	10	2	6
25-29	3	8	1	10
30-34	0	0	0	12
35+	0	0	0	8

	Home W	Home L	Road W	Road L
Edge In Assists				
Below -15	0	0	0	4
-10 to -14	0	1	0	9
-5 to -9	0	4	0	7
0 to -4	2	6	1	8
1-4	0	7	1	7
5-9	10	4	1	2
10-14	3	1	0	1
15-	3	0	0	0
Personal Fouls				
0-14	1	0	0	0
15-19	1	2	0	3
20-24	5	10	2	6
25-29	10	4	1	14
30-34	1	6	0	14
35+	0	1	0	1
Opp. Personal Fouls				
0-14	0	0	0	0
15-19	1	8	0	4
20-24	8	5	2	23
25-29	7	8	1	8
30-34	1	2	0	3
35+	1	0	0	0
Personal Fouls Edge				
Below -15	0	0	0	0
-10 to -14	1	0	0	0
-5 to -9	3	1	0	2
0 to -4	6	6	1	8
1-4	5	8	2	13
5-9	3	6	0	11
10-14	0	1	0	4
15+	0	1	0	0
Steals				
0-5	1	1	0	2
6-7	3	0	1	2
8-9	1	4	0	7
10-11	1	10	0	9
12-13	3	4	0	7
14+	9	4	2	11
Opp. Steals				
0-5	3	1	0	0
6-7	2	4	0	2
8-9	1	7	1	7
10-11	5	3	1	10
12-13	3	6	1	8
14+	4	2	0	11
Edge In Steals				
Below -7	1	0	0	4
-4 to -6	3	2	1	9
0 to -3	3	8	0	9
1-3	2	9	0	10
4-6	4	3	1	3
7-	5	1	1	3
Turnovers				
0-14	4	4	0	5
15-19	4	11	1	5
20-24	4	5	2	15
25-29	6	3	0	10
30-34	0	0	0	2
35+	0	0	0	1
Opp. Turnovers				
0-14	1	1	1	1
15-19	4	10	0	17

	Home W	L	Road W	L
20-24	7	8	0	15
25-29	4	4	1	4
30-34	2	0	1	1
35+	0	0	0	0
Edge In Turnovers				
Below -15	0	0	0	0
-10 to -14	2	2	1	3
-5 to -9	6	5	0	3
0 to -4	5	10	1	7
1-4	2	3	0	12
5-9	1	3	1	9
10-14	2	0	0	1
15+	0	0	0	3
Blocks				
1-2	2	3	0	6
3-4	5	13	2	8
5-6	6	4	0	11
7-8	4	2	0	10
9-10	1	1	1	2
11+	0	0	0	1

	Home W	L	Road W	L
Opp. Blocks				
0-2	5	3	0	0
3-4	5	6	1	6
5-6	3	3	0	10
7-8	4	6	1	5
9-10	1	3	0	12
11+	0	2	1	5
Edge In Blocks				
Below -7	0	2	0	6
-4 to -6	2	3	2	8
0 to -3	8	13	1	16
1-3	2	4	0	8
4-6	4	1	0	0
7+	2	0	0	0
Three-Pointers Attempted				
0-2	9	6	1	15
3-5	8	9	2	14
6-8	1	7	0	9
9-11	0	0	0	0
12-14	0	1	0	0
15+	0	0	0	0

	Home W	L	Road W	L
Three-Pointers Made				
0-2	16	21	3	37
3-5	2	2	0	1
6-8	0	0	0	0
9-11	0	0	0	0
12-14	0	0	0	0
15+	0	0	0	0
Three-Pointers Pct				
.000-.099	9	10	2	22
.100-.149	2	1	0	4
.150-.199	1	2	0	4
.200-.249	0	0	0	0
.250-.299	0	1	0	0
.300-.349	2	7	1	6
.350-.399	0	1	0	0
.400-.449	0	0	0	1
.450-.499	0	0	0	0
.500-	4	1	0	1
Opp. Three-Point Attempts				
0-2	1	3	0	4
3-5	7	10	2	11

	Home W	L	Road W	L
6-8	3	7	1	13
9-11	2	2	0	7
12-14	3	1	0	1
15+	2	0	0	2
Opp. Three-Pointers Made				
0-2	11	15	2	21
3-5	5	8	1	16
6-8	2	0	0	1
9-11	0	0	0	0
12-14	0	0	0	0
15+	0	0	0	0
Opp. Three-Pointer Pct				
.000-.099	8	9	1	11
.100-.149	0	0	0	0
.150-.199	2	1	0	5
.200-.249	0	0	0	0
.250-.299	1	0	0	1
.300-.349	2	3	0	8
.350-.399	2	2	1	2
.400-.449	2	4	1	2
.450-.499	0	0	0	2
.500-	1	4	0	7

San Antonio Spurs
1988–89 Power Chart

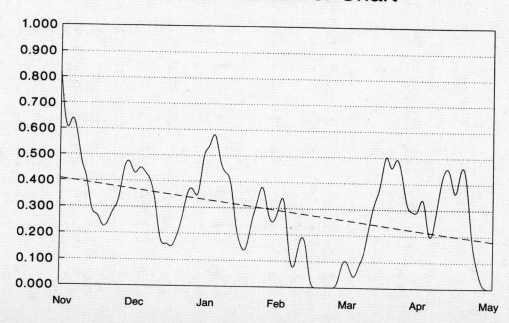

San Antonio Spurs

	GP	GS	Min	FGM	FGA	FG%	2GM	2GA	2G%	3GM	3GA	3G%	FTM	FTA	FT%	Off	Tot	Ast	PF	Stl	TO	Blk	Pts	HGS
Greg Anderson	82	56	2401	460	914	0.503	460	911	0.505	0	3	0.000	207	403	0.514	255	421	676	221	102	183	102	1127	1165
Per GP			29.3	5.6	11.1		5.6	11.1		0.0	0.0		2.5	4.9		3.1	5.1	8.2	2.7	1.2	2.2	1.2	13.7	14.2
Per 48			50.0	9.2	18.3		9.2	18.2		0.0	0.1		4.1	8.1		5.1	8.4	13.5	4.4	2.0	3.7	2.0	22.5	23.3
Michael Anderson	36	12	730	73	175	0.417	72	168	0.429	1	7	0.143	57	82	0.695	44	45	89	64	44	84	4	204	293
Per GP			20.3	2.0	4.9		2.0	4.7		0.0	0.2		1.6	2.3		1.2	1.3	2.5	1.8	1.2	2.3	0.1	5.7	8.1
Per 48			15.2	4.8	11.5		4.7	11.0		0.1	0.5		3.7	5.4		2.9	3.0	5.9	4.2	2.9	5.5	0.3	13.4	19.3
Willie Anderson	81	79	2738	640	1285	0.498	636	1264	0.503	4	21	0.190	224	289	0.775	152	265	417	295	150	261	59	1508	1391
Per GP			33.8	7.9	15.9		7.9	15.6		0.0	0.3		2.8	3.6		1.9	3.3	5.1	3.6	1.9	3.2	0.7	18.6	17.2
Per 48			57.0	11.2	22.5		11.1	22.2		0.1	0.4		3.9	5.1		2.7	4.6	7.3	5.2	2.6	4.6	1.0	26.4	24.4
Anthony Bowie	18	5	438	72	144	0.500	71	139	0.511	1	5	0.200	10	15	0.667	25	31	56	43	18	22	4	155	139
Per GP			24.3	4.0	8.0		3.9	7.7		0.1	0.3		0.6	0.8		1.4	1.7	3.1	2.4	1.0	1.2	0.2	8.6	7.7
Per 48			9.1	7.9	15.8		7.8	15.2		0.1	0.5		1.1	1.6		2.7	3.4	6.1	4.7	2.0	2.4	0.4	17.0	15.2
Frank Brickowski	64	60	1822	337	654	0.515	337	652	0.517	0	2	0.000	201	281	0.715	148	258	406	252	102	165	37	875	890
Per GP			28.5	5.3	10.2		5.3	10.2		0.0	0.0		3.1	4.4		2.3	4.0	6.3	3.9	1.6	2.6	0.6	13.7	13.9
Per 48			38.0	8.9	17.2		8.9	17.2		0.0	0.1		5.3	7.4		3.9	6.8	10.7	6.6	2.7	4.3	1.0	23.1	23.4
Dallas Comegys	67	10	1119	166	341	0.487	166	339	0.490	0	2	0.000	106	161	0.658	111	122	233	160	42	84	64	438	483
Per GP			16.7	2.5	5.1		2.5	5.1		0.0	0.0		1.6	2.4		1.7	1.8	3.5	2.4	0.6	1.3	1.0	6.5	7.2
Per 48			23.3	7.1	14.6		7.1	14.5		0.0	0.1		4.5	6.9		4.8	5.2	10.0	6.9	1.8	3.6	2.7	18.8	20.7
Darwin Cook	36	0	757	147	315	0.467	141	284	0.496	6	31	0.194	46	56	0.821	21	38	59	77	43	62	4	346	271
Per GP			21.0	4.1	8.8		3.9	7.9		0.2	0.9		1.3	1.6		0.6	1.1	1.6	2.1	1.2	1.7	0.1	9.6	7.5
Per 48			15.8	9.3	20.0		8.9	18.0		0.4	2.0		2.9	3.6		1.3	2.4	3.7	4.9	2.7	3.9	0.3	21.9	17.2
Johnny Dawkins	32	30	1083	177	400	0.442	177	397	0.446	0	3	0.000	100	112	0.893	32	69	101	64	55	111	0	454	466
Per GP			33.8	5.5	12.5		5.5	12.4		0.0	0.1		3.1	3.5		1.0	2.2	3.2	2.0	1.7	3.5	0.0	14.2	14.6
Per 48			22.6	7.8	17.7		7.8	17.6		0.0	0.1		4.4	5.0		1.4	3.1	4.5	2.8	2.4	4.9	0.0	20.1	20.7
David Greenwood	38	15	912	105	247	0.425	105	247	0.425	0	0	0.000	84	105	0.800	92	146	238	123	30	55	24	294	372
Per GP			24.0	2.8	6.5		2.8	6.5		0.0	0.0		2.2	2.8		2.4	3.8	6.3	3.2	0.8	1.4	0.6	7.7	9.8
Per 48			19.0	5.5	13.0		5.5	13.0		0.0	0.0		4.4	5.5		4.8	7.7	12.5	6.5	1.6	2.9	1.3	15.5	19.6
Albert King	46	11	791	141	327	0.431	133	295	0.451	8	32	0.250	37	48	0.771	33	107	140	97	27	74	7	327	261
Per GP			17.2	3.1	7.1		2.9	6.4		0.2	0.7		0.8	1.0		0.7	2.3	3.0	2.1	0.6	1.6	0.2	7.1	5.7
Per 48			16.5	8.6	19.8		8.1	17.9		0.5	1.9		2.2	2.9		2.0	6.5	8.5	5.9	1.6	4.5	0.4	19.8	15.8
Vernon Maxwell	79	36	2065	357	827	0.432	325	698	0.466	32	129	0.248	181	243	0.745	49	153	202	136	86	175	8	927	775
Per GP			26.1	4.5	10.5		4.1	8.8		0.4	1.6		2.3	3.1		0.6	1.9	2.6	1.7	1.1	2.2	0.1	11.7	9.8
Per 48			43.0	8.3	19.2		7.6	16.2		0.7	3.0		4.2	5.6		1.1	3.6	4.7	3.2	2.0	4.1	0.2	21.5	18.0
Alvin Robertson	65	65	2287	465	962	0.483	456	916	0.498	9	46	0.196	183	253	0.723	158	226	384	259	197	228	36	1122	1241
Per GP			35.2	7.2	14.8		7.0	14.1		0.1	0.7		2.8	3.9		2.4	3.5	5.9	4.0	3.0	3.5	0.6	17.3	19.1
Per 48			47.6	9.8	20.2		9.6	19.2		0.2	1.0		3.8	5.3		3.3	4.7	8.1	5.4	4.1	4.8	0.8	23.5	26.0
Scott Roth	47	3	464	52	143	0.364	50	133	0.376	2	10	0.200	52	76	0.684	20	36	56	55	19	33	4	158	151
Per GP			9.9	1.1	3.0		1.1	2.8		0.0	0.2		1.1	1.6		0.4	0.8	1.2	1.2	0.4	0.7	0.1	3.4	3.2
Per 48			9.7	5.4	14.8		5.2	13.8		0.2	1.0		5.4	7.9		2.1	3.7	5.8	5.7	2.0	3.4	0.4	16.3	15.6
Mike Smrek	43	18	623	72	153	0.471	72	153	0.471	0	0	0.000	49	76	0.645	42	87	129	102	13	48	58	193	248
Per GP			14.5	1.7	3.6		1.7	3.6		0.0	0.0		1.1	1.8		1.0	2.0	3.0	2.4	0.3	1.1	1.3	4.5	5.8
Per 48			13.0	5.5	11.8		5.5	11.8		0.0	0.0		3.8	5.9		3.2	6.7	9.9	7.9	1.0	3.7	4.5	14.9	19.1
Jay Vincent	24	3	551	91	219	0.416	91	218	0.417	0	1	0.000	35	51	0.686	36	56	92	52	5	37	3	217	146
Per GP			23.0	3.8	9.1		3.8	9.1		0.0	0.0		1.5	2.1		1.5	2.3	3.8	2.2	0.2	1.5	0.1	9.0	6.1
Per 48			11.5	7.9	19.1		7.9	19.0		0.0	0.1		3.0	4.4		3.1	4.9	8.0	4.5	0.4	3.2	0.3	18.9	12.7
Jerome Whitehead	52	4	580	69	176	0.392	69	176	0.392	0	0	0.000	30	45	0.667	49	80	129	107	22	22	4	168	171
Per GP			11.2	1.3	3.4		1.3	3.4		0.0	0.0		0.6	0.9		0.9	1.5	2.5	2.1	0.4	0.4	0.1	3.2	3.3
Per 48			12.1	5.7	14.6		5.7	14.6		0.0	0.0		2.5	3.7		4.1	6.6	10.7	8.9	1.8	1.8	0.3	13.9	14.2
Petur Gudmundsson	5	3	70	9	25	0.360	9	25	0.360	0	0	0.000	3	4	0.750	5	11	16	15	1	8	1	21	17
Shelton Jones	7	0	92	9	25	0.360	9	25	0.360	0	0	0.000	8	13	0.615	6	10	16	8	2	7	2	26	27
Mike Mitchell	2	0	33	2	9	0.222	2	9	0.222	0	0	0.000	1	4	0.250	1	2	3	2	1	4	0	5	0
Calvin Natt	10	0	185	25	66	0.379	25	66	0.379	0	0	0.000	35	48	0.729	16	16	32	19	2	19	2	85	68
Keith Smart	2	0	12	0	2	0.000	0	1	0.000	0	1	0.000	2	2	1.000	0	1	1	0	0	2	0	2	2
John Stroeder	1	0	2	0	0	0.000	0	0	0.000	0	0	0.000	0	0	0.000	0	0	0	2	0	1	0	0	-1

The Sonics probably expected to be in third place last year, behind the Lakers and Trail Blazers. Well, the Lakers got there, but the surprising Suns were the other team keeping Seattle down. Forty-seven wins is nothing to sneeze at, even for this once powerful team, which posted its best mark since the 48-win campaign of 1982–83. They parlayed their draft choice into Michael Cage, who gave the team over 2500 minutes, starting nearly every game until the end of the season. His rebounding was off from his league-leading year, but when you look at the stats, you have to believe that Seattle is ahead on this deal right now.

The team also responded positively to the departure of oft-maligned scorer Tom Chambers. He had such a dark cloud hanging over him in the Emerald City that no one even seemed to mind that they got nothing for him. All things considered, however, they'd probably like to have James Donaldson back, with or without his knees (Donaldson and Chambers were the prinicpals in the 1983 trade). It's hard to pick out one big star on Seattle, not due to a lack of talent, but because they're simply a good team in its prime. You want us to choose one anyway? Okay, by a nose, Xavier McDaniel was the most important player on this team. He had his minutes cut through the course of the season, and his scoring dropped accordingly as he nonetheless performed admirably as a sixth man. Late in the season, after coach Bickerstaff's ulcer healed, the X-Man cracked the starting lineup and went on a tear, averaging 30.5 ppg over the last ten games of the season.

The McDaniel promotion was the only move this team made all year; no other team had such a stable, unchanging starting lineup. Ellis, McKey, and Lister each started all 82 games for the Sonics; only Houston duplicated this feat. Considering that in the fourth starting position, Cage and McDaniel split 81 games, and McMillan started 74 of the 75 games in which he appeared, the Sonics led the league, by far, in total games started by their top five players.

Although McDaniel was probably the most important Sonic, Dale Ellis was probably the one player you'd most like to start a team with. He might be the most fearless, unflappable player in the league, and with his guts, he shoots and makes the three-pointer as well as any other player in the league. In fact, he led the league in total points gained by shooting the three, with 142.3.

Even with these two players out there, a case

Seattle Supersonics

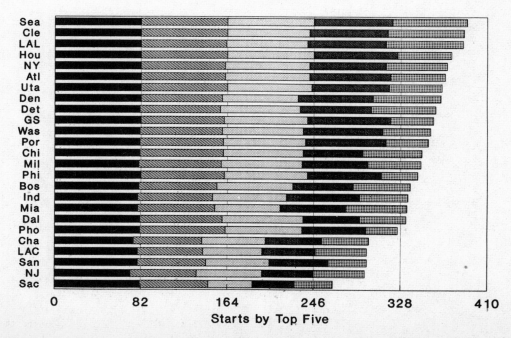

could be made for Derrick McKey being the most versatile player on the court, with three-point range as well as great driving skills and good defense. His presence nearly filled Chambers's high-tops, and he added dimensions that his predecessor never even dreamed of.

Michael Cage slumped last year, but it was somewhat deceptive. He had 173 fewer rebounds than the previous year in L.A., but his teammates had 267 more, so he simply didn't have to be as single-minded. Unfortunately, his other offensive stats were also off, so it wasn't all due to his environs. Although it appeared he was being benched in the late season, the team was suffering through a desperate slump, and it was more a matter of getting McDaniel back in. Both players got going in April, and the team pulled out of its nosedive, helping keep the wraps on Bickerstaff's ulcer.

Are we gushing over too many players here? The Sonics do have a young team whose nucleus is solid and in their prime. They tend to play too much on instinct at times, but a year or two of seasoning should calm them down. The biggest question mark on the team is at center, where Alton Lister and Olden Polynice split time. Lister isn't very consistent, and at times he looks like Benoit Benjamin without the attitude problems. He should do a lot more for the team, but can't night after night.

When Polynice comes off the bench, someone usually gets hurt. Although he's not a polished scorer, he gets his share off the offensive boards on tips, and he has the desire to stick for a few years. If Bickerstaff can get his centers into a good rotation, and extract a full year of production out of a platoon situation, the Sonics should continue to improve, and will be serious challengers for the home court advantage in the playoffs come 1990.

Seattle Supersonics

	Home W	L	Road W	L
By Month				
November	3	3	3	4
December	6	0	2	5
January	10	1	2	2
February	3	2	4	4
March	5	2	1	9
April	4	2	4	1
Playoffs				
Home/Away	31	10	16	25
Overtime	1	0	2	1
Offense				
0-89	0	0	1	1
90-99	1	2	2	5
100-109	5	5	6	11
110-119	7	3	6	7
120-129	12	0	0	1
130-	6	0	1	0
Defense				
0-89	1	0	4	0
90-99	6	1	5	0
100-109	12	1	5	8
110-119	10	6	1	7
120-129	1	2	0	7
130-	1	0	1	3
Over/Under				
0-189	1	0	3	0
190-199	3	1	3	2
200-209	1	0	4	6
210-219	3	4	2	5
220-229	9	3	2	4
230-239	4	1	1	5
240-	10	1	1	3
Margin Of Victory				
0-3	5	4	4	3
4-6	7	3	1	7
7-10	5	1	7	3
11-15	4	0	1	4
16-20	3	1	1	6
21-	7	1	2	2
Field Goal Attempts				
0-69	0	0	0	0
70-79	2	1	5	2
80-89	11	4	7	6
90-99	12	2	2	10
100-109	6	3	1	5
110+	0	0	1	2
Field Goals Made				
0-34	1	0	0	3
35-39	2	5	4	4
40-44	9	2	9	10
45-49	9	2	2	7
50-54	8	1	0	1
55+	2	0	1	0
Field Goal Pct.				
.000-.399	0	2	1	5
.400-.424	4	3	1	2
.425-.449	0	1	1	6
.450-.474	5	2	4	3
.475-.499	6	1	3	9
.500-.524	4	1	1	0
.525-.549	5	0	2	0
.550-.574	2	0	2	0

	Home W	L	Road W	L
.575-.599	4	0	1	0
.600-	1	0	0	0
Opp. Field Goal Attempts				
0-69	1	0	1	1
70-79	6	4	3	4
80-89	12	4	7	10
90-99	10	2	4	8
100-109	1	0	1	1
110+	1	0	0	1
Opp. Field Goal Made				
0-34	2	1	5	1
35-39	8	2	5	3
40-44	13	4	3	9
45-49	6	3	2	6
50-54	2	0	1	4
55+	0	0	0	2
Opp. Field Goal Percentage				
.000-.399	0	0	1	0
.400-.424	2	0	4	0
.425-.449	6	0	4	2
.450-.474	9	1	1	5
.475-.499	6	5	3	2
.500-.524	3	1	1	7
.525-.549	4	1	1	3
.550-.574	0	2	0	5
.575-.599	1	0	1	1
.600-	0	0	0	0
Free Throw Attempts				
0-9	0	0	0	0
10-19	4	1	1	8
20-29	5	4	8	10
30-39	13	4	7	5
40-49	8	1	0	2
50+	1	0	0	0
Free Throws Made				
0-9	1	0	0	3
10-19	6	5	7	11
20-29	15	3	9	8
30-39	8	2	0	3
40-49	1	0	0	0
50+	0	0	0	0
Free Throw Pct.				
.000-.549	0	0	0	0
.550-.599	1	0	1	1
.600-.649	3	1	0	3
.650-.699	3	3	3	5
.700-.749	3	3	2	5
.750-.799	13	2	6	6
.800-.849	7	0	3	7
.850-.899	0	1	0	1
.900-.949	1	0	0	0
.950-	0	0	1	1
Opp. Free Throw Attempts				
0-9	0	0	0	0
10-19	2	1	2	2
20-29	14	3	9	9
30-39	12	3	3	9
40-49	3	3	2	5
50+	0	0	0	0
Opp. Free Throws Made				
0-9	1	0	0	0
10-19	13	2	7	6
20-29	10	2	7	14

	Home W	L	Road W	L
30-39	7	6	2	5
40-49	0	0	0	0
50+	0	0	0	0
Opp. Free Throw Pct.				
.000-.549	1	0	1	0
.550-.599	3	0	0	1
.600-.649	1	0	1	3
.650-.699	4	0	3	3
.700-.749	5	1	2	0
.750-.799	9	2	4	4
.800-.849	3	5	1	7
.850-.899	0	2	3	6
.900-.949	3	0	0	1
.950-	2	0	1	0
Offensive Rebounds				
0-9	1	1	2	0
10-14	9	2	6	3
15-19	13	7	4	13
20-24	7	0	3	6
25+	1	0	1	3
Total Rebounds				
0-39	1	0	0	0
40-44	1	2	1	2
45-49	4	0	3	6
50-54	0	0	0	0
55-59	13	6	9	13
60-64	10	2	1	3
65-	2	0	2	1
Opp. Offensive Rebounds				
0-9	6	3	2	2
10-14	10	4	7	9
15-19	11	2	5	8
20-24	3	1	2	5
25+	1	0	0	1
Opp. Total Rebounds				
0-39	3	0	1	1
40-44	5	1	3	2
45-49	8	4	2	4
50-54	0	0	0	0
55-59	12	2	9	10
60-64	2	3	1	5
65-	1	0	0	3
Offensive Rebound Pct.				
Below 25%	5	2	4	1
25-29.99%	4	5	7	10
30-34.99%	11	3	2	6
35-39.99%	8	0	1	5
40-44.99%	3	0	1	2
45% and up	0	0	1	1
Assists				
0-14	0	1	0	1
15-19	2	0	1	2
20-24	8	4	7	13
25-29	9	4	5	8
30-34	7	1	3	1
35+	5	0	0	0
Opp. Assists				
0-14	1	0	1	0
15-19	8	3	3	2
20-24	16	1	7	8
25-29	2	5	4	6
30-34	4	1	0	7
35+	0	0	1	2

	Home W	L	Road W	L
Edge In Assists				
Below-15	0	1	0	1
-10 to -14	0	0	0	5
-5 to -9	2	2	2	9
0 to -4	6	3	3	2
1-4	6	1	5	4
5-9	8	2	4	4
10-14	5	0	2	0
15-	4	1	0	0
Personal Fouls				
0-14	1	0	0	0
15-19	8	3	1	2
20-24	6	0	8	8
25-29	13	3	4	9
30-34	3	3	3	5
35+	0	1	0	1
Opp. Personal Fouls				
0-14	0	0	0	2
15-19	5	3	5	10
20-24	9	3	7	5
25-29	10	3	3	6
30-34	6	1	1	2
35+	1	0	0	0
Personal Fouls Edge				
Below-15	0	0	0	0
-10 to -14	3	0	0	0
-5 to -9	6	1	2	1
0 to -4	9	0	6	4
1-4	9	6	3	5
5-9	3	2	4	11
10-14	1	1	1	2
15+	0	0	0	2
Steals				
0-5	1	3	0	3
6-7	2	1	3	5
8-9	4	2	1	7
10-11	10	2	5	4
12-13	7	0	3	1
14+	7	2	4	5
Opp. Steals				
0-5	4	3	2	5
6-7	9	3	6	3
8-9	7	1	5	7
10-11	9	3	3	5
12-13	1	0	0	1
14+	1	0	0	4
Edge In Steals				
Below-7	0	0	0	2
-4 to -6	1	0	1	3
0 to -3	8	3	3	10
1-3	7	6	1	2
4-6	7	1	5	7
7-	8	0	6	1
Turnovers				
0-14	8	3	5	6
15-19	17	6	8	7
20-24	4	1	3	7
25-29	1	0	0	5
30-34	1	0	0	0
35+	0	0	0	0
Opp. Turnovers				
0-14	4	4	2	8
15-19	11	3	8	10

	Home W	L	Road W	L
20-24	11	2	6	6
25-29	3	1	0	1
30-34	2	0	0	0
35+	0	0	0	0

Edge In Turnovers

	Home W	L	Road W	L
Below-15	1	0	0	0
-10 to -14	3	0	1	0
-5 to -9	8	4	3	4
0 to -4	11	2	8	7
1- 4	6	4	3	4
5- 9	2	0	1	7
10-14	0	0	0	2
15+	0	0	0	1

Blocks

	Home W	L	Road W	L
1-2	2	1	1	5
3-4	3	5	6	5
5-6	10	1	2	3
7-8	7	3	5	9
9-10	2	0	2	1
11+	7	0	0	2

Opp. Blocks

	Home W	L	Road W	L
0-2	6	2	1	2
3-4	14	3	7	4
5-6	6	3	5	10
7-8	3	2	2	7
9-10	1	0	1	1
11+	1	0	0	1

Edge In Blocks

	Home W	L	Road W	L
Below-7	1	0	0	2
-4 to -6	2	1	2	2
0 to -3	5	5	7	10
1-3	11	3	4	7
4-6	6	1	3	3
7+	6	0	0	1

Three-Pointers Attempted

	Home W	L	Road W	L
0-2	0	1	0	0
3-5	4	1	1	3
6-8	9	1	10	5
9-11	11	3	4	6
12-14	7	3	1	7
15+	0	1	0	4

Three-Pointers Made

	Home W	L	Road W	L
0-2	9	4	4	7
3-5	13	4	12	11
6-8	9	2	0	7
9-11	0	0	0	0
12-14	0	0	0	0
15+	0	0	0	0

Three-Pointers Pct.

	Home W	L	Road W	L
.000-.099	2	1	0	1
.100-.149	1	2	2	1
.150-.199	0	0	0	3
.200-.249	2	1	2	2
.250-.299	1	1	1	2
.300-.349	7	3	4	2
.350-.399	3	0	0	1
.400-.449	4	1	4	4
.450-.499	2	0	0	2
.500-	9	1	3	7

Opp. Three-Point Attempts

	Home W	L	Road W	L
0-2	5	1	1	3
3-5	11	2	5	7

	Home W	L	Road W	L
6-8	10	2	4	8
9-11	3	2	4	5
12-14	1	3	1	2
15+	1	0	1	0

Opp. Three-Pointers Made

	Home W	L	Road W	L
0-2	23	6	11	16
3-5	8	2	4	8
6-8	0	2	1	0
9-11	0	0	0	1
12-14	0	0	0	0
15+	0	0	0	0

Opp. Three-Pointer Pct.

	Home W	L	Road W	L
.000-.099	7	4	4	7
.100-.149	0	1	1	2
.150-.199	3	0	2	1
.200-.249	1	0	0	0
.250-.299	6	1	1	1
.300-.349	9	0	4	6
.350-.399	0	1	1	1
.400-.449	1	1	2	3
.450-.499	2	0	0	0
.500-	2	2	1	4

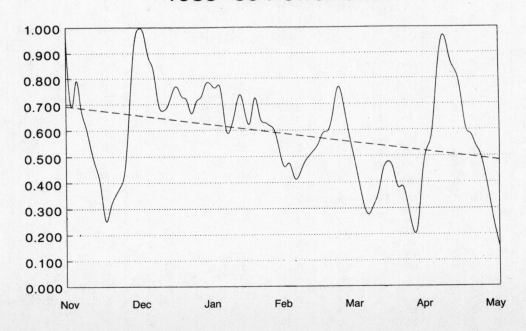

Seattle Supersonics
1988–89 Power Chart

Seattle Supersonics

	GP	GS	Min	FGM	FGA	FG%	2GM	2GA	2G%	3GM	3GA	3G%	FTM	FTA	FT%	Off	Tot	Ast	PF	Stl	TO	Blk	Pts	HGS
Greg Ballard	2	0	15	1	8	0.125	1	7	0.143	0	1	0.000	4	4	1.000	2	5	7	3	0	0	0	6	5
Per GP			7.5	0.5	4.0		0.5	3.5		0.0	0.5		2.0	2.0		1.0	2.5	3.5	1.5	0.0	0.0	0.0	3.0	2.5
Per 48			0.3	3.2	25.6		3.2	22.4		0.0	3.2		12.8	12.8		6.4	16.0	22.4	9.6	0.0	0.0	0.0	19.2	16.0
Michael Cage	80	71	2536	314	630	0.498	314	626	0.502	0	4	0.000	197	265	0.743	276	489	765	184	92	124	52	825	1118
Per GP			31.7	3.9	7.9		3.9	7.8		0.0	0.0		2.5	3.3		3.4	6.1	9.6	2.3	1.1	1.5	0.6	10.3	14.0
Per 48			52.8	5.9	11.9		5.9	11.8		0.0	0.1		3.7	5.0		5.2	9.3	14.5	3.5	1.7	2.3	1.0	15.6	21.2
Mike Champion	2	0	4	0	3	0.000	0	2	0.000	0	1	0.000	0	0	0.000	0	0	0	2	0	1	0	0	-3
Per GP			2.0	0.0	1.5		0.0	1.0		0.0	0.5		0.0	0.0		0.0	0.0	0.0	1.0	0.0	0.5	0.0	0.0	-1.5
Per 48			0.1	0.0	36.0		0.0	24.0		0.0	12.0		0.0	0.0		0.0	0.0	0.0	24.0	0.0	12.0	0.0	0.0	-36.0
Dale Ellis	82	82	3190	857	1710	0.501	695	1371	0.507	162	339	0.478	377	462	0.816	156	186	342	197	108	218	22	2253	1419
Per GP			38.9	10.5	20.9		8.5	16.7		2.0	4.1		4.6	5.6		1.9	2.3	4.2	2.4	1.3	2.7	0.3	27.5	17.3
Per 48			66.5	12.9	25.7		10.5	20.6		2.4	5.1		5.7	7.0		2.3	2.8	5.1	3.0	1.6	3.3	0.3	33.9	21.4
Avery Johnson	43	0	291	29	83	0.349	28	73	0.384	1	10	0.100	9	16	0.562	11	13	24	34	21	18	3	68	117
Per GP			6.8	0.7	1.9		0.7	1.7		0.0	0.2		0.2	0.4		0.3	0.3	0.6	0.8	0.5	0.4	0.1	1.6	2.7
Per 48			6.1	4.8	13.7		4.6	12.0		0.2	1.6		1.5	2.6		1.8	2.1	4.0	5.6	3.5	3.0	0.5	11.2	19.3
Alton Lister	82	82	1806	271	543	0.499	271	543	0.499	0	0	0.000	115	178	0.646	207	338	545	310	28	117	176	657	911
Per GP			22.0	3.3	6.6		3.3	6.6		0.0	0.0		1.4	2.2		2.5	4.1	6.6	3.8	0.3	1.4	2.1	8.0	11.1
Per 48			37.6	7.2	14.4		7.2	14.4		0.0	0.0		3.1	4.7		5.5	9.0	14.5	8.2	0.7	3.1	4.7	17.5	24.2
John Lucas	74	8	842	119	299	0.398	101	231	0.437	18	68	0.265	54	77	0.701	22	57	79	53	60	66	1	310	428
Per GP			11.4	1.6	4.0		1.4	3.1		0.2	0.9		0.7	1.0		0.3	0.8	1.1	0.7	0.8	0.9	0.0	4.2	5.8
Per 48			17.5	6.8	17.0		5.8	13.2		1.0	3.9		3.1	4.4		1.3	3.2	4.5	3.0	3.4	3.8	0.1	17.7	24.4
Xavier McDaniel	82	10	2385	677	1385	0.489	666	1349	0.494	11	36	0.306	312	426	0.732	177	256	433	231	84	210	40	1677	1219
Per GP			29.1	8.3	16.9		8.1	16.5		0.1	0.4		3.8	5.2		2.2	3.1	5.3	2.8	1.0	2.6	0.5	20.5	14.9
Per 48			49.7	13.6	27.9		13.4	27.1		0.2	0.7		6.3	8.6		3.6	5.2	8.7	4.6	1.7	4.2	0.8	33.8	24.5
Derrick McKey	82	82	2804	487	970	0.502	457	881	0.519	30	89	0.337	301	375	0.803	167	297	464	264	105	188	70	1305	1255
Per GP			34.2	5.9	11.8		5.6	10.7		0.4	1.1		3.7	4.6		2.0	3.6	5.7	3.2	1.3	2.3	0.9	15.9	15.3
Per 48			58.4	8.3	16.6		7.8	15.1		0.5	1.5		5.2	6.4		2.9	5.1	7.9	4.5	1.8	3.2	1.2	22.3	21.5
Nate McMillan	75	74	2341	199	485	0.410	184	415	0.443	15	70	0.214	119	188	0.633	143	245	388	236	156	211	42	532	1212
Per GP			31.2	2.7	6.5		2.5	5.5		0.2	0.9		1.6	2.5		1.9	3.3	5.2	3.1	2.1	2.8	0.6	7.1	16.2
Per 48			48.8	4.1	9.9		3.8	8.5		0.3	1.4		2.4	3.9		2.9	5.0	8.0	4.8	3.2	4.3	0.9	10.9	24.9
Olden Polynice	80	0	835	91	180	0.506	91	178	0.511	0	2	0.000	51	86	0.593	98	108	206	164	37	46	30	233	326
Per GP			10.4	1.1	2.3		1.1	2.2		0.0	0.0		0.6	1.1		1.2	1.3	2.6	2.0	0.5	0.6	0.4	2.9	4.1
Per 48			17.4	5.2	10.3		5.2	10.2		0.0	0.1		2.9	4.9		5.6	6.2	11.8	9.4	2.1	2.6	1.7	13.4	18.7
Jerry Reynolds	56	0	737	149	357	0.417	146	342	0.427	3	15	0.200	127	167	0.760	49	51	100	58	53	57	26	428	384
Per GP			13.2	2.7	6.4		2.6	6.1		0.1	0.3		2.3	3.0		0.9	0.9	1.8	1.0	0.9	1.0	0.5	7.6	6.9
Per 48			15.4	9.7	23.3		9.5	22.3		0.2	1.0		8.3	10.9		3.2	3.3	6.5	3.8	3.5	3.7	1.7	27.9	25.0
Russ Schoene	69	1	774	135	349	0.387	93	239	0.389	42	110	0.382	46	57	0.807	58	107	165	136	37	48	24	358	278
Per GP			11.2	2.0	5.1		1.3	3.5		0.6	1.6		0.7	0.8		0.8	1.6	2.4	2.0	0.5	0.7	0.3	5.2	4.0
Per 48			16.1	8.4	21.6		5.8	14.8		2.6	6.8		2.9	3.5		3.6	6.6	10.2	8.4	2.3	3.0	1.5	22.2	17.2
Sedale Threatt	63	0	1220	235	476	0.494	224	446	0.502	11	30	0.367	63	77	0.818	31	86	117	155	83	77	4	544	582
Per GP			19.4	3.7	7.6		3.6	7.1		0.2	0.5		1.0	1.2		0.5	1.4	1.9	2.5	1.3	1.2	0.1	8.6	9.2
Per 48			25.4	9.2	18.7		8.8	17.5		0.4	1.2		2.5	3.0		1.2	3.4	4.6	6.1	3.3	3.0	0.2	21.4	22.9

UTAH JAZZ

How long does it take for a rock-solid team to suddenly disintegrate and look like Swiss cheese? Sometimes a year, sometimes two or three. In Utah's case, however, it took about three games against Golden State for them to suddenly realize that they were *not* necessarily the heirs apparent to the Lakers in the West.

In a way, this team is one of the most complete in the league, since they have players who could do just about anything. However, most of the same players can *only* do one thing. Have you ever seen a team stocked with players gaudy in just one statistic? John Stockton gets assists. Mark Eaton blocks. Karl Malone scores and rebounds. No one else scores except Thurl Bailey. The Warriors exposed this flaw by forcing them to play an up tempo game. They dared Stockton to shoot, and he quickly lost his confidence, falling into a bad funk. Mark Eaton had a blocking slump, as the Warriors bombers drew him out of the middle. Golden State was the sixth most blocked team in the NBA during the regular season; Eaton managed only two in three games.

Where this team is at its worst is on the bench. Thurl Bailey is a premier sixth man, but he's really a starter—Marc Iavaroni is more of a tenth man than a starter (he finished dead last in the league in HGS).

Not to stretch the comparison, but Bill Russell played the same role as Bailey—off the bench for a majority of minutes, giving an infusion of instant offense. We know you don't doubt this fact, but just in case you might, imagine Iavaroni coming off the bench to replace Bailey. You'd be scouring the waiver wires for a replacement in a minute.

When Eaton was in foul trouble, which was often (he averaged 4.8 fouls per 48 minutes), who came in? Yup, Eric Leckner. Imagine Eaton with no defensive skills or reactive ability, and you've got Leckner. His offense is a bit sharper though (he shot .083 better than Eaton).

No, the bench is not the strength of this team. Take away Bailey, Eaton, Stockton, Malone, and Griffith, and what's left? Stiffs. Their defense was so good that you tended not to notice, but they averaged only 19.8 ppg from the bench, last in the league.

Still, given the choice, we'd rather have a great starting five than an average quintet and a great bench. It's not quite as bad as we make it sound. A quality small forward off the bench, maybe a scorer, and Utah could lead the whole conference next year. If not, well, then maybe Layden got out just in time.

Utah Jazz

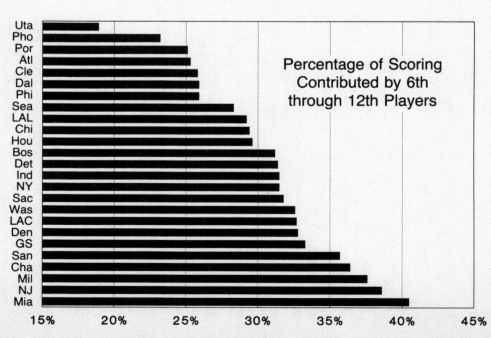

Percentage of Scoring Contributed by 6th through 12th Players

Utah Jazz

By Month	Home W	L	Road W	L
November	8	1	1	3
December	5	1	3	7
January	3	1	6	3
February	7	2	1	4
March	7	1	3	3
April	4	1	3	4
Playoffs				
Home/Away	34	7	17	24
Overtime	0	1	0	0

Offense	Home W	L	Road W	L
0-89	0	3	1	6
90-99	5	3	5	7
100-109	9	1	8	9
110-119	12	0	3	1
120-129	7	0	0	1
130-	1	0	0	0

Defense	Home W	L	Road W	L
0-89	8	1	5	0
90-99	17	4	8	2
100-109	6	2	3	7
110-119	2	0	1	11
120-129	1	0	0	3
130-	0	0	0	1

Over/Under	Home W	L	Road W	L
0-189	7	5	5	3
190-199	4	0	3	3
200-209	9	1	5	5
210-219	6	1	3	8
220-229	3	0	1	2
230-239	3	0	0	2
240-	2	0	0	1

Margin Of Victory	Home W	L	Road W	L
0-3	2	3	4	4
4-6	1	1	4	2
7-10	2	3	2	4
11-15	10	0	4	3
16-20	8	0	1	7
21-	11	0	2	4

Field Goal Attempts	Home W	L	Road W	L
0-69	1	0	1	3
70-79	12	3	8	13
80-89	14	2	6	7
90-99	6	2	2	1
100-109	1	0	0	0
110+	0	0	0	0

Field Goals Made	Home W	L	Road W	L
0-34	3	3	3	10
35-39	10	4	7	7
40-44	13	0	3	5
45-49	6	0	4	1
50-54	2	0	0	1
55+	0	0	0	0

Field Goal Pct.	Home W	L	Road W	L
.000-.399	3	3	0	1
.400-.424	1	1	0	3
.425-.449	1	3	2	5
.450-.474	4	0	4	8
.475-.499	4	0	3	2
.500-.524	11	0	4	0
.525-.549	3	0	2	1
.550-.574	5	0	1	2
.575-.599	0	0	0	1
.600-	2	0	1	1

Opp. Field Goal Attempts	Home W	L	Road W	L
0-69	1	0	0	0
70-79	4	1	2	5
80-89	11	5	8	10
90-99	15	1	7	9
100-109	3	0	0	0
110+	0	0	0	0

Opp. Field Goal Made	Home W	L	Road W	L
0-34	14	0	3	1
35-39	12	7	10	8
40-44	6	0	3	8
45-49	1	0	1	4
50-54	1	0	0	3
55+	0	0	0	0

Opp. Field Goal Percentage	Home W	L	Road W	L
.000-.399	14	1	5	1
.400-.424	11	0	2	1
.425-.449	4	3	5	1
.450-.474	2	2	4	8
.475-.499	2	0	0	4
.500-.524	1	1	1	6
.525-.549	0	0	0	2
.550-.574	0	0	0	0
.575-.599	0	0	0	0
.600-	0	0	0	1

Free Throw Attempts	Home W	L	Road W	L
0-9	0	0	0	0
10-19	0	0	3	1
20-29	9	5	7	8
30-39	11	0	3	10
40-49	13	2	4	5
50+	1	0	0	0

Free Throws Made	Home W	L	Road W	L
0-9	0	0	0	0
10-19	2	5	6	4
20-29	18	0	7	16
30-39	13	2	4	4
40-49	1	0	0	0
50+	0	0	0	0

Free Throw Pct.	Home W	L	Road W	L
.000-.549	0	0	0	0
.550-.599	0	0	0	1
.600-.649	1	0	0	1
.650-.699	2	2	1	4
.700-.749	2	1	2	5
.750-.799	14	3	4	10
.800-.849	8	1	5	1
.850-.899	5	0	4	2
.900-.949	2	0	1	0
.950-	0	0	0	0

Opp. Free Throw Attempts	Home W	L	Road W	L
0-9	0	0	0	0
10-19	5	1	4	0
20-29	13	4	9	10
30-39	14	2	4	7
40-49	2	0	0	7
50+	0	0	0	0

Opp. Free Throws Made	Home W	L	Road W	L
0-9	0	0	2	0
10-19	16	2	9	6
20-29	14	4	6	10
30-39	4	1	0	8
40-49	0	0	0	0
50+	0	0	0	0

Opp. Free Throw Pct.	Home W	L	Road W	L
.000-.549	2	0	0	0
.550-.599	3	0	1	2
.600-.649	0	0	4	0
.650-.699	3	0	5	2
.700-.749	4	0	1	4
.750-.799	9	3	5	8
.800-.849	8	1	0	4
.850-.899	5	2	1	3
.900-.949	0	1	0	0
.950-	0	0	0	1

Offensive Rebounds	Home W	L	Road W	L
0-9	7	1	5	5
10-14	13	2	9	13
15-19	11	3	3	6
20-24	3	1	0	0
25+	0	0	0	0

Total Rebounds	Home W	L	Road W	L
0-39	0	0	1	0
40-44	1	0	0	8
45-49	4	0	2	3
50-54	0	0	0	0
55-59	15	6	11	12
60-64	7	1	3	1
65-	7	0	0	0

Opp. Offensive Rebounds	Home W	L	Road W	L
0-9	3	1	2	1
10-14	14	2	4	11
15-19	12	3	9	9
20-24	3	1	2	3
25+	2	0	0	0

Opp. Total Rebounds	Home W	L	Road W	L
0-39	2	0	1	1
40-44	6	1	3	2
45-49	5	2	4	3
50-54	0	0	0	0
55-59	16	3	8	14
60-64	4	0	1	4
65-	1	1	0	0

Offensive Rebound Pct.	Home W	L	Road W	L
Below 25%	14	2	9	11
25-29.99%	10	2	5	9
30-34.99%	5	2	2	3
35-39.99%	3	1	1	1
40-44.99%	2	0	0	0
45% and up	0	0	0	0

Assists	Home W	L	Road W	L
0-14	0	0	0	0
15-19	2	1	0	2
20-24	8	6	7	10
25-29	12	0	7	10
30-34	9	0	3	2
35+	3	0	0	0

Opp. Assists	Home W	L	Road W	L
0-14	1	0	2	0
15-19	18	2	5	3
20-24	8	4	5	6
25-29	6	1	4	10
30-34	1	0	1	5
35+	0	0	0	0

Edge In Assists	Home W	L	Road W	L
Below -15	0	0	0	0
-10 to -14	0	0	1	2
-5 to -9	0	2	0	5
0 to -4	3	3	2	6
1-4	11	0	6	7
5-9	7	2	6	4
10-14	9	0	0	0
15-	4	0	2	0

Personal Fouls	Home W	L	Road W	L
0-14	2	0	1	0
15-19	6	3	5	1
20-24	14	2	7	8
25-29	11	1	4	9
30-34	1	0	0	6
35+	0	1	0	0

Opp. Personal Fouls	Home W	L	Road W	L
0-14	0	0	0	0
15-19	1	2	5	1
20-24	10	3	5	10
25-29	12	0	4	11
30-34	9	1	3	2
35+	2	1	0	0

Personal Fouls Edge	Home W	L	Road W	L
Below -15	2	0	0	0
-10 to -14	4	1	3	0
-5 to -9	13	0	1	4
0 to -4	10	5	8	10
1-4	5	0	1	5
5-9	0	1	4	4
10-14	0	0	0	1
15+	0	0	0	0

Steals	Home W	L	Road W	L
0-5	3	1	1	7
6-7	4	3	2	5
8-9	7	2	9	6
10-11	9	0	4	4
12-13	10	1	1	2
14+	1	0	0	0

Opp. Steals	Home W	L	Road W	L
0-5	5	2	1	2
6-7	5	1	5	5
8-9	8	1	5	4
10-11	6	1	3	3
12-13	5	1	2	7
14+	5	1	1	3

Edge In Steals	Home W	L	Road W	L
Below -7	2	1	1	3
-4 to -6	5	1	0	6
0 to -3	11	3	7	12
1-3	6	2	8	2
4-6	6	0	1	1
7-	4	0	0	0

Turnovers	Home W	L	Road W	L
0-14	8	1	5	3
15-19	13	4	7	6
20-24	12	2	5	12
25-29	1	0	0	2
30-34	0	0	0	1
35+	0	0	0	0

Opp. Turnovers	Home W	L	Road W	L
0-14	9	3	7	10
15-19	18	4	9	10

	Home W	L	Road W	L
20-24	5	0	1	3
25-29	2	0	0	1
30-34	0	0	0	0
35+	0	0	0	0
Edge In Turnovers				
Below -15	0	0	0	0
-10 to -14	1	0	0	0
-5 to -9	6	0	2	1
0 to -4	7	1	6	4
1-4	11	5	5	7
5-9	8	1	2	8
10-14	1	0	1	3
15+	0	0	1	1
Blocks				
1-2	1	0	1	3
3-4	2	1	2	8
5-6	5	3	4	6
7-8	6	3	6	5
9-10	11	0	3	2
11+	9	0	1	0

	Home W	L	Road W	L
Opp. Blocks				
0-2	4	1	2	4
3-4	5	1	5	5
5-6	10	0	3	4
7-8	11	4	3	3
9-10	2	1	3	5
11+	2	0	1	3
Edge In Blocks				
Below -7	2	0	0	4
-4 to -6	0	0	1	4
0 to -3	8	5	8	7
1-3	11	0	5	7
4-6	4	2	3	2
7+	9	0	0	0
Three-Pointers Attempted				
0-2	5	0	3	3
3-5	18	1	10	15
6-8	9	6	3	5
9-11	2	0	1	1
12-14	0	0	0	0
15+	0	0	0	0

	Home W	L	Road W	L
Three-Pointers Made				
0-2	30	6	13	22
3-5	4	1	4	2
6-8	0	0	0	0
9-11	0	0	0	0
12-14	0	0	0	0
15+	0	0	0	0
Three-Pointers Pct.				
.000-.099	10	2	8	7
.100-.149	1	2	0	0
.150-.199	7	3	0	1
.200-.249	1	0	0	0
.250-.299	1	0	0	3
.300-.349	6	0	1	3
.350-.399	0	0	0	0
.400-.449	2	0	4	3
.450-.499	0	0	0	0
.500-	6	0	4	7
Opp. Three-Point Attempts				
0-2	3	1	3	2
3-5	8	3	5	7

	Home W	L	Road W	L
6-8	8	1	4	6
9-11	10	0	3	5
12-14	4	2	2	1
15+	1	0	0	3
Opp. Three-Pointers Made				
0-2	20	5	9	15
3-5	13	2	8	6
6-8	1	0	0	1
9-11	0	0	0	2
12-14	0	0	0	0
15+	0	0	0	0
Opp. Three-Pointer Pct.				
.000-.099	9	4	9	8
.100-.149	0	0	0	2
.150-.199	2	0	0	0
.200-.249	2	1	1	0
.250-.299	2	1	1	1
.300-.349	9	1	2	6
.350-.399	3	0	0	0
.400-.449	3	0	1	2
.450-.499	3	0	0	0
.500-	1	0	3	5

Utah Jazz
1988–89 Power Chart

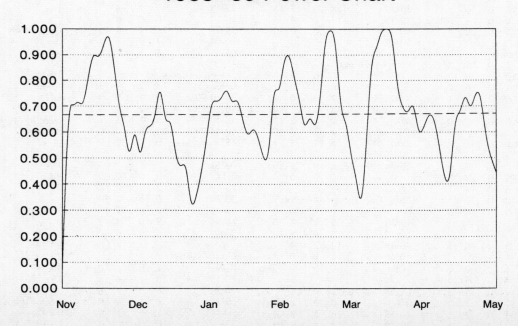

Utah Jazz

	GP	GS	Min	FGM	FGA	FG%	2GM	2GA	2G%	3GM	3GA	3G%	FTM	FTA	FT%	Off	Tot	Ast	PF	Stl	TO	Blk	Pts	HGS
Thurl Bailey	82	3	2777	615	1272	0.483	613	1267	0.484	2	5	0.400	363	440	0.825	115	332	447	185	48	208	91	1595	1241
Per GP				33.9	7.5	15.5		7.5	15.5		0.0	0.1		4.4	5.4		1.4	4.0	5.5	2.3	0.6	2.5	1.1	19.5	15.1
Per 48				57.9	10.6	22.0		10.6	21.9		0.0	0.1		6.3	7.6		2.0	5.7	7.7	3.2	0.8	3.6	1.6	27.6	21.5
Mike Brown	66	16	1051	104	248	0.419	104	248	0.419	0	0	0.000	92	130	0.708	92	166	258	132	25	78	17	300	340
Per GP				15.9	1.6	3.8		1.6	3.8		0.0	0.0		1.4	2.0		1.4	2.5	3.9	2.0	0.4	1.2	0.3	4.5	5.2
Per 48				21.9	4.7	11.3		4.7	11.3		0.0	0.0		4.2	5.9		4.2	7.6	11.8	6.0	1.1	3.6	0.8	13.7	15.5
Mark Eaton	82	82	2914	188	407	0.462	188	407	0.462	0	0	0.000	132	200	0.660	227	616	843	290	43	142	315	508	1218
Per GP				35.5	2.3	5.0		2.3	5.0		0.0	0.0		1.6	2.4		2.8	7.5	10.3	3.5	0.5	1.7	3.8	6.2	14.9
Per 48				60.7	3.1	6.7		3.1	6.7		0.0	0.0		2.2	3.3		3.7	10.1	13.9	4.8	0.7	2.3	5.2	8.4	20.1
Jim Farmer	37	0	412	57	142	0.401	48	122	0.393	9	20	0.450	29	41	0.707	22	33	55	41	9	26	0	152	109
Per GP				11.1	1.5	3.8		1.3	3.3		0.2	0.5		0.8	1.1		0.6	0.9	1.5	1.1	0.2	0.7	0.0	4.1	2.9
Per 48				8.6	6.6	16.5		5.6	14.2		1.0	2.3		3.4	4.8		2.6	3.8	6.4	4.8	1.0	3.0	0.0	17.7	12.7
Darrell Griffith	82	73	2382	466	1045	0.446	405	849	0.477	61	196	0.311	142	182	0.780	77	253	330	175	86	141	22	1135	773
Per GP				29.0	5.7	12.7		4.9	10.4		0.7	2.4		1.7	2.2		0.9	3.1	4.0	2.1	1.0	1.7	0.3	13.8	9.4
Per 48				49.6	9.4	21.1		8.2	17.1		1.2	3.9		2.9	3.7		1.6	5.1	6.6	3.5	1.7	2.8	0.4	22.9	15.6
Bob Hansen	46	9	964	140	300	0.467	121	246	0.492	19	54	0.352	42	75	0.560	29	99	128	105	37	45	6	341	276
Per GP				21.0	3.0	6.5		2.6	5.3		0.4	1.2		0.9	1.6		0.6	2.2	2.8	2.3	0.8	1.0	0.1	7.4	6.0
Per 48				20.1	7.0	14.9		6.0	12.2		0.9	2.7		2.1	3.7		1.4	4.9	6.4	5.2	1.8	2.2	0.3	17.0	13.7
Marc Iavaroni	77	50	796	72	163	0.442	72	162	0.444	0	1	0.000	36	44	0.818	41	91	132	99	11	52	13	180	182
Per GP				10.3	0.9	2.1		0.9	2.1		0.0	0.0		0.5	0.6		0.5	1.2	1.7	1.3	0.1	0.7	0.2	2.3	2.4
Per 48				16.6	4.3	9.8		4.3	9.8		0.0	0.1		2.2	2.7		2.5	5.5	8.0	6.0	0.7	3.1	0.8	10.9	11.0
Bart Kofoed	19	0	176	12	33	0.364	12	32	0.375	0	1	0.000	6	11	0.545	5	7	12	22	9	13	0	30	37
Per GP				9.3	0.6	1.7		0.6	1.7		0.0	0.1		0.3	0.6		0.3	0.4	0.6	1.2	0.5	0.7	0.0	1.6	1.9
Per 48				3.7	3.3	9.0		3.3	8.7		0.0	0.3		1.6	3.0		1.4	1.9	3.3	6.0	2.5	3.5	0.0	8.2	10.1
Eric Leckner	75	0	779	120	220	0.545	120	220	0.545	0	0	0.000	79	113	0.699	48	151	199	174	8	66	22	319	305
Per GP				10.4	1.6	2.9		1.6	2.9		0.0	0.0		1.1	1.5		0.6	2.0	2.7	2.3	0.1	0.9	0.3	4.3	4.1
Per 48				16.2	7.4	13.6		7.4	13.6		0.0	0.0		4.9	7.0		3.0	9.3	12.3	10.7	0.5	4.1	1.4	19.7	18.8
Jim Les	82	0	781	40	133	0.301	39	119	0.328	1	14	0.071	57	73	0.781	23	64	87	88	27	88	5	138	287
Per GP				9.5	0.5	1.6		0.5	1.5		0.0	0.2		0.7	0.9		0.3	0.8	1.1	1.1	0.3	1.1	0.1	1.7	3.5
Per 48				16.3	2.5	8.2		2.4	7.3		0.1	0.9		3.5	4.5		1.4	3.9	5.3	5.4	1.7	5.4	0.3	8.5	17.6
Karl Malone	80	80	3126	809	1559	0.519	804	1543	0.521	5	16	0.312	703	918	0.766	259	594	853	286	144	285	70	2326	2136
Per GP				39.1	10.1	19.5		10.0	19.3		0.1	0.2		8.8	11.5		3.2	7.4	10.7	3.6	1.8	3.6	0.9	29.1	26.7
Per 48				65.1	12.4	23.9		12.3	23.7		0.1	0.2		10.8	14.1		4.0	9.1	13.1	4.4	2.2	4.4	1.1	35.7	32.8
Jose Ortiz	51	15	327	55	125	0.440	55	124	0.444	0	1	0.000	31	52	0.596	30	28	58	40	8	36	7	141	106
Per GP				6.4	1.1	2.5		1.1	2.4		0.0	0.0		0.6	1.0		0.6	0.5	1.1	0.8	0.2	0.7	0.1	2.8	2.1
Per 48				6.8	8.1	18.3		8.1	18.2		0.0	0.1		4.6	7.6		4.4	4.1	8.5	5.9	1.2	5.3	1.0	20.7	15.6
Scott Roth	16	0	72	7	24	0.292	6	18	0.333	1	6	0.167	8	11	0.727	0	8	8	14	5	7	1	23	19
Per GP				4.5	0.4	1.5		0.4	1.1		0.1	0.4		0.5	0.7		0.0	0.5	0.5	0.9	0.3	0.4	0.1	1.4	1.2
Per 48				1.5	4.7	16.0		4.0	12.0		0.7	4.0		5.3	7.3		0.0	5.3	5.3	9.3	3.3	4.7	0.7	15.3	12.7
John Stockton	82	82	3171	497	923	0.538	481	857	0.561	16	66	0.242	390	452	0.863	83	165	248	241	260	308	14	1400	2134
Per GP				38.7	6.1	11.3		5.9	10.5		0.2	0.8		4.8	5.5		1.0	2.0	3.0	2.9	3.2	3.8	0.2	17.1	26.0
Per 48				66.1	7.5	14.0		7.3	13.0		0.2	1.0		5.9	6.8		1.3	2.5	3.8	3.6	3.9	4.7	0.2	21.2	32.3
Tony White	1	0	2	0	1	0.000	0	1	0.000	0	0	0.000	0	0	0.000	0	0	0	1	0	0	0	0	-1
Per GP				2.0	0.0	1.0		0.0	1.0		0.0	0.0		0.0	0.0		0.0	0.0	0.0	1.0	0.0	0.0	0.0	0.0	-1.0
Per 48				0.0	0.0	24.0		0.0	24.0		0.0	0.0		0.0	0.0		0.0	0.0	0.0	24.0	0.0	0.0	0.0	0.0	-24.0

Coach of the year? How about coach of the century? In 1987–88, Wes Unseld took over a team that was floundering at 8–19, and got them to fill that enormous ditch, going 30–25 under him and nearly dispatching the Pistons in the first round of the playoffs. This past season started out even worse for the Bullets. Looking back through our notes, we found a comment Josh wrote to himself in December: "This team is worse than the Hornets!" It is truly remarkable that Unseld got this seriously undermanned team to gel, challenging Boston until the last weekend of the season. It's a tribute to Unseld's will and personality, and he's done it two seasons in a row.

Unseld affected his team more than any other head coach last year. Moses Malone wanted to play the game his way, so Wes shipped him out. Unseld wanted to see some grit, the team showed grit. There are fears that the Bullets may have reached maximum potential last year, which is certainly possible unless Bob Ferry starts to make some moves aimed at plugging the holes that Unseld was able to patch over last year.

When Moses and Manute hit the Beltway, the talk around town was that any team with a player above 5'8" would cream the Bullets inside. Their lack of height was treated as a given, for one thing. Instead of belaboring the deficiency, they allowed nature to take its course and concentrated on the outside game. If you can't do anything about the big men, try to funnel the game away from them as much as possible, because when it does get into the paint, you're doomed.

Still, opposing centers had more than a field day against Washington in most games. Only Charlotte, San Antonio, and the Clippers were poorer at defending against starting centers, as shown in the chart below.

A lot of the next season hinges on the infusion of talent given the Bullets by their draft picks. Depending on their play, the Bullets could either breeze past .500, or duke it out with the Nets in the cellar. More than one player's status is up in the air right now. Although Bernard King is the heart of the team, he's not the player he once was, and must rely increasingly on his smarts to stay ahead of the competition. If they don't do something about their front line, opposing centers will run roughshod over them again this year. A gift at point guard would also certainly help. Nothing against Steve Colter, but he was only OK. The Bullets are only going to win when Jeff Malone is "on."

Washington Bullets

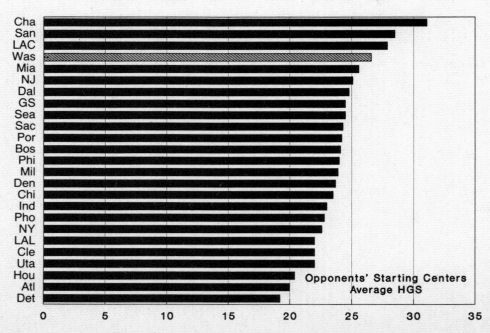

Opponents' Starting Centers
Average HGS

They could be the season's surprise team (the poor-man's Cleveland), or they could go into the dumpster. We'll know more once some of the nagging questions are answered. For a potentially weak team like this, though, they couldn't find a better coach.

There's one more note we have, which we realize is completely irrelevant, but is slightly less so in the team comments for a Washington squad. During his trial, Oliver North was quoted as providing the following testimony, describing the arms-for-hostages dealings with Iran:

> Slowly, more and more of the responsibility was passed to me. Basically, like a handoff in basketball, I suppose, we've got the ball and we run with it.

Now . . . we hope this doesn't sound partisan. And we're sure North is a great patriot and all. But any red-blooded American knows that you hand the ball off in *football,* not in basketball. Can you imagine if this guy had been captured by his own troops in World War II?

Sergeant: It's no use trying to escape from us, Nazi spy.

North: I am not a Nazi spy, sir, I am Lieutenant Colonel Oliver North of the United State Marine Corps.

Sergeant: If you're an American, who won the NL pennant in 1941?

North: The Red Wings, *sir!*

Sergeant: Like I said, it's no use trying to escape from us, Nazi spy.

Washington Bullets

	Home W	L	Road W	L
By Month				
November	2	4	2	4
December	3	2	1	9
January	8	3	0	3
February	3	1	3	6
March	9	0	2	6
April	5	2	2	2
Playoffs				
Home/Away	30	12	10	30
Overtime	2	1	1	2
Offense				
0-89	0	1	0	0
90-99	1	3	1	7
100-109	9	4	5	15
110-119	11	2	0	8
120-129	8	2	4	0
130-	1	0	0	0
Defense				
0-89	2	0	0	0
90-99	4	2	5	1
100-109	17	0	2	6
110-119	6	4	2	13
120-129	1	4	1	8
130-	0	2	0	2
Over/Under				
0-189	1	2	0	1
190-199	2	0	3	1
200-209	4	1	3	3
210-219	9	1	0	6
220-229	6	4	1	13
230-239	7	2	2	4
240-	1	2	1	2
Margin Of Victory				
0-3	7	2	1	3
4-6	6	1	4	5
7-10	7	2	4	6
11-15	5	3	1	7
16-20	4	1	0	6
21-	1	3	0	3
Field Goal Attempts				
0-69	0	0	0	0
70-79	2	0	0	1
80-89	13	4	7	8
90-99	12	5	3	18
100-109	2	2	0	3
110+	1	1	0	0
Field Goals Made				
0-34	1	0	0	2
35-39	1	5	1	11
40-44	12	3	5	12
45-49	10	4	2	3
50-54	6	0	1	2
55+	0	0	1	0
Field Goal Pct.				
.000-.399	2	1	0	5
.400-.424	1	2	0	4
.425-.449	2	5	3	10
.450-.474	5	3	1	5
.475-.499	3	0	3	3
.500-.524	10	1	0	3
.525-.549	2	0	1	0
.550-.574	5	0	2	0

	Home W	L	Road W	L
.575-.599	0	0	0	0
.600-	0	0	0	0
Opp. Field Goal Attempts				
0-69	0	0	0	0
70-79	5	4	0	6
80-89	10	3	6	7
90-99	12	4	4	16
100-109	3	1	0	1
110+	0	0	0	0
Opp. Field Goal Made				
0-34	3	1	0	0
35-39	12	1	2	4
40-44	6	4	8	13
45-49	7	4	0	9
50-54	2	2	0	4
55+	0	0	0	0
Opp. Field Goal Percentage				
.000-.399	1	0	0	0
.400-.424	6	0	2	0
.425-.449	4	2	2	3
.450-.474	7	1	1	3
.475-.499	6	3	3	9
.500-.524	4	3	1	8
.525-.549	1	0	1	4
.550-.574	1	0	0	2
.575-.599	0	3	0	1
.600-	0	0	0	0
Free Throw Attempts				
0-9	0	0	0	0
10-19	4	3	2	4
20-29	8	4	3	16
30-39	14	4	5	7
40-49	4	1	0	3
50+	0	0	0	0
Free Throws Made				
0-9	0	2	0	1
10-19	9	4	3	13
20-29	15	4	7	11
30-39	6	2	0	5
40-49	0	0	0	0
50+	0	0	0	0
Free Throw Pct				
.000-.549	0	0	0	1
.550-.599	1	0	1	0
.600-.649	5	1	0	1
.650-.699	4	2	0	6
.700-.749	1	0	1	5
.750-.799	10	3	4	2
.800-.849	5	4	2	7
.850-.899	2	2	2	7
.900-.949	1	0	0	1
.950-	1	0	0	0
Opp. Free Throw Attempts				
0-9	0	0	0	0
10-19	3	1	2	1
20-29	17	1	4	11
30-39	8	7	3	10
40-49	2	3	1	7
50+	0	0	0	1
Opp. Free Throws Made				
0-9	1	0	0	0
10-19	14	1	5	8
20-29	9	6	3	12

	Home W	L	Road W	L
30-39	6	5	2	10
40-49	0	0	0	0
50+	0	0	0	0
Opp. Free Throw Pct				
.000-.549	1	0	1	0
.550-.599	0	0	1	3
.600-.649	2	0	3	0
.650-.699	4	1	0	4
.700-.749	6	1	1	3
.750-.799	5	4	2	11
.800-.849	8	4	1	2
.850-.899	1	1	1	6
.900-.949	3	0	0	1
.950-	0	1	0	0
Offensive Rebounds				
0-9	1	2	0	2
10-14	14	4	6	8
15-19	7	4	3	16
20-24	5	1	1	4
25+	3	1	0	0
Total Rebounds				
0-39	0	1	0	0
40-44	0	1	0	2
45-49	4	4	1	7
50-54	0	0	0	0
55-59	19	2	8	17
60-64	5	4	1	3
65-	2	0	0	1
Opp. Offensive Rebounds				
0-9	4	2	1	6
10-14	12	5	5	12
15-19	9	4	3	9
20-24	5	1	1	3
25+	0	0	0	0
Opp. Total Rebounds				
0-39	0	0	0	0
40-44	6	1	2	2
45-49	10	2	1	3
50-54	0	0	0	0
55-59	6	3	5	14
60-64	5	4	2	9
65-	3	2	0	2
Offensive Rebound Pct.				
Below 25%	9	6	1	16
25-29.99%	4	3	5	5
30-34.99%	10	1	3	7
35-39.99%	7	2	1	2
40-44.99%	0	0	0	0
45% and up	0	0	0	0
Assists				
0-14	0	0	0	0
15-19	1	1	4	8
20-24	11	4	1	9
25-29	12	3	3	7
30-34	5	2	1	6
35+	1	2	1	0
Opp. Assists				
0-14	0	0	0	0
15-19	6	1	1	0
20-24	16	3	2	7
25-29	5	5	7	12
30-34	1	3	0	9
35+	2	0	0	2

	Home W	L	Road W	L
Edge In Assists				
Below -15	0	1	0	2
-10 to -14	2	1	2	3
-5 to -9	1	1	1	7
0 to -4	7	3	5	10
1-4	6	3	0	3
5-9	10	2	1	5
10-14	3	1	1	0
15-	1	0	0	0
Personal Fouls				
0-14	0	0	0	0
15-19	9	0	2	3
20-24	10	2	3	6
25-29	11	5	4	12
30-34	0	4	1	7
35+	0	1	0	2
Opp. Personal Fouls				
0-14	0	0	0	1
15-19	6	3	3	7
20-24	8	4	3	9
25-29	14	4	4	10
30-34	2	1	0	3
35+	0	0	0	0
Personal Fouls Edge				
Below -15	0	0	0	0
-10 to -14	0	0	0	0
-5 to -9	9	0	0	4
0 to -4	11	2	6	4
1-4	5	4	2	7
5-9	5	4	1	11
10-14	0	2	1	4
15+	0	0	0	0
Steals				
0-5	2	4	1	10
6-7	6	0	3	4
8-9	9	3	1	10
10-11	6	3	3	4
12-13	5	1	0	0
14+	2	1	2	2
Opp. Steals				
0-5	8	1	3	7
6-7	8	8	3	4
8-9	7	1	1	8
10-11	4	0	1	5
12-13	1	1	2	5
14+	2	1	0	1
Edge In Steals				
Below -7	1	1	0	3
-4 to -6	2	3	0	4
0 to -3	9	3	6	15
1-3	9	0	0	5
4-6	8	4	2	2
7-	1	1	2	1
Turnovers				
0-14	16	3	4	10
15-19	9	7	5	13
20-24	4	2	1	5
25-29	0	0	0	2
30-34	1	0	0	0
35+	0	0	0	0
Opp. Turnovers				
0-14	8	4	3	9
15-19	11	2	4	16

	Home W	L	Road W	L
20-24	11	5	3	4
25-29	0	1	0	1
30-34	0	0	0	0
35+	0	0	0	0

Edge In Turnovers

	Home W	L	Road W	L
Below -15	0	0	0	0
-10 to -14	2	0	1	1
-5 to -9	10	4	1	3
0 to -4	8	3	5	13
1-4	4	2	3	7
5-9	5	3	0	5
10-14	1	0	0	1
15+	0	0	0	0

Blocks

	Home W	L	Road W	L
1-2	9	5	3	10
3-4	7	2	2	13
5-6	8	5	4	6
7-8	4	0	1	1
9-10	1	0	0	0
11+	1	0	0	0

Opp. Blocks

	Home W	L	Road W	L
0-2	6	2	0	2
3-4	3	3	3	7
5-6	9	1	3	7
7-8	8	2	3	6
9-10	1	4	1	2
11+	3	0	0	6

Edge In Blocks

	Home W	L	Road W	L
Below -7	0	1	1	7
-4 to -6	10	3	1	6
0 to -3	13	5	7	12
1-3	6	3	1	5
4-6	0	0	0	0
7+	1	0	0	0

Three-Pointers Attempted

	Home W	L	Road W	L
0-2	24	6	9	7
3-5	5	3	0	15
6-8	1	3	0	6
9-11	0	0	1	2
12-14	0	0	0	0
15+	0	0	0	0

Three-Pointers Made

	Home W	L	Road W	L
0-2	29	12	9	28
3-5	1	0	1	2
6-8	0	0	0	0
9-11	0	0	0	0
12-14	0	0	0	0
15+	0	0	0	0

Three-Pointers Pct

	Home W	L	Road W	L
.000-.099	26	9	8	20
.100-.149	1	0	0	1
.150-.199	0	1	0	3
.200-.249	0	0	0	0
.250-.299	1	0	0	1
.300-.349	0	1	0	3
.350-.399	0	0	0	0
.400-.449	0	0	0	0
.450-.499	0	0	0	0
.500-	2	1	2	2

Opp. Three-Point Attempts

	Home W	L	Road W	L
0-2	0	6	0	5
3-5	12	3	5	11

	Home W	L	Road W	L
6-8	14	1	2	8
9-11	2	0	2	2
12-14	1	1	0	3
15+	1	1	1	1

Opp. Three-Pointers Made

	Home W	L	Road W	L
0-2	23	9	6	19
3-5	6	3	4	7
6-8	0	0	0	4
9-11	1	0	0	0
12-14	0	0	0	0
15+	0	0	0	0

Opp. Three-Pointer Pct

	Home W	L	Road W	L
.000-.099	10	7	3	10
.100-.149	6	1	1	1
.150-.199	4	1	1	3
.200-.249	0	0	0	1
.250-.299	0	0	1	1
.300-.349	4	1	1	2
.350-.399	1	1	0	0
.400-.449	4	0	0	3
.450-.499	0	0	0	1
.500-	1	1	3	8

Washington Bullets
1988–89 Power Chart

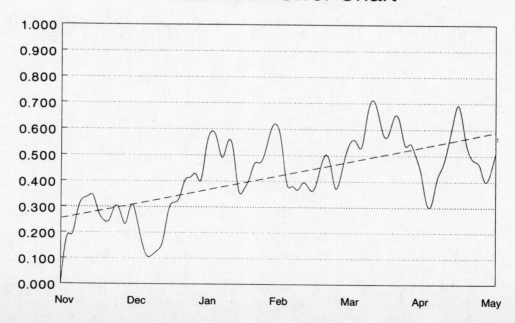

Washington Bullets

	GP	GS	Min	FGM	FGA	FG%	2GM	2GA	2G%	3GM	3GA	3G%	FTM	FTA	FT%	Off	Tot	Ast	PF	Stl	TO	Blk	Pts	HGS
Mark Alarie	74	5	1141	206	431	0.478	193	393	0.491	13	38	0.342	73	87	0.839	103	152	255	160	25	62	20	498	456
Per GP			15.4	2.8	5.8		2.6	5.3		0.2	0.5		1.0	1.2		1.4	2.1	3.4	2.2	0.3	0.8	0.3	6.7	6.2
Per 48			23.8	8.7	18.1		8.1	16.5		0.5	1.6		3.1	3.7		4.3	6.4	10.7	6.7	1.1	2.6	0.8	21.0	19.2
Terry Catledge	79	77	2077	334	681	0.490	333	676	0.493	1	5	0.200	153	254	0.602	230	342	572	250	46	120	28	822	843
Per GP			26.3	4.2	8.6		4.2	8.6		0.0	0.1		1.9	3.2		2.9	4.3	7.2	3.2	0.6	1.5	0.4	10.4	10.7
Per 48			43.3	7.7	15.7		7.7	15.6		0.0	0.1		3.5	5.9		5.3	7.9	13.2	5.8	1.1	2.8	0.6	19.0	19.5
Steve Colter	80	5	1425	203	457	0.444	200	432	0.463	3	25	0.120	125	167	0.749	62	120	182	158	69	64	14	534	632
Per GP			17.8	2.5	5.7		2.5	5.4		0.0	0.3		1.6	2.1		0.8	1.5	2.3	2.0	0.9	0.8	0.2	6.7	7.9
Per 48			29.7	6.8	15.4		6.7	14.6		0.1	0.8		4.2	5.6		2.1	4.0	6.1	5.3	2.3	2.2	0.5	18.0	21.3
Ledell Eackles	80	6	1459	318	732	0.434	309	692	0.447	9	40	0.225	272	346	0.786	100	80	180	156	41	128	4	917	661
Per GP			18.2	4.0	9.1		3.9	8.6		0.1	0.5		3.4	4.3		1.3	1.0	2.3	1.9	0.5	1.6	0.0	11.5	8.3
Per 48			30.4	10.5	24.1		10.2	22.8		0.3	1.3		8.9	11.4		3.3	2.6	5.9	5.1	1.3	4.2	0.1	30.2	21.7
Dave Feitl	57	36	828	116	266	0.436	116	265	0.438	0	1	0.000	54	65	0.831	69	133	202	136	17	65	18	286	278
Per GP			14.5	2.0	4.7		2.0	4.6		0.0	0.0		0.9	1.1		1.2	2.3	3.5	2.4	0.3	1.1	0.3	5.0	4.9
Per 48			17.2	6.7	15.4		6.7	15.4		0.0	0.1		3.1	3.8		4.0	7.7	11.7	7.9	1.0	3.8	1.0	16.6	16.1
Harvey Grant	71	1	1193	181	390	0.464	181	389	0.465	0	1	0.000	34	57	0.596	75	88	163	145	35	28	21	396	392
Per GP			16.8	2.5	5.5		2.5	5.5		0.0	0.0		0.5	0.8		1.1	1.2	2.3	2.0	0.5	0.4	0.3	5.6	5.5
Per 48			24.9	7.3	15.7		7.3	15.7		0.0	0.0		1.4	2.3		3.0	3.5	6.6	5.8	1.4	1.1	0.8	15.9	15.8
C.A. Jones	42	0	506	38	81	0.469	37	78	0.474	1	3	0.333	31	51	0.608	54	83	137	48	17	18	16	108	188
Per GP			12.0	0.9	1.9		0.9	1.9		0.0	0.1		0.7	1.2		1.3	2.0	3.3	1.1	0.4	0.4	0.4	2.6	4.5
Per 48			10.5	3.6	7.7		3.5	7.4		0.1	0.3		2.9	4.8		5.1	7.9	13.0	4.6	1.6	1.7	1.5	10.2	17.8
Charles Jones	54	45	1164	60	126	0.476	60	125	0.480	0	1	0.000	18	27	0.667	77	183	260	188	40	42	71	138	368
Per GP			21.6	1.1	2.3		1.1	2.3		0.0	0.0		0.3	0.5		1.4	3.4	4.8	3.5	0.7	0.8	1.3	2.6	6.8
Per 48			24.2	2.5	5.2		2.5	5.2		0.0	0.0		0.7	1.1		3.2	7.5	10.7	7.8	1.6	1.7	2.9	5.7	15.2
Bernard King	81	81	2559	654	1369	0.478	649	1339	0.485	5	30	0.167	361	441	0.819	133	251	384	219	64	224	12	1674	1282
Per GP			31.6	8.1	16.9		8.0	16.5		0.1	0.4		4.5	5.4		1.6	3.1	4.7	2.7	0.8	2.8	0.1	20.7	15.8
Per 48			53.3	12.3	25.7		12.2	25.1		0.1	0.6		6.8	8.3		2.5	4.7	7.2	4.1	1.2	4.2	0.2	31.4	24.0
Jeff Malone	76	75	2418	677	1410	0.480	676	1391	0.486	1	19	0.053	296	340	0.871	55	124	179	155	39	166	14	1651	1058
Per GP			31.8	8.9	18.6		8.9	18.3		0.0	0.3		3.9	4.5		0.7	1.6	2.4	2.0	0.5	2.2	0.2	21.7	13.9
Per 48			50.4	12.4	28.0		13.4	27.6		0.0	0.4		5.9	6.7		1.1	2.5	3.6	3.1	0.8	3.3	0.3	32.8	21.0
Dominick Presslev	10	0	107	8	25	0.320	8	25	0.320	0	0	0.000	5	9	0.556	3	11	14	9	4	11	0	21	31
Per GP			10.7	0.8	2.5		0.8	2.5		0.0	0.0		0.5	0.9		0.3	1.1	1.4	0.9	0.4	1.1	0.0	2.1	3.1
Per 48			2.2	3.6	11.2		3.6	11.2		0.0	0.0		2.2	4.0		1.3	4.9	6.3	4.0	1.8	4.9	0.0	9.4	13.9
Darrell Walker	79	78	2565	286	681	0.420	286	672	0.426	0	9	0.000	142	186	0.763	135	372	507	217	155	182	23	714	1143
Per GP			32.5	3.6	8.6		3.6	8.5		0.0	0.1		1.8	2.4		1.7	4.7	6.4	2.7	2.0	2.3	0.3	9.0	14.5
Per 48			53.4	5.4	12.7		5.4	12.6		0.0	0.2		2.7	3.5		2.5	7.0	9.5	4.1	2.9	3.4	0.4	13.4	21.4
John Williams	82	1	2413	438	940	0.466	419	869	0.482	19	71	0.268	225	288	0.781	158	415	573	213	142	157	69	1120	1348
Per GP			29.4	5.3	11.5		5.1	10.6		0.2	0.9		2.7	3.5		1.9	5.1	7.0	2.6	1.7	1.9	0.8	13.7	16.4
Per 48			50.3	8.7	18.7		8.3	17.3		0.4	1.4		4.5	5.7		3.1	8.3	11.4	4.2	2.8	3.1	1.4	22.3	26.8

THE EXPANSION TEAMS

MINNESOTA TIMBERWOLVES
ORLANDO MAGIC

When you're an expansion team you automatically become the butt of endless jokes—and with reason. With every loss the team inevitable comes thatmuchcloser to some NBA record for ineptness.

Victories are welcome, of course, but difficult to come by when the roster is made up of journeymen. In cases like this, a positive attitude is as valuable as the ability to execute a play because fragile egos get shattered very easily as the losses start to pile up.

The nucleus of the expansion squads are veteran players, cast-offs from other teams, players who didn't quite have the skill to stick. Of course, the surprise of last season's expansion draft was the number two pick, Rick "The Bad Boy" Mahorn from the Pistons. Just minutes after leading the soon-to-be-forgotten "Bad Boy" cheer at the NBA championship party at the Palace in Auburn Hills, bussing all of his teammates, and then thanking GM Jack McCloskey for encouraging him to lose weight and become a better player, Mahorn was told that he, and not center James Edwards, was being awarded the Bad Boy franchise in Minnesota. Mahorn was speechless.

Joining coach Bill Musselman's troops in the north this season will be one (Gulp!) double-figure scorer, center Steve Johnson (10.0 ppg) from Portland. You can be sure Musselman already has Johnson working on his abysmal free-throw shooting. Brad Lohaus (6.5 ppg) was cut loose from Sacramento and might add some offensive substance with his new team. Other notable standouts are Tyrone Corbin (8.2 ppg), the top offensive board man for the Suns, and David Rivers, (2.9 ppg) from the Lakers.

Coach Matt Guokas of the Orlando Magic may have more talent to work with than the Timberwolves. This means that he can hope to be competitive with his intra-state rival, the Miami Heat. Three double-digit scorers come from the expansion draft—Reggie Theus (15.8 ppg); Terry Catledge (10.4 ppg); and Otis Smith (10.0 ppg)—but the team still has no solid center. Mark Acres, at

6'11'' and 2.2 ppg, would be welcomed with open arms in Milan, but is hardly a solid foundation for Orlando. Sidney Green, the #1 pick overall in the expansion draft, will hopefully be the inside man with boards and points for this, his fourth team in seven seasons. However, if Reggie Theus holds true to form, he'll be heaving the ball at record pace. His career 18.8 ppg scoring dipped last year with the Hawks, but you can be sure he'll try his best to rectify the problem in Orlando.

Orlando Magic

	GP	Reb	Ast	PPG	HT	POS	PREV TEAM
Sidney Green	82	4.8	0.9	6.3	6-9	f	New York
Reggie Theus	81	3.0	4.7	15.8	6-7	g	Atlanta
Terry Catledge	79	7.2	0.9	10.4	6-8	f	Washington
Sam Vincent	70	2.7	4.8	9.4	6-2	g	Chicago
Otis Smith	80	4.1	1.8	10.0	6-5	g	Golden St.
Scott Skiles	80	1.9	4.9	6.8	6-1	g	Indiana
Jerry Reynolds	56	1.8	1.1	7.6	6-8	g-f	Seattle
Marc Acres	62	2.4	0.3	2.2	6-11	f-c	Boston
Morlon Wiley	51	0.9	1.5	2.2	6-4	g	Dallas
Jim Farmer	37	1.5	0.8	4.1	6-6	g	Utah
Keith Lee	57	4.5	0.7	4.8	6-10	f	New Jersey
Frank Johnson	67	1.2	2.7	4.4	6-3	g	Houston

Minnesota Timberwolves

	GP	Reb	Ast	PPG	HT	POS	PREV TEAM
Rick Mahorn	72	6.9	0.8	7.3	6-10	f-c	Detroit
Tyrone Corbin	77	5.2	1.5	8.2	6-6	g-c	Phoenix
Steve Johnson	72	5.0	1.5	10.0	6-10	f-c	Portland
Brad Lohaus	77	3.3	0.9	6.5	7-0	c	Sacramento
David Rivers	47	0.9	2.3	2.9	6-0	g	L.A. Lakers
Mark Davis	33	1.1	0.4	3.8	6-5	g	Milwaukee
Scott Roth	63	1.0	0.9	2.9	6-8	f	San Antonio
Shelton Jones	49	2.3	0.8	4.9	6-9	f	Philadelphia
Eric White	38	1.8	0.4	4.2	6-8	f	L.A. Clippers
Maurice Martin		did not play			6-6	g	Denver
Gunther Behnke		did not play			7-2	c	Cleveland

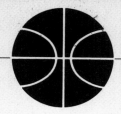

CHAPTER SEVEN

Player Analysis by Position

CENTERS

Akeem Olajuwon
Houston Rockets
36.6 HGS

College:	Houston
Age (1/1/1990):	27
Height:	7'0''
Weight:	250
Scoring:	0.539
Rebounding:	10.65
Playmaking:	0.10
Defense:	13.90
Gun Rating:	4.28
HoopStat Grade:	36.60
Minutes/Game:	36.88

Probably the best pure athlete in the NBA, and one of the best overall talents. Akeem can dominate a game as well as anyone, which has its drawbacks—he dominates not just the opponents, but his teammates at times. Although he's one of the highest-rated defensive players in the league, it's due to his superior shot-blocking abilities and quickness. He takes too many defensive chances, and sometimes it burns him, but he's banking on his ability to get back and overcompensate for mistakes. Besides, he only has to stop his opponent occasionally to come out on the long end of the stick, since he can score on any player in the league. It will be interesting, though, to see if he loses a step in a few years, and whether it affects his defense.

He tends to dominate his team's play, perhaps too much. Is he selfish? Or does he not understand the benefits of a team game? We'd like to think it was the latter, although his widely publicized feuds with teammates are not a positive sign. If you want to lead by virtue of being the best player on the team, you have to act like a leader.

Patrick Ewing
New York Knicks
32.6 HGS

College:	Georgetown
Age (1/1/1990):	28
Height:	7'0"
Weight:	240
Scoring:	0.594
Rebounding:	7.37
Playmaking:	0.15
Defense:	10.85
Gun Rating:	2.51
HoopStat Grade:	32.60
Minutes/Game:	36.20

Forget Mark Jackson. Forget Charles Oakley. Patrick Ewing is the absolute heart of this Knicks team. After a couple of oft-injured years, he's developed into a great player, even better than he was thought to be at Georgetown. He's also made a concerted effort to improve his public image; he was seen as a scary, hulking figure when he was a Hoya, and his relative shyness once he reached New York City meant it took longer for fans to get to "know" him.

One of Patrick's unique qualities is his "small" play. He seems at times to be a 6'6" small forward trapped in a center's body. He makes plays, he goes after the ball on the floor, he dives out of bounds to save a deflection. This same "smallness," however, sometimes keeps him from using his body to full advantage, as other centers are able to muscle him outside, altering his game slightly. Don't confuse this with a lack of toughness, however. The Knick trap would be dead in the water without him guarding against the free player breaking up the middle. He's learning how to rebound more effectively, although his defensive boards still outshadow his play in the paint. His defensive presence is much greater now that he knows he doesn't have to do it all for the Knicks. Opponents used to be able to pick up a lot of cheap fouls on him, but he doesn't get as frustrated on the floor now. He gets the benefit of the whistle less than he did as a rookie and soph, but only by a slight margin. He still draws about 1½ foul shots per foul he gives, a good bit above average for the league, but less than many superstars.

Oddly, the Knicks seemed to play better *without* Ewing, at least over the short haul. *Why* that is, is anybody's guess. Here's another fact that's anyone's guess. When Ewing had only one foul in a game, he played, on average, 33 minutes. However, the Knicks were 5–0 in those games and won by an average of 17 points.

Ewing averaged more rebounds when he had one or two fouls, highlighting his tentativeness when he was in foul trouble. When he fouled out, the Knicks lost by an average of over a point per game; when he drew only one foul, they won by 18.

Patrick's best line: He was never that poor when he was growing up. His family always had enough food on the table and enough air in the basketballs.

PATRICK EWING
Personal Fouls vs. Total Line

Patrick's Fouls	His Average Stats								The Final Score			
	Min	FGM	FGA	FTM	FTA	ORb	TRb	Pts	Opp	NY	Marg of Vict	W-L
6	35	9	20	5	6	3	8	24	113	111	−1	3–2
5	35	8	14	4	6	2	9	20	112	116	4	14–9
4	38	10	18	4	6	3	9	24	114	117	3	11–8
3	36	10	16	4	6	2	9	23	116	116	0	9–7
2	38	11	18	6	7	4	12	28	112	119	8	5–2
1	33	8	16	5	7	2	10	21	105	123	17	5–0

Robert Parish
Boston Celtics
29.3 HGS

College:	Centenary
Age (1/1/1990):	37
Height:	7'0''
Weight:	230
Scoring:	0.595
Rebounding:	10.44
Playmaking:	0.17
Defense:	8.81
Gun Rating:	4.15
HoopStat Grade:	29.30
Minutes/Game:	35.50

When Larry Bird went down, it wasn't McHale who came through for the Celtics. It wasn't Ainge, or D.J., or any of the rookies. The player who carried Boston on his back all year was Robert Parish. Unfortunately, he's hitting the downside of his career, and back-to-back games will place more of a strain on him over the next two years than ever before.

The Celtics scored 3.2 more points in the second of back-to-back games last year.

Ever notice how much Parish looks like New Hampshire's "Old Man in the Mountain"? It's scary.

Moses Malone
Atlanta Hawks
28.8 HGS

College:	None
Age (1/1/1990):	35
Height:	6'10''
Weight:	255
Scoring:	0.562
Rebounding:	10.23
Playmaking:	0.10
Defense:	7.74
Gun Rating:	1.51
HoopStat Grade:	28.80
Minutes/Game:	35.53

Moses had a good year for himself with Atlanta. The Hawks, however, are limited in what they can do with him. He won't run the floor, and this season he gave new life to the words "ball hog." He's gone through four teams now, sometimes for the money, sometimes because teams just give up trying to coach him. Like many of the Hawks, he hears, but doesn't care to listen. A lot depends on whether a team's game plan suits his style—if it does, he can hang around for a while. If not, he's a zero-sum proposition, for all his talent. With Moses as center this year, Atlanta stagnated, while Washington, with no center, improved slightly.

Although we have no figures on it, we're convinced that Malone gets away with the most traveling violations in the NBA.

Benoit Benjamin
Los Angeles Clippers
27.7 HGS

College:	Creighton
Age (1/1/1990):	26
Height:	7'0''
Weight:	250
Scoring:	0.579
Rebounding:	7.53
Playmaking:	0.17
Defense:	10.10
Gun Rating:	3.62
HoopStat Grade:	27.70
Minutes/Game:	32.72

Even if he hadn't come up with a good year, he'd get the money he was looking for. (Can you imagine his reaction upon reading that last statement? Something like: "You mean I didn't need to work as hard as I did? Damn, I wish I'd known that beforehand!") So much of this league is built on potential. Benoit is the King of Potential Land, and until he's well into his thirties, owners will be paying for it. When a 7'1'' player shows his undeniable flashes of brilliance, you'd be a fool not to try him out. But then again, you could be a fool to think he's going to turn the flashes into stretches. Look for him to get really lazy next year.

Danny Schayes
Denver Nuggets
25.9 HGS

College:	Syracuse
Age (1/1/1990):	31
Height:	6'11"
Weight:	245
Scoring:	0.596
Rebounding:	7.50
Playmaking:	0.17
Defense:	7.56
Gun Rating:	1.63
HoopStat Grade:	25.90
Minutes/Game:	25.22

Despite his high rating, he'd be better as a backup center. He's got decent fundamentals (shooting, passing), but his defense isn't his strong point, despite his work. Much of his game relies on back picks and making himself the open man on any particular play.

Brad Daugherty
Cleveland Cavaliers
25.6 HGS

College:	North Carolina
Age (1/1/1990):	25
Height:	7'0"
Weight:	245
Scoring:	0.578
Rebounding:	7.10
Playmaking:	0.28
Defense:	6.41
Gun Rating:	0.46
HoopStat Grade:	25.60
Minutes/Game:	36.17

Daugherty runs hot and cold. At times, you'll hear talk about how he's one of the top three centers in the league. Then he'll have a bad week or two, and he suddenly drops out of contention. On the whole, he's a player who's already damn good, and he's still got room to improve. If you were building a franchise from scratch, you'd have to flip a coin to decide whether you'd want to take Ewing or Daugherty first. Both are unselfish, possess fine fundamentals, and are young enough to build around.

Daugherty can pass better than most centers, (only Jack Sikma's play was better than Brad's 0.28) rebound fairly well (although he only rated 19th among centers), thread the needle on the outlet, and play pick and roll. See how far you get trying to convince Olajuwon to do that. Our scouts can't find any major weaknesses, notwithstanding his speed (and what center is really fast?) and his average shot blocking (but he's teamed with Larry Nance and Tree Rollins). His body is so big that he can stand nearly anywhere on the baseline and clog up the entire lane.

Rik Smits
Indiana Pacers
24.4 HGS

College:	Marist
Age (1/1/1990):	24
Height:	7'4"
Weight:	250
Scoring:	0.547
Rebounding:	7.40
Playmaking:	0.09
Defense:	8.13
Gun Rating:	1.92
HoopStat Grade:	24.40
Minutes/Game:	24.89

What do you see for Rik five years down the road? The prognosis before the season started varied widely from analyst to analyst—anywhere from the top center in the league to a CBA towel holder. Despite his lack of experience against major colleges (and don't tell us LIU is a major college), he was a surprisingly decent "project" last year. One could actually watch his play improve as Versace tossed him to the wolves in his first season. He's got a surprising mean streak, which showed in his 14 foulouts.

He blocks shots extremely well, and with the return of Stipanovich, a decision will have to be made. Smits could conceivably become a power forward, but he may get lost if players lure him out too far on the court. If he gets the ball, he can shoot over anybody (except maybe Manute).

The jury's still out, but Rik should be closer to the top of the NBA heap than the bottom within those five years.

Mike Gminski

Philadelphia 76ers

24.4 HGS

College:	Duke
Age (1/1/1990):	31
Height:	6'11"
Weight:	260
Scoring:	0.526
Rebounding:	8.04
Playmaking:	0.12
Defense:	7.48
Gun Rating:	−0.27
HoopStat Grade:	24.40
Minutes/Game:	33.40

Does anyone else think that the G-Man looks like he should be singing "Faith"? After an eight-year stint with the Nets (basketball's equivalent of paying your dues), he was allowed to start fresh in 1988 . . . with the worst Philly team in 13 years. With a slightly better team last year, Gminski got more credit for his perimeter game, and his stamina wasn't as much of a topic as in the past. Maybe it's just not as wearing to play for a decent team, but maybe Gminski is a player who can be good if he's just surrounded by some talent.

Alton Lister

Seattle Supersonics

24.2 HGS

College:	Arizona St.
Age (1/1/1990):	32
Height:	7'0"
Weight:	240
Scoring:	0.520
Rebounding:	9.17
Playmaking:	0.10
Defense:	9.91
Gun Rating:	6.75
HoopStat Grade:	24.20
Minutes/Game:	22.02

Alton is in a fortunate situation in Seattle. As NBA centers go, he's just average. He's inconsistent, although he can block shots and run the floor well. But he's surrounded by good players in Seattle, and that raises his level a bit.

He's foul-prone (8.2 per 48), and just isn't a great scorer. However, his defense and rebounding are both fifth among all centers, so he's doing *something* right. His biggest negative is his age right now. He'll be 31 during the 1989–90 season, so don't look for him to improve from where he is now. More sooner than later, Seattle will be looking for a new center.

Frank Brickowski

San Antonio Spurs

23.5 HGS

College:	Penn State
Age (1/1/1990):	31
Height:	6'10"
Weight:	240
Scoring:	0.550
Rebounding:	6.71
Playmaking:	0.20
Defense:	7.06
Gun Rating:	0.40
HoopStat Grade:	23.50
Minutes/Game:	28.47

Although he's too small to be a real center, Frank has improved himself over the years, to the point where he's at least passable. He runs the floor well and isn't all that bad when he's not facing the basket. But he ranked fifth on the Spurs in overall defense, behind Robertson, Greg Anderson, Comegys, and Smrek.

Mark West
Phoenix Suns
22.8 HGS

College:	Old Dominion
Age (1/1/1990):	30
Height:	6'10"
Weight:	230
Scoring:	0.628
Rebounding:	7.92
Playmaking:	0.10
Defense:	9.82
Gun Rating:	8.63
HoopStat Grade:	22.80
Minutes/Game:	24.62

Bill Laimbeer
Detroit Pistons
22.5 HGS

College:	Notre Dame
Age (1/1/1990):	33
Height:	6'11"
Weight:	260
Scoring:	0.527
Rebounding:	7.93
Playmaking:	0.20
Defense:	8.55
Gun Rating:	2.35
HoopStat Grade:	22.50
Minutes/Game:	32.59

A hard worker, but very limited in what he can do for a team. You could consider him the Suns' weak link last year, but he was still in the top half of all starting centers. His offensive game is *very* strange. Scouts say he can't hit the net from two feet, which may be true, but you'd never know it from his .635 shooting percentage. So if he can hit 63% from the field, just imagine what he can do from the line, right? Wrong. He made only 53.5% of his free throws! Only two regulars (Larry Smith from Golden State was the other) managed to do better from the field.

His great floor percentage meant that he led the league in scoring percentage, with 0.628, meaning he made over a point per game more than an average center would have, given the exact same number of shots from anywhere. (He made 83 points more, in fact.) Not bad for a guy who can't shoot and never got the benefit of the calls, either (his Draw rating was only 0.74, eleventh best amongst all players who put on a Phoenix uniform last year). He wasn't particularly effective under the boards: Phoenix was 19th overall in total offensive rebounds with 1095. Only 300 more and they'd have had as many as Seattle, the leaders.

Okay, let's not beat around the bush here. You hate him. We hate him. What are you going to do about it, beat him up? No, you just have to hope that your team gets the better of his team when they play, and that's not going to happen. Other than that, you can take solace in the fact that he lost his Ironman streak because he was suspended a game for fighting.

You know, lots of other players are just as dirty, you just don't notice them as much. It's not even that which gets you irritated, though, is it? It's the denial of said dirtiness. Take, for instance, this snow job (from *Inside Sports*):

IS: Will you say that you bend the rules?

BL: That's the way you get by in the game. You bend the rules as much as possible. And when I break the rules, referees call fouls; that's part of the game.
IS: But they called fewer before '85 [the year the Pistons played the Celtics in the playoffs]?
BL: Oh, sure. And I was playing the same way then as I play now.

Well, here's the truth of the matter. Laimbeer's fouls per game have dropped sharply since he entered the league, and have gone down *every* year since 1985, and only because 1984 was a blip in the trend.

Yeah, we can see your point there, Bill. They're sure cracking down on you because the Boston media told them to.

BILL LAIMBEER'S COMPLAINTS NO BASIS IN FACT

Year	GP	Min	PF	DQ	PF/48	Change from Previous
1989	81	2640	259	2	4.71	−0.00
1988	82	2897	284	6	4.71	−0.05
1987	82	2854	283	4	4.76	−0.07
1986	82	2891	291	4	4.83	−0.28
1985	82	2892	308	4	5.11	+0.53
1984	82	2864	273	4	4.58	−0.77
1983	82	2871	320	9	5.35	−2.42
1982	80	1829	296	5	7.77	+1.29
1981	81	2460	332	14	6.48	——

In eight seasons, he's only twice been whistled more often than the year before. *Not every year since 1985.*

Jack Sikma
Milwaukee Bucks
22.0 HGS

College:	Illinois Wesleyan
Age (1/1/1990):	35
Height:	7'0"
Weight:	260
Scoring:	0.490
Rebounding:	6.70
Playmaking:	0.35
Defense:	7.16
Gun Rating:	2.21
HoopStat Grade:	22.00
Minutes/Game:	32.34

Sikma was hurt by a few factors last year. As centers go, he was the least prototypical in the league, sending up three-pointers with frequency and actually demonstrating (gasp!) passing skills. The Bucks were hoping to reduce Sikma to about 25 minutes per game, where he could produce regularly without wearing down, but without feeling like a bench player. Their plans were shot, however, when Randy Breuer decided to sulk around and refuse to play. Breuer ended up with only 10.69 minutes per game played, while Sikma was called upon to play 32.34, which was far too much for a 33-year-old with 900+ games behind him. He's showing his age now, especially in his speed, but his game relies more on finesse and positioning rebounding than it used to. Although he's changed his game to adapt to his diminished physical skills, he needs some help from the other centers on the team.

Before last season, Sikma had taken 68 three-pointers in his career, making 7 (less than one per year). Last year he took 216 and made 82, a .381 percentage. For a man who's played center his whole career, a sudden adjustment to the perimeter, and the ability to shoot so *well* from there, speaks volumes about his shot, not to mention his grit.

Ralph Sampson
Golden State Warriors
21.4 HGS

College:	Virginia
Age (1/1/1990):	30
Height:	7'4"
Weight:	230
Scoring:	0.472
Rebounding:	8.41
Playmaking:	0.21
Defense:	8.57
Gun Rating:	4.02
HoopStat Grade:	21.40
Minutes/Game:	17.80

You know, we thought about giving Manute Bol the Warriors' starting center listing, but Sampson started more games. For a player who once held such awesome potential, a rating this low is simply depressing. Scouts say he avoids all responsibility of making his team good, which is why he ended up having to fight Bol for his spot on the team. Although Sampson is widely portrayed as an underachiever and one with a tendency to disappear in big games, his playoff stats are actually slightly *better* than his regular-season stats.

Sampson was the second worst center in converting scoring chances into points, as he came through only 47.2% of the time.

Kevin Duckworth
Portland Trail Blazers
21.0 HGS

College:	Eastern Illinois
Age (1/1/1990):	26
Height:	7'0"
Weight:	280
Scoring:	0.520
Rebounding:	7.28
Playmaking:	0.05
Defense:	5.38
Gun Rating:	−4.84
HoopStat Grade:	21.00
Minutes/Game:	33.70

Everyone expected Kevin to come into his own this year, after he was rewarded with a $2 million contract for his 1988 season. He didn't come through and ended up as a mild disappointment. His strength lies in his offense, but he's abandoned a good hook in favor of an average turnaround jumper, so he's had more shots blocked. He also doesn't know when to get rid of the ball, trying to shoot over a double-team. He managed to dish off only one assist per 19 shots taken. When you consider that Clyde Drexler, never known as a big passing threat, passed off once every 3.7 shots, Duckworth's effort comes up pretty weak. Duck couldn't even find the open man once per game, as he had only 61 assists all season. Moses Malone had 112. Akeem Olajuwon had 149. It earned him the Gunner's low-ball championship award, as his true

RALPH SAMPSON
REGULAR SEASON VS. PLAYOFF STATS

	FG%	FT%	Reb	Blk	PPG	PP48
Regular/48	.495	.668	14.36	2.64	19.3	26.58
Playoffs/48	.501	.707	14.66	2.09	19.7	26.24

Joe Barry Carroll

New Jersey Nets

20.9 HGS

Kareem Abdul-Jabbar

Los Angeles Lakers

20.1 HGS

College:	Purdue	College:	UCLA
Age (1/1/1990):	32	Age (1/1/1990):	43
Height:	7'1''	Height:	7'2''
Weight:	255	Weight:	267
Scoring:	0.490	Scoring:	0.503
Rebounding:	6.68	Rebounding:	5.75
Playmaking:	0.13	Playmaking:	0.11
Defense:	7.92	Defense:	6.75
Gun Rating:	−0.80	Gun Rating:	−1.06
HoopStat Grade:	20.90	HoopStat Grade:	20.10
Minutes/Game:	31.19	Minutes/Game:	22.91

worth was 4.8 points per 48 fewer than his scoring would have indicated.

All year long, Arvidas Sabonis was rumored to be coming over to play center. Sabonis is being sold as the second coming of Chamberlain in the Northwest, but we're probably looking at the second coming of Mark Eaton. He's about the same size, but he's a perimeter player, not effective at the low post. Remember Georgi Glouchkov? Neither do we, so take that as a lesson.

Is it unfair to say that the Nets are going nowhere with the team they've put together? JBC's been around for eight years, and his teams have made the playoffs twice. Meanwhile, his rebounds have dropped steadily since his rookie season, as has his shooting percentage. His foul shooting *has* gone up considerably, showing that he probably puts in his time at practice. But in a game? It's just not clicking.

Sometime during the All-Star weekend, someone mentioned that Kareem should have been playing in the Legends game on Saturday, not the All-Star Game on Sunday. Well, he got his time, sunk the last basket of the game (a sky hook), and made everyone happy. As for Doug Moe—well, Fat will get another chance; you only get one last chance to honor a player like Kareem.

Doug Collins and former Knick coach Rick Pitino are both younger than Kareem; Mike Fratello is about three months older.

During the Farewell Tour (really the Farewell Tour II, if you count the one three years ago), you may have noticed that he picked up some loot. *Voilà*, his gift registry:

Team Gift(s)

Atl	Complete jazz library of Warner Brothers records
Bos	Piece of parquet floor, Boston-area jazz CDs
Cha	Custom-made rocking chair
Chi	Painting of Kareem in All-Star Game, VCR, jazz CDs, fishing rod with 20,000 hooks (he's hit 20,000 sky hooks)

Mark Eaton
Utah Jazz
20.1 HGS

Rony Seikaly
Miami Heat
20.1 HGS

Eaton	
College:	UCLA
Age (1/1/1990):	33
Height:	7'4"
Weight:	290
Scoring:	0.501
Rebounding:	8.25
Playmaking:	0.20
Defense:	10.97
Gun Rating:	11.70
HoopStat Grade:	20.10
Minutes/Game:	35.54

Seikaly	
College:	Syracuse
Age (1/1/1990):	25
Height:	6'11"
Weight:	230
Scoring:	0.459
Rebounding:	8.46
Playmaking:	0.07
Defense:	7.69
Gun Rating:	−0.62
HoopStat Grade:	20.10
Minutes/Game:	25.15

Cle Persian rug, set of conga drums

Dal African sculpture of an elephant

Den A gold nugget

Det Painted portrait, key to the city

GS Twenty-four foot sailboat

Hou Display from the NASA Space Center

Ind Sax, flute, key to the city, named a "Sagamore of the Wabash"

LAC Donation to the UCLA scholarship fund

Mia Haitian marble sculpture

Mil Champagne, gold motorcycle, painting, $1,000 contribution to favorite charity

NJ Portrait painting, jazz CDs

NY Silver "Big Apple," framed uniforms of his 4 teams

Phi Mobile phone, CD player, Philadelphia-area jazz CDs

Pho Golf clubs

Por Custom-made glass backgammon table

SA Collage of Kareem in action

Sac $4,000 donation to Cal State Univesity, Sacramento in the name of Kareem Abdul-Jabbar Scholarship Fund

Sea Stratford rocker recliner chair

Uta Rattlesnake belt, boots, shotgun, cowboy hat, named honorary SLC deputy

Was Jukebox, 45s donated by fans

When you look objectively at the Def ratings for centers, Eaton comes in second, behind Akeem. But when you look at his scoring output, the negatives balance out. He didn't get called much for fouls when he blocked shots, but evidently refs were even more intimidated from blowing the whistle on opponents, and he had only 69% as many free throws as he drew fouls. His intimidation ability alone earned him an 11.70 Gun rating, the best among centers. His offense dropped him to 20th among starters. That's what you get when you're one-dimensional, even if that dimension is overpowering.

Still, it beats the money he'd be making as an auto mechanic.

It's obvious, when you watch him, that basketball wasn't Rony's first sport. The Heat really thought he'd be a good NBA player, but he has a dearth of offensive skills. He wasn't just the worst foul shooter among all league starters, he was the worst foul shooter *among all Syracuse alumni in the league*. It all added up to a .459 scoring percentage, the very worst among all centers, and very close to last in the league.

When opponents can foul your center with impunity, what are you going to do when you need someone in the middle as a "go-to" player? If he gets position, opponents can just foul him—chances are he'll make only one of two. This isn't a league of morons, and that's exactly what happened to Seikaly, who drew 1.37 free throws per foul he picked up, the highest amongst Heat regulars.

It was only his first year in the league, and he's probably got the raw athletic talent, but he needs some time to learn. Quite a few ingredients are lacking from his low-post game: a hook shot, a jumper, the ability to read double-teaming. But first, 500 foul shots per day might help. Overall, Miami might think it went with youth over cheap experi-

James Donaldson
Dallas Mavericks
20.0 HGS

College:	Washington St.
Age (1/1/1990):	33
Height:	7'2"
Weight:	278
Scoring:	0.603
Rebounding:	9.36
Playmaking:	0.11
Defense:	8.55
Gun Rating:	6.79
HoopStat Grade:	20.00
Minutes/Game:	32.94

Jim Petersen
Sacramento Kings
19.5 HGS

College:	Minnesota
Age (1/1/1990):	28
Height:	6'10"
Weight:	235
Scoring:	0.488
Rebounding:	7.31
Playmaking:	0.13
Defense:	7.67
Gun Rating:	−0.27
HoopStat Grade:	19.50
Minutes/Game:	24.74

ence the first couple of years, but when it's iffy as to the youth's future contributions, why bother?

You can't really blame Dallas for many of their problems last year. They lost two centers within a week, after their starter, Roy Tarpley, was gone nearly all year with arthroscopic drug surgery or something. Donaldson got the most starts, and he was a decent rebounder who benefited from a decent team around him. His career could well be over, owing to patellar tendon damage, and if not, he'll be gone for a good portion of this season because of rehab.

Although Donaldson isn't gifted offensively, he did what he could, and he played his talents to a .603 scoring percentage, the second best among all NBA regulars. He had a tendency to miss a lot of shots up close and didn't pick up an extraordinary number of offensive boards. He had good, but not great hands for a center, as demonstrated by his Hands rating (0.95).

The problem with a poor team, the Kings, for example, is that no one's role is quite clear, because of trades and movement. You're often content to have a player like Petersen start, when he'd be better suited to be a backup center/forward on a good team, perhaps the third man off the bench. Far be it from us to criticize anyone, especially someone who genuinely works hard, but Jim's lack of quickness hurt him badly last year. He often was beaten to position and ended up being awarded only 0.65 foul shot per foul called against him, just over half of what an average center drew.

Earl Cureton

Charlotte Hornets
17.3 HGS

Bill Cartwright

Chicago Bulls
17.2 HGS

College:	Detroit	College:	San Francisco
Age (1/1/1990):	33	Age (1/1/1990):	33
Height:	6'9''	Height:	7'1''
Weight:	215	Weight:	245
Scoring:	0.505	Scoring:	0.524
Rebounding:	7.26	Rebounding:	6.45
Playmaking:	0.28	Playmaking:	0.12
Defense:	6.12	Defense:	5.07
Gun Rating:	4.81	Gun Rating:	−2.64
HoopStat Grade:	17.30	HoopStat Grade:	17.20
Minutes/Game:	24.96	Minutes/Game:	29.91

The closest thing Charlotte had to a genuine center last year, which is more an indictment of their expansion draft actions than of Cureton. Earl did everything well except score and, well, play defense. Defensively, he was in the class of Kevin Duckworth and Bill Cartwright, while, offensively, Mark Eaton comes to mind. Granted, the Hornets couldn't have expected him to be too much, since he was often giving up 15 or 20 pounds to the opponent's starting forwards. He weighs the same as Dale Ellis (215 pounds), and towers over him by only 2 inches.

Once maligned by New Yorkers, Mr. Elbows has finally found a new home to be maligned in. Despite mild playoff heroics, his year-long play wasn't particularly strong. He *was*, however, a big step up from Dave Corzine, a fact often lost on critics. He's expected to be a strong inside player, when in truth he wants to be a perimeter player like Sikma, Laimbeer, and Gminski.

Cartwright supposedly has good foot speed and an ability to beat his man to position and draw fouls, but that talent has taken a nosedive of late. When he came into the league, his foul Draw rating was around 2.0, but every fracture his feet sustained has slowed him more, and last year he dropped a full 0.5 shot per call to only 1.32. As his speed deserted him, he was being beaten, and he couldn't get the calls he did when he was young.

BILL CARTWRIGHT'S DECLINING FOOT SPEED MEASURED BY THE FOULS HE DRAWS

Season	FTA	PF	Draw
1988–89	308	234	1.32
1987–88	426	234	1.82
1986–87	438	188	2.33
1985–86	10	6	1.67
1983–85	(DNP–Injury)		
1983–84	502	262	1.92
1982–83	511	315	1.62
1981–82	337	208	1.62
1980–81	518	259	2.00
1979–80	566	279	2.03

Charles Jones
Washington Bullets
15.2 HGS

College:	Albany St.
Age (1/1/1990):	33
Height:	6'9''
Weight:	215
Scoring:	0.493
Rebounding:	6.47
Playmaking:	0.34
Defense:	8.35
Gun Rating:	9.49
HoopStat Grade:	15.20
Minutes/Game:	21.56

The Bullets lost Moses Malone, one of the best centers in the league, to Atlanta, and ended up with a patchwork starting lineup, featuring either Jones (CJones, not CAJones, if you follow box scores) or Dave Feitl in the middle. Charles Jones is simply a less skilled version of his older brother, Caldwell. Feitl is in the league because he's 7' tall.

Jones started only 45 games and wasn't even with the team all year, but still, he played over 1100 minutes, and only managed 5.7 pp48. His defense was good, about the league average for centers (8.35 Def rating), but he went to the line only 27 times all year, while giving 188 fouls! When you've got inferior height and strength playing center, these things happen. You need to foul to get the ball, and it still doesn't work. Unless a center suddenly walks into camp, count on the Bullets to turn into Blanks.

GUARDS

Michael Jordan
Chicago Bulls
39.1 HGS

College:	North Carolina
Age (1/1/1990):	27
Height:	6'6''
Weight:	195
Scoring:	0.587
Rebounding:	5.58
Playmaking:	0.36
Defense:	8.10
Gun Rating:	0.25
HoopStat Grade:	39.10
Minutes/Game:	40.19

Jordan was the HGS most valuable player in 1988–89, and if you don't know why, you were napping during too many games. If anyone still seriously claims that he can't be the best because he doesn't make his team better, have them look at the performances of Scottie Pippen, Horace Grant, and anyone else on this team. When Jordan moved to point guard, he reeled off an incredible streak of triple doubles, something like ten in a row. What we'd like to know is: is a 10–10–10 game any more valuable than a 35–18–9 game? If we're going to be fair here, we need a better triple double measurement.

The TDI, or triple double index, is what we've designed to fill this void. It's simple. Just multiply the three parts of the triple together! If you have a 10–10–10 game, that's 1000. Therefore, the lowest TDI you can have and still get a triple is 1000. If you get 20 points with 10 rebounds and assists, your TDI is 2000. However, if your triple double category stats are 35–18–9, your TDI is 5670, or 5.67 times as good as a 10–10–10 game.

Jordan's top ten TDI games last year?

Michael Jordan's Top Ten TDI Performances

Date	Pts	Reb	Ast	TDI
4/13	47	11	13	6721
1/21	53	14	8	5931
4/21	34	14	11	5236
4/9	40	10	12	4800
4/2	27	14	12	4536
3/28	33	12	11	4356
1/10	48	10	9	4320
3/13	21	14	14	4116
4/6	31	13	10	4030
11/26	52	11	7	4004

Imagine. He's such a god that we have to measure his performance in multiples of a triple double now.

Earvin "Magic" Johnson

Los Angeles Lakers
37.3 HGS

College:	Michigan St.
Age (1/1/1990):	31
Height:	6'9"
Weight:	226
Scoring:	0.572
Rebounding:	5.69
Playmaking:	0.87
Defense:	6.79
Gun Rating:	8.55
HoopStat Grade:	37.30
Minutes/Game:	37.48

John Stockton

Utah Jazz
32.3 HGS

College:	Gonzaga
Age (1/1/1990):	28
Height:	6'1"
Weight:	175
Scoring:	0.592
Rebounding:	2.32
Playmaking:	1.21
Defense:	5.40
Gun Rating:	11.12
HoopStat Grade:	32.30
Minutes/Game:	38.67

For much of the year, Magic was the best player in the league, outperforming even Jordan. The latter's late-season move to point guard took the title away, however. If this were a normal league, without Jordan, Magic would have been the best guard by a full 5.0 HGS points. Instead, he trailed by nearly 2. The two players' lines are things of beauty, even for those of us who aren't turned on by raw numbers. Jordan had a 10.0 pp48 scoring edge (indeed, Magic was only the eighth most prolific center if you're looking at points). Magic rebounded a wee bit better and simply demolished Jordan in Play rating. Jordan came up with the ball a shade more often (a 0.27 edge in Hands), and played a better defense, but no one, not even Air, was able to get the calls better.

What does it all come down to? Magic had an 8.50 Gun to Jordan's 0.30. Right now, it's safe to say that the former is the more complete player, yet the latter also adds value to his game with the peripherals. It's the scoring that makes the difference. It's nice to know that two of the three or four greatest guards ever to play the game are in the league right now. But sorry Magic, you were edged out for best in a photo finish.

This is just about where you'd rate Stockton subjectively, third among guards, but well behind Jordan and Magic. His passing skills are better than anyone's—Jordan's throws often went where he thought his teammates would be, while Stockton's nearly always went to where they *were*.

If you think of a point guard as simply the player who brings the ball upcourt and gets it to the right man, Stockton's absolutely the best in the league. Only four regular players (Stockton, Muggsy Bogues, Nate McMillan, and Jim Les) gathered more assists than shot attempts last season. Stockton was a far better shooter than any of them, and he scored over 21 points per 48. He was also far superior to the others in his handiwork, actually getting the ball cleanly (with blocks, fouls) more often than he was whistled.

If you want to learn the fundamentals of running a team on the floor, it would pay to watch this man before you turned on anyone else. He can really control the ball, never turns it over, gets it to the right shooter, and when he feels he's got the shot, he takes it. His instincts for getting the good shot are marvelous—his .592 scoring per-

centage topped all guards. Had he taken as many shots as Jordan, he would actually have scored a whisker more, but all of Jordan's shots had a potential to score 4481 points last year (on 1795 FGA, 98 3GA, and 793 FTA), 2117 more than Stockton's. But had Stockton taken those extra shots, he probably wouldn't have been half the guard he was.

Clyde Drexler
Portland Trail Blazers
31.9 HGS

College:	Houston
Age (1/1/1990):	28
Height:	6'7''
Weight:	215
Scoring:	0.531
Rebounding:	6.40
Playmaking:	0.27
Defense:	6.72
Gun Rating:	−1.32
HoopStat Grade:	31.90
Minutes/Game:	39.31

Kevin Johnson
Phoenix Suns
31.1 HGS

College:	UC–Berkeley
Age (1/1/1990):	24
Height:	6'1''
Weight:	180
Scoring:	0.578
Rebounding:	2.81
Playmaking:	0.88
Defense:	4.62
Gun Rating:	6.18
HoopStat Grade:	31.10
Minutes/Game:	39.25

Lafayette "Fat" Lever
Denver Nuggets
29.8 HGS

College:	Arizona St.
Age (1/1/1990):	30
Height:	6'3''
Weight:	175
Scoring:	0.494
Rebounding:	6.93
Playmaking:	0.46
Defense:	7.91
Gun Rating:	5.18
HoopStat Grade:	29.80
Minutes/Game:	38.66

A major talent, one of the top ten in the entire league. There's something about going to the University of Houston, however, that seems to toy with a player's work ethic and team play. When you think of the current Phi Slamma Jammas in the league—Olajuwon, Greg Anderson, Drexler—they've all developed negative raps at the pro level.

Drexler's personal rap is that of a prima donna, a no-defense player who plays when *he* wants to. People who watch him in practice say he's absolutely terrible, since he doesn't care. This can be detrimental to a team, especially when you need to work on certain plays for the benefit of the rest of the guys.

He's undeniably strong in the stat department, though, and does everything during a game that makes a great player. He's finished in the top ten of HGS for two years straight, due to his remarkable inside game. His OR/DR was 0.89, highest in the league among guards. Does that mean he's strong *inside*, or weak *outside?* Judging from his .255 three-point percentage, it looks as if he's got trouble from outside 15 feet. He tried 106 threes, about 100 more than he should have.

K.J. was undeniably the biggest surprise of the 1988–89 season. Sending Nance to Cleveland to obtain him was a great move, because it gave both teams just the piece they needed to become a powerhouse. He came from out of nowhere to prominence as one of the best team leaders in the NBA, and he already appears to be one of the smartest players at the point. He really runs the show, knows when to shoot, and knows when he doesn't need to handle the ball. He's what you would get if you made Stockton shoot a bit more, and he was still learning the angles just a bit. With this guy, the Suns are going to be tough the next few years.

Then again, didn't we say that about Houston a few years ago?

You know the Nuggets are going nowhere when a 6'3'' guard leads the team in rebounds. This is no complaint about Fat, who's an all-around talent, but you really need a center here. Lever was the third most prolific scorer on the Nuggets, but the other two, Alex English and Walter Davis, were content to score (they combined for a −20.43 Gun). Fat was far better on defense than either of them, had better hands, rebounded as well as the two of them combined (and twice as well as your average guard), passed better, logged more time, and basically did everything but lead the team in scoring. There's no way to support anyone else as the Nuggets' MVP.

Alvin Robertson
Milwaukee Bucks
26.0 HGS

College:	Arkansas
Age (1/1/1990):	28
Height:	6'4''
Weight:	190
Scoring:	0.505
Rebounding:	5.19
Playmaking:	0.41
Defense:	7.26
Gun Rating:	2.50
HoopStat Grade:	26.00
Minutes/Game:	35.18

A much better player when the other team has the ball. Robertson's about as close to an average guard in scoring production as you can get (0.2 difference in pp48, same scoring percentage), but his defensive rating was second highest among Spurs starters behind Greg Anderson, and third in the league for guards. His playmaking wasn't superb, but when you're looking at Vernon Maxwell, it starts to impress. Robertson's stuck as a 'tweener, an off guard who plays like a point guard, too, so none of his stats stand out as they would were he to concentrate on one position's requirements.

Glenn "Doc" Rivers
Atlanta Hawks
25.5 HGS

College:	Marquette
Age (1/1/1990):	29
Height:	6'4''
Weight:	185
Scoring:	0.505
Rebounding:	3.40
Playmaking:	0.64
Defense:	6.21
Gun Rating:	5.38
HoopStat Grade:	25.50
Minutes/Game:	32.39

Are you tired of pro athletes nicknamed "Doc"? Reverse it for a second. Would you want your family doctor to be nicknamed "Slugger" or "Magic"?

Other than that, it must have been mighty confusing for Rivers, what with all those teammates yelling that they were free all year. Even he was a bit more selfish than the average point guard, garnering a Play rating of only 0.64. He wasn't the weak link for the Hawks, but he wasn't the strongest loop in the chain.

I'd give you more dirt on Glenn, but I have to call my dentist, Slugger Levine, to see if he can fill my cavity this week.

Mark Jackson
New York Knicks
25.5 HGS

College:	St. John's
Age (1/1/1990):	25
Height:	6'3''
Weight:	205
Scoring:	0.478
Rebounding:	4.02
Playmaking:	0.60
Defense:	5.11
Gun Rating:	1.91
HoopStat Grade:	25.50
Minutes/Game:	34.40

Mark's sort of a, well, touchy issue in New York right now. In two years, he's developed a classic love-hate relationship with the hometown fans, cheered as an All-Star, then booed as a hot dog. The more you watch him, the more confusing it gets. He's got all the skills that make a great point guard—he's smart enough to know exactly who needs the ball, and his passing can be fun to watch. But he wants to be the hero all too often, and many fans think he lost the first game of the playoffs against Chicago, and therefore the series. Sometimes he tries to take over a game when it's not appropriate, when a better percentage play is open.

He's young, often acts young, but plays like a vet. He's a better rebounder than most guards (a Rbdg rating of 4.02 is no negative), and when in the right situation, he *can* carry the team. When he was off the court two years ago, the opponents usually mounted their charges; this year he had a capable backup in Rod Strickland, so he could afford to rest a bit. Strickland actually had a higher HGS, but over many fewer minutes (often during garbage time). Either way, the Knicks got nearly 48 minutes of outstanding point play

Mark Price
Cleveland Cavaliers
25.2 HGS

College:	Georgia Tech
Age (1/1/1990):	26
Height:	6'1"
Weight:	175
Scoring:	0.562
Rebounding:	2.28
Playmaking:	0.63
Defense:	3.71
Gun Rating:	0.34
HoopStat Grade:	25.20
Minutes/Game:	36.37

Nate McMillan
Seattle Supersonics
24.9 HGS

College:	North Carolina St.
Age (1/1/1990):	26
Height:	6'5"
Weight:	195
Scoring:	0.433
Rebounding:	5.00
Playmaking:	1.44
Defense:	6.57
Gun Rating:	13.94
HoopStat Grade:	24.90
Minutes/Game:	31.21

per game. Next year's coach will have to find some way to move one or the other to two guard, probably Strickland, and let them develop into one of the best backcourts in the league.

The fifth best Cleveland starter, which says a lot about the Cleveland starters. He would have been the best starter on Dallas last year. He's not quite the best in the league, but he's got good hands and a simply incredible shot. A guard shooting .526? Including .441 from three-point range? And over 90% from the line? Pretty impressive for a guy with over 600 assists. He's the poor man's John Stockton, but even that's not bad. When the game is on the line, nobody wants the ball more than Price. He'll do whatever it takes to score and more often than not comes up with the deuce.

Absolutely great peripheral skills that belie his low scoring average. Although he netted only 10.9 pp48, his HGS was nearly 14 points higher, the largest edge in the league. Why? He never shoots! He dished off 1.44 assists per shot attempted last year, third to Muggsy Bogues and Jim Les. When he did keep the ball, he could convert only 43.3% of his chances, worst among all guards. Besides his shoddy shooting (.410 FG%, .633 FT%), he had more rebounds, assists, steals, and blocks and fewer turnovers than Dale Ellis, who is usually rated much more highly in people's minds. Which is why Nate's overall play was worth about 3.5 points per game more than Dale's. Take the 7.6 ppg and toss it out the window. Scoring isn't Nate's thing.

Terry Porter
Portland Trail Blazers
24.9 HGS

College:	Wisc. – Stevens Pt.
Age (1/1/1990):	27
Height:	6'3''
Weight:	195
Scoring:	0.505
Rebounding:	3.30
Playmaking:	0.67
Defense:	4.56
Gun Rating:	2.71
HoopStat Grade:	24.90
Minutes/Game:	38.30

Mitch Richmond
Golden State Warriors
24.4 HGS

College:	Kansas St.
Age (1/1/1990):	25
Height:	6'5''
Weight:	225
Scoring:	0.517
Rebounding:	5.11
Playmaking:	0.24
Defense:	4.42
Gun Rating:	– 6.31
HoopStat Grade:	24.40
Minutes/Game:	34.39

Lester Conner
New Jersey Nets
24.3 HGS

College:	Oregon St.
Age (1/1/1990):	31
Height:	6'4''
Weight:	185
Scoring:	0.508
Rebounding:	4.03
Playmaking:	0.89
Defense:	5.92
Gun Rating:	8.36
HoopStat Grade:	24.30
Minutes/Game:	30.88

Yeah, yeah, another one of those Talent Blazers. Porter did many things last year, none of them poorly, but none of them eye-openingly well. They don't like the three-pointer in Portland; the two starting guards shot them only half as often as the rest of the league's starters did.

Okay, so we've kidded around about the "talent" in Portland. It's still a fact that their guards are ranked at 4th and 12th out of 52. The league is top-heavy, too. The first 18 are above the average for the group, the other 34 are below. Only Golden State and Portland had both guards in the top 18, and both Warriors are below Porter. Can you argue that the Blazers have the best backcourt in the league now? There's no reason not to, but no one will believe it except you.

It's usually the kiss of death to compare a rookie to an All-Star by name. However, when you hold up Mitch Richmond next to a young Sidney Moncrief, you can see where it might fit. He's got the confidence, which should only increase if he takes the time to look back and see how he changed the Warriors around completely last season. The differences between him and Moncrief? Richmond shoots more often than he did, but didn't hit quite as great a percentage. For a rookie to draw more fouls than he's whistled for, by a 2.3 to 1 ratio, is remarkable. Evidently, most of those fouls were while driving to the hoop, as his Hands rating, at 0.43, was lowest on the team.

He deserved the Rookie of the Year award—although Strickland rated higher—because he was a starter. We know he can score, and if he can boost the other elements of his game, the hard play that he's shown so far could put him right in the top 10 players in the league.

Believe it or not (and we know you won't), Lester was the best player on the Nets last year. After five years as a journeyman guard, he popped up in the Meadowlands as a tag-along in the Joe Barry Carroll trade, took the starting job away from John Bagley a fourth of the way into the season, and proceeded to lead the squad with a 24.3 HGS. It wasn't close either, as Roy Hinson managed only a 21.8 for second place. Conner was the only Net with a triple double last year, and he had two. He even led the league in something, the first time in 23 years a Net had done so (well, maybe not 23). No guard had a better Hands mark than Lester's 1.40. He got 7 blocks and steals for every five fouls charged, fourth in the league behind three shot blockers (Manute Bol, Larry Nance, and Akeem Olajuwon). With only five blocks, Conner was the only leader to do it with steals. The best pick-pocket in the league? Certainly one of them.

So why is Buck Williams considered the only tradable? One word sums it up: history. Although he's slipping, Buck's proven his worth year after year, surrounded by hordes of CBA grads. Lester's performance might have been his career

Player Analysis by Position

Gary Grant
Los Angeles Clippers
23.6 HGS

College:	Michigan
Age (1/1/1990):	25
Height:	6'3"
Weight:	195
Scoring:	0.459
Rebounding:	3.68
Playmaking:	0.61
Defense:	5.78
Gun Rating:	2.51
HoopStat Grade:	23.60
Minutes/Game:	27.10

Isiah Thomas
Detroit Pistons
23.5 HGS

College:	Indiana
Age (1/1/1990):	29
Height:	6'1"
Weight:	185
Scoring:	0.498
Rebounding:	2.52
Playmaking:	0.54
Defense:	4.35
Gun Rating:	− 0.47
HoopStat Grade:	23.50
Minutes/Game:	36.55

year, or it might have been an example of a player coming into his own when given just one chance. If it's the latter, the Nets have one fewer roster spot to fret over.

During the day that was supposed to put the Clippers over the top (of the .500 mark, anyway), they traded with Seattle, getting Gary Grant for Michael Cage. Okay, so it didn't exactly put either club over the top. Grant was slightly better last year. But is he going to be a key in the Clippers of the future? Stay tuned.

When you look at the players on Detroit, not one of them rated in the top 15 at his position. You'd hardly expect this to be a power team. The difference is players like Isiah. No matter how much you dislike his choirboy pretensions, you know he wins. If you can take just one moment in time (the pass Bird stole in 1987, for instance), and draw resolve from it until you've won the championship, you'd be a suitable Piston.

Isiah was slightly worse than his scoring would have you believe last year. He couldn't get points as well as the average guard, and his other stats were very vanilla. What doesn't show up is the stifling effect his defense had on opponents, forcing them to miss their shots.

No matter what he claims, Isiah's a strong enough leader on this team of toughs to actually get one of them traded for a lifetime friend. If Aguirre continues to hold his own in Detroit, Thomas deserves as much credit for him as anyone.

Terry Teagle
Golden State Warriors
23.3 HGS

College:	Baylor
Age (1/1/1990):	30
Height:	6'5"
Weight:	195
Scoring:	0.513
Rebounding:	5.20
Playmaking:	0.11
Defense:	5.28
Gun Rating:	− 7.34
HoopStat Grade:	23.30
Minutes/Game:	23.77

When Don Nelson benched Terry for 14 games, he didn't gripe, he just went along with his business. When he got a chance to play, he proved himself worthy, finishing with the third best HGS on the Warriors. He wasn't that much in terms of passing or perimeter play; his 0.72 OR/DR ratio was tied with Larry Smith for highest among Warrior regulars. He played in deep, more so than your average guard.

Paul Pressey
Milwaukee Bucks
23.0 HGS

College:	Tulsa
Age (1/1/1990):	32
Height:	6'5"
Weight:	205
Scoring:	0.512
Rebounding:	3.46
Playmaking:	0.68
Defense:	5.70
Gun Rating:	5.00
HoopStat Grade:	23.00
Minutes/Game:	32.39

Pressey was injured for part of the season and productivity fell off. Still, a good all-around player. Good defender; he's part of the point-forward corps that Don Nelson started at Milwaukee and later instituted at Golden State with Chris Mullin. Only liability is that Pressey would rather take the ball to the basket than take an outside jumper. He's never been a real consistent outside shooter, but he has improved somewhat in that area. Good off the dribble, a solid passer who sees the floor very well. He's getting up in age and could be on the trading block.

Maurice Cheeks
Philadelphia 76ers
22.8 HGS

College:	West Texas St.
Age (1/1/1990):	34
Height:	6'1"
Weight:	180
Scoring:	0.515
Rebounding:	2.20
Playmaking:	0.78
Defense:	4.05
Gun Rating:	5.61
HoopStat Grade:	22.80
Minutes/Game:	32.37

Remember how *good* Mo was when Dr. J played with him? He had it all—the ability to read the floor, defense, scoring, leadership. His age, however, has caught up with him, and he can't do it like he used to. He won't get a farewell tour, probably has no shot at the Hall of Fame, either. But when he was in his prime, he was the best on the East Coast.

Vern Fleming
Indiana Pacers
22.8 HGS

College:	Georgia
Age (1/1/1990):	29
Height:	6'5"
Weight:	195
Scoring:	0.554
Rebounding:	3.47
Playmaking:	0.61
Defense:	3.79
Gun Rating:	2.40
HoopStat Grade:	22.80
Minutes/Game:	33.58

Considering the state of the Pacers last year, Fleming didn't do so badly. He was the sixth most deadly scorer (0.554 scoring percentage), a well-above-average playmaker, and just a shade better rebounder than you'd expect.

A better scorer than point guard. The Pacers aren't real happy with this since they need someone directing operations. Fleming would be a good third guard on many teams. In limited minutes he can play both positions, but running the show full time is not really his forte.

Eric "Sleepy" Floyd
Houston Rockets
22.8 HGS

College:	Georgetown
Age (1/1/1990):	30
Height:	6'3"
Weight:	175
Scoring:	0.487
Rebounding:	2.92
Playmaking:	0.79
Defense:	4.54
Gun Rating:	2.85
HoopStat Grade:	22.80
Minutes/Game:	34.01

The third best player on the Rockets, which also means the last good player on the team. His game was limited to passing off and perimeter shooting, as yours would be if you had Akeem in the middle.

Floyd still has yet to fully make the transition from a scoring guard to a point guard. He's a talented player, but he doesn't have the quickness or court savvy to be a top-flight point man. Floyd has great range, not bad off the dribble, but he doesn't create enough for the rest of his teammates. He's prone to turnovers under pressure. He can score and make plays (similar to Terry Porter), but he has trouble doing the two together. One night it might be only scoring, the next night only assists. At this point in his career, he's probably as good as he'll get. And that's not good news for the Rockets who need a real point man.

Quintin Dailey
Los Angeles Clippers
22.8 HGS

College:	San Francisco
Age (1/1/1990):	29
Height:	6'3"
Weight:	180
Scoring:	0.501
Rebounding:	3.54
Playmaking:	0.16
Defense:	4.59
Gun Rating:	−8.29
HoopStat Grade:	22.80
Minutes/Game:	24.96

Gaining 20 pounds during a season is just silly. Most players get lucrative sneaker contracts. Quintin, however, was rumored to have inked a pact with Hostess, ensuring that he would be seen eating only Twinkies on the bench during games.

He *did* slim down quite a bit after Casey took over, midseason. And he *did* average 31.1 pp48, best on the team. But all he can do *is* score. His −8.29 Gun was putrid, unless you like high offense/no defense players. The Clippers represent the end of the line for Dailey, who's always played for losers. A trade to a winner where he could come off the bench firing would do him and his new team a world of good.

Jeff Hornacek
Phoenix Suns
22.6 HGS

College:	Iowa St.
Age (1/1/1990):	27
Height:	6'4"
Weight:	190
Scoring:	0.517
Rebounding:	3.07
Playmaking:	0.52
Defense:	4.51
Gun Rating:	2.27
HoopStat Grade:	22.60
Minutes/Game:	31.88

Hornacek's nothing spectacular, but last season he rated slightly above the alternatives for the Suns, Dan Majerle and Tyrone Corbin. Majerle will be expected to justify his preseason hype next year, and health will help here. He declined significantly from the season before, but some of that is undoubtedly due to Kevin Johnson's increased output. Hornacek didn't need to play point, and his Play rating dropped from 1.03 as a rookie to 0.89 to 0.52 last year. He now passes off half as often as he did only three years ago. Two years ago he led the team in assists; last year he was second, but had fewer than half as many as the leader (guess who).

Derek Harper
Dallas Mavericks
22.5 HGS

College:	Illinois
Age (1/1/1990):	29
Height:	6'4"
Weight:	203
Scoring:	0.499
Rebounding:	2.10
Playmaking:	0.51
Defense:	4.92
Gun Rating:	−0.16
HoopStat Grade:	22.50
Minutes/Game:	36.64

His value tumbled a bit owing to his lack of concentration, but when he's on, he can be *really* on. He was the best of a weak playmaking crew in Dallas, with a lousy (for a point guard) 0.51 Play rating. He was durable, though, logging the most games started and played, and total minutes on the team. He has excellent range, and he had the green light to shoot from outside (3.05 2:3 rating), where he hit over 35%.

Michael Adams
Denver Nuggets
22.4 HGS

College:	Boston College
Age (1/1/1990):	27
Height:	5'11"
Weight:	165
Scoring:	0.471
Rebounding:	2.87
Playmaking:	0.45
Defense:	4.87
Gun Rating:	−2.09
HoopStat Grade:	22.40
Minutes/Game:	36.19

At 50, no one had heard about it. By 60, it was a big sports story. At 69, it was snapped. And so went the least important streak of the year, Adams's consecutive games hitting a three-point shot. It was his allotted fifteen minutes of fame. Once it was over, he had a decent but undistinguished season. It just goes to show the different type of player who can find a home under Doug Moe's system.

His range tends to spread out defenses, which suits the Nuggets' style just fine. He was the second best playmaker on the Nuggets last year and led nearly the whole league in 2:3 ratio, with 1.33. He got plenty of chances to shoot fouls (393, only 9 off the team lead). Doesn't that strike you as a bit strange for someone who takes 43% of his shots from beyond 23'9"? Even though he was awarded the second most free throws on the team, he was *eighth* in personal fouls. The guy's getting a lot of calls, especially for an open floor player.

Winston Garland

Golden State Warriors

22.3 HGS

College:	SW Missouri St.
Age (1/1/1990):	26
Height:	6'2''
Weight:	170
Scoring:	0.469
Rebounding:	3.60
Playmaking:	0.47
Defense:	5.44
Gun Rating:	1.67
HoopStat Grade:	22.30
Minutes/Game:	33.68

Do we want our children to idolize a player named after a brand of cigarettes?

Garland has developed into a decent player. Offense has improved. He can make tough shots off the dribble. He's great at penetrating. A good shooter from 10–15 feet. He had a nice year for Nelson at Golden State. He is in a perfect situation because so much of what the Warriors do is in the passing game: moving, running the ball. Garland is active. Not blessed with blinding speed, but he gets around a lot of people.

Reggie Theus

Minnesota Timberwolves

22.0 HGS

College:	UNLV
Age (1/1/1990):	33
Height:	6'7''
Weight:	213
Scoring:	0.513
Rebounding:	2.88
Playmaking:	0.36
Defense:	3.85
Gun Rating:	–2.74
HoopStat Grade:	22.00
Minutes/Game:	30.70

No one wanted to play with him when he was in Sacramento—no one even wanted his old uniform number when he left. Atlanta could have been a good atmosphere for him, because all the other players were too concerned with themselves to worry about him. Nothing stood out on his record last year, and he was the fourth rated Hawk. Perhaps the most telling part of the entire Hawk season was the post-season, when he said that the team would be better off if they left Fratello in the locker room for the fourth period. This from a player on a team that was 16–16 when they trailed entering those fourth quarters. You can't do that with inferior coaching down the stretch. Cleveland, no shoddy team, was 7–13 in the same situation. Theus takes his game to yet another team. Bombs away!

Danny Ainge

Sacramento Kings

21.7 HGS

College:	BYU
Age (1/1/1990):	31
Height:	6'5''
Weight:	185
Scoring:	0.484
Rebounding:	3.08
Playmaking:	0.38
Defense:	3.90
Gun Rating:	–4.12
HoopStat Grade:	21.70
Minutes/Game:	32.56

They didn't exactly send the Welcome Wagon from Sacramento to pick him up, but with a year of stability, he should be the basis of a pretty decent franchise in the years to come. Among all players still there at year's end, he trailed only Wayman Tisdale in HGS. He can't come through every night, but he's been an overachiever during his career. Every peripheral stat was below average last year, except for his scoring numbers. This is an indication that he takes shots in volume, not only when it's a particularly good idea.

Brian Shaw made him expendable back in Boston, because they didn't need two big backups. Wisely, they went for the young one. In one way, the Kings got the worst of the deal, but on the other hand, you can't win with players who don't have the experience on top. His experiences with the Celts could alter the mood of the Kings just enough to jump-start the others.

Dale Ellis
Seattle Supersonics
21.4 HGS

College:	Tennessee
Age (1/1/1990):	30
Height:	6'7''
Weight:	215
Scoring:	0.534
Rebounding:	3.39
Playmaking:	0.10
Defense:	3.36
Gun Rating:	−12.55
HoopStat Grade:	21.40
Minutes/Game:	38.90

As a defender, he's a great scorer. As a rebounder, he's a great scorer. As a playmaker, well, he's a great scorer. Dale's offensive game took great strides last year, but his consider this: he outscored Xavier McDaniel by 7.0 ppg, but when you adjust that for time played, he beat the X-Man by only 0.1 pp48.

Dale's always been a prolific scorer. Last season he added points to his game by shooting the three, the most in the NBA. When he first entered the league, he could only take the jumper, and defenders would be able to slack off on him. His ability to drive the lane has improved over the years, and his Draw ratio has gone up accordingly.

Perhaps a lot of the improvement is a direct result of being let loose in Seattle.

Dale Ellis
Increasing Ability to
Draw Fouls

Year	Draw
1983–84	1.02
1984–85	0.79
1985–86	1.05
1986–87	1.83
1987–88	1.79
1988–89	2.35

Darrell Walker
Washington Bullets
21.4 HGS

College:	Arkansas
Age (1/1/1990):	29
Height:	6'4''
Weight:	180
Scoring:	0.459
Rebounding:	5.63
Playmaking:	0.73
Defense:	6.81
Gun Rating:	8.02
HoopStat Grade:	21.40
Minutes/Game:	32.47

Disappointing. The Knicks spent a first-round draft pick on him in 1983, and it looked like a good move when he was named to the All-Rookie team. But his .517 college shooting percentage has evaporated into a .435 lifetime pro mark, and nothing else is improving quickly enough to offset it. All told, he converts only 45.9% of his points, making you wonder why he didn't just pass the ball to Jeff Malone a bit more.

Sidney Moncrief
Milwaukee Bucks
21.3 HGS

College:	Arkansas
Age (1/1/1990):	33
Height:	6'4''
Weight:	180
Scoring:	0.547
Rebounding:	3.07
Playmaking:	0.35
Defense:	4.22
Gun Rating:	−1.38
HoopStat Grade:	21.30
Minutes/Game:	25.71

Closer to the end than the beginning. He's no longer the force he once was, as age and injuries have dropped him. But wait until you see how quickly the Bucks drop once Moncrief and Sikma are done. Not offered a contract with the Bucks, look for Moncrief as a role player on his new squad.

Jeff Malone
Washington Bullets
21.0 HGS

College:	Mississippi St.
Age (1/1/1990):	29
Height:	6'4''
Weight:	205
Scoring:	0.519
Rebounding:	2.16
Playmaking:	0.16
Defense:	2.28
Gun Rating:	−11.78
HoopStat Grade:	21.00
Minutes/Game:	31.82

Why did he bother to try 19 threes last year? He *did* make one, sure, but what is someone thinking when he sets up outside, after going 1 for his last 18? Does he think that this one is going in? That the dry spell's almost over? That he's helping the team?

You can't do things like that when your team is struggling to keep its collective head above water. The difference between Malone and Dale Ellis was the three-pointer. Ellis took them, made them, and looked good despite his −12.50 Gun. Malone didn't take them, didn't make them when he did, and suddenly wasn't the rising young star anymore, but garnered a −11.80 Gun for his efforts. Give him another point or two per game, and you'd have Ellis. Give him a good screen though, and the ball is up. He's always looking for that extra point.

Joe Dumars
Detroit Pistons
21.0 HGS

College:	McNeese St.
Age (1/1/1990):	27
Height:	6'3''
Weight:	190
Scoring:	0.554
Rebounding:	2.11
Playmaking:	0.43
Defense:	2.50
Gun Rating:	−2.64
HoopStat Grade:	21.00
Minutes/Game:	34.91

Dumars knows how to score, as evidenced by his .554 scoring percentage. The fact that his scoring average is low just shows where the ball *doesn't* go while everyone else on the team sets themselves up. Joe isn't selfish by any means; his Play rating was nearly average for *all* guards (point and off included), so he passes it a lot more often than an average two guard. In the finals Joe passed, but he also let loose for 27 ppg, good enough for MVP and a salary raise to $2 million per season. With defensive and offensive skills like his, it will be increasingly harder for Quiet Joe to remain so quiet in the Piston scheme of things.

Michael Holton
Charlotte Hornets
20.4 HGS

College:	UCLA
Age (1/1/1990):	29
Height:	6'4''
Weight:	185
Scoring:	0.475
Rebounding:	1.78
Playmaking:	0.84
Defense:	3.27
Gun Rating:	4.79
HoopStat Grade:	20.40
Minutes/Game:	25.31

A good spot-up shooter from the perimeter. Holton has range from 20 feet in. Not a true point guard because he's not good enough off the dribble to control the team. However, he will do whatever he's asked to do, which is why Portland still regrets not having protected him in the expansion draft. He's a real positive player who never complains. This is an intangible that means so much over the course of a season.

Jay Humphries

Milwaukee Bucks
20.3 HGS

College:	Colorado
Age (1/1/1990):	28
Height:	6'3''
Weight:	185
Scoring:	0.502
Rebounding:	2.57
Playmaking:	0.57
Defense:	4.46
Gun Rating:	2.02
HoopStat Grade:	20.30
Minutes/Game:	30.41

A player who showed that he is much better than people thought he was. Stocky, but powerful and quick. He gets to the hoop real well. Finishes off plays at the basket and can make threes as well. Drawback might be his tendency to go one-on-one too much, bogging down the team's movement.

Kenny Smith

Sacramento Kings
20.0 HGS

College:	North Carolina
Age (1/1/1990):	25
Height:	6'3''
Weight:	170
Scoring:	0.492
Rebounding:	1.99
Playmaking:	0.52
Defense:	3.01
Gun Rating:	− 1.40
HoopStat Grade:	20.00
Minutes/Game:	38.83

Even with Mark Jackson's off year, you didn't hear Kenny compared to him as much as the previous season.

Quickness is his middle name. Flies up and down the floor. He's a marginal shooter with a terrible release on his jumper. Ever want to see a ball spin sideways? Watch Kenny hoist up a J. A good penetrator from UNC who's fundamentally sound in skills. His one drawback may be his inability to consistently make outside shots. Defense plays him for his drives.

Sam Vincent

Chicago Bulls
20.0 HGS

College:	Michigan St.
Age (1/1/1990):	31
Height:	6'7''
Weight:	220
Scoring:	0.513
Rebounding:	3.04
Playmaking:	0.59
Defense:	3.97
Gun Rating:	1.54
HoopStat Grade:	20.00
Minutes/Game:	24.33

Sam has all the qualities of a journeyman: he hasn't met his potential, freelances too much, can't shoot that well, and doesn't spread defenses. Jerry Krause might be lulled just a bit by the fact that they're winning with him in the lineup, but make no mistake: Jordan's the point guard of the future here. That is, if he wants the position.

Brian Shaw
Boston Celtics
20.0 HGS

College:	UC – Santa Barbara
Age (1/1/1990):	24
Height:	6'6"
Weight:	190
Scoring:	0.463
Rebounding:	4.79
Playmaking:	0.69
Defense:	4.87
Gun Rating:	5.35
HoopStat Grade:	20.00
Minutes/Game:	28.06

Behind his deficient scoring, he's hiding some good skills. There's a big swing between his Gun and Ainge's, nearly 9.5 to be exact. Neither one made much of what they shot, although Shaw was even worse (a .464 scoring percentage). The jury's still out, until "Exhibit B" (as in Bird) returns to the lineup next season. But with a year's experience at directing his Celtic teammates, only good things are expected from this triple double threat.

Byron Scott
Los Angeles Lakers
19.9 HGS

College:	Arizona St.
Age (1/1/1990):	29
Height:	6'4"
Weight:	195
Scoring:	0.514
Rebounding:	3.25
Playmaking:	0.19
Defense:	4.66
Gun Rating:	– 6.73
HoopStat Grade:	19.90
Minutes/Game:	35.20

Just because you're good enough to win with a player doesn't mean you should keep him around, trying to prove it. Watch for the Lakers to try to move Scott, even before you read this. The Lakers would like to weasel a center from another team; any halfway decent team would probably be crazy to give them one right now. Let them sweat for a year, see what they can find from the scrap heap.

But if they *do* make a trade for a center, Scott will probably be the easiest player to replace. He has the worst peripheral statistics of any Laker (a – 6.73 Gun rating), and although his scoring is okay, his HGS drops him to sixth or seventh on the team.

Rolando Blackman
Dallas Mavericks
19.0 HGS

College:	Kansas St.
Age (1/1/1990):	31
Height:	6'6"
Weight:	194
Scoring:	0.519
Rebounding:	2.62
Playmaking:	0.23
Defense:	3.04
Gun Rating:	– 6.01
HoopStat Grade:	19.00
Minutes/Game:	37.77

The Mavericks were thought to have the best young backcourt two years ago. So why is Rolando now rated so low? He's just one more example of a player content to score. Sure, he had a higher ppg average, but everything that Blackman did, Derek Harper did better. Injuries slowed Blackman last season and the turmoil and losses certainly didn't help his psyche. Look for better numbers from Rolando this season.

Reggie Miller
Indiana Pacers
19.0 HGS

College:	UCLA
Age (1/1/1990):	25
Height:	6'7''
Weight:	190
Scoring:	0.526
Rebounding:	3.25
Playmaking:	0.27
Defense:	4.38
Gun Rating:	− 3.39
HoopStat Grade:	19.00
Minutes/Game:	34.27

One of the big three-point shooters in the league. Reggie tried 244 and made over 40%, netting him about 50 points benefit from the outside.

A spot-up shooter with unlimited range. He doesn't beat people off the dribble. A solid player who's been labeled soft by coaches because he lurks on the outside of the action. He never will be a big scorer until he starts getting around people and getting to the hoop.

Dennis Johnson
Boston Celtics
18.6 HGS

College:	Pepperdine
Age (1/1/1990):	36
Height:	6'4''
Weight:	200
Scoring:	0.474
Rebounding:	2.20
Playmaking:	0.74
Defense:	4.04
Gun Rating:	3.56
HoopStat Grade:	18.60
Minutes/Game:	32.07

Some advice: Retire. Johnson's numbers were down and the Celts floundered. With his best years behind him, all that remains are the memories of a successful career.

Gerald Wilkins
New York Knicks
18.6 HGS

College:	Tenn. – Chattanooga
Age (1/1/1990):	27
Height:	6'6''
Weight:	190
Scoring:	0.471
Rebounding:	3.09
Playmaking:	0.27
Defense:	4.21
Gun Rating:	− 4.47
HoopStat Grade:	18.60
Minutes/Game:	29.80

Finally received some credit this year, instead of living in his brother's spotlight. He'll never be the player Dominique is, but he filled his role on the Knicks well. Gerald started slightly more games than Trent Tucker, so he gets the starting rating for the Knicks at shooting guard. His offense increased, however, when he was relegated to the bench and Tucker started. He averaged 22.1 pp48 in his starts, 26.7 off the bench.

Kevin Edwards
Miami Heat
18.6 HGS

College:	DePaul
Age (1/1/1990):	25
Height:	6'3"
Weight:	200
Scoring:	0.448
Rebounding:	3.28
Playmaking:	0.32
Defense:	5.16
Gun Rating:	−3.74
HoopStat Grade:	18.60
Minutes/Game:	29.73

A rookie who could develop into a very good player. Good at coming off picks. He was always competitive, which is a trait that usually goes first when you're constantly losing. Look for him to guide the Heat to a few more wins this season.

Vernon Maxwell
San Antonio Spurs
18.0 HGS

College:	Florida
Age (1/1/1990):	25
Height:	6'4"
Weight:	180
Scoring:	0.458
Rebounding:	2.75
Playmaking:	0.36
Defense:	3.96
Gun Rating:	−3.53
HoopStat Grade:	18.00
Minutes/Game:	26.14

Maxwell's problem is that he started out playing for a real bad team. It's extremely difficult to know the actual extent of his talents. He can hit the jumper, or else put his head down and take it to the hoop and get fouled. Luckily, he's decent from the line. It will be interesting to see how he holds up if the Spurs continue their downward slide this season.

Hersey Hawkins
Philadelphia 76ers
17.9 HGS

College:	Bradley
Age (1/1/1990):	25
Height:	6'3"
Weight:	190
Scoring:	0.499
Rebounding:	2.43
Playmaking:	0.25
Defense:	4.55
Gun Rating:	−4.46
HoopStat Grade:	17.90
Minutes/Game:	32.56

One of the bigger disappointments coming out of the draft, Hersey appeared to be in a year-long slump. His terrible playoff shooting probably swung the series in favor of the Knicks, as he had three consecutive one-fer games, going 3 for 24 overall. Hersey was the scorer in college, leading the nation in 1988. Something was lost, however, in the move to the pros. The Sixers are hoping it's not a permanent one . . . or they're all in trouble.

Robert Reid
Charlotte Hornets
17.6 HGS

College:	St. Mary's
Age (1/1/1990):	35
Height:	6'8''
Weight:	215
Scoring:	0.451
Rebounding:	4.01
Playmaking:	0.13
Defense:	4.08
Gun Rating:	−9.29
HoopStat Grade:	17.60
Minutes/Game:	26.24

His versatility was a big plus for the undermanned Hornets, as he could start at any position where they needed a body. His defense isn't what it used to be. His lifetime Def is 554; last year he had a defense rating of 4.08, and his other numbers weren't that high either. He kept his scoring up as well as he could, but the other categories suffered.

What's the biggest difference between a largely veteran expansion team, such as Charlotte, and Miami's commitment to newer players? From what we've seen, the older players are more likely to try to pad their own statistics than to work together as a team. Proof comes from this year's final Gun rating. The top four Hornet scorers, Tripucka, Chapman, Reid, and Curry, combined for a −42.08 Gun. The top four Heat scorers, Edwards, Sparrow, Long, and Seikaly were a cumulative −3.55. The numbers say a lot about who was trying to pad his stats.

Rory Sparrow
Miami Heat
16.8 HGS

College:	Villanova
Age (1/1/1990):	32
Height:	6'2''
Weight:	175
Scoring:	0.466
Rebounding:	2.34
Playmaking:	0.44
Defense:	3.70
Gun Rating:	−1.54
HoopStat Grade:	16.80
Minutes/Game:	32.66

Given up for dead by the Knicks, Sparrow came back to life (sort of) for the Heat. Although he wasn't great by any stretch of the imagination, he was a veteran presence, which a team full of bad young players needs to keep stability. He wasn't responsible for many wins, but he kept the team in the running. Until they can find a good young guard that they can bring along slowly, look for Sparrow to fill the gap for the Heat.

Mike Woodson
Houston Rockets
16.6 HGS

College:	Indiana
Age (1/1/1990):	32
Height:	6'5''
Weight:	198
Scoring:	0.476
Rebounding:	2.44
Playmaking:	0.22
Defense:	3.79
Gun Rating:	−5.64
HoopStat Grade:	16.60
Minutes/Game:	27.89

Once a Net, always a Net.

Woodson was really slowed down by his knee injury of a few years ago. He has range from 19 feet. Uses picks well, but not good off the dribble anymore because he's lost his lateral quickness to the surgeon's scalpel. Might be one step away from Minnesota.

Rex Chapman
Charlotte Hornets
16.3 HGS

College:	Kentucky
Age (1/1/1990):	23
Height:	6'4"
Weight:	185
Scoring:	0.433
Rebounding:	2.58
Playmaking:	0.14
Defense:	3.30
Gun Rating:	−11.07
HoopStat Grade:	16.30
Minutes/Game:	29.59

Rex should be a good player in the next few years, but he *really* shouldn't have come out early. A 16.3 HGS is just not adequate for an NBA player, much less a starter. He shows flashes of brilliance (who can forget that great drive against Sacramento? Well, uh . . .), but as a whole, he was weak.

Darrell Griffith
Utah Jazz
15.6 HGS

College:	Louisville
Age (1/1/1990):	32
Height:	6'4"
Weight:	190
Scoring:	0.460
Rebounding:	3.87
Playmaking:	0.12
Defense:	4.73
Gun Rating:	−7.30
HoopStat Grade:	15.60
Minutes/Game:	29.05

Joe Barry Carroll and Darrell Griffith were chosen 1–2 in the 1980 draft. Both have missed a lot of time with injuries. But where we're all still looking for Carroll to fulfill his promise, Griffith's been on the decline since he missed an entire season with injury. The past two seasons, however, has accelerated the fall, and Jazz management is reportedly showing discontent with his play.

DARRELL GRIFFITH CAREER PP48

Year	PTS/MINS	PP48
1981	1671/2867	27.98
1982	1582/2597	29.24
1983	1709/2787	29.43
1984	1636/2650	29.63
1985	1764/2776	30.50
1987	1142/1843	29.74
1988	589/1052	26.87
1989	1135/2382	22.87

Mike McGee
New Jersey Nets
14.9 HGS

College:	Michigan
Age (1/1/1990):	31
Height:	6'5"
Weight:	207
Scoring:	0.465
Rebounding:	2.84
Playmaking:	0.13
Defense:	3.55
Gun Rating:	−9.70
HoopStat Grade:	14.90
Minutes/Game:	25.34

McGee garnered the worst rating for *any* player who put on a Nets uniform for at least one game. And he was given 49 starts. Isn't that all you need to know?

FORWARDS

Charles Barkley
Philadelphia 76ers
35.0 HGS

College:	Auburn
Age (1/1/1990):	27
Height:	6'6"
Weight:	263
Scoring:	0.604
Rebounding:	9.86
Playmaking:	0.27
Defense:	7.52
Gun Rating:	3.33
HoopStat Grade:	35.00
Minutes/Game:	39.09

Barkley didn't dominate his position as Jordan and Olajuwon did, but he still blew past Karl Malone for the lead by 2.2 HGS. Every number of his was well above average, but the most impressive was his .604 scoring percentage. Had an average player been taking his shots, it would have worked out to a 3.0 ppg difference. Karl Malone outscored Barkley, got more MVP votes, but Malone had help from Stockton. Barkley was his own man. He took players outside and shot over them when they gave him room. Pity the team that lets him loose in the paint. He's not averse to hauling three bodies up to the rim if he has to.

Karl Malone
Utah Jazz
32.8 HGS

College:	Louisiana Tech
Age (1/1/1990):	27
Height:	6'9"
Weight:	254
Scoring:	0.574
Rebounding:	7.94
Playmaking:	0.14
Defense:	7.85
Gun Rating:	-2.92
HoopStat Grade:	32.80
Minutes/Game:	39.08

In these days of the perimeter guard, Malone was a throwback to the tough post-up style that won games years ago. He just pounded, and pounded, and scored, and drew fouls, and pounded some more. That he shot 3.21 FTs for every foul he was called for is a good demonstration of his game. In fact, he was awarded 921 attempts, the most in the league. That's over 14 per 48 minutes, and it certainly didn't hurt the Jazz's chances to win. He was the leading scorer among all forwards, second only to Air Jordan in scoring rate, with 35.7 pp48. Malone never takes a day off in the off-season, he's constantly working to improve his fitness and on-court performance. For his efforts, he was voted in a poll of his NBA peers as the top in the league.

Chris Mullin
Golden State Warriors
29.1 HGS

College:	St. John's
Age (1/1/1990):	27
Height:	6'7"
Weight:	220
Scoring:	0.556
Rebounding:	4.57
Playmaking:	0.25
Defense:	5.90
Gun Rating:	−4.64
HoopStat Grade:	29.10
Minutes/Game:	37.72

Okay, we'll admit that he's a heart-warming success story.

Mullin is a great shooter who finally has his confidence back. He's not exceptionally quick, but he makes up for it with court smarts. He doesn't have many offensive weaknesses. He has good moves without the ball, and he understands what has to be done when he's overplayed. This opens up the court for Golden State. Finally off alcohol and in shape, he's now blossomed into an All-Star performer. Mullin is perhaps one of the fittest players in the game today. Works out six hours a day in the off season on conditioning and during the season he rides a stationary bike 45 minutes daily. Never appears to be tired.

Larry Nance
Cleveland Cavaliers
27.8 HGS

College:	Clemson
Age (1/1/1990):	31
Height:	6'10"
Weight:	215
Scoring:	0.578
Rebounding:	6.56
Playmaking:	0.17
Defense:	9.04
Gun Rating:	3.87
HoopStat Grade:	27.80
Minutes/Game:	34.60

Nance just might have been the scariest guy in the East last year, as he went around rejecting shots with alarming frequency. His 1.41 Hands was highest among all forwards, and this tough defense more than made up for the ex–slam dunk champion's below-average scoring. But that's what Cleveland got him to do two years ago.

Tom Chambers
Phoenix Suns
26.8 HGS

College:	Utah
Age (1/1/1990):	31
Height:	6'10"
Weight:	230
Scoring:	0.525
Rebounding:	6.27
Playmaking:	0.14
Defense:	6.60
Gun Rating:	−6.58
HoopStat Grade:	26.80
Minutes/Game:	37.06

For someone widely considered one of the top gunners in the NBA, Chambers had surprising difficulty finding the net last year (his scoring percentage was only .525). No doubt, however, he was one of the many key ingredients in the Suns' resurgence. At 6'10", he did battle with the league giants down in the paint, and scored. If they followed him outside, he'd burn them from two- or three-point range, or else power back inside.

Ron Harper
Cleveland Cavaliers
26.8 HGS

College:	Miami, Ohio
Age (1/1/1990):	26
Height:	6'6"
Weight:	205
Scoring:	0.537
Rebounding:	4.16
Playmaking:	0.38
Defense:	6.78
Gun Rating:	1.13
HoopStat Grade:	26.80
Minutes/Game:	34.77

The least selfish forward in the league, as he garnered a Play rating of 0.38, exactly double the average for forwards. His Cont rating was by far the best, also, indicating that he wasn't prone to turnovers. Numbers five through seven on the list of forwards are basically interchangeable, ratings-wise, although their games are all very different. Chambers is a gunner, McHale a high-percentage "classic Celtic" player, and Harper is, well, a Cleveland cog. Even so, he's probably one of the top guards playing. He's great in transition. Can take it to the hoop or hit the open man; can stay outside and pop. His problem is that he's in Cleveland and not too many hoop legends are made there by the press.

Kevin McHale
Boston Celtics
26.8 HGS

College:	Minnesota
Age (1/1/1990):	33
Height:	6'10"
Weight:	225
Scoring:	0.594
Rebounding:	6.62
Playmaking:	0.14
Defense:	5.51
Gun Rating:	−2.55
HoopStat Grade:	26.80
Minutes/Game:	36.87

Next to Charles Barkley, Kevin McHale was the highest-percentage scorer among forwards. But where Barkley got a lot of his easy points through stuffs and inside moves, McHale got his with "easy" jumpers.

Terry Cummings
Milwaukee Bucks
26.3 HGS

College:	DePaul
Age (1/1/1990):	29
Height:	6'9"
Weight:	235
Scoring:	0.508
Rebounding:	7.20
Playmaking:	0.13
Defense:	6.11
Gun Rating:	−4.79
HoopStat Grade:	26.30
Minutes/Game:	35.30

Terry Cummings has found, lost, and refound his form more often than one of the spirits from *Ghostbusters II*.

One of the better one-on-one players in the league. He'll work hard to get the ball for himself, especially in the low post. A selfish player, the ball most likely won't get kicked out once he gets his hands on it.

Dominique Wilkins
Atlanta Hawks
26.2 HGS

Wayne Cooper
Denver Nuggets
25.4 HGS

College:	Georgia	College:	New Orleans
Age (1/1/1990):	30	Age (1/1/1990):	34
Height:	6'8''	Height:	6'10''
Weight:	200	Weight:	220
Scoring:	0.507	Scoring:	0.521
Rebounding:	5.86	Rebounding:	9.88
Playmaking:	0.12	Playmaking:	0.18
Defense:	5.09	Defense:	11.59
Gun Rating:	−7.38	Gun Rating:	12.03
HoopStat Grade:	26.20	HoopStat Grade:	25.40
Minutes/Game:	37.46	Minutes/Game:	23.61

Long a flashy fixture in the Omni, there were, probably for the first time, postseason rumblings about trading him while he still had value. He sure *looks* like he still does, although he didn't convert nearly enough opportunities last year.

A volume shooter who throws up a ton of shots. He makes a lot of hard shots, but he takes a lot of hard shots that no one else would attempt. Wilkins is a gifted athlete who could get 20 ppg just by running and jumping over the opposition. Sometimes when it comes down to actual execution of a play, he gets a little wild at times. If he harnessed his game and became more efficient, he'd really be unstoppable. Granted the man is talented, but he doesn't involve his teammates as much as he should. Once he lures the defense to him, he needs to dish it off to someone cutting the hoop. Not Dominique, though. He'll try to go over two or three defenders if he can. If he's on fire, he'll score. If he's not, then his teammates stand around watching, and this is deadly.

The Nuggets own the next two spots on the list, with Wayne Cooper and Alex English. Both are highly rated and have skills highly complementary to each others. In fact, they are the two most opposite forwards in the league. Alex English has the lowest Gun rating, −9.80, while Cooper has the very highest, at 12.00, among all forwards.

If you're going to have two players who, combined, have all the skills, this might not be the best way to do it. In one sense, you have two players who, combined, could do everything. However, if you managed to stop English from scoring one night, would Cooper be able to jump-start your offense as well as another guy might?

There's no mistake that arrangements like this can be dangerous, since if one player is stopped, the other can't chip in. But on the whole, it would beat two average forwards, say a Michael Cage and Johnny Newman. If you ever get the choice, take two players at this level, with slightly more equalized skills. But if you don't, this pair is far better than you need to be competitive.

Despite all the candidates, Cooper was by far the highest-rated defensive forward in the league, with a Def rating more than 2.5 ahead of Larry Nance. You don't hear about Wayne all that much, at least not out here in the East.

Alex English
Denver Nuggets
25.1 HGS

College:	South Carolina
Age (1/1/1990):	36
Height:	6'7"
Weight:	190
Scoring:	0.524
Rebounding:	3.45
Playmaking:	0.20
Defense:	2.68
Gun Rating:	−9.77
HoopStat Grade:	25.10
Minutes/Game:	36.46

One of the all-time best-scoring hands in the league, based as much on volume as anything else. English just keeps rolling along, with a prolific scoring game, and absolutely no defense. None. His 2.68 Def was the lowest of any forward and positively paled next to court mate Wayne Cooper's 11.59. Only Johnny Newman and Kelly Tripucka kept him out of the basement in rebounding rating, too. So does this guy do anything but shoot?

It doesn't look like it. His −9.80 Gun was the lowest of all forwards', meaning his value was diminished by his inability to do anything but score. Eleventh out of 51 isn't exactly an unenviable spot, however, and it's due to his scoring. And nothing else.

Jerome Kersey
Portland Trail Blazers
24.8 HGS

College:	Longwood
Age (1/1/1990):	28
Height:	6'7"
Weight:	222
Scoring:	0.499
Rebounding:	7.08
Playmaking:	0.21
Defense:	7.27
Gun Rating:	1.33
HoopStat Grade:	24.80
Minutes/Game:	35.74

The Blazers had only one permanent starting center last year, owing to many factors. Jerome Kersey was decent, but his scoring was slightly deficient for a starter. He was within 0.5 pp48 of average, but he had to take a lot of shots to get there, as he put down only 49.9% of his possible points. He more than made up for it with his other talents, such as rebounding and defense.

James Worthy
Los Angeles Lakers
24.6 HGS

College:	North Carolina
Age (1/1/1990):	29
Height:	6'9"
Weight:	235
Scoring:	0.570
Rebounding:	4.92
Playmaking:	0.22
Defense:	5.25
Gun Rating:	−2.25
HoopStat Grade:	24.60
Minutes/Game:	36.54

Nothing spectacular, but you need only above-average talent to fit in with the experience of the Lakers. He produced virtually the same as Wayman Tisdale (rated next), except that Worthy was a bit more of a finesse player, whereas Tisdale was a rebounder/power forward type.

He's not exactly one of the "top two or three" forwards in the NBA, as Phoenix radio man Al McCoy feels, but he's probably top-ten material, year in and year out. If a top center is on the block any time soon, don't be surprised if Jerry West uses James as bait to pry him loose.

Wayman Tisdale
Sacramento Kings
24.6 HGS

College:	Oklahoma
Age (1/1/1990):	26
Height:	6'9"
Weight:	240
Scoring:	0.556
Rebounding:	7.30
Playmaking:	0.12
Defense:	6.27
Gun Rating:	-2.63
HoopStat Grade:	24.60
Minutes/Game:	30.81

Despite the problems he's had in the league, Tisdale still has a great chance to succeed as a top-notch pro. His situation will be more settled in Sacramento, where he'll be playing on a team on its way up, not down. His offense was way above average last year, but we've all known that since he was at Oklahoma.

Charles Smith
Los Angeles Clippers
24.4 HGS

College:	Pittsburgh
Age (1/1/1990):	25
Height:	6'10"
Weight:	230
Scoring:	0.537
Rebounding:	6.51
Playmaking:	0.12
Defense:	6.73
Gun Rating:	-1.21
HoopStat Grade:	24.40
Minutes/Game:	30.44

Unlimited potential. Smith has a nice future, too bad it's with the Clippers. He's talented enough to play power forward/small forward. Runs the floor well, jumps well, can put the ball on the floor away from the basket. Can shoot over people or take them to the hoop.

Willie Anderson
San Antonio Spurs
24.4 HGS

College:	Georgia
Age (1/1/1990):	23
Height:	6'7"
Weight:	190
Scoring:	0.524
Rebounding:	4.59
Playmaking:	0.29
Defense:	5.99
Gun Rating:	-2.06
HoopStat Grade:	24.40
Minutes/Game:	33.80

Another player with a nice future. Anderson can play three positions, 1, 2, or 3. A shooter who has three-point range. A legitimate 6'7" who should be a big-time offensive player with the Spurs. Watch him.

A. C. Green
Los Angeles Lakers
24.3 HGS

College:	Oregon St.
Age (1/1/1990):	27
Height:	6'9"
Weight:	230
Scoring:	0.575
Rebounding:	8.79
Playmaking:	0.14
Defense:	7.45
Gun Rating:	3.47
HoopStat Grade:	24.30
Minutes/Game:	30.61

A.C. was just one in a line of great Lakers, and although he was a shade under average in scoring, he provided much needed rebounding in the vacuum created by Kareem's continuing play.

Kurt Rambis
Charlotte Hornets
24.1 HGS

College:	UC – Santa Clara
Age (1/1/1990):	32
Height:	6'8"
Weight:	213
Scoring:	0.553
Rebounding:	9.58
Playmaking:	0.25
Defense:	8.04
Gun Rating:	6.23
HoopStat Grade:	24.10
Minutes/Game:	29.77

Kurt Rambis and Kelly Tripucka both got chances to redeem their careers in Charlotte last year, and both made the most of them. Rambis showed that he could survive without scoring, with the toughest defense on the team. Tripucka showed that he could survive by just scoring, with a 33.5 pp48 average. Both were above the league average for forwards, which is impressive, considering the Hornets were built around their guards.

Kelly Tripucka
Charlotte Hornets
24.1 HGS

College:	Notre Dame
Age (1/1/1990):	31
Height:	6'6"
Weight:	225
Scoring:	0.531
Rebounding:	3.36
Playmaking:	0.18
Defense:	4.13
Gun Rating:	−9.43
HoopStat Grade:	24.10
Minutes/Game:	32.42

When he arrived in Charlotte, Tripucka was escaping two years of benching. It wasn't so much a doghouse as it was his inability to crack the lineup with Malone and Thurl Bailey in the way. He produced nearly identical numbers to those of Kurt Rambis, but as we just mentioned, Tripucka almost seemed to be padding his stats, taking a lot of shots and raising his scoring average. Rambis was well above the league average in scoring percentage; Tripucka, the scorer, was just below it.

Bernard King
Washington Bullets
24.0 HGS

College:	Tennessee
Age (1/1/1990):	34
Height:	6'7"
Weight:	205
Scoring:	0.522
Rebounding:	4.47
Playmaking:	0.21
Defense:	3.78
Gun Rating:	−7.36
HoopStat Grade:	24.00
Minutes/Game:	31.59

Reggie Lewis
Boston Celtics
23.6 HGS

College:	Northeastern
Age (1/1/1990):	25
Height:	6'7"
Weight:	195
Scoring:	0.521
Rebounding:	4.14
Playmaking:	0.18
Defense:	5.88
Gun Rating:	−3.46
HoopStat Grade:	23.60
Minutes/Game:	32.80

LaSalle Thompson
Indiana Pacers
23.4 HGS

College:	Texas
Age (1/1/1990):	29
Height:	6'10"
Weight:	253
Scoring:	0.534
Rebounding:	9.01
Playmaking:	0.10
Defense:	8.66
Gun Rating:	1.56
HoopStat Grade:	23.40
Minutes/Game:	30.64

Although he'll never be quite the player he was before the injury, Bernard has bounced back much better than anyone thought he could. We knew he had come full circle when a caller to a radio talk show in NYC suggested that the Knicks should pick him up "to solve their problems at forward."

Come to think of it, Bernard *did* have a better season than either of the two starting Knick forwards.

One of the Celtics' upstarts last year, Lewis was given a chance to crack the starting lineup and came through with a halfway decent season. He's been in the league for two years, but the first year was basically a wash, as he saw only 405 minutes.

You know, it's the excitement of a Sacramento-Indiana trade, and the leaguewide interest in the results, that makes basement teams so special. Sports bars nationwide were abuzz; feelings were split over which team got the better of the Thompson/Wittman for Tisdale deal.

Well, it wasn't *that* thrilling, but both teams started the long road back to respectability by swapping stars in February. LaSalle Thompson is a decent power forward, able to muscle home rebounds with regularity, and giving Indiana a pretty good frontcourt for the next few years.

Greg Anderson
San Antonio Spurs
23.3 HGS

College:	Houston
Age (1/1/1990):	26
Height:	6'10"
Weight:	230
Scoring:	0.504
Rebounding:	8.54
Playmaking:	0.07
Defense:	8.29
Gun Rating:	0.76
HoopStat Grade:	23.30
Minutes/Game:	29.28

An unknown quantity. If he had shown some signs of dominance in the low post, San Antonio would have won more than 20 games. Anderson is a great athlete with a somewhat questionable work ethic on the court. He shows flashes of competence in the low post on offense, but has no game away from the hoop. Depending on how hard he's willing to work at his game, he could have a bright future in Milwaukee as a backup to Sikma.

Ken Norman
Los Angeles Clippers
22.4 HGS

College:	Illinois
Age (1/1/1990):	26
Height:	6'8"
Weight:	215
Scoring:	0.512
Rebounding:	6.66
Playmaking:	0.22
Defense:	6.07
Gun Rating:	−0.61
HoopStat Grade:	22.40
Minutes/Game:	37.75

Norman worked himself into being a player. He's a tough kid who legitimately improved his outside shot over his first year. He's actually now a threat to make a 20-footer, whereas before the defense was more than willing to let him launch a long one.

Adrian Dantley
Dallas Mavericks
22.4 HGS

College:	Notre Dame
Age (1/1/1990):	34
Height:	6'5"
Weight:	210
Scoring:	0.565
Rebounding:	3.95
Playmaking:	0.18
Defense:	3.09
Gun Rating:	−5.37
HoopStat Grade:	22.40
Minutes/Game:	33.18

Need we remind anyone, after Dantley's late arrival in Dallas, and the stories that circulated about his aloofness in locker rooms, that his name is an anagram for "tardy and alien"?

This year, at least, Dallas got the better of the deal. Aguirre was lower-rated, although there are quite a few players bunched together in the middle. The difference between the two was 1.2 points HGS, but 9 slots in the ratings. It's not even enough to worry about, and Aguirre's much younger. Dallas is ahead right now, but in a few seasons they'll have nothing to show for it. For now, Dantley will content himself with holding the ball a little too long and mystifying anybody 6'5" to 7'5" who tries to stop him from scoring on them down low. A proven performer embittered by his exile from Detroit, look for Dantley to extract his pound of flesh . . . from Isiah.

Charles Oakley
New York Knicks
22.3 HGS

College:	Virginia Union
Age (1/1/1990):	27
Height:	6'8"
Weight:	225
Scoring:	0.538
Rebounding:	10.15
Playmaking:	0.22
Defense:	6.95
Gun Rating:	2.76
HoopStat Grade:	22.30
Minutes/Game:	31.76

Not quite as good as they'd have you believe here in New York, but he was a definite factor in the Knicks' improvement. He led the league in rebounding two years ago, on a team with Dave Corzine at center. Last year he didn't do as much, but was still intimidating under the boards. One of his unseen skills is his ability to make great breakout passes, which often got the team running. If he can get the thought out of his mind that he can score from the outside (he can't) and concentrate on boards and down-low offensive work, he and the Knicks will be better off.

Armon Gilliam
Phoenix Suns
22.1 HGS

College:	UNLV
Age (1/1/1990):	26
Height:	6'9"
Weight:	230
Scoring:	0.539
Rebounding:	7.43
Playmaking:	0.06
Defense:	6.07
Gun Rating:	−4.50
HoopStat Grade:	22.10
Minutes/Game:	28.65

The highlight of Armon's season was his well-publicized tiff with Pearl Washington in the Miami showers. He was one of only two forwards (with Larry Smith) not to attempt a three-pointer all year. In addition, he was the worst passer of all forwards, and actually had a negative Cont rating (more turnovers than steals and assists combined).

Otis Thorpe
Houston Rockets
22.0 HGS

College:	Providence
Age (1/1/1990):	28
Height:	6'11"
Weight:	236
Scoring:	0.577
Rebounding:	7.48
Playmaking:	0.21
Defense:	5.80
Gun Rating:	1.07
HoopStat Grade:	22.00
Minutes/Game:	38.23

They both started all 82 games, but Otis Thorpe actually got more minutes than his teammate Akeem Olajuwon. Was there a good reason for this? He was expected to be a real find for Houston and was at one time considered to be one of the league's most underrated players, but last year he plummeted into the second division of front courters. Both he and teammate Buck Johnson were excellent when they got the ball (their scoring percentages were .577 and .550, respectively), but Akeem wasn't about to let them have it.

Scottie Pippen
Chicago Bulls
21.8 HGS

College:	Central Arkansas
Age (1/1/1990):	25
Height:	6'8''
Weight:	210
Scoring:	0.496
Rebounding:	5.39
Playmaking:	0.30
Defense:	6.99
Gun Rating:	0.95
HoopStat Grade:	21.80
Minutes/Game:	33.05

Hurt by his poor shooting, Pippen was an undistinguished but adequate perimeter forward last year for the Bulls. He actually split time between guard and forward, but started up front more often. He played small, however, shooting lots of threes, not showing up under the boards, but controlling the ball well.

Bill Thompson
Miami Heat
21.6 HGS

College:	Louisville
Age (1/1/1990):	27
Height:	6'7''
Weight:	220
Scoring:	0.515
Rebounding:	7.82
Playmaking:	0.25
Defense:	6.90
Gun Rating:	3.56
HoopStat Grade:	21.60
Minutes/Game:	28.76

Surprise! The two Miami starters at forward ranked together, just ahead of the two Seattle starters, and both ahead of both Detroit starters! Does it mean anything? Probably not. Both Thompson and Long were underrated, in part because they didn't average many points per game. True, you'd want to have Aguirre and Mahorn before these two, but much of that preference is due solely to their proven qualities.

If you're in Miami, don't laugh at this assessment of your talent. We're just trying to cheer you up.

Grant Long
Miami Heat
21.6 HGS

College:	Eastern Michigan
Age (1/1/1990):	24
Height:	6'8''
Weight:	225
Scoring:	0.544
Rebounding:	7.05
Playmaking:	0.22
Defense:	6.38
Gun Rating:	2.35
HoopStat Grade:	21.60
Minutes/Game:	29.65

Although they were close in most categories, Grant Long provided a bit better offense than Thompson, although his peripherals weren't quite as sharp.

Derrick McKey
Seattle Supersonics
21.5 HGS

College:	Alabama
Age (1/1/1990):	24
Height:	6'9''
Weight:	205
Scoring:	0.543
Rebounding:	4.97
Playmaking:	0.23
Defense:	5.54
Gun Rating:	−0.86
HoopStat Grade:	21.50
Minutes/Game:	34.20

McKey is one of the great young talents in the league. He's more versatile in some ways than Dale Ellis or X-Man. McDaniel doesn't have McKey's 3 point range, and Ellis doesn't go to the hoop as well as McKey. He also can rebound well, put the ball on the floor, run, and play tough defense. His time for recognition will soon be arriving.

Michael Cage
Seattle Supersonics
21.2 HGS

College:	San Diego St.
Age (1/1/1990):	28
Height:	6'9''
Weight:	235
Scoring:	0.540
Rebounding:	9.07
Playmaking:	0.20
Defense:	7.35
Gun Rating:	5.54
HoopStat Grade:	21.20
Minutes/Game:	31.70

Cage isn't needed to lead the league in rebounds anymore, but he's still pulling down a ton for the Sonics. Seattle led the league in offensive rebounding, but their two forwards were just average in that respect. Their guards and center made up the difference.

Mark Aguirre
Detroit Pistons
21.2 HGS

College:	DePaul
Age (1/1/1990):	31
Height:	6'6''
Weight:	235
Scoring:	0.486
Rebounding:	4.51
Playmaking:	0.22
Defense:	3.72
Gun Rating:	−6.69
HoopStat Grade:	21.20
Minutes/Game:	32.46

This was the year of the head case, what with Reggie Williams refusing to enter a game, Mark Aguirre dodging it, Adrian Dantley being traded for him and then disappearing, locker room fights. Aguirre is the most famous of the head cases, but if anyone will benefit from a trade, he will. Detroit is probably the only team in the league where players like this won't get out of line, or else they risk being clotheslined in practice.

Aguirre's play dipped last year, but it can probably be discounted as a fluke, due to all the turbulence in his season. Hell, half the time in Dallas, he wasn't even trying.

Sam Perkins
Dallas Mavericks
20.7 HGS

College:	North Carolina
Age (1/1/1990):	29
Height:	6'9''
Weight:	235
Scoring:	0.512
Rebounding:	7.14
Playmaking:	0.13
Defense:	6.65
Gun Rating:	1.09
HoopStat Grade:	20.70
Minutes/Game:	36.67

Quiet. Solid fundamentally (UNC, of course). Perkins can hit from 20 feet or play in the post. A starter who'll just never be a dominant player. He'll get 12 to 14 points, 7 rebounds a night, and not make too many mistakes. Unfortunately, he's not the rebounder that Dallas would like him to be. He was bothered by a foot problem for a good part of the year, and he added to the medical woes in Dallas last season.

Buck Williams
New Jersey Nets
20.6 HGS

College:	Maryland
Age (1/1/1990):	30
Height:	6'8''
Weight:	225
Scoring:	0.555
Rebounding:	8.54
Playmaking:	0.11
Defense:	6.29
Gun Rating:	1.76
HoopStat Grade:	20.60
Minutes/Game:	33.05

Buck Williams is the Ernie Banks of the NBA.

Williams is buried in a losing situation in New Jersey. Here's a man who can be counted on getting double figures in points and boards who's wasting away in the Meadowlands. Not really a go-to player because of his limited offensive skills, Williams gets his points off hard work and effort. His numbers were down this year. Could be age creeping up. The Nets have been reluctant to trade him in the past. His value might be slipping and soon no one will want him for a front liner.

Chris Morris
New Jersey Nets
20.3 HGS

College:	Auburn
Age (1/1/1990):	24
Height:	6'8''
Weight:	210
Scoring:	0.480
Rebounding:	6.05
Playmaking:	0.13
Defense:	6.10
Gun Rating:	-4.34
HoopStat Grade:	20.30
Minutes/Game:	27.58

Chris Morris had a decent, underrated rookie season, which was camouflaged in part by the talent around him. He was a big factor under the boards on offense, as proven by his 0.90 OR/DR rating, highest among starters in the league, and lower than only that of Dallas Comegys (a Net castoff). He wasn't the rebounder that Buck Williams was, but he was much closer than you would have guessed at the beginning of the season.

Larry Smith
Golden State Warriors
20.2 HGS

College:	Alcorn St.
Age (1/1/1990):	32
Height:	6'8''
Weight:	235
Scoring:	0.535
Rebounding:	10.66
Playmaking:	0.30
Defense:	7.67
Gun Rating:	8.65
HoopStat Grade:	20.20
Minutes/Game:	23.71

Larry Smith didn't take many shots, which hurt his offense, but he was a better rebounder than any other forward. Usually, when you have a game based on the boards, powering other players away, you'd expect a player to draw some fouls. But for some reason, he only garnered one quarter as many foul shots as fouls, *worst* among forwards. He has much the same game as Wayne Cooper does in Denver, but at a somewhat lower level.

Chuck Person
Indiana Pacers
20.0 HGS

College:	Auburn
Age (1/1/1990):	26
Height:	6'8''
Weight:	225
Scoring:	0.506
Rebounding:	4.91
Playmaking:	0.20
Defense:	4.57
Gun Rating:	−7.58
HoopStat Grade:	20.00
Minutes/Game:	37.65

For someone who mouths off as often as Chuck does about his teammates, he's just not that great a player. Late in the 1987–88 season, he reportedly told then coach Jack Ramsay where to stick his game plan, and word of behavior such as this makes the league rounds quickly. Ramsay eventually quit, and Person's stuck in Indiana now, because it would be tough to get full value for him. It seems the Rifleman has shot himself in the foot with his outbursts.

Larry Krystkowiak
Milwaukee Bucks
19.9 HGS

College:	Montana
Age (1/1/1990):	26
Height:	6'9''
Weight:	220
Scoring:	0.537
Rebounding:	7.27
Playmaking:	0.14
Defense:	5.98
Gun Rating:	0.13
HoopStat Grade:	19.90
Minutes/Game:	30.90

Krystkowiak's career could be over after a particularly grisly injury in the playoffs. The doctor who performed the surgery on his knee after K. went down just one minute into a game against the Pistons said that it was the worst he had ever seen, including automobile accidents. You don't need details. Neither did we, but we got them anyway. Ick. More next year, if he's able to return that is.

Cliff Levingston
Atlanta Hawks
19.7 HGS

College:	Wichita St.
Age (1/1/1990):	29
Height:	6'8"
Weight:	220
Scoring:	0.551
Rebounding:	6.96
Playmaking:	0.13
Defense:	7.03
Gun Rating:	3.59
HoopStat Grade:	19.70
Minutes/Game:	27.30

Horace Grant
Chicago Bulls
19.6 HGS

College:	Clemson
Age (1/1/1990):	25
Height:	6'10"
Weight:	215
Scoring:	0.538
Rebounding:	7.25
Playmaking:	0.22
Defense:	6.31
Gun Rating:	3.34
HoopStat Grade:	19.60
Minutes/Game:	35.56

Terry Catledge
Washington Bullets
19.5 HGS

College:	South Alabama
Age (1/1/1990):	27
Height:	6'8"
Weight:	230
Scoring:	0.507
Rebounding:	8.47
Playmaking:	0.11
Defense:	5.66
Gun Rating:	0.49
HoopStat Grade:	19.50
Minutes/Game:	26.29

Cliff's hanging on after seven seasons in the pros. He's not really bad enough to dump, but he's not good enough to emerge from Dominique's shadow, even if he could.

Much of Levingston's low output can be traced to the frequency of his shooting, for he had an excellent .551 scoring percentage. When you play on this Hawks team, however, you're not going to get the ball.

Most analysts now feel that the Bulls got a good deal with the Cartwright trade, because they filled a need, and the hole that was created was filled with Horace Grant as power forward. However, Grant did *not* do as good a job as Oakley, and both positions involved (center and power forward) were weaker for the Bulls than the Knicks last year.

An okay rebounder, but below average when shots need to be made. Catledge is also a subpar defensive forward, which doesn't mean that he's bad, just not as good as most other players. Wes Unseld got only 26 minutes per game out of him, so he was well rested, at least.

Johnny Newman
New York Knicks
19.4 HGS

College:	Richmond
Age (1/1/1990):	27
Height:	6'7"
Weight:	190
Scoring:	0.507
Rebounding:	2.79
Playmaking:	0.17
Defense:	3.91
Gun Rating:	−7.22
HoopStat Grade:	19.40
Minutes/Game:	28.84

Rodney McCray
Sacramento Kings
19.4 HGS

College:	Louisville
Age (1/1/1990):	29
Height:	6'8"
Weight:	235
Scoring:	0.498
Rebounding:	6.05
Playmaking:	0.40
Defense:	5.47
Gun Rating:	2.55
HoopStat Grade:	19.40
Minutes/Game:	35.81

Rick Mahorn
Detroit Pistons
18.6 HGS

College:	Hampton Institute
Age (1/1/1990):	32
Height:	6'10"
Weight:	255
Scoring:	0.554
Rebounding:	7.95
Playmaking:	0.15
Defense:	7.58
Gun Rating:	4.69
HoopStat Grade:	18.60
Minutes/Game:	24.93

J. New was a favorite in the Garden, and he started nearly every game last year. The New York sports lens, which can be either a microscope or a magnifying glass, was kind to him. He had many weaknesses, defense and rebounding to name two, which were hidden by his offense and the unique nature of the Knicks' press.

Offense was by far his strength, reflected by his −7.20 Gun rating. He was one of the Knicks' many perimeter/three-point men, and tried the long shot more often than any other forward (a three for every 2.33 twos). Management evidently doesn't feel that the Knicks can win with him, because they went all out to get Kiki Vandeweghe to bolster their halfcourt game in midseason. The move, designed to replace a popular player, started the ball rolling toward the late-season dissension and disillusionment that touched MSG.

No matter that McCray ranked 45th of 51 forwards.

The death of his daughter and nagging injuries no doubt affected his play last year. Whether he'll ever recoup remains to be seen.

Strictly a role player, and that role often consisted of busting a guy's head. His Draw rating of 0.75 was exceptionally low, but it far outstrips his career average of 0.57. As any observer can tell you, his fouls have a history of being unduly flagrant. As a rookie in Washington, Mahorn actually had a Christmas list, consisting of opponents he had laid out for medical care before his first Christmas in the league. Classy act—wonder how he ended up on a team like Detroit. Wonder how he'll do in Minnesota.

RODNEY McCRAY
DEFENSIVE RATINGS SINCE 1983–84

Year	Min	DReb	Stl	Blk	Def
1983–84	2081	277	53	54	8.86
1984–85	3001	338	90	75	8.05
1985–86	2610	361	50	58	8.63
1986–87	3136	388	88	53	8.10
1987–88	2689	399	57	51	9.05
1988–89	2435	371	57	35	5.47

Derek Smith
Philadelphia 76ers
18.6 HGS

College:	Louisville
Age (1/1/1990):	29
Height:	6'6''
Weight:	218
Scoring:	0.469
Rebounding:	3.89
Playmaking:	0.26
Defense:	4.41
Gun Rating:	−2.48
HoopStat Grade:	18.60
Minutes/Game:	19.92

Sacramento saw Derek as a trouble child, and maybe he was when he was out there. Philadelphia, who had coveted him on and off for years, made their move when he was released, and for the time being, they've gotten an okay if undistinguished forward. Perhaps his problem out in California was that he needed contacts; he shot terribly from everywhere (.435 FG%, .226 3G%, .686 FT%).

Buck Johnson
Houston Rockets
17.4 HGS

College:	Alabama
Age (1/1/1990):	26
Height:	6'7''
Weight:	190
Scoring:	0.550
Rebounding:	4.74
Playmaking:	0.25
Defense:	4.77
Gun Rating:	0.61
HoopStat Grade:	17.40
Minutes/Game:	27.35

Buck suffered from Akeemitis, as he was denied much of his offensive potential because of the presence of Olajuwon. He was one of the least productive scorers, although his scoring percentage, at .550, was excellent. Would Buck be better had he not been intimidated by his own center's presence?

Mike Sanders
Cleveland Cavaliers
15.8 HGS

College:	UCLA
Age (1/1/1990):	30
Height:	6'6''
Weight:	210
Scoring:	0.474
Rebounding:	4.30
Playmaking:	0.18
Defense:	5.14
Gun Rating:	−1.62
HoopStat Grade:	15.80
Minutes/Game:	25.63

Sanders wasn't a very strong player for the Cavs, as reflected by his low rating. For a player who plays strong defense, Sanders's lack of offense wouldn't be as bad. However, he was a third less productive than average, and his defense was below the norm, too. His only real positive, relative to the league, was that he didn't turn the ball over very much.

Caldwell Jones
Portland Trail Blazers
15.3 HGS

Marc Iavaroni
Utah Jazz
11.0 HGS

College:	Albany St.	College:	Virginia
Age (1/1/1990):	40	Age (1/1/1990):	34
Height:	6'11"	Height:	6'10"
Weight:	225	Weight:	225
Scoring:	0.472	Scoring:	0.485
Rebounding:	6.79	Rebounding:	4.85
Playmaking:	0.32	Playmaking:	0.20
Defense:	8.07	Defense:	4.19
Gun Rating:	7.75	Gun Rating:	0.13
HoopStat Grade:	15.30	HoopStat Grade:	11.00
Minutes/Game:	17.76	Minutes/Game:	10.34

He's still around because he's a very known quantity, an old guy who can come off the bench and play great D. His scoring was simply invisible, at 7.6 pp48, but it's not expected of him, so who cares? He was largely a situational player and played less than 18 minutes per game, but he had the most starts among candidates for Portland's rating, so he stays.

The lowest rated regular in the NBA last year. Marc was on the Jazz for one purpose, to test out the court, see which way the wind was blowing, and then to keep Thurl Bailey's seat warm for the rest of the night. He was the lowest regular in the league in ppg, too, although there were others (Caldwell Jones, for instance) who scored fewer points per minute.

BENCH

Rod Strickland
New York Knicks
27.0 HGS

College:	DePaul
Age (1/1/1990):	24
Height:	6'3"
Weight:	180
Scoring:	0.506
Rebounding:	3.46
Playmaking:	0.56
Defense:	5.50
Gun Rating:	1.49
HoopStat Grade:	27.00
Minutes/Game:	16.77

Although he was the highest-rated nonstarter, he wouldn't be in contention for a "Sixth Man" award, simply because he was a backup, not a go-to player off the bench. He had a couple of faults, such as attempting to do too much after he left his feet, and getting stuck in the air. Considering his position, however, he had a great season, stepping in adequately when Mark Jackson went down for a few games, and his misfortune of being on the same team as another point guard with one more year's experience might very well have kept him from winning the Rookie of the Year award. The Knicks have two options right now: they can either keep him, hope his head stays on straight, and try to play him and Jackson together, or trade him and hope he's not the next Kevin Johnson story. Either way, two options like this are better than none.

John Williams
Washington Bullets
26.8 HGS

College:	Tulane
Age (1/1/1990):	29
Height:	6'11"
Weight:	230
Scoring:	0.500
Rebounding:	6.80
Playmaking:	0.38
Defense:	8.32
Gun Rating:	4.53
HoopStat Grade:	26.80
Minutes/Game:	29.43

We admit it's silly to have two players called John Williams rated together, but we don't make the choices. *This* John Williams rated second among nonstarters, despite his lack of what one scout called "intensity." He managed to get 29½ minutes per game off the bench, although he started only one game for the Bullets, and had statistics nearly as good as Strickland's (see above), but in 78% more minutes. Williams's strong suits were his defense and ball control (Cont of 7.41), while his rebounding (6.80) was also well above average. He gave many more positives than negatives.

John Williams
Cleveland Cavaliers
25.2 HGS

College:	Louisiana St.
Age (1/1/1990):	24
Height:	6'9"
Weight:	235
Scoring:	0.552
Rebounding:	6.77
Playmaking:	0.15
Defense:	8.18
Gun Rating:	3.83
HoopStat Grade:	25.20
Minutes/Game:	25.91

Now, *this* John Williams was given some starts at the end of the year, when he had a hot hand and no one else was healthy. Hot Rod (one of two Hot Rods in the top three bench leaders) was a deadly scorer from everywhere (a .552 scoring ratio), and added good rebounding and defense to his game as well. He also had a great Hands rating (1.12), matched only by one other reserve. Combined with his Draw of 1.67, it seemed that Hot Rod had a great ball sense.

Tyrone "Muggsy" Bogues
Charlotte Hornets
25.0 HGS

College:	Wake Forest
Age (1/1/1990):	25
Height:	5'3"
Weight:	140
Scoring:	0.451
Rebounding:	2.76
Playmaking:	1.48
Defense:	4.73
Gun Rating:	13.40
HoopStat Grade:	25.00
Minutes/Game:	22.22

Although he's really cute, and fun to watch out there, there's not much of a future for Muggsy in the league. He got 22 minutes per game because Charlotte was stuck for players, and many of his HGS points came because they had no other choice. He was battered alive by any player taller than, say, Spud Webb, and it was so easy to guard him that he managed a scoring percentage of only .451. You didn't need to foul him to stop him (he had a 0.62 Draw), and he got a few rebounds, but only when they bounced first. Of course, he was smart enough to know that he'd have to do something other than score to succeed, so he passed to a 1.48 Play rating, the highest in the entire league.

Once Charlotte starts to improve, they won't need an attraction like Muggsy, but until then, he won't make them any worse than they already are.

Ed Pinckney
Boston Celtics
24.5 HGS

College:	Villanova
Age (1/1/1990):	27
Height:	6'9"
Weight:	215
Scoring:	0.574
Rebounding:	6.74
Playmaking:	0.19
Defense:	6.93
Gun Rating:	2.57
HoopStat Grade:	24.50
Minutes/Game:	25.15

This might be Ed's last chance in Boston, but he seems to be making the most of it so far. Last year he had a .574 scoring percentage, did a bit of everything, and made the trade work out, at least in the short run. Kleine and Pinckney would appear to be better players than Ainge and Lohaus, especially when you look five years down the road. Ainge's value was inflated because he played on the Celtics, but then again, who knows what Bill Russell was thinking?

Xavier McDaniel
Seattle Supersonics
24.5 HGS

College:	Wichita St.
Age (1/1/1990):	27
Height:	6'7''
Weight:	205
Scoring:	0.519
Rebounding:	5.60
Playmaking:	0.10
Defense:	5.07
Gun Rating:	-9.21
HoopStat Grade:	24.50
Minutes/Game:	29.09

Eddie Johnson
Phoenix Suns
23.5 HGS

College:	Illinois
Age (1/1/1990):	31
Height:	6'9''
Weight:	218
Scoring:	0.523
Rebounding:	4.34
Playmaking:	0.13
Defense:	3.79
Gun Rating:	-11.76
HoopStat Grade:	23.50
Minutes/Game:	29.19

Dennis Rodman
Detroit Pistons
23.3 HGS

College:	SE Oklahoma St.
Age (1/1/1990):	29
Height:	6'8''
Weight:	210
Scoring:	0.592
Rebounding:	10.88
Playmaking:	0.19
Defense:	7.69
Gun Rating:	7.30
HoopStat Grade:	23.30
Minutes/Game:	26.91

The greatest NBA player ever whose initials are X.M. Near the end of the year, they finally figured out that maybe playing X-Man off the bench wasn't such a great idea after all. He was reinstated to starter, and the Sonics started to take off after that. Xavier did a lot of scoring, but that was pretty much the extent of his game, as his Gun was -9.21 overall. As most of the Sonics did, he worked the offensive boards much better than the rest of the league, in his case to a 0.69 OR/DR ratio (league average is usually about 0.50). A little streaky at times, but once he gets going he's hard to stop. A few bounces to his right, spins back, and two points from his left. Mild-mannered off-court, he undergoes a personality transformation on-court.

The Vinnie Johnson of forwards. A big, big scorer, Eddie averaged 35.3 pp48 en route to garnering the NBA's "Sixth Man" award last season. He popped in over 86% of his free throws and hoisted a bunch of three-pointers (his 2:3 was 6.13). The threes helped his scoring average by nearly half a point, as he gained 37.47 points on his total from them. Scoring was the end of the line for Eddie, though. His Gun was -11.76, a sure sign that he was doing too much shooting and not enough looking for open teammates.

But that's not his job. He's a scoring machine and Cotton can't get him in fast enough.

The Worm was a terrific, underrated shooter last year. He scored 59.2% of his possible points, including a .613 percentage from two-point range. As usual, though, his foul shooting was foul, only .013 better than his two-shooting.

Had Dennis had taken the same number of shots as Eddie Johnson, he'd have scored 290 more points than Eddie did. Some of the effort that E.J. put into scoring, however, Rodman distributed among the other facets of his game. His rebounding and defense numbers were both way higher than Johnson's, and he had 73% as many offensive as defensive rebounds, typical for him. One number says it all: the difference in their Gun ratings was 19.06 points. Rodman may act like a hot dog for most of the game, infuriating opposition and fans, but any opposing coach would take him without question. He's a human pogo stick who has an uncanny knack for getting his hands on loose balls. Don't ask him to score—he can't throw a ball through a hula hoop—just retrieve. He's a smaller version of Ray Tarpley, only he can't shoot. He's not upset either if he only shoots once a game.

Ricky Pierce
Milwaukee Bucks
23.0 HGS

College:	Rice
Age (1/1/1990):	31
Height:	6'4"
Weight:	222
Scoring:	0.556
Rebounding:	2.94
Playmaking:	0.15
Defense:	3.52
Gun Rating:	−7.39
HoopStat Grade:	23.00
Minutes/Game:	27.71

Sedale Threatt
Seattle Supersonics
22.9 HGS

College:	WV Tech
Age (1/1/1990):	29
Height:	6'2"
Weight:	177
Scoring:	0.514
Rebounding:	2.73
Playmaking:	0.50
Defense:	5.11
Gun Rating:	1.49
HoopStat Grade:	22.90
Minutes/Game:	19.37

Otis Smith
Golden State Warriors
22.6 HGS

College:	Jacksonville
Age (1/1/1990):	26
Height:	6'5"
Weight:	210
Scoring:	0.477
Rebounding:	6.31
Playmaking:	0.20
Defense:	6.88
Gun Rating:	−1.53
HoopStat Grade:	22.60
Minutes/Game:	19.96

Ricky Pierce is just one more reason to pity the Clippers. In 1984 they traded him, along with Terry Cummings and Craig Hodges, for Harvey Catchings, Junior Bridgeman, and Marques Johnson. The Bucks later got Jay Humphries for Hodges. Last season the Bucks got 7122 minutes from their three players, the Clippers got 0. More study is needed, but right now it seems that Milwaukee is ahead on this trade, by about three players.

Ricky, despite coming off the bench, posted his second best scoring season so far. After winning the NBA "Sixth Man" award in 1987, then losing a lot of time in 1987–88, he came back to play 75 games, although his shooting touch was a bit off from the three previous seasons in Milwaukee. Still, he scored over 55% of his possible points, not bad by any standard.

Not bad for a former sixth-round draft choice, but one can't help but think that the 1986 playoffs, where he scored 13.3 ppg, will be the high point of his career. After a career where he scored 20.7 ppg in four years of varsity college play, he's never hit 10.0 in the pros. Last year he managed 8.6 ppg, which translated into 21.4 pp48. He seems to be allowed to take the shot more often in Seattle, although his strength still lies setting up others (his Play was 0.50). Since he never shot, teams never fouled him in the act, so he drew only 0.50 as many foul shots as he gave fouls.

Otis had a disappointing season, not being able to put points on the board, but not making up for it in other categories such as rebounding. His scoring percentage, .477, wasn't anything to write home about, but his defense was good (not eye-opening).

Detlef Schrempf
Indiana Pacers
22.5 HGS

College:	Washington
Age (1/1/1990):	27
Height:	6'10"
Weight:	214
Scoring:	0.537
Rebounding:	6.27
Playmaking:	0.31
Defense:	5.36
Gun Rating:	1.04
HoopStat Grade:	22.50
Minutes/Game:	26.81

Steve Johnson
Portland Trail Blazers
22.2 HGS

College:	Oregon St.
Age (1/1/1990):	33
Height:	6'10"
Weight:	235
Scoring:	0.524
Rebounding:	7.35
Playmaking:	0.19
Defense:	5.70
Gun Rating:	-1.24
HoopStat Grade:	22.20
Minutes/Game:	20.51

Tyrone Corbin
Phoenix Suns
22.2 HGS

College:	DePaul
Age (1/1/1990):	28
Height:	6'6"
Weight:	222
Scoring:	0.580
Rebounding:	7.56
Playmaking:	0.26
Defense:	5.97
Gun Rating:	3.87
HoopStat Grade:	22.20
Minutes/Game:	21.49

If you're a foreign-born player, Germany has become the chic place to hail from. Currently, four players are from West Germany: Schrempf, Uwe Blab, Chris Welp, and Kiki Vandeweghe. At this point in their careers, Detlef is probably the best of the four, although Kiki's had a better career. Detlef is better defensively, but it's still a question of how he'll react to his new surroundings in Indiana. Dallas had made a commitment to a core of players before the whole plan went haywire last year, and Detlef was one of the casualties. To go from a key in a "family" team to a journeyman shrugged off to Indiana might take some of his heart away, unless he's accepted well at Market Square. Adrian Dantley was in much the same psychological situation, and it's still unsettled as to how well he'll do in Dallas.

Steve Johnson had an amazing season. It's not often that you find a player who doesn't attempt even a single three-pointer, and even rarer to come across one who shoots free throws only .003 better than two-pointers. Either he pulled up and took a lot of field goals from the foul line, or there were a lot of hands in his face when he lined up to take a one-and-one.

Johnson's never been a particularly good shooter from the line; his career FT% is only .647, just awful for someone who shoots 58.0% from the field. In 1982–83, his second year in the league, he managed to shoot .050 *better* from the field. Maybe practice alone *doesn't* always help.

Phoenix never looked for much from Corbin.

Cotton Fitzsimmons left Tyrone for dead a few times, but he managed to play himself back into the lineup each time. There seemed to be no set role for him on the team, which can't have helped his consistency. His minutes varied wildly, from 5 to 34 minutes in a game. Sometimes he was a guard, sometimes a forward.

When he was in, he was, on the whole, a decent offensive performer. His .580 scoring percentage was among the best for all reserves. The problem is, he didn't get to shoot that often (only 13.1 FGA per 48). He swept the boards much better than average, and he had enough of an effect on the game when he did play, but he never earned the starting job at any position conclusively. He never quite played himself out of it, either, but he wasn't firmly entrenched. That's why he was let loose in the expansion.

Walter Davis
Denver Nuggets
22.1 HGS

Manute Bol
Golden State Warriors
21.9 HGS

College:	North Carolina
Age (1/1/1990):	36
Height:	6'6''
Weight:	206
Scoring:	0.524
Rebounding:	2.32
Playmaking:	0.18
Defense:	3.41
Gun Rating:	−10.66
HoopStat Grade:	22.10
Minutes/Game:	22.93

College:	Bridgeport
Age (1/1/1990):	28
Height:	7'6''
Weight:	225
Scoring:	0.372
Rebounding:	7.37
Playmaking:	0.08
Defense:	14.19
Gun Rating:	13.36
HoopStat Grade:	21.90
Minutes/Game:	22.11

Davis was a great scorer, averaging 32.7 pp48. That's all that you need to know about him, because that's all there *is* to know. His Gun was −10.66, meaning that his peripheral stats pulled his scoring average down by over 10 points. It's what he's been doing his whole career (his lifetime average is 32.5), so it's worked well enough for him to last for 12 years.

Who cares that he threw a spear well enough to kill a lion once? Who cares that he practiced it over and over? There is absolutely no reason to let Manute take a single three-point shot. Ever. EVER. There is no possible way you can claim that his newfound three-point "ability" helps this team. He shoots only .423 from two-point range. Even those shots don't help. So you give him an extra 91 shots from outside? One for every 2.77 two-point shots? The first time Don Nelson saw him try a three in practice, he shouldn't have told him he could try it in a game. He should have told him just to get the idea out of his head forever. Oh, he lost 16.97 points with the three last year, by the way.

Not only does Manute have more blocks than points in his career, he's had more in every single season he's played. Last year was no different, as he had 339 blocks and 314 points, a 1.08 ratio. However, every year the gap has narrowed. Last year was the closest it's been since he entered the league. At this rate, look for him to score more than he blocks by 1991.

In case you didn't notice, the shortest and tallest players both have the initials M.B. Just a piece of trivia we thought you'd find useful.

MANUTE'S BLOCKS:POINTS

	Blocks	Points	Blk:Pts
1985–86	397	298	1.33
1986–87	302	251	1.20
1987–88	208	176	1.18
1988–89	339	314	1.08

Roy Hinson
New Jersey Nets
21.8 HGS

College:	Rutgers
Age (1/1/1990):	29
Height:	6′9″
Weight:	220
Scoring:	0.530
Rebounding:	5.93
Playmaking:	0.07
Defense:	6.44
Gun Rating:	−2.94
HoopStat Grade:	21.80
Minutes/Game:	31.00

Orlando Woolridge
Los Angeles Lakers
21.8 HGS

College:	Notre Dame
Age (1/1/1990):	31
Height:	6′9″
Weight:	215
Scoring:	0.537
Rebounding:	5.26
Playmaking:	0.12
Defense:	6.10
Gun Rating:	−1.17
HoopStat Grade:	21.80
Minutes/Game:	20.15

Ledell Eackles
Washington Bullets
21.7 HGS

College:	New Orleans
Age (1/1/1990):	24
Height:	6′5″
Weight:	215
Scoring:	0.496
Rebounding:	4.11
Playmaking:	0.17
Defense:	2.80
Gun Rating:	−8.42
HoopStat Grade:	21.70
Minutes/Game:	18.24

As long as we're on the subject of bad three-point shooters, let's not forget Roy Hinson's yeoman efforts. Entering the 1988–89 season, he sported an 0 for 10 lifetime mark from three-point range. This year he boasted an 0 for 2 mark, improving his lifetime record to 0 for 12. 0 for 12. Perfection.

Roy Hinson started the season on the bench. After Walter Berry played himself out of the job, Roy got to start some games at forward, before he himself was effectively deposed by Chris Morris's good rookie play. After that, he saw some starting action when Buck Williams couldn't make it, as well as some spot action at center, whenever Joe Barry Carroll injured himself. At year's end, he had seen 39 starts. Unfortunately, they were spread between two positions, and he didn't have the most at either, so he's been relegated to the reserve list. Talented performer for the Nets, but big numbers on a bad team don't carry much weight. Better off as a role-player on a good team.

The Lakers were in a no-lose situation when they picked up Orlando, the only player in the league who wears his first initial as a uniform number. They didn't give anything up for him, and he was bound to want to stay in Los Angeles, where his drug rehab support group is located.

Woolridge proved that he still has moves left in him, although he's not one half the guard Magic is. Still, he's elusive enough to garner a Draw rating of 2.64, best among all reserves and tied for 13th among all regulars. One would be tempted to say that it was because the Lakers got preference from the refs, but that's not at all the case. Kareem's Draw was 0.84, Coop's was 0.50, Byron Scott's was 1.25. The Lakers weren't given any more benefit than any other team.

Ledell had been spotted sporting some extra pounds at predraft tryout camps, but evidently he got himself pulled together, and he had a surprising rookie season. Despite his important role on a team of "parts," he tossed up a surprising amount of shots, hitting for only a .496 scoring percentage, but averaging over 30 pp48. For his efforts, he was granted a Gun of −8.42, which reflected the fact that his defense was just putrid (2.80 Def), and his rebounding was mushy, especially on the defensive end (he had more offensive than defensive boards). If he can keep his weight down and learn his shots a bit better (two questions of discipline), he'll be able to stick with the Bullets under Unseld's system. Although as wild as a March hare and uncontrollable at times, he's a gifted, up-and-coming player.

Vinnie Johnson
Detroit Pistons
21.7 HGS

College:	Baylor
Age (1/1/1990):	34
Height:	6'2"
Weight:	200
Scoring:	0.492
Rebounding:	3.84
Playmaking:	0.24
Defense:	3.75
Gun Rating:	−4.43
HoopStat Grade:	21.70
Minutes/Game:	25.28

Micro heats up fast. Vinnie's been coming off the bench for years, so this is nothing new for him. He's been remarkably consistent throughout his career, shooting .465 or so from the field, .770 or so from the line, giving you between 79 and 82 games, 220 to 250 rebounds, maybe 20 blocks. He's great for the Pistons, simply because he's such a known quantity to them.

The Pistons acquired Vinnie from Seattle in exchange for Greg Kelser. The next time you hear credit heaped on the Sonics for the Dale Ellis for Al Wood steal, just remember that they don't always come up smelling like roses.

Thurl Bailey
Utah Jazz
21.4 HGS

College:	North Carolina St.
Age (1/1/1990):	29
Height:	6'11"
Weight:	222
Scoring:	0.534
Rebounding:	4.56
Playmaking:	0.11
Defense:	5.27
Gun Rating:	−6.13
HoopStat Grade:	21.40
Minutes/Game:	33.87

Thurl really got the starter's minutes for the Jazz, but Marc Iavaroni actually started most of the games because, well, that's just the way things are done in Utah.

Bailey has never been that spectacular a scorer, usually shooting about 47.5% from the field, but he's always made up for it from the foul line, where he has shot over 80% every year since he was an NBA sophomore. His percentage through college and his NBA rookie season was .747 in five years. In his sophomore year, it jumped to .842, a 90-point difference. In the past five years, he's shot .826.

Now somewhere he found a way to tack 79 points on what had been his established level. There's no way your free-throw shooting takes a 10.5% leap and remains at the higher plateau over the next five years, unless you've dedicated a lot of time and effort to addressing the problem. He's taken his natural level of .750 and worked hard enough at it to elevate it to .820. If nothing else, the guy's got a great work ethic.

David Greenwood
Denver Nuggets
21.3 HGS

College:	UCLA
Age (1/1/1990):	33
Height:	6'9"
Weight:	225
Scoring:	0.482
Rebounding:	8.55
Playmaking:	0.24
Defense:	7.87
Gun Rating:	5.36
HoopStat Grade:	21.30
Minutes/Game:	20.94

After nine years, David's closer to the end than the beginning. The Spurs got maximum value for an aging George Gervin by acquiring him from Chicago four years ago, but it's hard to figure who made out better in the Natt/Vincent for Greenwood/Cook trade. All four are aging veterans, and since the trade, one has already been waived. These aren't the trades that win championships for either side. Either team should have tried to bundle their two players for one underachieving prospect, to at least make things interesting.

Steve Colter
Washington Bullets
21.3 HGS

College:	New Mexico St.
Age (1/1/1990):	28
Height:	6'3"
Weight:	175
Scoring:	0.483
Rebounding:	3.80
Playmaking:	0.49
Defense:	4.82
Gun Rating:	3.30
HoopStat Grade:	21.30
Minutes/Game:	17.81

Sidney Green
New York Knicks
21.2 HGS

College:	UNLV
Age (1/1/1990):	29
Height:	6'9"
Weight:	220
Scoring:	0.508
Rebounding:	9.47
Playmaking:	0.18
Defense:	6.90
Gun Rating:	1.76
HoopStat Grade:	21.20
Minutes/Game:	15.57

Rod Higgins
Golden State Warriors
21.1 HGS

College:	Fresno St.
Age (1/1/1990):	30
Height:	6'7"
Weight:	205
Scoring:	0.515
Rebounding:	5.77
Playmaking:	0.25
Defense:	5.38
Gun Rating:	−0.67
HoopStat Grade:	21.10
Minutes/Game:	23.30

The year 1988–89 was a prototypical Steve Colter season, a 1400-minute backup-player sort of season. He showed good numbers for a guard, and his lifetime Play rating is around 0.50 (he takes twice as many shots as he gets assists). He's had a three-year slump from three-point range—when he was in Portland, he shot 53 for 157 (.338) in two years. Since then, he's been given the red light and has gone only 10 for 52 (.192). Who says coaching accounts for nothing in the NBA?

Sidney Green was the fifth pick overall in the 1983 draft. Kenny Walker was the fifth pick overall in the 1986 draft. The Knicks have two fifth-overall draft choices, who combined for only 2200 minutes last year. That should tell you something about the value of potential.

Actually, Sidney was underutilized, mostly because he was used as a backup for Ewing. He was a power rebounder, but he couldn't hold on to the ball very well (125 turnovers, only 47 steals). He was one of the few players in the league who played in every game, yet started none (John Battle and Jim Les were the others). Meanwhile, he was nominated more often than any other Knick as Most Likely to Be Lost in the Expansion Draft. He starts a new career in the cellar with Orlando.

If you search hard enough, every player holds *some* league record. Rod Higgins started his career with the Bulls, until Kevin Loughery reduced his minutes to seconds. In his fourth year in the league (1985–86), he was waived by Chicago. Seattle signed him and released him a month later. He sat around until San Antonio gave him a ten-day contract, which expired (we're still in February, remember). Once he was free, New Jersey signed him for two weeks, and once that contract was complete, he ended up back in Chicago. *That* ten-day contract expired, and the Bulls re-signed him, then released him three days later.

So what was Rod Higgins's personal record? He's the only player ever to play for four different teams in one season. In fact, he played with five teams in one calendar year, as Golden State signed him in October. Considering he's stuck with the Warriors since then, it's strange that not one of those four other teams could use him for more than ten days.

Rod was one of the most prolific three-point shooters in the league,

Dwayne Washington
Miami Heat
20.9 HGS

College:	Syracuse
Age (1/1/1990):	26
Height:	6'2"
Weight:	195
Scoring:	0.466
Rebounding:	3.53
Playmaking:	0.59
Defense:	5.11
Gun Rating:	2.49
HoopStat Grade:	20.90
Minutes/Game:	19.81

Jon Koncak
Atlanta Hawks
20.7 HGS

College:	SMU
Age (1/1/1990):	27
Height:	7'0"
Weight:	260
Scoring:	0.527
Rebounding:	8.71
Playmaking:	0.21
Defense:	9.56
Gun Rating:	9.90
HoopStat Grade:	20.70
Minutes/Game:	20.69

lofting one every 2.77 two-pointers, and hitting 39.3% of them (a 28.19-point gain).

If the Pearl continues to have weight problems, will he be known as the Miami Pound Machine? Pearl's a decent point guard, but he might never find success in the league if he hasn't up to now. He was horrid when he tried to score last year, hitting only .429 from the field (including 1 for 14 from three). He could be gone from the league in two years, or he could stumble into a good situation somewhere, for a team that gives him the desire to win. Expansion teams probably won't do it for him, although if his play will be forgiven anywhere, it would be here. Overall, he's been a major NBA disappointment.

You can't worry that Jon scores only 10 points per 48 minutes. He's a project player who's worked out fairly well for the Hawks, providing them with over 450 rebounds and 98 blocks—not Manute-like numbers, but respectable for 1500 minutes played. He needs to be chained to the foul line in practice, however, until he can make more than 55% of his shots there. He's a 62% lifetime shooter there, but he dropped off badly last year. Opponents failed to take advantage of his slump, as he maintained a Draw of only 0.48. Had they fouled him a lot, that value would be up around 2.0 or so. In past seasons, his Draw has been in the 0.80s, but he just stopped drawing the fouls last year and got only 3.6 FTA per 48.

Dallas Comegys
San Antonio Spurs
20.7 HGS

College:	DePaul
Age (1/1/1990):	26
Height:	6'9"
Weight:	205
Scoring:	0.518
Rebounding:	6.66
Playmaking:	0.09
Defense:	7.16
Gun Rating:	1.94
HoopStat Grade:	20.70
Minutes/Game:	16.70

Strictly a spot player at forward for the Spurs, Dallas still saw action in 10 starts last season, when Cadillac Anderson needed a breather. He was one of the more effective offensive rebounds in the league, having nearly as many under his own boards as under the opponents'. He saw only about 16 minutes per game, however, and it doesn't look as if he's one of the larger cogs in the Spurs' future plans.

Johnny Dawkins
San Antonio Spurs
20.6 HGS

College:	Duke
Age (1/1/1990):	27
Height:	6'2"
Weight:	165
Scoring:	0.496
Rebounding:	2.73
Playmaking:	0.56
Defense:	3.97
Gun Rating:	0.53
HoopStat Grade:	20.60
Minutes/Game:	33.84

Johnny had been the Spurs' starting point guard before he went out for the year. He started 30 of 32 games while he was healthy, but it wasn't enough to be rated as a starter. Vernon Maxwell received some of Johnny's starts, as did Albert King and Michael Anderson. Things were so bad around San Antonio that Larry Brown used 22 players in all, and Dawkins's absence certainly didn't help matters. He was compiling a free-throw percentage in the top five in the league, for one thing, and he was drawing fouls with regularity. Without his abilities, the Spurs were a significantly weaker team.

Walter Berry
Houston Rockets
20.3 HGS

College:	St. John's
Age (1/1/1990):	26
Height:	6'8"
Weight:	215
Scoring:	0.531
Rebounding:	5.80
Playmaking:	0.15
Defense:	5.93
Gun Rating:	−1.28
HoopStat Grade:	20.30
Minutes/Game:	19.64

What was Don Chaney thinking when he opened his arms to this guy? The last thing you need on your team is a guy who pulls knives on teammates, who was described by the Nets as a "cancer" after his release. When a player is outrighted at midseason, especially one who was getting 20 minutes per game, there's usually a pretty solid reason.

There's no reason even to talk about Berry's skills, because he's not going to be around in a year or two. He'll get lazy, Houston will have problems with him, and he'll be either traded or released. His only chance to stick around any longer than that will be if he can get on a pro team coached by Lou Carnesecca.

John Salley

Detroit Pistons
20.3 HGS

College:	Georgia Tech
Age (1/1/1990):	26
Height:	7'0''
Weight:	230
Scoring:	0.541
Rebounding:	7.06
Playmaking:	0.23
Defense:	7.00
Gun Rating:	4.95
HoopStat Grade:	20.30
Minutes/Game:	21.76

It ain't easy being the comic relief for the Bad Boys. John Salley often was left out of the Pistons' offense, simply because the guards, Laimbeer, and Aguirre got all the play. He's got height and uncommon agility, which together cause big problems for opponents trying to set up against him; should you drive through him or shoot over him? It makes him a good defender, but being on a team of good ones, he doesn't get as much notice as he should.

Scott Skiles

Indiana Pacers
20.1 HGS

College:	Michigan St.
Age (1/1/1990):	26
Height:	6'1''
Weight:	200
Scoring:	0.495
Rebounding:	2.50
Playmaking:	0.88
Defense:	3.97
Gun Rating:	3.42
HoopStat Grade:	20.10
Minutes/Game:	19.64

Who can blame him for wanting to quit the Pacers? After all the acrimony at the beginning of the season, however, Scott ended up playing more games than he had over his entire career previous to last year. He was one of the weaker offensive rebounders in the entire league, grabbing only 21 in 80 games. It's a shame he's only 6'1''; if he were a bit bigger, he'd be better able to mix it up inside and get to the line more often, where he hits around 90%. Too bad height isn't an acquired skill.

Spud Webb

Atlanta Hawks
20.0 HGS

College:	North Carolina St.
Age (1/1/1990):	27
Height:	5'7''
Weight:	135
Scoring:	0.483
Rebounding:	2.71
Playmaking:	0.98
Defense:	5.00
Gun Rating:	7.48
HoopStat Grade:	20.00
Minutes/Game:	15.05

We think Muggsy's cuter, but Spud actually has NBA talent. In fact, Spud's a unique player, in that he's so small he can get underneath defenders, yet he can sky over them at the same time. He's also terrific at getting the fast break going, as his 0.98 Play would suggest. For a small player, though, he's not a great long-range shooter—he was 1 for 21 from three. (As we mentioned in the Jeff Malone comments, why would you take number 21, knowing you were already 1 for 20?)

Mychal Thompson
Los Angeles Lakers
19.9 HGS

College:	Minnesota
Age (1/1/1990):	35
Height:	6'10"
Weight:	235
Scoring:	0.580
Rebounding:	6.94
Playmaking:	0.09
Defense:	6.55
Gun Rating:	2.09
HoopStat Grade:	19.90
Minutes/Game:	24.93

The Lakers have real problems at center now, with a backup ready to step in, but at the age where his minutes need to be reduced. No one seems to know whether Mychal will, in fact, start next year, or whether they'll try to ship someone in and keep him as a backup. He can still score efficiently (55.9% field goal shooter), but his other power stats (rebounding, blocks) are lukewarm. Unless Kareem decides to come back *again*, things look interesting at center next year.

Antoine Carr
Atlanta Hawks
19.9 HGS

College:	Wichita St.
Age (1/1/1990):	29
Height:	6'9"
Weight:	235
Scoring:	0.532
Rebounding:	5.62
Playmaking:	0.19
Defense:	5.71
Gun Rating:	1.14
HoopStat Grade:	19.90
Minutes/Game:	19.08

Carr is a player who has had bright moments and everyone talks about how good he's going to be. Unfortunately, the day to be good has come and gone for Carr. He's a 10–12 minute player at best. Has the big wide body to take up space down low but he's limited offensively: He basically catches the ball and tries his best to score. He can't guard anybody and doesn't run the court very well.

Harold Pressley
Sacramento Kings
19.8 HGS

College:	Villanova
Age (1/1/1990):	27
Height:	6'8"
Weight:	210
Scoring:	0.453
Rebounding:	6.77
Playmaking:	0.20
Defense:	6.43
Gun Rating:	− 1.10
HoopStat Grade:	19.80
Minutes/Game:	28.21

Pressley had a poor year in Sacramento, but you would, too, playing out there. He *was*, however, a key ingredient in the Kings' three-point proliferation, shooting better than one third of his shots from outside. He was one of the biggest gainers in the league, improving his point total by about 87½ points with the three. He scored 20.9 pp48, which is no great average, but consider this: had he not shot any three-pointers, he would have only a 19.0 pp48 average, about 9% lower.

Dave Hoppen
Charlotte Hornets
19.4 HGS

College:	Nebraska
Age (1/1/1990):	26
Height:	6'11"
Weight:	235
Scoring:	0.590
Rebounding:	7.95
Playmaking:	0.16
Defense:	5.97
Gun Rating:	2.44
HoopStat Grade:	19.40
Minutes/Game:	18.43

Dave Hoppen was a light shooter who scored a high percentage of the time, a downscale Dennis Rodman. Neither had a scoring average over 10, although Rodman's was higher because of his larger share of minutes. Rebounding, Hoppen was also a minor version of the Worm. In fact, either player's stats wouldn't look out of line in the other's career line. The difference? Well, Hoppen's three inches taller, but Rodman makes it up by playing better.

Dennis Hopson
New Jersey Nets
19.3 HGS

College:	Ohio St.
Age (1/1/1990):	25
Height:	6'5"
Weight:	200
Scoring:	0.471
Rebounding:	4.11
Playmaking:	0.14
Defense:	4.84
Gun Rating:	-5.11
HoopStat Grade:	19.30
Minutes/Game:	25.02

You can't stick for too long in the NBA if you only make 43% of your two-pointers. Hopson's best skills come as a scorer, but he doesn't do even that particularly efficiently. His 24.4 pp48 was decent, but how many of the points came at the cost of others' shots? When you have a .471 scoring percentage, but a -5.11 Gun rating, it means you can't find the net that well, but you can't do much else. It's not a good sign, especially when you've established your low-percentage game over the two seasons you've been in the league. Hopson can go to the hoop, is quick on the open floor, and if he hits a few shots and gets his confidence, he can really do some damage. But his confidence hasn't been there, the defense has sagged off, thereby putting more pressure on him to score.

Craig Ehlo
Cleveland Cavaliers
19.2 HGS

College:	Washington St.
Age (1/1/1990):	29
Height:	6'7"
Weight:	185
Scoring:	0.481
Rebounding:	4.69
Playmaking:	0.51
Defense:	5.82
Gun Rating:	3.57
HoopStat Grade:	19.20
Minutes/Game:	22.77

He joined the team nearly three years ago as an emergency fill-in. Since then, he's become an important role player, whose role is small but steady. Lenny Wilkens had enough confidence in him to keep him on the floor in the end of some playoff games (okay, so he had no choice). He nearly won the Chicago playoff series when he executed a perfect play, the in-bound giveback, perfectly, but Jordan can't be beaten in a close game like that.

He shot only .607 from the stripe, about 90 points below his career average. Poor guy must have taken some pointers from Chris Dudley. Versatile, doesn't make too many mistakes. Fits in and does everything well, nothing spectacularly.

Sylvester Gray
Miami Heat
19.2 HGS

College:	Memphis St.
Age (1/1/1990):	23
Height:	6'6"
Weight:	230
Scoring:	0.460
Rebounding:	7.24
Playmaking:	0.29
Defense:	5.69
Gun Rating:	1.93
HoopStat Grade:	19.20
Minutes/Game:	22.18

Gray came out of Memphis State after two years, only to be sentenced to a year with the Heat. He wasn't a standout in any respect, although his rebounding was a bit better than average (7.24 Rbdg).

Mark Alarie
Washington Bullets
19.2 HGS

College:	Duke
Age (1/1/1990):	27
Height:	6'8"
Weight:	217
Scoring:	0.505
Rebounding:	6.88
Playmaking:	0.15
Defense:	5.09
Gun Rating:	−1.75
HoopStat Grade:	19.20
Minutes/Game:	15.42

Here's another player who could be a star, if only he had the natural physical attributes. Alarie has good skills and an understanding of the game that makes him a good specialist, but he's simply overmatched by the larger, stronger, and faster players. He's a weak 6'8".

Tim Kempton
Charlotte Hornets
19.1 HGS

College:	Notre Dame
Age (1/1/1990):	25
Height:	6'10"
Weight:	245
Scoring:	0.551
Rebounding:	6.58
Playmaking:	0.30
Defense:	5.78
Gun Rating:	1.74
HoopStat Grade:	19.10
Minutes/Game:	16.97

Tim Kempton played in nearly all the Hornets' games last year, but never got a start. He was good from the field, hitting over half his shots, and had halfway decent playmaking skills (a 0.30 Play), but just got lost in the shuffle somewhere.

Ron Anderson
Philadelphia 76ers
19.1 HGS

College:	Fresno St.
Age (1/1/1990):	32
Height:	6'7''
Weight:	215
Scoring:	0.523
Rebounding:	4.78
Playmaking:	0.12
Defense:	3.91
Gun Rating:	− 5.25
HoopStat Grade:	19.10
Minutes/Game:	31.99

One of the players you think of as a "pure" sixth man, who comes off the bench every night to put in as many minutes as a starter. In January he must have hired a press agent, because within the span of a week every wire service, sports show, and newspaper was doing a story on him. Then he disappeared again for the rest of the year.

Of course, we don't have to tell you that his job was to provide instant offense for the Sixers. But did you know that Dennis Hopson of the Nets scored at a higher rate? Per 48 minutes, Hopson scored 24.4 points, while Anderson scored only 24.3. There are enough players who could come off the bench every night to provide output similar to Anderson's. There aren't as many who would accept, or even want, to start every game on the pines, but Ron seemed to like it well enough.

Brad Lohaus
Sacramento Kings
19.0 HGS

College:	Iowa
Age (1/1/1990):	26
Height:	7'0''
Weight:	235
Scoring:	0.462
Rebounding:	6.22
Playmaking:	0.14
Defense:	6.80
Gun Rating:	− 0.89
HoopStat Grade:	19.00
Minutes/Game:	15.77

In the past, it probably would have been more devastating to be traded from Boston to Sacramento, but last year it just meant that Brad got to start his vacation about a week earlier. He was probably the lowest-impact player of the four involved in the trade, but he came up with 25 starts over the season. The trade didn't seem to affect his stats too radically; he got only one more minute per game for Sacramento than for Boston. Let's see what happens with his newest team. One hopes things can only get better.

Blair Rasmussen
Denver Nuggets
18.9 HGS

College:	Oregon
Age (1/1/1990):	28
Height:	7'0''
Weight:	250
Scoring:	0.472
Rebounding:	6.61
Playmaking:	0.09
Defense:	5.91
Gun Rating:	− 2.52
HoopStat Grade:	18.90
Minutes/Game:	16.99

He's rumored to be on the trading block. Stay tuned.

A good defensive player in the post with his turnaround jumper. He can also hit from the outside from 17 feet in. Can't be left unguarded outside because he'll fire it up. His biggest limitation is that he doesn't have the speed or quickness to keep up with a running team. He would be better suited with a team that relies on a half-court offense. He's a legitimate seven-footer who may end up on another team this season.

Kenny Walker
New York Knicks
18.8 HGS

College:	Kentucky
Age (1/1/1990):	26
Height:	6'8"
Weight:	210
Scoring:	0.513
Rebounding:	6.21
Playmaking:	0.10
Defense:	6.21
Gun Rating:	1.54
HoopStat Grade:	18.80
Minutes/Game:	14.72

After he won the NBA slam dunk competition, it looked as if Kenny might get more minutes for the Knicks. It wasn't to be, as his minutes were slashed drastically. He got only about 400 after the All-Star break, and there's a good chance he won't be with the team next year. The biggest factor in his low rating was his lack of playing time. He got fewer than 15 minutes per game, which made it hard to put together any consistent effort. If he hooks on with an expansion team, he'll be a decent power forward or small center.

James Edwards
Detroit Pistons
18.7 HGS

College:	Washington
Age (1/1/1990):	35
Height:	7'1"
Weight:	252
Scoring:	0.534
Rebounding:	5.33
Playmaking:	0.12
Defense:	4.80
Gun Rating:	−2.53
HoopStat Grade:	18.70
Minutes/Game:	16.50

He now has a ring on his finger. A great backup center for the Pistons. On a mediocre team with Edwards starting, you won't win with him. He did a great job at Detroit coming off the bench. His turnaround jumper from the low post is basically unstoppable. Edwards became a more aggressive defender in Detroit. But then again, who wouldn't if you got beat up in practice every day. You'd want to take it out on somebody. A good pick and roll player who was protected in the expansion because management knows that they now have a pretty good combination with Laimbeer and Edwards.

Scott Brooks
Philadelphia 76ers
18.7 HGS

College:	LaSalle
Age (1/1/1990):	32
Height:	6'7"
Weight:	220
Scoring:	0.444
Rebounding:	1.88
Playmaking:	0.82
Defense:	3.84
Gun Rating:	3.63
HoopStat Grade:	18.70
Minutes/Game:	16.67

A really dreadful shooter. Scott's .444 scoring percentage was only about 27% worse than that of his teammate Charles Barkley. However, his playmaking was a great plus for the Sixers, and his 16 minutes per game allowed an aging Mo Cheeks to catch his breath without the team's losing *too* much. It was obvious, however, that he wasn't guarded as hard as Mo, especially when you look at their Draw ratings: 1.71 for Cheeks vs. 0.59 for Brooks. When he was in, opponents were better able to fall off him and double-team Barkley or Gminski.

Vinnie Del Negro

Sacramento Kings
18.6 HGS

College:	North Carolina St.
Age (1/1/1990):	24
Height:	6'5''
Weight:	185
Scoring:	0.505
Rebounding:	3.16
Playmaking:	0.41
Defense:	4.33
Gun Rating:	1.02
HoopStat Grade:	18.60
Minutes/Game:	19.45

For a player many thought had no chance to make the NBA, Del Negro had a very good year. A three-point shooter who isn't bad off the dribble. He needs to get stronger physically. When the Kings opened their game after they got Ainge, the threes started raining and Del Negro had some pretty good games.

Brad Davis

Dallas Mavericks
18.5 HGS

College:	Maryland
Age (1/1/1990):	35
Height:	6'3''
Weight:	180
Scoring:	0.506
Rebounding:	2.03
Playmaking:	0.64
Defense:	3.89
Gun Rating:	1.39
HoopStat Grade:	18.50
Minutes/Game:	17.88

On a downhill slide now. He lost some quickness and now gets over-powered physically by some players. A good leader who may get sent away from Dallas as the Mavs start looking for younger legs.

Reggie Williams

Los Angeles Clippers
18.5 HGS

College:	Georgetown
Age (1/1/1990):	26
Height:	6'7''
Weight:	190
Scoring:	0.454
Rebounding:	4.20
Playmaking:	0.17
Defense:	6.06
Gun Rating:	−5.12
HoopStat Grade:	18.50
Minutes/Game:	20.68

Seemingly, an unhappy player on a losing team. He talks a good game but has yet to prove himself. He shoots (but who doesn't), he doesn't have an NBA body, and he can't guard his shadow. His time on the league is running out.

John Battle
Atlanta Hawks
18.4 HGS

College:	Rutgers
Age (1/1/1990):	28
Height:	6'2''
Weight:	175
Scoring:	0.510
Rebounding:	2.31
Playmaking:	0.31
Defense:	3.04
Gun Rating:	−3.99
HoopStat Grade:	18.40
Minutes/Game:	20.39

A mini-Vinnie Johnson. Comes in and can play one or two. He can help run the club and score when needed. Goes to the hoop a lot and gets fouled. Quick, so defense has a problem with him. A great third guard who gets better with better players around him.

John Bagley
New Jersey Nets
18.4 HGS

College:	Boston College
Age (1/1/1990):	30
Height:	6'0''
Weight:	192
Scoring:	0.439
Rebounding:	2.47
Playmaking:	0.81
Defense:	3.89
Gun Rating:	3.79
HoopStat Grade:	18.40
Minutes/Game:	24.15

Can't make an outside shot, doesn't defend very well, doesn't have the skills to be an NBA point guard.

Tom Garrick
Los Angeles Clippers
18.3 HGS

College:	Rhode Island
Age (1/1/1990):	24
Height:	6'2''
Weight:	185
Scoring:	0.529
Rebounding:	2.91
Playmaking:	0.68
Defense:	4.69
Gun Rating:	3.73
HoopStat Grade:	18.30
Minutes/Game:	21.11

Once Don Casey decided to keep him in as a starter, his game picked up. He has limited shooting range but likes to take it to the basket. He might end up being a decent guard off the bench for a good team, but he's more than adequate for the Clippers right now. Certainly an improvement over Reggie Williams, but the Clippers really need someone who can come in and light 'em up right away.

Pat Cummings
Miami Heat
18.0 HGS

College:	Cincinnati
Age (1/1/1990):	34
Height:	6'9''
Weight:	235
Scoring:	0.525
Rebounding:	7.44
Playmaking:	0.12
Defense:	6.37
Gun Rating:	−2.37
HoopStat Grade:	18.00
Minutes/Game:	20.68

Pat was nicknamed "Short" Cummings when he was in New York, and you can see why when you look at his numbers. He was the fourth worst in the league in Cont (ball control) rating, behind Kevin Duckworth, Rony Seikaly, and Manute Bol. He couldn't earn a starting job at Miami on a consistent basis, even with his nine years' experience. He seems to be a banger, a big player, but he now has only 166 blocks in his career, less than half of Manute Bol's total *last season*.

Darnell Valentine
Cleveland Cavaliers
17.9 HGS

College:	Kansas
Age (1/1/1990):	31
Height:	6'1''
Weight:	183
Scoring:	0.479
Rebounding:	2.62
Playmaking:	0.55
Defense:	4.62
Gun Rating:	1.73
HoopStat Grade:	17.90
Minutes/Game:	14.10

Darnell lucked into a good situation last year. He woke up on the day of the expansion draft in 1988 thinking he was a Clipper. Later in the day, he was a Heat (is that what you call a Miami player?). Finally, he ended up on the Cavs, where he filled in well as a small reserve guard. He wasn't going to get much time behind Mark Price, but he's played more than 2000 minutes in a season only once, back in 1985. Life as a reserve is still far preferable to life in the CBA.

Herb Williams
Dallas Mavericks
17.8 HGS

College:	Ohio St.
Age (1/1/1990):	32
Height:	6'11''
Weight:	242
Scoring:	0.463
Rebounding:	6.68
Playmaking:	0.17
Defense:	7.95
Gun Rating:	2.70
HoopStat Grade:	17.80
Minutes/Game:	32.50

In splitting his time between the Pacers and Mavs, Herb totaled 66 starts, but didn't lead either team at his position. Therefore, he's listed among the reserves, and not highly either. His minutes had been declining with Indiana, and the move was the best thing to freshen up both teams, and all players involved.

His biggest asset is his size, but at 6'11'', he's another one of the players who had no reason to shoot threes. Over his career, he was 4 for 54 entering last season. He tried 5 more, but didn't make any of them. Either he's demonstrated extremely poor judgment, or he gets stuck outside with time running down. Either way, there's no one else to blame.

Darwin Cook
Denver Nuggets
17.6 HGS

College:	Idaho St.
Age (1/1/1990):	34
Height:	6'10"
Weight:	215
Scoring:	0.472
Rebounding:	2.75
Playmaking:	0.27
Defense:	4.93
Gun Rating:	− 3.69
HoopStat Grade:	17.60
Minutes/Game:	17.32

Not a consistent offensive player. Some nights he looks good, but can't count on him every time out. He will make the big shot, however, and will look for the ball. His big strength has been his speed and quickness, but he's lost a little in that department over the years.

Derrick Chievous
Houston Rockets
17.6 HGS

College:	Missouri
Age (1/1/1990):	23
Height:	6'7"
Weight:	195
Scoring:	0.488
Rebounding:	5.24
Playmaking:	0.12
Defense:	4.05
Gun Rating:	− 5.80
HoopStat Grade:	17.60
Minutes/Game:	19.00

Derrick started the year as a fan favorite with the Houston fans, but that faded faster than the fortunes of the Rockets.

Joe Kleine
Boston Celtics
17.2 HGS

College:	Arkansas
Age (1/1/1990):	28
Height:	7'0"
Weight:	271
Scoring:	0.475
Rebounding:	7.91
Playmaking:	0.16
Defense:	6.23
Gun Rating:	0.76
HoopStat Grade:	17.20
Minutes/Game:	18.81

Kleine has the potential to be a good, beefy player for the Celts, but last year was a definite disappointment. His numbers show how weak he was in traffic—usually 7' players take shots in the paint, and when they do, they're expected to have a two-pointer percentage higher than .407. Normally, he's a good .470 shooter, and he improved considerably after the trade, so it's possible that much of his problem was in his unsettled season. He's improved his free-throw shooting every year but one since he was a sophomore in college, so it would make sense that he muscle it up inside more often, to draw some fouls.

Terry Tyler
Dallas Mavericks
17.1 HGS

College:	Detroit
Age (1/1/1990):	34
Height:	6'7"
Weight:	228
Scoring:	0.488
Rebounding:	5.92
Playmaking:	0.11
Defense:	5.93
Gun Rating:	−0.40
HoopStat Grade:	17.10
Minutes/Game:	15.10

A good support player who's bounced around the league. Tyler has the ability to come in and give his team a quick lift. He has a good turnaround jumper down low, and can hit from 15 feet. Tyler is aggressive on the boards and works hard at defending his man.

Ricky Berry
Sacramento Kings
17.1 HGS

College:	San Jose St.
Age (1/1/1990):	26
Height:	6'8"
Weight:	207
Scoring:	0.484
Rebounding:	4.04
Playmaking:	0.14
Defense:	4.40
Gun Rating:	−6.98
HoopStat Grade:	17.10
Minutes/Game:	21.97

Unlimited range, but he doesn't take it to the hoop as much as he should. Had a decent rookie year and should show marked improvement this season, especially if he adds some upper body muscle.

Dan Majerle
Phoenix Suns
17.0 HGS

College:	Central Michigan
Age (1/1/1990):	25
Height:	6'6"
Weight:	215
Scoring:	0.435
Rebounding:	4.47
Playmaking:	0.30
Defense:	5.34
Gun Rating:	0.48
HoopStat Grade:	17.00
Minutes/Game:	25.07

True, he had mono for most of the year. But even if you have *stereo*, you have to shoot better than Dan did last year. His .419 FG% was about average for reserves rated this low, but his .614 FT% didn't help him either. Still, a batter who will show better numbers in his sophomore season, and a highly valued addition to the new Suns.

Norm Nixon
Los Angeles Clippers
17.0 HGS

College:	Duquesne
Age (1/1/1990):	35
Height:	6'2''
Weight:	170
Scoring:	0.434
Rebounding:	1.59
Playmaking:	0.92
Defense:	2.86
Gun Rating:	3.79
HoopStat Grade:	17.00
Minutes/Game:	24.87

Gerald Henderson
Philadelphia 76ers
17.0 HGS

College:	Virginia Comm.
Age (1/1/1990):	34
Height:	6'2''
Weight:	180
Scoring:	0.457
Rebounding:	1.94
Playmaking:	0.40
Defense:	3.43
Gun Rating:	−3.65
HoopStat Grade:	17.00
Minutes/Game:	15.17

Purvis Short
Houston Rockets
16.9 HGS

College:	Jackson St.
Age (1/1/1990):	33
Height:	6'7''
Weight:	220
Scoring:	0.446
Rebounding:	4.66
Playmaking:	0.22
Defense:	4.61
Gun Rating:	−3.09
HoopStat Grade:	16.90
Minutes/Game:	17.80

Now retired, Norm couldn't make a successful comeback after two years on the sidelines. He used to be a workhorse, averaging 35.5 minutes per game over his career, even playing 64 minutes in one game (vs. Cleveland, in 1980). He had also been a remarkably consistent scorer, averaging 21.7 pp48 until last season, when he managed only 13.2. His scoring percentage was .507; last year it was .434. His passing skills were still sharp, but he knew when it was time to get out. Less than a month later he showed up in Italy on a team pushing for the title. Meanwhile, back at home his former team was mired in the Pacific cellar.

Gerald just missed playing 1000 minutes, but we let him slide. His career is in decline, obviously; he had never received fewer than 1500 minutes since his rookie year. Alas, the league is about to lose another good short guy.

. . . And speaking of short guys in decline, the only time Purvis played fewer minutes than last year was in 1987, when he appeared only in 34 games. Time to learn how to say "give me the ball" in Italian or Spanish.

Dave Corzine
Chicago Bulls
16.8 HGS

College:	DePaul
Age (1/1/1990):	34
Height:	6'11"
Weight:	260
Scoring:	0.487
Rebounding:	6.14
Playmaking:	0.23
Defense:	5.87
Gun Rating:	1.25
HoopStat Grade:	16.80
Minutes/Game:	18.31

Relegated to the bench with the acquisition of Bill Cartwright, Corzine was his usual soft touch when he did see action.

Michael Cooper
Los Angeles Lakers
16.7 HGS

College:	New Mexico
Age (1/1/1990):	34
Height:	6'7"
Weight:	176
Scoring:	0.455
Rebounding:	2.64
Playmaking:	0.64
Defense:	4.59
Gun Rating:	2.20
HoopStat Grade:	16.70
Minutes/Game:	24.29

It's quite a surprise that Coop was rated this low, but it's a sign of our inaccurate methods for measuring defense. If we were starting a team, we would almost definitely choose him over about nine-tenths of the reserves above him. He's a specialist who has been named to the NBA All-Defensive First or Second Team every year since 1981, and he gets the Jordan assignments when the Lakers play Chicago.

Bill Wennington
Dallas Mavericks
16.6 HGS

College:	St. John's
Age (1/1/1990):	26
Height:	7'0"
Weight:	245
Scoring:	0.468
Rebounding:	7.72
Playmaking:	0.17
Defense:	6.77
Gun Rating:	3.19
HoopStat Grade:	16.60
Minutes/Game:	16.52

He shows up for practice. He roots for his team. And for this he gets paid.

Scott Hastings
Miami Heat
16.5 HGS

College:	Arkansas
Age (1/1/1990):	30
Height:	6'10"
Weight:	235
Scoring:	0.487
Rebounding:	5.60
Playmaking:	0.18
Defense:	6.07
Gun Rating:	1.15
HoopStat Grade:	16.50
Minutes/Game:	16.08

Limited. A big guy who bangs guys around but nothing happens. Competitive, but not powerful enough to make an impact down low.

Fred Roberts
Milwaukee Bucks
16.2 HGS

College:	BYU
Age (1/1/1990):	30
Height:	6'10"
Weight:	220
Scoring:	0.534
Rebounding:	4.92
Playmaking:	0.21
Defense:	4.97
Gun Rating:	0.16
HoopStat Grade:	16.20
Minutes/Game:	17.62

The highlight of Fred's career was when he came off the bench to almost singlehandedly play the Pistons to a stalemate in the playoffs.

Richard Anderson
Portland Trail Blazers
16.2 HGS

College:	UC – Santa Barbara
Age (1/1/1990):	30
Height:	6'10"
Weight:	240
Scoring:	0.424
Rebounding:	6.09
Playmaking:	0.28
Defense:	6.23
Gun Rating:	– 0.22
HoopStat Grade:	16.20
Minutes/Game:	15.03

Anderson would rather shoot a three-pointer than get an open layup. A versatile player who runs the floor well. Can play 3 or 4. If played at 4, he can go outside and take the long shot. He defends well at times, but being from Southern California there are spells in the game in which he just doesn't seem to be there. He once received a birthday card that said, "Happy Birthday from the planet earth. Wish you were here."

Tim McCormick
Houston Rockets
16.2 HGS

College:	Michigan
Age (1/1/1990):	28
Height:	7'0''
Weight:	240
Scoring:	0.509
Rebounding:	6.15
Playmaking:	0.15
Defense:	4.89
Gun Rating:	−0.02
HoopStat Grade:	16.20
Minutes/Game:	15.52

A reserve player who has a big body to bang people around. He can't throw the ball in the ocean, and he can't be counted on to score too many points. His strong point is that he doesn't try to do things that he can't do.

Dave Feitl
Washington Bullets
16.1 HGS

College:	UTEP
Age (1/1/1990):	28
Height:	7'0''
Weight:	240
Scoring:	0.478
Rebounding:	7.26
Playmaking:	0.14
Defense:	5.88
Gun Rating:	−0.48
HoopStat Grade:	16.10
Minutes/Game:	14.53

Although it can be argued that he was the Bullets' "big man," Feitl is in the league only because he's tall.

Brad Sellers
Chicago Bulls
16.0 HGS

College:	Ohio St.
Age (1/1/1990):	28
Height:	7'0''
Weight:	210
Scoring:	0.520
Rebounding:	3.97
Playmaking:	0.21
Defense:	4.79
Gun Rating:	0.69
HoopStat Grade:	16.00
Minutes/Game:	21.65

A forward masquerading as a center. Plays small for a seven-footer. It's hard to believe he was a shot-blocker in college. Tends to shy away from physical contact in the Big League.

John Paxson
Chicago Bulls
16.0 HGS

College:	Notre Dame
Age (1/1/1990):	30
Height:	6'2"
Weight:	185
Scoring:	0.475
Rebounding:	1.42
Playmaking:	0.60
Defense:	2.75
Gun Rating:	0.31
HoopStat Grade:	16.00
Minutes/Game:	22.28

A three-point shooter who's also good off the dribble. Real competitive just like his brother, but a tad smaller. Paxson is well-liked in Chicago because he can make the open shot. His size is what's hurt him, especially when Jordan goes to the point and Paxson is left with bigger guards to handle.

Craig Hodges
Chicago Bulls
15.8 HGS

College:	UC – Long Beach
Age (1/1/1990):	30
Height:	6'3"
Weight:	195
Scoring:	0.482
Rebounding:	2.10
Playmaking:	0.34
Defense:	3.19
Gun Rating:	– 5.24
HoopStat Grade:	15.80
Minutes/Game:	20.41

The fact that three Chicago reserves are all grouped this low lends credence to the belief that the Bulls are just the Hornets plus Michael Jordan. All three of these players had deficiencies under the boards and on defense, and only Paxson showed a glimmer of passing ability. Paxson and Hodges were heavy three-shooters, but Sellers was a somewhat better scorer. When three of your reserves are in the bottom eleven of the league, and your top *four* non-starters are in the lowest twenty, you can't have a very good bench.

Harvey Grant
Washington Bullets
15.8 HGS

College:	Oklahoma
Age (1/1/1990):	25
Height:	6'8"
Weight:	200
Scoring:	0.473
Rebounding:	4.34
Playmaking:	0.21
Defense:	4.02
Gun Rating:	– 0.17
HoopStat Grade:	15.80
Minutes/Game:	16.80

Harvey's not progressing as quickly as twin brother Horace (Chicago Bulls). An inch shorter and 15 pounds lighter, Harvey played 17 minutes a game (35 for Horace), while averaging only 5.6 ppg for the late surging Bullets. A proven scorer at the University of Oklahoma (21 ppg 1988) and a 12th pick overall in the draft, the Bullets are expecting Grant to come through with much better numbers this season and not go the way of their other forgettable first picks. Anthony Jones, Kenny Green, Mel Turpin, and Wes Matthews are no longer in the league.

Jim Paxson
Boston Celtics
15.8 HGS

College:	Dayton
Age (1/1/1990):	33
Height:	6'6"
Weight:	210
Scoring:	0.484
Rebounding:	1.83
Playmaking:	0.24
Defense:	3.12
Gun Rating:	−4.94
HoopStat Grade:	15.80
Minutes/Game:	19.96

Hobbled by injuries the last few years. A legit 6'6" who goes to the hole. Works well with picks, which fits in well with Boston.

Mike Brown
Utah Jazz
15.5 HGS

College:	GWU
Age (1/1/1990):	27
Height:	6'10"
Weight:	260
Scoring:	0.479
Rebounding:	7.36
Playmaking:	0.17
Defense:	5.71
Gun Rating:	1.82
HoopStat Grade:	15.50
Minutes/Game:	15.92

A player with limited ability and an offensive game that's difficult for any observer to see. Brown is big, fast, and bangs people around. Not much of an offensive player, but he can usually be found lurking around the low post. Unfortunately, he doesn't have the offensive skills to get much done there. Jerry Sloan seemed to like him over Iavaroni because he was simply more physical.

Jon Sundvold
Miami Heat
14.5 HGS

College:	Missouri
Age (1/1/1990):	29
Height:	6'2"
Weight:	170
Scoring:	0.473
Rebounding:	1.79
Playmaking:	0.20
Defense:	2.24
Gun Rating:	−10.97
HoopStat Grade:	14.50
Minutes/Game:	19.68

A three-point shooter, and that's it. Not inviting him to the All-Star competition would be like not inviting Manute Bol to the NBA Shot-Blocking Contest, because it's all either of them can do. Sundvold gained 62.26 points with the three, which is not hard when you consider that he shot .522 from long range, only .444 from two-point range. Numbers like that are just silly.

Elston Turner
Denver Nuggets
13.8 HGS

College:	Mississippi
Age (1/1/1990):	31
Height:	6'5"
Weight:	200
Scoring:	0.438
Rebounding:	4.99
Playmaking:	0.41
Defense:	5.14
Gun Rating:	4.51
HoopStat Grade:	13.80
Minutes/Game:	22.38

Turner was an above-average play-maker, but his other numbers are weak. Only four other players averaged fewer points per 48 than his 9.3. He's not an intimidator, either. His eight blocks last season were a *career high*. He'll be 30 entering this season and doesn't look to be improving on defense.

Trent Tucker
New York Knicks
13.4 HGS

College:	Minnesota
Age (1/1/1990):	31
Height:	6'5"
Weight:	193
Scoring:	0.455
Rebounding:	2.82
Playmaking:	0.23
Defense:	4.07
Gun Rating:	−4.66
HoopStat Grade:	13.40
Minutes/Game:	22.52

Trent Tucker was the only player in the league who took more three-pointers than two-pointers. He drew the Knicks' "tough" defensive assignments by default, but most of his game consisted of setting up outside and tossing up threes for threes' sake (remember the last five seconds of the New York–Chicago playoffs?). He split starting time with Gerald Wilkins, although Gerald was a far better player last year. Tucker was the Knicks' elder, the player with what could pass for experience.

Joe Wolf
Los Angeles Clippers
13.2 HGS

College:	North Carolina
Age (1/1/1990):	26
Height:	6'11"
Weight:	230
Scoring:	0.438
Rebounding:	5.45
Playmaking:	0.28
Defense:	4.70
Gun Rating:	0.45
HoopStat Grade:	13.20
Minutes/Game:	21.97

Somehow Joe Wolf got 15 starts last season and averaged almost 22 minutes per game he played. Is there anything else you need to know about the Clippers? Has a nice baseline jumper, but can't score when pressured. No good off the boards. A real major bust, even for the Clippers.

Randy Wittman
Indiana Pacers
11.9 HGS

College:	Indiana
Age (1/1/1990):	31
Height:	6'6''
Weight:	210
Scoring:	0.470
Rebounding:	2.10
Playmaking:	0.39
Defense:	2.23
Gun Rating:	−0.61
HoopStat Grade:	11.90
Minutes/Game:	17.50

Wittman was a 6'6'' player who played like he was 5'10''. Sacramento was so fed up with Reggie Theus that they moved him for Wittman, but he didn't last very long at Arco. The Kings are probably better off with Wayman Tisdale than with Wittman and LaSalle Thompson, but Indiana spent the season shaking things up for the sake of it.

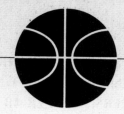

All-HoopStats Teams

THE JIM LUSCATOFF TROPHY
THE MOST PERSONAL FOULS PER 48
MINUTES PLAYED
(MINIMUM 900 MIN OR 70 GP)

C	Eric Leckner, Utah	10.72 (174 PF/779 Min)
F	Bill Wennington, Dallas	9.43 (211/1074)
F	Olden Polynice, Seattle	9.43 (164/835)
G	Ricky Berry, Sacramento	6.73 (197/1406)
G	Reggie Williams, LA Clippers	6.70 (182/1303)

THE ANDY ROONEY
ALL-OPINIONATED TEAM
THE MOST TECHNICAL FOULS

C	Bill Laimbeer, Detroit	9 (81 games)
F	Karl Malone, Utah	18 (80)
F	Rick Mahorn, Detroit	15 (72)
G	Derek Harper, Dallas	8 (81)
G	Glenn Rivers, Atlanta	6 (76)

Honorable Mention:

	Charles Barkley, Philadelphia	15 (79)
	Terry Catledge, Washington	12 (79)

THE GOLDEN ARCHES AWARD
THE MOST POINTS GAINED
BY SHOOTING THE THREE

C	Jack Sikma, Milwaukee.	+ 53.19 points
F	Harold Pressley, Sacramento	+ 87.52
F	Russ Schoene, Seattle	+ 40.39
G	Dale Ellis, Seattle	+142.30
G	Jon Sundvold, Miami	+ 62.26

THE BAD BOMBERS
THE MOST POINTS LOST
BY CHUCKING UP THE THREE

C	Manute Bol, Golden State	− 16.97 points
F	Charles Barkley, Philadelphia	− 98.05
F	Ron Harper, Cleveland	− 38.32
G	Chris Mullin, Golden State	− 36.49
G	Michael Jordan, Chicago	− 30.57

THE "FALL BACK! FALL BACK!" AWARD
THE LOWEST SHOOTING PERCENTAGES,
MINIMUM 100 ATTEMPTS

C	Paul Mokeski, Milwaukee	0.360 (59/164)
F	Scott Roth, San Antonio	0.353 (59/167)
F	Russ Schoene, Seattle	0.387 (135/349)
G	Jim Les, Utah	0.301 (40/133)
G	Allen Leavell, Houston	0.346 (65/188)

THE CLAY DUCK CLUB
THE HIGHEST SHOOTING PERCENTAGES,
MINIMUM 100 ATTEMPTS

C	Mark West, Phoenix	0.653 (243/372)
F	Dennis Rodman, Detroit	0.595 (316/531)
F	Charles Barkley, Philadelphia	0.579 (700/1208)
G	Kevin Gamble, Boston	0.551 (75/136)
G	Tyrone Corbin, Phoenix	0.541 (245/543)

THE SECOND CHANCE TROPHY
THE HIGHEST PERCENTAGE OF OFFENSIVE REBOUNDS, MINIMUM 100 TOTAL REBS.

C	Eddie Lee Wilkins, New York	48.6% (72 Off/76 Def)
F	Ledell Eackles, Washington	55.6% (100/80)
F	Jerry Reynolds, Seattle	49.0% (49/51)
G	Adrian Branch, Portland	47.7% (63/69)
G	Clyde Drexler, Portland	47.0% (289/326)

THE HOOVERS (FOR THOSE WHO VACUUM UP THE DEFENSIVE BOARDS) THE HIGHEST PERCENTAGE OF DEFENSIVE REBOUNDS, MINIMUM 100 TOTAL REBS.

C	Bill Laimbeer, Detroit	17.8% (138 Off/638 Def)
F	Michael Cooper, LA Lakers	17.3% (33/158)
F	Tom Chambers, Phoenix	20.9% (143/541)
G	Brad Davis, Dallas	13.0% (14/94)
G	Kevin Johnson, Phoenix	13.5% (46/294)

THE JOHNSON VS. WILLIAMS FAMILY FEUD PRESENTED BY RICHARD DAWSON

Johnsons	*Williamses*
C Steve, Portland	John, Cleveland
F Buck, Houston	Buck, New Jersey
F Eddie, Phoenix	John, Washington
G Magic, LA Lakers	Michael, Detroit
G Kevin, Phoenix	Reggie, LA Clippers
Dennis, Boston	Kevin, New Jersey
Vinnie, Detroit	Herb, Dallas

THE ALL-ANDERSON TEAM

The 1988–89 San Antonio Spurs

THE IRONMAN GIRDER
MOST MINUTES PER GAMES PLAYED

C	Akeem Olajuwon, Houston	36.88 (3024/82)
F	Charles Barkley, Philadelphia	39.09 (3088/79)
F	Karl Malone, Utah	39.08 (3126/80)
G	Michael Jordan, Chicago	40.19 (3255/81)
G	Clyde Drexler, Portland	39.31 (3066/78)

THE NRA "GUNNER" AWARD
MOST FIELD GOAL ATTEMPTS PER 48 MINUTES

C	Akeem Olajuwon, Houston	24.70 (1556 FGA/3024 Min)
F	Alex English, Denver	30.20 (1881/2990)
F	Eddie Johnson, Phoenix	28.80 (1226/2043)
G	Jeff Malone, Washington	27.99 (1410/2418)
G	Walter Davis, Denver	27.81 (1076/1857)

LOOKING FOR TROUBLE
MOST FREE THROWS DRAWN PER 48 MINUTES PLAYED

C	Moses Malone, Atlanta	11.86 (711 FTA/2878 Min)
F	Karl Malone, Utah	14.10 (918/3126)
F	Charles Barkley, Philadelphia	12.42 (799/3088)
G	Michael Jordan, Chicago	11.69 (793/3255)
G	Magic Johnson, LA Lakers	9.36 (563/2886)

THE PERCY ROSS PHILANTHROPY AWARD
MOST ASSISTS GIVEN PER SHOT TAKEN

C	Jack Sikma, Milwaukee	0.35 (289 Ast/835 FGA)
F	Vinnie Del Negro, Sacramento	0.41 (206/503)
F	Rodney McCray, Sacramento	0.40 (293/729)
G	Jim Les, Utah	1.62 (215/133)
G	Mugsy Bogues, Charlotte	1.48 (620/418)

THE HOG FUTURES AWARD
MOST SHOTS TAKEN PER ASSIST

C	Eddie Lee Wilkins, New York	35.00 (245 FGA/7 Ast)
F	Armon Gilliam, Phoenix	17.88 (930/52)
F	Greg Anderson, San Antonio	14.98 (914/61)
G	John Shasky, Miami	11.27 (248/22)
G	Dale Ellis, Seattle	10.43 (1710/164)

THE ILL STATE BAD HANDS AWARD
THE MOST TURNOVERS PER 48 MINUTES

C	Kevin Edwards, Miami	4.97 (243 TO/2349 Min)
F	Kelly Tripucka, Charlotte	4.92 (236/2302)
F	Chuck Person, Indiana	4.91 (308/3012)
G	Gary Grant, LA Clippers	6.44 (258/1924)
G	Dwayne Washington, Miami	5.47 (122/1070)

THE EARLY SHOWER AWARD
THE MOST TIMES DISQUALIFIED (6 FOULS)
PRORATED TO 82 GAMES

C	Rik Smits, Indiana	14.00 (14 Disq/82 GP)
F	Chuck Person, Indiana	13.33 (13/80)
F	LaSalle Thompson, Indiana	12.95 (12/76)
G	Scottie Pippen, Chicago	8.99 (8/73)
G	Willie Anderson, San Antonio	8.10 (8/81)

MONEY IN THE BANK
HIGHEST FREE THROW PERCENTAGE,
100 OR MORE ATTEMPTS

C	Jack Sikma, Milwaukee	0.905 (266 FTM/294 FTA)
F	Eddie Johnson, Phoenix	0.867 (215/248)
F	Kelly Tripucka, Charlotte	0.866 (440/508)
G	Magic Johnson, LA Lakers	0.911 (513/563)
G	Scott Skiles, Indiana	0.903 (130/144)

AAAAAAAAAAAAAAAAAIIIIIIIRBAAAAAAAAAAALL!
LOWEST FREE THROW PERCENTAGE
100 OR MORE ATTEMPTS

C	Chris Dudley, Cleveland*	0.364 (39 FTM/107 FTA)
F	Jerome Lane, Denver	0.384 (43/112)
F	Greg Anderson, San Antonio	0.514 (207/403)
G	Mike McGee, New Jersey	0.535 (77/144)
G	Craig Ehlo, Cleveland	0.607 (71/117)

Retires award

NBA Player Peripheral Stats by Position, 1988–89

(700 Min or 70 GP to qualify)

Beyond the normal statistics you read every day, there are certain combinations of stats that tell you more than you'd ever know with the straight numbers. These are the peripheral stats. Most people are still satisfied with the old standby, points per game, when it really has little bearing on a player's quality at all. However, it's easy to figure out, so people use it as a substitute for similar numbers that actually make a point.

The best part is, most of these numbers are not particularly complex. In fact, they take no more effort than the per-game stats we're all so accustomed to. We can start with the per-48 stats. The idea is simple. If one player averages 10.0 ppg in 20 minutes of play, he scores as much as one who averages 20.0 ppg in 40 minutes per play. They both score a point every 2 minutes. For every 48 minutes they play, they each come out with a 24.0 pp48 average.

On the next pages you will find a listing of the qualifiers at each position, and their peripheral stats. A fuller explanation of each number follows.

GP   Games played.
GS   Games started.
Min   Minutes played.

FG%   Percentage of all field goals made (two and three pointers).
3G%   Percentage of all three point shots made.
2G%   Percentage of all two point shots made.
FT%   Percentage of all free throws made.
PPG   Points per game played. This is the stat we all know and love, so you can see how it relates to the actual scoring *rate* of a player, indicated as pp48. The formula is **Pts/GP.**
PP48   Points per 48 minutes played. This is the number of points the player scores every 48 minutes of play (versus every game played). The formula is **(Pts × 48)/Min.**
HGS48   The player's HoopStat Grade per 48 minutes. This is a description of a player's "total" worth, comparable to his scoring average.
Score   The player's scoring percentage. It answers the question "What percentage of the points this player could have gotten did he actually make?" You divide the points he did get into those he could have gotten (two for each two-point attempt, three for each three-point attempt and one for each foul shot). The formula is: **(Pts/[(2 × FGA) + FTA + 3GA]).**
Rbdg   A player's combined rebounding rating, based on the HoopStat Grade values for offensive and defensive rebounds. It is meant to approximate the worth, in points, of a player's rebounding

per 48 minutes. To get the number, you must use the formula: **(0.85 × Off Reb) + (0.5 × Def Reb),** then prorate it for 48 minutes (divide by total minutes, then multiply by 48).

Play Designed to rate a player's pure playmaking, or unselfishness with the ball. It's simply the number of assists a player gives divided by the number of shots he attempts from the field. The formula is: **Ast/FGA.** Since it's a ratio, this stat isn't prorated.

Cont A rating of the player's ball control, taking into account assists, steals, and turnovers. The formula is: **(Ast + Stl −[0.8 × TO]),** prorated per 48 minutes.

Def The defensive rating of a player, taking into account the defensive stats readily available in a newspaper. The formula is: **(Def Reb + Stl + Blk),** pro-rated for 48 minutes.

M/GP Minutes per game played. We've put this in so you can see how much time a player was getting. The higher this is, the more he's utilized. Players like Jordan, who stay on the court for most of the game, will approach 40.0 here. The formula is simply **Min/GP.**

2:3 The two-to-three ratio for the player. It's the number of normal shots a player attempts, on average, between three-point attempts. The lower this number, the more a player tries the three. The higher the stat, the more of an inside player he is (usually). Centers can have numbers in the hundreds here (one three-point attempt per 100 two-point shots) while guards often dip below 2.0 (one out of three shots a three-pointer, a 2 to 1 ratio of twos). The formula is **(FGA − 3GA)/3GA,** since FGA − 3GA will give you the two-point shots attempted, or 2GA. Another way to say this is 2GA/3GA.

3Gain The number of points a player gained or lost by shooting three pointers. It's figured by pretending all their three-point attempts were taken as twos instead, and figuring out how many point they would have scored with the higher percentage shot. The exact formula is: **(3 × 3GM) − (2 × 2G% × 3GA).**

Draw The foul-drawing rating, based on the number of free-throw attempts per foul the player is charged with. When a player's number is 2.0, it means he averages two foul shots every time he fouls someone else. In general, a high number (over 1.0), means a player is good at drawing fouls without getting them charged to him. The formula is: **FTA/PF.**

Hands This rates how well a player can get his mitts on the ball (through steals and blocks) without getting them on the ball handler (and drawing a foul). The formula here is: **(Stl + Blk)/PF.**

OR/DR Offensive rebound ratio, or how many offensive rebounds a player gets for every defensive rebound. If he gets five of each, the ratio will be 1.0. It's interesting how widely this varies from team to team, and from fast to slow players. The formula is: **OReb/DReb.**

Gun The world-famous Gun rating. Since HGS is a measure of a player's overall skills, and PP48 shows only how much they can score, the difference between the two is how much a player is worth when he's *not* scoring. The formula is: **HGS48 − PP48.** It's called Gun, basically, because it shows who can score but nothing else, and who can do more. If a player has a rep as a scoring machine (Tom Chambers), his Gun will be below zero, because his scoring average overestimates his worth in points to a team. If he's a defensive gem, or a good playmaker, his Gun will be high, because his worth is greater than just his scoring output.

HoopStats '89 Rated Player Statistics

Qualifiers - 41 starts (or team high at position), or 1000 minutes played

Centers	Team	GP	GS	MIN	FG%	3G%	2G%	FT%	PPG	PP48	HGS48	Score	Rbdg	Play	Cont	Def	M/GP	2:3	3Gain	Draw	Hands	OR/DR	Gun
Olajuwon,Akeem	HOU	82	82	3024	0.508	0.000	0.511	0.696	24.8	32.3	36.6	0.539	10.65	0.10	2.25	13.90	36.88	154.60	-10.22	1.98	1.50	0.44	4.28
Ewing,Patrick	NY	80	80	2896	0.567	0.000	0.570	0.746	22.7	30.1	32.6	0.594	7.37	0.15	1.53	10.85	36.20	212.67	-6.84	1.56	1.26	0.40	2.51
Parish,Robert	BOS	80	80	2840	0.570	----	0.570	0.719	18.6	25.1	29.3	0.595	10.44	0.17	1.59	8.81	35.50	----	0.00	1.96	0.93	0.52	4.15
Malone,Moses	ATL	81	80	2878	0.491	0.000	0.496	0.789	20.2	27.3	28.8	0.562	10.23	0.10	-0.08	7.74	35.53	90.33	-11.91	4.62	1.16	0.68	1.51
Benjamin,Benoit	LAC	79	62	2585	0.541	0.000	0.543	0.744	16.4	24.1	27.7	0.579	7.53	0.17	0.45	10.10	32.72	452.50	-2.17	1.93	1.26	0.31	3.62
Schayes,Danny	DEN	76	64	1917	0.522	0.333	0.525	0.826	12.8	24.3	25.9	0.596	7.50	0.17	0.48	7.56	25.22	66.44	-0.45	1.26	0.38	0.40	1.63
Daugherty,Brad	CLE	78	78	2821	0.538	0.333	0.538	0.737	18.9	25.1	25.6	0.578	7.10	0.28	2.76	6.41	36.17	336.33	-0.23	2.99	0.58	0.30	0.46
Smits,Rik	IND	82	71	2041	0.517	0.000	0.518	0.719	11.7	22.5	24.4	0.547	7.40	0.09	0.07	8.13	24.89	745.00	-1.04	0.83	0.61	0.59	1.92
Gminski,Mike	PHI	82	82	2739	0.477	0.000	0.479	0.871	17.2	24.7	24.4	0.526	8.04	0.12	1.42	7.48	33.40	193.33	-5.75	2.40	1.05	0.38	-0.27
Lister,Alton	SEA	82	82	1806	0.499	----	0.499	0.646	8.0	17.5	24.2	0.520	9.17	0.10	-0.31	9.91	22.02	----	0.00	0.57	0.66	0.61	6.75
Brickowski,Frank	SAN	64	60	1822	0.515	0.000	0.517	0.715	13.7	23.1	23.5	0.550	6.71	0.20	2.66	7.06	28.47	326.00	-2.07	1.12	0.55	0.57	0.40
West,Mark	PHO	82	32	2019	0.653	----	0.653	0.535	7.2	14.1	22.8	0.628	7.92	0.10	-0.20	9.82	24.62	----	0.00	0.74	0.81	0.44	8.63
Laimbeer,Bill	DET	81	81	2640	0.499	0.345	0.515	0.840	13.7	20.1	22.5	0.527	7.93	0.20	2.24	8.55	32.59	9.34	0.32	0.82	0.58	0.22	2.35
Sikma,Jack	MIL	80	80	2587	0.431	0.380	0.449	0.905	13.4	19.8	22.0	0.490	6.70	0.35	4.77	7.16	32.34	2.87	51.98	0.98	0.48	0.29	2.21
Sampson,Ralph	GS	61	36	1086	0.449	0.375	0.451	0.653	6.4	17.4	21.4	0.472	8.41	0.21	1.59	8.57	17.80	44.63	1.78	0.56	0.55	0.52	4.02
Duckworth,Kevin	POR	79	79	2662	0.477	0.000	0.478	0.757	18.1	25.8	21.0	0.520	7.28	0.05	-0.79	5.38	33.70	579.50	-1.91	1.43	0.35	0.63	-4.84
Carroll,Joe Barry	NJ	64	62	1996	0.448	----	0.448	0.800	14.1	21.7	20.9	0.490	6.68	0.13	1.48	7.92	31.19	----	0.00	1.14	0.79	0.33	-0.80
Abdul-Jabbar,Kareem	LAL	74	74	1695	0.475	0.000	0.477	0.739	10.1	21.2	20.1	0.503	5.75	0.11	1.02	6.75	22.91	218.67	-2.86	0.84	0.63	0.45	-1.06
Eaton,Mark	UTA	82	82	2914	0.462	----	0.462	0.660	6.2	8.4	20.1	0.501	8.25	0.20	0.20	10.97	35.54	----	0.00	0.69	1.23	0.37	11.70
Seikaly,Ron	MIA	78	62	1962	0.448	0.250	0.449	0.511	10.9	20.7	20.1	0.459	8.46	0.07	-1.42	7.69	25.15	185.00	-0.59	1.37	0.55	0.59	-0.62
Donaldson,James	DAL	53	53	1746	0.573	----	0.573	0.766	9.1	13.2	20.0	0.603	9.36	0.11	-0.12	8.55	32.94	----	0.00	1.12	0.95	0.38	6.79
Petersen,Jim	SAC	66	40	1633	0.459	0.000	0.465	0.747	10.2	19.7	19.5	0.488	7.31	0.13	0.31	7.67	24.74	74.75	-7.44	0.65	0.49	0.41	-0.27
Cureton,Earl	CHA	82	41	2047	0.501	0.000	0.502	0.537	6.5	12.5	17.3	0.505	7.26	0.28	2.08	6.12	24.96	464.00	-1.00	0.53	0.48	0.63	4.81
Cartwright,Bill	CHI	78	76	2333	0.475	0.000	0.475	0.766	12.4	19.9	17.2	0.524	6.45	0.12	-0.79	5.07	29.91	125.00	0.00	1.32	0.26	0.41	-2.64
Jones,Charles	WAS	54	45	1164	0.476	0.000	0.480	0.667	2.6	5.7	15.2	0.493	6.47	0.34	2.04	8.35	21.56	125.00	-0.96	0.14	0.59	0.42	9.49
Average Center		**75**	**67**	**2234**	**0.503**	**0.315**	**0.507**	**0.737**	**13.3**	**21.5**	**24.0**	**0.540**	**7.96**	**0.15**	**1.05**	**8.37**	**29.71**	**49.31**	**-1.06**	**1.27**	**0.74**	**0.44**	**2.55**

Forwards	Team	GP	GS	MIN	FG%	3G%	2C%	FT%	PPG	PP48	HGS48	Score	Rbdg	Play	Cont	Def	M/GP	2:3	3Gain	Draw	Hands	OR/DR	Gun
Barkley,Charles	PHI	79	79	3088	0.579	0.219	0.635	0.753	25.8	31.7	35.0	0.604	9.86	0.27	3.85	7.52	39.09	6.55	-98.05	3.06	0.74	0.69	3.33
Malone,Karl	UTA	80	80	3126	0.519	0.313	0.521	0.766	29.1	35.7	32.8	0.574	7.94	0.14	2.07	7.85	39.08	96.44	-1.67	3.21	0.75	0.44	-2.92
Mullin,Chris	GS	82	82	3093	0.509	0.230	0.527	0.892	26.5	33.8	29.1	0.556	4.57	0.25	5.47	5.90	37.72	15.30	-36.49	3.11	1.21	0.46	-4.64
Nance,Larry	CLE	73	72	2526	0.539	0.000	0.541	0.799	17.2	23.9	29.1	0.578	6.27	0.17	2.33	9.04	34.60	229.00	-4.33	1.80	1.41	0.37	3.87
Chambers,Tom	PHO	81	81	3002	0.471	0.326	0.479	0.851	25.7	33.3	26.8	0.525	4.16	0.14	2.13	6.60	37.06	18.10	1.59	2.21	0.52	0.26	-6.58
Harper,Ron	CLE	82	82	2851	0.511	0.250	0.540	0.751	18.6	25.7	26.8	0.537	6.62	0.38	7.32	6.78	34.77	8.91	-38.32	1.92	1.16	0.43	1.13
McHale,Kevin	BOS	78	74	2876	0.546	0.000	0.548	0.818	22.5	29.3	26.8	0.594	7.20	0.14	0.69	5.51	36.87	241.20	-5.48	2.39	0.55	0.54	-2.55
Cummings,Terry	MIL	80	78	2824	0.467	0.467	0.467	0.787	22.9	31.1	26.3	0.508	5.86	0.13	2.43	6.11	35.30	103.20	6.99	1.74	0.66	0.76	-4.79
Wilkins,Dominique	ATL	80	80	2997	0.464	0.276	0.475	0.844	26.2	33.6	26.2	0.507		0.12	2.93	5.09	37.46	15.72	-12.85	3.80	1.22	0.86	-7.38
Cooper,Wayne	DEN	79	72	1865	0.495	0.250	0.498	0.745	6.6	13.4	25.4	0.521	9.88	0.18	1.43	11.59	23.61	110.00	-0.98	0.35	0.82	0.52	12.03
English,Alex	DEN	82	82	2990	0.491	0.250	0.492	0.858	26.5	34.9	25.1	0.524	3.45	0.20	4.67	2.68	36.46	234.13	-1.88	2.18	0.45	0.83	-9.77
Kersey,Jerome	POR	76	76	2716	0.469	0.286	0.472	0.694	17.5	23.5	24.8	0.499	7.08	0.21	4.35	7.27	35.74	53.14	-1.83	1.34	0.79	0.64	1.33
Worthy,James	LAL	81	81	2960	0.548	0.087	0.556	0.782	20.5	26.9	24.6	0.570	4.92	0.22	4.06	5.25	36.54	54.74	-19.58	1.83	0.94	0.53	-2.25
Tisdale,Wayman	SAC	79	35	2434	0.514	0.000	0.516	0.773	17.5	27.2	24.6	0.556	7.30	0.12	0.90	6.27	30.81	258.00	-4.12	1.41	0.37	0.44	-2.63
Smith,Charles	LAC	71	56	2161	0.496	0.000	0.498	0.725	16.3	25.7	24.4	0.537	6.51	0.12	1.20	6.73	30.44	291.33	-2.99	1.44	0.58	0.59	-1.21
Anderson,Willie	SAN	81	79	2738	0.498	0.190	0.503	0.775	18.6	26.4	24.4	0.524	4.59	0.29	5.49	5.99	33.80	60.19	-9.13	0.98	0.71	0.57	-2.06
Green,A.C.	LAL	82	82	2510	0.529	0.235	0.536	0.786	13.3	20.8	24.3	0.575	8.79	0.14	1.98	7.45	30.61	43.59	-6.22	2.10	0.87	0.54	3.47
Rambis,Kurt	CHA	75	75	2233	0.518	0.000	0.521	0.734	11.1	17.9	24.1	0.553	9.58	0.25	3.02	8.04	29.77	208.00	-3.13	1.19	0.75	0.62	6.23
Tripucka,Kelly	CHA	71	65	2302	0.467	0.357	0.476	0.866	22.6	33.5	24.1	0.531	3.36	0.18	2.57	4.13	32.42	13.46	10.08	2.59	0.53	0.42	-9.43
King,Bernard	WAS	81	81	2559	0.478	0.167	0.485	0.819	20.7	31.4	24.0	0.522	4.47	0.21	3.35	3.78	31.59	44.63	-14.08	2.01	0.35	0.53	-7.36
Lewis,Reggie	BOS	81	57	2657	0.486	0.136	0.493	0.787	18.5	27.0	23.6	0.521	4.14	0.18	4.13	5.88	32.80	55.45	-12.68	1.40	0.76	0.44	-3.46
Thompson,LaSalle	IND	76	71	2329	0.489	0.000	0.490	0.808	13.9	23.4	23.4	0.534	9.01	0.10	0.35	8.66	30.64	849.00	-0.98	0.99	0.61	0.45	1.56
Anderson,Greg	SAN	82	56	2401	0.503	0.000	0.505	0.514	13.7	22.5	23.3	0.504	8.54	0.07	0.33	8.29	29.28	303.67	-3.03	1.82	0.92	0.61	0.76
Norman,Ken	LAC	80	79	3020	0.502	0.190	0.507	0.630	18.1	23.0	22.4	0.512	6.66	0.22	3.47	6.07	37.75	59.52	-9.30	1.21	0.77	0.58	-0.61
Dantley,Adrian	DAL	73	67	2422	0.493	0.000	0.493	0.810	19.2	27.7	22.4	0.565	3.95	0.18	1.66	3.09	33.18	953.00	-0.99	3.05	0.30	0.59	-5.37
Oakley,Charles	NY	82	82	2604	0.510	0.000	0.526	0.773	12.9	19.6	22.3	0.538	10.15	0.22	1.71	6.95	31.76	16.40	-14.50	0.94	0.44	0.66	2.76
Gilliam,Armon	PHO	74	60	2120	0.503	----	0.503	0.743	15.9	26.6	22.1	0.539	7.43	0.06	-0.16	6.07	28.65	---	-14.50	1.84	0.45	0.44	-4.50
Thorpe,Otis	HOU	82	82	3135	0.542	0.000	0.543	0.729	16.7	21.0	22.0	0.577	7.48	0.21	1.62	5.80	38.23	479.50	-2.17	1.74	0.47	0.53	1.07
Pippen,Scottie	CHI	73	56	2413	0.476	0.273	0.496	0.668	14.4	20.8	21.8	0.496	5.39	0.30	4.69	6.99	33.05	10.26	-13.42	1.15	0.76	0.45	0.95
Thompson,Bill	MIA	79	58	2272	0.487	0.000	0.489	0.696	10.8	18.0	21.6	0.515	7.82	0.25	1.71	6.90	28.76	237.67	-2.94	0.86	0.62	0.73	3.56
Long,Grant	MIA	82	73	2431	0.486	0.000	0.489	0.751	11.9	19.3	21.6	0.544	7.05	0.22	2.18	6.38	29.65	137.40	-4.89	1.20	0.50	0.78	2.35
McKey,Derrick	SEA	82	82	2804	0.502	0.337	0.519	0.803	15.9	22.3	21.5	0.543	4.97	0.23	2.97	5.54	34.20	9.90	-2.33	1.42	0.66	0.56	-0.86
Cage,Michael	SEA	80	71	2536	0.498	0.000	0.502	0.743	10.3	15.6	21.2	0.540	9.07	0.20	2.25	7.35	31.70	156.50	-4.01	1.44	0.78	0.56	5.54
Aguirre,Mark	DET	80	76	2597	0.464	0.293	0.488	0.733	18.9	27.9	21.2	0.486	4.51	0.22	2.89	3.72	32.46	6.30	-16.87	1.72	0.35	0.61	-6.69
Perkins,Sam	DAL	78	77	2860	0.464	0.184	0.476	0.833	15.0	19.7	20.7	0.512	7.14	0.13	1.57	6.65	36.67	24.24	-15.14	1.47	0.75	0.51	1.09
Williams,Buck	NJ	74	72	2446	0.531	0.000	0.534	0.666	13.0	18.8	20.6	0.555	8.54	0.11	0.50	6.29	33.05	233.00	-3.20	1.43	0.43	0.56	1.76
Morris,Chris	NJ	76	48	2096	0.457	0.366	0.479	0.717	14.1	24.6	20.3	0.480	6.05	0.13	1.58	6.10	27.58	4.17	24.19	1.02	0.65	0.90	-4.34
Smith,Larry	GS	80	78	1897	0.552	----	0.552	0.310	5.7	11.5	20.2	0.535	10.66	0.30	2.18	7.67	23.71	---	0.00	0.23	0.46	0.72	8.65
Person,Chuck	IND	80	79	3012	0.489	0.307	0.519	0.792	21.6	27.5	20.0	0.506	4.91	0.20	2.00	4.57	37.65	6.09	-23.88	1.08	0.35	0.39	-7.58
Krystkowiak,Larry	MIL	80	77	2472	0.473	0.333	0.475	0.823	12.7	19.7	19.9	0.537	7.27	0.14	1.62	5.98	30.90	62.83	0.60	1.60	0.47	0.48	0.13
Levingston,Cliff	ATL	80	52	2184	0.528	0.200	0.531	0.696	9.2	16.1	19.7	0.551	6.96	0.13	1.95	7.03	27.30	112.60	-2.31	0.71	0.62	0.64	3.59
Grant,Horace	CHI	79	79	2809	0.519	0.000	0.522	0.704	12.0	16.2	19.6	0.538	7.25	0.22	2.59	6.31	35.56	155.20	-5.22	0.79	0.59	0.54	3.34
Catledge,Terry	WAS	79	79	2077	0.490	0.200	0.493	0.602	10.4	19.0	19.5	0.507	8.47	0.11	0.58	5.66	26.29	135.20	-1.93	1.02	0.30	0.67	0.49
Newman,Johnny	NY	81	80	2336	0.475	0.338	0.534	0.815	16.0	26.6	19.4	0.507	2.79	0.17	3.13	3.91	28.84	2.33	-15.70	1.36	0.52	0.82	-7.22
McCray,Rodney	SAC	68	65	2435	0.466	0.227	0.474	0.722	12.6	16.8	19.4	0.498	6.05	0.40	4.25	5.47	35.81	32.14	-5.85	1.95	0.77	0.39	2.55
Mahorn,Rick	DET	72	61	1795	0.517	0.000	0.519	0.748	7.3	14.0	18.6	0.554	7.95	0.15	0.57	7.58	24.93	195.50	-2.08	0.75	0.51	0.40	4.69
Smith,Derek	PHI	65	38	1295	0.435	0.226	0.449	0.686	8.7	21.1	18.6	0.469	3.89	0.26	3.73	4.41	19.92	15.00	-6.87	1.15	0.40	0.58	-2.48
Johnson,Buck	HOU	68	51	1860	0.528	0.111	0.535	0.754	9.6	16.8	17.4	0.550	4.74	0.25	2.70	4.77	27.35	56.67	-6.64	0.63	0.46	0.67	0.61
Sanders,Mike	CLE	82	82	2102	0.453	0.300	0.455	0.719	9.3	17.4	15.8	0.474	4.30	0.18	3.17	5.14	25.63	72.30	-0.10	0.59	0.53	0.48	-1.62
Jones,Caldwell	POR	72	40	1279	0.421	0.000	0.423	0.787	2.8	7.6	15.3	0.472	6.79	0.32	0.62	8.07	17.76	182.00	-0.85	0.37	0.66	0.42	7.75
Iavaroni,Marc	UTA	77	50	796	0.442	0.000	0.444	0.818	2.3	10.9	11.0	0.485	4.85	0.20	0.08	4.19	10.34	162.00	-0.89	0.44	0.24	0.45	0.13
Average Forward		**78**	**70**	**2458**	**0.497**	**0.280**	**0.506**	**0.765**	**15.8**	**24.0**	**23.2**	**0.533**	**6.53**	**0.19**	**2.58**	**6.19**	**31.57**	**22.51**	**-7.06**	**1.49**	**0.63**	**0.55**	**-0.80**

Guards	Team	GP	GS	MIN	FG%	3G%	2G%	FT%	PPG	PP48	HGS48	Score	Rbdg	Play	Cont	Def	M/GP	2:3	3Gain	Draw	Hands	OR/DR	Gun
Jordan,Michael	CHI	81	81	3255	0.538	0.265	0.554	0.850	32.5	38.8	39.1	0.587	5.58	0.36	9.61	8.10	40.19	17.32	-30.57	3.21	1.21	0.30	0.25
Johnson,Earvin	LAL	77	77	2886	0.509	0.314	0.548	0.911	22.5	28.8	37.3	0.572	5.69	0.87	14.67	6.79	37.48	5.05	-29.03	3.27	0.93	0.22	8.55
Stockton,John	UTA	82	82	3171	0.538	0.242	0.561	0.863	17.1	21.2	32.3	0.592	2.32	1.21	17.13	5.40	38.67	12.98	-26.09	1.88	1.14	0.50	11.12
Drexler,Clyde	POR	78	78	3066	0.496	0.255	0.512	0.799	27.2	33.2	31.9	0.531	6.40	0.27	7.25	6.72	39.31	14.77	-27.57	2.04	0.99	0.89	-1.32
Johnson,Kevin	PHO	81	81	3179	0.505	0.091	0.514	0.882	20.4	24.9	31.1	0.578	2.81	0.88	13.11	4.62	39.25	50.27	-16.60	2.56	0.70	0.16	6.18
Lever,Lafayette	DEN	71	71	2745	0.457	0.348	0.463	0.785	19.8	24.6	29.8	0.494	6.93	0.46	10.97	7.91	38.66	17.50	7.86	1.93	1.21	0.39	5.18
Robertson,Alvin	SAN	65	65	2287	0.483	0.196	0.498	0.723	17.3	23.5	26.0	0.505	5.19	0.41	8.55	7.26	35.18	19.91	-18.80	0.98	0.90	0.70	2.50
Rivers,Glenn	ATL	76	76	2462	0.455	0.347	0.474	0.861	13.6	20.1	25.5	0.505	3.40	0.64	11.30	6.21	32.39	5.58	11.45	1.09	0.84	0.45	5.38
Jackson,Mark	NY	72	72	2477	0.467	0.338	0.507	0.698	16.9	23.6	25.5	0.478	4.02	0.60	11.19	5.11	34.40	3.27	-0.36	1.58	0.90	0.45	1.91
Price,Mark	CLE	75	74	2728	0.526	0.441	0.548	0.901	18.9	24.9	25.2	0.562	2.28	0.63	10.14	3.71	36.37	3.77	47.56	2.98	1.24	0.27	0.34
McMillan,Nate	SEA	75	74	2341	0.410	0.214	0.443	0.633	7.1	10.9	24.9	0.433	5.00	1.44	14.01	6.57	31.21	5.93	-17.07	0.80	0.84	0.58	13.94
Porter,Terry	POR	81	81	3102	0.471	0.361	0.497	0.840	17.7	22.1	24.9	0.505	3.30	0.67	11.10	4.56	38.30	4.23	19.18	1.73	0.82	0.30	2.71
Richmond,Mitch	GS	79	79	2717	0.468	0.367	0.475	0.810	22.0	30.8	24.4	0.517	5.11	0.24	3.53	4.42	34.39	14.40	13.44	2.30	0.43	0.51	-6.31
Conner,Lester	NJ	82	63	2532	0.457	0.351	0.463	0.788	10.3	16.0	24.3	0.508	4.03	0.89	12.13	5.92	30.88	17.27	4.72	2.04	1.40	0.52	8.36
Grant,Gary	LAC	71	48	1924	0.435	0.227	0.441	0.735	11.9	21.1	23.6	0.459	3.68	0.61	11.07	5.78	27.10	36.73	-4.39	0.95	0.90	0.52	2.51
Thomas,Isiah	DET	80	76	2924	0.464	0.273	0.485	0.818	18.2	23.9	23.5	0.498	2.52	0.54	9.18	4.35	36.55	9.14	-18.28	1.68	0.73	0.22	-0.47
Teagle,Terry	GS	66	41	1569	0.476	0.167	0.481	0.809	15.2	30.7	23.3	0.513	5.20	0.11	2.56	5.28	23.77	70.58	-5.53	1.30	0.55	0.72	-7.34
Pressey,Paul	MIL	67	62	2170	0.474	0.218	0.497	0.776	12.2	18.0	23.0	0.512	3.46	0.68	9.09	5.70	32.39	10.78	-18.72	1.09	0.74	0.39	5.00
Cheeks,Maurice	PHI	71	70	2298	0.483	0.077	0.490	0.774	11.6	17.2	22.8	0.515	2.20	0.78	11.66	4.05	32.37	52.54	-9.75	1.71	1.07	0.27	5.61
Fleming,Vern	IND	76	69	2552	0.515	0.130	0.526	0.799	14.3	20.4	22.8	0.554	3.47	0.61	7.85	3.79	33.58	34.39	-15.19	1.43	0.42	0.38	2.40
Floyd,Eric	HOU	82	82	2789	0.443	0.373	0.478	0.845	14.2	20.0	22.8	0.487	2.92	0.79	10.78	4.54	34.01	2.06	48.12	1.58	0.69	0.19	2.85
Dailey,Quintin	LAC	69	51	1722	0.465	0.111	0.468	0.759	16.1	31.1	22.8	0.501	3.54	0.16	4.08	4.59	24.96	106.11	-5.43	1.88	0.63	0.50	-8.29
Hornacek,Jeff	PHO	78	73	2487	0.495	0.333	0.511	0.826	13.5	20.3	22.6	0.517	3.07	0.52	9.80	4.51	31.88	9.98	-1.80	0.95	0.73	0.39	2.27
Harper,Derek	DAL	81	81	2968	0.477	0.356	0.517	0.806	17.3	22.7	22.5	0.499	2.10	0.51	9.35	4.92	36.64	3.05	9.50	1.30	0.97	0.25	-0.16
Adams,Michael	DEN	77	77	2787	0.433	0.357	0.489	0.819	18.5	24.5	22.4	0.471	2.87	0.45	8.82	4.87	36.19	1.33	42.80	2.64	1.19	0.33	-2.09
Garland,Winston	GS	79	79	2661	0.434	0.233	0.442	0.809	14.5	20.7	22.3	0.469	3.60	0.47	9.55	5.44	33.68	23.98	-8.04	1.16	0.87	0.44	1.67
Theus,Reggie	ATL	82	82	2517	0.466	0.288	0.476	0.851	15.8	24.7	22.0	0.513	2.88	0.36	6.48	3.85	32.56	17.08	-5.19	1.42	0.53	0.55	-2.74
Ainge,Danny	SAC	73	54	2377	0.457	0.380	0.488	0.854	17.5	25.9	21.7	0.484	3.08	0.38	7.65	3.90	32.56	2.45	50.36	1.29	0.54	0.39	-4.12
Ellis,Dale	SEA	82	82	3190	0.501	0.478	0.507	0.816	27.5	33.9	21.4	0.534	3.39	0.10	1.47	3.36	38.90	4.04	142.30	2.35	0.66	0.84	-12.55
Walker,Darrell	WAS	79	78	2565	0.420	0.000	0.426	0.763	9.0	13.4	21.4	0.459	5.63	0.73	9.44	6.81	32.47	74.67	-7.66	0.86	0.82	0.36	8.02
Moncrief,Sidney	MIL	62	50	1594	0.491	0.342	0.514	0.865	12.1	22.6	21.3	0.547	3.07	0.35	5.40	4.22	25.71	6.29	-0.07	2.08	0.68	0.37	-1.38
Malone,Jeff	WAS	76	75	2418	0.480	0.053	0.486	0.871	21.7	32.8	21.0	0.519	2.16	0.16	2.49	2.28	31.82	73.21	-15.47	2.19	0.34	0.50	-11.78
Dumars,Joe	DET	69	67	2409	0.505	0.483	0.506	0.850	17.2	23.6	21.0	0.554	2.11	0.43	6.19	2.50	34.91	30.14	12.67	2.97	0.66	0.50	-2.64
Holton,Michael	CHA	67	60	1696	0.427	0.214	0.433	0.839	8.3	15.7	20.4	0.475	1.78	0.84	11.17	3.27	25.31	35.00	-3.11	0.87	0.47	0.40	4.79
Humphries,Jay	MIL	73	50	2220	0.483	0.266	0.516	0.816	11.6	18.2	20.3	0.502	2.57	0.57	9.09	4.46	30.41	6.60	-22.03	0.84	0.79	0.59	2.02
Smith,Kenny	SAC	81	81	3145	0.462	0.359	0.475	0.737	17.3	21.4	20.0	0.492	1.99	0.52	7.99	3.01	38.83	8.24	16.43	2.06	0.63	0.28	-1.40
Vincent,Sam	CHI	70	56	1703	0.484	0.118	0.495	0.822	9.4	18.5	20.0	0.513	3.04	0.59	7.73	3.97	24.33	32.29	-10.85	1.04	0.51	0.22	1.54
Shaw,Brian	BOS	82	54	2301	0.433	0.000	0.441	0.826	8.6	14.7	20.0	0.463	4.79	0.69	8.35	4.87	28.06	51.77	-11.47	0.63	0.46	0.45	5.35
Scott,Byron	LAL	74	73	2605	0.491	0.399	0.508	0.863	19.6	26.7	19.9	0.514	3.25	0.19	3.99	4.66	35.20	5.21	34.74	1.25	0.76	0.31	-6.73
Blackman,Rolando	DAL	78	78	2946	0.476	0.353	0.485	0.854	19.7	25.0	19.0	0.519	2.62	0.23	3.61	3.04	37.77	13.69	7.63	2.70	0.62	0.34	-6.01
Miller,Reggie	IND	74	70	2536	0.479	0.402	0.511	0.844	16.0	22.4	19.0	0.526	3.25	0.27	3.89	4.38	34.27	2.41	44.60	2.00	0.72	0.33	-3.39
Johnson,Dennis	BOS	72	72	2309	0.434	0.140	0.459	0.821	10.0	15.0	18.6	0.474	2.20	0.74	8.86	4.04	32.07	11.76	-24.92	0.92	0.55	0.19	3.56
Wilkins,Gerald	NY	81	58	2414	0.452	0.297	0.483	0.756	14.3	23.1	18.6	0.471	3.09	0.27	5.05	4.21	29.80	4.95	-13.14	1.48	0.83	0.64	-4.47
Edwards,Kevin	MIA	79	62	2349	0.425	0.270	0.431	0.746	13.8	22.4	18.6	0.448	3.28	0.32	5.98	5.16	29.73	28.86	-1.87	1.25	0.48	0.32	-3.74
Maxwell,Vernon	SAN	79	36	2065	0.432	0.248	0.466	0.745	11.7	21.5	18.0	0.458	2.75	0.36	5.74	3.96	26.14	5.41	-24.13	1.79	1.06	0.32	-3.53
Hawkins,Hersey	PHI	79	79	2572	0.455	0.428	0.461	0.831	15.1	22.3	17.9	0.499	2.43	0.25	4.34	4.55	32.56	4.85	59.99	1.58	0.69	0.29	-4.46
Reid,Robert	CHA	82	54	2152	0.428	0.327	0.432	0.776	14.7	26.9	17.6	0.451	4.01	0.13	2.70	4.08	26.24	22.35	6.07	0.83	0.85	0.37	-9.29
Sparrow,Rory	MIA	80	79	2613	0.452	0.243	0.469	0.879	12.5	18.4	16.8	0.466	2.34	0.44	6.84	3.70	32.66	12.27	-15.44	0.64	0.72	0.34	-1.54
Woodson,Mike	HOU	81	79	2259	0.438	0.348	0.447	0.823	12.9	22.2	16.6	0.476	2.44	0.22	3.97	3.79	27.89	9.52	13.35	1.22	0.55	0.36	-5.64
Chapman,Rex	CHA	75	44	2219	0.414	0.314	0.431	0.795	16.9	27.4	16.3	0.433	2.58	0.14	3.39	3.30	29.59	5.65	15.17	1.17	0.55	0.65	-11.07
Griffith,Darrell	UTA	82	73	2382	0.446	0.311	0.477	0.780	13.8	22.9	15.6	0.460	3.87	0.12	2.08	4.73	29.05	4.33	-4.00	1.04	0.62	0.30	-7.30
McGee,Mike	NJ	80	49	2027	0.473	0.365	0.515	0.535	13.0	24.6	14.9	0.465	2.84	0.13	2.29	3.55	25.34	2.60	16.30	0.78	0.50	0.63	-9.70
Average Guard		**76**	**68**	**2488**	**0.470**	**0.341**	**0.487**	**0.815**	**15.9**	**23.3**	**23.0**	**0.505**	**3.44**	**0.45**	**7.96**	**4.75**	**32.64**	**7.57**	**5.66**	**1.56**	**0.76**	**0.40**	**-0.33**

Reserves	Team	GP	GS	MIN	FG%	3G%	2G%	FT%	PPG	PP48	HGS48	Score	Rbdg	Play	Cont	Def	M/GP	2:3	3Gain	Draw	Hands	OR/DR	Gun
Strickland,Rod	NY	81	10	1358	0.467	0.322	0.484	0.745	8.9	25.5	27.0	0.506	3.46	0.56	10.58	5.50	16.77	8.61	-0.14	1.63	0.71	0.47	1.49
Williams,John	WAS	82	1	2413	0.466	0.268	0.482	0.781	13.7	22.3	26.8	0.500	6.80	0.38	7.41	8.32	29.43	12.24	-11.47	1.35	0.99	0.38	4.53
Williams,John	CLE	82	10	2125	0.509	0.250	0.510	0.748	11.6	21.5	25.2	0.552	6.77	0.15	2.34	8.18	25.91	174.00	-1.08	1.67	1.12	0.58	3.83
Bogues,Tyrone	CHA	79	21	1755	0.426	0.077	0.437	0.750	5.4	11.6	25.0	0.451	2.76	1.48	17.25	4.73	22.22	31.15	-8.36	0.62	0.83	0.47	13.40
Pinckney,Ed	BOS	80	33	2012	0.513	0.000	0.518	0.800	11.5	21.9	24.5	0.574	6.74	0.19	2.52	6.93	25.15	31.15	-6.21	1.73	0.74	0.59	2.57
McDaniel,Xavier	SEA	82	10	2385	0.489	0.306	0.494	0.732	20.5	33.8	24.5	0.519	5.60	0.10	1.01	5.07	29.09	37.47	-2.55	1.84	0.54	0.69	-9.21
Johnson,Eddie	PHO	70	7	2043	0.496	0.413	0.509	0.867	21.5	35.4	23.5	0.523	4.34	0.13	2.62	3.79	29.19	6.13	37.74	1.24	0.27	0.42	-11.76
Rodman,Dennis	DET	82	8	2207	0.595	0.240	0.613	0.626	9.0	16.1	23.3	0.592	10.88	0.19	1.16	7.69	26.91	20.24	-12.63	0.53	0.45	0.73	7.30
Pierce,Ricky	MIL	75	4	2078	0.518	0.222	0.529	0.859	17.6	30.5	23.0	0.556	2.94	0.15	3.39	3.52	27.71	27.28	-14.05	1.54	0.49	0.71	-7.39
Threatt,Sedale	SEA	63	0	1220	0.494	0.367	0.502	0.818	8.6	21.3	22.9	0.514	2.73	0.50	10.21	5.11	19.37	14.87	-2.87	0.50	0.56	0.36	1.49
Smith,Otis	GS	80	5	1597	0.435	0.194	0.448	0.798	10.0	24.0	22.5	0.477	6.31	0.20	3.58	6.88	19.96	18.86	-11.24	1.32	0.78	0.63	-1.53
Schrempf,Detlef	IND	69	13	1850	0.474	0.200	0.492	0.780	12.0	21.5	22.2	0.537	6.27	0.31	3.26	5.36	26.81	15.51	-13.42	1.59	0.33	0.47	-1.04
Johnson,Steve	POR	72	11	1477	0.524	---	0.524	0.527	10.0	23.4	22.2	0.524	7.35	0.19	0.42	5.70	20.51	225.50	0.00	0.96	0.25	0.61	-1.24
Corbin,Tyrone	PHO	77	30	1655	0.541	0.290	0.543	0.788	8.2	18.3	22.1	0.580	7.56	0.26	3.67	5.97	21.49	14.59	-2.17	0.81	0.43	0.79	3.87
Davis,Walter	DEN	81	0	1857	0.498	0.220	0.512	0.879	15.6	32.7	21.9	0.524	2.32	0.18	4.04	3.41	22.93	2.78	-10.71	1.06	0.41	0.37	-10.66
Bol,Manute	GS	80	4	1769	0.369	0.000	0.423	0.606	3.9	8.5	21.8	0.372	7.37	0.08	-0.75	14.19	22.11	511.00	-16.97	0.29	1.55	0.34	13.36
Hinson,Roy	NJ	82	39	2542	0.483	0.000	0.484	0.757	16.0	24.8	21.8	0.530	5.93	0.07	-0.49	6.44	31.00	493.00	-1.94	1.41	0.52	0.41	-2.94
Woolridge,Orlando	LAL	74	0	1491	0.468	0.000	0.469	0.738	9.7	23.1	21.7	0.537	5.26	0.12	0.18	6.10	20.15	17.30	-0.94	2.64	0.73	0.43	-1.17
Eackles,Ledel	WAS	80	6	1459	0.434	0.225	0.447	0.786	11.5	30.3	21.7	0.496	4.11	0.17	2.03	2.80	18.24	21.64	-8.72	2.22	0.29	1.25	-8.42
Johnson,Vinnie	DET	82	21	2073	0.464	0.295	0.472	0.734	13.8	26.2	21.4	0.492	3.84	0.24	5.33	3.75	25.28	253.40	-2.50	1.70	0.57	0.75	-4.43
Bailey,Thurl	UTA	82	3	2777	0.483	0.400	0.484	0.825	19.5	27.6	21.3	0.534	4.56	0.11	0.34	5.27	33.87	17.28	1.16	2.38	0.75	0.35	-6.13
Greenwood,David	SAN	67	18	1403	0.423	---	0.423	0.750	7.0	16.0	21.3	0.482	8.55	0.24	2.43	7.87	20.94	139.67	0.00	0.88	0.49	0.53	5.36
Colter,Steve	WAS	80	5	1425	0.444	0.120	0.463	0.749	6.7	18.1	21.2	0.483	3.80	0.49	8.18	4.82	17.81	2.77	-14.15	1.06	0.53	0.52	3.30
Green,Sidney	NY	82	0	1277	0.460	0.000	0.463	0.759	6.3	19.4	21.2	0.508	9.47	0.18	0.86	6.90	15.57	26.29	-2.78	0.99	0.38	0.66	1.76
Higgins,Rod	GS	81	1	1887	0.476	0.393	0.505	0.821	10.6	21.8	21.1	0.515	5.77	0.25	3.47	5.38	23.30	88.67	28.19	1.33	0.46	0.42	-0.67
Washington,Dwayne	MIA	54	8	1070	0.429	0.071	0.443	0.788	7.6	18.4	20.9	0.466	3.53	0.59	9.03	5.11	19.81	169.50	-9.40	1.03	0.76	0.66	2.49
Koncak,Jon	ATL	74	22	1531	0.524	0.000	0.530	0.553	4.7	10.9	20.7	0.527	8.71	0.21	1.94	9.56	20.69	132.33	-3.18	0.48	0.64	0.48	9.90
Comegys,Dallas	SAN	67	10	1119	0.487	0.048	0.490	0.658	6.5	18.7	20.7	0.518	6.66	0.09	0.21	7.16	16.70	249.50	-1.96	1.01	0.66	0.91	1.94
Dawkins,Johnny	SAN	32	30	1083	0.443	0.000	0.446	0.893	14.2	20.1	20.6	0.496	2.73	0.56	8.43	3.97	33.84	165.50	-2.68	1.75	0.86	0.46	0.53
Berry,Walter	HOU	69	31	1355	0.507	0.000	0.507	0.699	8.8	21.5	20.3	0.531	5.80	0.15	1.23	5.93	19.64	4.89	0.97	0.78	0.42	0.48	-1.28
Salley,John	DET	67	21	1458	0.498	0.500	0.502	0.692	7.0	15.4	20.3	0.541	7.06	0.23	1.15	7.00	21.76	12.81	-2.01	0.99	0.57	0.67	4.95
Skiles,Scott	IND	80	13	1571	0.448	0.000	0.485	0.903	6.8	16.6	20.1	0.495	2.50	0.88	9.55	3.97	19.64	469.00	-12.75	0.95	0.44	0.16	3.42
Webb,Spud	ATL	81	6	1219	0.459	0.267	0.491	0.867	3.9	12.4	20.0	0.483	2.71	0.98	11.32	5.00	15.05	1.96	-17.61	0.58	0.73	0.21	7.48
Thompson,Mychal	LAL	80	8	1994	0.559	0.000	0.560	0.678	9.2	17.7	19.9	0.580	6.94	0.09	0.68	6.55	24.93	175.50	-1.12	1.03	0.52	0.51	2.09
Carr,Antoine	ATL	78	12	1488	0.481	0.403	0.482	0.855	7.5	18.9	19.8	0.532	5.62	0.19	1.82	5.71	19.08	25.44	-0.96	0.69	0.42	0.63	1.14
Pressley,Harold	SAC	80	25	2257	0.439	0.500	0.457	0.780	12.3	20.9	19.4	0.453	6.77	0.20	3.55	6.43	28.21	4.24	87.52	0.57	0.78	0.80	-1.10
Hoppen,Dave	CHA	77	2	1419	0.564	0.148	0.564	0.727	6.5	16.9	19.3	0.590	7.95	0.16	0.69	5.97	18.43	17.94	0.74	0.58	0.19	0.47	2.44
Hopson,Dennis	NJ	62	36	1551	0.419	0.390	0.429	0.849	12.7	24.4	19.2	0.471	4.11	0.14	2.86	4.84	25.02	98.50	-11.19	1.46	0.67	0.82	-5.11
Ehlo,Craig	CLE	82	4	1867	0.475	0.250	0.495	0.607	7.4	15.6	19.2	0.481	4.69	0.51	7.28	5.82	22.77	10.34	17.94	0.73	0.80	0.51	3.57
Gray,Sylvester	MIA	55	15	1220	0.420	0.250	0.421	0.673	8.0	17.3	19.2	0.460	7.24	0.29	2.81	5.69	22.18	334.00	-0.37	1.08	0.42	0.69	1.93
Alarie,Mark	WAS	74	5	1141	0.478	0.342	0.491	0.839	6.7	20.9	19.1	0.505	6.88	0.15	1.62	5.09	15.42	103.73	1.68	0.54	0.28	0.68	-1.75
Kempton,Tim	CHA	79	0	1341	0.510	0.000	0.512	0.686	6.1	17.3	19.1	0.551	6.58	0.30	1.65	5.78	16.97	43.18	-1.02	0.96	0.26	0.43	1.74
Anderson,Ron	PHI	82	12	2623	0.491	0.182	0.494	0.856	16.2	24.3	19.0	0.523	4.78	0.12	2.06	3.91	31.99	16.80	-4.87	1.38	0.57	0.70	-5.25
Lohaus,Brad	SAC	77	25	1214	0.432	0.091	0.440	0.786	6.5	19.8	19.0	0.462	6.22	0.14	1.36	6.80	15.77	—	-6.68	0.64	0.53	0.49	-0.89
Rasmussen,Blair	DEN	77	22	1308	0.445	---	0.445	0.852	7.6	21.4	18.9	0.472	6.61	0.09	1.46	5.91	16.99	—	0.00	0.42	0.36	0.58	-2.52
Walker,Kenny	NY	79	2	1163	0.489	0.250	0.503	0.776	5.3	17.3	18.8	0.513	6.21	0.10	1.76	6.21	14.72	—	-5.12	0.45	0.46	0.78	1.54
Edwards,James	DET	76	1	1254	0.500	0.000	0.502	0.686	7.3	21.2	18.7	0.534	5.33	0.12	0.17	4.80	16.50	210.00	-2.01	0.86	0.19	0.42	-2.53
Brooks,Scott	PHI	82	6	1367	0.420	0.359	0.463	0.884	5.2	15.0	18.7	0.444	1.88	0.82	11.34	3.84	16.67	1.42	23.23	0.59	0.62	0.25	3.63
Del Negro,Vinnie	SAC	80	2	1556	0.475	0.300	0.482	0.850	7.1	17.5	18.6	0.505	3.16	0.41	6.76	4.33	19.45	24.15	-1.30	0.63	0.49	0.39	1.02
Davis,Brad	DAL	78	4	1395	0.483	0.317	0.543	0.805	6.4	17.2	18.5	0.506	2.03	0.64	7.42	3.89	17.88	2.75	-13.72	0.81	0.44	0.15	1.39
Williams,Reggie	LAC	63	17	1303	0.438	0.288	0.469	0.754	10.2	23.7	18.5	0.454	4.20	0.17	3.42	6.06	20.68	4.71	-7.63	0.67	0.60	0.64	-5.12
Battle,John	ATL	82	0	1672	0.457	0.324	0.465	0.815	9.5	22.4	18.4	0.510	2.31	0.31	4.47	3.04	20.39	17.47	1.40	1.90	0.41	0.27	-3.99
Bagley,John	NJ	68	20	1642	0.416	0.204	0.443	0.724	7.4	14.7	18.4	0.439	2.47	0.31	9.87	3.89	24.15	7.91	-14.80	1.05	0.68	0.33	3.79
Garrick,Tom	LAC	71	20	1499	0.490	0.000	0.509	0.803	6.4	14.6	18.3	0.529	2.91	0.81	7.31	4.69	21.11	26.62	-13.23	0.90	0.62	0.31	3.73
Cummings,Pat	MIA	53	28	1096	0.500	0.000	0.503	0.742	8.8	20.4	18.0	0.525	7.44	0.12	-0.56	6.37	20.68	196.00	-2.01	0.61	0.29	0.43	-2.37
Valentine,Darnell	CLE	77	4	1086	0.426	0.214	0.436	0.813	4.8	16.3	17.9	0.479	2.62	0.55	7.28	4.62	14.10	21.79	-3.21	1.27	0.73	0.27	1.73
Williams,Herb	DAL	76	66	2470	0.436	0.342	0.439	0.686	10.2	15.1	17.8	0.463	6.68	0.17	0.99	7.95	32.50	146.80	-4.39	0.82	0.76	0.29	2.70
Cook,Darwin	DEN	66	4	1143	0.456	0.195	0.481	0.808	7.7	21.3	17.6	0.472	2.75	0.27	5.36	4.93	17.32	10.66	-15.41	0.64	0.67	0.47	-3.69
Chievous,Derrick	HOU	81	1	1539	0.437	0.208	0.446	0.783	9.3	23.5	17.6	0.488	5.24	0.12	0.51	4.05	19.00	25.42	-6.40	1.52	0.37	0.80	-5.80

Reserves (Cont'd)	Team	GP	GS	MIN	FG%	3G%	2G%	FT%	PPG	PP48	HGS48	Score	Rbdg	Play	Cont	Def	M/GP	2:3	3Gain	Draw	Hands	OR/DR	Gun
Kleine,Joe	BOS	75	13	1411	.405	.000	.407	.882	6.5	16.5	17.2	.475	7.91	0.16	0.57	6.23	18.81	215.00	-1.63	0.79	0.29	0.49	0.76
Tyler,Terry	DAL	70	11	1057	.469	.111	.479	.758	5.5	17.5	17.1	.488	5.92	0.11	1.05	5.93	15.10	39.00	-5.62	0.69	0.70	0.55	-0.40
Berry,Ricky	SAC	64	21	1406	.450	.406	.467	.789	11.0	24.1	17.1	.484	4.04	0.14	1.75	4.40	21.97	2.54	45.61	0.84	0.30	0.41	-6.98
Majerle,Dan	PHO	54	5	1354	.419	.329	.440	.614	8.6	16.6	17.0	.435	4.47	0.30	5.45	5.34	25.07	4.27	8.84	0.91	0.55	0.42	0.48
Nixon,Norm	LAC	53	30	1318	.414	.276	.425	.738	6.8	13.2	17.0	.434	1.59	0.92	10.58	2.86	24.87	11.76	-0.66	0.94	0.67	0.20	3.79
Henderson,Gerald	PHI	65	0	986	.414	.308	.461	.819	6.5	20.7	17.0	.457	1.94	0.40	5.97	3.43	15.17	2.25	0.44	1.05	0.37	0.33	-3.65
Short,Purvis	HOU	65	16	1157	.413	.273	.423	.875	7.4	20.0	16.9	.446	4.66	0.22	3.82	4.61	17.80	13.55	-0.91	0.76	0.47	0.57	-3.09
Corzine,Dave	CHI	81	7	1483	.461	.250	.465	.740	5.9	15.5	16.8	.487	6.14	0.23	1.86	5.87	18.31	54.00	-1.44	0.72	0.52	0.41	1.25
Cooper,Michael	LAL	80	13	1943	.431	.381	.468	.871	7.3	14.5	16.7	.455	2.64	0.64	7.75	4.59	24.29	1.35	43.31	0.50	0.58	0.21	2.20
Wennington,Bill	DAL	65	9	1074	.433	.111	.444	.744	4.6	13.4	16.6	.468	7.72	0.17	0.70	6.77	16.52	29.56	-4.98	0.39	0.24	0.42	3.19
Hastings,Scott	MIA	75	6	1206	.436	.321	.447	.841	5.1	15.3	16.5	.487	5.60	0.18	1.46	6.07	16.08	10.71	1.99	0.53	0.36	0.45	1.15
Roberts,Fred	MIL	71	3	1251	.486	.214	.498	.806	5.9	16.0	16.2	.534	4.92	0.21	1.46	4.97	17.62	21.79	-4.95	1.02	0.47	0.48	0.16
Anderson,Richard	POR	72	3	1082	.417	.348	.464	.865	5.2	16.5	16.2	.424	6.09	0.28	4.38	6.23	15.03	1.47	16.22	0.37	0.56	0.37	-0.22
McCormick,Tim	HOU	81	0	1257	.481	.000	.487	.674	5.2	16.2	16.2	.509	6.15	0.15	0.64	4.89	15.52	86.75	-3.90	0.67	0.21	0.50	-0.02
Feitl,Dave	WAS	57	36	828	.436	.000	.438	.831	5.0	16.6	16.1	.478	7.26	0.14	0.06	5.88	14.53	265.00	-0.88	0.48	0.26	0.52	-0.48
Sellers,Brad	CHI	80	25	1732	.485	.500	.485	.851	6.9	15.3	16.0	.520	3.97	0.21	2.12	4.79	21.65	78.33	3.18	0.57	0.58	0.60	0.69
Paxson,John	CHI	78	20	1738	.480	.338	.529	.861	7.3	15.7	16.0	.475	1.42	0.60	8.40	2.75	22.28	2.86	-5.70	0.22	0.36	0.16	0.31
Hodges,Craig	CHI	59	6	1204	.472	.417	.512	.842	9.0	21.1	15.8	.482	2.10	0.34	5.72	3.19	20.41	1.39	40.68	0.63	0.52	0.35	-5.24
Grant,Harvey	WAS	71	1	1193	.464	.000	.465	.596	5.6	15.9	15.8	.473	4.34	0.21	3.73	4.02	16.80	389.00	-0.93	0.39	0.39	0.85	-0.17
Paxson,Jim	BOS	57	7	1138	.454	.167	.470	.816	8.6	20.8	15.8	.484	1.83	0.24	4.19	3.12	19.96	17.54	-10.57	1.07	0.48	0.32	-4.94
Brown,Mike	UTA	66	16	1051	.419	---	.419	.708	4.5	13.7	15.5	.479	7.36	0.17	0.16	5.71	15.92	---	0.00	0.98	0.32	0.55	1.82
Sundvold,Jon	MIA	68	8	1338	.455	.522	.444	.825	10.4	25.4	14.5	.473	1.79	0.20	3.44	2.24	19.68	6.34	62.26	0.73	0.36	0.26	-10.97
Turner,Elston	DEN	78	12	1746	.428	.286	.431	.589	4.3	9.3	13.8	.438	4.99	0.41	5.09	5.14	22.38	49.43	-0.03	0.27	0.47	0.61	4.51
Tucker,Trent	NY	81	24	1824	.454	.399	.512	.782	8.5	18.1	13.4	.455	2.82	0.23	4.55	4.07	22.52	0.96	50.68	0.34	0.58	0.45	-4.66
Wolf,Joe	LAC	66	15	1450	.423	.143	.433	.688	5.8	12.8	13.2	.438	5.45	0.28	2.31	4.70	21.97	27.71	-6.12	0.42	0.32	0.44	0.45
Wittman,Randy	IND	64	13	1120	.455	.500	.454	.683	4.5	12.5	11.9	.470	2.10	0.39	4.65	2.23	17.50	46.67	3.56	0.95	0.58	0.48	-0.61
Average Reserve		**73**	**13**	**1535**	**.467**	**.332**	**.480**	**.767**	**8.7**	**19.7**	**19.6**	**.500**	**5.07**	**0.27**	**3.74**	**5.42**	**21.05**	**10.96**	**1.57**	**0.94**	**0.52**	**0.51**	**-0.12**

Top 1989 Draft Picks

Here's a brief run-down on some of the rookies this season and what can be expected.

FORWARDS

Stacey King, 6'11'', 230 pounds. King was an All-American selection who played center in college but will be moved to power forward in the big league. Averaged 26 ppg and will be expected to hit for double figures his first season. (Oklahoma)

Nick Anderson, 6'6'', 200 pounds. Anderson has the size and skill to score points. Can also play guard. (Illinois)

Sean Elliott, 6'8'', 205 pounds. Elliott is a versatile player who can put the ball on the floor, has great range, and can score points in a hurry. Plays every spot but center. (U. Arizona)

Pervis Ellison, 6'9'', 210 pounds. A lightweight who knocks back shots on a regular basis. Deadly in close with the ball. His .615 shooting percentage is an asset. (U. Louisville)

Danny Ferry, 6'10'', 230 pounds. Ferry's been tutored in hoops since childhood and his court savvy is highly sought after. Will do well only with the right team. (Duke)

Tom Hammonds, 6'9'', 215 pounds. Hammonds hits the boards and can score from the foul line in. (Georgia Tech)

J.R. Reid, 6'9'', 260 pounds. Reid takes up a lot of space down low. Leaving UNC a year early with decreased stats leaves room for wonder about his rookie impact. (UNC)

Glen Rice, 6'7'', 215 pounds. Outstanding in Michigan's NCAA title season. Hit for 25 a game with plenty of range. Can go guard or forward. (Michigan)

Cliff Robinson, 6'11'', 225 pounds. UConn's blue-chipper has size but the question remains: Will he be able to produce in the NBA? (U. Conn)

Randy White, 6'8'', 260 pounds. Scored 21 ppg for Louisiana Tech. Tough under the boards. (Louisiana Tech)

Vlade Divac, 6'11'', 225 pounds. A Yugoslav with vintage Bill Walton passing and low post moves. Questionable: He doesn't speak English and has prima donna tendencies. (Yugoslavia National Team)

GUARDS

B.J. Armstrong, 6'2'', 170 pounds. Skilled as a passer and defender. Scored 18.6 ppg for Iowa. (Iowa)

Mookie Blaylock, 6'1'', 185 pounds. A Sooner considered to be the top point man for 1988–89. (Oklahoma)

Tim Hardaway, 5'11'', 175 pounds. Top player in the land under six feet, but will he be able to steal the ball and deal assists in the bigs remains the question. (UTEP)

George McCloud, 6'6'', 200 pounds. McCloud (23.1 ppg) likes to score from the outside. Last year with Florida State he averaged close to four three-pointers a game. (Florida State)

CENTERS

Gary Leonard, 7'1'', 235 pounds. Just barely got double figures for Missouri in scoring and was anemic off the glass with 5.5 rpg. A big project. (Missouri)

Miroslav Pecarski, 6'11'', 230 pounds. Hit for 20 a game for Marist but needs work. A lot of work. (Marist)

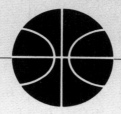

APPENDIX 4

Team Draft Selections, 1989

1989 NBA COLLEGIATE DRAFT

Pick	Team	Player	Height	Pos	College
		FIRST ROUND			
1	Sacramento	Pervis Ellison	6'9"	F	Louisville
2	LA Clippers	Danny Ferry	6'11"	F	Duke
3	San Antonio	Sean Elliot	6'8"	F/G	Arizona
4	Miami	Glen Rice	6'7"	G	Michigan
5	Charlotte	J.R. Reid	6'9"	F	North Carolina
6	Chicago	Stacey King	6'11"	C	Oklahoma
7	Indiana	George McCloud	6'6"	G	Florida State
8	Dallas	Randy White	6'7"	F	Louisiana Tech
9	Washington	Tom Hammonds	6'8"	F	Georgia Tech
10	Minnesota	Pooh Richardson	6'1"	G	UCLA
11	Orlando	Nick Anderson	6'6"	F	Illinois
12	New Jersey	Mookie Blaylock	6'1"	G	Oklahoma
13	Boston	Michael Smith	6'10"	F	Brigham Young
14	Golden State	Tim Hardaway	5'11"	G	Texas, El Paso
15	Denver	Todd Lichti	6'4"	G	Stanford
16	Seattle	Dana Barros	5'11"	G	Boston College
17	Seattle	Shawn Kemp	6'10"	F	Trinity Valley CC
18	Chicago	B.J. Armstrong	6'2"	G	Iowa
19	Philadelphia	Kenny Payne	6'8"	F	Louisville
20	Chicago	Jeff Sanders	6'9"	F	Georgia Southern
21	Utah	Blue Edwards	6'5"	G	East Carolina
22	Portland	Byron Irvin	6'5"	G	Missouri
23	Atlanta	Roy Marble	6'6"	G	Iowa
24	Phoenix	Anthony Cook	6'9"	F	Arizona
25	Cleveland	John Morton	6'3"	G	Seton Hall
26	LA Lakers	Vlade Divac	6'11"	F	Yugoslavia
27	Detroit	Kenny Battle	6'6"	F	Illinois

1989 NBA COLLEGIATE DRAFT

Pick	Team	Player	Height	Pos	College
		SECOND ROUND			
28	Miami	Sherman Douglas	6'0"	G	Syracuse
29	Charlotte	Dyron Nix	6'7"	F	Tennessee
30	Milwaukee	Frank Kornet	6'9"	F	Vanderbilt
31	LA Clippers	Jeff Martin	6'6"	F	Murray State
32	New Jersey	Stanley Brundy	6'7"	F	DePaul
33	LA Clippers	Jay Edwards	6'5"	G	Indiana
34	Minnesota	Gary Leonard	7'1"	C	Missouri
35	Dallas	Pat Durham	6'7"	F	Colorado State
36	Portland	Cliff Robinson	6'10½"	F	Connecticut
37	Orlando	Michael Ansley	6'7"	F	Alabama
38	Minnesota	Doug West	6'6"	G	Villanova
39	Washington	Ed Horton	6'8"	F	Iowa
40	Boston	Dino Radja	6'8"	F	Yugoslavia
41	Washington	Doug Roth	7'0"	C	Tennessee
42	Denver	Michael Cutright	6'4"	G	McNeese State
43	Cleveland	Chucky Brown	6'8"	F	North Carolina State
44	Philadelphia	Reggie Cross	6'8"	F	Hawaii
45	Miami	Scott Hafner	6'3"	G	Evansville
46	Phoenix	Ricky Blanton	6'7"	F	Louisiana State
47	Denver	Reggie Turner	6'8"	F	Alabama, Birmingham
48	Utah	Junie Lewis	6'3"	G	South Alabama
49	Atlanta	Haywoode Workman	6'3"	G	Oral Roberts
50	New York	Brian Quinnett	6'8"	F	Washington State
51	Phoenix	Mike Morrison	6'4"	G	Loyola, Maryland
52	Phoenix	Greg Grant	5'7"	G	Trenton State
53	Dallas	Jeff Hodge	6'2"	G	South Alabama
54	Philadelphia	Toney Mack	6'5"	G	Georgia

CHANGING PLACES

In a postseason effort to shore up holes in their lineups, team GMs started pounding the phones right after the Pistons popped champagne corks in Los Angeles. All-Star performer Buck Williams was finally freed up by the Nets and sent to Portland, immediately bolstering the Blazers' frontcourt. Oft-injured center Sam Bowie was sent to the Meadowlands in exchange. Vicious rumors then started flying that Bowie came only after the Bill Walton deal fell through for the Nets. From all appearances it seems Portland got the better of the deal and will certainly be pushing the Lakers for the Pacific crown.

In other trades, backup center Dave Corzine was banished from Chicago to Orlando, while Indiana's backup center, Stuart Gray, was sent to Charlotte. Other trades will certainly be made but our presses are running...

Joshua Trupin has been a long-time sports statistician, going back as far as high school. While at Yale University, he managed the varsity hockey team and spearheaded statistical operations for the Sports Information Office. Currently he works as a computer services assistant for a Connecticut-based firm. He lives in Norwalk, Connecticut with his fiancée Laura and dogs Basil and Valdis. In his spare time he takes naps.

Gerald Secor Couzens is a hoop nut who's been throwing up jumpers since 1962 . . . and will continue to do so. Shortly after receiving his university diploma (thereby officially ending his collegiate hoop career), he was on a plane bound for France, where he played for a local Paris team for the next few years. Finally back on American hardwood, he was one of the founding members of the New York Thursday Night Pro League, a pick-up game for older guys who can still shoot, or think they can. He also organized the first basketball camp for players over 30, and authored two other books on roundball. He lives near a playground with a full court in New York City with his wife and four children.